W9-CRT-451

Passion . . .

Violence . . .

Ribald Humor . . .

HERE is the fictional world of Erskine Caldwell—
the farmers, drummers, sharecroppers, Negroes,
loose women, and lusty men who are brought to
life in a fascinating panorama of rural life in New
England and the Deep South.

You will meet bold women on the prowl for a
man; poverty-stricken farmers struggling for sur-
vival; hen-pecked husbands on riotous sprees,
curious adolescents as they awaken to an adult
world—a mighty procession of unforgettable char-
acters straight out of the fabric of American life.

If you are one of the millions who have already
enjoyed such Caldwell classics as *Tobacco Road,*
and *God's Little Acre,* or if you have yet to savor
his earthy artistry, humor, and compassionate understanding, you will want to read and own *The
Complete Stories of Erskine Caldwell.*

". . . these . . . stories present Erskine Caldwell
as an artist without any superiors in his field of
modern writing."   —*Atlanta Journal*

THIS IS A REPRINT OF THE ORIGINAL HARDCOVER
EDITION PUBLISHED BY LITTLE, BROWN & CO.

TO OUR READERS

We welcome your comments about SIGNET, SIGNET KEY,
and MENTOR Books, as well as your suggestions for new
reprints. If your dealer does not have the books you
want, you may order them by mail, enclosing the list
price plus 5c a copy to cover mailing costs. Send for a
copy of our complete catalog. The New American Library
of World Literature, Inc., 501 Madison Avenue, New
York 22, New York.

The
Complete Stories
of
ERSKINE CALDWELL

A SIGNET BOOK

Published by THE NEW AMERICAN LIBRARY

Published as a SIGNET BOOK
By Arrangement with Little, Brown & Company

FIRST PRINTING, APRIL, 1955

SIGNET BOOKS are published by
The New American Library of World Literature, Inc.
501 Madison Avenue, New York 22, New York

PRINTED IN THE UNITED STATES OF AMERICA

Contents

Country Full of Swedes

THERE I was, standing in the middle of the chamber, trembling like I was coming down with the flu, and still not knowing what God-awful something had happened. In all my days in the Back Kingdom, I never heard such noises so early in the forenoon.

It was about half an hour after sunrise, and a gun went off like a cofferdam breaking up under ice at twenty below, and I'd swear it sounded like it wasn't any farther away than my feet are from my head. That gun shot off, pitching me six-seven inches off the bed, and, before I could come down out of the air, there was another roar like somebody coughing through a megaphone, with a two-weeks cold, right in my ear. God-helping, I hope I never get waked up like that again until I can get myself home to the Back Kingdom where I rightfully belong to stay.

I must have stood there ten-fifteen minutes shivering in my nightshirt, my heart pounding inside of me like a ramrod working on a plugged-up bore, and listening for that gun again, if it was going to shoot some more. A man never knows what's going to happen next in the State of Maine; that's why I wish sometimes I'd never left the Back Kingdom to begin with. I was making sixty a month, with the best of bed and board, back there in the intervale; but like a God-damn fool I had to jerk loose and came down here near the Bay. I'm going back where I came from, God-helping; I've never had a purely calm and peaceful day since I got here three-four years ago. This is the damnedest country for the unexpected raising of all kinds of unlooked-for hell a man is apt to run across in a lifetime of traveling. If a man's born and raised in the Back Kingdom, he ought to stay there where he belongs; that's what I'd done if I'd had the sense to stay out of this down-country near the Bay, where you don't ever know, God-helping, what's going to happen next, where, or when.

But there I was, standing in the middle of the upstairs chamber, shaking like a ragweed in an August windstorm, and not knowing what minute, maybe right at me, that gun was going to shoot off again, for all I knew. Just then, though, I heard Jim and Mrs. Frost trip-trapping around downstairs in their bare feet. Even if I didn't know what God-awful something

9

had happened, I knew things around the place weren't calm and peaceful, like they generally were of a Sunday morning in May, because it took a stiff mixture of heaven and hell to get Jim and Mrs. Frost up and out of a warm bed before six of a forenoon, any of the days of the week.

I ran to the window and stuck my head out as far as I could get it, to hear what the trouble was. Everything out there was as quiet and peaceful as midnight on a back road in middle-most winter. But I knew something was up, because Jim and Mrs. Frost didn't make a practice of getting up and out of a warm bed that time of forenoon in the chillish Maytime.

There wasn't any sense in me standing there in the cold air shivering in my nightshirt, so I put on my clothes, whistling all the time through my teeth to drive away the chill, and trying to figure out what God-damn fool was around so early shoot-ing off a gun of a Sunday morning. Just then I heard the down-stairs door open, and up the steps, two at a time, came Jim in his breeches and his shirttail flying out behind him.

He wasn't long in coming up the stairs, for a man sixty-seven, but before he reached the door to my room, that gun went off again: Boom! Just like that; and the echo came rolling back through the open window from the hills: Boom! Boom! Like fireworks going off with your eyes shut. Jim had busted through the door already, but when he heard that Boom! sound he sort of spun around, like a cockeyed weathervane, five-six times, and ran out of the door again like he had been shot in the hind parts with a moose gun. That Boom! so early in the forenoon was enough to scare the daylights out of any man, and Jim wasn't any different from me or anybody else in the town of East Joloppi. He just turned around and jumped through the door to the first tread on the stairway like his mind was made up to go somewhere else in a hurry, and no fooling around at the start.

I'd been hired to Jim and Mrs. Frost for all of three-four years, and I was near about as much of a Frost, excepting name, as Jim himself was. Jim and me got along first-rate together, doing chores and haying and farm work in general, because neither one of us was ever trying to make the other do more of the work. We were hitched to make a fine team, and I never had a kick coming, and Jim said he didn't either. Jim had the name of Frost, to be sure, but I wouldn't ever hold that against a man.

The echo of that gunshot was still rolling around in the hills and coming in through the window, when all at once that God-awful coughlike whoop through a megaphone sounded again right there in the room and everywhere else, like it might have been, in the whole town of East Joloppi. The man or beast or whatever animal he was who hollered like that ought to be locked up to keep him from scaring all the women and children to death, and it wasn't any stomach-comforting sound for a grown man who's used to the peaceful calm of the Back Kingdom all his life to hear so early of a Sunday forenoon, either.

I jumped to the door where Jim, just a minute before, leaped through. He didn't stop till he got clear to the bottom of the stairs. He stood there, looking up at me like a wild-eyed cow moose surprised in the sheriff's corn field.

"Who fired that God-awful shot, Jim?" I yelled at him, leaping down the stairs quicker than a man of my years ought to let himself do.

"Good God!" Jim said, his voice hoarse, and falling all to pieces like a stump of punkwood. "The Swedes! The Swedes are shooting, Stan!"

"What Swedes, Jim—those Swedes who own the farm and buildings across the road over there?" I said, trying to find the buttonholes in my shirt. "Have they come back here to live on that farm?"

"Good God, yes!" he said, his voice croaking deep down in his throat, like he had swallowed too much water. "The Swedes are all over the place. They're everywhere you can see, there's that many of them."

"What's their name, Jim?" I asked him. "You and Mrs. Frost never told me what their name is."

"Good God, I don't know. I never heard them called anything but Swedes, and that's what it is, I guess. It ought to be that, if it ain't."

I ran across the hall to look out a window, but it was on the wrong side of the house, and I couldn't see a thing. Mrs. Frost was stepping around in the downstairs chamber, locking things up in the drawers and closet and forgetting where she was hiding the keys. I could see her through the open door, and she was more scared-looking than Jim was. She was so scared of the Swedes she didn't know what she was doing, none of the time.

"What made those Swedes come back for, Jim?" I said to him. "I thought you said they were gone for good, this time."

"Good God, Stan," he said, "I don't know what they came back for. I guess hard times are bringing everybody back to the land, and the Swedes are always in the front rush of everything. I don't know what brought them back, but they're all over the place, shooting and yelling and raising hell. There are thirty-forty of them, looks like to me, counting everything with heads."

"What are they doing now, Jim, except yelling and shooting?"

"Good God," Jim said, looking behind him to see what Mrs.

Frost was doing with his things in the downstairs chamber. "I don't know what they're not doing. But I can hear them, Stan! You hurry out right now and lock up all the tools in the barn and bring in the cows and tie them up in the stalls. I've got to hurry out now and bring in all of those new cedar fence posts across the front of the yard before they start pulling them up and carrying them off. Good God, Stan, the Swedes are everywhere you look outdoors! We've got to make haste, Stan!"

Jim ran to the side door and out the back of the house, but I took my time about going. I wasn't scared of the Swedes, like Jim and Mrs. Frost were, and I didn't aim to have Jim putting me to doing tasks and chores, or anything else, before breakfast and the proper time. I wasn't any more scared of the Swedes than I was of the Finns and Portuguese, anyway. It's a God-awful shame for Americans to let Swedes and Finns and the Portuguese scare the daylights out of them. God-helping, they are no different than us, and you never see a Finn or a Swede scared of an American. But people like Jim and Mrs. Frost are scared to death of Swedes and other people from the old countries; Jim and Mrs. Frost and people like that never stop to think that all of us Americans came over from the old countries, one time or another, to begin with.

But there wasn't any sense in trying to argue with Jim and Mrs. Frost right then, when the Swedes, like a fired nest of yellow-headed bumblebees, were swarming all over the place as far as the eye could see, and when Mrs. Frost was scared to death that they were coming into the house and carry out all of her and Jim's furniture and household goods. So while Mrs. Frost was tying her and Jim's shoes in pillowcases and putting them out of sight in closets and behind beds, I went to the kitchen window and looked out to see what was going on around that tall yellow house across the road.

Jim and Mrs. Frost both were right about there being Swedes all over the place. God-helping, there were Swedes all over the country, near about all over the whole town of East Joloppi, for what I could see out of the window. They were as thick around the barn and pump and the woodpile as if they had been a nest of yellow-headed bumblebees strewn over the countryside. There were Swedes everywhere a man could see, and the ones that couldn't be seen could be heard yelling their heads off inside the yellow clapboarded house across the road. There wasn't any mistake about there being Swedes there, either; because I've never yet seen a man who mistakes a Swede or a Finn for an American. Once you see a Finn or a Swede you know, God-helping, that he is a Swede or a Finn, and not a Portugee or an American.

There was a Swede everywhere a man could look. Some of them were little Swedes, and women Swedes, to be sure; but little Swedes, in the end, and women Swedes too, near about, grow up as big as any of them. When you come right down to it, there's no sense in counting out the little Swedes and the women Swedes.

Out in the road in front of their house were seven-eight autos and trucks loaded down with furniture and household goods. All around, everything was Swedes. The Swedes were yelling and shouting at one another, the little Swedes and the women Swedes just as loud as the big Swedes, and it looked like none of them knew what all the shouting and yelling was for, and when they found out, they didn't give a damn about it. That was because all of them were Swedes. It didn't make any difference what a Swede was yelling about; just as long as he had leave to open his mouth, he was tickled to death about it.

I have never seen the like of so much yelling and shouting anywhere else before; but down here in the State of Maine, in the down-country on the Bay, there's no sense in being taken back at the sights to be seen, because anything on God's green earth is likely and liable to happen between day and night, and the other way around, too.

Now, you take the Finns; there's any God's number of them around in the woods, where you least expect to see them, logging and such. When a Finn crew breaks a woods camp, it looks like there's a Finn for every tree in the whole State, but you don't see them going around making the noise that Swedes do, with all their yelling and shouting and shooting off guns. Finns are quiet about their hell-raising. The Portugu' se are quiet, too; you see them tramping around, minding their own business, and working hard on a river dam or something, but you never hear them shouting and yelling and shooting off guns at five-six of a Sunday morning. There's no known likeness to the noise that a houseful of Swedes can make when they get to yelling and shouting at one another early in the forenoon.

I was standing there all that time, looking out the window at the Swedes across the road, when Jim came into the kitchen with an armful of wood and threw it into the wood box behind the range.

"Good God, Stan," Jim said, "the Swedes are everywhere you can look outdoors. They're not going to get that armful of wood, anyway, though."

Mrs. Frost came to the door and stood looking like she didn't know it was her business to cook breakfast for Jim and me. I made a fire in the range and put on a pan of water to boil for the coffee. Jim kept running to the window to look out, and there wasn't much use in expecting Mrs. Frost to start cooking unless somebody set her to it, in the shape she was in, with all the Swedes around the place. She was so upset, it was a downright pity to look at her. But Jim and me had to eat, and I went and took her by the arm and brought her to the range and left her standing there so close she would get burned if she didn't stir around and make breakfast.

"Good God, Stan," Jim said, "those Swedes are into everything. They're in the barn, and in the pasture running the cows, and I don't know what else they've been into since I looked last. They'll take the tools and the horses and cows, and the cedar posts, too, if we don't get out there and put everything under lock and key."

"Now, hold on, Jim," I said, looking out the window. "Them you see are little Swedes out there, and they're not going to make off with anything of yours and Mrs. Frost's. The big Swedes are busy carrying in furniture and household goods. Those Swedes aren't going to tamper with anything of yours and Mrs. Frost's. They're people just like us. They don't go around stealing everything in sight. Now, let's just sit here by the window and watch them while Mrs. Frost is getting breakfast ready."

"Good God, Stan, they're Swedes," Jim said, "and they're moving into the house across the road. I've got to put everything under lock and key before—"

"Hold on, Jim," I told him. "It's their house they're moving into. God-helping, they're not moving into your and Jim's house, are they, Mrs. Frost?"

"Jim," Mrs. Frost said, shaking her finger at him and looking at me wild-eyed and sort of flustered-like, "Jim, don't you sit there and let Stanley stop you from saving the stock and tools. Stanley doesn't know the Swedes like we do. Stanley came down here from the Back Kingdom, and he doesn't know anything about Swedes."

Mrs. Frost was partly right, because I've never seen the things in my whole life that I've seen down here near the Bay; but there wasn't any sense in Americans like Jim and Mrs. Frost being scared of Swedes. I've seen enough Finns and Portuguese in my time in the Back Kingdom, up in the intervale, to know that Americans are no different from the others.

"Now, you hold on a while, Jim," I said. "Swedes are no different than Finns. Finns don't go around stealing another man's stock and tools. Up in the Back Kingdom the Finns are the finest kind of neighbors."

"That may be so up in the Back Kingdom, Stan," Jim said, "but Swedes down here near the Bay are nothing like anything that's ever been before or since. Those Swedes over there across the road work in a pulp mill over to Waterville three-four years, and when they've got enough money saved up, or when they lose it all, as the case may be, they all move back here to East Joloppi on this farm of theirs for two-three years at a time. That's what they do. And they've been doing it for the past thirty-forty years, ever since I can remember, and they haven't changed none in all that time. I can recall the first time they came to East Joloppi; they built that house across the road then, and if you've ever seen a sight like Swedes building a house in a hurry, you haven't got much else to live for. Why! Stan, those Swedes built that house in four-five days—just like that! I've never seen the equal of it. Of course now, Stan, it's the damnedest-looking house a man ever saw, because it's not a farmhouse, and it's not a city house, and it's no kind of a house an American would erect. Why! Those Swedes threw that house together in four-five days—just like that! But whoever saw a house like that before, with three stories to it, and only six rooms in the whole building! And painted yellow, too; Good God, Stan, white is the only color to paint a house, and those Swedes went and painted it yellow. Then on top of that, they went and painted the barn red. And of all of the shouting and yelling, at all times of the day and night, a man never saw or heard before. Those Swedes acted like they were purely crazy for the whole of four-five days, and they were, and they still are. But what gets me is the painting of it yellow, and the making of it three stories high, with only six rooms in the whole building. Nobody but Swedes would go and do a thing like that; an American would have built a farmhouse, here in the country, resting square on the ground, with one story, maybe a story and a half, and then painted it lead-white. But Good God, Stan, those fool Swedes had to put up three stories, to hold six rooms, and then went and painted the building yellow."

"Swedes are a little queer, sometimes," I said. "E 't Finns and Portuguese are too, Jim. And Americans sometimes—"

"A little queer!" Jim said. "Why! Good God, Stan, the Swedes are the queerest people on the earth, if that's the right word for them. You don't know Swedes, Stan. This is the first time you've ever seen those Swedes across the road, and that's why you don't know what they're like after being shut up in a pulpwood mill over to Waterville for four-five years. They're purely wild, I tell you, Stan. They don't stop for anything they set their heads on. If you was to walk out there now and tell them to move their autos and trucks off of the town road so the travelers could get past without having to drive around through the brush, they'd tear you apart, they're that wild, after being shut up in the pulp mill over to Waterville these three-four, maybe four-five, years."

"Finns get that way, too," I tried to tell Jim. "After Finns have been shut up in a woods camp all winter, they make a lot

of noise when they get out. Everybody who has to stay close to
the job for three-four years likes to act free when he gets out
from under the job. Now, Jim, you take the Portuguese—"

"Don't you sit there, Jim, and let Stanley keep you from
putting the tools away," Mrs. Frost said. "Stanley doesn't
know the Swedes like we do. He's lived up in the Back Kingdom most of his life, tucked away in the intervale, and he's
never seen Swedes—"

"Good God, Stan," Jim said, standing up, he was that
nervous and upset, "the Swedes are overrunning the whole
country. I'll bet there are more Swedes in the town of East
Joloppi than there are in the rest of the country. Everybody
knows there's more Swedes in the State of Maine than there
are in the old country. Why! Stan, they take to this state like
potato bugs take to—"

"Don't you sit there and let Stanley keep you back, Jim,"
Mrs. Frost put in again. "Stanley doesn't know the Swedes like
we do. Stanley's lived up there in the Back Kingdom most
of his life."

Just then one of the big Swedes started yelling at some of
the little Swedes and women Swedes. I'll swear, those big
Swedes sounded like a pastureful of hoarse bulls, near the end
of May, mad about the black flies. God-helping, they yelled
like they were fixing to kill all the little Swedes and women
Swedes they could get their hands on. It didn't amount to anything, though; because the little Swedes and the women Swedes
yelled right back at them just like they had been big Swedes
too. The little Swedes and women Swedes couldn't yell hoarse
bull bass, but it was close enough to it to make a man who's
lived most of his life up in the Back Kingdom, in the intervale, think that the whole town of East Joloppi was full of big
Swedes.

Jim was all for getting out after the tools and stock right
away, but I pulled him back to the table. I wasn't going to let
Jim and Mrs. Frost set me to doing tasks and chores before
breakfast and the regular time. Forty dollars a month isn't
much to pay a man for ten-eleven hours' work a day, including Sundays, when the stock has to be attended to like any
other day, and I set myself that I wasn't going to work twelve-
thirteen hours a day by them, even if I was practically one of
the Frosts myself, except in name, by that time.

"Now, hold on awhile, Jim," I said. "Let's just sit here by the
window and watch them carry their furniture and household
goods inside while Mrs. Frost's getting the cooking ready to
eat. If they start taking off any of you and Mrs. Frost's things,
we can see them just as good from here by the window as we
could out there in the yard and road."

"Now, Jim, I'm telling you," Mrs. Frost said, shaking all over, and not even trying to cook us a meal, "don't you sit there and let Stanley keep you from saving the stock and tools. Stanley doesn't know the Swedes like we do. He thinks they're like everybody else."

Jim wasn't for staying in the house when all of his tools were lying around in the yard, and while his cows were in the pasture unprotected, but he saw how it would be better to wait where we could hurry up Mrs. Frost with the cooking, if we were ever going to eat breakfast that forenoon. She was so excited and nervous about the Swedes moving back to East Joloppi from the pulp mill in Waterville that she hadn't got the beans and brown bread fully heated from the night before, and we had to sit and eat them cold.

We were sitting there by the window eating the cold beans and brown bread, and watching the Swedes, when two of the little Swedes started running across Jim and Mrs. Frost's lawn. They were chasing one of their big yellow tomcats they had brought with them from Waterville. The yellow tom was as large as an eight-months collie puppy, and he ran like he was on fire and didn't know how to put it out. His great big bushy tail stuck straight up in the air behind him, like a flag, and he was leaping over the lawn like a devilish calf, newborn.

Jim and Mrs. Frost saw the little Swedes and the big yellow tomcat at the same time I did.

"Good God," Jim shouted, raising himself part out of the chair. "Here they come now!"

"Hold on now, Jim," I said, pulling him back to the table. "They're only chasing one of their tomcats. They're not after taking anything that belongs to you and Mrs. Frost. Let's just sit here and finish eating the beans, and watch them out the window."

"My crown in heaven!" Mrs. Frost cried out, running to the window and looking through. "Those Swedes are going to kill every plant on the place. They'll dig up all the bulbs and pull up all the vines in the flower bed."

"Now you just sit and calm yourself, Mrs. Frost," I told her. "Those little Swedes are just chasing a tomcat. They're not after doing hurt to your flowers."

The big Swedes were unloading the autos and trucks and carrying the furniture and household goods into their three-story yellow clapboarded house. None of them was paying any attention to the little Swedes chasing the yellow tom over Jim and Mrs. Frost's lawn.

Just then the kitchen door burst open, and the two little Swedes stood there looking at us, panting and blowing their heads off.

Mrs. Frost took one look at them, and then she let out a yell, but the kids didn't notice her at all.

"Hey," one of them shouted, "come out here and help us get the cat. He climbed up in one of your trees."

By that time, Mrs. Frost was all for slamming the door in their faces, but I pushed in front of her and went out into the yard with them. Jim came right behind me, after he had finished calming Mrs. Frost, and telling her we wouldn't let the Swedes come and carry out her furniture and household goods.

The yellow tom was all the way up in one of Jim's young maple shade trees. The maple wasn't strong enough to support even the smallest of the little Swedes, if he should take it into his head to climb to the top after the cat, and neither Jim nor me was hurting ourselves trying to think of a way to get the feline down. We were all for letting the cat stay where he was, till he got ready to come down of his own free will, but the little Swedes couldn't wait for anything. They wanted the tom right away, then and there, and no wasting of time in getting him.

"You boys go home and wait for the cat to come down," Jim told them. "There's no way to make him come down now, till he gets ready to come down of his own mind."

But no, those two boys were little Swedes. They weren't thinking of going back home till they got the yellow tom down from the maple. One of them ran to the tree, before Jim or me could head him off, and started shinnying up it like a pop-eyed squirrel. In no time, it seemed to me like, he was up amongst the limbs, jumping around up there from one limb to another like he had been brought up in just such a tree.

"Good God, Stan," Jim said, "can't you keep them out of the trees?"

There was no answer for that, and Jim knew there wasn't. There's no way of stopping a Swede from doing what he has set his head on doing.

The boy got almost to the top branch, where the yellow tom was clinging and spitting, when the tree began to bend towards the house. I knew what was coming, if something wasn't done about it pretty quick, and so did Jim. Jim saw his young maple shade tree begin to bend, and he almost had a fit looking at it. He ran to the lumber stack and came back dragging two lengths of two-by-fours. He got them set up against the tree before it had time to do any splitting, and then we stood there, like two damn fools, shoring up the tree and yelling at the little Swede to come down out of there before we broke his neck for being up in it.

The big Swedes across the road heard the fuss we were making, and they came running out of that three-story, six-room house like it had been on fire inside.

"Good God, Stan," Jim shouted at me, "here comes the Swedes!"

"Don't turn and run off, Jim," I cautioned him, yanking him back by his coattail. "They're not wild beasts; we're not scared of them. Hold on where you are, Jim."

I could see Mrs. Frost's head almost breaking through the window glass in the kitchen. She was all for coming out and driving the Swedes off her lawn and out of her flowers, but she was too scared to unlock the kitchen door and open it.

Jim was getting ready to run again, when he saw the Swedes coming towards us like a nest of yellow-headed bumblebees, but I wasn't scared of them, and I held on to Jim's coattail and told him I wasn't. Jim and me were shoring up the young maple, and I knew if one of us let go, the tree would bend to the ground right away and split wide open right up the middle. There was no sense in ruining a young maple shade tree like that, and I told Jim there wasn't.

"Hey," one of the big Swedes shouted at the little Swede up in the top of the maple, "come down out of that tree and go home to your mother."

"Aw, to hell with the Old Lady," the little Swede shouted down. "I'm getting the cat by the tail."

The big Swede looked at Jim and me. Jim was almost ready to run again by that time, but I wasn't, and I held him and told him I wasn't. There was no sense in letting the Swedes scare the daylights out of us.

"What in hell can you do with kids when they get that age?" he asked Jim and me.

Jim was all for telling him to make the boy come down out of the maple before it bent over and split wide open, but I knew there was no sense in trying to make him come down out of there until he got good and ready to come, or else got the yellow tom by the tail.

Just then another big Swede came running out of that three-story, six-room house across the road, holding a double-bladed ax out in front of him, like it was a red-hot poker, and yelling for all he was worth at the other Swedes.

"Good God, Stan," Jim said, "don't let those Swedes cut down my young maple!"

I had lots better sense than to try to make the Swedes stop doing what they had set their heads on doing. A man would be purely a fool to try to stop it from raining from above when it got ready to, even if he was trying to get his corn crop planted.

I looked around again, and there was Mrs. Frost all but popping through the window glass. I could see what she was thinking, but I couldn't hear a word she was saying. It was good and plenty though, whatever it was.

"Come down out of that tree!" the Swede yelled at the boy up in Jim's maple.

Instead of starting to climb down, the little Swede reached up for the big yellow tomcat's tail. The tom reached out a big fat paw and harried the boy five-six times, just like that, quicker than the eye could follow. The kid let out a yell and a shout that must have been heard all the way to the other side of town, sounding like a whole houseful of Swedes up in the maple.

The big Swede covered the distance to the tree in one stride, pushing everything behind him.

"Good God, Stan," Jim shouted at me, "we've got to do something!"

There wasn't anything a man could do, unless he was either a Swede himself, or a man of prayer. Americans like Jim and me had no business getting in a Swede's way, especially when he was swinging a big double-bladed ax, and he just out of a pulp mill after being shut up making paper four-five years.

The big Swede grabbed the ax and let go at the trunk of the maple with it. There was no stopping him then, because he had the ax going, and it was whipping around his shoulders like a cow's tail in a swarm of black flies. The little maple shook all over every time the ax blade struck it, like wind blowing a cornstalk, and then it began to bend on the other side from Jim and me where we were shoring it up with the two-by-fours. Chips as big as dinner plates were flying across the lawn and pelting the house like a gang of boys stoning telephone insulators. One of those big dinner-plate chips crashed through the window where Mrs. Frost was, about that time. Both Jim and me thought at first she had fallen through the window, but when we looked again, we could see that she was still on the inside, and madder than ever at the Swedes.

The two-by-fours weren't any good any longer, because it was too late to get to the other side of the maple in time to keep it from bending in that direction. The Swede with the double-bladed ax took one more swing, and the tree began to bend towards the ground.

The tree came down, the little Swede came down, and the big yellow tom came down on top of everything, holding for all he was worth to the top of the little Swede's head. Long before the tree and the boy struck the ground, the big yellow tom had sprung what looked like thirty feet, and landed in the middle of Mrs. Frost's flowers and bulbs. The little Swede let out a yell and a whoop when he hit the ground that brought out six-seven more Swedes from that three-story, six-room house, piling out into the road like it was the first time they had ever heard a kid bawl. The women Swedes and the little Swedes and the big Swedes piled out on Jim and Mrs. Frost's front lawn like they had been dropped out of a dump truck and didn't know which was straight up from straight down.

I thought Mrs. Frost was going to have a fit right then and there in the kitchen window. When she saw that swarm of Swedes coming across her lawn, and the big yellow tomcat in her flower bed among the tender plants and bulbs, digging up the things she had planted, and the Swedes with their No. 12 heels squashing the green shoots she had been nursing along—well, I guess she just sort of caved in, and fell out of sight for the time being. I didn't have time to run to see what was wrong with her, because Jim and me had to tear out behind the tom and the Swedes to try to save as much as we could.

"Good God, Stan," Jim shouted at me, "go run in the house and ring up all the neighbors on the line, and tell them to hurry over here and help us before the Swedes wreck my farm and buildings. There's no telling what they'll do next. They'll be setting fire to the house and barn the next thing, maybe. Hurry, Stan!"

I didn't have time to waste talking to the neighbors on the telephone line. I was right behind Jim and the Swedes to see what they were going to do next.

"I pay you good pay, Stan," Jim said, "and I want my money's worth. Now, you go ring up the neighbors and tell them to hurry."

The big yellow tom made one more spring when he hit the flower bed, and that leap landed him over the stone wall. He struck out for the deep woods with every Swede on the place behind him. When Jim and me got to the stone wall, I pulled up short and held Jim back.

"Well, Jim," I said, "if you want me to, I'll go down in the woods and raise hell with every Swede on the place for cutting down your young maple and tearing up Mrs. Frost's flower bed."

We turned around and there was Mrs. Frost, right behind us. There was no knowing how she got there so quick after the Swedes had left for the woods.

"My crown in heaven," Mrs. Frost said, running up to Jim and holding on to him. "Jim, don't let Stanley make the Swedes mad. This is the only place we have got to live in, and they'll be here a year now this time, maybe two-three, if the hard times don't get better soon."

"That's right, Stan," he said. "You don't know the Swedes like we do. You would have to be a Swede yourself to know what to tell them. Don't go over there doing anything like that."

"God-helping, Jim," I said, "you and Mrs. Frost ain't scared of the Swedes, are you?"

"Good God, no," he said, his eyes popping out, "but don't go making them mad."

(First published in the *Yale Review*)

Man and Woman

THEY came slowly up the road through the colorless dawn like shadows left behind by the night. There was no motion in their bodies, and yet their feet scuffed up dust that settled behind them as quickly as it was raised. They lifted their eyes with each step they took, peering toward the horizon for the first red rays of the sun.

The woman held her lower lip clamped tightly between her teeth. It hurt her to do that, but it was the only way she could urge herself forward step after step. There was no other way to drag her feet one behind the other, mile after mile. She whimpered occasionally, but she did not cry out.

"It's time to stop and rest again," Ring said.

She did not answer him.

They kept on.

At the top of the hill, they came face to face with the sun. It was a quarter of the way up, cut like a knife by the treeless horizon. Down below them was a valley lying under a cover of mist that was rising slowly from the earth. They could see several houses and farms, but most of them were so far away they were almost indistinguishable in the mist. There was smoke rising from the chimney of the first house.

Ruth looked at the man beside her. The red rays of the sun had begun to color his pale face like blood. But still his eyes were tired and lifeless. He looked as if he were balancing himself on his two feet with great effort, and as if the next moment he might lose his balance and fall to the ground.

"We'll be able to get a little something to eat at that first house," she said, waiting minute after minute for him to reply.

"We'll get something there," she said, answering for him. "We will."

The sun came up above the horizon, fast and red. Streaks of gray clouds, like layers of woodsmoke, swam across the face of it. Almost as quickly as it had risen, the sun shrank into a small fiery button that seared the eyes until it was impossible to look at it any longer.

"Let's try, anyway," Ruth said.

Ring looked at her in the clear daylight, seeing her for the first time since the sun had set the night before. Her face was paler, her cheeks more sunken.

Without words, he started forward down the hill. He did not turn his head to see if she was following him, but went down the road drawing one foot from behind and hurling it in front of him with all his might. There was no other way he could move himself over the ground.

He had stopped at the front of the house, looking at the smoke that floated overhead, when she caught up with him at last.

"I'll go in and try," she said. "You sit down and rest, Ring."

He opened his mouth to say something, but his throat became choked and no words came. He looked at the house, with its worn doorstep and curtain-filled windows and its smoke-filled chimney, and he did not feel like a stranger in a strange country as long as he kept his eyes upon those things.

Ruth went through the gate, and around the side of the house, and stopped at the kitchen door. She looked behind her and saw Ring coming across the yard from the road.

Someone was watching them from behind a curtain at the window.

"Knock," Ring said.

She placed the knuckles of her right hand against the side of the house and rapped on the clapboards until her hand began to hurt.

She turned around and glanced quickly at Ring, and he nodded his head.

Presently the kitchen door opened a few inches and a woman's head could be seen through the crack. She was middle-aged and brown-faced and had a long, thick scar on her forehead that looked as if it might have been made by a bursting fruit jar.

"Go away," she told them.

"We won't bother you," Ruth said as quickly as she could. "All we wanted was to ask you if you could give us a little something to eat. Just a potato, if you have any, or bread, or something."

"I don't know what you are doing here," the woman said. "I don't like to have strange people around my house."

She almost closed the door, but in a moment the crack widened, and her face could be seen once more.

"I'll feed the girl," she said finally, "but I can't let the man have anything. I don't have enough for both of you, anyway."

Ruth turned quickly around, her heels digging into the sandy earth. She looked at Ring. He nodded his head eagerly.

He could see the word forming on her lips even though he could not hear it. She shook her head.

Ring went several steps toward her.

"We'll try somewhere else," she said.

"No," he said. "You go in and eat what she'll give you. I'll try at the next house we come to."

She still did not wish to go into the house without him. The woman opened the door a foot or more, and waited for her to come up the steps.

Ring sat down on a bench under a tree.

"I'm going to sit here and wait until you go in and get something to eat for yourself," he said.

Ruth went up the steps slowly to the porch and entered the door. When she was inside, the woman pointed out a chair by a table, and Ruth sat down.

There were potatoes, warmed over from the night before, and cold biscuits. These were put on the table in front of her, and then the woman poured a cup of hot coffee and set it beside the plate.

Ruth began to eat as quickly as she could, sipping the hot black coffee and chewing the potatoes and bread while the brown-faced woman stood behind her at the door, where she could watch Ring and her by turns.

Twice Ruth managed to slip pieces of bread into her blouse, and finally she got half a potato into the pocket of her skirt. The woman eyed her suspiciously when she was not watching Ring in the yard outside.

"Going far?" the woman asked.

"Yes," Ruth answered.

"Come far?" the woman asked.

"Yes," Ruth said.

"Who is that man with you?"

"He's my husband," Ruth told her.

The woman looked out into the yard again, then back at Ruth. She did not say anything more for a while.

Ruth tried to put another piece of potato into her skirt pocket, but by then the woman was watching her more closely than ever.

"I don't believe he is your husband," the woman said.

"Well," Ruth answered, "he is."

"I wouldn't call him much of a husband to let you walk through the country begging food like you did just a little while ago."

"He's been sick," Ruth said quickly, turning in the chair to face the woman. "He was sick in bed for five weeks before we started out."

"Why didn't you stay where you were, instead of making

tramps out of yourselves? Can't he hold a job, or don't he want to work?"

Ruth got up, dropping the bread in her hand.

"Thank you for the breakfast," she said. "I am going now."

"If you take my advice," the woman said, "you'll leave that man the first chance you get. If he won't work at a job, you'll be a fool—"

"He had a job, but he got sick with a kind of fever."

"I don't believe you. I'd put you down for lying about him."

Ruth went to the door, opened it herself, and went outside. She turned around on the porch and looked at the woman who had given her something to eat.

"If he was sick in bed, like you said," the woman asked, following her past the door, "why did he get up and start tramping like this with nothing for you and him to eat?"

Ruth saw Ring sitting on the bench under the tree, and she was not going to answer the woman, but she could not keep from saying something.

"The reason we started out walking like this was because my sister wrote and told me that our baby had died. When my husband first got sick, I sent the baby to my sister's. Now we're going to see the grave where she's buried."

She ran down the steps and walked across the yard as rapidly as she could. When she reached the corner of the house, Ring got up and followed her to the road. Neither of them said anything, but she could not keep from looking back at the house, where the woman was watching them through the crack in the door.

After they had gone a hundred feet or more, Ruth unfastened her blouse and pulled out the pieces of bread she had carried there. Ring took them from her without a word. When he had eaten all there was, she gave him the potato. He ate it hungrily, talking to her with his eyes while he chewed and swallowed.

They had walked for nearly half an hour before either of them spoke again.

"She was a mean old woman," Ruth said. "If it hadn't been for the food, I'd have got up and left before I ate what she gave me."

Ring did not say anything for a long time. They had reached the bottom of the valley and were beginning to go up the grade on the other side before he spoke again. "Maybe if she had known where we were going, she might not have been so mean to you," Ring said.

Ruth choked back a sob.

"How much farther is it, Ring?"

"About thirty or forty miles."

"Will we get there tomorrow?"

He shook his head.

"The day after?"

"I don't know."

"Maybe if we get a ride, we might get there tonight?" she asked, unable to hold back any longer the sobs that choked her throat and breast.

"Yes," he said. "If we could get a ride, we would get there a lot sooner."

He turned his head and glanced down the road behind them, but there was nothing in sight. Then he looked down at the ground he was walking on, counting the steps he took with his right foot, and then his left.

(First published in the *New Yorker*)

Candy-Man Beechum

IT was ten miles out of the Ogeechee swamps, from the saw-mill to the top of the ridge, but it was just one big step to Candy-Man. The way he stepped over those Middle Georgia gullies was a sight to see.

"Where you goin', Candy-Man?"

"Make way for these flapping feet, boy, because I'm going for to see my gal. She's standing on the tips of her toes waiting for me now."

The rabbits lit out for the hollow logs where those stomping big feet couldn't get nowhere near them.

"Don't tread on no white-folks' toes, Candy-Man," Little Bo said. "Because the white-folks is first-come."

Candy-Man Beechum flung a leg over the rail fence just as if it had been a hoe handle to straddle. He stood for a minute astride the fence, looking at the black boy. It was getting dark in the swamps, and he had ten miles to go.

"Me and white-folks don't mix," Candy-Man told him, "just as long as they leave me be. I skin their mules for them, and I snake their cypress logs, but when the day is done, I'm long gone where the white-folks ain't are."

Owls in the trees began to take on life. Those whooing birds were glad to see that setting sun.

The black boy in the mule yard scratched his head and watched the sun go down. If he didn't have all those mules to feed, and if he had had a two-bit piece in his pocket, he'd have liked to tag along with Candy-Man. It was Saturday night, and there'd be a barrelful of catfish frying in town that evening. He wished he had some of that good-smelling cat.

"Before the time ain't long," Little Bo said, "I'm going to get me myself a gal."

"Just be sure she ain't Candy-Man's, boy, and I'll give you a helping hand."

He flung the other leg over the split-rail fence and struck out for the high land. Ten miles from the swamps to the top of the ridge, and his trip would be done. The bushes whipped around his legs, where his legs had been. He couldn't be waiting for the back-strike of no swamp-country bushes. Up the log road, and across the bottom land, taking three corn rows at a stride, Candy-Man Beechum was on his way.

There were some colored boys taking their time in the big road. He was up on them before they had time to turn their heads around.

"Make way for these flapping feet, boys," he shouted. "Here I come!"

"Where you going, Candy-Man?"

They had to do a lot of running to keep up with him. They had to hustle to match those legs four feet long. He made their breath come short.

"Somebody asked me where I'm going," Candy-Man said. "I got me a yellow gal, and I'm on my way to pay her some attention."

"You'd better toot your horn, Candy-Man, before you open her door. Yellow gals don't like to be taken by surprise."

"Boy, you're tooting the truth, except that you don't know the whyfor of what you're saying. Candy-Man's gal always waits for him right at the door."

"Saturday-night bucks sure have to hustle along. They have to strike pay before the Monday-morning whistle starts whipping their ears."

The boys fell behind, stopping to blow and wheeze. There was no keeping up, on a Saturday night, with the seven-foot mule skinner on his way.

The big road was too crooked and curvy for Candy-Man. He struck out across the fields, headed like a plumb line for a dishful of frying catfish. The lights of the town came up to meet him in the face like a swarm of lightning bugs. Eight miles to town, and two more to go, and he'd be rapping on that yellow gal's door.

Back in the big road, when the big road straightened out, Candy-Man swung into town. The old folks riding, and the young ones walking, they all made way for those flapping feet. The mules to the buggies and the sports in the middle of the road all got aside to let him through.

"What's your big hurry, Candy-Man?"

"Take care my dust don't choke you blind, niggers. I'm on my way."

"Where to, Candy-Man?"

"I got a gal what's waiting right at her door. She don't like for to be kept waiting."

"Better slow down and cool those heels, Candy-Man, because you're coming to the white-folks' town. They don't like niggers stepping on their toes."

"When the sun goes down, I'm on my own. I can't be stopping to see what color people be."

The old folks clucked, and the mules began to trot. They didn't like the way that big coon talked.

"How about taking me along, Candy-Man?" the young bucks begged. "I'd like to grab me a chicken off a hen-house roost."

"Where I'm going I'm the cock of the walk. I gouge my spurs in all strange feathers. Stay away, black boy, stay away."

Down the street he went, sticking to the middle of the road. The sidewalks couldn't hold him when he was in a hurry like that. A plateful of frying catfish, and he would be on his way. That yellow gal was waiting, and there was no time to lose. Eight miles covered, and two short ones to go. That sawmill fireman would have to pull on that Monday-morning whistle like it was the rope to the promised land.

The smell of the fish took him straight to the fish-house door. Maybe they were mullets, but they smelled just as good. There wasn't enough time to order up a special dish of fins.

He had his hand on the restaurant door. When he had his supper, he would be on his way. He could see that yellow gal waiting for him only a couple of miles away.

All those boys were sitting at their meal. The room was full of hungry people just like him. The stove was full of frying fish, and the barrel was only halfway used. There was enough good eating for a hundred hungry men.

He still had his hand on the fish-house door, and his nose was soaking it in. If he could have his way about it, some of these days he was going to buy himself a whole big barrel of catfish and eat them every one.

"What's your hurry, Candy-Man?"

"No time to waste, white-boss. Just let me be."

The night policeman snapped open the handcuffs, and reached for his arms. Candy-Man stepped away.

"I reckon I'd better lock you up. It'll save a lot of trouble. I'm getting good and tired of chasing fighting niggers all over town every Saturday night."

"I never hurt a body in all my life, white-boss. And I sure don't pick fights. You must have the wrong nigger, white-boss."

You sure has got me wrong. I'm just passing through for to see my gal."

"I reckon I'll play safe and lock you up till Monday morning just the same. Reach out your hands for these cuffs, nigger."

Candy-Man stepped away. His yellow gal was on his mind. He didn't feel like passing her up for no iron-bar jail. He stepped away.

"I'll shoot you down, nigger. One more step, and I'll blast away."

"White-boss, please just let me be. I won't even stop to get my supper, and I'll shake my legs right out of town. Because I just got to see my gal before the Monday-morning sun comes up."

Candy-Man stepped away. The night policeman threw down the handcuffs and jerked out his gun. He pulled the trigger at Candy-Man, and Candy-Man fell down.

"There wasn't no cause for that, white-boss. I'm just a big black nigger with itching feet. I'd a heap rather be traveling than standing still."

The people came running, but some of them turned around and went the other way. Some stood and looked at Candy-Man while he felt his legs to see if they could hold him up. He still had two miles to go before he could reach the top of the ridge.

The people crowded around, and the night policeman put away his gun. Candy-Man tried to get up so he could be getting on down the road. That yellow gal of his was waiting for him at her door, straining on the tips of her toes.

"White-boss, I sure am sorry you had to go and shoot me down. I never bothered white-folks, and they sure oughtn't bother me. But there ain't much use in living if that's the way it's going to be. I reckon I'll just have to blow out the light and fade away. Just reach me a blanket so I can cover my skin and bones."

"Shut up, nigger," the white-boss said. "If you keep on talking with that big mouth of yours, I'll just have to pull out my gun again and hurry you on."

The people drew back to where they wouldn't be standing too close. The night policeman put his hand on the butt of his gun, where it would be handy, in case.

"If that's the way it's to be, then make way for Candy-Man Beechum, because here I come."

(First published in *Kneel to the Rising Sun*)

Saturday Afternoon

TOM DENNY shoved the hunk of meat out of his way and stretched out on the meat block. He wanted to lie on his back and rest. The meat block was the only comfortable place in the butcher shop where a man could stretch out and Tom just had to rest every once in a while. He could prop his foot on the edge of the block, swing the other leg across his knee and be fairly comfortable with a hunk of rump steak under his head. The meat was nice and cool just after it came from the icehouse. Tom did that. He wanted to rest himself a while and he had to be comfortable on the meat block. He kicked off his shoes so he could wiggle his toes.

Tom's butcher shop did not have a very pleasant smell. Strangers who went in to buy Tom's meat for the first time were always asking him what it was that had died between the walls. The smell got worse and worse year after year.

Tom bit off a chew of tobacco and made himself comfortable on the meat block.

There was a swarm of flies buzzing around the place; those lazy, stinging, fat and greasy flies that lived in Tom's butcher shop. A screen door at the front kept out some of them that tried to get inside, but if they were used to coming in and filling up on the fresh blood on the meat block they knew how to fly around to the back door where there had never been a screen.

Everybody ate Tom's meat, and liked it. There was no other butcher shop in town. You walked in and said, "Hello, Tom. How's everything today?" "Everything's slick as a whistle with me, but my old woman's got the chills and fever again." Then after Tom had finished telling how it felt to have chills and fever, you said, "I want a pound of pork chops, Tom." And Tom said, "By gosh, I'll git it for you right away." While you stood around waiting for the chops Tom turned the hunk of beef over two or three times businesslike and hacked off a pound of pork for you. If you wanted veal it was all the same to Tom. He slammed the hunk of beef around several times making a great to-do, and got the veal for you. He pleased everybody. Ask Tom for any kind of meat you could name, and Tom had it right there on the meat block waiting to be cut off and weighed.

Tom brushed the flies off his face and took a little snooze. It was midday. The country people had not yet got to town. It was laying-by season and everybody was working right up to twelve o'clock sun time, which was half an hour slower than railroad time. There was hardly anybody in town at this time of day, even though it was Saturday. All the town people who had wanted some of Tom's meat for Saturday dinner had already got what they needed, and it was too early in the day to buy Sunday meat. The best time of day to get meat from Tom if it was to be kept over until Sunday was about ten o'clock Saturday night. Then you could take it home and be fairly certain that it would not turn bad before noon the next day—if the weather was not too hot.

The flies buzzed and lit on Tom's mouth and nose and Tom knocked them away with his hand and tried to sleep on the meat block with the cool hunk of rump steak under his head. The tobacco juice kept trying to trickle down his throat and Tom had to keep spitting it out. There was a cigar box half full of sawdust in the corner behind the showcase where livers and brains were kept for display, but he could not quite spit that far from the position he was in. The tobacco juice splattered on the floor midway between the meat block and cigar box. What little of it dripped on the piece of rump steak did not really matter: most people cleaned their meat before they cooked and ate it, and it would all wash off.

But the danged flies! They kept on buzzing and stinging as mean as ever, and there is nothing any meaner than a lazy, well-fed, butcher-shop fly in the summertime, anyway, Tom knocked them off his nose and spat them off his mouth the best he could without having to move too much. After a while he let them alone.

Tom was enjoying a good little snooze when Jim Baxter came running through the back door from the barbershop on the corner. Jim was Tom's partner and he came in sometimes on busy days to help out. He was a great big man, almost twice as large as Tom. He always wore a big wide-brimmed black hat and a blue shirt with the sleeves rolled up above his elbows. He had a large egg-shaped belly over which his breeches were always slipping down. When he walked he tugged at his breeches all the time, pulling them up over the top of his belly. But they were always working down until it looked as if they were ready to drop to the ground any minute and trip him. Jim would not wear suspenders. A belt was more sporty-looking.

Tom was snoozing away when Jim ran in the back door and grabbed him by the shoulders. A big handful of flies had gone to sleep on Tom's mouth. Jim shooed them off.

"Hey, Tom, Tom!" Jim shouted breathlessly. "Wake up, Tom! Wake up quick!"

Tom jumped to the floor and pulled on his shoes. He had become so accustomed to people coming in and waking him up to buy a quarter's worth of steak or a quarter's worth of ham that he had mistaken Jim for a customer. He rubbed the back of his hands over his mouth to take away the fly stings.

"What the hell!" he sputtered, looking up and seeing Jim standing there beside him. "What you want?"

"Come on, Tom! Git your gun! We're going after a nigger down the creek a ways."

"God Almighty, Jim!" Tom shouted, now fully awake. He clutched Jim's arm and begged: "You going to git a nigger, sure enough?"

"You're damn right, Tom. You know that gingerbread nigger what used to work on the railroad, a long time back? Him's the nigger we're going to git. And we're going to git him good and proper, the yellow-face coon. He said something to Fred Jackson's oldest gal down the road yonder about an hour ago. Fred told us all about it over at the barbershop. Come on, Tom. We got to hurry. I expect we'll jerk him up pretty soon now."

Tom tied on his shoes and ran across the street behind Jim. Tom had his shotgun under his arm, and Jim had pulled the cleaver out of the meat block. They'd get the God-damn nigger all right—God damn his yellow hide to hell!

Tom climbed into an automobile with some other men. Jim jumped on the running board of another car just as it was leaving. There were thirty or forty cars headed for the creek bottom already and more getting ready to start.

They had a place already picked out at the creek. There was a clearing in the woods by the road and there was just enough room to do the job like it should be done. Plenty of dry brushwood nearby and a good-sized sweetgum tree in the middle of the clearing. The automobiles stopped and the men jumped out in a hurry. Some others had gone for Will Maxie. Will was the gingerbread Negro. They would probably find him at home laying his cotton by. Will could grow good cotton. He cut out all the grass first, and then he banked his rows with earth. Everybody else laid his cotton by without going to the trouble of taking out the grass. But Will was a pretty smart Negro. And he could raise a lot of corn too, to the acre. He always cut out the grass before he laid his corn by. But nobody liked Will. He made too much money by taking out the grass before laying by his cotton and corn. He made more money than Tom and Jim made in the butcher shop selling people meat.

Doc Cromer had sent his boy down from the drugstore

with half a dozen cases of Coca-Cola and a piece of ice in a
wash tub. The tub had some muddy water put in it from the
creek, then the chunk of ice, and then three cases of Coca-
Cola. When they were gone the boy would put the other three
cases in the tub and give the dopes a chance to cool. Everybody likes to drink a lot of dopes when they are nice and cold.

Tom went out in the woods to take a drink of corn with
Jim and Hubert Wells. Hubert always carried a jug of corn
with him wherever he happened to be going. He made the
whisky himself at his own still and got a fairly good living
by selling it around the courthouse and the barbershop. Hubert made the best corn in the county.

Will Maxie was coming up the big road in a hurry. A couple
of dozen men were behind him poking him with sticks. Will
was getting old. He had a wife and three grown daughters, all
married and settled. Will was a pretty good Negro too, minding
his own business, stepping out of the road when he met a
white man, and otherwise behaving himself. But nobody liked
Will. He made too much money by taking the grass out of
his cotton before it was laid by.

Will came running up the road and the men steered him
into the clearing. It was all fixed. There was a big pile of
brushwood and a trace chain for his neck and one for his feet.
That would hold him. There were two or three cans of gasoline, too.

Doc Cromer's boy was doing a good business with his Coca-
Colas. Only five or six bottles of the first three cases were left
in the wash tub. He was getting ready to put the other cases
in now and give the dopes a chance to get nice and cool. Everybody likes to have a dope every once in a while.

The Cromer boy would probably sell out and have to go
back to town and bring back several more cases. And yet
there was not such a big crowd today, either. It was the hot
weather that made people have to drink a lot of dopes to stay
cool. There were only a hundred and fifty or seventy-five there
today. There had not been enough time for the word to get
passed around. Tom would have missed it if Jim had not run
in and told him about it while he was taking a nap on the
meat block.

Will Maxie did not drink Coca-Cola. Will never spent his
money on anything like that. That was what was wrong with
him. He was too damn good for a Negro. He did not drink
corn whisky, nor make it; he did not carry a knife, nor a
razor; he bared his head when he met a white man, and he
lived with his own wife. But they had him now! God damn
his gingerbread hide to hell! They had him where he could not
take any more grass out of his cotton before laying it by.
They had him tied to a sweet-gum tree in the clearing at the

creek with a trace chain around his neck and another around his knees. Yes, sir, they had Will Maxie now, the yellow-face coon! He would not take any more grass out of his cotton before laying it by!

Tom was feeling good. Hubert gave him another drink in the woods. Hubert was all right. He made good corn whisky. Tom liked him for that. And Hubert always took his wife a big piece of meat Saturday night to use over Sunday. Nice meat, too. Tom cut off the meat and Hubert took it home and made a present of it to his wife.

Will Maxie was going up in smoke. When he was just about gone they gave him the lead. Tom stood back and took good aim and fired away at Will with his shotgun as fast as he could breech it and put in a new load. About forty or more of the other men had shotguns too. They filled him so full of lead that his body sagged from his neck where the trace chain held him up.

The Cromer boy had sold completely out. All of his ice and dopes were gone. Doc Cromer would feel pretty good when his boy brought back all that money. Six whole cases he sold, at a dime a bottle. If he had brought along another case or two he could have sold them easily enough. Everybody likes Coca-Cola. There is nothing better to drink on a hot day, if the dopes are nice and cool.

After a while the men got ready to draw the body up in the tree and tie it to a limb so it could hang there, but Tom and Jim could not wait and they went back to town the first chance they got to ride. They were in a big hurry. They had been gone several hours and it was almost four o'clock. A lot of people came downtown early Saturday afternoon to get their Sunday meat before it was picked over by the country people. Tom and Jim had to hurry back and open up the meat market and get to work slicing steaks and chopping soupbones with the cleaver on the meat block. Tom was the butcher. He did all the work with the meat. He went out and killed a cow and quartered her. Then he hauled the meat to the butcher shop and hung it on the hooks in the icehouse. When somebody wanted to buy some meat, he took one of the quarters from the hook and threw it on the meat block and cut what you asked for. You told Tom what you wanted and he gave it to you, no matter what it was you asked for.

Then you stepped over to the counter and paid Jim the money for it. Jim was the cashier. He did all the talking, too. Tom had to do the cutting and weighing. Jim's egg-shaped belly was too big for him to work around the meat block. It got in his way when he tried to slice you a piece of tenderloin steak, so Tom did that and Jim took the money and put it into the cashbox under the counter.

Tom and Jim got back to town just in time. There was a big crowd standing around on the street getting ready to do their weekly trading, and they had to have some meat. You went in the butcher shop and said, "Hello, Tom. I want two pounds and a half of pork chops." Tom said, "Hello, I'll get it for you right away." While you were waiting for Tom to cut the meat off the hunk of rump steak you asked him how was everything.

"Everything's slick as a whistle," he said, "except my old woman's got the chills and fever pretty bad again."

Tom weighed the pork chops and wrapped them up for you and then you stepped over to Jim and paid him the money. Jim was the cashier. His egg-shaped belly was too big for him to work around the meat block. Tom did that part, and Jim took the money and put it into the cashbox under the counter.

(First published in *Nativity*)

The Strawberry Season

EARLY in the spring when the strawberries began to ripen, everybody went from place to place helping the farmers gather them. If it had been a good season for the berries and if there were many berries to pick, there would sometimes be as many as thirty-five or forty people in one field. Some men brought their families along, going from one farm to the next as fast as the berries could be gathered. They slept in barns or any place they could find. And, because the season was so short, everybody had to work from sunrise to sunset.

We used to have the best times picking strawberries. There were always a lot of girls there and it was great fun teasing them. If one of them stooped over a little too far and showed the least bit of herself, whoever saw her first shouted as loudly as he could. The rest of us would take up the yell and pass it all over the field. The other girls would giggle among themselves and pull their skirts down. The girl who had caused the shouting would blush and hurry away to the packing shed with a tray of baskets. By the time she returned some other girl had stooped over too far and everybody was laughing at her.

There was a girl named Fanny Forbes who was always showing some of herself by stooping over too far. Everybody liked Fanny.

Another thing we had a lot of fun out of was what we called "strawberry-slapping." One of us would slip up behind a girl while she was stooping over filling her baskets and drop a big juicy ripe strawberry down her dress. It usually stopped midway of her back and there we slapped it good and hard. The mashed strawberry made a mess. The red juice oozed through the cloth and made a big round stain. If the berry was against the skin it was even worse. Very few girls minded that though. Everybody wore his old clothes in the fields and it did not matter about the stain. The worst part was being laughed at. Everybody stopped picking berries to laugh. When that was over, everybody went back to work and forgot it until somebody else got strawberry-slapped. We had a lot of fun picking strawberries.

Fanny Forbes got more strawberry-slappings than any other girl. All the boys and men liked her and she never became angry. Fanny was good-looking, too.

One day I went to a field where I knew the strawberry crop was good. It was a small field of only two or three acres and few people ever bothered to go there. I decided to go before somebody else did.

When I reached the field, Fanny was finishing the first two rows. She had thought of having the whole field to herself, just as I had thought of doing. We did not mind the other being there as long as no one else came.

"Hello, Fanny," I said. "What made you think of coming over here to Mr. Gunby's place today?"

"The same thing that made you think of it, I guess," she answered, blowing the sand off a handful of berries and putting them into her mouth.

We started off side by side. Fanny was a fast picker and it was all I could do to keep up with her.

About an hour before noon the sun came out hot and the sky became cloudless. The berries were ripening almost as fast as we could gather them. Fanny filled a dozen boxes from her next row. She could pick all day and never have a single piece of vine among her berries. She used only the thumb and the next two fingers, making a kind of triangle that grasped the berry close to the stem and lifted it off. She never mashed a berry like some people were forever doing.

I had never before noticed it in any other field, but today Fanny was barelegged. In the afternoon it was much cooler without stockings, of course, and it was the best way to keep from wearing them out in the knees. She saw me looking at her bare legs and smiled just a little. I wanted to tell her how nice-looking they were but I did not dare to.

The midafternoon was even hotter than it had been at twelve o'clock. The slight breeze we had felt in the morning was gone and the sun hung over us like a burning glass. Fanny's legs were burned brown.

Before I knew what I was doing I stole up behind Fanny and dropped a great big juicy berry down the open neck of her dress. It frightened her at first. Believing that I was several rows away she thought it was a bug or insect of some kind that had fallen down the opening of her dress. When she jumped up and saw me standing behind her however she laughed and reached down into the bosom of her waist for the berry. I was certain I saw it under her dress. Before she could reach it with her hand I slapped it as hard as I could. I thought surely she would laugh as she had always done when somebody strawberry-slapped her, but this time she did not laugh. She sat down quickly, hugging herself tightly. I then realized something was wrong. She looked up at me and there were tears in her eyes. I fell on my knees beside her. I had slapped her breasts.

"What's the matter, Fanny?" I begged. "Did I hurt you? I didn't mean to. Honest, I didn't mean to."

"I know you didn't mean to," she said, the tears falling on her lap, "but it did hurt. You mustn't hit me there."

"I'll never do it again, Fanny. I promise I won't."

"It's all right now," she smiled painfully. "It still hurts a little though."

Her head fell on my shoulder. I put my arms around her. She wiped the tears from her eyes.

"It's all right now," she repeated. "It will stop hurting soon."

She lifted her head and smiled at me. Her large round blue eyes were the shade of the sky when the sun has begun to rise.

"I'll never strawberry-slap you again as long as I live, Fanny," I pleaded, hoping she would forgive me.

Fanny unbuttoned the dress down to her waist. The berry was mashed beneath her underclothes. The scarlet stain looked like a morning-glory against the white cloth.

"I'll have to unfasten this too, to get the berry out," she said.

"Let me get it," I urged. "You don't want the juice all over your fingers."

She unfastened the undergarment. The berry lay crushed between her breasts. They were milk-white and the center of
each was stained like a mashed strawberry. Hardly knowing
what I was doing I hugged her tightly in my arms and kissed
her lips for a long time. The crushed strawberry fell to the
ground beside us.

When we got up, the sun was setting and the earth was becoming cool. We found our boxes and baskets of berries and
walked across the fields to the barn. When we got there, Mr.
Gunby counted them and paid us the money we had earned.

We went through the barnyard to the front of the house
and stood at the gate looking at each other for several minutes.
Neither of us said anything. Fanny had once said she had
never had a sweetheart. I wish she had been mine.

Fanny turned and went down the road in one direction and
I went up the road in another. It was the end of the strawberry
season.

(First published in *Pagany*)

Maud Island

UNCLE MARVIN was worried. He got up from the log and
walked toward the river.

"I don't like the looks of it, boys," he said, whipping off
his hat and wiping his forehead.

The houseboat was drifting downstream at about three miles
an hour, and a man in a straw hat and sleeveless undershirt
was trying to pole it inshore. The man was wearing cotton
pants that had faded from dark brown to light tan.

"It looks bad," Uncle Marvin said, turning to Jim and me.
"I don't like the looks of it one whit."

"Maybe they are lost, Uncle Marvin," Jim said. "Maybe
they'll just stop to find out where they are, and then go on
away again."

"I don't believe it, son," he said, shaking his head and
wiping the perspiration from his face. "It looks downright bad
to me. That kind of a houseboat never has been out for no
good since I can remember."

On a short clothesline that stretched along the starboard
side, six or seven pieces of clothing hung waving in the breeze.

"It looks awful bad, son," he said again, looking down at
me.

We walked across the mud flat to the river and waited to see what the houseboat was going to do. Uncle Marvin took out his plug and cut off a chew of tobacco with his jackknife. The boat was swinging inshore, and the man with the pole was trying to beach it before the current cut in and carried them back to mid-channel. There was a power launch lying on its side near the stern, and on the launch was a towline that had been used for upstream going.

When the houseboat was two or three lengths from the shore, Uncle Marvin shouted at the man poling it.

"What's your name, and what do you want here?" he said gruffly, trying to scare the man away from the island.

Instead of answering, the man tossed a rope to us. Jim picked it up and started pulling, but Uncle Marvin told him to drop it. Jim dropped it, and the middle of the rope sank into the yellow water.

"What did you throw my rope in for?" the man on the houseboat shouted. "What's the matter with you?"

Uncle Marvin spat some tobacco juice and glared right back at him. The houseboat was ready to run on the beach.

"My name's Graham," the man said. "What's yours?"

"None of your business," Uncle Marvin shouted. "Get that raft away from here."

The houseboat began to beach. Graham dropped the pole on the deck and ran and jumped on the mud flat. He called to somebody inside while he was pulling the rope out of the water.

The stern swung around in the backwash of the current, and Jim grabbed my arm and pointed at the dim lettering on the boat. It said *Mary Jane,* and under that was *St. Louis.*

While we stood watching the man pull in the rope, two girls came out on the deck and looked at us. They were very young. Neither of them looked to be over eighteen or nineteen. When they saw Uncle Marvin, they waved at him and began picking up the boxes and bundles to carry off.

"You can't land that shantyboat on this island," Uncle Marvin said threateningly. "It won't do you no good to unload that stuff, because you'll only have to carry it all back again. No shantyboat's going to tie up on this island."

One of the girls leaned over the rail and looked at Uncle Marvin.

"Do you own this island, Captain?" she asked him.

Uncle Marvin was no river captain. He did not even look like one. He was the kind of man you could see plowing cotton on the steep hillsides beyond Reelfoot Lake. Uncle Marvin glanced at Jim and me for a moment, kicking at a gnarled root on the ground, and looked at the girl again.

"No," he said, pretending to be angry with her. "I don't

own it, and I wouldn't claim ownership of anything on the Mississippi, this side of the bluffs."

The other girl came to the rail and leaned over, smiling at Uncle Marvin.

"Hiding out, Captain?" she asked.

Uncle Marvin acted as though he would have had something to say to her if Jim and I had not been there to overhear him. He shook his head at the girl.

Graham began carrying off the boxes and bundles. Both Jim and I wished to help him so we would have a chance to go on board the houseboat, but we knew Uncle Marvin would never let us do that. The boat had been beached on the mud flat, and Graham had tied it up, knotting the rope around a young cypress tree.

When he had finished, he came over to us and held out his hand to Uncle Marvin. Uncle Marvin looked at Graham's hand, but he would not shake with him.

"My name's Harry Graham," he said. "I'm from up the river at Caruthersville. What's your name?"

"Hutchins," Uncle Marvin said, looking him straight in the eyes, "and I ain't hiding out."

The two girls, the dark one and the light one, were carrying their stuff across the island to the other side where the slough was. The island was only two or three hundred feet wide, but it was nearly half a mile long. It had been a sandbar to begin with, but it was already crowded with trees and bushes. The Mississippi was on the western side, and on the eastern side there was a slough that looked bottomless. The bluffs of the Tennessee shore were only half a mile in that direction.

"We're just on a little trip over the week end," Graham said. "The girls thought they would like to come down the river and camp out on an island for a couple of days."

"Which one is your wife?" Uncle Marvin asked him.

Graham looked at Uncle Marvin a little surprised for a minute. After that he laughed a little, and began kicking the ground with the toe of his shoe.

"I didn't quite catch what you said," he told Uncle Marvin.

"I said, which one is your wife?"

"Well, to tell the truth, neither of them. They're just good friends of mine, and we thought it would be a nice trip down the river and back for a couple of days. That's how it is."

"They're old enough to get married," Uncle Marvin told him, nodding at the girls.

"Maybe so," Graham said. "Come on over and I'll introduce you to them. They're Evansville girls, both of them. I used to work in Indiana, and I met them up there. That's where I got this houseboat. I already had the launch."

Uncle Marvin looked at the lettering on the *Mary Jane,* spelling out *St. Louis* to himself.

"Just a little fun for the week end," Graham said, smiling. "The girls like the river."

Uncle Marvin looked at Jim and me, jerking his head to one side and trying to tell us to go away. We walked down to the edge of the water where the *Mary Jane* was tied up, but we could still hear what they were saying. After a while, Uncle Marvin shook hands with Graham and started along up the shore towards our skiff.

"Come on, son, you and Milt," he said. "It's time to look at that taut line again."

We caught up with Uncle Marvin, and all of us got into the skiff, and Jim and I set the oarlocks. Uncle Marvin turned around so he could watch the people behind us on the island. Graham was carrying the heavy boxes to a clearing, and the two girls were unrolling the bundles and spreading them on the ground to air.

Jim and I rowed to the mouth of the creek and pulled alongside the taut line. Uncle Marvin got out his box of bait and began lifting the hooks and taking off catfish. Every time he found a hook with a catch, he took the cat off, spat over his left shoulder, and dropped it into the bucket and put on a new bait.

There was not much of a catch on the line that morning. After we had rowed across, almost to the current in the middle of the creek mouth, where the outward end of the line had been fastened to a cypress in the water, Uncle Marvin threw the rest of the bait overboard and told us to turn around and row back to Maud Island.

Uncle Marvin was a preacher. Sometimes he preached in the schoolhouse near home, and sometimes he preached in a dwelling. He had never been ordained, and he had never studied for the ministry, and he was not a member of any church. However, he believed in preaching, and he never let his lack of training stop him from delivering a sermon whenever a likely chance offered itself. Back home on the mainland, people called him Preacher Marvin, not so much for the fact that he was a preacher, but because he looked like one. That was one reason why he had begun preaching at the start. People had got into the habit of calling him Preacher Marvin, and before he was forty he had taken up the ministry as a calling. He had never been much of a farmer, anyway—a lot of people said that.

Our camp on Maud Island was the only one on the river for ten or fifteen miles. The island was only half a mile from shore, where we lived in Tennessee, and Uncle Marvin brought us out to spend the week end five or six times during the summer. When we went back and forth between the mainland and the island, we had to make a wide circle, nearly two miles out of the way, in order to keep clear of the slough. The slough was a mass of yellow mud, rotting trees, and whatever drift happened to get caught in it. It was almost impossible to get through it, either on foot or in a flat-bottomed boat, and we kept away from it as far as possible. Sometimes mules and cows started out in it from the mainland to reach the island, but they never got very far before they dropped out of sight. The slough sucked them down and closed over them like quicksand.

Maud Island was a fine place to camp, though. It was the highest ground along the river for ten or fifteen miles, and there was hardly any danger of its being flooded when the high water covered everything else within sight. When the river rose to forty feet, however, the island, like everything else in all directions, was covered with water from the Tennessee bluffs to the Missouri highlands, seven or eight miles apart.

When we got back from baiting the taut line, Uncle Marvin told us to build a good fire while he was cleaning the catch of catfish and cutting them up for frying. Jim went off after an armful of driftwood while I was blowing the coals in the camp-fire. Jim brought the wood and built the fire, and I watched the pail of water hanging over it until Uncle Marvin was ready to make the coffee.

In the middle of the afternoon Uncle Marvin woke up from his midday nap and said it was too hot to sleep any longer. We sat around for ten or fifteen minutes, nobody saying much, and after a while Uncle Marvin got up and said he thought he would walk over to the other camp and see how the people from Caruthersville, or Evansville, or wherever they came from, were getting along.

Jim and I were up and ready to go along, but he shook his head and told us to stay there. We could not help feeling that there was something unusual about that, because Uncle Marvin had always taken us with him no matter where he went when we were camping on the island. When Jim said something about going along, Uncle Marvin got excited and told us to do as he said, or we would find ourselves being sorry.

"You boys stay here and take it easy," he said. "I've got to find out what kind of people they are before we start in to mix with them. They're from up the river, and there's no telling what they're like till I get to know them. You boys just stay here and take it easy till I get back."

After he had gone, we got up and picked our way through the dry underbrush toward the other camp. Jim kept urging me to hurry so we would not miss seeing anything, but I was afraid we would make so much noise Uncle Marvin would hear us and run back and catch us looking.

"Uncle Marvin didn't tell them he's a preacher," Jim said. "Those girls think he's a river captain, and I'll bet he wants them to keep on thinking so."

"He doesn't look like a river captain. He looks like a preacher. Those girls were just saying that for fun."

"The dark one acted like she's foolish about Uncle Marvin," Jim said. "I could tell."

"That's Jean," I said.

"How do you know what their names are?"

"Didn't you hear Graham talking to them when they were carrying their stuff off that houseboat?"

"Maybe he did," Jim said.

"He called that one Jean, and the light one Marge."

Jim bent down and looked through the bushes.

"Uncle Marvin's not mad at them now for coming here to camp," he said.

"How can you tell he's not?" I asked Jim.

"I can tell by the way he's acting up now."

"He told Graham to get the houseboat away from here, didn't he?"

"Sure he did then," Jim whispered, "but that was before those two girls came outside and leaned over the railing and talked to him. After he saw them a while he didn't try to stop Graham from landing, did he?"

We had crawled as close as we dared go, and fifty feet away we could see everything that was going on in Graham's camp. When Uncle Marvin walked up, Graham was sitting against the trunk of a cypress trying to untangle a fishing line, and the two girls were lying in hammocks that had been hung up between trees. We could not see either of them very well then, because the sides of the hammocks hid them, but the sun was shining down into the clearing and it was easy to see them when they moved or raised their arms.

Five or six cases of drinks were stacked up against one of the trees where the hammocks were, and several bottles had already been opened and tossed aside empty. Graham had a bottle of beer beside him on the ground, and every once in a while he stopped tussling with the tangled fishing line and grabbed the bottle and took several swallows from it. The dark girl, Jean, had a bottle in her hand, half full, and Marge was juggling an empty bottle in the air over her head. Everybody looked as if he was having the best time of his life.

None of them saw Uncle Marvin when he got to the clearing. Graham was busy fooling with the tangled fishing line, and Uncle Marvin stopped and looked at all three of them for almost a minute before he was noticed.

"I'll bet Uncle Marvin takes a bottle," Jim said. "What do
you bet?"

"Preachers don't drink beer, do they?"

"Uncle Marvin will, I'll bet anything," Jim said. "You know
Uncle Marvin."

Just then Graham raised his head from the line and saw
Uncle Marvin standing not ten feet away. Graham jumped up
and said something to Uncle Marvin. It was funny to watch
them, because Uncle Marvin was not looking at Graham at
all. His head was turned in the other direction all the time,
and he was looking where the girls lay stretched out in the
hammocks. He could not take his eyes off them long enough
to glance at Graham. Graham kept on saying something, but
Uncle Marvin acted as though he was on the other side of the
river beyond earshot.

Jean and Marge pulled the sides of the hammocks over
them, but they could not make Uncle Marvin stop looking at
them. He started to grin, but he turned red in the face instead.

Graham picked up a bottle and offered it to Uncle Marvin.
He took it without even looking at it once, and held it out in
front of him as if he did not know he had it in his hand. When
Graham saw that he was not making any effort to open it, he
took it and put the cap between his teeth and popped it off as
easily as he could have done with a bottle opener.

The beer began to foam then, and Uncle Marvin shoved the
neck of the bottle into his mouth and turned it upside down.
The foam that had run out on his hand before he could get the
bottle into his mouth was dripping down his shirt front and
making a dark streak on the blue cloth.

Jean leaned out of her hammock and reached to the ground
for another bottle. She popped off the cap with a bottle opener
and lay down again.

"Did you see that, Milt?" Jim whispered, squeezing my arm.
He whistled a little between his teeth.

"I saw a lot!" I said.

"I didn't know girls ever did like that where everybody
could see them," he said.

"They're from up the river," I told him. "Graham said they
were from Evansville."

"That don't make any difference," Jim said, shaking his
head. "They're girls, aren't they? Well, whoever saw girls lie
in hammocks naked like that? I know I never did before!"

"I sure never saw any like those before, either," I told him.

Uncle Marvin had gone to the tree at the foot of one of the
hammocks, and he was standing there, leaning against it a
little, with the empty bottle in his hand, and looking straight
at them.

Graham was trying to talk to him, but Uncle Marvin would

not pay attention to what Graham was trying to say. Jean had turned loose the sides of the hammock, and Marge, too, and they were laughing and trying to make Uncle Marvin say something. Uncle Marvin's mouth was hanging open, but his face was not red any more.

"Why doesn't he tell them he's a preacher?" I asked Jim, nudging him with my elbow.

"Maybe he will after a while," Jim said, standing on his toes and trying to see better through the undergrowth.

"It looks to me like he's not going to tell them," I said. "It wouldn't make any difference, anyway, because Uncle Marvin isn't a real preacher. He only preaches when he feels like doing it."

"That doesn't make any difference," Jim said.

"Why doesn't it?"

"It just doesn't, that's why."

"But he calls himself a preacher, just the same."

"He doesn't have to be a preacher now if he doesn't want to be one. If he told them he was a preacher, they'd all jump up and run and hide from him."

Uncle Marvin was still standing against the tree looking at the dark girl, and Graham was a little to one side of him, looking as if he didn't know what to do next.

Presently Uncle Marvin jerked himself erect and turned his head in all directions listening for sounds. He looked towards us, but he could not see us. Jim got down on his hands and knees to be out of sight, and I got behind him.

The three others were laughing and talking, but not Uncle Marvin. He looked at them a while longer, and then he reached down to the top case against the cypress and lifted out another bottle. Graham reached to open it for him, but Uncle Marvin bit his teeth over the cap and popped it off. The beer began to foam right away, but before much of it could run out, Uncle Marvin had turned it up and was drinking it down.

When the bottle was empty, he wiped his mouth with the back of his hand and took three or four steps towards the dark girl in the hammock. Jean kicked her feet into the air and pulled the sides of the hammock around her. The other girl sat up to watch Uncle Marvin.

All at once he stopped and looked towards our camp on the other side of the island. There was not a sound anywhere, except the sucking sound in the slough that went on all the time, and the sharp slap of water against the sides of the houseboat. He listened for another moment, cocking his head like a dog getting ready to jump a rabbit, and broke into a run, headed for our camp. Jim and I just barely got there before Uncle Marvin. We were both puffing and blowing after running so fast, but Uncle Marvin was blowing even harder and he did not notice how short our breath was. He stopped and looked down at the dead fire for a while before he spoke to us.

"Get ready to go home, son, you and Jim," he said. "We've got to leave right now."

He started throwing our stuff into a pile and stamping out the ashes at the same time, He turned around and spat some tobacco juice on the live coals and grabbed up an armful of stuff. He did not wait for us to help him, but started for our skiff on the mud flat right away with a big load of stuff in both arms. Jim and I had to hurry to catch up with him so he would not forget and leave us behind.

He took the oars from us and shoved off without waiting for us to do it for him. When we were out of the mouth of the creek, he took his hat off and threw it on the bottom of the skiff and bent over the oars harder than ever. Jim and I could not do a thing to help, because there were only two oars and he would not turn either one of them loose.

Nobody said a thing while we were rowing around the slough. When we got within a hundred feet of shore, Uncle Marvin started throwing our stuff into a heap in the stern. We had no more than dragged bottom on shore when he picked up the whole lot and threw the stuff on the dried mud. The pans and buckets rolled in every direction.

Both of us were scared to say a word to Uncle Marvin because he had never acted like that before. We stood still and watched him while he shoved off into the river and turned the skiff around and headed around the slough. We were scared to death for a while, because we had never seen anybody cut across so close to the slough. He knew where he was all the time, but he did not seem to care how many chances he took of being sucked down into the slough. The last we saw of him was when he went out of sight around Maud Island.

We picked up our things and started running with them towards home. All the way there we were in too much of a hurry to say anything to each other. It was about a mile and a half home, and upgrade every step of the way, but we ran the whole distance, carrying our heavy stuff on our backs.

When we reached the front gate, Aunt Sophie ran out on the porch to meet us. She had seen us running up the road from the river, and she was surprised to see us back home so soon. When we left with Uncle Marvin early that morning, we thought we were going to stay a week on Maud Island. Aunt Sophie looked down the road to see if she could see anything of Uncle Marvin.

Jim dropped his load of stuff and sank down on the porch steps panting and blowing.

"Where's your Uncle Marvin, Milton?" Aunt Sophie asked

us, standing above me and looking down at us with her hands on her hips. "Where's Marvin Hutchins?"

I shook my head the first thing, because I did not know what to say.

"Where's your Uncle Marvin, James?" she asked Jim.

Jim looked at me, and then down again at the steps. He tried to keep Aunt Sophie's eyes from looking straight into his.

Aunt Sophie came between us and shook Jim by the shoulder. She shook him until his hair tumbled over his face, and his teeth rattled until they sounded as if they were loose in his mouth.

"Where is your Uncle Marvin, Milton?" she demanded, coming to me and shaking me worse than she had Jim. "Answer me this minute, Milton!"

When I saw how close she was to me, I jumped up and ran out into the yard out of her reach. I knew how hard she could shake when she wanted to. It was lots worse than getting a whipping with a peach-tree switch.

"Has that good-for-nothing scamp gone and taken up with a shantyboat wench again?" she said, running back and forth between Jim and me.

I had never heard Aunt Sophie talk like that before, and I was so scared I could not make myself say a word. I had never heard her call Uncle Marvin anything like that before, either. As a rule she never paid much attention to him, except when she wanted him to chop some stovewood, or something like that.

Jim sat up and looked at Aunt Sophie. I could see that he was getting ready to say something about the way she talked about Uncle Marvin. Jim was always taking up for him whenever Aunt Sophie started in on him.

Jim opened his mouth to say something, but the words never came out.

"One of you is going to answer me!" Aunt Sophie said. "I'll give you one more chance to talk, Milton."

"He didn't say where he was going or what he was going to do, Aunt Sophie. Honest, he didn't!"

"Milton Hutchins!" she said, stamping her foot.

"Honest, Aunt Sophie!" I said. "Maybe he went off somewhere to preach."

"Preach, my foot!" she cried, jamming her hands on her hips. "Preach! If that good-for-nothing scalawag preached half as many sermons as he makes out like he does, he'd have the whole country saved for God long before now! Preach! Huh! Preach, my foot! That's his excuse for going off from home whenever he gets the notion to cut-up-jack, but he never fools me. And I can make a mighty good guess where he is this very minute, too. He's gone chasing off after some shantyboat wench! Preach, my foot!"

Jim looked at me, and I looked at Jim. To save our life we could not see how Aunt Sophie had found out about the two girls from Evansville on Maud Island.

Aunt Sophie jammed her hands on her hips a little harder and motioned to us with her head. We followed her into the house.

"We're going to have a house cleaning around this place," she said. "James, you bring the brooms. Milton, you go start a fire under the wash-pot in the back yard and heat it full of water. When you get it going good, come in here and sweep down the cobwebs off the ceilings."

Aunt Sophie went from room to room, slamming doors behind her. She began ripping curtains down from the windows and pulling the rugs from the floor. A little later we could hear the swish of her broom, and presently a dense cloud of dust began blowing through the windows.

(First published in the *Brooklyn Eagle*)

Warm River

THE driver stopped at the suspended footbridge and pointed out to me the house across the river. I paid him the quarter fare for the ride from the station two miles away and stepped from the car. After he had gone I was alone with the chill night and the star-pointed lights twinkling in the valley and the broad green river flowing warm below me. All around me the mountains rose like black clouds in the night, and only by looking straight heavenward could I see anything of the dim afterglow of sunset.

The creaking footbridge swayed with the rhythm of my stride and the momentum of its swing soon overcame my pace. Only by walking faster and faster could I cling to the pendulum as it swung in its wide arc over the river. When at last I could see the other side, where the mountain came down abruptly and slid under the warm water, I gripped my hand-bag tighter and ran with all my might.

Even then, even after my feet had crunched upon the gravel path, I was afraid. I knew that by day I might walk the bridge without fear; but at night, in a strange country, with dark mountains towering all around me and a broad green river flowing beneath me, I could not keep my hands from trembling and my heart from pounding against my chest.

I found the house easily, and laughed at myself for having run from the river. The house was the first one to come upon after leaving the footbridge, and even if I should have missed it, Gretchen would have called me. She was there on the steps of the porch waiting for me. When I heard her familiar voice calling my name, I was ashamed of myself for having been frightened by the mountains and the broad river flowing below.

She ran down the gravel path to meet me.

"Did the footbridge frighten you, Richard?" she asked excitedly, holding my arm with both of her hands and guiding me up the path to the house.

"I think it did, Gretchen," I said; "but I hope I outran it."

"Everyone tries to do that at first, but after going over it once, it's like walking a tightrope. I used to walk tightropes when I was small—didn't you do that, too, Richard? We had a rope stretched across the floor of our barn to practice on."

"I did, too, but it's been so long I've forgotten how to do it now."

We reached the steps and went up to the porch. Gretchen took me to the door. Someone inside the house was bringing a lamp into the hall, and with the coming of the light I saw Gretchen's two sisters standing just inside the open door.

"This is my little sister, Anne," Gretchen said. "And this is Mary."

I spoke to them in the semidarkness, and we went on into the hall. Gretchen's father was standing beside a table holding the lamp a little to one side so that he could see my face. I had not met him before.

"This is my father," Gretchen said. "He was afraid you wouldn't be able to find our house in the dark."

"I wanted to bring a light down to the bridge and meet you, but Gretchen said you would get here without any trouble. Did you get lost? I could have brought a lantern down with no trouble at all."

I shook hands with him and told him how easily I had found the place.

"The hack driver pointed out to me the house from the other side of the river, and I never once took my eyes from the light. If I had lost sight of the light, I'd probably be stumbling around somewhere now in the dark down there getting ready to fall into the water."

He laughed at me for being afraid of the river.

"You wouldn't have minded it. The river is warm. Even in winter, when there is ice and snow underfoot, the river is as warm as a comfortable room. All of us here love the water down there."

"No, Richard, you wouldn't have fallen in," Gretchen said, laying her hand in mine. "I saw you the moment you got out of the hack, and if you had gone a step in the wrong direction, I was ready to run to you."

I wished to thank Gretchen for saying that, but already she was going to the stairs to the floor above, and calling me. I went with her, lifting my handbag in front of me. There was a shaded lamp, lighted but turned low, on the table at the end of the upper hall, and she picked it up and went ahead into one of the front rooms.

We stood for a moment looking at each other, and silent.

"There is fresh water in the pitcher, Richard. If there is anything else you would like to have, please tell me. I tried not to overlook anything."

"Don't worry, Gretchen," I told her. "I couldn't wish for anything more. It's enough just to be here with you, anyway. There's nothing else I care for."

She looked at me quickly, and then she lowered her eyes. We stood silently for several minutes, while neither of us could think of anything to say. I wanted to tell her how glad I was to be with her, even if it was only for one night, but I knew I could say that to her later. Gretchen knew why I had come.

"I'll leave the lamp for you, Richard, and I'll wait downstairs for you on the porch. Come as soon as you are ready."

She had left before I could offer to carry the light to the stairhead for her to see the way down. By the time I had picked up the lamp, she was out of sight down the stairs.

I walked back into the room and closed the door and bathed my face and hands, scrubbing the train dust with brush and soap. There was a row of hand-embroidered towels on the rack, and I took one and dried my face and hands. After that I combed my hair, and found a fresh handkerchief in the handbag. Then I opened the door and went downstairs to find Gretchen.

Her father was on the porch with her. When I walked through the doorway, he got up and gave me a chair between them. Gretchen pulled her chair closer to mine, touching my arm with her hand.

"Is this the first time you have been up here in the mountains, Richard?" her father asked me, turning in his chair towards me.

"I've never been within a hundred miles of here before, sir. It's a different country up here, but I suppose you would think the same about the coast, wouldn't you?"

"Oh, but Father used to live in Norfolk," Gretchen said. "Didn't you, Father?"

"I lived there for nearly three years."

There was something else he would say, and both of us waited for him to continue.

"Father is a master mechanic," Gretchen whispered to me. "He works in the railroad shops."

"Yes," he said after a while, "I've lived in many places, but here is where I wish to stay."

My first thought was to ask him why he preferred the mountains to other sections, but suddenly I was aware that both he and Gretchen were strangely silent. Between them, I sat wondering about it.

After a while he spoke again, not to me and not to Gretchen, but as though he were speaking to someone else on the porch, a fourth person whom I had failed to see in the darkness. I waited, tense and excited, for him to continue.

Gretchen moved her chair a few inches closer to mine, her motions gentle and without sound. The warmth of the river came up and covered us like a blanket on a chill night.

"After Gretchen and the other two girls lost their mother," he said, almost inaudibly, bending forward over his knees and gazing out across the broad green river, "after we lost their mother, I came back to the mountains to live. I couldn't stay in Norfolk, and I couldn't stand it in Baltimore. This was the only place on earth where I could find peace. Gretchen remembers her mother, but netiher of you can yet understand how it is with me. Her mother and I were born here in the mountains, and we lived here together for almost twenty years. Then after she left us, I moved away, foolishly believing that I could forget. But I was wrong. Of course I was wrong. A man can't forget the mother of his children, even though he knows he will never see her again."

Gretchen leaned closer to me, and I could not keep my eyes from her darkly framed profile beside me. The river below us made no sound; but the warmth of its vapor would not let me forget that it was still there.

Her father had bent farther forward in his chair until his arms were resting on his knees, and he seemed to be trying to see someone on the other side of the river, high on the mountain top above it. His eyes strained, and the shaft of light that came through the open doorway fell upon them and glistened there. Tears fell from his face like fragments of stars, burning into his quivering hands until they were out of sight.

Presently, still in silence, he got up and moved through the doorway. His huge shadow fell upon Gretchen and me as he stood there momentarily before going inside. I turned and looked towards him but, even though he was passing from sight, I could not keep my eyes upon him.

Gretchen leaned closer against me, squeezing her fingers

into the hollow of my hand and touching my shoulder with her cheeks as though she were trying to wipe something from them. Her father's footsteps grew fainter, and at last we could no longer hear him.

Somewhere below us, along the bank of the river, an express train crashed down the valley, creaking and screaming through the night. Occasionally its lights flashed through the openings in the darkness, dancing on the broad green river like polar lights in the north, and the metallic echo of its steel rumbled against the high walls of the mountains.

Gretchen clasped her hands tightly over my hand, trembling to her fingertips.

"Richard, why did you come to see me?"

Her voice was mingled with the screaming metallic echo of the train that now seemed far off.

I had expected to find her looking up into my face, but when I turned to her, I saw that she was gazing far down into the valley, down into the warm waters of the river. She knew why I had come, but she did not wish to hear me say why I had.

I do not know why I had come to see her, now. I had liked Gretchen, and I had desired her above anyone else I knew. But I could not tell her that I loved her, after having heard her father speak of love. I was sorry I had come, now after having heard him speak of Gretchen's mother as he did. I knew Gretchen would give herself to me, because she loved me; but I had nothing to give her in return. She was beautiful, very beautiful, and I had desired her. That was before. Now, I knew that I could never again think of her as I had come prepared.

"Why did you come, Richard?"

"Why?"

"Yes, Richard; why?"

My eyes closed, and what I felt was the memory of the star-pointed lights twinkling down in the valley and the warmth of the river flowing below and the caress of her fingers as she touched my arm.

"Richard, please tell me why you came."

"I don't know why I came, Gretchen."

"If you only loved me as I love you, Richard, you would know why."

Her fingers trembled in my hand. I knew she loved me. There had been no doubt in my mind from the first. Gretchen loved me.

"Perhaps I should not have come," I said. "I made a mistake, Gretchen. I should have stayed away."

"But you will be here only for tonight, Richard. You are leaving early in the morning. You aren't sorry that you came for just this short time, are you, Richard?"

"I'm not sorry that I am here, Gretchen, but I should not have come. I didn't know what I was doing. I haven't any right to come here. People who love each other are the only ones—"

"But you do love me just a little, don't you, Richard? You couldn't possibly love me nearly so much as I love you, but can't you tell me that you do love me just a little? I'll feel much happier after you have gone, Richard."

"I don't know," I said, trembling.

"Richard, please—"

With her hands in mine I held her tightly. Suddenly I felt something coming over me, a thing that stabbed my body with its quickness. It was as if the words her father had uttered were becoming clear to me. I had not realized before that there was such a love as he had spoken of. I had believed that men never loved women in the same way that a woman loved a man, but now I knew there could be no difference.

We sat silently, holding each other's hands for a long time. It was long past midnight, because the lights in the valley below were being turned out; but time did not matter.

Gretchen clung softly to me, looking up into my face and laying her cheek against my shoulder. She was as much mine as a woman ever belongs to a man, but I knew then that I could never force myself to take advantage of her love, and to go away knowing that I had not loved her as she loved me. I had not believed any such thing when I came. I had traveled all that distance to hold her in my arms for a few hours, and then to forget her, perhaps forever.

When it was time for us to go into the house, I got up and put my arms around her. She trembled when I touched her, but she clung to me as tightly as I held her, and the hammering of her heart drove into me, stroke after stroke, like an expanding wedge, the spears of her breasts.

"Richard, kiss me before you go," she said.

She ran to the door, holding it open for me. She picked up the lamp from the table and walked ahead up the stairs to the floor above.

At my door she waited until I could light her lamp, and then she handed me mine.

"Good night, Gretchen," I said.

"Good night, Richard."

I turned down the wick of her lamp to keep it from smoking, and then she went across the hall towards her room.

"I'll call you in the morning in time for you to catch your train, Richard."

"All right, Gretchen. Don't let me oversleep, because it leaves the station at seven-thirty."

"I'll wake you in plenty of time, Richard," she said.

The door was closed after her, and I turned and went into my room. I shut the door and slowly began to undress. After I had blown out the lamp and had got into bed, I lay tensely awake. I knew I could never go to sleep, and I sat up in bed and smoked cigarette after cigarette, blowing the smoke through the screen at the window. The house was quiet. Occasionally, I thought I heard the sounds of muffled movements in Gretchen's room across the hall, but I was not certain.

I could not determine how long a time I had sat there on the edge of the bed, stiff and erect, thinking of Gretchen, when suddenly I found myself jumping to my feet. I opened the door and ran across the hall. Gretchen's door was closed, but I knew it would not be locked, and I turned the knob noiselessly. A slender shaft of light broke through the opening I had made. It was not necessary to open the door wider, because I saw Gretchen only a few steps away, almost within arm's reach of me. I closed my eyes tightly for a moment, thinking of her as I had all during the day's ride up from the coast.

Gretchen had not heard me open her door, and she did not know I was there. Her lamp was burning brightly on the table.

I had not expected to find her awake, and I had thought surely she would be in bed. She knelt on the rug beside her bed, her head bowed over her arms and her body shaken with sobs.

Gretchen's hair was lying over her shoulders, tied over the top of her head with a pale blue ribbon. Her nightgown was white silk, hemmed with a delicate lace, and around her neck the collar of lace was throw open.

I knew how beautiful she was when I saw her then, even though I had always thought her lovely. I had never seen a girl so beautiful as Gretchen.

She had not heard me at her door, and she still did not know I was there. She knelt beside her bed, her hands clenched before her, crying.

When I had first opened the door, I did not know what I was about to do; but now that I had seen her in her room, kneeling in prayer beside her bed, unaware that I was looking upon her and hearing her words and sobs, I was certain that I could never care for anyone else as I did for her. I had not known until then, but in the revelation of a few seconds I knew that I did love her.

I closed the door softly and went back to my room. There I found a chair and placed it beside the window to wait for the coming of day. At the window I sat and looked down into the bottom of the valley where the warm river lay. As my eyes grew more accustomed to the darkness, I felt as if I were coming closer and closer to it, so close that I might have reached out and touched the warm water with my hands.

Later in the night, towards morning, I thought I heard someone in Gretchen's room moving softly over the floor as one who would go from window to window. Once I was certain I heard someone in the hall, close to my door.

When the sun rose over the top of the mountain, I got up and dressed. Later, I heard Gretchen leave her room and go downstairs. I knew she was hurrying to prepare breakfast for me before I left to get on the train. I waited awhile, and after a quarter of an hour I heard her coming back up the stairs. She knocked softly on my door, calling my name several times.

I jerked open the door and faced her. She was so surprised at seeing me there, when she had expected to find me still asleep, that she could not say anything for a moment.

"Gretchen," I said, grasping her hands, "don't hurry to get me off—I'm not going back this morning—I don't know what was the matter with me last night—I know now that I love you—"

"But, Richard—last night you said—"

"I did say last night that I was going back early this morning, Gretchen, but I didn't know what I was talking about. I'm not going back now until you go with me. I'll tell you what I mean as soon as breakfast is over. But first of all I wish you would show me how to get down to the river. I have got to go down there right away and feel the water with my hands."

(First published in *Pagany*)

Snacker

FRIDAY morning classes were over, and Snacker was walking down the third-floor hall of the dormitory to leave his books in his room when Pete Downs saw him. There were a couple of other fellows in Pete's room, and the door was open. Snacker saw them. He owed Pete forty cents, and he thought Pete was going to say he had to have the money right then.

"Hey, Snacker!" Pete yelled. "Come here a minute."

Snacker went back to the door and looked inside. Tom and Jack Phillips were sitting on a trunk whistling, and Pete was motioning to him to come inside.

"I haven't got a nickel on me, Pete," he said. "But just as soon as I can get it, I'll pay you back."

"Forget it, Snacker," Pete said. "Come over here. I want to show you a sight you've never seen before."

Snacker sat down on the bed beside him and looked at the picture Pete held in front of him.

"Who's that?" Snacker asked.

"My girl," Pete said. "Ever see anything in your life to beat that?"

Snacker shook his head.

"She's all right, Pete," he said.

"All right!" Pete said. "She's going to be the best-looking honeybunch at the banquet tomorrow night. That's how 'all right' she is!"

Tom and Jack Phillips were whistling louder than ever. Every time they looked at Pete they began whistling in a higher key.

Pete nodded towards them.

"Don't let them worry you, Snacker," he said. "They might think they're going to have better-looking girls at the dinner, but they'll be whistling a different tune after they see my girl. She's coming all the way from the old home town just to show this school what a pretty girl looks like."

Snacker had forgotten that the football banquet was only one day off. It was the week after Thanksgiving, and the annual football banquet was always given the Saturday night after the holidays.

Tom stopped whistling.

"Who's your girl, Snacker?" he asked. "Who are you bringing to the banquet?"

"Me?" Snacker said. "I haven't got a girl, Tom. I'll have to go by myself."

Everybody stared at Snacker.

"You can't do that, Snacker," Jack Phillips said. "They won't let you in at the door unless you have a girl with you."

Snacker looked at Pete and then at Tom. They nodded. Snacker began to worry. He had forgotten all about that rule.

"You can't go without a girl," Tom said. "Don't you know somebody to bring?"

Jack leaned forward and frowned at Snacker.

"Haven't you got a girl, Snacker?" he asked.

"Gee-my-nettie!" Snacker said aloud. "I never had a girl in all my life."

Tom whistled through his teeth, and Pete laughed. They looked at Snacker curiously for a moment.

"That's too bad, Snacker," Pete said finally. "You put in a lot of hard work on the squad this season. It would be a shame for you not to go to the banquet and get all you want to eat."

"You played a full quarter in the Riverside game, didn't

you, Snacker?" Jack Phillips said. "Didn't you go in at left tackle the last quarter when Chuck Harris got knocked out?"

"Sure," Snacker said. "And I never missed a day's practice, either. I was on the scrubs all the rest of the time, but I tried like the dickens to make the first team."

"You've got as much right to go to the banquet as the captain," Pete said. "It's a shame you have to stay away just because you don't have a girl like the rest of us fellows."

"Maybe I could ask one of the girls in town to go with me?" Snacker suggested eagerly.

Everybody looked at the floor. Pete shook his head. Tom and Jack Phillips shook their heads, too. Snacker knew at once what they were thinking.

"All the town girls have been dated up for the banquet ever since school opened in September," Pete said. "It's too late to try to get hold of a girl anywhere else now. I wish we had thought about it sooner, Snacker."

Snacker sat up.

"How about that Harper girl?" he asked. "You know the one I mean—Frances Harper."

They looked at Snacker rather hard for a moment, and then they shook their heads and stared at the floor.

"Frances Harper is Chuck's girl, Snacker. She's going to sit at the head of the table with Chuck—at the captain's end."

"Well," Snacker said, slamming his books on the table, "if I had known about it in time, I'd have had the prettiest girl in the state here tomorrow night. You can bet your life I would."

Jack Phillips jumped up.

"The prettiest girl in the state?" he said, laughing. "Stop your joking, Snacker. The prettiest girl in the state lives in Saunderstown."

"What's her name?" Snacker asked.

"I don't know what her name is, but I saw her once in my life. I tried to get introduced to her, but it was at a dance in Saunderstown and there were about forty ahead of me in the line, and I never got within ten yards of her. But when I say she's the prettiest, I mean just that. Ask anybody if you don't believe me. If you ever got a chance to see her for yourself, you'd know exactly what I mean. If Saunderstown wasn't so far away—"

Tom and Pete nodded, looking out the window.

"What's her last name, Jack?" Snacker asked.

"I think it's Hampton, but I'm not sure. But it doesn't matter, because—"

Snacker got up and went to the window and looked out over the campus for a while. It was almost time for lunch.

"I'll have a girl for you next year, Snacker," Pete said. "If I had known about it in time this year—"

Snacker paid no attention to what they were saying. He began talking to himself.

"I went out for the team the first day of practice and never missed a single minute all season. I thought sure I could go to the banquet. And, besides, I played a whole quarter in the Riverside game Thanksgiving Day, even if I was on the scrubs the rest of the time."

Tom heard some of the things he said, and he went to the window beside Snacker.

"It's too bad, Snacker," he said, putting his arm over his shoulder. "You've got as much right to go to the banquet as I have. But—but they wouldn't even let the captain of the team in at the door if he didn't bring a girl. That's a rule of some kind or other."

Snacker went out and walked down the hall to his room and left his books on the table. He did not feel like staying there, even until lunch was served, and he went back down the stairs and out of the dormitory. By the time he had reached the Yard, he had made up his mind to do something. He kept on walking toward town, but by the time he reached the campus gate he was running.

The bank on the corner was open. He ran inside and asked how much money he had on deposit. It was four dollars, even. He wrote a check for three dollars and asked for it in silver pieces. He wanted to be able to hold the money in his pocket and feel it there, because if he lost one of the dollars he knew he would never be able to do what he had decided on.

As soon as he left the bank, he went to the barbershop and got into the chair for a haircut. He would have to have his hair cut, because it was nearly three weeks since the last time he had had it trimmed. While sitting in the chair, he began figuring out in his mind how much it would cost to go to Saunderstown and back. The train fare was ninety cents each way. That would leave a dollar and twenty cents. If he ate any meals at all, he knew he would probably spend half of that before he got back. And, besides, he might have to spend some money while he was in Saunderstown.

When the barber had finished, Snacker decided he would have to use the other dollar in the bank. He asked the barber to cash a check. When he handed it to the barber, the man said he would have to send it to the bank to get the change. Snacker sat down and waited while the shoeshine boy was taking it there.

"Going away over the week end?" the barber asked. "Isn't tomorrow night the time for the big football banquet?"

"I'm going away, but I'll be back in time for the banquet," Snacker said. "I played on the scrubs all season, and I got into the Riverside Academy game for a full quarter when Chuck Harris got knocked out."

"That Chuck Harris is the best tackle Forrest Grove ever had," the barber said.

The shoeshine boy came back, but instead of handing over the change, he handed the barber the check Snacker had written for one dollar.

"What's this?" the barber asked.

"The bank man said the check wasn't any good at all," the boy told him.

The barber looked at Snacker, nodding his head sideways. "What's the idea?" he said. "Trying to gyp me?"

Snacker tried his best to explain about the money. It was almost time for the train to leave. Snacker told him that he went to the bank and asked for his balance. It was four dollars, even. He drew out three dollars, leaving one dollar on deposit. That dollar, Snacker kept on saying, was the one he had given the check for. The barber stopped listening and led him to the door. They went across the street to the bank on the corner.

When they got inside, Snacker asked the cashier if he did not have a dollar in his account. The cashier looked at his books for a minute and shook his head.

"There's a check here that just came in," he said. "It's a dollar check, and it wipes out your account."

Everybody, the cashier and the barber included, was right. Snacker was wrong. He did not see how he could be, but he knew he could not be right if everybody else said he was wrong. He tore up the check and paid the barber forty cents for cutting his hair. That left him eighty cents, not counting the round-trip fare.

He caught the train just in time and got a seat in the smoker. After he had sat down, he remembered that nobody on the football squad was supposed to break training until the night of the banquet, and he was glad he remembered it, because it would keep him from spending ten cents for a cigar.

It was about seven o'clock in the evening when the train reached the Saunderstown depot. He hopped off the train and made for the restaurant the first thing. He ordered a sliced-chicken sandwich and a glass of milk. That left him with only fifty-five cents.

The telephone book listed fifteen or twenty Hamptons. At five cents a call . . . He decided to write down on a piece of paper two or three of the Hampton addresses, and to try some way to find out where the prettiest Hampton daughter lived. He was certain that most of them would be related, and in that way he could find out where the one he was looking for lived.

He found the first Hampton address. It was about nine

blocks from the depot, and it was nearly eight o'clock when he got to the house.

A Negro maid answered the bell. Snacker slipped her a dime in a casual sort of way. That set him back to forty-five cents.

"What's this for?" she asked, looking curiously at the ten-cent piece.

"I just got into town on an important trip," Snacker said huskily, "and I've got to find Miss Hampton."

"Which Miss Hampton?" the maid asked. "There's a heap of young Hampton girls in Saunderstown. Don't none of them live here, but they live in all other directions."

Snacker felt around in his pants pocket. He slipped another dime into the Negro girl's hand when she was not looking. He was down to thirty-five cents.

"I don't know her first name," Snacker said, "but I've got an important message for her, anyway. She ought to be the prettiest one of them all."

"Most of the young Hampton girls are good-looking," the Negro maid said. "I don't know exactly—"

"The best-looking one there is," Snacker urged.

"I'll bet you mean Miss Sally Hampton," she said quickly. "She's might pretty."

"Where does she live?"

The maid went to the corner of the porch and pointed down the street. There were about four or five turns to make, and the house was three stories and painted white. Snacker forgot all about the turns to make, but he kept his eyes open for the three-story white house.

When he got to the one which he was certain the Negro maid had described, he ran up the steps and was about to ring the bell at the door. Before he could ring it, he heard someone at the end of the porch get up and come toward him. The porch was dark, and the street lights were too faint to help much.

"I'm calling on Miss Sally Hampton," Snacker said.

"You are? That's funny."

"Why is it funny?" Snacker asked.

"Because I'm Sally Hampton. But—but who are you?"

"Snacker," he said. "I mean—I mean—Snacker. But my name is—I'm Russell Sherman. I'm—I'm Snacker."

"And you came to see me?" the girl asked.

"All the way from Forrest Grove Academy—I mean—yes. That's what I came for. I came to see you."

"Did you bring a message from somebody I know, or did somebody send you for something, or—?"

"Not exactly," Snacker said, peering at her intently in the

faint street light. "I just came to see you because some fellows told me you were—"

"But I don't know a single person at Forrest Grove," she said. "You must be mistaken. I know lots of boys at Riverside, but I never met anybody from your school."

"We beat them 21 to 0 last week," Snacker said. "If Chuck Harris hadn't got knocked out, we would have beat them more than that. I played the last quarter when Chuck got hurt and had to leave the game."

"And you came all the way from Forrest Grove to tell me that?" she asked, laughing a little.

"No, not exactly," Snacker said. "But it's got something to do with it. We're having a banquet tomorrow night, because we always celebrate the end of the football season with a lot to eat."

"Are you going to the banquet?" Sally asked him.

"You bet!" Snacker said. "I mean—well, I'd like to go. Would you?"

"Me?"

"Sally Hampton," he said, nodding his head jerkily. "I thought you might like to go. That's why I came over to Saunderstown to ask you."

"I don't know," she said uneasily. "Mother might not like for me to go. And, besides, I don't know you."

"I'm Snacker," he said. "It would be all right for you to go with me."

She laughed.

"Maybe if you knew someone I know—Mother might let me. Do you know Ralph Carroll at Riverside? He plays on the football team."

"Sure, I know him," Snacker said. "He was in the line against me Thanksgiving Day, in the last quarter."

"I'll go ask Mother," Sally said. "She might let me go."

She went into the house and Snacker sat down in the swing to wait for her to come back and tell him. She was gone a long time. Snacker thought for a while that she had used that as an excuse to get away from him. It was nearly ten minutes before she came back to the porch. He jumped up to meet her.

"I've got a date for tomorrow night," Sally said.

"Aw, gee-my-nettie!" Snacker said.

She sat down in the swing, at one end. Snacker sat down beside her.

"But I think I'll break it and go to Forrest Grove," she said, looking at him a little. "Mother says it will be all right. She'll take me over, and we'll stay at the hotel."

"Gee-my-nettie!" Snacker said. "Do you mean it?"

"Of course," Sally said, rocking the swing.

"And you'll go with me to the banquet?"

"I'd love to."

"Well," Snacker said, "I guess I'll have to be going."

"So soon?" she said.

"It's getting pretty late for a football player to be up," he said. "We don't break training, in earnest, till tomorrow night."

She got up and went with him to the steps. She held out her hand.

"Good night, Mr.—"

"Snacker," he said.

"Good night, Snacker," she said.

"I'll come for you at the hotel at nine o'clock sharp tomorrow night," he said.

He backed down the steps. He was trying to see her in the flashes of the street light when she moved. He had backed almost to the gate and still had not seen her plainly.

It was between nine and ten o'clock when he got back to the depot. A Negro porter was sweeping out the waiting room. The restaurant across the street was still open, and Snacker went over to it and ordered a sliced-chicken sandwich and a glass of milk. When he paid for it, he did not bother to think if he had any money left.

When he got back to the depot, the lights had been turned off. He went into the waiting room and sat down on a bench. In a few minutes the porter came along and locked the doors. The next train to Forrest Grove would not leave until nine-thirty the next morning.

After Snacker had taken off his coat and spread it over him, he closed his eyes and, because he was so tired, he dropped off to sleep even before he could think about the football banquet the next night.

It was late the next afternoon when Snacker got back to Forrest Grove. On his way across the campus to the dormitory he saw Tom and Pete coming across the Yard from the gym. They waved at him and cut across the campus to meet him.

"Where've you been ever since yesterday noon?" Pete asked anxiously. "We were awfully scared something had happened to you. I thought you might have taken it a little too hard— you know, about the banquet tonight in the gym. I sure am glad to see you, Snacker. Are you all right?"

"Took what too hard?" Snacker said.

"You know, Snacker," Pete said; "about the banquet to-night, and getting cut out of going, and all that. All the fellows feel sorry about it. They'd give anything to have you there, but you know how hard it is to get rules changed. But next year we'll be looking for you."

Tom put his arm around Snacker's shoulder and nodded sympathetically.

"We'll be seeing you some other time, Snacker," he said.

"Don't forget to come out for basketball practice next Monday. Coach has posted the call, and he wants all men out Monday. We ought to have a fine basketball team this year, and I hope you make the squad, Snacker."

Before he could say anything to them, they had turned and gone towards the study hall. Snacker started to call them back, but they appeared to be in a hurry to get away. By the way they acted, Snacker was afraid his name had been posted for the doorkeeper to keep him out of the banquet room that night. He went to the notice board, and to the banquet-hall door, but he could not find anything like that posted. He climbed the dormitory stairs to the third floor on a run. He was in a hurry to begin getting ready for the banquet.

That evening at ten after eight Snacker could not sit still another minute, so he left his room and started to the hotel after Sally Hampton. When he reached Pete's room, he saw Pete and Tom brushing their hair and straightening their ties. When he passed, they would not look his way at all.

Sally and her mother were in the lobby of the hotel when Snacker got there at a few minutes to nine. He had waited outside as long as he could stand it, and then he had rushed into the lobby looking for Sally. There were girls everywhere. Fellows were rushing in and out of the hotel every second or so, trying to find violets, or something or other, at the last minute. Snacker saw Jack Phillips, but both of them were too excited to recognize each other then.

When Snacker saw Sally for the first time, in full view and in the strong light of the hotel lobby, he was not certain who she was. When she smiled at him, he rushed up to her and tried to recognize her. Then he was certain, and he saw that Tom and Pete and Jack Phillips knew what they were talking about when they had said she was the prettiest girl in the state. The other fellows in the lobby turned around and looked at her, and even when they were talking to their own girls, they could not keep their eyes off her. Nobody appeared to notice Snacker.

When they got to the banquet hall, the doorkeeper did not even look at Snacker. His eyes followed Sally Hampton as long as she was within sight. Snacker felt better once he was inside the hall.

It was not until the first course had been served that anybody took his eyes off Sally long enough to recognize Snacker. Pete saw him first. He dropped his spoon into his plate, and the soup splashed all over the front of his clothes. Pete's girl nudged him with her elbow, but Pete continued to stare first at Snacker and then at Sally. His lips were moving all the time as if he were saying to himself: "For gosh sakes! That's Snacker!"

After nearly a quarter of an hour, Pete called across the table to Jack Phillips, and Jack began to stare too. When the other fellows caught on to what had happened, they began to strain their necks to see Snacker and the girl beside him. The other girls fell back into themselves, or something, because most of them kept their heads turned in the other direction.

Up at the head of the table, at the captain's seat, Chuck Harris was glaring down at Snacker. The girl beside him, Frances Harper, nudged him with her elbow every once in a while, but he did not pay any attention to her. He looked for a while as if he might at any moment pick up a plate of something and hurl it down the table at Snacker.

Sally Hampton was having the best time of all. The fellows all around were trying to talk to her at the same time. Snacker finished up each course as it was laid before him. He did not stop to talk or to look around at anybody at the table until the final course had been served.

On the way out, when it was after eleven o'clock, Snacker got an awful hard kick in the rear. When he turned around to see who had done it, Chuck Harris and Frances Harper were glaring at him. Snacker wanted to stop and ask Chuck what he had kicked him like that for, but he had to see Sally back to the hotel and he did not want to waste any time.

He left Sally in the hotel lobby and went back across the campus to the dormitory. It looked as if most of the other fellows had hurried back too, because the doorway and lower hall were jammed. Somebody caught Snacker's arm and jerked him inside.

"What's the matter with you, Froggy?" Snacker asked in surprise.

Froggy dragged him towards the stairway.

"What's the matter!" Froggy repeated. "I want to know what's the matter with you! You brought the prettiest girl in the state to the banquet and sat there all night without saying a word to her!"

"Well, gee-my-nettie, Froggy," Snacker said, "I just had to get something to eat! I played on the scrubs all season, and a full quarter in the Riverside game besides, and I was so hungry I didn't know what to do. All I've had to eat since yesterday morning was two sliced-chicken sandwiches and a couple glasses of milk. I just had to eat, Froggy."

Pete took Snacker by the arm and pushed him up the stairway. When they had got away from the crowd downstairs, Pete began slapping Snacker on the back. On the way to Pete's room, Snacker kept on trying to tell them that he was nearly starved and just had to eat.

Tom and Jack Phillips were waiting for them at the door. Before any of the other fellows could come up from downstairs

to hear Snacker tell how it all had happened, Pete pushed him
inside the room with Tom and Jack. They locked the door
with the key and shoved the thumb bolt all the way across
the slot.

(First published in *Cosmopolitan*)

The Empty Room

THE first time I saw her was something more than a year after
they had become married. The funeral was over and all the
people had left and we were in the house alone. There was
nothing I could say to her, and she had not spoken since the
morning before. She and Finley had been married only a little
more than a year, and she was still far from being twenty.
Her body was in the beauty of girlhood, but she was only a
child.

She had sat by the window, looking out at the gathering
dusk until late in the evening, and night was coming. I had
not turned on the lights, and she had not moved from her
chair for several hours. From where I was, I could see her
darkly framed profile motionless against the gray evening
like an ebony cameo. It was then that I knew that there could
be beauty even in sorrow.

Finley was the only brother I had ever had, and before his
death he was the only kinsman I had left in the world, and
now she was his widow.

Her name was Thomasine, but I had not yet called her by
it. I had not become used to it, and there is something about
an unfamiliar name that guards itself against a stranger's
thoughtless intrusion. When the time came for me to call her
by her name, I knew I would be speaking a sound that was
hers alone.

I was a stranger in the house and we had not yet spoken to
each other. Finley had been her husband, and my brother, and
I was not then certain what our relationship became thereby.
I knew, though, that we could not for long stay in the house
alone without an understanding of her place and mine becoming clear.

The twilight was chill, and the dark room was an expanding void, receding into its wall-less immensity. Her profile was
becoming softer as the gray dusk fell away to the obscurity of

night. The walls retreated and the room became a place made without them. The room was immense and her profile against the gray dusk melted into the growing darkness of the house.

While she sat across the room she had not fully realized her loneliness. The curve of her head and shoulders drooped with the enveloping shadows, but she was not thinking of even her own presence. Finley had been dead such a short time.

When she got up to go, I got up also, and walked across the room towards her. I went to her side and stood at arm's length from her, but the distance between us could only have been measured by the bounds of the room's infinite space. I wished to put my arms around her and comfort her as I would have comforted the one I loved, but she was Finley's widow, and the room with its walls made distance immeasurable. The room in which we stood was hollow and wide, and it swam in the darkness of its vast space. A spark from a flint would have struck us blind with the intensity of its light, and the certain conflagration would have consumed us to ashes.

Before I came to the house I had given no thought to a girl whose name would be Thomasine, and now she was my brother's widow.

Some of the flowers in the room had curled for the night, but petals from the roses fell gently to the floor.

Suddenly she whispered, turning in the darkness towards me.

"Did you feed Finley's rabbits tonight?"

"Yes, I fed them," I told her. "I gave them all they can eat. They have everything they want for the night."

Her hair had fallen over her shoulders, boiling thickly about her head. Her hair was citrus color, and it strangely matched the darkness of the room and the blackness of her clothes. Its color made her sorrow more uncomfortable, because hers was the head that bowed the deepest in the darkness of the immense room. When I stared at the inky blackness of the walls not within sight, I could somehow see the quickness of her citrus hair tousled on my brother's chest while he kissed the smoothness of her profile and caressed the softness of her limbs. The beauty and richness of their year of love was yielding, though slowly, to the expanding darkness. It was in the darkness of the hollow room that I was able to believe in the finality of death, and to believe the sorrow I felt in her heart. Lovers for a year cannot believe the finality of death, and she least among them. I wished to tell her all I knew of it, but my words would have told only the triviality. Her love was not to be confused with death, and she would not have wished to understand it.

It was then to be the beginning of night.

I could not see her go, but I felt her leave the chair by the window. I walked behind her, touching the unfamiliar furniture, and guiding myself through the room and around it time after time by the direction of the citrus scent of her hair.

She stopped then, and I realized that I was in the bedroom. I found myself standing in the doorway knowing only one direction, and that was the fragrant citrus scent which came from her hair. When she went from corner to corner, I stood in the doorway of the room waiting for her to speak, for a word to send me away until morning. If there was anything else she wished, or if there was nothing I could do, she had not told me.

The lonely walk from corner to corner and back again, and the still coldness of her bed, echoed through the hollow room. I could hear her walk across the floor to the bed, touch it with her fingers, and walk back across the carpeted floor to the window. She stood by the window looking out at the nothing of night, the black nothing, while I waited for her to tell me to close the door and go away and leave her alone.

Though she was in the room, and I was in the doorway, and the rabbits were just outside the window, the emptiness about us descended upon the house like the stillness of night without stars and the moon. When I reached out my arms, they stretched to regions unknown, and when I looked with my eyes, they seemed to be searching for light in all corners of the dark heavens.

She knew I was waiting in the doorway for a word to send me away, but she was helpless in her loneliness. She knew she could not bear to be alone in the room whose walls could not be seen at such a great distance. She knew her loneliness could not be dispelled with a word uttered in the hollow darkness, and she knew herself alone could not be propelled from the immensity of the house.

My brother had written to me of her with a feeling of regret because I did not have someone like her to love. He had been with her a year, sharing this house and sharing this bed. Each night they had gone side by side into this room where she was now but for me alone. Then it was that I could feel the loneliness of this night, because he had been taken away from her; while I, who had never known such love, was never to be made a part of it.

Once more she went to the bed and touched it. The room was dark and the bed was still. She knew now that she was to be alone.

She began to cry softly, as a girl cries.

Her slippers dropped from her feet, and the echo was like the throwing of a man's solid-heeled shoes against the floor.

When she touched a comb on the table and it fell to the floor in the darkness, it might have been a man's clumsy hands feeling in the night and knocking clocks and mirrors from their places.

Her knees touched a chair, but the sound was like a man walking blindly in a dark room, stumbling over furniture and cursing hoarsely under his breath.

The clothes she removed were laid on a chest at the foot of the bed, but it was as if a man were tossing his heavy-laden coat and trousers across the room towards a chair.

Noiselessly she raised the window, but it was as if a man had thrown it open, impatient with delay.

She sat on the side of the bed and lay down upon it, but it was like a man hurling himself there and jerking the cover over him.

Softly she turned over and lay her arm across the far pillow, but it sounded in the hollow room as if a man were tossing there, beating the pillows with his fists.

Her body began to tremble with her sobs, faintly shaking the springs of the bed and the mattress, but it was like the ruthless action of a man quick with his uncontrolled strength.

I do not know how long I had stood in the doorway waiting for a word from her to send me away. Time in the pitch blackness of the house of hollow darkness had passed quickly at first, and then slowly. It may have been an hour, it may have been five.

I parted my lips and spoke to her. The sounds of my words seemed to be without an end in their echo.

"Good night, Thomasine," I said, trembling.

She screamed with fright and with pain. Had someone cut her heart with a knife, she could not have screamed more loudly.

Then slowly she turned over in bed and lay on her other side.

"My God! My God! My God!"

The pillow she had been clutching fell from the far side of the bed to the floor, crashing in the darkness like a felled tree deep in a forest.

Evening gave way, and night in the empty room began.

(First published in *Pagany*)

The Day the Presidential Candidate
Came to Ciudad Tamaulipas

THE presidential candidate's special train was due to arrive from Monterrey at nine o'clock, and it was expected to come into the station at eleven. The track was in poor condition farther west, but the General had taken that into consideration and had started the journey three hours ahead of schedule in order to arrive in Ciudad Tamaulipas not more than two hours late.

Three weeks earlier one of the other candidates had made the fatal mistake of not thinking about the poor condition of the track, merely leaving Monterrey on schedule. Consequently, he arrived in Ciudad Tamaulipas five hours late, and by that time all the people had decided to go home and eat and take the siesta.

The bands, cheated out of their opportunity to play three weeks before, were practicing all over town that morning. They had been up since sunrise. Three of them, along with some of the shoeshine boys and lottery-ticket vendors, were marching up and down in the dusty arroyo behind the bull ring.

In the plaza two more bands were practicing bars and scales and getting a feeling for the pitch. Several other bands were riding through the streets in trucks and practicing at the same time.

The special train bearing the General and his party suddenly puffed up to the station, the engineer tooting the whistle a long and two shorts only when it was a mere dozen raillengths away. Everybody was caught unprepared. It had arrived an hour and a half late, but a full thirty minutes before it was expected.

As it was, the only persons on the station platform when the General's train puffed up and stopped were some shoeshine boys and lottery-ticket vendors, and they would have been there even if the special had not been coming that day at all.

The official welcoming committee was still in the cantina two blocks away, and the chauffeur of the limousine in which the General was to ride to the bull ring for the speech was

69

sitting comfortably in a restaurant across the street eating fried beans. The limousine itself, however, was parked at the station platform.

The General and his party bought up all lottery tickets on which the numeral 5 appeared in the serial numbers and went directly to the limousine. Somebody blew the horn three sharp blasts. The chauffeur came running out of the restaurant with his mouth full of hot beans, thinking somebody was playing with it. When he recognized the General on the back seat, he swallowed the beans, saluted, and slid under the steering wheel.

News of the General's arrival had already begun to spread through the town. Shopkeepers began pulling down the steel blinds over their plateglass windows, expecting the crowds to jam the streets at any moment.

One of the bands in the plaza heard the news and opened up right away, the bandsmen pulling out all the stops in their instruments so the sound would carry four blocks across town to the station, where the General could hear and appreciate it.

But before the music reached the General's ears, he and his party were off in a burst of scudding speed and billowy dust. Six of his rangers who could not find space inside the limousine clung to the outside along with five or six shoeshine boys, several lottery-ticket vendors, and a delegate from an *ejido*, who happened to be at the station early because he had misjudged the time.

Halfway to the bull ring a shoeshine boy and the *ejido* delegate fell off when the limousine struck a bounce in the street.

When the General arrived at the bull ring there were seven or eight thousand men in the stands, filling them to capacity, and two or three thousand more were on the outside trying vainly to gain entrance by scaling the adobe walls and tunneling with their machetes under the concrete stands.

Just as he and his party were about to enter the bull ring a squad of soldiers that had been detailed to protect the life of the presidential candidate came forward and forcibly disarmed his rangers, taking all their automatics and dumping them into a canvas sack.

The rangers resented the attitude of the soldiers, who were comrades of the revolution, too, but the General laughed and beckoned to half a dozen of the prettiest girls around him. He requested the girls to precede him through the passageway, and then they all entered the bull ring together. The rangers stayed behind and argued with the soldiers while all of them took advantage of the opportunity to get their shoes shined and buy some lottery tickets.

The General mounted the platform that had been erected in the middle of the bull ring while an *ejido* delegate was delivering an introductory speech to the crowd over the loud-speaker system. When the people recognized the General, their voices drowned out the words of the delegate and he had to resign himself to leaving his speech half unread.

As the clamor was dying down, two bands arrived and began playing as they marched around the platform several times. In the meantime several shoeshine boys and lottery-ticket vendors made a dash for the platform, making it safely while everyone's attention was being held by the performance of the band.

After a while there was less noise and commotion, and the General went to the microphone and greeted the people. He was able to speak only a few words before the shouting of the crowd made it impossible to continue.

"What did the General say?" we asked one of the lottery-ticket vendors beside us.

"The General said it has made him happy to be here, because now he has seen the most beautiful girls and the strongest men in all Mexico!"

After a while the General was able to resume his address. He spoke one full sentence and half of another into the microphone before the shouts of the people again drowned out his voice.

"Viva el General!"

"Viva Mexico!"

"Viva el General!"

In wave after wave the shouts of many thousands of voices thundered through the bull ring.

"What did the General say?" we asked excitedly.

"The General said it has made him happy to come here where all the land is rich and fertile—even the mountain-sides!" the lottery-ticket vendor said, excitedly waving his arms in a gesture that took in the whole world.

Just as the General was getting ready to attempt to speak again, two more bands arrived. They began playing the marches they knew, circling the platform time after time. While they were playing, the arena gates suddenly burst open and dozens of men on horseback swarmed across the bull ring. They were carrying banners of the revolution and flags of the republic, but they had no musical instruments, and soon nobody noticed them any more.

There was a period of comparative calm in the bull ring, and the General stepped briskly to the microphone and spoke rapidly to the people. This time he completed two sentences before the crowd's shouts of approval stilled his voice once more. He stepped back, wiped his face, and waited patiently for the din to subside.

"What did he say this time?" we asked eagerly.

"The General said he wished all the people in the world could have the good fortune to come to Ciudad Tamaulipas!"

During an unaccountable lull, the General hurried back to the microphone, but before he could utter any sound another band arrived and struck up its music as it began circling the platform. When it was all over, the General grasped the microphone firmly in both hands and quickly resumed his speech. This time he raced through several sentences before the swelling roar of the crowd forced him to pause.

"*Viva el General!*"

"*Viva Mexico!*"

"*Viva el General!*"

The clamor lasted for a long time, and the vendors around us had joined in so enthusiastically that it was several minutes before we could secure anyone's attention.

"What did the General say that pleased the people so much?"

The lottery-ticket vendor gripped us excitedly by the arm, shouting into our ears.

"The General said it is a beautiful day!"

In the excitement of the moment we had failed to be aware that one of the shoeshine boys was polishing our shoes, and he startled us by raising his voice and repeating what the General had said. We looked up into the cloudless, pale blue desert sky. It was one of the most beautiful days we had ever seen in Mexico. The sun beamed down upon us like the smile of a benevolent friend, warming us to the core. We stood there in its kindly glow, feeling in the depths of our hearts that no truer words had ever before been uttered. There in the heat and clamor, breathing deeply of the pungent aroma of the scorched desert sand, we repeated to ourselves the hope that the General, who had made us aware of the beauty of the day, would secure all the votes and become the next president of his country.

(First published in *Town and Country*)

Over the Green Mountains

Was reading a piece in the Boston paper last night about the smartest people in the whole country coming from the State of Maine. Said at the time, and I'm still here to say it: you can take your pick of any ten men in the whole Union, and

I'll back one Varmonter of my own choosing against them any day. Take ten men from any of the states you can find them in, and all of them put together won't have the smartness that my lone Varmonter has got. Have lived in the State of Maine all my life, ninety-odd years of it, but I've always said that if you want some smartness you shall have to go to Varmont to get it. Varmont is where it comes from.

Now, you take the farmers. Varmont farmers is that smart they can't keep from making money while the farmers in other places is all losing money. And here is why they are so smart: not so long ago there was a Varmont farmer over here, riding around in his big auto having a good time and laughing at us farmers here because we hadn't made enough money to retire and maybe take a trip to Florida on, in even years. I asked this Varmont farmer how it was he had made so much money running a farm.

And this is what he told me: "Friend," he said, "the secret of making money out of a farm is this: Sell all you can; what you can't sell, feed to the hogs; what the hogs won't eat, eat yourself."

After he finished telling me that, he drove off laughing in his big auto to look at some more Maine farmers working and sweating in the fields because they ain't got sense enough to make money to retire on, and maybe take a winter trip to Florida, in even years.

That sporting farmer wasn't the first Varmonter I'd known, though. I used to know another one when I was a young man on the Penobscot.

This was a young fellow we called Jake Marks, one of them old-time Varmonters who used to come over here to the State of Maine driving teams of oxen before the railroads was built across the mountains. This Jake Marks was a smart one, if there ever was a Varmonter who warn't. He used to drive his oxen over here hauling freight back and forth all the time. It was a long haul in them days, when you stop to think how slow them brutes travel, and Jake had a lot of mountain to cross coming and going. I don't recall how long it took him to make one of his trips, but it was quite a time in them days when there warn't no State roads, only trails wide enough for a yoke of oxen.

Jake was a real young man at that time, I should say about twenty-five, maybe twenty-seven. He warn't married then, neither. But pretty soon he took a liking to a young and handsome filly who cooked his meals for him at the house in Bangor where he put up while he was changing cargo between trips. She was just the kind of young filly that Jake wanted, too. She used to come into the room where he sat waiting for his meal and make herself real frisky in his presence. Jake, he was tormented something awful by the way she cut up in front of him, and he used to have to get up out of his chair sometimes and walk real fast around the house three-four times to get control over himself.

But this Jake Marks was a cautious man, and he never undertook a deal until he had thought it out a lot beforehand and saw that he had everything on his side. Then, when he had thought it all through, he turned loose and went after whatever it was he wanted like a real Varmonter. All them old-time Varmonters was like that, I guess; anyway, the ones who used to drive ox freights over here to the State of Maine was, and Jake was just like all the rest of them.

This young filly of Jake's got so she pestered him about marrying of her all the time he was resting up between trips. Jake, he wanted her, all right. That was one thing he was wanting all the time he was over here. But Jake, he was taking his own good time about it, I'm telling you. He was figuring the thing out like all them Varmonters who drove ox freights did. He had to be real certain that everything was on his side before he made any signs. He took the rest of the season for figuring the thing out, and he didn't make motions of a move toward the young filly that year at all.

The next spring when the frost had thawed out of the ground and when he could make his first trip of the year over the mountains, Jake he called at the house where this young filly stayed and told her to get ready to be married to him when he got back to Bangor on his next trip. That suited the young filly first-rate. She had been uneasy all winter about Jake, taking too much at heart all the gossip that was talked about them Varmont ox freighters. But when Jake told her to get ready for marrying, she knew he would keep his promise right down to the last letter and come and marry her like he said he would.

So, Jake he went back to Varmont with his freight, promising to be ready to marry the young filly the same day he got back to Bangor on his next trip.

And just as he promised, Jake came back to get married to the young filly. He went straight to the house where she stayed, and there she was all waiting for him. Jake told her to get ready right away for the marriage, and then he went out to find a preacher somewhere. When he got back to the house with the preacher, he called her down to the room where all the guests had gathered to see the ceremony performed.

The minute she stepped into the room where Jake and the rest of the people was, Jake took one look at the young filly and told her to go back upstairs to her room and take off her dress. Well, that was all right and proper, because in those days there was a law in the State of Maine to the effect that a man could make what was called a shift-marriage. That was to say, the man could make the woman take off the dress she was wearing while the ceremony was being performed, and in that case he could not be held legally responsible for her past debts and would not have to pay them for her if he didn't have a mind to. Well, Jake he had heard all about this shift-law in Maine, and he was taking full advantage of its benefits. That was what he had been figuring out all the time he was driving them slow-footed oxen back and forth between Bangor and Varmont. Jake, he warn't no man's fool. Jake, he was a Varmonter.

After a while Jake's young filly came downstairs dressed according to this here shift-law. She had on what women wore under their dresses in those days, and that was all she had on. But Jake, he warn't satisfied, not completely. He told her to go back upstairs and take off everything she had on. Jake, he was a hardheaded ox freighter from Varmont, all right. He had figured all this out while he was driving them slow-footed oxen back and forth across the mountains.

In a little while his young filly came into the room again where Jake and the preacher and all the guests was, and she didn't have nothing on, except that she had a bedsheet wrapped around her, which was a good thing, I tell you. She was a handsome-looking filly if there ever was one.

They all got ready again for the ceremony, the preacher telling them where to stand and what to say to the questions he was getting ready to ask them. Then, just when they was beginning to get married, Jake he told his young filly to drop the bedsheet on the floor. Now, Jake he warn't taking no chances over here in the State of Maine. That shift-law said that if a woman was married without her dress on, her husband couldn't be held liable for her past debts, and Jake he figured that if the young filly didn't have nothing at all on her, there wouldn't be a chance in the whole world for to dun him for what she might owe, while if she had clothes on that he didn't know the true and legal names of, a storekeeper might try to say her underclothes was her overdress. Jake, he was thinking that he might by chance get cheated out of his rights to the full benefits of the shift-law if he didn't take care, and Jake he warn't after taking no chances whatsoever over here in the State of Maine when he was so far away from Varmont. He was as cautious where he sat his foot as the next ox freighter from Varmont.

"Drop the bedsheet on the floor," Jake he told the young filly again.

The young filly was getting ready to turn loose the bedsheet and let it drop on the floor like Jake told her to do, when the preacher he grabbed the bedsheet and held to it tight around her so she wouldn't show none of her naked self to him and Jake and the rest of the people in the house.

"No! No! No!" he yelled, getting red in the face and shaking his head at Jake. "That won't do, my man—that won't do at all! That would be indecent here before all of us! That can't be done! I'll never allow it!"

But the preacher he didn't know Jake Marks. Jake was one of them Varmont ox freighters, and he was as hardheaded about what he wanted as the next one to come along. Jake, he told the young filly again to drop the bedsheet on the floor, and to drop it quick if she wanted to get married.

The handsome young filly was getting ready to let go of it like Jake said to, because she was that crazy about Jake she would have stood on her head right then and there if Jake had told her to do it, but just when she was getting ready to let go of it, the preacher he grabbed the bedsheet again and held it fast with both hands.

The preacher started in trying to argue with Jake about it being indecent for the handsome young filly to stand there naked while she was being married, but Jake he had his head set on getting the full benefits of the shift-law and he wouldn't give in an inch.

Then the preacher said he warn't going to perform the ceremony if that was what Jake was set on doing, and Jake he told the preacher he warn't going to get married at all without the bedsheet being dropped on the floor so that none of the cloth was touching the young filly.

Everybody got excited when Jake said that, and the people talked back and forth for an hour or more, arguing first on Jake's side, because they knew the law on the books, and then on the preacher's side, because they realized how it might upset the preacher if the handsome young filly stood there naked like Jake was set on having her do. The young filly didn't care which way the ceremony was done, just so long as Jake married her. She was willing to drop the bedsheet for Jake the minute the preacher let her. She was all excited about getting married, just like Jake had been all the time.

After a while the preacher gave in to Jake just a little. He saw what a fool he was, trying to argue with a Varmont ox freighter.

"If she'll go inside the closet and shut the door so nobody can see her nakedness, I'll perform the ceremony," the preacher told Jake.

"That's all right by me," Jake said, "but I'll be compelled to have some witnesses on my side in case anybody tries to dispute me about us being married under the shift-law or not."

They finally settled that part when the preacher agreed to allow two of the older women to go in the closet with the young filly, just to make sure that everything was done in a legal manner. The preacher he didn't like to have Jake going in a closet with the naked filly, but he was pretty well worn out by that time after arguing for nearly two hours with a Varmont ox freighter, and he said he would have to allow Jake to go in the closet, too.

Jake went in the closet where the filly and the two older women were.

"Now, you just look once, Jake," the preacher said, shaking his head back and forth, "and then you shut your eyes and keep them shut."

Jake was in the closet saying something to the young filly, but nobody in the room could hear what it was. The preacher he reached over and made a bit of a crack in the door while he was marrying them so he could hear their answers to the questions. And all that time Jake he was in there striking matches to make sure that the young filly was not putting the bedsheet on again, and to be certain that he was getting the full benefits of the shift-law.

When it was all done, the preacher he took the money Jake handed him and went off home without waiting to see what shape the young and handsome filly was in when the closet door was opened. When they came out into the room, the bedsheet was all twisted up into a knot; Jake handed it to her, and she didn't lose no time in getting upstairs where her clothes were. Jake he had told her to hurry and get dressed, because he wanted to get started with his ox freight back to Varmont.

They started home to Varmont right away, the handsome young filly all dressed up in her wedding clothes and sitting on top of the freight cargo while Jake he walked along beside the wagon bellowing at the oxen.

When Jake came back to Bangor on his next trip, a storekeeper tried to present him a bill for a hundred and forty dollars. The storekeeper told Jake that the young filly had bought a lot of dresses and things just before she got married, and he wanted to know if Jake had married her under the shift-law.

Jake just laughed a little, and started unloading his cargo.

"Well, was you married that way, or the other way?" the storekeeper asked him.

"You tell me this first," Jake said, "and then I'll answer your question. Does the State of Maine have a shift-law on the books?"

"Well, yes; but the shift-law says that the woman has to—"

"Never mind about explaining it to me," Jake said. "If the shift-law is on the statute books, then that's the law I married her with."

(First published in *Contact*)

The People's Choice

GUS was leaning against the fount in the drugstore Saturday morning when Ed Wright, one of the elders, came in and told Gus that the church had made him a deacon. Laying aside the election itself, that was the first of the blunders that were made between then and noon Sunday; Ed Wright should have had the sense not to notify Gus of the election until about midnight Saturday, or better still, until just before preaching time Sunday morning. All the blame for what took place cannot be put off on Ed, though; Gus Streetman should be held just as responsible for what happened as anyone else in town.

After Ed had told Gus about the church election, Gus just stood there looking at Ed and at the boy behind the fount for several minutes. He was feeling so good about it, he didn't know what to say. He was as pleased about it as he ever was when he heard the county returns on election night.

"You're a deacon now, Gus," Ed said, leaning against the fount and waiting for Gus to set him up. "Don't let the boys in the back seats slip any suspender buttons over on you."

"You know, Ed," he said, "I'd rather be elected deacon in the church than to get any other office in the county—except tax assessor. By George, it's a big thing to be a deacon in the church."

Gus was the county tax assessor. He had held the office against all opposition for the past ten or fifteen years, and, from the way things looked then, he would continue being the assessor as long as men went to the polls and saw Gus Streetman's name printed on the ballot.

"Well, Gus," Ed said, "everybody's glad about it, too. There wasn't any doubt about you being elected after your name was put up. It was unanimous, too."

Gus was feeling so good he didn't know what to say. He waited for Ed to tell him more about the election, when the minister and all the elders voted for him; but Ed was licking the corners of his mouth for a drink.

"Let's have a drink, Gus," he suggested.

"Oh, sure, sure!" Gus said, waking up. "What'll you have, Ed?"

"Make mine a lime Coke," he told the boy behind the fount.

"Give me another Coke, son," Gus said, "with three big squirts of ammonia."

That was the fifth Coke-and-ammonia Gus had drunk since eight-thirty that morning, and it was still two hours until noon.

He and Ed stood at the fount drinking their Coca-Colas silently. Gus was busy thinking about his election as a deacon, and he was too busy thinking about it to say anything. After a while, Ed said he had to hurry back to the hardware store to see if any customers had come in, and he left Gus leaning against the fount drinking his Coke-and-ammonia.

"You'll have to help take up the collection tomorrow morning, Gus," Ed said at the door. "You'd better wear some shoes that don't squeak so much, because everybody will be looking at you."

"Oh, sure, sure," Gus said. "I'll be there all right. I'm a deacon now."

Gus was so busy thinking about his being a deacon in the church that he hardly knew what he was saying, or what Ed was talking about. He was busy thinking about celebrating in some way, too. He had never won an election yet that he hadn't celebrated, and he was just as proud of being a deacon as he was of being county tax assessor. He walked out of the drugstore and started for the barbershop.

In the back room of the barbershop there was a little closet where he kept some of his corn and gin. He intended making the celebration this time as big as, or bigger than, any he had ever undertaken before. Usually, he had the chance to celebrate only each four years, when he was re-elected tax assessor, and this was an extra time, like an unexpected holiday.

People said that Gus Streetman was as big-hearted as a man can be, and that a man just couldn't help liking him. You could walk up to Gus on the street on a Saturday afternoon and ask Gus for anything you wished, and Gus would give it to you if he had it or if he knew where he could lay his hands on it. You could ask Gus to lend you his new automobile to take a ride out to the country in, and Gus would slap his hand on your shoulder, just as if you were doing him a big favor, and say: "Oh, sure, sure! Go ahead and use it, Joe. Why, by George, all I've got in the world is yours for the asking. Sure, go ahead and drive it all you want, Joe."

After you had thanked Gus for the use of his new automobile, he would silence you and say: "Now, don't start talking like that, Joe. You make me think I ain't doing enough for you. Drive down to the filling station and fill her up with gas, and charge it to me. Just tell Dick I said to make out a ticket for whatever you want, and I'll come by and take it up the first of the week."

That's how Gus Streetman was about everything. It never mattered to him what a man wished. If you thought you would like to have something, all you had to do was to ask Gus, and if he had it, or knew where he could lay his hands on it, it was yours until you got good and ready to hand it back to him. Sometimes people took advantage of Gus, but not often. Nearly everyone knew where to draw the line, and he had so many friends to look out for him that he was taken care of. In the spring of that year Vance Young had stopped Gus one morning and said he was going up to Atlanta that week-end on a short business trip and that he would like to take Gus's wife along for company. Gus told him to go ahead and take her along, and he meant it, too; but just before train time somebody broke down and told Gus that Vance was only fooling, and it turned out to be a joke the barbershop crowd was playing on him.

That was one of the main reasons why Gus got re-elected tax assessor time after time. He had been tax assessor for about fifteen years already, and no man who had ever tried to run against Gus in the primaries had a dog's chance of taking the office away from him. Just before a primary, Gus would load his automobile up with three or four dozen of those big Senator Watson watermelons, and start out electioneering. He would come to a house beside the road, stop, and get out carrying two of those big melons under his arms. When he reached the front porch, he would roll the Senator Watsons up to the door and take out his pearl-handled pocket-knife and rap on the boards until somebody came out.

"Well, how's everything, Harry?" Gus would say, thumping the Senator Watsons with his knuckles, and cocking his head sideways to hear the *thump! thump!* "How are you satisfied with your tax assessment, Harry?"

Nobody was ever satisfied, of course, and that was all there would be to Gus getting another vote for the primary. Being a Democrat, he never had to worry about the Republicans at election time. The Lily-whites never bothered with county politics; the mail carriers knew perfectly well which side their bread was buttered on.

"Reckon we can get the assessment changed, Gus?" the man would say.

Gus would never answer that question, because by that time he was always busy splitting open one of those big Senator Watsons. When he had got the heart cut out, and had passed it around, he would wipe the blade of his pearl-handled knife on his pants leg and shake hands all around.

"We need a little rain, don't we?" Gus would say, starting back to the road where his car was. "Maybe we'll get a shower before sundown."

That's how Gus got elected county tax assessor the first time, and that's how he was re-elected every four years following. He never made any promises; therefore he never violated any. But he got the votes, nearly all there were in the whole county.

When Gus had first started out to be elected deacon, he went about his campaign the same way he did when he was running for political office. He filled up the minister on those big Senator Watsons, day after day, and all the elders, too. When the church election was held during the last week in July, Gus's name was the first one put up for deacon, and there was only one ballot taken. Gus got all the votes.

But when Gus wasn't canvassing for votes, political or otherwise, and when he wasn't out in some part of the county assessing property, he was usually drinking corn and gin. He kept a store of it in the back room of the barbershop, another supply in the garage at home where his wife wouldn't be likely to find it, and a third one at the courthouse, in the coal box in his office, where he could reach it at any time of the day or night.

Gus never got too drunk to walk; that is to say, Fred Jones, the marshal, never had to lock him up. Gus was always on his feet, no matter how much he had been drinking, or for how long a time. He could hold his corn and gin with never an outward sign of drunkenness, unless you happened to look him in his eyes, or to measure his stride.

That Saturday morning, though, after Ed Wright had notified him of the election, Gus went down to the barbershop and cleaned out all his liquor there, and then he walked over to the courthouse and started on the bottles he kept in the coal box in his office on the second floor.

Nobody saw much of him again that day, until a little after eight o'clock that night when he came out of the courthouse and walked across the square for another Coke-and-ammonia at the fount in the drugstore. Even then nobody paid much attention to Gus, because he was walking in fairly even strides, and he wasn't talking unduly loud for a Saturday night. The marshal watched Gus for a few minutes, and then left the square and went back down the alley to pick up a few more drunks in front of the Negro fish houses for the lockup.

There had been a traveling carnival in town all that week, and nearly everyone went to the show grounds that night to see the carnival close up and move off to the next town. Gus started out there with two or three of his friends at about ten-thirty or eleven. All of them were well liquored, and Gus was shining. When they got to the show grounds, Gus started out to wind up his celebration. He let loose that Saturday night. He took in all the side shows, and he had a big crowd of men and boys following him around the grounds, whooping it up with him.

Just before midnight, when the carnival was getting ready to close and move on to the next town down the road, Gus saw a show he had missed. It was a little tent off to itself, with a big red-painted picture of a girl, pretty much naked, dancing on it. There was no name on the show, as there were on the others, but down in one corner of the big red picture, just under the girl's feet, was a little sign that said: *For Men Only*.

As soon as somebody told Gus it was a hoochie-coochie show, he dashed for it, pushing people out of his way right and left. He ran up to the ticket seller, bought three or four dozen tickets, and waved his arms at everybody who wished to go in with him and see the show. After they had crowded inside, the show went to pieces so quickly that no one knew what had happened.

Nobody yet tells exactly what Gus said or did when he got inside with the hoochie-coochie girl, but whatever it was, the show was a complete wreck inside of two minutes. It might have been Gus who jerked out the center pole, bringing the tent down on top of everybody, and it might not have been Gus who grabbed the girl around her waist and made her yell as though she were being squeezed to death by a maniac. But anyway, the tent came down; the dancer yelled and screamed, first for help, next for mercy; the ticket seller shouted for the stake drivers; and some fool down under the tent struck a match to the canvas. When the crowd got the blazing tent off the girl and the bunch of men, they found her and Gus down on the bottom of the pile struggling with each other. Fred Jones, the marshal, came running up just then all excited, deputizing citizens right and left, and got everybody herded out of the show grounds and closed up the carnival.

What happened to Gus after that, nobody knows exactly, because some of his friends pried him loose from the little dark-skinned hoochie-coochie dancer, and carried him away in an automobile to cool off. Later that night they brought him back to town and locked him in the barbershop so he couldn't get out where the marshal was certain to get him if he showed himself on the street again that night.

Gus didn't go home to his wife that night, because he was in the back room of the barbershop pulling on two or three new bottles at three o'clock when the rest of the crowd decided it was time to call it a night and to go home and get some sleep. They locked Gus in the back room to sleep it off.

Early the next morning, Clyde Young, the barber, went down and shaved Gus and patched up his clothes a little; and at about eleven-fifty, ten or fifteen minutes before the sermon at the church was due to end, Gus walked in and sat down in a rear pew.

Gus was supposed to be there, all right, because he was a deacon then, and it was his duty to help take up the morning offering. But Gus was not supposed to be there in the shape he was in, all liquored up again fresh that morning in the barbershop. Clyde Young had brought Gus an eye opener when he went down to shave him and to get him ready to take up collection at the church.

Nobody paid much attention to Gus when he walked into the church and took a seat in the back. The minister saw Gus, and likewise a dozen or more of the congregation who turned around to see who was coming to church so late. But nobody knew the condition Gus was in. He did not show it any more than he ever did. He looked to be as sober as the minister himself.

Gus sat still and quiet in the back of the church until the sermon was over. It was then time to take up the morning offering. It was customary for the deacons to walk down to the front of the pulpit, pick up the collection baskets, take up the money, and then to march back down the aisles while one of the women in the choir sang a solo.

Gus went down and got his basket all right, and took up all the money on his side of the aisle without missing a dime. Then, when all the deacons had got to the rear of the church, they began marching in step, slowly, down the aisles towards the pulpit where the minister was waiting to say a prayer over the money and to pronounce the benediction. The girl singing the solo was supposed to time herself so she would get to the end of the piece just as the deacons laid the collection baskets on the table in front of the pulpit.

Everything worked smoothly enough, until just about the time that the rest of the deacons got about halfway down the aisles on their way back to the pulpit. The soloist was standing up in the choir singing her piece, the organist was playing the accompaniment, when Gus stopped dead in his tracks, playing havoc with all the ritual.

The elders and the minister should have had better sense than to have made Gus Streetman a deacon, to begin with; but Gus had carried them off their feet, just as he did the voters when he was canvassing for re-election for county tax assessor. It wasn't Gus's fault any more than it was the fault of the people who made him a deacon; they were the ones upon whom most of the blame should be put. And on the other hand, even if he was to be a deacon, somebody connected with the church should have hunted up Gus that morning before preaching started and made sure that he was in condition to enter a house of worship. But things were never done that way. People liked Gus, and they let him do as he pleased.

When Gus came stomping down the aisle that morning, rattling the collection basket as though he were warming up a crap game, he was as drunk as a horse trader on court day. But it was the people's fault; they should never have made Gus a deacon to begin with, unless some arrangement to keep him sober on Sunday was agreed upon.

Gus was standing there in the aisle by himself. The other deacons had marched down to the table in front of the pulpit, glancing back over their shoulders to see what the matter was with Gus, but scared to go back and get him. They didn't know what he might say or do if they tried to make him follow them.

By that time, the church was rank with the smell of Gus's liquor, and all the people were sniffing the air, and turning around in their pews to look at him. Gus was staring at the girl singing the solo in the choir, and shaking the dimes and quarters in the collection basket as if it had been a kitty pot in a Saturday night crap game in the barbershop.

Then, suddenly, Gus shouted. He must have been heard all the way across town in the Baptist church, disrupting their service, too.

"Shake it up!" Gus yelled at the girl singing the solo.

The church was buzzing like a beehive in no time. The congregation was standing up, sniffing Gus's whisky-smell; the organist stopped playing the accompaniment for the solo, the girl stopped singing, and everybody, including the minister, was staring openmouthed at Gus Streetman. During all that time, Gus was standing there in the aisle rattling the money and looking at the soloist. It was a strange thing to happen, but she did look a lot like the hoochie-coochie dancer with the carnival.

When everybody was hoping that the worst was over, Gus shouted again.

"Shake it up!" he yelled at the girl. "Shake it up, baby!"

Nearly everyone in the church knew what Gus was talking about, because most of the men had been to the show grounds the week before, and either had seen, or had been told about the little brown-skinned hoochie-coochie dancer in the tent for men only, and all the women, of course, had heard about her.

Gus was getting ready to yell again, and maybe do something shocking, but before he could do it, a bunch of the elders and deacons jumped on him and hustled him out of the church in a hurry.

The minister pronounced a hurried and short benediction, and ran out the back door and around to the street to see what was happening to Gus in front of the church.

The elders and deacons hustled Gus into an automobile and drove off with him at fifty miles an hour. The minister and the rest of the congregation came running down the street behind the car.

When they reached the jail, nearly everybody in town was down there by that time to see Gus Streetman get locked up. The Baptist church had turned out, and all the Baptists were there on their way home to see what was taking place. There was a delay of ten or fifteen minutes while somebody was going for Fred Jones, the marshal; Fred wasn't a member of any church, and he was always at home Sunday morning reading the Sunday *Journal* and the *Atlanta Constitution*. The marshal had the only key to the jail there was, and Gus couldn't be put inside until he came and unlocked the doors.

While everybody was standing around looking and talking, Gus climbed up on the radiator of an automobile and held out his hands for silence. People standing off at a distance pushed closer, saying, "Shhh!" in order to hear what Gus was about to say.

"Citizens of Washington County," Gus shouted, waving his hands and looking the crowd over just as he did when he took the stump for the county primary. "Citizens of Washington County, I'm not here today to ask you if you are satisfied with your tax assessments; I'm not here today, folks, to ask if you believe there is a better man in the county than Gus Streetman —citizens of Washington County, I'm here today, folks, to ask if you think there's another man in the entire county who can increase the membership and attendance and double the collection in a church like the man you are now facing!"

The marshal came running up just then and opened the doors of the lockup. He walked over to the car and jerked Gus down from the radiator and hustled him inside the little brick building. The crowd pressed around the lockup, trying to see what Gus looked like on the inside. A lot of the ones who were not engaged in pushing and shoving and elbowing towards the windows were shouting: "Hooray for Gus! Hooray for Gus! Hooray for Gus Streetman."

While the crowd was milling around the windows of the lockup, Gus's face suddenly appeared behind the bars of one of them. He shouted for attention and raised his hands for silence just as if he were canvassing the county for the Democratic White Primary.

"Go home and think it over, folks!" he yelled, "and when

election day comes around, bring out the family and let's pile up a landslide for Gus Streetman!"

Somebody in the crowd shouted: "Hooray for Gus!"

Gus held up his hands again, silencing the crowd outside the windows.

"Vote for Gus Streetman, folks!" he yelled. "Everybody votes for Gus Streetman! Gus Streetman for deacon!"

Just then the marshal came up behind Gus and hustled him away from the window and pushed him into one of the lockup cages. After that there was nothing to stay for any longer, because Gus was locked out of sight, and the crowd turned away and started home for Sunday dinner. Everybody was hoping, though, that Gus would get bailed out of the lockup in time to take up the collection again the following week, the second Sunday in August.

(First published in *Folk-say, IV: The Land Is Ours*)

Return to Lavinia

AT first she did not know what had awakened her. She was not certain whether it had been à noise somewhere about the house, or whether it was the metallike burning of her feverish skin. By the time her eyes were fully open she could hear a bedlam of crowing, the sounds coming from every direction. For an hour at midnight the roosters crowed continually; from the chicken yards in town and from the farms surrounding the town, the sounds filled the flat country with an almost unbearable din.

Lavinia sat up in bed, wide awake after three hours of fitful sleep. She pressed the palms of her hands against her ears to shut out the crowing, but even that did not help any. She could still hear the sounds no matter what she did to stop it.

"I'll never be able to go to sleep again," she said, holding her hands tight to the sides of her head. "I might as well stop trying."

When she looked up, there was a light shining through the rear windows and doors. The illumination spread over the back porch and cast a pale moonlike glow over the walls of her room. She sat tensely awake, holding her breath while she listened.

Presently the screen door at the end of the hall opened,

squeaked shrilly, and slammed shut. She shivered while the small electric fan on the edge of her dresser whirred with a monotonous drone. In her excitement she clutched her shoulders in her arms, still shivering while the fan blew a steady stream of sultry air against her face and neck.

The footsteps became inaudible for a moment, then distinct. She would know them no matter where she heard them. For three years she had heard them, night and day since she was fifteen. Some footsteps changed from year to year; strides increased, strides decreased; leather-and-nail heels were changed to rubber, heel-and-toe treads became flat-footed shufflings; most footsteps changed, but his had remained the same during all that time.

Phil Glenn crossed the porch to the kitchen, the room next to hers, and snapped on the light. She shivered convulsively in the fan draft, gasping for breath in the sultry air.

Through the wall she could hear him open the icebox, chip off several chunks of ice, and drop them into a tumbler. When he dropped the lid of the icebox and crossed to the spigot, she could hear the flow of water until the tumbler filled and overflowed. Everything he did, every motion he made, was taking place before her eyes as plainly as if she were standing beside him while he chipped the ice and filled the tumbler to overflowing.

When he had finished, he turned off the light and went back out on the porch. He stood there, his handkerchief in hand, wiping his face and lips spasmodically while he listened as intently as she was listening.

There was a sound of someone else's walking in the front of the house. It was an unfamiliar sound, a sound that both of them heard and listened to for the first time.

When she could bear it no longer, Lavinia threw herself back upon the bed, covering her face with the pillow. No matter how hard she tried, she could not keep from sobbing into the pillow. As regularly as midnight came, she had cried like that every night since he had been away.

The next thing she knew, he was sitting on the edge of her bed trying to say something to her. She could not understand a word he was saying. Even after she had sat up again, she still did not know what it was. Long after he had stopped speaking, she stared at his features in the pale glow of reflected light. She tried to think of something either of them would have to say.

"We just got back," he said.

After he had spoken, she laughed at herself for not having known he would say exactly that.

"We went down to the beach for a few days when we left here," he finished.

Lavinia stared at him while she wondered what he expected her to say by way of comment or reply.

All she could do was nod her head.

"I thought I told you where we were going, but after I left I remembered I hadn't. If we hadn't been halfway there, I'd have turned around and come back to tell you. I wouldn't want you to think—"

She laughed.

"—I wouldn't want you to think—" he said over again.

Lavinia threw her head back and laughed out loud. Her voice sounded soft and deep.

"Well, anyway," she said, "it was a mighty short honeymoon. But it was nice on the beach."

She laughed again, but the sound of her laughter was all but drowned out in the drone of the electric fan.

"It was just what you would expect," he said casually.

The electric fan was blowing her gown against her back with rippling motions. She moved sidewise to the fan so that nothing would prevent her from hearing every word he said. After she had settled down, he crossed his legs.

"I guess it's going to be all right," he said, looking through the window and back again at her. "It'll be all right."

Before he had finished, both of them turned to listen to the sound of footsteps in the front of the house. The sound echoed through the night.

In the closeness of the room, Lavinia could feel his heavy breathing vibrate the air. She wanted to say something to him, but she was afraid. She did not know what she could say. If she said the wrong thing, it would be a lot worse than not saying anything. She held her breath in perplexity.

He got up, went to the window, looked out into the darkness for a moment, and came back to stand beside her. She could feel him looking down at her even though she could not see him distinctly in the shadow he made when his back was to the door. She had to restrain herself from reaching out to feel if he were there beside her.

"Hannah is quite a girl," he said finally, laughing a little to hide his uneasiness.

She knew he would have to say something like that sooner or later. It was the only way to get it over with. After that she waited for him to go on.

"We'll get along all right," he said. "There won't be any trouble."

She shook her hair in the draft of the fan. All at once the fan seemed as if it were going faster than ever. The draft became stronger, the whirring sound rose in volume to an ear-splitting pitch, and her shoulders shook involuntarily in the fan's chill breeze.

"I thought I would have a hard time of it," he said, "but now that it's over, it wasn't half as bad as I thought it was going to be. We'll get along all right."

Lavinia reached out and found his hand in the dark. He sat down on the side of the bed while she tried to think what to say.

"What's the matter, Lavinia?" he asked her. "What's wrong?"

"Let me go, Phil," she begged, beginning to cry in her soft deep voice. "I want to go."

He shook his head unmistakably.

"I couldn't let you go now, Lavinia," he said earnestly. "We agreed about that before this business took place the other day. You promised me. If I hadn't believed you would keep your promise, I wouldn't have gone ahead and done it."

"Please, Phil," she begged, crying brokenly until her soft deep voice filled the room. "Please let me go."

He kept on shaking his head, refusing to listen to her. Suddenly, there rose once more the bedlam of crowing that lasted for an hour in intermittent bursts every midnight. Neither of them tried to say anything while the crowing was at its height.

After several minutes the drone of the fan and the sobs in her breast drowned out the roosters' crowing.

"I've got to go, Phil," she said, holding back her sobs while she spoke.

"I can't let you go," he said. "I just can't let you go, Lavinia."

She stopped crying and sat up more erectly, almost on her knees. He gazed at her wonderingly.

"I'm a nigger, Phil," she said slowly. "I'm a nigger—a cooking, cleaning, washing nigger."

"Shut up, Lavinia!" he said, shaking her until she was in pain. "Shut up, do you hear?"

"I am, and you know I am," she cried. "I'm a nigger—a cooking, cleaning, washing nigger—just like all the rest are."

She brushed the tears from her eyes and tried to look at him clearly in the half-light. She could see his deep, serious expression and she knew he meant every word he had said.

"You'll get over it in a few days," he told her. "Just wait awhile and see if everything doesn't turn out just like I say it will."

"You know what I am, though," she said uncontrollably.

"Shut up, Lavinia!" he said, shaking her some more. "You're not! You're a white girl with colored blood—and little of that. Any of us might be like that. I have colored blood in me, for all I know. Even *she* might have some."

He jerked his head toward the front of the house. Forgetting everything else momentarily, they both listened for a while.

There was no sound whatever coming from that part of the building.

"She'll order me around just like she would anybody else," Lavinia said. "She'll treat me like the blackest washwoman you ever saw. She'll be as mean to me as she knows how, just to keep me in my place. She'll even call me 'nigger' sometimes."

"You're just excited now," he said. "It won't be like that tomorrow. You know as well as I do that I don't care what you are. Even if you looked like a colored girl, I wouldn't care. But you don't look like one—you look like a golden girl. That's all there is to it. If she ever says anything different, just don't pay any attention to her."

"She'll keep me in my place," Lavinia said. "I don't mind staying in my place, but I can't live here and have her tell me about it a dozen times a day. I want to go. I am going."

Phil got up, went to the door, and closed it. He came back and stood beside her.

"You're going to stay here, Lavinia," he said firmly. "If anybody goes, she'll have to go. I mean that."

Lavinia lay back on the pillow, closing her eyes and breathing deeply. She would rather have heard him say that than anything else he had said that night. She had been waiting five days and nights to hear him say it, and at last she could relax with the relief he had given her.

"I got married for a pretty good reason," he told her, "but I'm not going to let it ruin everything. I thought you understood all about it before it happened. You even told me to go ahead and marry her, so it would put a stop to all the talk about you living here as my housekeeper. It was hurting business at the store. We had to do something like that. And now you say you are going to leave."

There was silence for a long time after he had finished. Only the drone of the electric fan could be heard, and that for the first time sounded subdued.

"I won't leave," Lavinia said slowly, her voice so low he had to lean closer to her in order to hear. "The only way to make me leave is to throw me out. And I'd come back even if you did that. I want to stay, Phil."

As she lay on her back, she felt herself dropping into unconsciousness. For a while she made no effort to keep herself awake. She lay with her eyes closed and a smile on her lips.

She knew nothing else until he got up from the side of the bed. She opened her eyes as wide as she could in order to see if he was still there.

"I've got to go now," he said.

She sat up, shaking her head from side to side in the breeze of the electric fan. The air that blew through her hair was warm and clinging, and it began making her drowsy once more.

"Phil," she asked, "will you tell me something before you go?"

"Sure," he said, laughing. "What?"

"Phil, did you have a good time on your honeymoon?"

He laughed at her for a moment. After he had stopped there was a pause, and he laughed again.

"I had a great time on the beach," he said hesitatingly.

She laughed at him then, with motions of her head, in her soft deep voice.

"And with that old-maid schoolteacher you married, too?" she said, her words trailing off into soft deep laughter that filled the room.

He did not answer her. He went to the door to open it, but for several moments he did not turn the knob. He turned back to look at her again, her laughter filling his ears.

After a while he jerked open the door, stepped out on the porch, and closed the door as quickly as he could. He waited there for a moment to find out if Hannah had heard the laughter in Lavinia's room. When she did not come out into the hall after that length of time, he walked quickly down the porch to the hall door.

Lavinia's laughter swam through the hot night air, pouring into his ears until he could not hear even the sound of his own footsteps. The soft deep notes followed him like a familiar sound that was so close to him he could not find its source.

(First published in *Esquire*)

After-Image

I DON'T know how the thing came about. It just happened that way. One moment I was standing beside her with my hand on her arm, and the next moment she was gone. A thing like that can be an occurrence, an event, a tragedy, or merely the final act of living. I don't know what this was; but she was gone.

She had been standing beside me, her hands on the rail, looking out across the water. There was no mist in the air, and the stars were near and bright; but the lights on the shore seemed to be a long way off.

"They told me I could never see her again," she said. "Then

they shut the door and left me alone on the porch. I couldn't stay there forever. I left."

But there is no sense in my trying to repeat what she said. I can't remember everything, and most of it was unspoken. She had not even started at the beginning. The first words she said were: "I was nineteen when the baby was born." And when she spoke again, it was about something else. It would be foolish for me to try to arrange her sentences in any kind of order, and it would be impossible. Even if it were possible to take the words she uttered that night and arrange them in some kind of order, the things would have no meaning. A thousand things could be made of the words and sentences, but there is no one who knows what the logical sequence should be. In the end, we could with just as much purpose shake several thousand words in a hat and put them together in the order in which they were drawn.

I am not trying to repeat the things she said. It would be impossible to do that. I did not even try to hear much of what was being said, and most of what I did hear was all but inaudible.

"The house they live in has two stories and an attic. The roof has been covered with tin painted red. In the yard are three elm trees."

I heard her say that, but put those sentences after "I was nineteen when the baby was born," and almost everyone would suppose that she had given birth to a child in a house with two stories and a tin roof painted red. And that in the yard were elm trees. But that is not true, because the baby was born in a hospital. That's why I am not going to repeat what she said, at least not much of it. Some would be inclined to believe one thing, and some another. But the fact is that nothing someone else would be inclined to believe is true. What actually happened was that she said several things to me and stood beside me at the rail. That's why I don't know how the thing came about.

She had told me everything there was to tell. That was all she wished to talk about. The baby had been taken away from her, and her husband had left her. "I have never been dishonest with him," she had said. "But he was tired of me, and he wanted to live with someone else. That was all right, if he wished to do that. I loved him, but if he wanted to go, I did not wish to make him stay. I really wanted him to go and be happy. But they had no right to take the baby. She was mine. I am her mother."

I am not going to tell a lie about this thing. A lie is told with words, and the words in this have nothing whatever to do with what I am telling.

The proper thing for me to have done was to offer to help

her in some way, and to promise her that I would try to raise some money for a lawyer to take the matter to court. Or this or that. But I made no offer. I merely stood and looked at her, and waited to see what was going to happen next.

"The baby is mine," she said. "She is mine! I am her mother, and I have not been dishonest with him."

People were strolling past us, laughing and talking. There were three hundred people behind us.

"I'll never see the baby again. She will never see me. They will teach her that someone else is her mother. But she is my baby, and I'm her mother."

There is no reason why I should pretend not to be sentient about this. I have heard women many times before talk about their children, about their lovers, about nearly everything under the sun that women live for. And yet, in a case like this, when a woman says, "He begged me to marry him so we could live together and have a baby," I never know what to say or to think. Usually I stand and look at her and wonder how such things happen. That was what she had said: "He begged me to marry him."

"This other woman he fell in love with made him happier than I could. If I had known, I would have given him everything she did."

We were not at the rail then. We were in her cabin eating some sandwiches she had brought with her, and drinking coffee. Oh, the whole thing was mixed up. Nothing took place in logical order, and nothing had been said one moment that had any bearing on what was said the moment before. The whole thing was a hopeless cutout puzzle with an unknown number of parts missing. It would never come out in a way that made sense. I knew that. I knew that even when the whole thing was over, when the puzzle was finished except for the missing pieces, it would be unrecognizable. Neither I nor anyone else would know how the whole should appear.

She was on her way back home. At any rate, it had been her destination. But when she got there, there was nothing she could have done. She had no money for rent and food and clothes. She did not even know where she could find a job. When she reached home, she would have been forced to walk from house to house asking for something to eat and for some work to do. If she had had her baby, she could have undertaken to do that. But alone, with no family to help her, and with nothing left to live for, it would have been more than she could have endured. There is a breaking point. There is a place which is the end. After that, going back is the only way left. She could not go back. They had shut the door in her face, and had told her not to come there again.

"I don't care what happens to me," she said. "Nothing matters now. I want to forget everything for a few moments. If I could only be happy for a little while, I would be satisfied. I have never talked like this before, because this is the first time in my life I have ever thought of such things. I have always been honest with my husband. I did not deceive him. I have never been unfaithful. I have not even wished to be. I have never done anything that I knew he did not like for me to do. Now, I don't care what happens. I only want to be happy for a few short minutes. Perhaps I could get some liquor and drink until I am senseless. But that's foolish. I couldn't be happy that way. I would only be asleep. I want to feel happy, and to know that I am."

I'm not going to lie about this thing. I could make the whole thing a lie, perhaps, by pretending that I tried this way and that to comfort her. Perhaps I might have told her that if she stopped thinking about it so much and went to sleep that everything would be all right the next day. But I said nothing like that. I did nothing of the kind. I put the empty cups on the floor, in the corner of the cabin so the roll and pitch of the ship wouldn't upset them, and at the same time looked at her while she tried to talk.

"This woman he loved drank a certain kind of liquor with him and then they lay down together. My love was stronger than anything like that can be. I would have gladly torn myself open for him."

When she first began talking like that, I didn't know what to do. She had given up all hope of ever seeing either her husband or her baby again, and she knew that what happened after that night would not concern her. And she knew there was a way to forget and to feel happy, even if it was so short in time. She must have known that when she began telling me that she wished to forget for a few moments.

"He used to come home, after being away for two or three weeks, and tell me to leave him alone. He never knew how much he hurt me, but I could stand it because I had my baby then. But there were times when I wanted him so much. No one will ever know how I loved him. I loved him and my baby more than my own life."

What could I have said? What could a man, accustomed to doing the things he wished to do, say to a woman who had told him that? How could I understand what she was talking about? How can a man know how a woman feels when she is forced to live mute and alone?

Oh, the whole thing was a jumble. It was the framework of an image, indistinct and unbelievable. When she asked me what time it was, she knew and I knew that time did not matter. Time had nothing to do with who we were, what we were doing, and what we were talking about. The face of a clock is merely the reminder of the past. One o'clock, ten o'clock or five, it would still have been time for her to go in and see if the baby had tossed off the cover and to tuck her in for the night.

But why did my hands tremble, and why did my heart quiver? This thing was real. There she was, sitting before me, crying this moment and laughing the next. She had a wedding ring on her finger. The woodwork creaked under the stress and strain of the sea and the engines. It was real. I could feel it with my hands. I could touch it, scratch it, mar it with the nails in my shoes.

"I went down to the dock and bought a ticket. I had to wait nearly half an hour because there was such a crowd ahead of me. It took a long time for me to get aboard."

How did all this happen? How did it come about that I, who had never seen her before and who would never see her again, went with her and sat down in front of her? There were other things to do. This was not the only cabin on the ship. She was not the only person. It would be so easy to tell what might have happened, rather than to tell what actually did. It would be easier than doing this.

"Hurt me—ruin me—kill me!" she whispered. "Look! You won't have to suffer!"

A thousand lies could be told about the whole thing. I could say I said this-and-that; I could say I did this-that-and-the-other. A thousand things might have happened, but only one did. This only happened. This one thing. That's why I do not know how it came about. That's why I can't repeat, in logical sequence, what was said. Everything was in a hopeless jumble. This second she said one thing, and the next moment something else. Putting the two together made no sense.

I put my hand over her mouth. She had begun to scream. Screams such as I had never before heard pounded against my ears. The scratching at my face and shoulders I could partly endure and partly evade, but the screams had to be stopped. I tied a heavy bath towel over her mouth. What else could I have done? She lay there and scratched me and tried to scream until her face was as discolored as a bruise. She had to scream. It mattered nothing to her that there were three hundred people on the boat. If three hundred people heard her, or if no one heard her, she did not care. If the door were battered down, showing us there, the blood from my face and shoulders dripping upon her white body, she did not care. But I tied a heavy bath towel over her mouth. She tried to jerk it off, but I held it there. If she had torn it away and screamed, I could have forced it into her throat and choked her. She would have stopped breathing then. She wished me to kill her. She had said so. She had begged me to kill her. She had scratched the blood from my face and shoulders, begging me to kill her. But

first she wished to be happy. She wished to feel happiness
within her body. She wanted to forget herself in happiness.
There was a way. We were both covered with my blood by
then. It had dripped from my chest and smeared her face and
body.

All that was before. Everything seemed to be before anything else. Everything had happened before anything else had.
That was why it was such a hopeless jumble. Time, place, and
events had neither a beginning nor an end. I actually do not
know what the sequence of events was. I am only trying to
tell about them. There is no possible way of placing them in
the order of their origin. That's why the thing can't be told
with any order. That's why I can't lie about what happened.
They will have to be put down just as they are. The things she
said will have to be put down as she said them. If she had
spoken with order, things would perhaps be clear. And if
nothing comes out right in the end, it will be because I tried
to put the whole thing down with respect for her. She had said
things and done things with no regard for the way they would
look and sound when re-enacted and repeated. She didn't care
about that. She wished to be happy, and to feel the happiness
within herself, for a few moments.

She had said: "He wanted me to marry him. He begged me
to do it. He cried like a baby when I said I wanted to wait a
while longer. He cried like a baby. A great big strong man
like him cried like a baby."

She had said: "We lived in a six-room house with a pump on
the back porch. We had a collie puppy named Spot. Oh, we
were so happy together, all the time, day and night. Don't look
at me when I cry; I can't help it."

I don't know what I said. That is the truth. But what in
God's name could I have said? She did not want me to talk to
her. Only to listen now.

"Oh, I loved him so! And we loved each other like nothing
else in the world for nearly two years. Then one night he came
home and said he was going to leave me. He told me about
the other woman. He told me what she looked like and how
she wore her clothes. He told me what she looked like when
they slept together. Oh, he told me everything about her. He
told me of many things I had never heard about before. He
said she knew all those things. Then he went away and left me.
Someone came and took the baby away from me. They jerked
her out of my arms and ran out of the house and out of sight
before I could stop them. I did not know how to stop them.
I did not know what to do. Then I went up there, where his
home was. His sisters and mother had my baby, holding her
in their arms. They would not even let me touch her, or kiss
her. When I tried to reach for her, they pushed me back and

shut the door. They left me standing there on the porch, shutting the door and locking it to keep me out."

And then about the first week of their marriage. But what was it she said? Something about how they loved each other. The way he had of waking her up in the morning. And something else. What was that? But he loved her then, almost as much as she loved him.

Oh, there were hundreds of things she had said. I remember everything, but I can't recall the words she used. I can't repeat them. She uttered them in a jumble of things. They had come from her lips like the jumbled parts of a cutout puzzle. There was no man wise enough or patient enough to put the words in their correct order. If I attempted to put them together, there would be too many "ands" and "buts" and "theys" and thousands of other words left over. They would make no sense in human ears. They were messages from her heart. Only feeling is intelligible there. Sounds that words make never reach that deep. Only feeling reaches those depths. The words from her lips were never intended to be reassembled in the first place. Let them go. Let them resound their poor meanings upon trivial ears.

All that was before. It was before anything had happened. Nothing had yet taken place. All that was to be, was yet to come. There had been words, movements, and glances; but nothing at all had happened. You feel such things. Sounds cannot talk like that. Sounds in ears have only the sensation of loudness and softness. All that is unimportant. It is trivial. What I love and hate is the feeling of things. I felt her. I am not lying about it. I did feel her. And I am going to tell of what I felt. It was the quiver of her heart against my heart.

All that was before those quick movements when she looked at me once more, and left. It was the last of them all. There was nothing more to come afterward. Everything else had been before, and now it had happened.

The rail was before us. Her hands were resting on it, then gripping it tightly, so tightly that the tips of her fingers became white. A tightening of her fingers over the varnished rail was the beginning of it all. Nothing had happened until then. I can't lie about this thing.

The lights on the shore were a long way off. They were farther away than ever. There was no background of land, only the dim lights hanging over the foreside like fireflies caught and pinned to the bare limbs of weather-whipped trees.

She did not say she was going. We knew that. She did not pause to remind me of herself. She did not expect me to think of her as one who was going. That's all it was. She had been standing beside me this moment, the next she was gone. It was a moment of unhurried simplicity. She leaned over the rail, far over, balancing herself before my eyes. Then with no effort, only the weight of her unbalancing body to carry her, she went over the boatside out of sight.

I could have stopped her. Of course I could have stopped her. I am not denying that. And lies could be told about that, too. But I can't lie about it. I did not try to stop her. My hands did not move. But who would have wished to stop her? Is there anyone who would have done that? Only a coward would have grasped her, held her, and called for help. But we do not wish to be cowards. I'm sure of that. And I know. I was there. That's why I'm so certain about it. Only a coward would have caught her and pulled her away from the rail. But we do not want to be cowards. We try our hardest to keep from it. All of us wish to be brave, and we try our best to be above cowardice. We believe we are brave, and we attempt to act the part.

I was brave. I let her go. I stood with my arms within reach of her, watching her go. I even had to move my left arm out of the way so she could go. If I had not moved it out of the way, she would have had to exert herself to get past me. So I stood there, brave, watching her go over the boatside. When she had gone, I began to count. One, two, three, four, five, six, seven—

What was it she had said about her husband? Something about his hair. Its color. Blond. His hair was blond. She had told me that. But what was the color of her hair? She had not told me that. I had seen it with my own eyes. What was it? Blond? No. Brown? No. Red? No. Black? No. Then what was it! I don't know. I can't remember. I've forgotten. But it was her color. That was all it should have been. That is enough.

I was counting—forty-seven, forty-eight, forty-nine—*fifty!* That's enough. She has gone. *Gone!*

What were all those things I could have done? The things I might have done? There were so many I can't recall most of them now. But it doesn't matter. But do something! Jump after her? No. Call for help? No. What then? Nothing! I did not want to become a coward. I was not afraid to see a woman die. If she was not afraid to die, why should I be afraid to witness the death? Only the brave can take themselves into death. Life is too precious for the most miserable of us—when we are cowards. Only the brave can walk to death without a blindfold. The cowards fight for the last breath, for the last glimpse, for the final touch. Cowards do not wish to die. But she was not afraid. Then why should I be afraid to witness her death? Am I a coward beside a brave woman? She did not expect me to be a coward. I could not deceive her.

Oh, I might have done many things. I could first of all have stopped her from going. Then what? Notify the Captain? Report it to the police at the dock? Make an effort to reach her husband through the newspapers? Why? Why should I have done anything? The death of a brave woman could not make me become a coward.

The time to act was when she had leaned over the rail. Before she went over. But I didn't. I wanted her to feel her happiness in the act. We are only happy when we can do the thing we desire above all others. I was not afraid to stand and watch her. I was afraid to be a coward in the presence of a brave woman, a woman who was not afraid to be happy for a few moments.

That was all. And now this doesn't make much sense. The words are a jumble. The sounds they make are sometimes loud, sometimes soft. None of them is of any importance whatever. Only feeling matters. It is of that which has been told. I have been telling of feeling, the quiver of her heart against my heart.

(First published in *Pagany*)

Squire Dinwiddy

MY wife and I moved to the country toward the end of June, hopefully looking forward to a long restful summer in the Connecticut hills. But we soon discovered that we had been overly optimistic. It seemed that we were too far back in the hills to interest maids, housemen, or even tree surgeons. Nobody from the agencies wanted to work that distance from Stamford or Bridgeport.

We had been doing our own housework for a week when we looked up one morning while cooking breakfast to see a big shiny black limousine drive up and stop. A Negro man about thirty years old and wearing what appeared to be the remnants of a ragbag after it had been picked over came around to the kitchen door and knocked lightly.

"Good morning, boss," he said, peering through the door. "How you folks making out?"

My wife was all for sending him away without more ado, but by that time he had opened the screen door and had stepped into the kitchen.

"Good morning," I replied civilly. "Lost?"

"No, sir, boss," he said, his lips rolling back from two neat rows of the whitest teeth I had ever seen. "I'm right here. I ain't lost one bit."

"What do you want?" my wife asked him.

"I'se come to take hold," he said.

"Take hold of what?" I asked, concerned.

"Take hold the work, boss," he answered, grinning.

"Who sent you?" my wife and I asked simultaneously.

"Nobody sent me," he said. "I just heard about it and come."

My wife and I looked at each other, each wondering if the other were going to be able to think of something to say. Our attention was drawn back to the Negro when he opened the screen door and. shooed a stray fly out of the kitchen.

"What can you do?" my wife asked at last.

"Anything you or the boss wants done, Missy," he said respectfully. "Eating, drinking, clotheses, driving, laundering—anything at all. Now, you folks just go sit down in comfort at the table and make yourself feel at ease, and I'll have your breakfast in front of you in no time at all. I'll fix up my extra special omelette and see how you folks take to it."

We moved toward the dining room.

"How much do you want in wages?" I asked.

"Would it hurt you to pay fifteen a week, boss?"

"Well," I said hesitatingly, "maybe we can stand it."

"I'll take thirteen and a half," he said almost obligingly, "if that'll help you out any."

We backed through the door.

"What's your name?" my wife asked.

"Squire," he said, grinning until his white teeth gleamed from ear to ear. "Squire Dinwiddy."

When my wife and I reached the hall, we stopped and looked at each other questioningly for a moment. All we could do was to nod our heads.

"Squire," I called through the door, "now that you've got a new job, don't you think you ought to return that limousine to your former employer—"

"Boss," he spoke up proudly, "that there's my machine. I'se the lawful solitary owner."

We backed carefully into the dining room, watching our step.

All went well until one morning about a week later. It happened to be the Fourth of July. My wife and I had been out late the evening before, and at seven o'clock we were sound asleep. But not for long. There was a terrific explosion on the lawn just outside our window. I rushed from bed, threw open the screen, and looked out. There squatted Squire Dinwiddy, holding a lighted match under the fuse of the biggest firecracker I had ever seen. The fuse began to spew, and Squire dashed away and got behind a tree. The salute went off, charring the grass and blowing a hole in the earth. My wife screamed.

"Squire!" I yelled. "What are you doing?"

Squire stuck his head cautiously around the trunk of the tree and looked up at me in the window.

"It's the Fourth of July, boss," he said, grinning happily. "Did you forget all about that?"

"No, I didn't forget," I said. "And it's not up to you to remind me at this time of morning, either."

"I still got one more to shoot off, boss," Squire said, striking a match and setting the fuse on another giant cracker to spewing.

"Hold your ears!" I shouted to my wife just in time.

The cracker went off while Squire was still running from it. When the report sounded, it caught him by surprise, and he jumped two feet off the ground. Then he stopped and looked around.

"It makes celebrating best when they go off when you ain't expecting them to, don't it, boss?" he said, grinning up at the window.

"Maybe," I said.

Three weeks later, just when we had accustomed ourselves to Squire's manner of running the house, he came in one morning and said he was sorry to have to do it, but that he had to go away for several days on a business trip.

We were upset by his sudden announcement, and my wife protested vigorously.

"Can't you postpone your trip for a while, Squire?" she said. "We can't get anybody to take your place on such short notice."

"I'm sorry about the notice I didn't give," Squire said apologetically, "but the time crept up on me while I wasn't paying attention."

"At least," my wife said, "you can wait a day or two. Maybe by then we—"

"No, ma'am!" he said, emphatically, "I just naturally can't wait. I'se got to be in Washington by six o'clock this very day."

"Six o'clock!" I said. "How do you expect to get to Washington by six o'clock!"

"On the plane, boss," he said. "I'se flying down on the two o'clock plane from New York."

My wife and I looked at each other helplessly.

"That costs a lot of money, Squire," she said, hoping to discourage him. "Do you realize what it costs?"

"Yes, ma'am," Squire said, "but I add it to my expenses."

"What expenses?" I asked. "What expenses are you talking about?"

"The expenses of doing business," Squire said.

My wife and I stared at each other bewilderedly.

"What kind of business?" I asked, wondering.

"I kind of forgot to mention it to you, I reckon," Squire said sheepishly. "I has to go to Washington once every month to collect the rents."

"What rents?" I asked. "Whose rents?"

"My rents," he answered. "I'se got twenty-seven families living in my tenements down there, and I can't afford to let the rents fall behind. The rents just can't be collected, not in Washington, noway, if you let them run over. Because the renters will let you get an eviction against them, and after that they have the law on their side. They don't have to pay the past-due rent at all after that. So that's why I never let the renters get that far along. I stay just one jump ahead of what they're thinking in their heads down there while I'm up here."

My wife and I could only stare at Squire for a long time after he had finished. He began to grin then, his lips rolling back from his straight white teeth.

"Why, that makes you an absentee landlord, Squire," I said finally, shaking my head.

"It sure does, boss," he said, his whole face agrin. "That's why I'm taking the plane this afternoon. I don't aim to be absent when the rents come due. No, sir, boss!"

Squire bowed, backing toward his shiny black limousine with the silver speaking tube. He grinned broadly as he got in and started the motor. As he rolled away, he stuck an arm out and waved to us.

"Good-by, boss!" he called. "I'll be right back again as soon as I collect the rents!"

We raised our arms and waved until he was out of sight. After that we turned and stared at each other, wondering what there was to say.

(First published in *Esquire*)

Picking Cotton

ABOUT an hour after sunrise every morning during the cotton-picking season, people began coming towards the Donnie Williams farm from all directions. They came walking over the fields from four and five miles away, following the drain ditches, wading waist-high through the brown broom sedge in the fallow land, and shuffling through the yellow road dust. They came in pairs, in families, and in droves.

There were nearly five hundred acres of cotton to gather, and the Williamses were paying fifty cents a hundred pounds. Besides that, though, there were good-sized watermelons for every man, woman, and child, both white and colored, at dinnertime. Everybody liked to pick cotton at the Donnie Williams place, even though some of the farmers who could not find enough hands were offering seventy-five a hundred pounds, and even up as high as a dollar a hundred. But none of them had free watermelons for everybody.

Even though everyone liked to pick cotton for Donnie Williams, it was unusual to find the same people in the fields for two consecutive days. A man, with his family, would work for Donnie a day, and then stay at home a day to pick his own crop, or to just lie around the house and rest. Then there were the drifters who never stayed at one farm longer than a day. They had no homes to go to at night, so they slept in field houses and went to the next farm the following day. There were always new pickers arriving, and usually there were just as many people coming as there were leaving.

It had been a custom at Donnie Williams's place for the pickers to work in pairs. Donnie had tried out all kinds of schemes to get his crop gathered as quickly as he could before the price began to fall, and he had found out that people could, and would, pick better if they worked in pairs. Sometimes, otherwise, when there were crowds of twenty and thirty together, all of them would stop picking to laugh at a joke, and stand up to talk with the others. Ten or fifteen minutes wasted of every hour cut down the number of pounds a man could gather in a day, and Donnie was trying to get his crop through the gins as soon as possible.

I sometimes paired off with a Negro boy named Sonny. He and I had a lot to talk about, because he worked as a houseboy for Mrs. Williams when he was not needed in the fields, and he knew a lot that I was anxious to hear.

Three or four times I had paired off with a redhaired girl from across the country. Her name was Gertie. She was about fifteen, and she knew more riddles than anybody I ever saw. She used to ask me riddles all the time we were picking, and when I could not answer them and had to give up, she would sit down, lift her calico skirt, and fan her face with it while she laughed at me for not knowing the answers.

Once she asked me if I knew what was the age of consent. I was not certain that I did know.

"Come on and tell me, Gertie," I begged her.

"You think it over tonight, Harry," she said, "and if you don't know by tomorrow, I'll tell you."

Gertie had a habit of giggling when she asked me something like that, and now she was giggling again. All that time she was fanning her face with her skirt, drawing the calico higher and higher above her waist while she laughed at me.

"It's real funny," she giggled.

There was nothing funny to me about a riddle I could not answer, nor even guess, but no amount of begging would ever make Gertie tell me the answer to that one. She would always sit down on her cotton-bag, cross her slender round legs under her, and fan her face with her skirt while she giggled because I did not know what to say.

It was all right for her to do that if she wished to, but I was never able to pick much cotton and look at her naked from the waist down at the same time. She would sit there and giggle about the riddle, fanning herself furiously, and smile at me. It would even have been all right for her to sit down on her cotton-bag and lift her skirt like that if only she had worn something under the one-piece calico wrapper. As long as I knew Gertie though, she never did.

"Why does an old maid look under the bed at night before she puts out the light, Harry?"

"God damn it, Gertie!" I shouted at her. "Why don't you keep your dress down where it belongs!"

I could not pick cotton when she did like that, and it made me angry.

"You can make up good riddles, too, can't you, Harry?" she said.

I was just getting ready to jump over to her row and throw her down when I looked around and saw Donnie Williams walking across the field not far away, and I had to go back to work right away.

After picking with one of the Johnsons for two days, I again paired off one morning with Gertie. We started off at a fast pace, each of us trying his best to get ahead of the other. Gertie had thought up a lot of new riddles to ask me, but we were so busy trying to leave each other behind that she did not have time to say anything to me for several hours.

It was about dinnertime when I heard her whistle to me. I turned around to see what she wished.

"Harry," she said, straightening up and packing the cotton in her bag with her feet, "do you see that black-haired girl over there with the old woman?"

She pointed over the rows towards them.

"What about her?" I asked.

"She was paired off yesterday with that Dennis boy, and last night she weighed in four hundred pounds, and the boy had only fifty pounds."

"Hell, Gertie," I said, "that's no riddle. Can't you think up a better one than that? She's not the first to weigh in more than a man. You can see them stripping over in the broom sedge almost any time that Donnie's not around."

"I don't suppose she is," Gertie said, sitting down and fanning her face with the calico skirt, "because I weighed in three-fifty myself the other night when I was picking with Sonny. He didn't have much more than forty pounds at quitting time, either."

That made me angry. I threw off the strap over my shoulder and jumped over the row beside her.

"God damn you, Gertie," I shouted, grabbing her by the arms, "did you let that damn nigger—"

"Let him do what?" she asked, giggling a little and pulling her skirt above her waist. "Did I let him give me some of his cotton?"

"Yes—"

"Sonny gave me only a hundred pounds, Harry."

"I'm going to beat hell out of him," I told her. "He ought to have better sense than to pair off with a white girl. And anyway, he ought to have given you two hundred pounds—"

Gertie twisted her shoulders from side to side and her heavy breasts shook until I thought that they would surely burst.

"I've just thought of a good riddle, Harry!" she said, naked again from her waist down. "Listen to this: If Sonny offered me a hundred pounds and you offered me two hundred, which one of you would I rather have take me?"

"Any fool knows that two hundred is twice as much as one hundred, Gertie. And anyway, Sonny is a nigger!"

"When are you ever going to learn how to answer riddles, Harry?" she said, fanning herself faster and faster. "Two hundred is twice as much as one hundred, but you're not Sonny."

She had begun to giggle, but before she could laugh at me, I caught her and threw her down, and began stuffing cotton into her mouth.

"That damn nigger, Sonny, won't ever—"

I said that much, but I never finished saying all I had meant to tell her when I jumped on her. I could see by looking into her eyes that she had thought of a new riddle, and that as soon as I took the cotton from her mouth she would ask me another one that I could not answer.

(First published in *Contempo*)

The Girl Ellen

ELLEN was nice enough about it. She said she would never have come over to spend the night with Doris if her family had not suddenly left town for the week end, because she knew Doris and Jim had planned to go swimming that evening. No one could have been more considerate than Ellen.

Finally, she begged them to let her stay at the house while they went without her.

It was late in summer, and it had already turned dark. The street lights had just been switched on, but on the porch a dim twilight still lingered.

"Honest, I'd lots rather stay here," Ellen insisted.

"Forget it," Jim said. "Sometimes it takes three to have a good time, anyway. This might be one of those times."

Under his breath he muttered something. It was the first night in almost a month that he had not had to work, and it would probably be the last time that summer he and Doris could go swimming together. He turned his head from the girl and glared at the street light that twinkled intermittently through the restless, breeze-blown maple leaves.

Jim Gregory did not feel in high spirits anyway. The fellow who worked next to him in the plant had been turned off, and Jim could not help wondering if that were a sign that some of the rest of them would be discharged, too. He had thought about it all the way home, and then he got there and found Ellen with Doris saying that she was afraid to stay by herself while her family was away.

"I'll find something to read," Ellen was saying then, "and I'll have just as good a time right here."

Doris did not have much to say. She liked Ellen a lot, but she was a little sorry it had to happen on just the one night in the month that Jim had off from work.

"I wouldn't think of letting you and Jim take me along," Ellen said for the third or fourth time. "I'd rather stay here."

Jim started to tell her to stay there, but to hush up about it.

"That's different," he said. "If you don't like our company, we probably wouldn't like yours, either."

Ellen jumped off the railing and began tousling Jim's hair. When he found that he could not push her away, he succeeded in catching her hands and pulling her to the arm of the chair.

When he got her there, he was sorry he had touched her. He was on the verge of telling her that she was as sticky as molasses.

"Nothing in the world could make me go along with you now," Ellen said. "I wouldn't do anything with a person who talked so mean."

"How do you know I'd like your company?" he said.

She tried to pull away from him. He caught both of her hands in his.

Doris got up and moved towards the door.

"Of course you are going with us," she said with finality. "All three of us are going swimming."

Doris went into the house to get ready, and Ellen got down from the arm of the chair. Her hands slipped through Jim's like silk.

Before he knew what had happened, Ellen had turned around and kissed him lightly on the mouth. The momentary brushing of her lips on his drew him towards her as if to a magnet. When he finally realized what had taken place, she had already turned and had run into the house. He sat upright for a moment, staring after her in a daze. Slowly he sank back into the chair.

When the sound of her had died away in the house, he drew the back of his hand across his lips several times, roughly, until the last trace of her kiss had been wiped away.

While she and Doris were getting ready, he remained on the porch. He had never liked Ellen; she was always running over to see Doris and getting in the way. The longer he thought about it, the more he wished he had worked that night. When he stopped wiping his mouth with the back of his hand, his lips felt bruised, and he was more angry than ever with Ellen for having kissed him.

Doris and Ellen finally came downstairs ready to leave. When the porch light was turned on, he got up and went to the door. Ellen came out first, smiling a little, and Jim could not keep from staring at her again. He felt then, in spite of himself, that he was glad she was going along. Ellen was taller than Doris and, he saw for the first time, prettier. He wondered why he had never noticed that before. He drew the back of his hand over his mouth, quickly, when the touch of her lips came back to him.

When they got to the street where the car was standing, all of them waited indecisively to see who would sit in the middle. Ellen hung back until Doris could decide.

"You sit in the middle," Doris said finally, taking Ellen by the arm and pushing her to the door.

Ellen said nothing, but she hesitated for a moment.

"It's all the same to me," Jim said, trying to appear indifferent.

He made no effort to get into the car until Doris and Ellen had made up their minds. When Ellen got in, Jim opened the door on his side and sat down beside her. He could not see Doris's face then.

He started the motor, turned around in the street, and drove off faster than usual. It was only nine o'clock and there was plenty of time to reach the swimming pool in the country. However, he was in a hurry to get there.

During the first few minutes of driving, Ellen sat away from him as far as she could, but after they had gone a mile or more, he could feel her close beside him. She was as yielding as he had remembered her being on the porch at home.

After several more minutes he felt that he could not keep from looking at her. Taking his eyes from the road for a moment, he turned and looked at her. Ellen refused to let her eyes meet his. He leaned nearer, hoping to make her look at him.

"You'd better watch where you are going, Jim," Doris said, not turning her head.

He jerked around just in time to keep from running off the road. It made him feel like a fool to have Doris speak like that, but for some reason he did not care. Ellen drew away from him again, and she and Doris began talking together in low tones. After a while, Jim finally stopped trying to overhear what they were saying.

Just before they reached the swimming pool, Jim drew the back of his hand over his mouth several times. His lips still felt bruised where he had mashed them with his knuckles while on the porch at home. But when he closed his eyes, he could still feel, through the numbness and bruise, the brushing of Ellen's lips against his.

"What in the world are you doing, Jim?" Doris cried.

He opened his eyes just in time to jam on the brakes. He turned into the parking lot beside the swimming pool. If Doris had not stopped him, they would have passed it. Jim tried to laugh about it, but he felt like a fool just the same. He wondered what Doris was thinking.

When he stopped the car, Doris jumped out and started for the bathhouse without a word. She did not even wait for Ellen.

"I've got to lock up the car, Doris," he said crossly. "Can't you wait a minute?"

Doris stopped and watched him lock the car. When he put the keys into his pocket and started towards her, she turned and walked away. Ellen ran and caught up with her, and they entered the bathhouse together.

When Jim got there, they had gone into a locker room, and he did not see them again.

It did not take him long to change into his bathing suit, and he was in the water ten or fifteen minutes before Doris and Ellen came out of the bathhouse. They came together towards him in the pool.

There was so much shouting and splashing of water all around them that Jim could not make them understand what he was trying to say. Giving up, he swam across the pool towards them.

Just before he got to the side of the pool, Doris dived in, plunging out of sight into the ten-foot depth. He and Ellen watched her until she came up. Instead of swimming back to where they were, Doris turned and struck out across the pool to the opposite side. Jim motioned to her with his hands to come back, but Doris did not even shake her head in reply.

"Can't you dive?" he said to Ellen.

"You don't have to snap my head off," she said.

She dived but did not come up for several seconds. Just when he was becoming uneasy, her head appeared thirty feet away, near the center of the pool.

He swam to her.

"You'd better go talk to Doris," Ellen said, backing away from him.

They were both treading water.

"Let's dive off the tower," Jim said.

Ellen shook her head and began swimming towards the shallow end. He followed her.

"Doris won't like it if you don't go over there where she is," Ellen said. "You'd better go, Jim."

He did not look in Doris's direction.

Ellen backed away. Reaching for her hand, Jim caught her and pulled her to him. Even under the water her hands were as yielding as they had been on the porch at home. More than ever he felt that she was like soft rubber in his hands.

"You shouldn't do that," she said. "Jim, I—"

Somebody splashed water near by, and a wave broke over their heads. Ellen came up choking. Quickly grasping her around the waist, Jim lifted her so no more water could reach her head. She was all right after a moment, but he did not release her. Once he had her in his arms, he felt he could never turn her loose again. It was like holding a wild rabbit in his arms, knowing the frightened, panting animal would make a break for freedom at the slightest chance. He squeezed her all the more tightly.

"Don't do that, Jim," she said.

She strained to break away from him, but Jim's arms were like iron bands around her. Once, for a moment, she relaxed in his arms. He crushed her more tightly than ever.

"Jim," she said, "Jim, we can't . . ."

Out of the corner of his eye he saw Doris jump to her feet from the bench where she had been sitting and walk to the edge of the pool. He did not look long enough to see whether she had dived in or whether she went back to the bench.

"Please don't hold me any more," Ellen said. "Let's go with Doris. I can't let you hold me like this."

"She's all right," Jim heard himself say. "Don't worry about her."

"But you've got to stop, Jim. Please don't hold me any more. I'm going with Doris."

He pulled her with him to the other side of the pool, ignoring her protests. When they got to the rim, Ellen broke away from him and dived under the water. He plunged after her.

When he came up, he could see neither Ellen nor Doris. For a while he thought they were ducking out of sight, and he went under again himself, swimming along the side of the pool with his eyes open in the water. He could see neither of them.

After thirty or forty seconds under the water he came up for breath. He came up just in time to see Ellen climbing the ladder out of the water. He splashed after her.

"Where's Doris?" Ellen asked him.

He climbed out and stood beside her, looking around the pool. Doris was not to be seen among the fifteen or twenty persons in the water.

"Maybe she's gone into the bathhouse," he said.

Ellen's fingers caught his, closing over his hand.

"No," she said, trembling all over. "No, she didn't go into the bathhouse. She couldn't have, because I've been watching all the time."

Jim walked hurriedly around the pool, searching each face in the crowd. When he got back, he sat down on a bench. Ellen dropped beside him.

"Where is she, Jim?" Ellen said.

"She's all right," he said. "She'll show up in a minute."

"But she wouldn't go off like this, Jim."

Jim laughed.

"Maybe she didn't like it because I was in the water with you so long," he said. "She'll be back as soon as she gets over it."

Ellen drew away from him, moving to the other end of the bench.

"I shouldn't have let you," she said, covering her face with her hands. "I didn't know what I was doing. It was my fault. I should have known better."

He got up and left her to go to the refreshment stand. He brought back two cones of ice cream and sat down on the bench.

"I wouldn't have hurt Doris for anything in the world," Ellen said, covering her face.

"You didn't hurt her," Jim insisted. "She just went into the bathhouse."

Ellen tried to eat the ice cream, but she could not swallow it. She handed the cone back to Jim and ran into the bathhouse. She was back in less than a minute.

"Doris isn't in the locker room, Jim, but her clothes are!" she cried.

Jim ran to the pool and tried to see down into the bottom of it. The people all around him were diving and splashing in the water.

He began to tremble.

"Jim!" Ellen cried. "Something has happened to Doris!"

"How could anything happen to her? She can swim as good as I can. What makes you think something happened?"

Ellen screamed.

The guard who had been sitting in a chair reading a magazine jumped to his feet and ran towards them.

"What's the matter with you people?" he said.

"A girl is missing!" Ellen cried excitedly. "Doris isn't here. I haven't seen her for nearly half an hour."

The guard ran to the drain tap and opened the outlet. The water began to sink immediately.

By that time a dozen or more persons had begun diving and searching in the ten-foot depth. Jim and Ellen stood on the edge, leaning over as far as they could, watching.

When the water had drained to the four-foot mark, somebody said something. He went under the water and came up slowly. Jim jumped into the pool and felt under the water with his hands. Together they brought up the body of a girl. It was Doris.

When she had been carried out of the pool and stretched on the ground, Ellen began crying. The guard had already begun working over Doris, and somebody had thought to call an ambulance.

Doris's rubber bathing cap had slipped off her head, and her long brown hair was tangled around her. Jim jumped into the water and began searching frantically for the rubber cap while the guard worked over Doris. Jim could think of nothing else to do.

In spite of the guard's determined attempt to resuscitate her, Doris was already dead when they lifted her on the stretcher and placed her in the ambulance.

Jim slumped down in a corner of the bathhouse. No one saw him there, and long after everybody else had hurriedly dressed and left, he was still there. The lights had been turned off when he opened his eyes.

Feeling his way outside, he did not think of changing into his clothes. He walked outside into the parking lot where his car was standing. When he remembered that his keys were in his clothes inside the bathhouse, he started walking towards town without another thought. If the keys had been anyplace else, he would have gone for them; but he could not turn his face again in the direction of the swimming pool.

He finally got home, but he could not remember how he had managed to find his way when he could recall nothing that had taken place since leaving the parking lot. The hall light was burning as they had left it, and he found an unlocked window through which he managed to climb inside.

Stumbling through the house from room to room, he at last fell on his hands and knees on the floor, and a moment later he felt himself fall over on his side. The last thing he remembered doing was wondering if Ellen would be there when he woke up.

(First published in *Kneel to the Rising Sun*)

A Woman in the House

MAX CLOUGH was getting along well enough until Elam went away over the week end. Max had his winter's wood in, his house was sawdust-banked against the frost, and there was a good supply of pumpkin wine in the cellar. He had settled himself for a good three months' rest and he thought Elam had done the same. Both of them knew that winter was coming, as the ground was frozen every morning, and the sun was already beginning to set in the intervale by two o'clock.

But Elam went away over the week end. He went off without coming to tell Max about it, and he left early Saturday morning before it was light enough for Max to see him go.

Only a few days before, Max had gone across the road and talked for an hour or longer, but Elam had not said a word about going away. He had not even said that he was thinking of taking a short trip. They had talked about how dear money was getting to be, and how much improved the mail delivery was since Cliff Stone had taken over the route through the intervale, and about the prospects for a new State highroad through the town. But Elam had said nothing about his going away over the week end. That was the reason why Max was upset Saturday morning when he went across the road to see Elam a moment, and found that the house was locked and that the shades were drawn.

"When a man gets to be thirty-six years old," Max said, looking sharply at the closed dwelling, "he ought to have sense enough to stay at home, instead of going off for week ends in Lewiston and throwing away dear money for lodging and what-not. Elam might possess a little sense about minor things, but he hasn't got the sense he was born with when it comes to throwing away dear money in Lewiston. Nobody but a plain fool would go to Lewiston and give a woman five-ten dollars for her bed."

He went back across the road and up the slope to his own house, glancing up the intervale and down it, as if he expected to see Elam coming home. But he knew Elam would not come home until Sunday afternoon. He had gone away before like that, and each time he had stayed the two whole days. He knew Elam would not return until the next afternoon.

Max's farm and buildings were on the eastern slope of the intervale, and Elam Stairs' were on the western slope. Between them was the Yorkfield town road. The only advantage Elam had, Max admitted, was longer sunlight in winter. The sun set on Max's house by two o'clock in midwinter, while Elam had an hour's longer sun. But Max was well enough pleased with his place, because he knew that his eastern slope grew better green peas. His land was well watered the year around; in midsummer, Elam's fields became dry.

For the rest of the afternoon and far into the evening, Max could not get off his mind Elam's trip. He did not envy him the week end in Lewiston, because he knew exactly how much it would cost, but he did not wish for Elam to slip off as he did three or four times a year. It upset his carefully planned living. He could do nothing while Elam was absent from home. He had become accustomed to seeing Elam somewhere about his farm at almost any hour of the day when he looked over at the western slope, and when Elam was not there, Max was at a loss to know how to continue doing his work. And, besides that, when Elam was away, there was always the possibility that he would not come back alone. He knew he could never get over Elam's bringing home somebody with him.

They had talked such things over many times. Each time Elam went to Lewiston, he came home talking about the women he had seen on the streets and in the lodginghouses. That was one reason why Max did not like for Elam to go there. Sooner or later, he knew Elam would bring home a woman.

"The women aren't suited to our lives, Elam," Max told him once. "You on your western slope, and me on my eastern slope, live as people ought to live. Just as soon as a man brings home a woman, his house is too small a space for him to live in, eight rooms or twelve rooms. Married, or housekeeper, there's no difference. It's a woman, and there's always trouble under a roof when you mix the two sexes. I wish to stay just as I am. I wish to live peacefully, and my wish is to die the same way."

"Can't somehow always agree with you, Max," Elam said, shaking his head. "You've got a lot of sense; good, sane, horse sense, Max. But God was required to make woman. Why! do you know that before there were any women, the men were fixing to tear the world to pieces unless women were provided?"

"Why?" Max asked.

"Why?" Elam said. "Why! because the men wouldn't stand for it any longer, that's why. They had to have housekeepers, or if they couldn't be had, just wives. There's a world of difference between the two, but at bottom they both are women, and that's what man had to have. Otherwise, us men would have to do all the sewing and cooking."

"Have always got along fairly well doing my own labor," Max said. "Never had a woman to do my work for me. I don't wish to have one in the house to cause trouble."

"Well," Elam said, "they may cause some trouble. I'm willing to grant you that. But taking all in all, their good points pretty well overbalance the bad ones. God was compelled to make them, and I don't aim to disuse anything that is provided. Guess I wish to get all there is in this life to make use of. No sense in letting it go to waste, or to have somebody else take my share, and his too. I wish to have all of everything that's due me."

Max was not convinced then, and he was still firm in his belief that a man could live more happily and peacefully in his house alone. None of the times when Elam tried to make Max admit that women were a necessary part of existence did he succeed. Max was steadfast in his determination to live his life apart from women.

Now that Elam had gone away on another of his quarterly trips to Lewiston, Max was afraid once again that he would bring home a housekeeper. On each occasion before, he had been on edge the whole time Elam was away, and he was never able to calm himself until he could go over and see that Elam had not brought back a housekeeper. He would not even take Elam's word for it. He would first ask Elam if he came home alone, and then he would go from room to room, looking behind doors and into closets, until he was satisfied in his own mind that there was no woman in the house. After that, he would feel better. He could then go back to his own house with a calm mind.

But Elam was away again for the week end, and Max could

not sit still. He could not eat his meals, and he could not sleep. He sat beside his window looking across to the western slope, his window raised several inches in case there should be the sound of an automobile in the intervale. He sat by the window all day Saturday, Saturday evening, and Sunday.

Late Sunday afternoon, when Max knew it was time for Elam to come back home, he heard Elam's automobile coming up the intervale. He knew it was Elam's car, and he knew he could not sit there another minute. He jumped up and found his hat and coat and started down the front doorstep.

The road was not within sight of Max's house, as there was a grove of birch trees down there, and he could not see the automobile. He heard Elam drive into his lane, however, and he waited and listened until the sound of the motor stopped abruptly in the barn.

There was something about the abruptness of the sound's stopping that caused him to pause on the doorstep. The motor was shut off the moment the car entered the barn, and then there was complete silence again in the intervale. Not even the rumbling sound of Elam closing the barn doors could be heard. Max wondered if Elam could be in such a hurry to get into his house that he had not waited to close the barn doors. He could not think of any reason to explain that. A man who was in such a great hurry to get into his house would certainly have something of importance coming up. Max thought about that, but he could think of no reason why a man would fail to close the barn doors.

He sat down on the doorstep and waited. He turned his head from side to side, allowing each ear to try to detect some sound in the intervale. Surely, he thought to himself, Elam had not gone and lost his mind. But he could think of no other reason for Elam's failure to close the barn doors. A man who drove his automobile into the barn and then left the doors open would certainly be foolish, and Elam had not been known theretofore as a foolish man. Elam knew better than to leave the barn doors open when evening was coming.

The sun in the intervale was dim and gray. A bank of gray clouds had risen in the northwest, and before long there would be no more sunshine. It was after three o'clock then, and the sun had already set on the western slope. Max had become accustomed to two o'clock sunsets on the eastern slope of the intervale, but when it set before three o'clock on the western slope, he was unprepared for it.

During all the time that he had been sitting on his doorstep, Max had hoped that Elam would come over to see him and tell him about the trip to Lewiston. Elam had always done that. Each time Elam had gone away for the week end in

Lewiston, he had come home Sunday afternoon, had slammed shut the barn doors, and then had walked down the lane and up the slope and told Max what he had seen and what he had done in Lewiston. It was long past the time for him to come, and he had not even closed the barn doors. Max could not sit still and wait for Elam any longer. He got up and started down the slope towards the road.

When he reached the road, he stopped a moment and looked up towards Elam's farm and buildings. The barn door was wide open, and the automobile stood there exposed to the weather. There was no one to be seen about the house, but the shades had been opened, and the entrance door was ajar. Something was wrong, Max thought. Something had happened to Elam this time on his trip to Lewiston.

Standing beside Elam's mail box, Max looked up the slope towards the house. It was only a few hundred yards away, and he could see everything as plainly as if he had been standing on the doorstep. The white paint was whiter than ever in the gray twilight of the intervale, and the green trim was brighter than the grass in midsummer. Max stood looking at the place, waiting.

He had been staring at the house for ten minutes without seeing a single sign of Elam, when suddenly Elam appeared at one of the windows. He raised the window with a single thrust of his arm, and stuck out his head. Immediately another window was raised, on the opposite corner of the house, and a woman stuck out her head. They looked at each other for a moment, and then both withdrew their heads and the windows were lowered so quickly that Max was certain that the glass had been cracked. For a few seconds he did not believe what his eyes had seen. He would not believe that he had actually seen a woman in Elam's house. But slowly the realization came to him that he had seen a woman there, a young woman with a full body and yellow hair, and he stepped backward off Elam's land into the public road.

After what he had seen, Max did not know whether to stand there looking at the house, or whether to turn and go back up the slope to his own place. He knew he would never again set foot on Elam's land, however; he had already made up his mind never to have anything more to do with Elam Stairs. He did not even wish to speak to him again. He could never forgive Elam for having brought home a woman from Lewiston.

While he stood in the road trying to make up his mind about what he was going to do, the woman he had first seen in the window came running around the corner of the house. Max stared unbelievingly. Then a moment later came Elam, running faster than Max thought it possible for anyone to run. He was overtaking the yellow-haired young woman, two strides to her one, and if they had not turned the other corner of the house at that moment, he would have seen Elam grab her. Elam had his coat off, and the woman's dress was open down her back all the way to her waist. The woman was laughing, but Elam was not.

Max waited another five minutes, wishing to be there in case they again ran around the house. Then he turned and walked slowly up the eastern slope of the intervale. The sight of a woman at Elam's house made him wish to go over there and drive her out of the intervale, but he knew he could never do that. Elam would not allow him to run her away. Elam would protect her, and send him back across the road.

By the time that Max had reached his own house, he had definitely made up his mind about what he was going to do. He was going to take a trip himself the following week end. He was going down to Lewiston Saturday morning and stay there until Sunday afternoon. And while he was there he would do the same things that Elam had done.

"Elam Stairs isn't the only man in the intervale who can bring home a woman," he said, taking his seat beside the window and looking over at the western slope where the sun had set. He raised the window several inches so that he might hear any sound that was audible in the intervale. "Will hire me a housekeeper in Lewiston and bring her back here, too. Elam Stairs has an hour's more sunshine because his farm and buildings are on the western slope, and he thinks he can have even more advantage with a housekeeper. But he shan't. I'll show him that I can go to Lewiston and maybe get a finer-looking housekeeper than he's got."

Max hitched his chair closer to the window.

"Guess I'll chase mine thrice around the house when I bring her here," he said. "And it might be a good plan to wait till she gets right in the middle of changing her clothes to start chasing her, instead of starting after her like Elam did when she only had her dress unfastened down her back. Guess Elam Stairs will see as how I made a pretty smart deal, when he looks out his window some fine day and sees me chasing a naked housekeeper, and gaining on her three strides to her one. He chased his woman once around the house, so I'll chase mine thrice around, with maybe an extra time to show him what I can do when I get good and started."

Max paused to look out across the intervale. While he watched Elam's house, he began going through the motions of washing his hands.

"Don't guess Elam's idea was so bad, after all. Can't think

of much to quarrel about with a Lewiston young woman in the house, and not having to pay her five-ten dollars for her bed over the week end."

(First published in *We Are the Living*)

The Automobile That Wouldn't Run

MAL ANDERSON made himself comfortable beside his dog on the back seat of the automobile and tuned up his banjo. Signe sat in a rocking chair on the front porch of the Penobscot Hotel listening to the music Mal made. It was midsummer and the weather was hot. It looked as if a thunderstorm might come from the west before the afternoon was over. Occasionally a gust of wind did come from that direction, blowing the dust down the street in balls like little yellow balloons.

Mal had a job in the spool mill in summer but he did not like to work the year 'round. He went into the woods in winter and did not come out until spring. In the summer he wanted to live in his shack with the dog and play his banjo when Signe sat on the hotel porch.

Mal strummed away on his banjo. Signe sat on the porch rocking faster and faster.

Plunkety plunk . . . plunkety plunk . . . plunkety plink!

Mal, who was called by everybody who did not like him "that damn Swede," was a fine woodsman. In the spool mill, though, he was not such a good workman. He did not like to work in the mill in summer. The mill made spools for electric wires, and Mal was supposed to be there now, checking the squares before they went through the turning-machines; but he did not like to work the year 'round.

Signe ran the Penobscot Hotel. It was a woodsman's hotel. The men used it when they came to town to spend the money they made up in the woods. Signe ran the hotel without help. She did not need any.

Plunkety plunk . . . plunkety plunk . . . plunkety plink!

Mal played his banjo for Signe. Neither of them ever spoke to the other. Mal might just as well have been born without the power of speech, for all the use he made of it. A man could talk to him an hour and he would not say a word.

Signe went to the kitchen and brought back a bone for Mal's dog. Mal opened the door and the dog jumped out after the

bone and hopped in again. The dog curled up on the seat beside Mal and licked the bone. Mal played a tune on his banjo
for Signe.

Plunkety plunk . . . plunkety plunk . . . plunkety plink!

At five o'clock Signe went into the hotel to start supper.
Mal laid his banjo on the seat and he and the dog got out and
pushed the automobile up the street to the shed beside his
shack. The car would not run. One winter while Mal was up
in the woods somebody broke into the shed and took the engine out. When Mal came back in the spring, he got into the
habit of pushing his automobile to the hotel where he played
his banjo for Signe.

Mal pushed his automobile up the street to the shed. His
boss was there waiting to see him. Mal did not like him at all.

"Hello there, Mal," Scott, the boss, said. "I got some good
news for you."

"I don't want to hear your news."

Mal knew that when Scott came to the shack he wanted to
get some more work out of him. Nobody in the woods liked
Scott.

"Get your stuff together, Mal. We're pushing up into the
woods tomorrow morning at four o'clock."

"To hell with you and the woods and all your damn spools,"
Mal shouted, slamming shut the shed door. The only way to
make Mal talk was to get him angry. But it was dangerous to
make him mad. He had run half a dozen boss woodsmen out
of the country. They went to Canada before he got a chance
to hurt them.

Scott went down the road without looking back once. Scott
was a brave boss woodsman.

Mal went into his shack and slammed shut the door behind
him. The dog curled up under the table waiting for supper.

Everybody in the woods had heard about Mal Anderson. He
was the best banjo player between Rangeley and Caribou, for
one thing. And he was one of the best woodsmen ever to lay
a tree down in the woods. He could stick a stake in the ground
where he wanted the tree to fall and make the tree drive the
stake into the earth. He took his two axes and went to work.
When one ax became too hot he laid it aside and took up the
other one. Give any two men the same start on a tree with a
saw, axes, or anything they wanted, and Mal would have his
tree on the ground before the other one was ready to fall.
That was one reason why Mal was paid for eight days' work
a week while the other men were getting paid for six.

It was summertime now and Mal did not want to go into the
woods until winter. In summer he liked to stay in town and
play his banjo in front of the Penobscot Hotel. The spool
mill was running short of squares, however, and Mal had to

help get the logs out of the woods. It was a hell of a time of year to make a man work.

Mal went up the river with the crew the next morning and went to work the following day felling trees for squares. He left his dog and banjo at home.

The crew worked in the woods three weeks and then the men began to grumble. When they left town, Scott had said they would be back by the end of two weeks. At the end of the third week Mal got mad. Scott was going to keep them there another month. And long before the end of the fourth week Scott had to watch himself pretty closely. He had to watch himself to keep from getting hurt. For instance, a tree might fall on him.

"Let's sink the son of a bitch in the river," one of the woodsmen suggested.

"Tie him to a stump and let the bobcats have him," another said. "You couldn't drown the yellow-backed bastard; he was born like a bullfrog."

"Mal'll catch him under a tree some of these days," Sanderson, who was the head teamster, said. "Let Mal have him."

Mal sat back on his haunches and said nothing.

Scott had enough sense to go into his shack every night after supper and not show himself until daylight. He could have been finished in five minutes in the dark, and he knew it.

But at the end of six weeks Scott was in as good condition as he had ever been. He watched himself pretty closely in the woods and he did not show himself after dark.

In the meantime two of the men got it into their heads that they were going out of the woods, Scott or no Scott. They said nothing about it and got ready to slip out alone. Scott was in his shack washing up for dinner when they ran down to the river and pushed off in a canoe.

Scott missed them a few minutes later when everybody sat down at the table to eat. Calling Mal and another man, they ran down to the river. The two men who had set their heads on going out of the woods were half a mile downstream paddling like mad. They were standing up in the canoe on the lookout for submerged logs and rocks. Their arms and paddles waved like a windmill in a cyclone.

"Get a canoe, Mal, and pick out a good man to help you and bring those God-damn Canucks back to me," Scott ordered, swearing and stamping around on the riverbank.

Mal motioned to one of the men nearest him and they shoved off without a word. Mal was the biggest and strongest man in camp. The other man was to help with the canoe.

The river lay in a straight course downstream for two miles or more. It was used for running logs to the spool mill in the spring and summer. In winter it was frozen over to a depth of three or four feet and the logging teams drove over it going and coming to the woods.

Scott sent a man to camp for his field glasses.

Mal and the other woodsman struck out down the river after the two runaway men. In both canoes the men worked frantically with their oars. Mal's canoe shot through the water at a terrific rate of speed. There was no doubt that he would overtake the other canoe within the next mile. He and the man in the stern squatted on their knees so they would be nearer the water. Their canoe shot down the river, leaving a foaming white wake spreading out to the shores behind.

The man came running back from camp with the field glasses for Scott.

"I'll break those God-damn Canucks of wanting to run away from the job," Scott shouted, snatching the glasses from the man's hand.

The two canoes looked only a dozen lengths apart now. The leading canoe was about a mile and a quarter downstream. Mal's canoe closed up on it with every powerful stroke of his blade. Scott thrust the glasses to his eyes and held them there. The woodsmen crowded down to the edge of the water straining their eyes to see Mal overtake the men. It would be a sight worth seeing. What he would probably do would be to hold their heads under the water until they were nearly drowned before hauling them into his canoe and bringing them back to Scott. Scott had already planned enough work to take all the fight out of them.

Mal's canoe closed up on the one that had had the first start. The men in the canoe were still paddling with all their might, but Mal was stroking faster and faster.

The next instant the two canoes were prow-and-prow, only an oar's length apart. And then, before anybody could see what had happened, Mal has passed them and the first canoe was a whole length behind.

"The God-damn son of a bloody—" Scott swore, smashing the field glasses against the rocks. He was so mad he was almost speechless. Mal had double-crossed him. He shouted at the men and kicked savagely at the broken field glasses on the shore. "The God-damn son of a bloody—" he shouted from the depths of his powerful lungs.

Both canoes were completely out of sight now. One canoe was actually half a mile ahead of the other.

Scott ordered the men back to the woods. After they had gone he walked slowly up the hillside to the camp. Mal Anderson had put one over on him.

Mal got home early the next afternoon and opened the door of his shack. His dog was sleeping under the shack and woke up when he sniffed Mal's scent inside. Mal made a fire and cooked something for the dog and himself to eat.

After they had finished eating Mal got his banjo and pushed his automobile out of the shed and down the street as far as the Penobscot Hotel. Signe was sitting on the front porch rocking in her chair. When she saw Mal coming down the street with his automobile, she leaned back in her chair and rocked faster and faster.

Mal pushed the car down the street and stopped it in front of Signe's hotel. He opened the door and he and the dog got into the back seat and sat down. Mal slammed shut the door and picked up his banjo. Then he began playing a tune for Signe.

The dog curled up and went to sleep. Mal strummed away on the banjo.

Plunkety plunk . . . plunkety plunk . . . plunkety plink!

Signe rocked back and forth, smiling out into the street at Mal sitting in his car and glad he was back in town again.

Mal settled down and propped his feet on the back of the driver's seat. Signe brought a bone for the dog and Mal opened the door. The dog jumped out after the bone and hopped in again and began licking it. Mal slammed shut the automobile door and took up his banjo again.

Plunkety plunk . . . plunkety plunk . . . plunkety plink!

The tune floated to the porch of the Penobscot Hotel and up the street and down it.

(First published in *Hound and Horn*)

The Negro in the Well

JULE ROBINSON was lying in bed snoring when his foxhounds struck a live trail a mile away and their baying woke him up with a start. He jumped to the floor, jerked on his shoes, and ran out into the front yard. It was about an hour before dawn.

Holding his hat to the side of his head like a swollen hand, he listened to the trailing on the ridge above the house. With his hat to deflect the sound into his ear, he could hear the dogs treading in the dry underbrush as plainly as his own breathing. It had taken him only a few seconds to determine that the hounds were not cold-trailing, and he put his hat back on his head and stooped over to lace his shoes.

"Papa," a frightened voice said, "please don't go off again now—wait till daybreak, anyway."

Jule turned around and saw the dim outline of his two girls. They were huddled together in the window of their bedroom. Jessie and Clara were old enough to take care of themselves, he thought, but that did not stop them from getting in his way when he wanted to go fox hunting.

"Go on back to bed and sleep, Jessie—you and Clara," he said gruffly. "Those hounds are just up on the ridge. They can't take me much out of hollering distance before sunup."

"We're scared, Papa," Clara said.

"Scared of what?" Jule asked impatiently. "There ain't a thing for two big girls like you and Jessie to be scared of. What's there to be scared of in this big country, anyway?"

The hounds stopped trailing for a moment, and Jule straightened up to listen in the silence. All at once they began again, and he bent down to finish tying his shoes.

Off in the distance he could hear several other packs of trailing hounds, and by looking closely at the horizon he could see the twinkle of campfires where bands of fox hunters had stopped to warm their hands and feet.

"Are you going, anyway, Papa?" Clara asked.

"I'm going, anyway," he answered.

The two girls ran back to bed and pulled the covers over their heads. There was no way to argue with Jule Robinson when he had set his head on following his foxhounds.

The craze must have started anew sometime during the holidays, because by the end of the first week in January it looked and sounded as if everybody in Georgia were trading foxhounds by day and bellowing "Whoo-way-oh!" by night. From the time the sun went down until the next morning when it came up, the woods, fields, pastures, and swamps were crawling with beggar-liced men and yelping hound-dogs. Nobody would have thought of riding horseback after the hounds in a country where there was a barbwire fence every few hundred yards.

Automobiles roared and rattled over the rough country roads all night long. The fox hunters had to travel fast in order to keep up with the pack.

It was not safe for any living thing with four legs to be out after sundown, because the hounds had the hunting fever too, and packs of those rangy half-starved dogs were running down and devouring calves, hogs, and even yellow-furred bobcats. It had got so during the past two weeks that the chickens knew enough to take to their roosts an hour ahead of time, because those packs of gaunt hunt-hungry hounds could not wait for sunset any more.

Jule finished lacing his shoes and went around the house.

The path to the ridge began in the back yard and weaved up the hillside like a cowpath through a thicket. Jule passed the well and stopped to feel in his pockets to see if he had enough smoking tobacco to last him until he got back.

While he was standing there he heard behind him a sound like water gurgling through the neck of a demijohn. Jule listened again. The sound came even more plainly while he listened. There was no creek anywhere within hearing distance, and the nearest water was in the well. He went to the edge and listened again. The well did not have a stand or a windlass; it was merely a twenty-foot hole in the ground with boards laid over the top to keep pigs and chickens from falling into it.

"O Lord, help me now!" a voice said.

Jule got down on his hands and knees and looked at the well cover in the darkness. He felt of the boards with his hands. Three of them had been moved, and there was a black oblong hole that was large enough to drop a calf through.

"Who's that?" Jule said, stretching out his neck and cocking his ear.

"O Lord, help me now," the voice said again, weaker than before.

The gurgling sound began again, and Jule knew then that it was the water in the well.

"Who's down there muddying up my well?" Jule said.

There was no sound then. Even the gurgling stopped.

Jule felt on the ground for a pebble and dropped it into the well. He counted until he could hear the *kerplunk* when it struck the water.

"Doggone your hide, whoever you are down there!" Jule said. "Who's down there?"

Nobody answered.

Jule felt in the dark for the water bucket, but he could not find it. Instead, his fingers found a larger pebble, a stone almost as big around as his fist, and he dropped it into the well.

The big rock struck something else before it finally went into the water.

"O Lord, I'm going down and can't help myself," the voice down there said. "O Lord, a big hand is trying to shove me under."

The hounds trailing on the ridge swung around to the east and started back again. The fox they were after was trying to back-trail them, but Jule's hounds were hard to fool. They had got to be almost as smart as a fox.

Jule straightened up and listened to the running.

"Whoo-way-oh!" he called after the dogs.

That sent them on yelping even louder than before.

"Is that you up there, Mr. Jule?" the voice asked.

Jule bent over the well again, keeping one ear on the dogs

on the ridge. He did not want to lose track of them when they were on a live trail like that.

"This is me," Jule said. "Who's that?"

"This is only Bokus Bradley, Mr. Jule," the voice said.

"What you doing down in my well, muddying it up like that, Bokus?"

"It was something like this, Mr. Jule," Bokus said. "I was coming down the ridge a while ago, trying to keep up with my hounds, and I stumbled over your well cover. I reckon I must have missed the path, somehow or other. Your well cover wouldn't hold me up, or something, and the first thing I knew, here I was. I've been here ever since I fell in. I reckon I've been down here most of the night. I hope you ain't mad at me, Mr. Jule. I just naturally couldn't help it at all."

"You've muddied up my well water," Jule said. "I ain't so doggone pleased about that."

"I reckon I have, some," Bokus said, "but I just naturally couldn't help it none at all."

"Where'd your dogs go to, Bokus?" Jule asked.

"I don't know, Mr. Jule. I haven't heard a sound out of them since I fell in here. They was headed for the creek when I was coming down the ridge behind them. Can you hear them anywhere now, Mr. Jule?"

Several packs of hounds could be heard. Jule's on the ridge was trailing east, and a pack was trailing down the creek toward town. Over toward the hills several more packs were running, but they were so far away it was not easy to tell to whom they belonged.

"Sounds to me like I hear your dogs down the creek, headed for the swamp," Jule said.

"Whoo-way-oh!" Bokus called.

The sound from the well struck Jule like a blast out of a megaphone.

"Your dogs can't hear you from 'way down there, Bokus," he said.

"I know they can't, Mr. Jule, and that's why I sure enough want to get out of here. My poor dogs don't know which way I want them to trail when they can't hear me talk to them. Whoo-way-oh!" Bokus shouted. "O Lord, help me now!"

Jule's dogs sounded as if they were closing in on a fox, and Jule jumped to his feet.

"Whoo-way-oh!" he shouted, cupping his hands around his mouth. "Whoo-way-oh!"

"Is you still up there, Mr. Jule?" Bokus asked. "Please, Mr. Jule, don't go away and leave me down here in this cold well. I'll do anything for you if you'll just only get me out of here. I've been standing neck-deep in this cold water near about all night long."

Jule threw some of the boards over the well.

"What you doing up there, Mr. Jule?"

Jule took off his hat and held the brim like a fan to the side of his head. He could hear the panting of the dogs while they ran.

"How many foxhounds have you got, Bokus?" Jule asked.

"I got me eight," Bokus said. "They're mighty fine fox trailers, too, Mr. Jule. But I'd like to get me out of this here well before doing much more talking with you."

"You could get along somehow with less than that, couldn't you, Bokus?"

"If I had to, I'd have to," Bokus said, "but I sure enough would hate to have fewer than my eight dogs, though. Eight is just naturally the right-sized pack for me, Mr. Jule."

"How are you figuring on getting out of there?" Jule said.

"I just naturally figured on you helping me out, Mr. Jule," he said. "Leastaways, that's about the only way I know of getting out of this here well. I tried climbing, but the dirt just naturally crumbles away every time I dig my toes into the sides."

"You've got that well so muddied up it won't be fit to drink out of for a week or more," Jule said.

"I'll do what I can to clean it out for you, Mr. Jule, if I ever get up on top of the solid ground again. Can you hear those hounds of mine trailing now, Mr. Jule?"

"They're still down the creek. I reckon I could lower the water bucket, and I could pull a little, and you could climb a little, and maybe you'd get out that way."

"That just naturally would suit me fine, Mr. Jule," Bokus said eagerly. "Here I is. When is you going to lower that water bucket?"

Jule stood up and listened to his dogs trailing on the ridge. From the way they sounded, it would not be long before they treed the fox they were after.

"It's only about an hour till daybreak," Jule said. "I'd better go on up the ridge and see how my hounds are making out. I can't do much here at the well till the sun comes up."

"Don't go away and leave me now, Mr. Jule," Bokus begged. "Mr. Jule, please, sir, just lower that water bucket down here and help me get out. I just naturally got to get out of here, Mr. Jule. My dogs will get all balled up without me following them. Whoo-way-oh! Whoo-way-oh!"

The pack of fox-trailing hounds was coming up from the creek, headed toward the house. Julie took off his hat and held it beside his ear. He listened to them panting and yelping.

"If I had two more hounds, I'd be mighty pleased," Jule said, shouting loud enough for Bokus to hear. "Just two is all I need right now."

"You wouldn't be wanting two of mine, would you, Mr. Jule?" Bokus asked.

"It's a good time to make a trade," Jule said. "It's a mighty good time, being as how you are down in the well and want to get out."

"Two, did you say?"

"Two is what I said."

There was silence in the well for a long time. For nearly five minutes Jule listened to the packs of dogs all around him, some on the ridge, some down the creek, and some in the far-off fields. The barking of the hounds was a sweeter sound to him than anything else in the world. He would lose a night's sleep any time just to stay up and hear a pack of foxhounds live-trailing.

"Whoo-way-oh!" he called.

"Mr. Jule!" Bokus shouted up from the bottom of the well.

Jule went to the edge and leaned over to hear what the Negro had to say.

"How about that there trade now, Bokus?"

"Mr. Jule, I just naturally couldn't swap off two of my hounds, I just sure enough couldn't."

"Why not?" Jule said.

"Because I'd have only just six dogs left, Mr. Jule, and I couldn't do much fox hunting with just that many."

Jule straightened up and kicked the boards over the top of the well.

"You won't be following even so few as one hound for a while," he said, "because I'm going to leave you down in the bottom where you stand now. It's another hour, almost, till daybreak, and I can't be wasting that time staying here talking to you. Maybe when I get back you'll be in a mind to do some trading, Bokus."

Jule kicked the boards on top of the well.

"O Lord, help me now!" Bokus said. "But, O Lord, don't make me swap off no two hounds for the help I'm asking for."

Jule stumbled over the water bucket when he turned and started across the yard toward the path up the ridge. Up there he could hear his dogs running again, and when he took off his hat and held it to the side of his head he could hear Polly pant, and Senator snort, and Mary Jane whine, and Sunshine yelp, and the rest of them barking at the head of the trail. He put on his hat, pulled it down hard all around, and hurried up the path to follow them on the ridge. The fox would not be able to hold out much longer.

"Whoo-way-oh!" he called to his hounds. "Whoo-way-oh!"

The echo was a masterful sound to hear.

(First published in the *Atlantic Monthly*)

Carnival

IT was more than she could bear any longer. Bess stumbled out of the pitch-dog stand and felt her way over ropes, pegs, and packing crates to their house-tent. She had told Hutch she wanted to comb her hair, but she knew that he knew as well as she did what the trouble was.

Bess did not cry. It had been a year since she had done anything like that. She had been with Hutch, following the carnival with a pitch-dog stand, for over two years, and it was at least a year since she had cried. She lay down on the cot, breathing heavily.

She could hear Hutch's voice occasionally above the din and the raucous roar of the midway. No matter how high rose the pitch of screaming voices in the Fun House, or of the metallic grind-music in the Cuban Cabaret, or of the amplified hoarseness of the try-your-luck barkers, Bess could always hear Hutch's familiar singsong spiel.

"Knock the little doggies off, and take home a brand-new silver dollar, folks!" She had said it so many times herself that Hutch's voice sounded as if the words were coming from her.

The dust raised by the carnival crowd's shuffling feet settled over her face and arms as she lay stiffly extended on the cot. The heat, the noise, the incessant glare of light settled on her like a heavy blanket.

"Knock the little doggies off, and take home a brand-new silver dollar, folks, a brand-new silver dollar."

Hutch's voice sounded mechanical again. Bess lay back on the cot. Hutch was talking to that girl who had been leaning against the railing in front of the stand for the past half hour. There was always a different ring in Hutch's voice when he was trying to do two things like that at once. She knew what he was up to as well as he knew himself. He was trying to make a date with the girl. When he succeeded, he would disappear, the girl would disappear, and Bess would not see Hutch again until the next morning. It had been that way so many times during the past two years that she had lost count.

Bess turned over, trying to shut out the glare of the midway lights that filtered through the thin canvas. She did not even know the name of the town they were in. It might have been something like Emporia, Fostoria, Peoria. It was a cotton town somewhere west of Birmingham, and that was about all she knew. Towns had been all the same lately, since Hutch had got into the habit of going off with a strange girl several times a week.

Bess got up, combed her hair, and brushed the dust from her dress. While she was brushing her clothes, she heard Hutch call her. She left the tent and stumbled towards the stand.

"Knock the little doggies off, and take home a brand-new silver dollar, folks!" Hutch said while she climbed under the railing. He turned around and winked at her. "Knock the little doggies off, folks! Only a dime!"

Before she saw Hutch, Bess saw the girl. It was the same girl, the one who had been leaning over the railing and talking to Hutch when she left.

"How about it, Bess?" Hutch began.

Bess turned and looked the girl up and down. She was a plain-looking creature with straight blond hair that needed shampooing. She did not seem much over twenty, but her hands were work-stained and a little wrinkled.

"Her?" Bess asked Hutch, futilely.

"What's the difference, this time?" he said a little impatiently.

"You seem to be a little less particular each time, Hutch."

"Now, let's not fall out, Bess," Hutch said, rubbing her nervously on her back and shoulders.

Hutch ducked under the railing and disappeared behind the stand. The milling mob of people was churning up a cloud of dust that looked like dense yellow smoke in the glare of lights. Bess could feel particles of dust and flakes of grit settle on her arms and face. She brushed it all away.

The girl looked up at her nervously two or three times. She was gradually receding into the crowd. All at once she turned and pushed her way around the side of the stand out of sight.

A party of men and women pushed up to the railing, filling the vacant space the girl had left. The people stared at Bess as if she were one of the freaks in the sideshow down the midway.

"What's the game?" one of the men asked her in a loud voice.

Bess stared down into the faces. Each one of them looked like Hutch and his girls.

Almost automatically Bess picked up a handful of battered balls and held them out in front of her.

"Knock the little doggies off, folks, and take home a brand-new silver dollar!"

"That's fair enough," one of the men said, handing her a dime.

The man threw the three balls, but knocked off only two of the three stuffed dogs. He turned away to leave.

"Wait a minute, Mister!" Bess cried after him. "I'll make you a better proposition!"

The man came back.

"I haven't any more dimes to throw away on a game like that," he said, shaking his head. "You people have got those dogs rigged up so they all won't fall off, even if I did hit them."

Bess leaned over the railing.

"Be a sport, Mister. Here's your chance of a lifetime. Look! I'm going to give you ten balls. If you knock off all three dogs, you can write your own ticket. Now, how's that for an offer?"

The man grabbed the balls, heaving them at the dogs. They all fell on the ground.

"You win the setup!" Bess cried, ducking under the railing. "It's all yours! Go on in there and take it!"

She pushed into the crowd, elbowing her way out of sight. Soon she was blinded by the dust that rose up from the ground, and before she had gone halfway down the midway, she was lost. Pushing her way out of the crowd, she crossed a vacant lot and began walking along a street that looked as if it would lead her out of town. She did not care in what direction she was going, as long as it led away from Emporia, Fostoria, Peoria, or whatever it was.

(First published in *Mid-Week Pictorial*)

The Windfall

WHEN Waldo Murdock, whose trade, when he felt like working at it, was rendering creatures, came into the unexpected inheritance, there had been no commotion in Brighton to equal it since the time when, eleven years before, one of the Perkins brothers, with no more forewarning than a stroke of summer lightning, ran away in broad daylight with the resident minister's wife.

As for the townspeople, none of them, not even Aunt Susie Shook, who told fortunes by reading tea leaves, or coffee grounds if necessary, had ever had the remotest idea that anything in the nature of sudden wealth would fall into Waldo

Murdock's scrawny lap, while at the same time, of course, people were quick to say that if he had not been sitting down, as usual, instead of being up and doing, there would have been no lap of his for it to fall into; and certainly Waldo himself, even though he daydreamed about almost everything else under the sun, had never entertained such a far-fetched thought in his mind.

Waldo did not even know he had a brother in Australia and, even if he had known it, he would never have imagined that he would be remembered in a will. From Bangor to Burlington, all the Murdocks, especially the home-owning branch of the family, were known throughout the entire region north of Boston for their trait, which relatives by marriage and other outsiders called cussedness, of not acknowledging kinship with one another. And as it was, it was all Waldo could do to force himself, after having cast aside pride of long standing, publicly to admit blood relationship with another Murdock, even if he had lived in Australia, long enough to go to the bank in Waterville and cash the check the lawyer from Portland had handed him.

"Pay no mind to what the people say," he told the clerk in the bank. "There may be others in the State of Maine bearing the name of Murdock, but there's not a single drop of mingling blood that I would own to. I'd sooner claim kinship with my old black cow than I would with a so-called Murdock."

Dessie, Waldo's wife, was, at the beginning, the most level-headed of all. She maintained her mental balance, if only at the start, much better than Waldo and some of the townspeople. Dessie, although afterward she regretted not having gone along, even remained at home and tended the house chores while Waldo was away in Waterville cashing the check. There was only one thing she did out of the ordinary that forenoon, and that was to make Justine, the hired girl, air the parlor and shake out the scatter rugs, even if it was not Saturday.

During all that time the neighbors were ringing her up on the phone and asking what she was going to do with all that money, but that, too, in the beginning, failed to veer the even measure of her thoughts.

"When the check is cashed, if it's not worthless, and it'll be a wonder if it's not, there'll be ample time at hand for me to go out of my way to think about it," she told them. "Right now, and likely forever after, it's nothing but a scrawl and a promise on a slip of paper."

Dessie went back to work with her lips a little tighter each time she finished talking to one of the neighbors on the phone. She was not exactly worried, she told Justine, but she was feeling impatient. Waldo failed to come home at the noon hour for dinner, and it was not long after that before she, like everybody else in Brighton who was working himself into a frenzy over Waldo's sudden windfall, began thinking of the things that could be done with the money.

Late that afternoon Waldo drove up to the dooryard and left the automobile standing there instead of putting it away in the shed where it belonged.

Justine came running to tell her.

Dessie was so on edge by that time that she jumped several inches off the chair seat when Justine, who was as excited as she by then, ran into the room where she was.

"Mr. Murdock's back!" Justine cried, twisting her fingers.

"He'd better be!" Dessie said. "If he hadn't got home when he did, he could have just kept on traveling, for all the concern I'd ever have."

"I guess Mr. Murdock has the real money," Justine said, looking over her shoulder. "He looked like he was feeling good about it when he got out of the auto."

Dessie leaped to her feet.

"Go on about your tasks, whatever they be, Justine," she said crossly. "It's none of your money, if there is any, anyway."

Justine went to the kitchen and watched Waldo come along the path to the side door.

Waldo came in, throwing his hat on the table. He looked at Dessie for a moment, cocking his head a little to one side. His coat pocket sagged heavily.

Neither Dessie nor Waldo spoke for a while.

Presently Dessie walked up to him and held out her hand.

"Guess I'll take charge for the time being," she said stiffly. "Hand it over."

Waldo reached into his coat pocket, drawing out a mostly empty bottle and handing it to her. She stepped back, looking at it severely. Then, without a word, she grabbed the bottle by the neck and slung it with all her might across the room. It struck the wall, shattering into dozens of pieces.

"I might have known it, and I would have, if I had only had the sense God has given most people!" she said, raising her voice. "I've got only myself to blame!"

Waldo reached for a chair.

"Now there's no cause for a human to take on so, Dessie," he said. "Everything turned out, from here to there and back again, like it was made to order."

He reached into his pants pocket and drew out a bulging roll of greenbacks. The bills were tied tightly around the center with a piece of heavy twine. Dessie forgot her anger the instant she saw the money. The scowling lines on her face disappeared completely while she watched Waldo bounce the roll up and down in his hand.

"All I've got to say," she began, "is that I never thought I'd live to breathe the air of the day when a deceasing Murdock would have the decency to do the honorable thing with his money, even if he couldn't find means of taking it along with him when he went, which would be a wonder if he didn't try to do, and he probably did, anyway."

Waldo leaned back and let her talk to her heart's content. He felt so good himself that he wanted her to have a good time, too. He let her speak what came to mind, without uttering a single grumble.

"Have you any more blood relations that we've neglected to remind ourselves of, Waldo?" she asked, leaning toward him. "It seems to me that I recall your second cousin in Skowhegan saying once some years ago that a Murdock went to California at the end of the Spanish-American War and prospected for gold. It might be that he struck it rich out there, which a lot of people did, so I've read, if reading can be believed. If we'd been more particular about your blood relations in the past, we wouldn't have to sit here now and wrack our brains trying to call them to mind at a time like this."

"Guess I have no blood relations of the name of Murdock," Waldo said firmly.

Dessie drew a deep breath and looked longingly at the large roll of greenbacks bouncing up and down in her husband's hand.

Suddenly she leaned forward and grasped the roll desperately.

Waldo snatched it from her.

"I think we ought to start making plans," she said.

"This is Murdock money, woman," he said quickly. "A Murdock made it, and a Murdock shall spend it."

Dessie sat up decisively.

"Well, anyway, we'll be sensible," she said calmly. "We won't throw it away on trifles like a lot of people would who I could mention, if I had a mind to."

"I've got it all settled, Dessie," Waldo told her, smiling as a kindly feeling came over him. "Guess we can afford to have a good time now at our age. Maybe we won't be lingering here much longer, which would be a shame if we hadn't taken full advantage of it by the time we went. Wouldn't be no sense in hoarding it only to have to pass it along to somebody else after we are gone."

Dessie nodded approvingly, her spirits rising again.

"I've always wanted a fur neckpiece, Waldo," she said, her face bright with hope.

Dessie did not sleep a single wink that night. For an hour

after they had gone to bed, she lay silently tense, listening. Waldo did not stir. He lay on his back listening to Dessie's labored breathing.

Just before midnight Dessie got up as quietly as she possibly could and tiptoed to the foot of the bed where Waldo had laid his pants over the back of a chair. It was dark in the room with the shades drawn, and she took care in feeling her way to the chair. She was trembling nervously when she touched it, and the jerking of her breath had started a pain in her chest. Without losing any more time she slid her hand into the pants pocket.

"Get your hand out of my pants, Dessie," Waldo said, rising up in bed. "Leave that money be."

Dessie dropped the pants without having touched the money, and went back to bed without a word. Neither of them spoke as she lay down again and tried to make herself as comfortable as possible for the remainder of the night. After that both of them lay staring into the blackness of the room.

Just as dawn was beginning to show the first signs of breaking, Dessie slid carefully from the bed and crawled on her hands and knees toward the chair. As she was rising up to reach the pants, Waldo sat up erectly.

"Don't want to have to mention it again about you putting your hand in my pants pocket," he said. "Leave that money be, Dessie."

Dessie dropped the pants and went to the window. She stood there watching a red dawn break in the east. After a while she began dressing, and as she was leaving the chamber she heard Justine starting a fire in the kitchen stove.

While she and Justine were preparing breakfast, she began to realize how uneasy she really was about the money. She had spent a sleepless night worrying over the wealth, and she was afraid she would not get a chance to spend a single penny of it herself.

"Mrs. Murdock," Justine said, coming and standing beside her, "Carl and I could get mated right away if we had the money for a chamber suite."

"Let Carl Friend make his own money," Dessie said sharply, turning on the girl. "Me and my husband have worked hard all our lives for what we possess. It won't hurt Carl Friend to do the same for you, if he wants a family."

"I couldn't sleep much last night for staying awake wondering if you and Mr. Murdock wouldn't want to help me out," Justine said persistently. "Especially because I've worked here for you six years without asking favors, and I didn't think you'd miss a little of all that big inheritance from Australia."

"Mind your own affairs, Justine!" she said sharply. "Besides, Carl Friend can get the money from his own family if he wants to furnish a house for you. Those Friends have made plenty of profit in roof tinning in the past."

"They won't help any, Mrs. Murdock," Justine said sadly. "And Carl and I don't want to have to wait and wait and wait."

"You don't have to hurry the marriage for any reason, do you?" Dessie asked suspiciously.

Justine looked at her for several moments, her thoughts racing through her mind.

"Not exactly," she admitted at last.

"Well, then," Dessie said, turning away, "in that case, you can afford to wait."

In turning abruptly she almost walked headlong into Waldo. He had come into the kitchen and was going toward the pantry. After Dessie had stepped out of the way, she watched him go into the pantry and pick up several cans off the shelf. He found an empty coffee can and left, going through the kitchen and out the door without a word being spoken. Dessie watched him leave, wondering what he was about to do. She went to the window and watched as he walked to the toolshed and came out a moment later carrying a spade. With the coffee can in one hand and the spade over his shoulder, he disappeared out of sight behind the barn.

It was not until almost ten minutes had passed that Dessie realized what Waldo was doing behind the barn.

Just as she was opening the door to run out there and observe him from the corner of the barn, Waldo walked into view. He came toward the house, carrying the spade but not the coffee can. Dessie's heart sank. He had buried the can, and the money with it, and she had failed to get out there in time to see where the wealth had been hidden. She walked back into the kitchen and placed breakfast on the table.

Waldo came in a few minutes later, washed his hands at the pump, and sat down at his place. He began eating as though nothing out of the ordinary had taken place out behind the barn. Neither she nor Waldo had anything to say to each other during the whole twenty minutes they were at the table. When he finished eating, he got up and put on his hat.

"Have some affairs to attend to in the village," he said shortly. "Will be away for the forenoon, the whole of it."

Dessie nodded. She had to grip her hands tightly in order to hide her impatience. She waited until Waldo had got out of sight, and then she grabbed Justine by the arm and pulled her through the door. Pushing Justine ahead, Dessie ran as fast as she could to the toolshed, where she quickly snatched up two spades, and then hurried toward the back of the barn.

She set Justine to digging right away, while she looked the ground over carefully, hoping to find evidence of a freshly covered hole. She searched for nearly half an hour without finding a single trace of the hole she was positive Waldo had dug, and after that she went to work, digging methodically.

After several hours, Justine slumped to the ground, completely exhausted. Dessie was tired, too, and the blisters on her hands made digging so painful that she could hardly bear to hold the spade. But she forced herself to keep on, allowing Justine to rest a few minutes.

"Get up and dig, Justine," she called breathlessly, not being able to bear seeing her idle any longer.

Justine crawled to her feet and tried to push the blade of her spade into the stony earth. She wanted to beg Dessie to let her rest some more, but when she glanced up and saw Dessie's closely clamped lips, she knew it would be useless to ask.

Dessie stopped for a moment to ease her back. When her eyes were raised from the ground, she saw Fred Paxton leaning over the stone wall beside the road a hundred feet away.

"Going fishing, Dessie?" he called. "See you're digging fishing worms."

Dessie thrust her hand against the small of her aching back and straightened up a little more.

"Thought I might," she said slowly. "It's been a long time since I went."

"Now that you and Waldo have all that money to falute on," Fred said, "I guess you and him can afford to spend all your time doing nothing but fish, if you have a mind to."

"Maybe," she said, tightening her lips.

The mere mention of the money inflamed her thoughts until she could not see clearly. She bent over the spade, thrusting the blade into the rough, stony ground with all her might. She kept doggedly at it until she was certain Fred had walked out of sight over the hill.

Later she sent Justine to the kitchen for some bread and potatoes left over from breakfast, and when Justine returned, Dessie sat down in the shade of the barn and ate hurriedly.

"While I was in the house, Mr. Murdock phoned and said he wouldn't be back in the forenoon," Justine said. "He told me to tell you he would be away in the afternoon, too, the whole of it."

Dessie leaped to her feet.

"Why didn't you tell me right away when you came back a minute ago?" she said angrily.

Justine glanced at the stony ground.

"We're not going to dig out here the whole afternoon, too, are we, Mrs. Murdock?" she inquired pleadingly. "My hands are raw with blisters, and—"

"Never mind that," Dessie said firmly. "We are going to dig this afternoon, the whole of it."

"But Mrs. Murdock—"

"Shut up, Justine, and do as you are told!"

When Dessie fell on the bed at dusk that evening, she had never before in all her life felt so thoroughly miserable. Not only had she spent the entire day digging in the stony ground behind the barn, but, moreover, she had not been able to find the coffee can. Her back felt as if she would never be able to use it again.

Once upon the bed, she moved her body carefully, easing herself into a prone position. Justine had gone out earlier in the evening with Carl Friend, and Waldo still had not returned. Dessie felt so tired and lonely that she wanted to cry. Just as she felt tears coming into her eyes, the phone began to ring. She lay motionless, listening to it ring for several minutes, hoping all the while that it would stop so she could begin crying.

The phone did not stop, and it sounded as if it never would as long as she lived. She got to her feet, pressing her hands over her ears in order to keep out the sound, and stumbled painfully to the hall. There she sat down in the chair beside the stand and lifted the receiver.

"Hello," she said unsteadily.

"Is this Waldo Murdock's wife?" a voice boomed.

"Yes," she answered, wondering who it could be.

"Then you'd better bestir yourself and fetch Waldo home where he belongs before it's too late. This is Charles Mason. Waldo is over here at my place, in the east part of town, annoying my household, and if he was a Democrat, I'd shoot him myself, instead of turning the job over to his wife. I've never in my life seen a man behave like he's doing. I guess it's public knowledge by now, otherwise I wouldn't be repeating it that sudden wealth has gone to his head, but that's still no excuse for the way he's doing."

"What's Waldo doing?" Dessie asked, shouting impulsively into the phone.

"He's befuddling Miss Wilson, the schoolteacher who boards at my house, into going away with him. He says he's going to set sail for Australia or somewhere."

"But he can't do that!" Dessie protested.

"That's what any average, normal, level-minded human being would think, too, but I don't know what's going to stop Waldo if you don't come and get him right away, because he's already befuddled Miss Wilson into going to Boston with him tonight, and starting out again from there the first thing in the morning. He's got Miss Wilson believing everything he says, the lies along with the common truth. Looks like she would be on her guard, knowing she's associating with a newly-rich, but she's too far gone to listen to reason. Waldo pulls out his wealth every few minutes and waves it in front of her, and the sight of that big roll of greenbacks acts on her just like chloroform would on an average being. I've done my best to—"

Dessie gripped the phone.

"Did you say Waldo has a big roll of money?" she shouted. "Greenbacks tied with a string around the middle?"

"He surely has, Mrs. Murdock. It's the biggest roll of money I've seen on a man since the Democrats took over."

Dessie, who had risen from the chair until she was almost erect, sat down, hard.

"Let him be!" she said coldly. "I don't want part or parcel of him. He had me digging in stony ground all day looking for that money in a coffee can, and it wasn't there at all. Let the schoolteacher take him. I've had my share, and more, of suffering, and now I'd be comforted to see somebody else have a goodly portion of it. Sudden wealth will show up a man's true nature every time, and I'm glad I found out the true size and shape of Waldo Murdock's nature before I wasted another single day of my life on him."

"You mean you're not going to try to stop Waldo from going away to the other end of the world with Miss Wilson?"

"No!" Dessie said emphatically. "Waldo Murdock has a free hand from now on!"

She hung up the receiver. A moment later she slumped brokenly in the chair. She called Justine several times before remembering that Justine had gone out with Carl Friend.

After that she hurried into her clothes and went back to the phone. She rang up Thornton Blanchard, her lawyer, and told him to come right away. He lived only a few miles distant, and he promised to be there within fifteen minutes.

While waiting for Thornton Blanchard, Dessie paced up and down the hallway, her face grim and determined. Her mind was made up, and she knew the sooner she acted the better she would feel.

After a few more minutes, he drove up to the house and stopped his car in the dooryard. Dessie went to the step, holding the door open for him. Thornton Blanchard hurried inside and went directly to the table in the center of the living room.

"Is there something wrong, Mrs. Murdock?" he asked anxiously.

"There is now, but it won't be much longer," she said, sitting down at the table, "not after I set things right I should have attended to twenty years ago."

Blanchard sat down and opened his briefcase, slipping out

a pad of ruled yellow writing paper and a pencil. He watched Dessie's face, waiting for her to begin.

"Are you ready?" she asked.

"Yes, Mrs. Murdock," he told her, adjusting the pad on the table.

"I want a divorce," she said quickly, "and I want it in a hurry. How soon can I get it, or do I have to go find myself a better lawyer?"

Blanchard sat up.

"Joking aside, Mrs. Murdock, right after you and your husband inherited all that wealth, you want a divorce?" he asked unbelievingly.

"That's what I said."

"But why?"

"Never mind my reasons," she answered. "When I go to the store and ask for a pound of sugar, I don't have to tell the clerk my reasons for wanting it, do I?"

"No, but—"

"Then go ahead and get me my divorce."

Blanchard fingered the writing pad nervously. After several moments he shook himself, and glanced across the table at Dessie.

"Have you any grounds, Mrs. Murdock?" he inquired cautiously.

"Of course, I've got grounds. I've got all the grounds needed and a plentiful supply to spare."

"What are to be the grounds on which the suit is to be based, Mrs. Murdock?" he asked, bending over the pad and gripping the pencil tightly.

"Cussedness," she said, leaning back.

Blanchard looked up.

"That's what I said," she nodded. "Cussedness!"

"The judge that hears this suit might not—"

"I don't care what the judge thinks," she retorted. "It's my divorce, and I'll have grounds of my own choosing whether the judge likes them or not."

Blanchard tapped the pencil on the table several times, his mind deep in thought.

"As your attorney, Mrs. Murdock," he said finally, "would you mind telling me in confidence on just what grounds you do base your contention?"

"Waldo Murdock tricked me," she said angrily, relieved to have an opportunity to talk about her troubles. "He went and made as if to bury the inheritance in a coffee can behind the barn, but didn't, and then went off and stayed from home all day while I broke my back, and Justine's, too, digging in stony ground for it."

Blanchard drew the palm of his right hand slowly over his

face. He leaned back after that and gazed professionally at the ceiling. He was doing his best to keep from saying, on the spur of the moment, anything of a rash nature.

"And I want alimony, too," Dessie spoke up. "I want all of it."

Blanchard sat up.

"What do you mean by all of it?"

"All the inheritance, of course," she replied.

Blanchard was silent for some time. He looked at the pad, studying the texture of the paper minutely. After a while he looked up at Dessie, fortifying himself with several deep breaths.

"It's going to be difficult, if not impossible," he said gravely. "Downright difficult, Mrs. Murdock."

"That's your job," Dessie told him. "I've worked hard for my living, too."

Blanchard expelled the breath from his lungs and took a fresh start.

"For one thing, Mrs. Murdock, we have no community property law in this state." He leaned back, rolling the pencil between the palms of his hands. "Naturally, that rules out automatically any possibility of a legal division of Waldo's wealth, whatever it may amount to. But let me put it another way. I'll review briefly the background of the whole matter. A wife is subject, more or less, to the will of the husband, all things being equal, of course. However, the marriage contract also subjects the husband to the will of the wife, placing the shoe on the other foot, so to speak. Now we arrive at the conclusion that the two members of the partnership are each and individually subject to the will of the other. But, and let me speak frankly, in our present society, it is the wife's own responsibility to devise, instate, and employ methods, means, and opportunities for enticement that will cause her spouse to desire of his own free will and accord to bestow, shall we say, a single largess, or, as the case often is, continuing largesses, upon her while united in wedlock. Now, as you no doubt realize, Mrs. Murdock, the average wife, to put it bluntly, by showering her favors upon her spouse obtains, in most instances, a bountiful portion of his goods, chattels, and wealth, in some cases benefits that, judged by worldly standards, are far out of proportion to the value—"

"No!" Dessie said emphatically.

Blanchard cleared his throat and bit his underlip.

"It might be best, in the long run, to let the presiding judge set the sum you might obtain from your present husband," he said wearily. "I'm afraid I won't be of much help in that connection. However, I can proceed with filing the divorce papers, and the matter of alimony can be taken up in due course."

"When can I see the judge about getting the money?" Dessie asked. "Tomorrow morning?"

"I'm afraid not," he said, shaking his head. "Your suit couldn't possibly come up for trial until the next term of court, come autumn."

"Come autumn!" Dessie cried.

Blanchard nodded.

"You mean wait all that time!" she cried excitedly. "Why, Waldo Murdock will have every penny of the wealth spent long before then. There wouldn't be anything left for me to sue for!"

"Well," Blanchard said, shaking his head, "I don't know what can be done, then. The terms of court are set by statute."

The side door burst open, and they both turned around to find Waldo standing in the doorway blinking his eyes in the bright light. After adjusting his vision, he walked into the room and went to the vacant chair between Dessie and Blanchard.

"How be you, Thornton?" Waldo said, reaching out and grasping Blanchard's hand. He shook it hard.

"Fair," Blanchard said uneasily. He glanced at Dessie. She was staring at Waldo. "Fair," he said again.

Waldo seated himself.

"Thought for a while today I needed to see you about a matter, but I changed my mind. There's no need, now."

"Well, I'm glad you handled the matter without needing any help," Blanchard said, stumbling over the words.

"Decided not to bother handling it," Waldo said, "so I just dropped it."

"That's fine," Blanchard said, wondering.

Waldo made himself comfortable.

"Was trying to figure out a way to have a good time and keep the money, too. Figured it couldn't be done. So I decided to get shet of it."

Dessie was about to leap from her chair when Waldo reached into his pants pocket and tossed the big roll of greenbacks across the table to her. The tightly bound roll of money tumbled into her lap.

For a moment Dessie looked as if she did not know what in the world had happened. Then slowly her eyes began to bulge and she looked down into her lap. She stared at the money dazedly.

"Waldo—" she said, her speech choked.

Tears began to flow down her cheeks, and Waldo squirmed uneasily in his chair. He dropped his head, glancing up at her from beneath his eyebrows every now and then.

"Waldo—" she began again. She could not continue.

Waldo wiped his mouth with the back of his hand.

"Figured a man with no more sense than I've got ought not be allowed to possess that much wealth," he said, still looking down. "So I decided there was only one thing to do and that was to get shet of it." He glanced from Dessie to Blanchard. "It makes me feel better to be shet of it, the whole three hundred and fifty dollars of it."

Her chair falling over backward as she jumped to her feet, Dessie ran to Waldo. She dropped on her knees beside him and threw her arms around him.

"Waldo—that schoolteacher—"

"The mind was weaker than the eye," he said, glancing up at Blanchard. "The mind was weaker than the eye until she said she wanted me to give her the money to carry."

He looked down admiringly at Dessie.

"Waldo," she said haltingly. "I needed that exercise out behind the barn." She looked up into his face. "It did me a lot of good."

Blanchard pushed back his chair as quietly as possible, gathering up his pad and pencil as he backed away from the table. He had almost reached the door when he was startled to hear somebody singing in the kitchen. He stopped and listened, and by that time Dessie had heard it, too. She raised her head and listened intently. It was Justine singing at the top of her voice. She had never sung like that before, not even during the day.

Dessie got up and went to the kitchen door. She threw it open and stood back.

"Come in here, Justine," she called into the next room.

Justine walked slowly past her and went as far as the table. She stood trembling, fearing she was going to be scolded for singing in such a loud voice at that time of night.

Dessie followed her to the table.

"What did you tell me this morning about not having cause to hurry marriage with Carl Friend, Justine?" she asked her.

Justine gripped her fingers tightly.

"That's what I said this morning, Mrs. Murdock," she replied after hesitating to answer for several moments. She glanced quickly around the room at Waldo and Blanchard. "But—"

Dessie nodded.

"You can't fool me when I hear such singing as I heard a minute ago, Justine," she said. "I think it would be a good thing if you and Carl Friend went ahead right away and bought that chamber suite you were speaking to me about this morning."

She handed Justine the roll of bills and walked around the table to the chair where Waldo sat. Justine looked at the greenbacks in her hand, gripping them tightly before she could bring herself to believe they were real.

"Thank you, Mrs. Murdock!" she said, tears beginning to trickle down her cheeks. "How did you know?"

"Never mind, Justine," Dessie said quickly.

Justine began backing toward the kitchen doorway.

"That money never was intended for us in the first place," Waldo said. "We couldn't have managed it, even if we had had a smart lawyer to help."

Dessie dropped on her knees beside Waldo, throwing her arms around him again. They both turned and looked toward the door where Blanchard was standing. Without a word he turned, opened the door quickly, and stepped out into the night.

(First published in *Story*)

John the Indian and George Hopkins

GEORGE HOPKINS, who was about ninety years old, died just in time to have his grave decorated on Memorial Day. Grace and Jessie, his two daughters, buried him on the hilltop behind the house and had an iron fence put around the plot. Grace Hopkins, who was several years the older, said she wanted the fence painted red. Jessie, the younger one, said it was going to be left just as it was. They argued about the fence for two days, and then Grace lost her temper and called Jessie ugly names and had the iron fence painted red anyway. Jessie took her half of the furniture from the house and moved to another part of town. Grace stayed where she was and had another coat of red paint put on the fence around George Hopkins's grave.

Nobody in the town paid much attention to what the Hopkins girls were doing, because the whole Hopkins family had been raising the devil for the past twenty years or more.

George Hopkins had been a selectman ever since anybody could remember and he had always scrapped with someone over something.

First it was over the question whether the town should buy a snowplow and keep the main roads open in winter. He had said "No!" the first time, and had kept on saying that at every town meeting.

"Let the snow be!" he shouted. "God melts it every spring and don't make no charge for it!"

Another time he was scrapping with one of the boys from the village who wanted to come and sit up evenings with one of his daughters.

"You get the hell away from here, Tom Peck's son," he told the boy, "and don't you come back unless you've got a marriage license in your pocket."

George Hopkins had been a mean old scoundrel.

Friday before Memorial Day, Jessie brought her lawn mower and hand scythe and went up the hill to where they had buried her father. She cut the grass with the mower and trimmed the edges of the plot where the grass grew against the fence. When she finished, she stuck a flag in the center of the mound and tied a wreath around the headstone.

Grace heard about Jessie going to the grave, so she got her lawnmower and grass clippers and went up the hill. The plot was in fine shape, but Grace went to work and mowed the grass over again and clipped around the edges where it grew between the iron palings of the fence. She jerked the wreath from the headstone and put one of her own making in its place. She pulled up Jessie's flag and stuck a larger one near the headstone and a smaller one near the footstone.

By nightfall Jessie had heard about Grace's going to the grave. She went over at once to John the Indian's. John lived by himself and wove baskets for sale.

She told John she wanted him to do some work for her and he agreed to help her by the hour. After supper that night he went over to Jessie's.

She brought John into the house and told him exactly what she wanted him to do. Then they went across the pasture to the hill where George Hopkins was buried. They carried a pick and shovel with them and began to open up the grave as soon as they got there. John worked for nearly two hours before he reached the coffin. George Hopkins had been buried deep so the frost would not reach him that winter.

It was hard work getting at the casket. There was no light to work by and John could not see very well after he had dug three or four feet into the ground. When he did get to the coffin, he said he would have to open it up where it was and lift George Hopkins out. It was the only thing to do. He could not get the casket out of the hole by himself.

John was a strong Indian and he got the body on top of the ground. Then he hoisted it on his shoulder and carried it to Jessie's house. Jessie came behind, bringing the pick and shovel.

Jessie told John to lay the body down by the icehouse while

she looked for a place to dig the new grave. She wanted the grave near the house so she could keep watch over it from her window. She stumbled around in the dark several minutes before deciding where the new grave should be.

"Dig it here," Jessie said, standing over the place she had decided upon. "Come here, John, and dig it here."

John spat on his hands and measured off the grave with the pick handle.

"George Hopkins a lot of damn trouble," he grunted, digging away in the dark.

John dug away in the dark. He worked for nearly an hour and then struck a ledge of rock. It was as deep as he could go without blasting. Jessie found another place for the grave and John started all over again. He dug to about the same depth in the ground and struck the same ledge. Jessie made him begin a third time, and he hit the ledge of rock again. By this time it was getting late. John was tired and Jessie said her feet were wet. She said she was afraid of catching cold and pneumonia. John said he was going home.

"What you do with that?" he asked, pointing toward the icehouse. George Hopkins sat propped up against it.

Jessie said she did not know what to do with it. She asked John what could she do with it.

"I take him home with me tonight and bring him back tomorrow night," he suggested.

"All right, John," Jessie said, much relieved. "You take it home with you and bring it back tomorrow evening after supper."

Jessie went into the house and went to bed.

John lifted the body on his shoulder and started home at a trot. The body was not too heavy for him, but it slipped around on his shoulder. It was difficult for him to keep it there. Whenever he grasped it tighter it slid away under the suit of clothes as if the skin were loose.

John got it home though. He laid it on the floor beside his bed and went to sleep.

The next morning, when he got up, he carried it to the kitchen while he cooked his breakfast.

"Want some fried potatoes for eating, George Hopkins?" John asked the body he had propped up against the wood box.

"Huh, huh," John chuckled, "George Hopkins, you don't eat much these days."

He went about getting his breakfast.

"Maybe you want to smoke your pipe, George Hopkins," John said. "Huh, huh, George Hopkins, I got fine tobacco."

Grace went to the hilltop that forenoon to see if Jessie had been back with another wreath of her own. Grace was determined to take them away as fast as Jessie brought them.

When she reached the top of the hill and saw the pile of fresh earth inside the fenced plot, she turned around and ran straight across the town to the village as fast as she could. She went straight for a warrant.

Grace got the warrant and the man to serve it on Jessie. They went in a hurry to Jessie's house. All the doors and windows were locked tightly and they could not get in. Jessie heard them banging on the door, but she would not come out. Grace and the man found the graves Jessie and John the Indian had started, but they could not find George Hopkins in any of them.

Grace came back again the next day and looked for the body but she could not find it anywhere on the place. Jessie still would not come out of the house.

John was becoming tired of waiting for Jessie to come out of the house so they could bury George Hopkins. He did not know what to do about it. He waited another two days for her to come out and by that time he was sorry he had taken the job to dig a new grave for George Hopkins. John's house was beginning to have a bad odor.

Early the next morning he went to Jessie's house and tried to make her open the door and tell him what to do. She did not make a sound. He knew she was inside because once he saw her looking at him from behind a curtain at the window.

John trotted back to his house and carried the body down to the lake and propped it up in a canoe. Then he towed it to the middle of the lake with his other canoe. He had some live bait with him and a fishing-pole.

When he reached the center of the lake he threw the baited fishing-line overboard, tied the pole securely to the canoe George Hopkins was in, and shoved away from it.

John paddled to the shore, leaving George Hopkins sitting up in the canoe salmon-fishing. He looked back just as he reached the shore and saw the canoe shoot down the lake fast as a speedboat. A big bull-headed salmon had hooked the line. The salmon was taking George Hopkins down the lake so fast the wind blew his hat overboard.

John the Indian waited on the shore chuckling to himself until they were out of sight. Then he went home to get himself some breakfast.

(First published in *Pagany*)

Yellow Girl

NELL stood at the kitchen window packing the basket of eggs. She arranged eleven white eggs carefully, placing the cotton-seed hulls between them and under them so that none would be broken. The last one to be put into the basket was large and brown and a little soiled. She dipped it into the pan of soap and warm water and wiped it dry with a fresh dish towel. Even then she was not pleased with the way it looked, because it was brown; all the other eggs in the basket were as white as September cotton bolls.

Behind her in the room, Myrtie was scouring the two frying pans with soapy water and a cloth dipped in sand. Nell laid down the brown egg and called Myrtie.

"Here's another of those big brown eggs, Myrtie," she said, pointing at the egg. "Do you have any idea where they come from? Have you seen any strange hens in the yard? There must be a visiting hen laying eggs in the chicken house."

Myrtie laid down the frying pan and came over to the little table by the window. She picked up the large brown egg and looked at it. The egg no longer looked brown. Nell looked at the egg again, wondering why in Myrtie's hands it had apparently changed color.

"Where do these brown eggs come from, Myrtie?" she asked. "There was one last week, and now today there's this. It was in the basket Mr. Willis brought in from the chicken house, but he said he forgot to notice which nest he took it from."

Myrtie turned the egg over in her hands, feeling the weight of it and measuring its enormous circumference with her fingers.

"Don't ask me, Miss Nell," Myrtie said, staring at the egg. "I've never seen a flock of Leghorns yet, though, that didn't lay a few brown eggs, sometime or other. Looks like it just can't be helped."

"What do you mean, Myrtie? What on earth are you talking about? Of course Leghorns lay white eggs; this is a brown egg."

"I'm not saying the Leghorns lay them, Miss Nell, and I'm not saying they don't. Those old Buff Orpingtons and Plymouth Rocks and Domineckers lay funny-looking eggs, too,

147

sometimes. I wouldn't take on so much about finding one measly brown egg, though. I've never seen anybody yet, white or colored, who knew how such things happen. But I wouldn't worry about it, Miss Nell. Brown eggs are just as good as white eggs, to my way of tasting."

Nell turned her back on Myrtie and looked out the window until the girl had returned to the other side of the kitchen. Nell disliked to talk to Myrtie, because Myrtie pretended never to know the truth about anything. Even if she did know, she would invariably evade a straightforward answer. Myrtie would begin talking, and talk about everything under the sun from morning to night, but she would never answer a question that she could evade. Nell always forgave her, though; she knew Myrtie was not consciously evading the truth.

While the girl was scouring the pans, Nell picked up the egg again and looked at it closely. Mrs. Farrington had a flock of Dominique chickens, and she gathered in her chicken house eggs of all sizes, shapes, and colors. But that was to be expected, Mrs. Farrington had said, because she had two old roosters that were of no known name or breed. Nell had told Mrs. Farrington that some of her Dominiques were mixed-bred, and consequently they produced eggs of varying sizes, shapes, and colors; but Mrs. Farrington continued to lay all the blame on her two roosters, because, she said, they were a mixture of all breeds.

Once more Nell dipped the brown egg into the pan of water and wiped it with the fresh dish towel, but the egg remained as brown as it was at first. The egg was clean by then, but soap and water would not alter its size or change its color. It was a brown egg, and it would remain brown. Nell gave up, finally; she realized that she could never change it in any way. If she had had another egg to put into the basket in its place, she would have laid it aside and substituted a white one; but she only had a dozen, counting the brown one, and she wished to have enough to make an even exchange with Mrs. Farrington when she went over after some green garden peas.

Before she finally placed the egg in the basket with the others she glanced out the window to see where Willis was. He was sitting in the crib door shelling red seed corn into an old wooden lard pail.

"I'm going over to Mrs. Farrington's now to exchange these eggs for some peas," she told Myrtie. "Keep the fire going good, and put on a pan of water to boil. I'll be back in a little while."

She turned around and looked at Myrtie.

"Suppose you mash the potatoes today, for a change, Myrtie. Mr. Willis likes them that way."

"Are you going to take that big egg, Miss Nell?" Myrtie

asked, looking down at it in the basket with the eleven white Leghorns.

"Certainly," she said. "Why?"

"Mrs. Farrington will be surprised to see it in with all those white ones, won't she, Miss Nell?"

"Well, what if she does see it?" Nell asked impatiently.

"Nothing, Miss Nell," Myrtie said. "But she might want to know where it came from. She knows we've got Leghorn hens, and she might think one of her Domineckers laid it."

"I can't help that," Nell said, turning away. "And, besides, she should keep her Dominiques at home if she doesn't want them to lay eggs in somebody else's chicken house."

"That's right, Miss Nell," Myrtie said. "She sure ought to do that. She ought to keep her Domineckers at home."

Nell was annoyed by the girl's comments. It was none of Myrtie's business, anyway. Myrtie was getting to be impertinent, and she was forgetting that she was a hired servant in the house. Nell left the kitchen determined to treat Myrtie more coldly after that. She could not allow a colored cook to tell her what to do and what not to do.

Willis was sitting in the crib door shelling the red seed corn. He glanced up when Nell came down the back steps, and looked at her. He stopped shelling corn for a moment to wipe away the white flakes of husk that clung to his eyes.

"I'm going over to Mrs. Farrington's now and exchange a basket of eggs for some green peas, Willis," she said. "I'll not be gone long."

"Maybe she won't swap with you today," Willis said. He stopped and looked up at her through the thin cloud of flying husk that hovered around him. "How do you know she will want to take eggs for peas today, Nell?"

"Don't be foolish, Willis," she said, smiling at him; "why wouldn't she take eggs in exchange today?"

"She might get to wondering where that big brown egg came from," he said, laughing. "She might think it is an egg one of her hens laid."

Nell stopped, but she did not turn around. She waited, looking towards the house.

"You're as bad as Myrtie, Willis."

"In which way is that?"

The moment he spoke, she turned quickly and looked at him. He was bending over to pick up an ear of seed corn.

"I didn't mean to say that, Willis. Please forgive what I said. I didn't mean anything like that."

"Like what?"

"Nothing," she said, relieved. "It wasn't anything; I've even forgotten what it was I said. Good-by."

"Good-by," he said, looking after her, wondering.

Nell turned and walked quickly out of the yard and went around the corner of the house towards the road. The Farrington house was half a mile away, but by taking the path through the cotton field it was two or three hundred yards nearer. She crossed the road and entered the field, walking quickly along the path with the basket of eggs on her arm.

Halfway to the Farringtons' Nell turned around and looked back to see if Willis was still sitting in the crib door shelling seed corn. She did not know why she stopped and looked back, but even though she could not see him there or anywhere else in the yard, she went on towards the Farringtons' without thinking of Willis again.

Mrs. Farrington was sitting on the back porch peeling turnips when Nell turned the corner of the house and walked across the yard. There was a bucket of turnips beside Mrs. Farrington's rocking chair, and long purple peelings were lying scattered on the porch floor around her, twisted into shapes like apple peelings when they were tossed over the shoulder. Nell ran up the steps and picked up the longest peeling she could find; she picked up the peeling even before she spoke to Mrs. Farrington.

"Sakes alive, Nell," Mrs. Farrington said; "why are you throwing turnip peelings over your shoulder? Doesn't that good-for-nothing husband of yours love you any more?"

Nell dropped the turnip peeling, and, picking it up again, tore it into short pieces and threw them into the bucket. She blushed and sat down in the chair beside Mrs. Farrington.

"Of course, he loves me," Nell said. "I suppose I did that so many time when I was a little girl that I still have the habit."

"You mean it's because you haven't grown up yet, Nell," the woman said, chuckling to herself. "I used to be just like that myself; but, sakes alive, it doesn't last, always, girl."

Both of them laughed, and looked away, one from the other. Over across the cotton field a cloud of white dust hung close to the earth. Mr. Farrington and the colored men were planting cotton, and the earth was so dry it rose up in the air when it was disturbed by the mules' hooves and the cotton planters. There was no wind to carry the dust away, and it hung over the men and mules, hiding them from sight.

Presently Mrs. Farrington dropped a peeled turnip into the pan and folded her hands in her lap. She looked at Nell, noting her neatly combed hair and her clean gingham frock and white hands. Mrs. Farrington turned away again after that and gazed once more at the cloud of dust where her husband was at work.

"Maybe you and Willis will always be like that," she said. "Seems like you and Willis are still in love with each other. As long as he stays at home where he belongs and doesn't run off at night, it's a pretty sure sign he isn't getting ready to chase after another woman. Sakes alive, men can't always be depended upon to stay at home at night, though; they go riding off when you are least looking for them to."

Nell sat up, startled by what Mrs. Farrington had said, terrified by the directness of her comments.

"Of course, Willis wouldn't do such a thing like that," she said confidently. "I know he wouldn't. Willis wouldn't do a thing like that. That's impossible, Mrs. Farrington."

Mrs. Farrington glanced at Nell, and then once more she looked across the field where the planting was being done. The cloud of white dust followed the men and mules, covering them.

"Seems like men are always saying something about being compelled to go to Macon on business, and even up to Atlanta sometimes," she said, ignoring Nell. "And then there are the times when they say they have to go to town at night. Seems like they are always going off to town at night."

Several Dominique hens came from under the porch and stopped in the yard to scratch on the hard white sand. They scratched listlessly; they went through the motions of scratching as if they knew of nothing else to do. They bent their long necks and looked down at the chicken-scrawls they had made with their claws, and they walked away aimlessly, neither surprised nor angry at not having unearthed a worm to devour. One of them began singing in the heat, drooping her wings until the tips of them dragged on the sand. The other hens paid no attention to her, strolling away without interest in the doleful music.

"You have pretty chickens, Mrs. Farrington," Nell said, watching the Dominiques stroll across the yard and sit down in the shaded dust holes as though they were nests.

"They're nothing but Domineckers," she said; "sakes alive, a body can't call them much of a breed, but they do get around to laying an egg or two once in a while."

Nell glanced down at the basket of eggs in her lap, covering the brown egg with her hand. She looked quickly at Mrs. Farrington to see if she had noticed what she had done.

"How are your Leghorns laying now, Nell?" she asked.

"Very well. Willis gathered sixteen eggs yesterday."

"My Domineckers seem to be taking a spell of resting. I only gathered two eggs yesterday, and that's not enough for a hungry man and a yard full of blacks. Sakes alive, we were saying only last night that we wished you would bring over some eggs in a day or two. And now here you are with them. Half an hour's prayer couldn't have done better."

"I thought you might let me have some green peas for dinner," Nell said, lifting the basket and setting it on the floor.

"Willis likes green peas at this time of year, and ours haven't begun to bear yet."

"You're as welcome to as many as you want," Mrs. Farrington said. "Just walk into the kitchen, Nell, and look on the big table and you'll find a bushel basket of them. Help yourself to all you think you and Willis will want. We've got more than we can use. Sakes alive, there'll be another bushel ready for picking tomorrow morning, too."

Nell went into the kitchen and placed the eleven Leghorn eggs and the big brown one in a pan. She filled the basket with green peas and came back to the porch, closing the screen noiselessly behind her.

"Sit down, Nell," Mrs. Farrington said, "and tell me what's been happening. Sakes alive, I sit here all day and never hear a word of what's going on."

"Why, I haven't heard of anything new," Nell said.

"What's Willis doing now?"

"He's getting ready to plant corn. He was shelling the seed when I left home. He should be ready to begin planting this afternoon. The planter broke down yesterday, and he had to send to Macon for a new spoke chain. It should be here in the mail today."

"Myrtie is still there to help you with the house, isn't she?"

"Yes, Myrtie is still there."

The hens lying in the dust holes in the shade of the sycamore tree stood up and flapped their wings violently, beating the dust from their feathers. They stretched, one leg after the other, and flapped their wings a second time. One of them spread her legs, bending her knees as if she were getting ready to squat on the ground, and scratched the hard white sand five or six times in quick succession. The other hens stood and watched her while she stretched her long neck and looked down at the marks she had made; and then, wiping her beak on her leg as one whets a knife blade, she turned and waddled back across the yard and under the porch out of sight. The other hens followed her, singing in the heat.

"Couldn't you find a black woman to help you with the house?" Mrs. Farrington asked.

"A black woman?" Nell said. "Why, Myrtie is colored."

"She's colored all right," Mrs. Farrington said; "but, sakes alive, Nell, she isn't black. Myrtie is yellow."

"Well, that's all right, isn't it?" Nell asked. "Myrtie is yellow, and she is a fairly good cook. I don't know where I could find a better one for the pay."

"I reckon I'd heap rather have a black girl and a poor cook, than to have a yellow girl and the finest cook in the whole country."

Nell glanced quickly at Mrs. Farrington, but her head was turned, and she did not look at Nell.

There was a long silence between them until finally Nell felt that she must know what Mrs. Farrington was talking about.

One of the Dominiques suddenly appeared on the bottom step. She came hopping up to the porch, a step at a time. When she reached the last one, Mrs. Farrington said, "Shoo!" The hen flew to the yard and went back under the porch.

"You don't mean—"

Mrs. Farrington began rocking slowly, backward and forward. She gazed steadily across the field where her husband was planting cotton with the colored men.

"You don't mean Willis and—"

One of the roosters strutted across the yard, his eye first upon the hens under the porch and next upon the two women, and stopped midway in the yard to stand and fix his eye upon Mrs. Farrington and Nell. He stood jerking his head from side to side, his hanging scarlet comb blinding his left eye, while he listened to the squeaking of Mrs. Farrington's chair. After a while he continued across the yard and went out of sight behind the smokehouse.

"Mrs. Farrington, Willis wouldn't do anything like that!" Nell said indignantly.

"Like what?" Mrs. Farrington asked. "Sakes alive, Nell, I didn't say he would do anything."

"I know you didn't say it, Mrs. Farrington, but I thought you said it. I couldn't help thinking that you did say it."

"Well, that's different," she replied, much relieved. "I wouldn't want you to go telling Willis I did say it. Menfolks never understand what a woman means, anyway, and when they are told that a woman says something about them, they sometimes fly off the handle something awful."

Nell got up and stood beside the chair. She wished she could run down the steps and along the path towards home without another second's delay, but she knew she could not jump up and leave Mrs. Farrington like that, after what had been said. She would have to pretend that she was not in such a great hurry to get home.

"You're not going so soon, are you, Nell? Why, sakes alive, it seems like you only got here two or three minutes ago, Nell."

"I know," she said, "but it's getting late, and I've got to go home and get these peas ready for dinner. I'll be back to see you soon."

She walked carelessly down the steps. Mrs. Farrington got up and followed her across the hard yard. When they reached the beginning of the path that led across the field, Mrs. Farrington stopped. She never went any farther than that.

"I'm afraid I must hurry home now and hull the peas in

time for dinner," Nell said, backing down the path. "I'll be back again in a few days, Mrs. Farrington. Thank you so much for the peas. Willis has wanted some for the past week or longer."

"It's as fair an exchange as I can offer for the Leghorn eggs," she said, laughing. "Because if there's anything I like better than those white Leghorn eggs, I don't know what it is. I get so tired of eating my old Dominecker's brown eggs I sometimes say I hope I may never see another one. Maybe I'll be asking you for a setting of them some day soon."

"Good-by," Nell said, backing farther and farther away. She turned and walked several steps. "I'll bring you another basket soon, Mrs. Farrington."

It seemed as if she would never reach the house, even though it was only half a mile away. She could not run, because Mrs. Farrington was in the yard behind her watching, and she could not walk slowly, because she had to get home as soon as possible. She walked with her eyes on the path in front of her, forcing herself to keep from looking up at the house. She knew that if she did raise her eyes and look at it, she would never be able to keep herself from running. If she did that, Mrs. Farrington would see her.

It was not until she had at last reached the end of the path that she was able to look backward. Mrs. Farrington had left her yard, and Nell ran across the road and around to the back of the house.

Willis was nowhere within sight. She looked first at the crib where she had hoped she would find him, but he was not there, and the crib door was closed and locked. She looked down at the barn, but he was not there, either. When she glanced hastily over the fields, she was still unable to see him anywhere.

She stopped at the bottom step on the back porch. There was no sound within the house that she could hear, and not even the sound of Myrtie's footsteps reached her ears. The place seemed to be entirely deserted, and yet she knew that could not be, because only half an hour before when she left to go to Mrs. Farrington's to exchange eggs, Willis was sitting in the crib door shelling seed corn, and Myrtie was in the kitchen scouring the two frying pans.

Nell's hands went out and searched for the railing that led up the porch steps. Her hands could not find it, and her eyes would not let her see it.

The thought of Mrs. Farrington came back to her again and again. Mrs. Farrington, sitting on her own back porch, talking. Mrs. Farrington, sitting in her rocking chair, looking. Mrs. Farrington, peeling purple-top turnips, talking about yellow girls.

Nell felt deathly sick. She felt as if she had been stricken with an illness that squeezed the core of her body. Deep down within herself, she was deathly ill. A pain that began by piercing her skull struck downward and downward until it became motionless in her stomach. It remained there, gnawing and biting, eating the organs of her body and drinking the flow of her blood. She sank limp and helpless upon the back porch steps. Although she did not know where she was, she could still see Mrs. Farrington. Mrs. Farrington, in her rocking chair, looking. Mrs. Farrington, peeling purple-top turnips, talking about yellow girls.

Nell did not know how much later it was when she opened her eyes. The day was the color of the red seed corn Willis had been shelling when she last saw him sitting in the crib door, and it swam in a sea so wide that she almost cried out in fear when she saw it. Slowly she remembered how she had come to be where she was. She got to her feet weakly, holding to the railing for support.

Stumbling up the steps and across the porch, she flung open the screen door and went into the kitchen. Myrtie was standing beside the table mashing the boiled Irish potatoes with a long fork that had seven tines. Myrtie looked up when Nell ran in, but she did not have an opportunity to speak. Nell ran headlong through the dining room and on into the front room. Myrtie looked surprised to see her running.

Nell paused a moment in the doorway, looking at Willis, at the room, at the daybed, at the floor, at the rugs, at the open door that led into their room. She stood looking at everything she could see. She looked at the pillows on the daybed, at the rugs on the floor, at the chairs against the wall, at the counterpane on their bed. Remembering, she looked at the carpet in their room. Willis sat in front of her reading the *Macon Telegraph* that had just come in the mail, and he was calmly smoking his pipe. She glanced once more at the daybed, at the pillows arranged upon it, and at the rug in front of it. Running, she went to their room and ran her hands over the counterpane of the bed. She picked up the pillows, feeling them, and laid them down again. She ran back into the other room where Willis was.

Willis looked up at her.

Nell ran and fell on her knees in front of him, forcing her body between his legs and locking her arms around him. She pressed her feverish face against his cool cheeks and closed her eyes tightly. She forced herself tightly to him, holding him with all her might.

"Did Mrs. Farrington exchange with you?" he asked. "I'll bet a pretty that she had something to say about that big brown egg in a basketful of Leghorns."

Nell felt her body shake convulsively, as if she were shivering with cold. She knew she had no control over herself now.

"Look here," he said, throwing aside the *Telegraph* and lifting her head and looking into her eyes. "I know where that brown egg came from now. I remember all about it. There was one of Mrs. Farrington's old Dominecker hens over here yesterday morning. I saw her scratching in the yard, and she acted like she didn't give a cuss whether she clawed up a worm or not. She would scratch awhile and then walk off without even looking to see if she had turned up a worm."

Nell felt herself shaking again, but she did not attempt to control herself. If she could only lie there close to Willis with her arms around him, she did not care how much she shivered. As long as she was there, she had Willis; when she got up and walked out of the room, she would never again be that certain.

(First published in *Story*)

The First Autumn

THEY sat on the lawn looking up at the fluttering leaves on the old maples. He was beside the wagon with his arm over the red wooden body; she was on the other side, sitting with her legs crossed under her and with her hands folded in her lap.

"That is the oldest tree over there," Elizabeth said, pointing across the lawn. "I know it's the oldest, because it's the one where the squirrels live."

"But that's not why it is the oldest, silly," Robert said. "It's the oldest because the leaves stay green the longest. The little trees turn red first."

A week ago all the trees were as green as the newly mown lawn, and then all of a sudden they had begun to turn. The grove of maples on the hill was orange and gold, the younger trees were the deeper color; and in the yard the old maples that had been there scores of years were turning yellow and purple. In a short while the leaves would begin to twirl and spin on the branches when the breezes blew, and then they would twist themselves off and come fluttering down. After that the grass would die, the flowers would shrivel, and the hills and fields would be a deep dark brown until the first snow fell.

"The sky was raining paint last night while we slept," Elizabeth said. "It rained a pot of paint on every tree."

"Daddy says it is the end of summer. He said that the trees turn red and orange and yellow every year when summer is over."

"I didn't see it last year."

"But Daddy said that last year all the trees were colored. They were yellow for a while, and then all of them were red. When the leaves turn red, that's when they are ready to fall almost any minute. That's because they are dead."

The front door opened. Robert dropped the wagon tongue and raced to the porch.

"Here's Daddy! Here's Daddy! Daddy's come out to play!"

Elizabeth ran after him. They clambered up on the porch steps as fast as they could.

"Now what?" Daddy said.

"Play!" said Robert, jumping up and down, swinging on his arm. "We're going to play!"

"Is this the end of the week, Daddy?" Elizabeth asked. "Are you going to stay two whole days now?"

"It's the end of the week. No more city for two whole days."

"Let's play," Robert said, pulling him down the steps. "Let's play everything!"

"We are tired of playing bear, aren't we?" Daddy asked. "We played bear last week-end. What'll we play this week?"

"Bear!" Robert cried. "Let's play bear again. It's more fun than anything else."

"I've just thought of a new game to play," Daddy said. "How would you like to play horse, Robert?"

"Oh, let's play bear first of all," Elizabeth begged, pulling him across the lawn. "Just for a little while, Daddy, and then we can play all the other games."

"All right, then," Daddy said. "Who's going to be the great big black bear this time?"

"You are!" Robert said. "You're always the bear, Daddy. Let's hear you growl!"

"Woof!" Daddy said, dropping down on his hands and knees. "Woof! Woof! Woof!"

"Oh, don't scare me so!" Elizabeth cried, crawling backward. "Please don't scare me so! I'm awfully scared of bears!"

"Woof! Woof! Woof!" Daddy said, pawing the lawn and waddling after her.

"You're missing me!" Robert said. "Here I am. Growl some at me."

"Woof! Woof! Woof!"

"Look! Here are some berries for the big black bear," Elizabeth said, holding out a handful of grass. "Would you like to have some berries?"

"Woof!" Daddy said, licking the short blades of grass from her hand. "Woof!"

"I'm going to ride the bear!" Robert cried. "Look at me! I'm going to ride the big black bear's back. I'm not afraid!"

Robert ran and climbed on Daddy's back, whipping the bear with a maple twig to make him get-up.

"Now, let's play horse," Daddy said. "This is a new game. We've never played horse before, have we, Elizabeth?"

"Oh, let's do!" she said. "Hurry, Robert! Get down off the bear's back so we can all play horse. It's going to be lots of fun, isn't it, Daddy?"

"It certainly is," said Daddy. "But who is going to be the horse?"

"Oh, you are!" Elizabeth cried. "You be the horse."

"All right. I'm the horse. Now look out! Here comes the wild white horse!"

"What's the horse going to do?" Robert asked.

"The horse would like some sugar," Daddy said. "The horse likes sugar better than anything else. He likes salt sometimes, but he would rather have sugar now. He hasn't had any sugar for a long time."

"Where's the horse going to get sugar?" Elizabeth asked. "We haven't any out here."

"Neigh! Neigh! Neigh!" Daddy said, galloping around in a circle on his hands and feet.

"The horse is looking for sugar," Robert said. "Look out! Don't let the wild horse kick you!"

Daddy stopped, twisted his head from side to side and raised his foot high into the air behind him.

"Look out!" Robert cried. "The horse is getting ready to kick!"

Daddy held his foot high up behind him a moment and kicked. He kicked so hard it made his shoe come tumbling off.

"The horse kicked his shoe off!" Elizabeth said. "Let's be careful, because the horse is angry with us for not giving him some sugar. Oh, where will we find some sugar!"

"I'm not afraid of the horse," Robert said. "Watch me! I'm going to ride him!"

"He'll throw you off," said Elizabeth. "You'd better wait until he gets some sugar first."

"Watch me! This is the way to catch a wild horse and ride him away!"

"Neigh! Neigh! Neigh!" Daddy said, galloping off. He stopped and kicked high into the air with his other foot. That shoe did not come off as the other one had.

"Here I go!" Robert said. "Watch me ride the wild horse all around the pasture!"

Daddy stood still until Robert had climbed on his back.

Then he shook his head from side to side, snorted, and pawed the lawn.

"Let me ride, too," Elizabeth begged. "I'd like to ride the wild horse."

She climbed on Daddy's back behind Robert and held Robert around the waist so she would not be thrown off when the horse bucked and reared.

"What are you getting down flat on the ground for, Daddy?" Robert asked. "We are all on. You may get up now, Daddy. Make the wild horse snort and buck!"

Daddy lay down flat on the lawn. Elizabeth got off, but Robert took a maple-tree twig and tried to make the horse get-up.

"The horse won't get-up," Robert said. "He wants to lie down."

"Why don't you play horse any more, Daddy?" Elizabeth asked. "If you are tired of playing horse, let's play another game. I know a good one called 'Hunting the Kitty.' Don't you wish to play that with us? It's lots of fun, Daddy."

Robert got up and walked towards the porch. He stopped and looked back at Daddy and Elizabeth on the lawn.

"I'm going to tell Mother you won't play with us any more, Daddy," he said. "She'll come out and make you play."

He ran into the house. Elizabeth moved closer to Daddy and began searching for four-leaf clovers in the grass.

The red leaves on the maples in the yard were falling to the lawn. When a sudden gust of wind blew, the leaves spun and twirled on their stems, fluttering to the ground like small pieces of torn red paper. Over on the hill the orange and gold trees rustled and bowed in the wind, shaking themselves until the underside of the leaves turned outward to the sun.

Mother and Robert came out the front door and walked across the lawn. Mother put her finger over her lips so that no one would make a sound. She came closer, tiptoeing softly on the smooth lawn, trying not to make any noise. Robert held her by the hand, holding his finger over his lips, too. Elizabeth put her hand over her mouth, nodding her head up and down, and opening her eyes wider and wider. In another moment they could all scare Daddy, because he did not know that Mother and Robert were there.

When Mother got almost in front of him, she took her finger from her lips and nodded at Robert and Elizabeth. He and Elizabeth were all but bursting with excitement.

"Boo!" Mother cried, falling down beside Daddy on the grass.

"Boo! Daddy!" Robert said.

"Boo!" said Elizabeth, jumping up and down.

Mother looked down at Daddy, waiting for him to raise his

head and smile at her. She waited another moment and bent
closer.

A small black ant was crawling over his nose. On the back
of his white shirt a big green grasshopper sat with his long
legs all ready to spring.

"Look at the funny grasshopper," Robert said, touching it
with a blade of grass. "He's resting on Daddy's shirt. Look at
him jump so high!"

"Shhh!" Mother said, putting her finger over her lips again.
"Don't make any sounds. Daddy is fast asleep."

"Then how can we play, if Daddy isn't going to be the wild
horse?" Elizabeth asked, pouting.

"Playing horse isn't much fun," Robert said. "I would like
to play something else when Daddy wakes up."

Mother sat down close to Daddy, taking one of his hands in
hers. She held his hand a moment, and dropped it.

"What's the matter?" Elizabeth asked, clutching Mother's
skirt. "Why did you scream, Mother?"

Mother was biting her lips and looking down at Daddy's
white shirt where the big grasshopper had been sitting. A
maroon maple leaf fluttered down, spinning over and over. It
fell on Daddy's shirt and lay there.

"Will Daddy play with us again when he wakes up?" Robert
asked. "We had almost finished playing horse, and there're
some other games we wish to play, too."

"Daddy kicked so hard while we were playing horse that
his shoe came off," Elizabeth said. "Look! Here it is!"

She picked it up, and Mother took it from her and held it in
both of her hands, pressing it against her breast. Her fingers
moved over it as if she were trying to feel what it was without
looking at it.

The little black ant on Daddy's nose crawled up on his forehead and stopped there to look at something.

"We must go into the house now," Mother said, taking
Elizabeth and Robert by the hands. "I want both of you to go
to the playroom and stay there until I call you. Look at the
pictures in your books, or build something with your blocks,
but do not look out of the window until I call you. Run along
now, Robert and Elizabeth. Mother will be busy for a long
time."

They went into the house and Mother waited at the bottom
of the stairs while they were going up to the playroom. She
leaned against the newel post, holding close to her breast the
shoe that Daddy had kicked off when he was the wild horse.

"It's a shame to stay indoors when it's so nice out there,"
Robert said. "All the red leaves will soon be gone."

"Will you call us the minute Daddy wakes up, Mother?"

Elizabeth asked. "Please do. We wish to finish playing horse —and we have some new games to play, too."

"Yes," Mother said, "I'll call you."

(First published in *Pagany*)

Savannah River Payday

A QUARTER of a mile down the river the partly devoured carcasses of five or six mules that had been killed during the past two weeks by the heat and overwork at the sawmill, lay rotting in the midafternoon sun. Of the hundred or more buzzards hovering around the flesh, some were perched drowsily on the cypress stumps, and some were strutting aimlessly over the cleared ground. Every few minutes one of the buzzards, with a sound like wagon-rumble on a wooden bridge, beat the sultry air with its wings and pecked and clawed at the decaying flesh. Dozens of the vultures glided overhead hour after hour in monotonous circles.

The breeze that had been coming up the river since early that morning shifted to the east and the full stench of sunrotted muleflesh settled over the swamp. The July sun blazed over the earth and shriveled the grass and weeds until they were as dry as crisp autumn leaves. A cloud of dense black smoke blew over from the other side of the river when somebody threw an armful of fat pine on the fire under the moonshine still.

Jake blew his nose on the ground and asked Red for a smoke. Red gave him a cigarette.

"What time's it now, Red?"

Red took his watch from his overalls pocket and showed it to Jake.

"Looks to me like it's about three o'clock," he told Red.

Red jerked the pump out of the dust and kicked at the punctured tire. The air escaped just as fast as he could pump it in. There was nothing in the old car to patch the tube with.

Jake spat at the Negro's head on the running board and grabbed Red's arm.

"That nigger's stinkin' worse than them mules, Red. Let's run that tire flat so we can git to town and git shed of him. I don't like to waste time around that smell."

Red was open to any suggestion. The sweat had been running down his face and over his chest and wetting his breeches. He had been pumping for half an hour trying to get some air into the tire. It had been flat when they left the sawmill.

Jake cranked up the engine and they got in and started up the road towards town. It was three miles to town from the sawmill.

The old automobile rattled up the road through the deep yellow dust. The sun was so hot it made the air feel like steam when it was breathed into the lungs. Most of the water had leaked from the radiator, and the engine knocked like ten-pound hammers on an anvil. Red did not care about the noise as long as he could get where he was going.

Half a mile up the road was Hog Creek. When they got to the top of the hill Red shut off the engine. The car rolled down to the creek and stopped on the bridge.

"Git some water for the radiator, Jake," Red said. He reached in the back seat and pulled out a tin can for Jake to carry the water in.

Jake crawled out of the car and stretched his arm and legs. He wiped the sweat off his face with his shirttail.

"Don't hurry me," Jake said, leaning against the car. "Ain't no hurry for nothin'."

Red got tired holding the can. He threw it at Jake. Jake dodged it and the can rolled off the bridge down into the creek. Red propped his feet on the windshield and got ready to take a nap while Jake was going for the water.

Jake walked around to the other side of the car and looked at the Negro. The hot sun had swollen the lips until they curled over and touched the nose and chin. The Negro had tripped up that morning when he tried to get out of the way of a falling cypress tree.

"What's this nigger's name?" he asked Red.

"Jim somethin'," Red grunted, trying to sleep.

Jake turned the head over with his foot so he could see the face. He happened to think that he might have known him.

"God Almighty!" he said, shaking Red by the arm. "Hand me that monkey wrench quick, Red."

Red lifted up the back seat and found the monkey wrench. He got out and handed it to Jake.

"What's the matter, Jake? What's the matter with the nigger?"

Jake picked up a stick and pushed back the Negro's lips.

"Look at them gold teeth, Red," he pointed.

Red squatted beside the running board and tried to count the gold teeth.

"Here, Red, you take this stick and hold his mouth open while I knock off that gold."

Red took the stick and pushed the lips away from the teeth.

Jake choked the monkey wrench halfway and tapped on the first tooth. He had to hit it about six or seven times before it broke off and fell on the bridge. Red picked it up and rubbed the dirt off on his overalls.

"How much is it worth, Jake?" he asked, bouncing the tooth in the palm of his hand trying to feel the weight.

"About two dollars," Jake said. "Maybe more."

Jake took the tooth and weighed it in his hand.

"Hold his mouth open and let me knock out the rest of them," Jake said. He picked up the monkey wrench and choked it halfway. "There's about three or four more, looks like to me."

Red pushed the Negro's lips away from the teeth while Jake hammered away at the gold. The sun had made the teeth so hot they burned his fingers when he picked them off the bridge.

"You keep two and give me three," Red said. "It's my car we're totin' him to town in."

"Like hell I will," Jake said. "I found them, didn't I? Well, I got the right to keep three myself if I want to."

Red jerked the monkey wrench off the running board and socked Jake on the head with it. The blow was only hard enough to stun him. Jake reeled around on the bridge like he was dead drunk and fell against the radiator. Red followed him up and socked him again. A ball of skin and hair fell in the dust. He took all the gold teeth and put them into his overalls pocket. Jake was knocked out cold. Red shook him and kicked him, but Jake didn't move. Red dragged him around to the back seat and threw him inside and shut the door. Then he cranked up the car and started to town. The tire that was punctured had dropped off the wheel somewhere down the road and there was nothing left except the rim to ride on.

Red had gone a little over a mile from the bridge when Jake came to himself and sat up on the back seat. He was still a little dizzy, but he knew what he was doing.

"Hold on a minute, Red," he shouted. "Stop this automobile."

Red shut off the engine and the car rolled to a stop. He got out in the road.

"What you want now, Jake?" he asked him.

"Look, Red," he pointed across the cotton field beside the road. "Look what's yonder, Red."

A mulatto girl was chopping cotton about twenty rows from the road. Red started across the field after her before Jake could get out. They stumbled over the cotton rows kicking up the plants with every step.

Jake caught up with Red before they reached the girl. When

they were only two rows away, she dropped her hoe and started running towards the woods.

"Hey, there!" Jake shouted. "Don't you run off!"

He picked up a heavy sun-baked clod and heaved it at her as hard as he could. She turned around and tried to dodge it; but she could not get out of the way in time, and it struck her full on the forehead.

Red got to her first. The girl rubbed her head and tried to get up. He pushed her down again.

Jake came running up. He tried to kick her dress above her waist with his foot.

"Wait a minute," Red said. He shoved Jake off his feet. "I got here first."

"That don't cut no ice with me," Jake said. He started for Red and butted him down. Then he stood over him and tried to stomp Red's head with his heels.

Red got away and picked up the girl's hoe and swung it with all his might at Jake's head. The sharp blade caught Jake on the right side of his head and sliced his ear off close to his face. Jake fell back and felt his face and looked at the ear on the ground.

Red turned around to grab the girl, but she was gone. She was nowhere in sight.

"Come on, Jake," he said. "She run off. Let's git to town and dump that nigger. I want 'bout a dozen good stiff drinks. I don't work all week and let payday git by without tankin' up good and plenty."

Jake tore one of the sleeves out of his shirt and made a bandage to tie around his head. It did not bleed so much after that.

Red went back to the car and waited for Jake. The dead Negro on the running board was a hell of a lot of trouble. If it had not been for him, the girl would not have got scared and run away.

They got into the car again and started to town. They had to get to the undertaker's before six o'clock, because he closed up at that time; and they did not want to have to carry the dead Negro around with them all day Sunday.

"What time's it now, Red?" Jake asked him.

Red pulled out his watch and showed it to Jake.

"Looks like it's about five o'clock," Jake told him.

Red put the watch back into his overalls pocket.

It was about a mile and a half to town yet, and there was a black cloud coming up like there might be a big thunderstorm. The old car had got hot again because they did not get the water at Hog Creek, and the engine was knocking so hard it could be heard half a mile away.

Suddenly the storm broke overhead and the water came down

in bucketfuls. There was no place to stop where they could get out of the rain and there was no top on the car. Red opened the throttle as wide as it would go and tried to get to town in a hurry. The rain cooled the engine and made the car run faster.

When they got to the edge of town, the old car was running faster than it ever had. The rain came down harder and harder all the time. It was a cloudburst, all right.

Then suddenly one of the cylinders went dead, and the machine slowed down a little. In a minute two more of the cylinders went dead at the same time, and the car could barely move on the one that was left. The rain would drown that one out, too, in a little while.

The car went as far as the poolroom and stopped dead. All the cylinders were full of water.

"Git out, Red," Jake shouted. "I'll bet you a quart of corn I can beat you five games of pool."

Red was right behind Jake. The rain had soaked every thread of their clothes.

The men in the poolroom asked Jake and Red where they got the Negro and what they were going to do with him.

"We're takin' him to the undertaker's when the shower's over," Red said. "He got tripped up down at the sawmill this mornin'. Right on payday, too."

Some of the hounds that were not too lazy went out in the rain and smelled the Negro on the running board.

One of the men told Jake he had better go to the drugstore and have his head fixed. Jake said he couldn't be bothered.

Jake beat Red the first four games, and then Red wanted to bet two quarts that he could win the last game. He laid a ragged five-dollar bill on the table, for a side bet. Jake covered that with a bill that was even more ragged.

Red had the break on the fifth game. He slammed away with his stick and lucked the eleven ball, the fifteen, the nine, and the four ball.

"Hell," Jake said, "I'll spot you that thirty-nine and beat you." He chalked his stick and got ready to make a run, after Red missed his next shot. "All I want is one good shot and I'll make game before I stop runnin' them. We shoot pool where I come from."

Jake made the one, two, three, and lucked the twelve ball. He chalked his cue again and got ready to run the five ball in.

Just as he was tapping the cue ball somebody on the other side of the table started talking out loud.

"He ain't no pool shot," the man laughed. "I bet he don't make that five ball."

Jake missed.

Before anybody knew what was happening, Jake had swung

the leaded butt-end of his cue stick at the man's head with all his might. The man fell against another table and struck his head on a sharp-edged spittoon. A four-inch gash had been opened on his head by the stick, and blood was running through a crack in the floor.

"I'll teach these smart guys how to talk when I'm shootin' pool," Jake said. "I bet he don't open his trap like that no more."

The man was carried down to the doctor's office to get his head sewed up.

Red took two shots and made game. Jake was ready to pay off.

They went out the back door and got the corn in a half-gallon jug. Jake took half a dozen swallows and handed the jug over to Red, Red drank till the jug was half full. Then they went back into the poolroom to shoot some more pool.

A man came running in from the street and told Jake and Red the marshal was outside waiting to see them.

"What does he want now?" Red asked him.

"He says he wants you-all to tote that nigger down to the undertaker's before he stinks the whole town up."

Jake took another half-dozen swallows out of the jug and handed it over to Red.

"Say," Jake said, falling against one of the tables, "you go tell that marshal that I said for him to take a long runnin' start and jump to hell.—Me and Red's shootin' pool!"

(First published in *American Earth*)

Here and Today

"WHAT was it?" Virginia remembered having said after dinner. "What was it we used to tell each other in a half-serious manner? Was it that when the time comes to drop the pilot we won't cry on his shoulder?"

That was an hour before, but she remembered very clearly that Don had looked her squarely in the eyes and said: "That was a long time ago. That's not here and today."

He had put on his coat and hat and left the house. She had wanted to run to the door and kiss him, but, even though he waited for her to come, he pretended he was looking for his gloves. She had let him go out without kissing him.

Virginia realized she had been crying for nearly an hour when she looked up at the clock. It was a quarter past eight.

"What does she have that I haven't got? What does she give Don that I couldn't give him?"

Before she had finished saying the words she realized that love could not be itemized that way. She knew she had to make herself believe that it was a circumstance that had to be either accepted or rejected. She was not willing to make a decision then.

At eight-thirty she looked at the clock again. It was just about the time Don would be walking into wherever it was he went. She did not know what part of town the place was, she did not know how many stories there were in the building, she did not know how many rooms there were in the apartment. She did not know anything for sure, except that the girl's name was Lois, that Lois was two years younger than she, and that Lois had dark brown bobbed hair.

The phone rang. It was Edna. Edna and Harry wanted Don and her to go to the movies with them. She told Edna that Don was not at home, and that she was staying in that night. It was not that easy to fool Edna. Edna told her she was a fool to stay in and cry herself sick over Don. Virginia said good-by and hung up.

It was all right for Edna to think like that and to talk like that, but she was not Edna. She loved Don, and she wanted to keep him no matter what happened. All she needed was some means to keep herself together until the time when he came back to her. It might be worth it in the end, no matter if the world crumbled to the ground in the meantime.

At five minutes to nine, she studied the face of the clock. Don and Lois. It was the time when they would be saying things to each other, kissing each other, holding each other. Don and Lois. From eight fifty-five to nine o'clock they would be deciding whether to stay in that evening, or whether to go out and dance or see a show for a while first. Don and Lois.

"I wouldn't mind it so much," she said partly aloud, "if he were not giving her things that I want myself. I want every kiss, every touch, every look, every minute."

No matter how hard she tried, she could not keep from looking at the clock again. What she saw was not numerals and time—she saw Don's face.

"Oh, God!" she cried.

When her eyes closed, she felt a leaden feeling that compressed her mind and body as surely as if it had been tons and tons of lead pressing against her. Under such an unbearable weight, she could feel her anger rise up within her to fight it off. It was a dull, steady ache by then. She tried to push the weight from her, she tried to keep the anger from overriding her thoughts, but in spite of herself it overcame her like a dark cloud which she was powerless to push away. The cloud sank around her, dragging her down with it. By then she did not know whether she was sitting, standing, or walking. She had reached the point where, numbed by misery and aching, she did not know what she was doing. She could have committed murder then, and not have known what she had done.

She went to the closet for her hat and cloak, not fully aware of what was taking place. She could not feel herself move, but she remembered seeing the walls of the room and the hall slide past her.

On the way down, the elevator boy smiled and bowed, and said: "It's a nice bright evening out, Mrs. Warner. I wish I had tonight off."

"I'm sorry you don't have it off, Frank," she said.

By then she knew where she was. It was a pleasant sensation to feel herself coming down to earth so swiftly.

It was much cooler outside than she had imagined. The wind was sharp. Her cloak was a little light for such weather.

Two blocks down the street a man bumped into her accidentally. Both of them had their heads down against the wind, and when they ran together she almost lost her balance. She caught herself before he had a chance to help her.

"I'm sorry," he said, taking off his hat.

She looked at him closely, studying his face from side to side. He looked about Don's age.

"Where are you going?" she asked impulsively.

"Why—I—have an appointment."

"A girl?"

"Yes," he said, smiling a little.

She hurried on down the street as fast as she could. She did not look back even once, because she was afraid by then that the man might try to catch up with her.

A block or more farther on she saw a movie house. She ran until she was in the midst of the crowd. When she looked back then she could see nothing of the man, and she felt relieved. She bought a ticket and got inside as quickly as she could.

Her eyes saw that an animated cartoon was on the screen. She noticed that, before she could accustom her eyes to the semidarkness enough to find a seat. She sat down where the usher told her to sit down.

The audience was howling. Men, women, and children were laughing so loud that it was difficult to hear anything else. Virginia could not make herself laugh at first, but as the cartoon went on and on, she forgot herself and began laughing. It was only a few minutes more until she was laughing as loud as anyone else in the theater. The short picture came to an end. The mirth lingered with her for a while, and she could not keep from smiling. Out of the corners of her eyes she watched a man and a girl next to her holding hands. That was all right, too. She had not felt so good in more than two months. After having been one with Don for all those years, it gave her a pleasant feeling to know that she was alone in the world, laughing and tingling in a strange body that was so new to her that she had not had time to become accustomed to it. It was a feeling more pleasant than she had ever imagined.

The feature picture was nearly half over before she saw it. She did not know what she had been looking at during all that time, because when she tried to recall, she had no memory of anything other than the strange new feeling in her body.

Suddenly there flashed across the screen another woman. She had not followed the story long enough to know that the picture had another woman in it, but Virginia recognized her the instant she saw her. There was no doubt about it. It was a woman in love with a man who was about to leave his wife for her.

Everything came back to Virginia at the precise point where it had left off. She could feel the heightened continuation of her misery and anger and hopelessness. She could feel the thing surge through her as if it had been liquid. She was bursting with it. She could not bear it another moment.

"I hope she chokes," she said in a loud voice.

Instantly there was a murmur of voices all around her. People as far ahead as eight or nine rows turned around and looked in her direction. The usher came down the aisle and flashed his light on her, asking her in a gentle way if she wished to leave the theater.

"I said, I hope she chokes to death!" Virginia said, louder, much louder than before.

At that moment the other woman on the screen turned and looked at Virginia. She was lovely to look at, but she was the other woman. Virginia could never forgive her for being that.

The usher had left in a hurry, and a moment later the manager came running down the aisle. She found herself being lifted out of her seat and carried up the aisle. The audience was in an uproar. Most of the people were standing up trying to get a glimpse of her in the semidarkness.

She was carried into a small room furnished like an office. The manager was dipping a towel in water, wringing it out, and applying it to her forehead. The two ushers were fanning her with newspapers.

"Do you feel better now, madam?" the manager asked, looking deeply into her face.

Virginia began to cry and laugh all at once.

"Get a doctor," the manager said. "I don't like the way she failed to come out of it."

In what seemed like a mere moment the usher came back with a doctor. She closed her eyes when she saw his face.

"Just a slight nervous shock," the doctor said later, getting to his feet and standing back to observe her.

All of twenty minutes had passed without her knowledge of time. She began to wonder if she had been lying on the couch in the manager's office for five minutes or five hours.

Virginia sat up.

"I'm all right now," she said, putting her feet on the floor.

"Have you been worrying lately over any matter?" the doctor asked professionally, stepping closer again.

"Don," she said without a thought.

The doctor turned around, nodded to the manager, and went out. The manager nodded to the two ushers, and went out. The two ushers looked at each other, winked, and held the door open for her.

"I want a taxi," she said, walking bravely but weakly through the door between them. "Get me a taxi right away. An orange-colored taxi!"

When she got home, Frank smiled, bowed, and said: "It has been a nice bright evening out, Mrs. Warner."

She looked at Frank, stiff and erect in his green uniform.

"Has it?" she said.

He left her at her door, waiting until she had found her key and let herself in.

The lights were on. She thought surely she would have turned them out when she left, no matter what her state of mind had been.

"Where have you been?" Don's voice said from somewhere in the room.

Virginia threw her hat and cloak off and ran to the other end of the room. He was lying back in his chair, a frayed newspaper across his knees.

"What time is it, Don? Why are you here now? What did you come back for?"

"It's about twelve," he said. "Where have you been?"

She sank down on the floor beside him.

"I've had a disgraceful experience, Don," she said, looking up at him.

"What did you do?"

"I went to a movie and talked out loud."

"Loud enough for everybody to hear you?"

"Yes."

"Did they put you out?"

"Yes."

"Have to carry you out?"

"Yes."

He laughed a little, looking down at her curiously and tenderly.

"Don't worry about that," he said, stroking her arm. "It happens all the time. No names are ever taken, and it never gets into the papers. Forget about it, Virginia."

She looked at him in amazement, shaking her head from side to side.

"Does it really happen—to other people, Don?"

"Of course."

"How do you know?"

"Because I've seen it happen myself two or three times in my life, and I don't go to movies often, either."

"What do they—we—say?"

"The same thing you probably said, or a variation of it."

" 'I hope she chokes'?"

"Exactly."

Virginia laid her head on the arm of his chair. It was a relief to know that Don was not angry with her for having behaved in public as she did. She was so happy about it that tears came into her eyes and rolled down her cheeks. She brushed them away quickly so she could talk to him.

"I'm not going to ask you to give her up—for a while, Don," she said calmly and slowly.

He sat up, to see her face better.

"Are you talking about Lois?" he asked her.

"Yes, Don."

"That's awfully decent of you, Virginia," he said. "What made you change your mind?"

"I didn't change it. I think I've just found out that there has never been but one answer since the world began."

"What's that?"

"That it is natural for you to go to the most attractive person, and that the battle is between her and me. I've been fighting you all this time, trying to take you from her and bring you back to me. I know now that it is up to me to make you think I'm the most attractive. It's a waste of time for me to fight you—it's like calling up the wrong grocer and bawling him out for not delivering the coffee. What fighting is to be done will take place between her and me from now on— to prove which is the most attractive."

He looked down at her, continuing to stroke her arm, and saw in her face something that he had known all their lives together. What he knew was that, no matter what happened to others in similar situations, no matter what happened to them temporarily, no matter what happened to her or to him separately, it was to be certain for them to come back together in the future on a foundation even more solid and firm than it had been in the beginning. The thing was so clear and satisfying to both of them that there was no need of either of them saying it. It was something they knew. It was a knowledge that the fulfillment was to be as inevitable as life itself.

(First published in *Harper's Bazaar*)

Horse Thief

I DIDN'T steal Lud Moseley's calico horse.

People all over have been trying to make me out a thief, but anybody who knows me at all will tell you that I've never been in trouble like this before in all my life. Mr. John Turner will tell you all about me. I've worked for him, off and on, for I don't know exactly how many years. I reckon I've worked for him just about all my life, since I was a boy. Mr. John knows I wouldn't steal a horse. That's why I say I didn't steal Lud Moseley's, like he swore I did. I didn't grow up just to turn out to be a horse thief.

Night before last, Mr. John told me to ride his mare, Betsy. I said I wanted to go off a little way after something, and he told me to go ahead and ride Betsy, like I have been doing every Sunday night for going on two years now. Mr. John told me to take the Texas saddle, but I told him I didn't care about riding saddle. I like to ride with a bridle and reins, and nothing else. That's the best way to ride, anyway. And where I was going I didn't want to have a squeaking saddle under me. I wasn't up to no mischief. It was just a little private business of my own that nobody has got a right to call me down about. I nearly always rode saddle Sunday nights, but night before last was Thursday night, and that's why I didn't have a saddle when I went.

Mr. John Turner will tell you I'm not the kind to go off and get into trouble. Ask Mr. John about me. He has known me all my life, and I've never given him or anybody else trouble.

When I took Betsy out of the stable that night after supper, Mr. John came out to the barnyard and asked me over again if I didn't want to take the Texas saddle. That mare, Betsy, is a little rawboned, but I didn't mind that. I told Mr. John I'd just as lief ride bareback. He said it was all right with him if I wanted to get sawn in two, and for me to go ahead and do

like I pleased about it. He was standing right there all the
time, rubbing Betsy's mane, and trying to find out where I was
going, without coming right out and asking me. But he knew
all the time where I was going, because he knows all about me.
I reckon he just wanted to have a laugh at me, but he couldn't
do that if I didn't let on where I was headed. So he told me
it was all right to ride his mare without a saddle if I didn't
want to be bothered with one, and I opened the gate and rode
off down the road towards Bishop's crossroads.

That was night before last—Thursday night. It was a little
after dark then, but I could see Mr. John standing at the barnyard gate, leaning on it a little, and watching me ride off. I'd
been plowing that day, over in the new ground, and I was
dog-tired. That's one reason why I didn't gallop off like I always did on Sunday nights. I rode away slow, letting Betsy
take her own good time, because I wasn't in such a big hurry,
after all. I had about two hours' time to kill, and only a little
over three miles to go. That's why I went off like that.

II

Everybody knows I've been going to see Lud Moseley's
youngest daughter, Naomi. I was going to see her again that
night. But I couldn't show up there till about nine-thirty. Lud
Moseley wouldn't let me come to see her but once a week, on
Sunday nights, and night before last was Thursday. I'd been
there to see her three or four times before on Thursday nights
that Lud Moseley didn't know about. Naomi told me to come
to see her on Thursday night. That's why I had been going
there when Lud Moseley said I couldn't come to his house
but once a week. Naomi told me to come anyway, and she
had been coming out to the swing under the trees in the front
yard to meet me.

I haven't got a thing in the world against Lud Moseley. Mr.
John Turner will tell you I haven't. I don't especially like him,
but that's to be expected, and he knows why. Once a week isn't
enough to go to see a girl you like a lot, like I do Naomi. And
I reckon she likes me a little, or she wouldn't tell me to come
to see her on Thursday nights, when Lud Moseley told me
not to come. Lud Moseley thinks if I go to see her more than
once a week that maybe we'll take it into our heads to go
get married without giving him a chance to catch on. That's
why he said I couldn't come to his house but once a week, on
Sunday nights.

He's fixing to have me sent to the penitentiary for twenty
years for stealing his calico horse, Lightfoot. I reckon he knows
good and well I didn't steal the horse, but he figures he's got
a good chance to put me out of the way till he can get Naomi

married to somebody else. That's the way I figure it all out, because everybody in this part of the country who ever heard tell of me knows I'm not a horse thief. Mr. John Turner will tell you that about me. Mr. John knows me better than that. I've worked for him so long he even tried once to make me out as one of the family, but I wouldn't let him do that.

So, night before last, Thursday night, I rode off from home bareback, on Betsy. I killed a little time down at the creek, about a mile down the road from where we live, and when I looked at my watch again, it was nine o'clock sharp. I got on Betsy and rode off towards Lud Moseley's place. Everything was still and quiet around the house and barn. It was just about Lud's bedtime then. I rode right up to the barnyard gate, like I always did on Thursday nights. I could see a light up in Naomi's room, where she slept with her older sister, Mary Lee. We had always figured on Mary Lee's being out with somebody else, or maybe being ready to go to sleep by nine-thirty. When I looked up at their window, I could see Naomi lying across her bed, and Mary Lee was standing beside the bed talking to her about something. That looked bad, because when Mary Lee tried to make Naomi undress and go to bed before she did, it always meant that it would take Naomi another hour or more to get out of the room, because she had to wait for Mary Lee to go to sleep before she could leave. She had to wait for Mary Lee to go to sleep, and then she had to get up and dress in the dark before she could come down to the front yard and meet me in the swing under the trees.

III

I sat there on Betsy for ten or fifteen minutes, waiting to see how Naomi was going to come out with her sister. I reckon if we had let Mary Lee in on the secret she would have behaved all right about it, but on some account or other Naomi couldn't make up her mind to run the risk of it. There was a mighty chance that she would have misbehaved about it and gone straight and told Lud Moseley, and we didn't want to run that risk.

After a while I saw Naomi get up and start to undress. I knew right away that that meant waiting another hour or longer for her to be able to come and meet me. The moon was starting to rise, and it was getting to be as bright as day out there in the barnyard. I'd been in the habit of opening the gate and turning Betsy loose in the yard, but I was scared to do it night before last. If Lud Moseley should get up for a drink of water or something, and happen to look out toward the barn and see a horse standing there, he would either think it was one of his and come out and lock it in the stalls, or else he would catch on it was me out there. Anyway, as soon as he saw Betsy, he would have known it wasn't his mare, and there would have been the mischief to pay right there and then. So I opened the barn door and led Betsy inside and put her in the first empty stall I could find in the dark. I was scared to strike a light, because I didn't know but what Lud Moseley would be looking out the window just at that time and see the flare of the match. I put Betsy in the stall, closed the door, and came back outside to wait for Naomi to find a chance to come out and meet me in the swing in the yard.

It was about twelve-thirty or one o'clock when I got ready to leave for home. The moon had been clouded, and it was darker than everything in the barn. I couldn't see my hand in front of me, it was that dark. I was scared to strike a light that time, too, and I felt my way in and opened the stall door and stepped inside to lead Betsy out. I couldn't see a thing, and when I found her neck, I thought she must have slipped her bridle like she was always doing when she had to stand too long to suit her. I was afraid to try to ride her home without a lead of some kind, because I was scared she might shy in the barnyard and start tearing around out there and wake up Lud Moseley. I felt around on the ground for the bridle, but I couldn't find it anywhere. Then I went back to the stall door and felt on it, thinking I might have taken it off myself when I was all excited at the start, and there was a halter hanging up. I slipped it over her head and led her out. It was still so dark I couldn't see a thing, and I had to feel my way outside and through the barnyard gate. When I got to the road, I threw a leg over her, and started for home without wasting any more time around Lud Moseley's place. I thought she trotted a little funny, because she had a swaying swing that made me slide from side to side, and I didn't have a saddle pommel to hold on to. I was all wrought up about getting away from there without getting caught up with, and I didn't think a thing about it. But I got home all right and slipped the halter off and put her in her stall. It was around one or two o'clock in the morning then.

The next morning after breakfast, when I was getting ready to catch the mules and gear them up to start plowing in the new ground again, Lud Moseley and three or four other men, including the sheriff, came riding lickety-split up the road from town and hitched at the rack. Mr. John came out and slapped the sheriff on the back and told him a funny story. They carried on like that for nearly half an hour, and then the sheriff asked Mr. John where I was. Mr. John told him I was getting ready to go off to the new ground, where we had planted a crop of corn that spring, and then the sheriff said he had a warrant for me. Mr. John asked him what for, a joke or something? And the sheriff told him it was for stealing Lud Moseley's calico horse, Lightfoot. Mr. John laughed at him, because he still thought it just a joke, but the sheriff pulled out the paper and showed it to him. Mr. John still wouldn't believe it, and he told them there was a mix-up somewhere, because, he told them, I wouldn't steal a horse. Mr. John knows I'm not a horse thief. I've never been in any kind of trouble before in all my life.

They brought me to town right away and put me in the cellroom at the sheriff's jail. I knew I hadn't stole Lud Moseley's horse, and I wasn't scared a bit about it. But right after they brought me to town, they all rode back and the sheriff looked in the barn and found Lud Moseley's calico horse, Lightfoot, in Betsy's stall. Mr. John said things were all mixed up, because he knew I didn't steal the horse, and he knew I wouldn't do it. But the horse was there, the calico one, Lightfoot, and his halter was hanging on the stall door. After that they went back to Lud Moseley's and measured my foot tracks in the barnyard, and then they found Betsy's bridle. Lud Moseley said I had rode Mr. John's mare over there, turned her loose, and put the bridle on his Lightfoot and rode him off. They never did say how come the halter came to get to Mr. John's stable, then. Lud Moseley's stall door was not locked, and it wasn't broken down. It looks now like I forgot to shut it tight when I put Betsy in, because she got out someway and came home of her own accord sometime that night.

Lud Moseley says he's going to send me away for twenty years where I won't have a chance to worry him over his youngest daughter, Naomi. He wants her to marry a widowed farmer over beyond Bishop's crossroads who runs twenty plows and who's got a big white house with fifteen rooms in it. Mr. John Turner says he'll hire the best lawyer in town to take up my case, but it don't look like it will do much good, because my footprints are all over Lud Moseley's barnyard, and his Lightfoot was in Mr. John's stable.

I reckon I could worm out of it someway, if I made up my mind to do it. But I don't like to do things like that. It would put Naomi in a bad way, because if I said I was there seeing her, and had put Betsy in the stall to keep her quiet, and took Lightfoot out by mistake in the dark when I got ready to leave —well, it would just look bad, that's all. She would just have to say she was in the habit of slipping out of the house to see me after everybody had gone to sleep, on Thursday nights, and it would just look bad all around. She might take it into her head some day that she'd rather marry somebody else than me, and by that time she'd have a bad name for having been mixed up with me—and slipping out of the house to meet me after bedtime.

Naomi knows I'm no horse thief. She knows how it all happened—that I rode Lud Moseley's calico horse, Lightfoot, off by mistake in the dark, and left the stall door unfastened, and Betsy got out and came home of her own accord.

Lud Moseley has been telling people all around the courthouse as how he is going to send me away for twenty years so he can get Naomi married to that widowed farmer who runs twenty plows. Lud Moseley is right proud of it, it looks like to me, because he's got me cornered in a trap, and maybe he will get me sent away sure enough before Naomi gets a chance to tell what she knows is true.

But, somehow, I don't know if she'll say it if she does get the chance. Everybody knows I'm nothing but a hired man at Mr. John Turner's, and I've been thinking that maybe Naomi might not come right out and tell what she knows, after all.

I'd come right out and explain to the sheriff how the mix-up happened, but I sort of hate to mention Naomi's name in the mess. If it had been a Sunday night, instead of night before last, a Thursday, I could—well, it would just sound too bad, that's all.

If Naomi comes to town and tells what she knows, I won't say a word to stop her, because that'll mean she's willing to say it and marry me.

But if she stays at home, and lets Lud Moseley and that widowed farmer send me away for twenty years, I'll just have to go, that's all.

I always told Naomi I'd do anything in the world for her, and I reckon this will be the time when I've got to prove whether I'm a man of my word, or not.

(First published in *Vanity Fair*)

Dorothy

WHEN I saw her for the first time, she was staring several hundred miles away. She was standing on the other side of the street near the corner, holding a folded newspaper in front of her. It had been folded until the want ads were the only print showing, and it looked like a paper printed without headlines. Suddenly she blinked her eyes several times and looked at the paper she was holding. Her knees and legs were rigidly stiff, but her body swayed backward and forward like someone weak from hunger. Her shoulders drooped downward and downward until they seemed to be merely the upper part of her arms.

She glanced at the ads every few moments and then searched half-heartedly for a number on one of the doors behind her. Once she opened her pocketbook and read something written on the back of a crumpled envelope. There were numbers on most of the doors, but either she could not see the numerals plainly enough, or she could not find the one she was looking for—I didn't know what the trouble was. I couldn't see her face. Her head had dropped forward, and her chin sank to the collar of her dress. She would look up for a moment, and then her head would suddenly drop downward again and hang there until she could raise it.

She was standing across the street within reach of one of the white-way poles. She could have leaned against the pole or else found a place to sit down. I didn't know why she did neither. I don't suppose she herself knew.

I was standing on the shady side of the street waiting for something. I don't know what I was waiting for. It wasn't important, anyway. I didn't have anything to do, and I wasn't going anywhere. I was just standing there when I looked across the street and saw her with the folded paper in her hands. There were hundreds of other people in the street, all of them hurrying somewhere. She and I were the only ones standing still.

It was between one and two o'clock in the afternoon. Men and women were coming out of the restaurants on both sides of the street, hurrying back to work. I had a quarter in my pocket, but I had not eaten any lunch. I was hungry for something to eat, but I was saving the quarter. I wanted to get up to Richmond where I was sure I could find a job. Things were quiet in New Orleans, and I had tried Atlanta. Now I wanted to get up to Richmond. It was July, and there were not many jobs anywhere. I had always been lucky in Richmond, though.

The girl on the other side of the street turned the newspaper over and read down another column of the closely printed page. There were several office buildings and a few banks on the street. Everywhere else there were retail stores of some kind. Most of them had displays of women's wear in the windows. It was hard for a man to find a job there, and not much easier for a woman, especially a girl, unless she were wearing the right kind of clothes.

The girl put the newspaper under her arm and started across the street. I was standing a few steps from the corner. She came across, holding the paper tightly under her arm and looking down at the pavement all the time. When she reached the curb, she turned down the street in my direction. She still did not look up. She was holding her head down all the time as if she were looking at her slippers.

The pavement was hot. It was July.

She walked past me, behind. I could hear the gritty sand and dust grind under her shoes. It made a sound like the sand-papering of an iron pipe. Then suddenly the sound stopped. I looked around and saw her standing almost beside me. She was so close I could have touched her with my hand. Her face was pale and her lips were whiter than her forehead. When she looked up at me, she did not raise her head, only her eyes saw me. Her eyes were damp. They were very blue. She did not want me to know that she had been crying.

I turned all the way around and looked at her. I did not know what to do. Until she spoke to me she held her mouth tightly against her teeth, but she could not stop her lips from quivering.

"Can you tell me where No. 67 Forsyth Street is?" she asked me.

I looked down at her. Her hands were clenched so tightly I could see only the backs of her fingers. They were stained as if she had been handling freshly printed newspapers all day. They were not dirty. They were just not clean. A sort of black-ish dust had settled on the backs of her hands. Dust is in the air of every city and some people wash their hands five or six times a day to keep them clean. I don't know, but maybe she had not had a chance to wash her hands for several days. Her face was not soiled, but it looked as if she had tried to keep it clean with a dampened handkerchief and a powdered chamois skin.

She had asked me where No. 67 Forsyth Street was. She had said, "Pardon me—" when she asked me. I knew she would say, "Thank you very much," when I told her where the address was.

I had to swallow hard before I could say anything at all. I knew where the number was. It was an employment agency. I had been there myself two or three times a day all that week. But there were no jobs there for anybody. It was July. I could look across the street and see the number in large gilt numerals on the door. The door was being constantly opened and closed by people going in and coming out again.

"What?" I asked her. It didn't sound like that, though, when I said it. When you talk to a girl who is very beautiful you say things differently.

I knew what she had said but I could not remember hearing her say it. I had been looking at her so long I forgot the question she asked.

She opened her pocketbook and put her hand inside, feeling for the crumpled envelope on which she had written the address. Her eyes were staring at me with the same faraway vagueness they had when I saw her for the first time on the other side of the street. She searched for the envelope without once looking at what she was doing. It had fallen to the pavement the moment she unclasped the pocketbook.

I picked up the letter. It was addressed to *Dorothy*—I couldn't read the last name. It had been sent in care of general delivery at the Atlanta post office from some little town down near the Florida border. It might have been from her mother or sister. It was a woman's handwriting. She jerked it from me before I could hand it to her. There was something in the way she reached for it that made me wonder about it. Maybe her father had died and she was trying to find a job so she could support her mother—I don't know. Things like that happen all the time. Or all of her family might have been killed in an accident and she had to leave home to make a living—things like that happen everywhere.

People were turning around to look at us. They walked past us and then turned around and stared. Peachtree Street was only around the corner from where we stood. It was a fashionable section.

I don't know what made me say what I did. I knew where No. 67 Forsyth Street was. I had been there myself only half an hour before. It was an employment agency. They said come in tomorrow morning. They told everybody the same thing—both men and women. It was the dull season. It was July.

I said, "No. 67 is about three blocks down the street, on the other side of the viaduct." I pointed down there, my arm over her head. She was very small beside me.

She looked down the street to the other side of the viaduct. There were half a dozen cheap hotels down there. They were the cheapest kind. Everybody has seen them. There are some in every city. They charge fifty cents, seventy-five, and a dollar. I thought I was doing right. There was no money in her pocketbook. Not a cent. I saw everything she had in it. I had a quarter and I would have to go all the way to Richmond before I found a job. There were no jobs across the street at No. 67. It was the dull season. Everybody was out of town for the summer. There were no jobs in July. And she was hungry. She had been trying to sleep in railroad stations at night, too . . . On the other side of the viaduct there were at least seven or eight hotels. The cheap kind. I had seen women in them, running down the corridors in kimonos after midnight. They always had some money, enough to buy something to eat when they were hungry. Everyone knows what it is to be hungry. A man can stand it for a while—a week, ten days, two weeks—but a woman—if you have ever seen the naked body of a starving woman you'll know why I thought I was doing right.

She had not moved.

"It's about three blocks down the street, on the other side of the viaduct," I told her again. She had heard what I said the first time.

She did not move.

She was standing there, looking at the dirty red-brick buildings. She knew the kind they were. Some of them had signs that could be read across the viaduct. HOTEL—75c & $1. She was reading the signs. My hand was in my pocket holding the quarter between the fingers. I don't know what she could have done with the money. I was ashamed to give it to her—it was only a quarter.

"All right," she said.

It was as if she was making up her mind about something of great importance, like a decision of life and death. It was as if she had said, "All right, I'll go." She was not thanking me for telling her where she could find the number. She knew No. 67 was on this side of the viaduct.

"All right," she said.

She turned and walked down the street toward the dirty red-brick buildings. The heels of her slippers had worn sideways. She tried to stand erectly on her feet and she had to walk stiffly so her ankles would not turn. If her legs had relaxed for a second she would have sprained her ankles.

She did not look back at me. Her blue flannel skirt was wrinkled far out of shape. It looked as if she had slept in it for several nights, maybe a week. It was covered with specks of dust and lint. Her white silk waist was creased and discolored. The dust had lodged in the folds, and the creases made horizontal smudges across her shoulders. Her hat looked as if it had been in a hard rain for several hours and then dried on a sharp peg of some kind. There was a peak in the crown that drew the whole hat out of shape.

I couldn't stand there any longer. She had gone almost a block toward the dirty red-brick buildings. I crossed over the street and ran down an alley towards Marietta Street.

I went to a garage on Marietta Street. A mechanic who worked in the garage had told me there was a good chance of getting a ride to Richmond if I would stay around long enough and wait until an automobile came along that was going through.

When I got to the garage, there was a car inside being greased. The man in the garage nodded at me and pointed toward the automobile. It was a big car. I knew it wouldn't take long to make the trip in a car like that. I asked the man who was driving it if he would take me to Richmond with him. He asked the man in the garage about me. They talked inside the office a while and then he came out and said he would take me up with him. He was leaving right away.

We drove up to Richmond. I started out to find a job somewhere. There's a wholesale district under the elevated railway tracks between the State Capitol and the river. I had been there before.

But there was something the matter with me. I didn't have the patience to look up a job. I was nervous. I had to keep moving all the time. I couldn't stand still.

A few days later I was in Baltimore. I applied for a job in an employment agency. They had plenty of jobs, but they took their time about giving them out. They wanted you to wait a week or two, to see if you would stick. Most everybody went on to Philadelphia. That's the way it is in summer. Everybody goes up. When the weather begins to get cold they come down again, stopping in Baltimore until the weather catches up, and then they move to the next city. Everybody ends up in New Orleans.

I couldn't stay in Baltimore. I couldn't stand still. I went on to Philadelphia like everybody else. From Philadelphia you move over into Jersey. But I didn't. I stayed in Philadelphia.

Then one day I was standing on Market Street, near the city hall, watching a new skyscraper go up. I saw a young woman on the other side of the street who looked like the girl I had talked to in Atlanta. She was not the same one, of course. But there was a close resemblance.

I could not think about anything else. I stood there all the afternoon thinking about the girl in Atlanta and wondering what I could do. I knew I had to think up some way to get to Atlanta and find her. I had sent her down Forsyth Street, across the viaduct. She knew where she was going, but she would not have gone if it had not been for me. I sent her down there. If I had only pointed across the street to No. 67! She knew where it was. She had been standing in front of it when I first saw her with the folded newspaper, reading the ads. But she knew it would be useless to go inside. They would have told her to come in again the next morning. That's what they told everybody. Maybe she thought I would give her some money. I don't know what she thought, to tell the truth. But she was up against it, just as I was. She was too proud to ask for money to buy something to eat, and yet she thought I might give her some. I had a quarter but I was ashamed to offer it to her, especially after I had sent her down the street toward those hotels. She had tried to find a job somewhere so she could have something to eat and a place to sleep. She knew there was always one way. She knew about Forsyth Street on the other side of the viaduct. Somebody had told her about it. A woman in one of the railroad stations, perhaps. Somebody told her, because she knew all about it.

I didn't send her there, she would have gone anyway. . . . That's what I think sometimes—but it's a lie! I told her to go down the street and cross the viaduct.

(First published in *Scribner's*)

The Medicine Man

THERE was nobody in Rawley who believed that Effie Henderson would ever find a man to marry her, and Effie herself had just about given up hope. But that was before the traveling herb doctor came to town.

Professor Eaton was a tall gaunt-looking man with permanent, sewn-in creases in his trousers and a high celluloid collar around his neck. He may have been ten years older than Effie, or he may have been ten years younger; it was no more easy to judge his age than it was to determine by the accent of his speech from what section of the country he had originally come.

He drove into Rawley one hot dusty morning in mid-August, selling Indian Root Tonic. Indian Root Tonic was a beady, licorice-tasting cure-all in a fancy green-blown bottle. The bottle was wrapped in a black and white label, on which the most prominent feature was the photographic reproduction of a beefy man exhibiting his expanded chest and muscles and his postage-stamp wrestler's trunks. Professor Eaton declared, and challenged any man alive to deny his statement, that his Indian Root Tonic would cure any ailment known to man, and quite a few known only to women.

Effie Henderson was the first person in town to give him a dollar for a bottle, and the first to come back for the second one.

The stand that Professor Eaton had opened up was the back seat of his mud-spattered touring car. He had paid the mayor ten ragged one-dollar bills for a permit to do business in Rawley, and he had parked his automobile in the middle of the weed-grown vacant lot behind the depot. He sold his medicine over the back seat of his car, lifting the green-blown bottles from a box at his feet as fast as the customers came up and laid down their dollars.

There had been a big crowd standing around in the weed-grown lot the evening before, but there were only a few people standing around him listening to his talk when Effie came back in the morning for her second bottle. Most of the persons there then were Negroes who did not have a dollar among them, but who had been attracted to the lot by the alcoholic fumes around the mud-caked automobile and who were willing to be convinced of Indian Root Tonic's marvelous curative powers. When Effie came up, the Negroes stepped aside, and stood at a distance watching Professor Eaton get ready to make another sale.

Effie walked up to the folded-down top in front of Professor Eaton and laid down a worn dollar bill that was as limp as a piece of wet cheesecloth.

"I just had to come back this morning for another bottle," Effie said, smiling up at Professor Eaton. "The one I took last night made me feel better than I have ever felt before in all my life. There's not another medicine in the whole country like it, and I've tried them all, I reckon."

"Pardon me, madam," Professor said. "There are hundreds of preparations on the market today, but there is only one Indian Root Tonic. You will be doing me a great favor if you will hereafter refer to my aid-to-human-life by its true and trade-marked name. Indian Root Tonic is the name of the one and only cure for ailments of any nature. It is particularly good for the mature woman, madam."

"You shouldn't call me 'madam,' Professor Eaton," Effie said, lowering her head. "I'm just a young and foolish girl, and I'm not married yet, either."

Professor Eaton wiped the perspiration from his upper lip and looked down at Effie.

"How utterly stupid of me, my dear young lady," he said. "Anyone can see by looking at your fresh young face that you are a mere girl. Indian Root Tonic is particularly good for the young maiden."

Effie turned around to see if any of the Negroes were close enough to hear what Professor Eaton had said. She hoped that some of the women who lived on her street would walk past the corner in time to hear Professor Eaton talk like that about her.

"I never like to talk about myself, but don't you think I am too young yet to get married, Professor Eaton?"

"My dear young lady," he continued after having paused long enough to relight his dead cigar, "Indian Root Tonic is particularly good for the unmarried girl. It is the greatest discovery known to medical science since the beginning of mankind. I personally secured the formula for this marvelous medicine from an old Indian chief out in our great and glorious

West, and I was compelled to promise him on my bended knee that I would devote the remainder of my life to traveling over this great nation of ours offering Indian Root Tonic to men and women like you who would be helpless invalids without it."

He had to pause for a moment's breath. It was then that he looked down over the folded top and for the first time looked at Effie face to face. The evening before in the glare of the gasoline torch, when the lot was crowded with people pushing and shoving to get to the medicine stand before the special introductory offer was withdrawn, he had not had time to look at everyone who came up to hand him a dollar for a bottle. But now when he looked down and saw Effie, he leaned forward to stare at her.

"Oh, Professor Eaton," Effie said, "you are such a wonderful man! Just to think that you are doing such a great work in the world!"

Professor Eaton continued to stare at Effie. She was as good-looking as the next girl in town, not over thirty, and when she fixed herself up, as she had done for nearly two hours that morning before leaving home, she usually had all the drummers in town for the day staring at her and asking the storekeepers who she was.

After a while Professor Eaton climbed out of the back seat of his car and came around to the rear where she was. He relit his cold cigar, and inspected Effie more closely.

"You know, Professor Eaton, you shouldn't talk like that to me," she said, evading his eyes. "You really don't know me well enough yet to call me 'dear girl.' This is the first time we have been alone together, and——"

"Why! I didn't think that a beautiful young girl like you would seriously object to my honorable admiration," he said, looking her up and down and screwing up his mouth when she plucked at her blouse. "It's so seldom that I have the opportunity of seeing such a charming young girl that I must have lost momentarily all sense of discretion. But, now that we are fully acquainted with each other, I'm sure you won't object to my devoted admiration. Will you?"

"Oh, Professor Eaton," Effie said excitedly, "do you really and truly think that I am beautiful? So many men have told me that before, I'm accustomed to hearing it frequently, but you are the first man to say it so thrillingly!"

She tried to step backward, but she was already standing against the rear of the car. Professor Eaton moved another step closer, and there was no way for her to turn. She would not have minded that if she had not been so anxious to have a moment to look down at her blouse. She knew there must be something wrong, surely something had slipped under the waist, because Professor Eaton had not raised his eyes from her bosom since he got out of the car and came down beside her. She wondered then if she should not have confined herself when she dressed that morning, putting on all the undergarments she wore to church on Sunday morning.

"My dear girl, there is not the slightest doubt in my mind concerning your beauty. In fact, I think you are the most charming young girl it has been my good fortune to encounter during my many travels over this great country of ours—from coast to coast, from the Lakes to the Gulf."

"You make me feel so young and foolish, Professor Eaton!" Effie said, smoothing her shirtwaist over her bosom. "You make me feel like—"

Professor Eaton turned abruptly and reached into the back seat for a bottle of Indian Root Tonic. He closed his teeth over the cork stopper and popped it out, and, with no further loss of time, handed it to Effie.

"Have this one on me, my dear girl," he said. "Just drink it down, and then see if it doesn't make you feel even better still."

Effie took the green-blown bottle, looking at the picture of the strong young man in wrestler's trunks.

"I drank the whole bottle I bought last night," she said. "I drank it just before going to bed, and it made me feel so good I just couldn't lie still. I had to get up and sit on the back porch and sing awhile."

"There was never a more beneficial—"

"What particular ailment is the medicine good for, Professor Eaton?"

"Indian Root Tonic is good for whatever ails you. In fact, merely as a general conditioner it is supreme in its field. And then on the other hand, there is no complaint known to medical science that it has yet failed to allevi—— to help."

Effie turned up the bottle and drank down the beady, licorice-tasting fluid, all eight ounces of it. The Negroes standing around the car looked on wistfully while the alcoholic fumes from the opened bottle drifted over the lot. Effie handed the empty bottle to Professor Eaton, after taking one last look at the picture on the label.

"Oh, Professor Eaton," she said, coming closer, "it makes me feel better already. I feel just like I was going to rise off the ground and fly away somewhere."

"Perhaps you would allow me—"

"To do what, Professor Eaton? What?"

He flicked the ashes from his cigar with the tip of his little finger.

"Perhaps you would allow me to escort you to your home," he said. "Now, it's almost dinnertime, and I was just getting ready to close up my stand until the afternoon, so if you will permit me, I'll be very glad to drive you home in my automobile. Just tell me how to get there, and we'll start right away."

"You talk so romantic, Professor Eaton," Effie said, touching his arm with her hand. "You make me feel just like a foolish young girl around you."

"Then you will permit me to see you home?"

"Of course, I will."

"Step this way, please," he said, holding open the door and taking her arm firmly in his grasp.

After they had settled themselves in the front seat, Effie turned around and looked at Professor Eaton.

"I'll bet you have had just lots and lots of love affairs with young girls like me all over the country."

"On the contrary," he said, starting the motor, "this is the first time I have ever given my serious consideration to one of your sex. You see, I apply myself faithfully to the promotion, distribution, and sale of Indian Root Tonic. But this occasion, of course, draws me willingly from the cares of business. In fact, I consider your presence in my car a great honor. I have often wished that I might—"

"And am I the first young girl—the first woman you ever courted?"

"Absolutely," he said. "Absolutely."

Professor Eaton drove out of the vacant weed-grown lot and turned the car up the street toward Effie's house. She lived only two blocks away, and during the time it took them to drive that distance neither of them spoke. Effie was busy looking out to see if people were watching her ride with Professor Eaton in his automobile, and he was busily engaged in steering through the deep white sand in the street. When they got there, Effie told him to park the machine in front of the gate where they could step out and walk directly into the house.

They got out and Effie led the way through the front door and into the parlor. She raised one of the shades a few inches and dusted off the sofa.

Professor Eaton stood near the middle of the room, looking uneasily through the small opening under the shade, and listening intently for sounds elsewhere in the house.

"Just sit down here on the sofa beside me," Effie said. "I know I am perfectly safe alone with you, Professor Eaton."

Effie closed her eyes and allowed herself the pleasure of feeling scared to death of Professor Eaton. It was an even nicer feeling than the one she had had the night before when she drank the first bottle of Indian Root Tonic and got into bed.

"And this is the ancestral home?" he asked.

"Don't let's talk about anything but you—and me," Effie said. "Wouldn't you just like to talk about us?"

Professor Eaton began to feel more at ease, now that it was evident that they were alone in the house.

"Perhaps," Professor Eaton said, sitting closer to Effie and looking down once more at her blouse, "perhaps you will permit me to diagnose your complaint. You see, I am well versed in the medical science, and I can tell you how many bottles of Indian Root Tonic you should use in your particular case. Naturally, some people require a greater number of bottles than others do."

Effie glanced out the window for a second, and then she turned to Professor Eaton.

"I won't have to——"

"Oh, no," he said, "that won't be at all necessary, though you may do as you like about it. I can just——"

"Are you sure it's perfectly all right, Professor Eaton?"

"Absolutely," he said. "Absolutely."

Effie smoothed her shirtwaist with her hands and pushed her shoulders forward. Professor Eaton bent towards her, reaching for her hand.

He held her hand for a few seconds, feeling her pulse, and then dropped it to press his ear against her bosom to listen to her heartbeat. While he listened, Effie tucked up a few loose strands of hair that had fallen over her temples.

"Perhaps," he said, raising his head momentarily, "perhaps if you will merely——"

"Of course, Professor Eaton," Effie said excitedly.

He bent closer after she had fumbled nervously with the blouse and pressed his head against her breasts. Her heartbeat jarred his eardrum.

After a while Professor Eaton sat up and loosened the knot in his necktie and wiped the perspiration from his upper lip with the back of his hand. It was warm in the room, and there was no ventilation with the door closed.

"Perhaps I have already told you——"

"Oh, no! You haven't told me!" she said eagerly, holding her hands tightly clasped and looking down at herself with bated breath. "Please go ahead and tell me, Professor Eaton!"

"Perhaps," he said, fingering the open needlework in her blouse, "perhaps you would like to know that Indian Root Tonic is the only complete aid for general health on the market today. And in addition to its general curative properties, Indian Root Tonic possesses the virtues most women find themselves in need of during the middle and later stages of life. In other words, it imparts a vital force to the glands that are in most need of new vitality. I am sure that once you discover for yourself the marvelous power of rejuvenation that Indian Root Tonic possesses, you will never again be alone in the house without it. In fact, I can say without fear of successful contradiction that—"

Effie laid her blouse aside.

"Do you want me to take—"

"Oh, yes; by all means," he replied hastily. "Now, as I was saying—"

"And this, too, Professor Eaton? This, too?"

Professor Eaton reached over and pinched her lightly. Effie giggled and passed her hands over her bosom as though she were smoothing her shirtwaist.

"I don't suppose you happen to have another bottle of that tonic in your pocket, do you, Professor Eaton?"

"I'm afraid I haven't," he said, "but just outside in my car there are several cases full. If you'll let me, I'll step out and—"

"Oh, no!" Effie cried, clutching at his arms and pulling him back beside her. "Oh, Professor Eaton, don't leave me now!"

"Very well," he said, sitting down beside her once more. "And now as I was saying, Indian Root Tonic's supernatural powers of re——"

"Professor Eaton, do you want me to take off all of this—like this?"

"Absolutely," he said. "And Indian Root Tonic has never been known to fail, whereas in so many—"

"You don't want me to leave anything—"

"Of course not. Being a doctor of the medical science, in addition to my many other activities, I need absolute freedom. Now, if you feel that you cannot place yourself entirely in my hands, perhaps it would be better if I—"

"Oh, please don't go!" Effie cried, pulling him back to the sofa beside her. "You know I have complete confidence in your abilities, Professor Eaton. I know you wouldn't—"

"Wouldn't do what?" he asked, looking down at her again.

"Oh, Professor Eaton! I'm just a young girl!"

"Well," he said, "if you are ready to place yourself entirely in my hands, I can proceed with my diagnosis. Otherwise—"

"I was only teasing you, Professor Eaton!" Effie said, squeezing his hand. "Of course I trust you. You are such a strong man, and I know you wouldn't take advantage of a weak young girl like me. If you didn't take care of me, I'd more than likely run away with myself."

"Absolutely," he said. "Now, if you will continue removing the—"

"There is only this left, Professor Eaton," Effie said. "Are you sure it will be all right?"

"Absolutely."

"But I feel so—so bare, Professor Eaton."

" 'Tis only natural to feel like that," he said, comforting her. "A young girl who has never before experienced the—"

"Experienced the what?"

"Well—as I was saying—"

"You make me feel so funny, Professor Eaton. And are you sure—"

"Absolutely," he said. "Absolutely."

"I've never felt like this before. It feels like—"

"Just place yourself completely in my hands, my dear young girl, and I promise nothing will—"

Without warning the parlor door was thrown open and Effie's brother, Burke, came in. Burke was the town marshal.

"Is dinner ready, Effie?" Burke asked, standing in the doorway and trying to accustom his eyes to the near-darkness of the parlor. "It's a quarter after twelve and—"

Burke stopped in the midst of what he was saying and stared at Effie and Professor Eaton. Effie screamed and pushed Professor Eaton away from her. He got up and stood beside Effie and the sofa, looking first at Burke and then at Effie. He did not know what to do. Effie reached for the things she had thrown aside. Professor Eaton bent down and picked up something and threw it at her.

The room suddenly appeared to Professor Eaton to be as bright as day.

"Well, I'll be damned!" Burke said, coming slowly across the floor. His holster hung from his right hip, and it swung heavily as he swayed from step to step. "I'll be damned!"

Professor Eaton stood first on one foot and then on the other. He was between Effie and her brother, and he knew of no way by which he could change his position in the room. He wished to get as far away from Effie as he possibly could. Until she had dressed herself, he hoped he would not be forced to look at her.

Burke stepped forward and pushed Professor Eaton aside. He looked at Effie and at the herb doctor, but he gave no indication of what he intended doing.

Professor Eaton shifted the weight of his body to his other foot, and Burke's hand dropped to the top of the holster, his fingers feeling for the pearl handle that protruded from it.

Effie snapped a safety pin and ran between Burke and Professor Eaton. She was still not completely dressed, but she was fully covered.

"What are you going to do, Burke?" she cried.

"That all depends on what the Professor is going to do," Burke said, still fingering the pearl handle on the pistol. "What is the Professor going to do?"

"Why, Professor Eaton and I are going to be married, Burke," she said. "Aren't we, Professor Eaton?"

"I had not intended making known the announcement of our engagement and forthcoming marriage at this time," he said, "but since we are to be married very shortly, Effie's brother should by all means be the first to know of our intentions."

"Thanks for telling me, Professor," Burke said. "It had better by a damn sight be forthcoming."

Effie ran to Professor Eaton and locked her arms around his neck.

"Oh, do you really mean it, Professor Eaton? I'm so happy I don't know what to do! But why didn't you tell me sooner that you really wanted to marry me? Do you really and truly mean it, Professor Eaton?"

"Sure," Burke said; "he means it."

"I'm the happiest girl in the whole town of Rawley," Effie cried, pressing her face against Professor Eaton's celluloid collar. "It was all so unexpected! I had never dreamed of it happening to me so soon!"

Burke backed across the room, one hand still around the pearl handle that protruded from the cowhide holster. He backed across the room and reached for the telephone receiver on the wall. He rang the central office and took the receiver from the hook.

"Hello, Janie," he said into the mouthpiece. "Ring up Reverend Edwards for me, will you, right away."

Burke leaned against the wall, looking at Effie and Professor Eaton while Janie at the central office was ringing the Reverend Edwards's number.

"Just to think that I'm going to marry a traveling herb doctor!" Effie said. "Why! all the girls in town will be so envious of me they won't speak for a month!"

"Absolutely," Professor Eaton said, pulling tight the loosened knot in his tie and adjusting it in the opening of his celluloid collar. "Absolutely. Indian Root Tonic has unlimited powers. It is undoubtedly the medical and scientific marvel of the age. Indian Root Tonic has been known to produce the most astounding results in the annals of medical history."

Effie pinned up a strand of hair that had fallen over her forehead and looked proudly upon Professor Eaton.

(First published in *We Are the Living*)

Back on the Road

WHEN Mr. Sears kissed his wife good-by at the trainside in Union Station, he had no more idea of going back on the road than he had of flying around the world in an airplane. Never for a moment in ten years' time had he regretted his decision to buy a seven-room house, to marry Mrs. Sears, and to accept the offer from the company to make him office manager.

"Good-by, Mr. Sears," his wife said, drying her eyes with the corners of her handkerchief as he boarded the St. Louis Express. "Don't sleep in a drafty room, and be sure to ask the hotel to fix up a bottle of hot milk for you to drink before you go to bed."

For the past ten years his wife had called him Mr. Sears. His name was Henry, but no one ever called him that any longer. Ever since the day he came in off the road and settled down as office manager he had been Mr. Sears. During the fifteen or sixteen years he had spent on the road as sales representative for the company, calling on the trade in the Southwest, people everywhere had called him Henry. Even Mrs. Sears had called him Henry then. But when he left the road and became office manager, she thought it was more dignified to address him in public and in private as Mr. Sears.

"Good-by," Mr. Sears said, pausing for a moment in the vestibule. "I'll be back tomorrow evening for dinner. The train gets in at seven-twenty."

His wife turned her handkerchief around until she found an unused corner, and dried a tear before going back through the station to the street.

Mr. Sears had been called into the president's office the day before and instructed to run up to St. Louis and attend to an important matter for the company. The home office and plant in Memphis, where Mr. Sears was office manager, were worried over the piling up of orders from the Missouri distributor in St. Louis. The orders for plows, hoes, rakes, pitchforks, cultivators, and miscellaneous farm implements were highly prized, and the company thought it best to send Mr. Sears up and have him explain that the delay in shipping was unavoidable, and that the orders would be filled and shipped by the end of the week.

The president had impressed upon Mr. Sears the importance

192

of the mission, and had urged him to handle the matter with great delicacy and tact. Orders for anything, the president had told him, were worth fighting for during such times, and if their company could not fill them with reasonable promptness, there were dozens of other companies that could. As special representative of the company, Mr. Sears was to exert a calming influence over the St. Louis jobbers and to promise them that the orders would be filled and in transit by the end of the week. Having served the company faithfully for twenty-five years, the president said, he knew he could rely upon Mr. Sears to forestall the threatened cancellations and to smooth the way for future orders from Missouri.

It was late in the afternoon when Mr. Sears arrived in St. Louis, and he went directly to his hotel. His appointment was set for ten o'clock the next morning, and he planned to devote the rest of the afternoon and a part of the evening to a study of the papers the president had given him before leaving Memphis. The papers themselves were of little importance; they were merely sheets of data that were to be laid before the St. Louis people to show that sales for the current quarter in the southwestern territory, and in Missouri particularly, were 12½ per cent greater than were those of the corresponding quarter of the preceding year. Mr. Sears did not know exactly how the figures had been arrived at, as the past three salary cuts had been based on the decline of carloadings, the president had explained at the time, but Mr. Sears was convinced that the figures as they stood were for the good of the company.

When Mr. Sears walked into the hotel, he had expected to see someone whom he knew. For fifteen years he had made St. Louis twice a month, stopping at the same hotel, and he had known everyone connected with the house. But during the ten years he had been off the road, everything had changed. The room clerks were new men, the bellboys were younger, the cashiers were behind grilled walls, and the lobby was filled with palm trees and lounging women. Mr. Sears called for the assistant manager, expecting to see at least one former friend in the strange place, but the new assistant manager bowed stiffly and assigned one of the sleek-haired clerks to place Mr. Sears in an outside tenth-floor room-and-shower. Stiffly, Mr. Sears rode up the elevator and was shown to his room. He tipped the boy a dime and slammed the door. He was glad he was off the road. He could not bear to think how he had been able to spend fifteen years of his life jumping from hotel to hotel, from train to train, with none of the comforts of home, and without the companionship of a wife. He was glad he would be able to get back to Memphis the next evening in time for dinner. Mrs. Sears was expecting him at seven-twenty.

Mr. Sears took off his coat, put it on a hanger in the closet, unbuttoned his vest, and got out his briefcase. He spread the president's papers on the writing desk and filled his pipe.

After an hour spent in looking out the window, he stood up and put the unread papers back into the case, and got ready to go down to the lobby. He thought he would go down there and sit in a quiet place until dinner. The room was uninviting, and the sooty jungle of chimney pots on the roofs below somehow reminded him of Mrs. Sears's flower garden. Fifteen years of living in hotel rooms was all he wished of it, he said to himself; a seven-room house, a kind and devoted wife, and comfortable overstuffed furniture soon show a man how empty and tragic life can be for the commercial traveler. He thought that again, it sounded so good. A wife, a seven-room house, and overstuffed furniture! What does the road have to offer now! He chuckled to himself as he washed his hands and dried them on a towel with too much starch in it. He hoped the president would not wish to send him to St. Louis again any time soon. Nor to Dallas, New Orleans, Tulsa, or Kansas City. All of them were like St. Louis now. Once there had been a difference, in his younger days. But a wife and a home make a man realize that to live and work in one place is the best that life has to offer. Let the others travel all they wish to. Let them go to New York, San Francisco, anywhere; but give him Memphis for the rest of his days. Mr. Sears locked the door and went down to the lobby.

After dinner he came back to his room. It was not quite seven o'clock then, but the lobby was filled with a noisy crowd of shoe salesmen and evening-gowned women, and Mr. Sears wished to finish studying the president's papers before he turned in for a good night's rest. He did not care to mingle with the crowd downstairs and undoubtedly be mistaken for one of them. He was not a commercial traveler; he was an office manager.

First of all, though, he decided to take a shower. He undressed hurriedly, throwing his clothes over the chairs, and turned on the water. He was busily engaged for a long time tempering the shower to suit his taste. He liked his showers just so—there was a certain temperature that suited him to perfection, and the delay in adjusting the hot and cold streams was worth the time and trouble. The moment when it was ready, he jumped into the spray of water, closing his eyes contentedly, and pretending that he was in his own house, with Mrs. Sears in the kitchen preparing dinner, and trying to forget that there was such a thing as southwestern sales territory.

Suddenly, in the midst of his shower, he heard an insistent knocking on the outside door. He stuck his head out from the spray and listened a moment. The knocking was loud and impatient. Mr. Sears stuck his head back into the spray of water smiling broadly to himself. He remembered how it had been when he was on the road. There had been quick knockings on doors in Dallas, Kansas City, Fort Worth—well, nearly everywhere he went in those days. Now he paid no attention to such a thing. He was not on the road now. He lived in Memphis, and he was married to Mrs. Sears. Drummers were forever making fools of themselves in one way or another, he said to himself. A settled businessman like himself could not afford to take notice of such things.

But the knocking continued. It grew louder; it became so loud that it could not possibly be ignored for any great length of time.

Mr. Sears stuck his head out from the shower to listen again. Someone was rapping angrily on the door—on his door. It was a mistake, he said, just as there had been mistakes in Houston, Shreveport, Kansas City. He had sent for no one, and there was no possible reason why anyone in St. Louis should wish to see him. He knew no one, and he was certain nobody he had previously known would try to look him up. He listened to the knocking on the door, listened with both ears above the spray, wondering how long it would continue.

The rapping on his door kept up, becoming louder and more insistent than ever. Mr. Sears smiled to himself, glancing into the mirror to give himself a sly wink. He didn't care if he did, he said. He would go and take one little look. No harm could possibly come from that. He wished to see.

Reaching for a towel, Mr. Sears turned off the shower and stepped out on the bath mat. He tied the towel around his waist, pulling it down over his legs as far as it would go.

He unlocked the door and opened it until there was a crack an inch wide he could see through. He took one look and shut the door as quickly as he could. The automatic lock behaved as though it would never bolt the door.

When he was certain that the door was securely locked, Mr. Sears took a deep breath and looked around him wild-eyed. He had not expected to see what he did. There was a young woman standing out there without a coat or cloak of any kind and, besides, she was wearing a slanting little red hat over her left ear. He had not expected that. It was all a mistake, he said to himself. It was a genuine mistake. The woman was knocking on the wrong door. She should go to some other door and knock. She was trying to enter the wrong room.

Before he could decide what to do about it, the knocking began again, louder and more determined than ever. Mr. Sears did not know what in the world to do. He stood looking down at himself for a moment, wondering how on earth he was ever going to get her away from his door.

"Open the door!" the woman said. "Open the door this minute!"

That, thought Mr. Sears, was extraordinary. He had never seen or heard of anything like it before in all his life, not even during his fifteen years on the road in the Southwest.

"Do you hear me!" she cried. "Open the door!"

"What do you want in here?" he asked hastily.

"I want to come in! Open the door!"

"But I don't want you in here," Mr. Sears said. "You mustn't come in. I can't allow you to come in."

"Open the door!" she said, raising her voice louder than ever. "Let me in! Open the door this minute!"

Mr. Sears was so nervous and upset by then that he could not stand without holding on to something. He leaned against the wall, trying to think of the proper course of action under the circumstances. While he was trying to think of something to do, it occurred to him that it would never in the world do for the woman to make so much noise out there in the corridor. People would surely hear her, and then they would come to see what the trouble was. If that should happen, someone would be certain to call the police, and the police would come and arrest both of them on some pretext. Then he would be taken to court, along with the young woman, and the thing would get into the newspapers. The Memphis papers would print everything that was sent out by the news agencies. He could already see the headlines in the *Press-Scimitar* at home: MEMPHIS MAN AND ST. LOUIS WOMAN ARRESTED IN HOTEL! Then below that would be his name in full, and, no doubt, his picture. The woman's picture would be there, too. What would Mrs. Sears say!

"Open the door!" the strange woman cried again, striking the panels with her hands. "Let me in!"

Mr. Sears promptly did the only thing he knew to do under the circumstances. He opened the door and ran for the bathroom.

The young woman ran into the room and began pulling out the bed and hurling chairs around as though she had suddenly lost something of great value. Mr. Sears was in the bathroom out of sight, but he knew by the sounds she made that she was searching for something she wished to find without delay. He knew she had no right to come into his room like that and tear things to pieces, and he believed he should stand up for his rights and order her out; but she was such an extraordinary young woman, and he had never been in such an embarrassing position before in all his life, so he just stood there in the bathroom not knowing what in the world to do about it all.

Presently she ran into the bathroom where Mr. Sears was hiding, completely ignoring his desire for privacy. He was more surprised and embarrassed than ever, and the young woman with the slanting little red hat was panting with anger.

"What are you doing in my room?" she demanded, staring through Mr. Sears from head to toe with an impatient up-and-down movement of her head. "Who let you in here?"

Mr. Sears drew the towel around his waist and reached for a second one. He decided that it was about time for him to stand up for his rights and put this impertinent and shameless young woman in her place.

"I engaged this room," he said, his voice not so strong as he wished it might have been. "This is my room. What are you doing here?"

"Your room!" she cried, stamping her foot on the tiled floor. "Your room! Why, I engaged this room myself yesterday! I slept here last night, and I worked here this morning. I told the clerk at the desk that I was not leaving until seven o'clock tonight."

"Well," Mr. Sears said, smiling faintly, "then that's the whole trouble. The people down at the desk evidently thought you had checked out when they assigned the room to me."

While Mr. Sears was explaining, the young woman was running back into the room, leaving him as suddenly as she had burst into his privacy a moment before. She found her two pieces of baggage and opened them to see if anything had been disturbed. Mr. Sears waited in the bathroom, glancing at himself in the mirror.

"Oh, I'm so sorry about all this," she said.

"I am, too," Mr. Sears said.

"I wouldn't have had it to happen for anything."

"Neither would I."

"Come here a minute," she said.

Mr. Sears took a last hasty glance at his appearance, hitched up the towels around his waist, and stepped into the room. She was bending over one of her bags when Mr. Sears saw her, and she turned around and beckoned him.

"What was it you wanted?" he asked weakly.

"Can you snap this lock for me, please?"

"I'll try," he said. "What seems to be the trouble with it?"

"I don't know. It just won't fasten for me. Maybe you can make it work. You are stronger than I am."

Mr. Sears straightened his shoulders and stepped across the floor to her side. He pushed the lock together and it snapped.

"That was all it needed," she said, smiling down at Mr.

Sears. "I don't know what I would have done if you had not been here to help me with it."

"Oh, that's all right," he said, taking a step backward to balance himself.

After that he had expected to see her turn and go toward the door, but instead she went over to the bed and sat down upon it. The chairs were covered with Mr. Sears's clothes, and he had not thought to remove them. She sat on the bed looking at Mr. Sears, wrapped insecurely in his towels, until he wished the floor would open and drop him out of her sight. He noticed the suggestion of a smile on her lips, but he was too much occupied with his thoughts just then to smile back at her. While he waited for some excuse to come to mind that would let him go back to the bathroom, she crossed her legs and took a cigarette and a box of matches from her handbag.

Mr. Sears stood in the middle of the room glancing from the door to her and back again. The door was closed, and it was locked.

"Come over here and sit down beside me," she said, smiling at Mr. Sears. "Maybe you can strike one of these matches for me. They break every time I try to light a cigarette."

He went to the bed and sat down on the pillow at the head. She was arm's length from him, but it was as close as he dared go. He wished more than ever that he had his trousers on.

"Are you on the road?" she asked, when he had struck a match for her.

"Not any longer. I was for fifteen years, and then I went into the home office. I just came up to St. Louis today on a small matter of business for the company."

"That's too bad," she said. "I know how much you miss the road. I'm awfully sorry."

"I—that—well, I like both."

"Oh, but the road is so much more thrilling than the office," she said. "I wouldn't leave it for any inducement now."

"Leave what?"

"The road, of course."

"Do you travel—I mean, are you a commercial traveler?"

"Certainly," she said. "I cover the Southwest."

"But I didn't know—I didn't know that—"

"You didn't know what?"

"Why! I didn't know that women were covering the territory now."

"That's because you have been shut up in the home office for—how long is it?"

"Ten years."

"Ten years! Then that's why you didn't know."

Mr. Sears moved uncomfortably on the pillow. The young woman talked as if she knew more about commercial traveling than he did. Then he realized that he was no longer a salesman. He was an office manager.

"Anyway," she said, "women travelers are the best representatives for my line."

"What's your line?" he asked quickly.

"Barbers' and beauty shop supplies," she said. "I travel out of Kansas City."

Mr. Sears sat looking off into space. The young woman beside him turned to say something else, but when she saw the expression on his face, she waited to hear what he was going to say. Mr. Sears looked as if he would burst open if he did not say something soon.

"When were you in Dallas last?" he asked suddenly, leaning towards her.

"About two weeks ago. Why?"

"Have the hotels there put up the summer doors yet?"

"Yes, I believe they have."

"Has the new railroad station in Houston been completed yet?"

"That was finished three years ago."

"Do the hotels in New Orleans still have runners to meet all the trains?"

"Yes. Runners were meeting the trains there last week."

"And in Kansas City—"

"Oh, in Kansas City the best hotels now employ girls for elevator operators. They wear trousers and coats just like boys."

"They do!" Mr. Sears said. "Just think of that! The last time I was in KC—"

"By the way," the young woman asked, "what did you say your name was?"

"Mr. Sears."

"The first name?"

"It's Henry, but—"

"Henry? That's a good name, Hen. Mine's Jancy. Jancy is sometimes short for Jeanette."

"Jeanette?" Mr. Sears said. "Why! That's my wife's name!"

"Your wife? You're not married, are you, Hen?"

"Certainly," Mr. Sears said. "Her name is Jeanette, but I don't call her Jancy. I call her Jeanette."

"You should call her Jancy, Hen. I'll bet she would like it."

"Maybe when I go back to Memphis I'll—"

"Where is she now, Hen? Is she here with you?"

"She's at home in Memphis."

"Well, that's better," Jancy smiled. "I don't care to be surprised in here with you, Hen. That wouldn't be so funny, would it?"

"No," Mr. Sears said. "My wife—"

"Oh, I know, Hen. All of them are alike. You don't have to tell me about her. I understand perfectly. Let's you and me just enjoy ourselves and have a good time. Do you know any new jokes? I heard a good one last night. A man in New Orleans took a sleeper for Chicago and when he got ready to—"

"But it's time for you to catch your train, isn't it, Miss—"

"Just Jancy, Hen," she said. "But forget about the train. I've changed my mind. I'm not going to Wichita Falls tonight. These sleeper jumps get on my nerves sometimes, and all I want is a nice soft bed in a quiet hotel. Don't you ever feel that way sometimes, Hen?"

"Well, I used to when I was on the road. I've got accustomed to living at home now. Even hotels—"

Mr. Sears glanced nervously at the door once more. The young woman had moved closer to him, and he was already as far as he could move. The bed frame was hurting his side even then.

Jancy began taking off her hat. Mr. Sears sat up and took notice.

"Lay this on the table for me, will you, Hen?" she asked, placing the slanting little red hat in his hands. "I want to take my hair down."

Mr. Sears hitched up his towels and stepped jauntily across the floor with the little red hat. When he came back to the bed, Jancy was sitting in his place and shaking out her curls. Mr. Sears stood first on one foot and then on the other.

"But you can't spend the night in this room," he said uneasily. "Though I suppose I could let you have it, and ask the desk downstairs to give me another one."

"Why do all that, Hen," Jancy said, pointing to a place on the bed where Mr. Sears could sit down. "You talk as if you were never on the road in your whole life. Don't you ever think of expense accounts?"

Mr. Sears felt something turn over in his head. It was like listening to the well-oiled machinery in the Memphis plant. Everything worked so smoothly when all the moving parts were well oiled and when the belts and bands were in place.

He found himself walking back to the bathroom to hang up the towels, and, more surprisingly, he was humming to himself.

"By the way, Jancy," he called through the door, "what's the best hotel in Oklahoma City now?"

She did not answer immediately. He waited, listening for her answer. He was getting ready to repeat the question when something impelled him to turn around. She was standing in the doorway looking at him. He whistled through his teeth.

"Why do you want to know that, Hen? I thought you said you were not on the road any longer."

"Well, I've been off the road for ten years now, but when I

get back to Memphis, I'm going to see the president and tell him I want my old territory back again. I'm not going to stand for the way I've been treated, no sir-ree! I'm going to tell the president that you can't take a commercial traveler off the road and stick him into an office and expect him to settle down there for the rest of his life. And besides, I'm tired of going to the same house every night. Why, Jancy, that house has only got seven rooms in it, and every damn one of them is cluttered up with overstuffed furniture!"

He followed Jancy through the door and into the room. She sat down on the bed and kicked off her slippers.

Mr. Sears reached for the phone on the writing desk.

"What are you going to do, Hen?"

"The first thing I'm going to do is to have some sandwiches and beer sent up. We're going to make—" he stopped abruptly and began shouting into the mouthpiece. After he had shouted himself red in the face, he hung up and threw the phone on the desk. "We're going to make a night of this," he finished.

(First published in *Metropolis*)

Daughter

AT sunrise a Negro on his way to the big house to feed the mules had taken the word to Colonel Henry Maxwell, and Colonel Henry phoned the sheriff. The sheriff had hustled Jim into town and locked him up in the jail, and then he went home and ate breakfast.

Jim walked around the empty cellroom while he was buttoning his shirt, and after that he sat down on the bunk and tied his shoelaces. Everything that morning had taken place so quickly that he had not even had time to get a drink of water. He got up and went to the water bucket near the door, but the sheriff had forgotten to put water into it.

By that time there were several men standing in the jailyard. Jim went to the window and looked out when he heard them talking. Just then another automobile drove up, and six or seven men got out. Other men were coming towards the jail from both directions of the street.

"What was the trouble out at your place this morning, Jim?" somebody said.

Jim stuck his chin between the bars and looked at the faces in the crowd. He knew everyone there.

While he was trying to figure out how everybody in town had heard about his being there, somebody else spoke to him.

"It must have been an accident, wasn't it, Jim?"

A colored boy hauling a load of cotton to the gin drove up the street. When the wagon got in front of the jail, the boy whipped up the mules with the ends of the reins and made them trot.

"I hate to see the State have a grudge against you, Jim," somebody said.

The sheriff came down the street swinging a tin dinner pail in his hand. He pushed through the crowd, unlocked the door, and set the pail inside.

Several men came up behind the sheriff and looked over his shoulder into the jail.

"Here's your breakfast my wife fixed up for you, Jim. You'd better eat a little, Jim boy."

Jim looked at the pail, at the sheriff, at the open jail door, and he shook his head.

"I don't feel hungry," he said. "Daughter's been hungry, though—awful hungry."

The sheriff backed out the door, his hand going to the handle of his pistol. He backed out so quickly that he stepped on the toes of the men behind him.

"Now, don't you get careless, Jim boy," he said. "Just sit and calm yourself."

He shut the door and locked it. After he had gone a few steps towards the street, he stopped and looked into the chamber of his pistol to make sure it had been loaded.

The crowd outside the window pressed in closer. Some of the men rapped on the bars until Jim came and looked out. When he saw them, he stuck his chin between the iron and gripped his hands around it.

"How come it to happen, Jim?" somebody asked. "It must have been an accident, wasn't it?"

Jim's long thin face looked as if it would come through the bars. The sheriff came up to the window to see if everything was all right.

"Now, just take it easy, Jim boy," he said.

The man who had asked Jim to tell what had happened elbowed the sheriff out of the way. The other men crowded closer.

"How come, Jim?" the man said. "Was it an accident?"

"No," Jim said, his fingers twisting about the bars. "I picked up my shotgun and done it."

The sheriff pushed towards the window again.

"Go on, Jim, and tell us what it's all about."

Jim's face squeezed between the bars until it looked as though only his ears kept his head from coming through.

"Daughter said she was hungry, and I just couldn't stand it no longer. I just couldn't stand to hear her say it."

"Don't get all excited now, Jim boy," the sheriff said, pushing forward one moment and being elbowed away the next.

"She waked up in the middle of the night again and said she was hungry. I just couldn't stand to hear her say it."

Somebody pushed all the way through the crowd until he got to the window.

"Why, Jim, you could have come and asked me for something for her to eat, and you know I'd have given you all I got in the world."

The sheriff pushed forward once more.

"That wasn't the right thing to do," Jim said. "I've been working all year and I made enough for all of us to eat."

He stopped and looked down into the faces on the other side of the bars.

"I made enough working on shares, but they came and took it all away from me. I couldn't go around begging after I'd made enough to keep us. They just came and took it all off. Then Daughter woke up again this morning saying she was hungry, and I just couldn't stand it no longer."

"You'd better go and get on the bunk now, Jim boy," the sheriff said.

"It don't seem right that the little girl ought to be shot like that," somebody said.

"Daughter said she was hungry," Jim said. "She'd been saying that for all of the past month. Daughter'd wake up in the middle of the night and say it. I just couldn't stand it no longer."

"You ought to have sent her over to my house, Jim. Me and my wife could have fed her something, somehow. It don't look right to kill a little girl like her."

"I'd made enough for all of us," Jim said. "I just couldn't stand it no longer. Daughter'd been hungry all the past month."

"Take it easy, Jim boy," the sheriff said, trying to push forward.

The crowd swayed from side to side.

"And so you just picked up the gun this morning and shot her?" somebody asked.

"When she woke up this morning saying she was hungry, I just couldn't stand it."

The crowd pushed closer. Men were coming towards the jail from all directions, and those who were then arriving pushed forward to hear what Jim had to say.

"The State has got a grudge against you now, Jim," somebody said, "but somehow it don't seem right."

"I can't help it," Jim said. "Daughter woke me up again this morning that way."

The jailyard, the street, and the vacant lot on the other side were filled with men and boys. All of them were pushing forward to hear Jim. Word had spread all over town by that time that Jim Carlisle had shot and killed his eight-year-old daughter, Clara.

"Who does Jim sharecrop for?" somebody asked.

"Colonel Henry Maxwell," a man in the crowd said. "Colonel Henry has had Jim out there about nine or ten years."

"Henry Maxwell didn't have no business coming and taking all the shares. He's got plenty of his own. It ain't right for Henry Maxwell to come and take Jim's, too."

The sheriff was pushing forward once more.

"The State's got a grudge against Jim now," somebody said. "Somehow it don't seem right, though."

The sheriff pushed his shoulder into the crowd of men and worked his way in closer.

A man shoved the sheriff away.

"Why did Henry Maxwell come and take your share of the crop, Jim?"

"He said I owed it to him because one of his mules died about a month ago."

The sheriff got in front of the barred window.

"You ought to go to the bunk now and rest some, Jim boy," he said. "Take off your shoes and stretch out, Jim boy."

He was elbowed out of the way.

"You didn't kill the mule, did you, Jim?"

"The mule dropped dead in the barn," Jim said. "I wasn't nowhere around. It just dropped dead."

The crowd was pushing harder. The men in front were jammed against the jail, and the men behind were trying to get within earshot. Those in the middle were squeezed against each other so tightly they could not move in any direction. Everyone was talking louder.

Jim's face pressed between the bars and his fingers gripped the iron until the knuckles were white.

The milling crowd was moving across the street to the vacant lot. Somebody was shouting. He climbed up on an automobile and began swearing at the top of his lungs.

A man in the middle of the crowd pushed his way out and went to his automobile. He got in and drove off alone.

Jim stood holding to the bars and looking through the window. The sheriff had his back to the crowd, and he was saying something to Jim. Jim did not hear what he said.

A man on his way to the gin with a load of cotton stopped to find out what the trouble was. He looked at the crowd in the vacant lot for a moment, and then he turned around and looked at Jim behind the bars. The shouting across the street was growing louder.

"What's the trouble, Jim?"

Somebody on the other side of the street came to the wagon. He put his foot on a spoke in the wagon wheel and looked up at the man on the cotton while he talked.

"Daughter woke up this morning again saying she was hungry," Jim said.

The sheriff was the only person who heard him.

The man on the load of cotton jumped to the ground, tied the reins to the wagon wheel, and pushed through the crowd to the car where all the shouting and swearing was being done. After listening for a while he came back to the street, called a Negro who was standing with several other Negroes on the corner, and handed him the reins. The Negro drove off with the cotton towards the gin, and the man went back into the crowd.

Just then the man who had driven off alone in his car came back. He sat for a moment behind the steering wheel, and then he jumped to the ground. He opened the rear door and took out a crowbar that was as long as he was tall.

"Pry that jail door open and let Jim out," somebody said. "It ain't right for him to be in there."

The crowd in the vacant lot was moving again. The man who had been standing on top of the automobile jumped to the ground, and the men moved towards the street in the direction of the jail.

The first man to reach it jerked the six-foot crowbar out of the soft earth where it had been jabbed.

The sheriff backed off.

"Now, take it easy, Jim boy," he said.

He turned and started walking rapidly up the street towards his house.

(First published in *Anvil*)

The Lonely Day

FOR a week the wet midsummer mists had been creeping over Maine from the south, from the coast; sheets of low-hanging gray vapor spread over the country like dirty steam and leveled the foothills into smooth fields, while the mountains had been wrapped in wet gray clouds and put away from sight towards the north, towards Canada. Yesterday the mists had lifted over the house top, almost over the tops of the elm trees; but today, Sunday, the lower air was so wet that the meshes of the window screens were filled with panes of opaque water.

Katherine hurried across the wet grass from the garden and went into the house. She opened the kitchen door quietly and closed it slowly as she stood back against it.

The old woman struck at her with the heavy end of the crutch and cursed her.

The girl jumped away and ran to the other side of the kitchen.

The room was wet with the midsummer mists. There were little balls of water in the dusty spider web over the stove and a thin stream of water trickled at intervals down the table legs to the floor.

"Go pick me some berries," the old woman cried at her. *"Go pick me some berries!"* she shouted. "Do you hear me? You damned little sneak! Bring me a pail of berries before I take this crutch and kill you!"

"All right," Katherine whimpered. "I'm going."

"Well, why don't you run? I'll break your head if you don't get out of here after those berries!"

Katherine took the berry pail from the kitchen table and ran outside before the old woman could strike her again. The wet mists clung to her hair as she ran towards the pasture, and tears fell on her dampened cheeks. The berry field was on the other side of the stream, beyond the sheep pasture. Bordering the field was the State road, running north and south.

She gathered the wet berries as quickly as she could. She knew the old woman was even then waiting at the kitchen door to strike her with the crutch because she had not returned sooner. She tried as hard as she could, but she could not pick them any faster.

Several hundred yards away automobiles passed in both directions, going up into the Provinces, coming back into Maine. All around her was the forest, the deep dark forest where men worked in winter, in the white frozen snow, cutting pulpwood. The men who worked there were French from Canada and she could not understand what they said. Now there was nobody near. The closest settlement was forty miles to the south and the only people who came through the woods were tourists, passing but never stopping. She had never gone so far as the road, but when she picked berries she could hear the roar of the speeding automobiles and occasionally the laughter of men and women. The old woman would not let her go near the road.

While she was gathering the wet berries she thought she

heard one of the automobiles stop. As she listened, there came shouts and laughter from the direction of the road, but she was too far away to hear what the people said. She bent over the berry bushes and tried to fill the pail as quickly as she could.

It was noon before the pail was full. She ran towards the house where the old woman sat waiting for the berries.

While she ran down the hillside toward the stream in the sheep pasture she heard again the shouts and laughter of several persons. When she reached the footbridge she could see them in dim outline through the mists. There were five or six men and girls farther down the stream toward the lower lake.

Katherine crossed the footbridge and went down the stream where the men and girls were. At first she thought they were fishing, but almost before she knew it, she was within a hundred yards of them; and then she saw that they were swimming and diving into the stream. The low-hanging cloud had cleared along the banks of the stream for a few moments and she saw them plainly only a short distance away.

She stared wild-eyed as she saw one of the men and a girl wade out of the water and stand on the bank a moment before diving in again.

She was so confused by what she saw that she could neither cry out nor run away. Her heart was beating madly and her body trembled with excitement.

While she stood in amazement before the scene, one of the girls climbed to the bank of the stream and ran out across the pasture. The girl turned and called to one of the men.

"You can't catch me, Jimmy!"

Laughing, the naked girl ran off and disappeared in the heavy mists.

The other men and girls were laughing and splashing water in the stream.

Katherine stood beside the stream, above them. She had never seen anything such as this happen before in her life, and she could barely believe that men and girls could have such a good time together. It was too incredible to be true, but she could hear everything they said and see everything they did. And still the scene was unreal to her. She had never been with men and girls of her own age, and she was bewildered with the strangeness of their behavior.

Her heart was racing so excitely that she could stand still no longer. She wanted to run as fast as she could and fall in the midst of those men and girls and laugh with them. Then suddenly she felt the weight of the berry pail in her hand, and she turned and ran as quickly as she could to the house where the old woman waited.

The old woman snatched the pail of berries from her hands

and began eating the fruit. Katherine went to her room and closed the door. She stood beside her bed trembling with excitement, remembering what she had seen and heard down at the stream in the sheep pasture. She ran from window to window trying to see through the wet mists. If only there had been no mists, she knew she could have seen the men and girls in the pasture. But she could see no further than the windows. The mists covered everything outside.

While the old woman sat in the kitchen eating the berries, Katherine slipped quietly from the front of the house and ran towards the stream. As she ran down the hillside she tried to hear the things the men and girls were saying. She wanted to run, just as they were, into their midst and throw herself on the grass beside them. She wanted to laugh and dive into the stream and splash water over everybody.

Running wildly towards the stream, she suddenly saw that the men and girls were not there. They had taken their clothes and gone back to the automobile to dress, and by now they were probably several miles away. Now there was nothing she could do. She did not want to stay at the stream alone. She wanted to be with someone, with men and girls who laughed and splashed water. Alone, she stood crying by the stream.

The wet mists chilled her body and she began to shiver. The warm tears fell cold and hard on her arms and hands.

Slowly she turned and walked up the hillside towards the house. She repeated over and over the words she thought she had heard as she was running so happily to the stream a few minutes before.

The old woman had not missed her. She still sat in the kitchen eating from the pail the berries Katherine had picked that morning.

Katherine sat on the bed in her room crying. She fell backward and crushed a pillow over her face so the old woman could not hear her.

Later in the afternoon she got up. She walked around the room, stopping at a window and trying to penetrate the gray mists that hung over the earth. There was no one to see her, there were no men and girls she could see. It was not what had happened in the sheep pasture that morning, when the gray mists were filled with laughter and the stream with splashing water. It was not the same thing. And she could not laugh aloud.

After supper, when the old woman had gone to bed, Katherine stole out of the house and ran through the wet dark night towards the pasture. When she reached the stream, she could see nothing, not even the grass at her feet. All about her she felt the clinging wet clouds of vapor. The black mists covered everything. Over the hill she thought she heard an automobile speed along the road towards the Provinces. She tried again, but she could not laugh aloud in the wet mists.

She ran across the berry field until she reached the road where the automobiles passed. When she got there, she stood in the road and waited. It was then after midnight. She waited but no car came from either direction.

While she stood in the center of the road she distinctly heard in the distance the same laughter that had made her so excited that afternoon. Clearly she heard a girl's voice. Someone was calling, "You can't catch me, Jimmy!" Almost immediately the voice of a man could be heard out in the far darkness somewhere. And then, all around her, men and girls were shouting and laughing, just as she had heard them that afternoon in the pasture. From the music of their voices she knew they were splashing water in a stream and lying naked on the grassy banks beside the water. But they were so far away she knew she could never find them while everything was so black and misty.

She waited and listened for an automobile to come up or down the road. But there was none. She wanted to stand in the center of the road and have the men and women see her.

The first light of day broke through the mists and found her lying in the road, her body made lifeless by an automobile that had shot through the darkness an hour before. She was without motion, but she was naked, and a smile that was the beginning of laughter made her the most beautiful woman that tourists speeding to the Provinces had ever seen.

(First published in *American Earth*)

Nine Dollars' Worth of Mumble

You couldn't see no stars, you couldn't see no moon, you couldn't see nothing much but a measly handful of sparks on the chimney spout. It was a mighty poor beginning for a courting on a ten o'clock night. Hollering didn't do a bit of good, and stomping up and down did less.

Youster swung the meal sack from his right shoulder to his left. Carrying around a couple of hobbled rabbits wasn't much fun. They kicked and they squealed, and they kept his mind from working on a way to get into that house where Sis was.

He stooped 'way down and felt around on the road for a handful of rocks. When he found enough, he pitched them at the house where they would make the most noise.

"Go away from here and stop pestering us, Youster Brown," that old pinch-faced woman said through the door. "I've got Sis right where my eyes can see her, and that's where she's going to stay. You go on and get yourself away from here, Youster Brown."

"Woman," Youster shouted, "you shut your big mouth and open up that door! I reckon you must be so pinched-faced, you scared of the nighttime."

"The nighttime is one time when I ain't scared, even when you're in it, Youster Brown. Now, go yourself on off somewhere and stop worrying Sis and me."

"Old pinched-faced woman, why you scared to open the door and let me see Sis?" he asked, creeping up closer to the house.

"Because Sis is saving up for a man her worth. She can't be wasting herself on no half-Jim nigger like you. Now, go on off, Youster Brown, and leave us be."

Youster crept a little closer to the door, feeling his way up the path from the road. All he wanted was to see that door unlatch just one little inch, and he would get his way in.

"I've got a little eating-present here for Sis," he said when he got to the doorstep. He waited to hear if that old pinched-faced Matty would come close to the door. "It'll make some mighty good eating, I'm telling you."

"Don't you go bringing no white-folks' stole chickens around here, Youster Brown," she said. "I don't have nothing to do with white-folks' stole chickens, and you know I don't."

"Woman, these here ain't chickens. They ain't nothing like chickens. They ain't even got feathers on them. These here is plump rabbits I gummed in my own cotton patch."

"Lay them on the doorsill, and then back off to the big road," she said. "I wouldn't leave you get a chance to come in that door for a big white mansion on easy street, Youster Brown."

"What you got so heavy against me, Matty?" he asked her. "What's eating on you, anyhow?"

There was no sight or sound for longer than he could hold his breath. When Matty wasn't at the hearth to poke the fire, the sparks stopped coming out of the chimney.

"If you so set on knowing what's the matter, you go ask Sally Lucky. She'll tell you in no time."

"Sally Lucky done give me a charm on Sis," Youster said. "I handed over and paid her three dollars and six bits only last week. I'm already sunk seven dollars in Sally Lucky, and all

the good she ever done me was to say to come see Sis on every
black night there was. That's why I'm standing out here now
like I am, because it's a black night, and Sally Lucky says to
come when it's like it is now."

"You go give Sally Lucky two dollars more right now, and
see what happens, Youster Brown. For all that money you'll
have a lot coming to you. But you won't never find out nothing
standing around here. Sally Lucky'll tell you, so you'll be told
for all time."

Youster laid the sack with the two hobbled rabbits in it
on the doorstep. Then he backed out to the road. It wasn't
long before the door opened a crack, then a foot. Matty's long
thin arm reached out, felt around, grabbed the meal sack, and
jerked it inside. When she closed the door and latched it, the
night was again as black as ever.

He waited around for a while, feeling the wind, and smelling
the chimney smoke. He couldn't see why Sis had to grow up
and live with an old pinched-faced woman like Matty.

When he got to thinking about Matty, he remembered what
she said. He cut across the field toward Sally Lucky's. It didn't
take him long when he had no time to lose. When he got to the
creek, he crossed it on the log and jogged up the hollow to
Sally Lucky's shack.

"Who's that?" Sally Lucky said, when he pounded on the
door.

"Youster Brown," he said as loud as he could.

"What you want, Youster?"

"I want a working charm on Sis, or something bad on that
old pinched-faced Matty. I done paid you seven, all told, dollars, and it ain't worked for me none yet. It's time it worked,
too. If I give you two more dollars, will you make the charm
work, and put something bad on Matty, too?"

The shriveled-up old Sally Lucky opened the door and stuck
her head out on her thin neck. She squinted at him in the dark,
and felt to see if he had a gun or knife in his pockets. She had
been putting up her hair for the night, and half was up on one
side of her head, and half down on the other. She looked all
wore out.

"You sure look like you is the right somebody to put things
on folks," Youster said, gulping and shaking. "If you is, now's
the time to prove it to me. Man alive, I'm needing things on
folks, if ever I did."

"Let me see your money, Youster," she said, taking him
inside and sitting down in her chair on the hearth. "What kind
of money you got on you?"

He took out all the money he had in the world—four half-
dollar pieces—and put it on the fingers of her hand.

"I'm getting dog-tired of handing you over all my money,

and not getting no action for it," Youster said. "Look here, now, woman, is you able to do things or ain't you?"

"You know Ham Beaver, don't you?"

"I reckon I know Ham. I saw him day before yesterday. What about him?"

"I gave him a charm on a yellow girl six miles down the creek, and he went and got her all for himself before the week was over."

"Maybe so," Youster said. "But I paid you seven dollars, all told, before now, for a charm on Sis, and I ain't got no sign of action for it. That old pinched-faced woman Matty just locks up the door and won't let me in when I want in."

"What you need is a curse on Matty," Sally Lucky said. "A curse is what you want, and for nine dollars, all told, you appear to be due one, Youster."

"It won't get me in no trouble with the law, will it?" he asked, shaking. "The law is one thing I don't want no trouble with no more at all."

"All my charms and curses are private dealings," she said, shaking her finger at him until he trembled more than ever. "As long as you do like I tell you, and keep your mouth shut, you won't have no trouble with the law. I see to that."

"I has bought charms before, and they didn't make no trouble for me. But I ain't never before in my life bought a curse on nobody. I just want to make sure I ain't going to get in no trouble with the law. I'm positive about that."

He studied the hickory-log fire for a while, and spat on an ember. He couldn't be afraid of the law as long as he had Sally Lucky on his side. And he figured nine dollars' worth was plenty to keep her on his side.

Sally Lucky picked up her poker and began sticking it into the fire. Sparks swirled in the fireplace and disappeared out of sight up the chimney. Youster watched her, sitting on the edge of his chair. He was in a big hurry, and he hoped it wouldn't take her long this time to see what she was looking for in the fire.

All at once she began to mutter to herself, saying things so fast that Youster could not understand what the words were. He got down on his hands and knees and peered into the blazing fire, trying to see with his own eyes what Sally Lucky saw. While he was looking so hard, Sally Lucky started saying things faster and faster. He knew then that she was talking to Matty, and putting the curse on her.

He was as trembly as Sally Lucky was by then. He crept so close to the fire that he could barely keep his eyes open in the heat. Then as suddenly as she had begun, Sally Lucky picked up a rusty tomato can partly filled with water, and dashed it into the fire. The water sizzled, and the logs smoked and hissed, and a sharp black face could be seen in the fire.

Youster got back on his chair and waited. Sally Lucky kept on mumbling to herself, but the double talk was dying down, and before long no sound came through her jerking lips.

"You sure must be real sure enough conjur, Sally Lucky," Youster said weakly.

She put a small tin snuff can into his hand, closing her fingers over it. He could feel that it was heavy, heavier than a can of snuff. It rattled, too, like it had been partly filled with BB shot.

Sally Lucky didn't say another thing until she took him to the door. There she pushed him outside, and said:

"Whenever you think the curse ain't working like it ought to, just take out that snuff can, Youster, and shake it a little."

"Like it was dice?"

"Just exactly like it was dice."

She shut the door and barred it.

Youster put the can into his pocket, and kept his hand in there with it so he wouldn't have a chance in the world to lose it. He ran down the creek as fast as he could, crossed it on the log, and cut across the field toward the big road where Sis and Matty lived.

There still was no light anywhere in the night. When he got closer to the house, he could see a handful of sparks come out the chimney spout every once in a while when Matty poked the hickory-log fire.

He strode up to the front door as big as a bill collector. There wasn't nothing to make him scared of that old pinched-faced Matty no more.

"Open up," he said, pounding on the door.

"That you, Youster Brown, again?" Matty said on the inside.

"I reckon it is," Youster said. "It ain't nobody else. Open this here door up, woman, before I take it off its hinges. I ain't got no time to lose."

"You sure do talk big for a half-Jim nigger, Youster Brown. Ain't you got no sense? Don't you know that big talk don't scare me none at all?"

"The talk maybe don't, but the conjur do," Youster said. "Woman, I got a curse on you."

"You is?"

"Don't you feel it none?"

"I don't feel nothing but a draft on my back."

Youster took the snuff can out of his pocket and shook it in his hand. He shook it like it was a pair of dice.

"Come on, can, do your work," he said to the snuffbox in his hand. "Get down on your knees and do your nine dollars' worth!"

While he waited for the can to put the curse into action, he listened through the door. There was no sound in there, except the occasional squeak of Matty's rocking chair on the hearth.

"I don't hear Sis in there," Youster said. "Where you at, Sis?"

"Sis is minding her own business," Matty told him. "You go on off somewhere and mind yours. Sis ain't studying about you, anyhow."

"Why ain't she?" Youster shouted. "Sis is my woman, and my woman ought to be studying about me all the time."

"You sure do talk like all the big-headed half-Jim niggers I ever knew," Matty said. "Just because you paid seven dollars to Sally Lucky for a charm on Sis, you get the notion in your head that Sis's your woman. Nigger, if I had only your sense, I wouldn't know which end to stand on."

"That talk don't fool me none," Youster told her. "The way that gal cut her eyes at me last Sunday showed me the way to go home. I reckon I know when the best is yet to come."

Youster rubbed the snuffbox in his hands, feeling its slick surface and good warmth. He held his breath while he listened through the door.

"I can afford to put off getting her for a while," he said through the cracks, "being as how this curse is going to be working on you."

"What curse?" Matty said.

"The curse I just a while ago got Sally Lucky to put on you for me, that's what. I paid her two dollars for it. That makes nine, all told, dollars I've paid out. All I don't feel right about is that I waited all this time before I got a curse put on you. I ought to have had it working on you all this past summer and fall."

"If you paid nine dollars to Sally Lucky for putting something on me, Youster Brown, all you got was just nine dollars' worth of mumble."

"How come?" Youster said.

"Because I paid Sally Lucky three dollars for a curse on you the first time I ever saw you, that's how come," Matty said. "And that's how come all your big talk about getting a charm on Sis and a curse on me won't never come to nothing. Charms and curses won't cross, Youster Brown, because it's the one that's taken out first that does the work, and that's how come the curse I took out on you took, and the ones you took out on Sis and me won't take. I saw you coming, Youster Brown, and I didn't lose no time taking out the curse on you."

Youster sat down on the step. He looked down the path toward the road and across the field toward Sally Lucky's. He fingered the snuff can for a while.

There came a squeak from the chair through the door, but there was no other sound. The black night was pulling down all around him. He couldn't see nothing, nowhere. There wasn't no sense in night being black like the bottom of a hole. After a while he got up and went off down the road. He was trying his best to think of some way to get his nine dollars back. Nine dollars was a lot of money to pay for mumble.

(First published in *Harper's Bazaar*)

The Cold Winter

AFTER I had been in town a week, I began going early in the evening to the room I had rented, to lie awake under the warmth of the blanket.

Out on the streets, when night fell, it was always cold. There was usually a chill wet wind from the river, and from the bare uplands the February winter descended hour after hour, freezing and raw. Even men with overcoats hurried through the icy streets with lowered heads fighting the cold, hurrying towards heated homes.

It was cold in the unheated room I had rented, but the warmth of the blanket was like the clinging arms of a girl.

By the third night of the week I had got accustomed to the unheated house. At first I could not sleep. But on that evening I took off my shoes as soon as I had reached the room and got into bed immediately. For the next five or six hours I lay awake, warm under the blanket, while frost on the window-panes formed slowly and precisely into fragile designs of cold beauty.

Out in the hall I could hear people passing quickly from room to room, hurrying through the cold corridor while the contracted boards of the floor creaked under their feet.

After a while I became conscious of warm air flowing through the cracks in the wall. A young woman and her small daughter lived in the room next to mine, on the right, and the heat they had was escaping into my room. I could smell the scorched air and the burned gas of their heater. I lay awake then, listening to the movements in the next room, while their slowly formed picture was melted into my memory. Towards midnight I fell asleep, remembering only that in the next room the young woman moved lightly when she walked and that the small girl spoke to her mother softly and lovingly.

After that night I began coming home much earlier in the evening to cover myself with the warmth of the blanket and to lie awake in the darkness listening to all that happened in the next-door room. The young woman prepared supper for the girl and herself, and then they sat at the small table by the window and ate slowly, laughing and talking. The little girl was about eight, and her mother was almost as young as she when they laughed and talked.

The cold of the unheated room was not so hard to bear as it had been before I came to know them.

I knew by the end of that second week how each of them looked even though I had never seen either of them. Through the thin plaster wall I could hear everything they said and did, and I followed the motions of their hands and the expressions on their faces from second to second, hour after hour. The young woman was not working, either; she remained in the room most of the day, going out only in the morning for half an hour to walk with the girl to school, and again in the afternoon to walk home with her. The rest of the day she sat in the room, by the window, looking out over the red-painted tin roof across the way, and waiting for midafternoon to come so she could walk to the school for her daughter.

There were other people in the house, many of them. The three floors of the building were rented, room by room, to men and women who came and went during all hours. Some of them worked during the day, some at night, and many had no jobs at all. But even though there were many people in the house, no one ever came to my door, and no one ever went to the young woman's door next to mine. Sometimes there would be the sound of a man walking heavily, coming hurriedly down the hall, and the young woman would jump from her chair by the window and run frantically to the door, leaning against it while her fingers held the key in the lock and listening to the sound of the man's stride. After he had passed, she went slowly back to her chair and sat down once more to look out over the red-painted tin roof across the way.

Into the month of February it became colder and colder, but I was warm when I lay under the blanket and listened to the sounds that came through the thin plaster wall.

It was not until I had become aware of her running to the door each time the sound of a man's footstep rang through the rooms that I realized something was about to happen. I did not know what the happening was to be, nor when, but each morning before leaving my room I waited and listened for several minutes to hear if she were standing against her door or sitting in her chair. When I came back in the evening, I pressed my ear against the cold wall to listen again.

That evening, after I had listened for nearly half an hour, I knew something was about to happen; and for the first time in my life, while I stood there shivering in the cold, I had the desire to be the father of a child. I did not stop to turn on the light, but climbed straightway into bed without even taking off my shoes. I lay tensely awake upon the bed for a long time listening to the movements on the other side of the wall. The young woman was quick and nervous, and her face was white and drawn. The little girl was put to bed as soon as they had finished eating supper and, without a word being spoken, the young woman went to her chair by the window to sit and wait. She sat silently, not even rocking, for a long time. I had raised my head from the pillow, and my neck was stiff and cold after the strain of holding my head horizontally without support.

It was eleven o'clock before I heard another sound in the room next to mine. During the three hours that I had lain awake on the bed waiting, she had not moved from her chair. But at eleven o'clock she got up and drank a glass of water and covered the girl with another blanket. When she had finished, she moved to her chair for a moment, and then she carried it to the door and sat down. She sat and waited. Before another hour had passed, a man came down the hall, walking heavily on the contracted boards of the floor. We both heard him coming, and we both jumped to our feet. I ran to the wall and pressed my ear against the cold white plaster and waited. The young woman leaned against the door, her fingers gripped around the key, and listened with bated breath. The little girl was sound asleep in bed.

After I had been standing for several minutes I felt the cold of the unheated room wither my hands and feet. Under the warmth of the blanket I had forgotten how cold it was, and the blood had raced through me while I waited still and tense and listened to the sounds in the building. But standing in the unheated room, with my face and ear pressed against the cold white plaster, I was shaking as though with a chill.

The man came to the door next to mine and stopped. I could hear the woman's trembling, and the breathing that jerked her body, and each moment I expected to hear her scream.

He knocked on the door once and waited. She did not open it. He turned the knob and shook it. She pressed with all her strength against the door, and held the key in its place with fingers of steel.

"I know you are in there, Eloise," he said slowly; "open the door and let me in."

She made no reply. I could hear through the thin wall the strain of her body against the frail door.

"I'm coming in," he said.

He had barely finished before there was a sudden thrust of his shoulder against the door that burst the lock and threw him inside. Even then there was no sound from her lips. She ran to the bed and threw herself upon it, hugging desperately in her arms the girl who had slept so soundly.

"I didn't come here to argue with you," the man said. "I came here to put an end to this mess. Get up off the bed."

It was then for the first time that evening that I heard the sound of the young woman's voice. She had sprung to her feet and was facing him. I pressed my face and ear against the cold white plaster and waited.

"She's as much mine as she is yours. You can't take her away from me."

"You took her away from me, didn't you? Well, it's my turn now. I'm her father."

"Henry!" she begged. "Henry, please don't!"

"Shut up," he said.

He strode to the bed and lifted the girl in his arms.

"I'll kill you, Henry, if you take her out of this room," she said slowly. "I mean that, Henry."

He walked with the girl to the door and stopped. He was not excited, and his breath was not even audible through the thin wall. But the woman was frantic, and my hands and feet were numbed with the cold and I could not move the muscles of my lips. The young woman had not begun to cry, but through the plaster wall I could hear her breathe, and I could feel the quick movements of her body.

He turned around.

"You'll do what?" he said.

"I'll kill you, Henry."

There was a moment's silence, complete and still. He stood at the door, the girl lying in his arms waking slowly from sleep, and waited. Each second seemed as though it were an hour long.

"No, you won't do that," he said after a while. "I'm going to beat you to it, Eloise."

Through the thin plaster wall I could hear the smooth slide of his hand into his coat pocket and out again. I could hear everything that was to happen.

When he pointed the pistol at her, she screamed. He waited until she had cried out, and then he pulled the trigger, not taking careful aim, but nevertheless closing one eye as though he were looking down the sights at her.

The echoes of the explosion drowned out the sound of his running down the hall and the creaking of the floor under his feet.

It was several minutes before the ringing in my ears had died out, and by that time there was the sound of people running through the house from top to bottom, flinging open the doors of the heated rooms and of the unheated rooms as they raced towards us on the second floor.

For a long time I lay against the white plastered wall, trembling because I who was the father had allowed without protest the taking away of the girl, and shaking because I was cold in the unheated room.

(First published in *Story*)

The Growing Season

THE heat was enough to drive anybody crazy.

The wire grass was growing faster than Jesse English could keep it chopped down and covered up. He had been going over the twelve acres of cotton for five days already, and he was just about ready to give up.

At noon when his wife called him to dinner, Jesse unhitched the mule from the scraper and turned him loose. The mule walked unsteadily towards the barn, stumbling over the rows as if he had blindstaggers. Jesse's eyes were bloodshot by the heat, and he was afraid he was going to get a sunstroke. He got to the house, but he could not eat anything. He stretched out on the porch, his straw hat over his face to shut out the glare of the sun, feeling as if he could never get up again as long as he lived.

Lizzie came to the door and told him to get up and eat the meal she had cooked. Jesse did not answer her, and after a while she went back inside out of sight.

The rattling of the trace chain in the yard woke Jesse up. He raised himself on his elbow and looked out under the chinaberry tree at Fiddler. Fiddler crawled around the tree, winding the chain around the trunk of the chinaberry. When Fiddler had wound the chain as far as he could, he lay down again.

Jesse stared at Fiddler with his bloodshot eyes burning into his head until he could not stand it any longer. He dug his knuckles into his eye sockets until the pain had left for a while.

Fiddler got up and made as if to stand. Instead, he pitched forward like a drunken man, falling into a mass. Jesse felt a new rush of blood in his head each time Fiddler rattled the chain. While watching him, he began to wonder what was going to happen to his crop of cotton. It had rained for a solid week just when the cotton was ready to hoe, and before he could catch up with it, the wire grass had got ahead of him. Lizzie had had a sunstroke the year before, and every time she stayed in the sun fifteen or twenty minutes she fainted. She could not help him hoe; there was nobody to help him. There was not even a Negro on the place.

When he looked out over the field, he realized how little he had accomplished since sunup that morning. He did not see how he would ever be able to clear out the grass before the cotton plants got choked out.

The trace chain rattled again. Jesse pushed himself on his hands and feet to the edge of the porch and sat there staring at Fiddler. Lizzie came to the door once more and told him to come and eat his dinner, but he did not hear her.

Fiddler turned over on the ground and lay with his head up against the trunk of the chinaberry tree.

Sitting on the edge of the porch with his feet swinging back and forth, Jesse rubbed his eyes with his knuckles and tried to reason clearly. The heat, even in the shade of the porch roof, was blinding him. His eyes burned like hot chestnuts in his head. When he heard Fiddler rattle the chain again, he tried to stare at him through the heat, but Fiddler was by then no more than a blue patch in the yard.

The crop was going to ruin because there was nobody to help him get the grass out before the cotton plants were choked to death by the wire grass.

Jesse eased himself off the edge of the porch and climbed the steps and went into the hall. His shotgun was standing in the corner behind the door. It was kept loaded all the time, and he did not stop to see if there were any shells in the barrels.

"Your dinner's getting spoiled, Jesse," his wife said somewhere in the house.

He did not answer her.

Outside in the sun and heat once more, Jesse could see the wire grass choking the life out of his crop of cotton. He ran to the far end of the yard and out into the field and began kicking the cotton plants and grass with his feet. Even then the wire grass sprang back like coils in a bedspring. The cotton plants he had kicked from their roots began slowly to wilt in the noonday heat. By the time he had turned away, the plants had shriveled up and died.

He went back into the yard and kicked the trace chain. One end was fastened to the chinaberry tree, and the other end was clamped around Fiddler's neck. He stood the shotgun against the tree and began fumbling with the clamp. While he was stooped over, Lizzie came to the porch again.

"What are you aiming to do with that shotgun, Jesse?" she asked, shading her eyes with her hands.

When he did not answer her, she ran down the steps and raced across the yard to the chinaberry.

The clamp was unfastened then. Jesse grabbed the gun and jerked the chain. He jerked the chain harder the next time, and Fiddler rolled to his feet and went wobbling across the yard like a drunken man trying to walk.

Lizzie tried to jerk the chain out of Jesse's hand. He pushed her aside.

"Jesse!" she screamed at him. "Jesse, what you going to do with Fiddler!"

He pushed her behind him. Fiddler wobbled on his undeveloped legs and Jesse poked him upright with the gunstock each time he looked as if he would fall. Lizzie came screaming after them and fell around her husband's legs. Jesse got away from her before she could lock her arms around his knees.

Fiddler had started running towards the barn. Jesse ran behind, holding the gun ahead so he could prod Fiddler in the direction he wanted him to go.

The crop was ruined. But he had forgotten all about the wire grass choking out the tender cotton plants. The grass had got ahead of him before he could stop it. If Lizzie had not been sunstruck, or if he had had anybody else to help him, he could have saved his cotton. The wire grass on twelve acres was too much for one man, once he fell behind.

His eyes were so bloodshot he could not see Fiddler very well. The heat and the throbbing in his head made him forget everything except that he had to get Fiddler out behind the barn where the gully was. He threw a corncob at the mule to get him out of Fiddler's way. The mule went into the barn.

Fiddler ran off in another direction, but Jesse headed him back to the gully with the butt end of the shotgun. He hit Fiddler again with the stock to keep him from going in the wrong direction.

Lizzie was screaming in the front yard. She did not have her sunbonnet on, and she had already got a touch of heat.

When they got to the gully, Jesse shoved Fiddler down into it. Fiddler lay on the bottom on the wash, digging at the sides and trying to get out.

Jesse raised his gun to sight down the barrels, and all he could see was a wiggling gray mass against the red clay gully-bank. He pulled the trigger anyway, and waited a moment. Without lowering the gun, he fired the second shell at Fiddler.

Fiddler was making more noise than he had ever made before. Jesse sat down on the side of the gully and rubbed his eyes with his knuckles. He felt the dried earth give way under his knees, and he moved back a little to keep from sliding down into the gully where Fiddler was floundering like a fish that had been tossed upon dry land.

"Stop that kicking and squealing, and die, damn you!" Jesse shouted. "Die! Damn you, die!"

He could not sit there any longer. He had waited as long as he could wait for Fiddler to stop thrashing around in the gully. The birdshot in the shells was strong enough to kill a mule at short range, but they had not been strong enough to kill Fiddler.

Lizzie screaming under the chinaberry tree and the heat and the blazing sun overhead sent Jesse running to the woodpile at the back of the house. He grabbed up the ax and came running back to the gully. Fiddler was still thrashing around on the bottom like a chicken with its head cut off. Jesse jumped down the bank and struck at Fiddler three or four times. When he stopped, blood was all over the ax handle and blade, and the bottoms of his overall legs were soaked with it.

After a while Fiddler lay still, and Jesse walked down to the lower end of the gully where the banks were not so steep and climbed to the top. On the way back to the house he could see Lizzie lying on the ground under the chinaberry tree where Fiddler had been kept chained.

He carried the ax to the woodpile and swung the blade into a hickory log. After that he sat down on the woodpile and wiped his face with his hands and tried to stop the burning of his eyeballs by digging at them with his knuckles.

From somewhere a breeze came up, and the wind against his hot face made him feel better all over. He ran his thumb under one overall strap and threw it off. The breeze blowing against his wet shirt and skin felt like a gentle rain.

One of the hounds that had been sleeping under the house got up and walked out to the woodpile and began licking the ax handle. Jesse watched him until he had finished. When the dog started licking his overall legs, Jesse kicked him with all his might. The hound tumbled to his feet and ran yelping back under the house.

Jesse wiped his face with his hands again, and got up. He found the hoe leaning against the side of the house. He carried it to the porch and pulled the rat-tailed file out of the weatherboarding where it had been stuck since the last time he used it.

He thought he heard his wife stumbling through the hall of the house.

Propping the hoe against the porch, Jesse began filing the blade until it was as keen as a corn knife. After that was done, he jabbed the file back into the weatherboarding and walked towards the cotton field, bareheaded in the hot sun, carrying the hoe over his shoulder.

Jesse was not certain, but he felt he might be able to save

his crop. The wire grass could not stand up under a sharp hoe blade, and he could go back and file his hoe with the rat-tailed file whenever it wanted sharpening.

(First published in *Kneel to the Rising Sun*)

The End of Christy Tucker

CHRISTY TUCKER rode into the plantation town on muleback late in the afternoon, whistling all the way. He had been hewing new pickets for the fence around his house all morning, and he was feeling good for having got so much done. He did not have a chance to go to the plantation town very often, and when he could go he did not lose any time in getting there.

He tied up the mule at the racks behind the row of stores, and the first thing he noticed was the way the other Negroes out there did not seem anxious to speak to him. Christy had been on friendly terms with all the colored people on the plantation ever since he and his wife had moved there three months before, and he could not understand why they pretended not to see him.

He walked slowly down the road toward the plantation office wondering why nobody spoke to him.

After he had gone a little farther, he met Froggy Miller. He caught Froggy by the arm before Froggy could dodge him.

"What's the matter with you folks today?" he said. Froggy Miller lived only a mile from his house in a straight line across the cotton field, and he knew Froggy better than anyone else on the plantation. "What's the matter, anyway, Froggy?"

Froggy, a big six-foot Negro with close-cropped hair, moved away.

He grabbed Froggy by the arm and shook him.

"Now look here!" Christy said, getting worried. "Why do you and everybody else act so strange?"

"Mr. Lee Crossman sent for you, didn't he?" Froggy said.

"Sure, he sent for me," Christy said. "I reckon he wants to talk to me about the farming. But what's that got to do with—"

Before he could finish, Froggy had pulled away from him and walked hurriedly up the road.

Without wasting any more time, Christy ran toward the plantation office to find out what the trouble was.

The plantation bookkeeper, Hendricks, and Lee Crossman's younger brother, Morgan, were sitting in the front office with their feet on the window sill when he ran inside. Hendricks got up when he saw Christy and went through the door into the back room. While the bookkeeper was in the other room, Morgan Crossman stared sullenly at the Negro.

"Come here, you," Hendricks said, coming through the door.

Christy turned around and saw Lee Crossman, the owner and boss of the plantation, standing in the doorway.

"Yes, sir," Christy said.

Lee Crossman was dressed in heavy gray riding breeches and tan shirt, and he wore black boots that laced to his knees. He stood aside while Christy walked into the back room, and closed the door on the outside. Christy walked to the middle of the room and stood there waiting for Lee Crossman.

Christy had moved to the Crossman plantation the first of the year, about three months before. It was the first time he had ever been in Georgia, and he had grown to like it better than Alabama, where he had always lived. He and his wife had decided to come to Georgia because they had heard that the land there was better for sharecropping cotton. Christy said he could not be satisfied merely making a living; he wanted to get ahead in life.

Lee Crossman still had not come, and Christy sat down in one of the chairs. He had no more than seated himself when the door opened. He jumped to his feet.

"Howdy, Mr. Lee," he said, smiling. "I've had a good chance to look at the land, and I'd like to be furnished with another mule and a gang plow. I figure I can raise twice as much cotton on that kind of land with a gang plow, because it's about the best I ever saw. There's not a rock or stump on it, and it's as clear of bushes as the palm of my hand. I haven't even found a gully anywhere on it. If you'll furnish me with another mule and a gang plow, I'll raise more cotton for you than any two sharecroppers on your plantation."

Lee Crossman listened until he had finished, and then he slammed the door shut and strode across the room.

"I sent for you, nigger," he said. "You didn't send for me, did you?"

"That's right, Mr. Lee," he said. "You sent for me."

"Then keep your black face shut until I tell you to open it."

"Yes, sir, Mr. Lee," Christry said, backing across the room until he found himself against the wall. Lee Crossman sat down in a chair and glared at him. "Yes, sir, Mr. Lee," Christy said again.

"You're one of these biggity niggers, ain't you?" Lee said.

"Where'd you come from, anyway? You ain't a Georgia nigger, are you?"

"No, sir, Mr. Lee," Christy said, shaking his head. "I was born and raised in Alabama."

"Didn't they teach you any better than this in Alabama?"

"Yes, sir, Mr. Lee."

"Then why did you come over here to Georgia and start acting so biggity?"

"I don't know, Mr. Lee."

Christy wiped his face with the palm of his hand and wondered what Lee Crossman was angry with him about. He began to understand why the other Negroes had gone out of their way to keep from talking to him. They knew he had been sent for, and that meant he had done something to displease Lee Crossman. They did not wish to be seen talking to anyone who was in disfavor with the plantation owner and boss.

"Have you got a radio?" Lee asked.

"Yes, sir."

"Where'd you get it?"

"I bought it on time."

"Where'd you get the money to pay on it?"

"I had a little, and my wife raises a few chickens."

"Why didn't you buy it at the plantation store?"

"I made a better bargain at the other place. I got it a little cheaper."

"Niggers who live on my plantation buy what they need at my plantation store," Lee said.

"I didn't want to go into debt to you, Mr. Lee," Christy said. "I wanted to come out ahead when the accounts are settled at the end of the year."

Lee Crossman leaned back in the chair, crossed his legs, and took out his pocketknife. He began cleaning his fingernails.

There was silence in the room for several minutes. Christy leaned against the wall.

"Stand up straight, nigger!" Lee shouted at him.

"Yes, sir," Christy said, jumping erect.

"Did you split up some of my wood to hew pickets for the fence around the house where you live?"

"Yes, sir, Mr. Lee."

"Why didn't you ask me if I wanted you to do it?"

"I figured the fence needed some new pickets to take the place of some that had rotted, and because I'm living in the house I went ahead and did it."

"You act mighty big, don't you?" Lee said. "You act like you own my house and land, don't you? You act like you think you're as good as a white man, don't you?"

"No sir, Mr. Lee," Christy protested. "I don't try to act any of those ways. I just naturally like to hustle and get things done, that's all. I just can't be satisfied unless I'm fixing a fence or cutting wood or picking cotton, or something. I just naturally like to get things done."

"Do you know what we do with biggity niggers like you in Georgia?"

"No, sir."

"We teach them to mind their own business and stay in their place."

Lee Crossman got up and crossed the room to the closet. He jerked the door open and reached inside. When he turned around, he was holding a long leather strap studded with heavy brass brads. He came back across the room, slapping the strap around his boot tops.

"Who told your wife she could raise chickens on my plantation?" he said to Christy.

"Nobody told her, Mr. Lee," Christy said. "We didn't think you'd mind. There's plenty of yard around the house for them, and I built a little hen house."

"Stop arguing with me, nigger!"

"Yes, sir."

"I don't want chickens scratching up crops on this plantation."

"Yes, sir," Christy said.

"Where did you get money to pay on a radio?"

"I snared a few rabbits and skinned them, and then I sold their hides for a little money."

"I don't want no rabbits touched on my plantation," Lee said.

He shook out the heavy strap and cracked it against his boots.

"Why haven't you got anything down on the books in the plantation store?" Lee asked.

"I just don't like to go into debt," Christy said. "I want to come out ahead when the accounts are settled at the end of the year."

"That's my business whether you come out owing or owed at the end of the year," Lee said.

He pointed to a crack in the floor.

"Take off that shirt and drop your pants and get down on your knees astraddle that crack," the white man said.

"What are you going to do to me, Mr. Lee?"

"I'll show you what I'm going to do," he replied. "Take off that shirt and pants and get down there like I told you."

"Mr. Lee, I can't let you beat me like that. No, sir, Mr. Lee. I can't let you do that to me. I just can't!"

"You black-skinned, back-talking coon, you!" Lee shouted, his face turning crimson with anger.

He struck Christy with the heavy, brass-studded strap. Christy backed out of reach, and when Lee struck him the second time, the Negro caught the strap and held on to it. Lee glared at him at first, and then he tried to jerk it out of his grip.

"Mr. Lee, I haven't done anything except catch a few rabbits and raise a few chickens and things like that," Christy protested. "I didn't mean any harm at all. I thought you'd be pleased if I put some new pickets in your fence."

"Shut your mouth and get that shirt and pants off like I told you," he said, angrier than ever. "And turn that strap loose before I blast it loose from you."

Christy stayed where he was and held on to the strap with all his might. Lee was so angry he could not speak after that. He ran to the closet and got his pistol. He swung around and fired it at Christy three times. Christy released his grip on the strap and sank to the floor.

Lee's brother, Morgan, and the bookkeeper, Hendricks, came running into the back room.

"What happened, Lee?" his brother asked, seeing Christy Tucker lying on the floor.

"That nigger threatened me," Lee said, blowing hard. He walked to the closet and tossed the pistol on the shelf.

"You and Hendricks heard him threaten to kill me. I had to shoot him down to protect my own life."

They left the back room and went into the front office. Several clerks from the plantation store ran in and wanted to know what all the shooting was about.

"Just a biggity nigger," Lee said, washing his hands at the sink. "He was that Alabama nigger that came over here two or three months ago. I sent for him this morning to ask him what he meant by putting new pickets in the fence around his house without asking me first. When I got him in here, he threatened me. He was a bad nigger."

The clerks went back to the plantation store, and Hendricks opened up his books and went to work on the accounts.

"Open up the back door," Lee told his brother, "and let those niggers out in the back see what happens when one of them gets as biggity as that coon from Alabama got."

His brother opened the back door. When he looked outside into the road, there was not a Negro in sight. The only living thing out there was the mule on which Christy Tucker had ridden to town.

(First published in *The Nation*)

Rachel

EVERY evening she came down through the darkness of the alley, emerging in the bright light of the street like the sudden appearance of a frightened child far from home. I knew that she had never reached the end of the alley before eight o'clock, and yet there were evenings when I ran there two hours early and waited beside the large green and red hydrant until she came. During all those months I had known her, she had been late only two or three times, and then it was only ten or fifteen minutes past eight when she came.

Rachel had never told me where she lived, and she would never let me walk home with her. Where the alley began, at the hydrant, was the door through which she came at eight, and the door which closed behind her at ten. When I had begged her to let me walk with her, she always pleaded with me, saying that her father did not allow her to be with boys and that if he should see us together he would either beat her unmercifully or make her leave home. For that reason I kept the promise I had given, and I never went any farther than the entrance to the alley with her.

"I'll always come down to see you in the evening, Frank," she said; and added hastily, "as long as you wish me to come. But you must remember your promise never to try to find where I live, or to walk home with me."

I promised again and again.

"Perhaps some day you can come to see me," she whispered, touching my arm, "but not now. You must never go beyond the hydrant until I tell you that you may."

Rachel had told me that almost every time I saw her, as if she wished to impress upon me the realization of some sort of danger that lay in the darkness of the alley. I knew there was no physical danger, because around the corner was our house and I was as familiar with the neighborhood as anyone else. And besides, during the day I usually walked through the alley to our back gate on my way home, because it was a short cut when I was late for supper. But after dark the alley was Rachel's, and I had never gone home that way at night for fear of what I might have seen or heard of her. I had promised her from the beginning that I would never follow her to find out where she lived, and that I would never at-

228

tempt to discover her real name. The promise I had made
was kept until the end.

I knew Rachel and her family were poor, because she had
been wearing the same dress for nearly a year. It was a worn
and fragile thing of faded blue cotton. I had never seen it
soiled, and I knew she washed it every day. It had been mend-
ed time after time, carefully and neatly, and each evening
when I saw her, I was worried because I knew that the weave
of the cloth would not stand much more wear. I was constantly
afraid that almost any day the dress would fall into shreds, and
I dreaded for that time ever to come. I wished to offer to buy
her a dress with the few dollars I had saved in my bank, but I
was afraid to even suggest such a thing to her. I knew she
would not have allowed me to give her the money, and I did
not know what we would do when the dress became completely worn out. I was certain that it would mean the end of
my seeing her. It was only the constant attention that she
gave it and the care with which she laundered it each day
that could have kept the dress whole as long as it had been.

Once Rachel had worn a pair of black silk stockings. From
the first she had come each night to the brightly lighted street
in her white cotton stockings, and for a year she had worn no
other kind. Then one evening she had on a pair of black silk
ones.

The next evening I expected to see her wearing them again,
but when she came out of the alley, she was wearing the stockings of white cotton. I did not ask her about it, because I had
learned never to say anything that might hurt her feelings,
but I was never able to understand why she wore black silk
stockings just that one time. She may have borrowed them
from her mother or sister, and there were dozens of other
ways she could have got them, and yet none of the reasons
I could think of ever seemed entirely conclusive. If I had
asked her, perhaps she would have laughed, touched my arm
as she did when we were together, and told me. But I was
afraid to ask her. There were so many ways of making her
feel badly, and of hurting her.

Each evening when she came out of the black alley I met
her there, and together we walked down the brightly lighted
street to the corner where there was a drugstore. On the opposite corner there was a moving-picture theater. To one or the
other we went each evening. I should have liked to have taken
her to both the show and to the drugstore, but I was never
able to earn enough money for both in the same evening. The
twenty cents I received every day for delivering the afternoon
paper on a house-to-house route was not enough to buy ice
cream at the drugstore and seats at the picture show, too. We
had to take our choice between them.

When we stood on the corner across from the drugstore and across from the theater, we could never decide at first whether to see the show or to eat ice cream. The good times we had there on the corner were just as enjoyable, to me, as anything else we did. Rachel would always try to make me tell her which I would rather do before she would commit herself. And of course I wished to do that which would please her the most.

"I'm not going a step in either direction until you tell me which you would rather do," I would say to her. "It doesn't matter to me, because being with you is everything I want."

"I'll tell you what let's do, Frank," she said, touching my arm, and pretending not to be serious; "you go to the drugstore, and I'll go to the movies."

That was Rachel's way of telling me which she preferred, although I didn't believe she ever suspected that I knew. But when she suggested that I go to the movies while she went to the drugstore, I knew it to mean that she would much rather have a dish of ice cream that evening. The enjoyment of the show lasted for nearly two hours, while the ice cream could never be prolonged for more than half an hour, so all but two or three evenings a week we went to the theater across the street.

There was where I always wished to go, because in the semi-darkness we sat close together and I held her hand. And if the house was not filled, we always found two seats near the rear, in one of the two corners, and there I kissed her when we were sure no one was looking at us.

After the show was over, we went out into the bright street and walked slowly towards the green and red hydrant in the middle of the block. There at the entrance to the alley we stopped awhile. If there were no other people in the street, I always put my arm around Rachel's waist while we walked slowly to the dark entrance. Neither of us spoke then, but I held her tighter to me, and she squeezed my fingers. When at last, after delaying as long as possible the time for her to go, we walked together a few steps into the darkness of the alley and stood in each other's arms, Rachel kissed me for the first time during the evening, and I kissed her for as long a time as I had wished to in the theater. Still not speaking, we drew apart, our fingers interwoven and warm.

When she was about to disappear into the darkness of the alley, I ran to her and caught her hands in mine.

"I love you, Rachel," I told her, squeezing her fingers tighter and tighter as she withdrew them.

"And I love you, too, Frank," she said, turning and running into the alley out of sight for another day.

After waiting awhile and listening until she had gone beyond hearing distance, I turned and walked slowly up the street towards home. Our house was only a block away: half a block to the corner, and another half block from there. When I had reached my room, I went to the window and stood there looking out into the night and listening for some sound of her. My window faced the alley behind the house, and the street lights cast a dim glow over the house tops, but I could never see down into the darkness of the alley. After waiting at the window for an hour or more I undressed and went to bed. Many times I thought I heard the sound of her voice somewhere in the darkness, but after I had sprung from bed and had listened intently at the window for a long time I knew it was some other sound I had heard.

Near the end of summer I received five dollars as a birthday present from an aunt. As soon as I got it, I began making plans for Rachel and me. I wanted to surprise her that evening with the money, and then to take her downtown on a streetcar. First we would go to a restaurant, and afterward to one of the large theaters. We had never been downtown together, and it was the first time I had ever had more than fifty cents at one time. That afternoon as soon as I could deliver all the papers on my route, I ran home and began thinking about the plans I had made for the evening.

Just before dark I went downstairs from my room to wait on the front porch for the time to come when I could meet Rachel. I sat on the porch steps, not even remembering to tell my mother that I was going downtown. She had never allowed me to go that far away from the house without my first telling her where I was going, with whom, and at what time I would come back.

I had been sitting on the porch steps for nearly an hour when my older sister came to the door and called me.

"We have a job for you, Frank," Nancy said. "Mother wants you to come to the kitchen before you leave the house. Now, don't forget and go away."

I told her I would come right away. I was thinking then how much the surprise would mean to Rachel, and I did forget about the job waiting for me in the kitchen for nearly half an hour. It was then almost time for me to meet Rachel at the hydrant, and I jumped up and ran to the kitchen to finish the task as quickly as I could.

When I reached the kitchen, Nancy handed me a small round box and told me to open it and sprinkle the powder in the garbage can. I had heard my mother talking about the way rats were getting into the garbage, so I went down to the back gate with the box without stopping to talk about it. As soon as I had sprinkled the powder on the refuse, I ran back into the house, found my cap, and ran down the street. I was angry with my sister for causing me to be late in meeting Rachel, even though the fault was my own for not having done the task sooner. I was certain, though, that Rachel would wait for me, even if I was a few minutes late in getting to the hydrant. I could not believe that she would come to the hydrant and leave immediately.

I had gone a dozen yards or more when I heard my mother calling me. I stopped unsteadily in my tracks.

"I'm going to the movies," I told her. "I'll be back soon."

"All right, Frank," she said. "I was afraid you were going downtown or somewhere like that. Come home as soon as you can."

I ran a few steps and stopped. I was so afraid that she would make me stay at home if I told her that I was going downtown that I did not know what to do. I had never told her a lie, and I could not make myself start then. I looked back, and she was standing on the steps looking at me.

"Mother, I am going downtown," I pleaded, "but I'll be back early."

Before she could call me again, I ran with all my might down the street, around the corner, and raced to the hydrant at the alley. Rachel was not within sight until I had reached it and had stood for a moment panting and blowing with excitement and exertion.

She was there though, waiting for me beside the fence, and she said she had just got there the second before. After we had started towards the corner where the drugstore was, I took the money from my watch pocket and showed it to her. She was even more excited than I had been when I first saw it. After she had looked at it awhile, and had felt it in the palm of her hand, I told her what I had planned for us to do that evening.

We heard a streetcar coming, and we ran to the corner just in time to get aboard. The ride downtown was too fast, even though it took us nearly half an hour to get there. We got off near the theaters.

First I had planned for us to go to a small restaurant, and later to a show. Just as we were passing a drugstore Rachel touched my arm.

"Please, Frank," she said, "I'm awfully thirsty. Won't you take me into that drugstore and get me a glass of water?"

"If you must have a drink right away, I will," I said, "but can't you wait a minute more? There's a restaurant a few doors below here, and we can get a glass of water there while we're waiting for our supper to be served. If we lose much time we won't have the chance to see a complete show."

"I'm afraid I can't wait, Frank," she said, clutching my arm. "Please—please get me a glass of water. Quick!"

We went into the drugstore and stood in front of the soda

fountain. I asked the clerk for a glass of water. Rachel waited close beside me, clutching my arm tighter and tighter.

In front of us, against the wall, there was a large mirror. I could see ourselves plainly, but there was something about our reflection, especially Rachel's, that I had never been aware of before. It's true that we had never stood before a mirror until then, but I saw there something that had escaped me for a whole year. Rachel's beauty was revealed in a way that only a large mirror can show. The curve of her cheeks and lips was beautiful as ever, and the symmetrical loveliness of her neck and arms was the same beauty I had worshiped hundreds of times before; but now for the first time I saw in the mirror before us a new and unrevealed charm. I strained my eyes once more against the surface of the mirror, and once again I saw there the new sinuous beauty of her body.

"Quick, Frank!" Rachel cried, clutching me desperately. "Water—please!"

I called to the clerk again, not looking, because I was afraid to take my eyes from the new beauty I saw in the mirror. I had never before seen such beauty in a girl. There was some mysterious reflection of light and shadow that had revealed the true loveliness of Rachel. The mirror had revealed in one short moment, like a flash of lightning in a dark room, the sinuous charm that had lain undiscovered and unseen during all the time I had known her. It was almost unbelievable that a woman, that Rachel, could possess such a new, and perhaps unique, beauty. My head reeled when the sensation enveloped me.

She clutched my arm again, breaking as one would a mirror, the reflection of my thoughts. The clerk had filled the glass with water and was handing it to her, but before he could place it in her hands, she had reached for it and had jerked it away from him. He looked as surprised as I was. Rachel had never before acted like that. Everything she did had always been perfect.

She grasped the glass as if she were squeezing it, and she swallowed the water in one gulp. Then she thrust the glass back towards the clerk, holding her throat with one hand, and screamed for more water. Before he could refill the glass, she had screamed again, even louder than before. People passing the door paused, and ran inside to see what was taking place. Others in the store ran up to us and stared at Rachel.

"What's the matter, Rachel?" I begged her, catching her wrists and shaking her. "Rachel, what's the matter?"

Rachel turned and looked at me. Her eyes were turned almost upside down, and her lips were swollen and dark. The expression on her face was horrible to see.

A prescription clerk came running towards us. He looked

quickly at Rachel, and ran back to the rear of the store. By that time she had fallen forward against the marble fountain, and I caught her and held her to keep her from falling to the floor.

The prescription clerk again came running towards us, bringing a glass filled with a kind of milk-white fluid. He placed the glass to Rachel's lips, and forced the liquid down her throat.

"I'm afraid it's too late," he said. "If we had known ten minutes sooner we could have saved her."

"Too late?" I asked him. "Too late for what? What's the matter with her?"

"She's poisoned. It looks like rat poison to me. It's probably that, though it may be some other kind."

I could not believe anything that was being said, nor could I believe that what I saw was real.

Rachel did not respond to the antidote. She lay still in my arms, and her face was becoming more contorted and darker each moment.

"Quick! Back here!" the clerk said, shaking me.

Together we lifted her and ran with her to the rear of the store. The clerk had reached for a stomach pump, and was inserting the tube in her throat. Just as he was about to get the pump started, a physician ran between us and quickly examined Rachel. He stood up a moment later, motioning the other man and myself aside.

"It's too late now," he said. "We might have been able to save her half an hour ago, but there is no heart action now, and breathing has stopped. She must have taken a whole box of poison—rat poison, I guess. It has already reached her heart and blood."

The clerk inserted the tube again and began working with the pump. The physician stood beside us all the time, giving instructions, but shaking his head. We forced stimulants down her throat and attempted to revive her by means of artificial respiration. During all of that time the doctor behind us was saying: "No, no. It's of no use. She's too far gone now. She'll never live again. She has enough rat poison in her system to kill ten men."

Some time later the ambulance came and took her away. I did not know where she was taken, and I did not try to find out. I sat in the little brown-paneled room surrounded by white-labeled bottles, looking at the prescription clerk who had tried so hard to save her. When at last I got up to go, the drugstore was empty save for one clerk who looked at me disinterestedly. Outside in the street there was no one except a few taxi drivers who never looked my way.

In a daze I started home through the deserted streets. The

way was lonely, and tears blinded my eyes and I could not see the streets I walked on. I could not see the lights and shadows of the streets, but I could see with a painful clarity the picture of Rachel, in a huge mirror, bending over our garbage can, while the reflection of her beauty burned in my brain and in my heart.

(First published in *Clay*)

The Midwinter Guest

IT was the first time in his whole life that Orland Trask had done such a thing. Even Orland's wife could not say afterward what had got into Orland to cause him to tell the strange man from the eastern country that he might remain in the house and stay for the night. And it was the last time. Both Orland and Emma knew better than to do a thing like that again.

The stranger from the eastern country knocked on the door that evening while Orland and his wife were eating supper. Orland heard him knock at the beginning, but he did not make an effort to get up from the table to answer a knocking on his door at suppertime.

"It's nobody I want dealings with," Orland said to his wife. "A man who would come knocking on a neighbor's door at mealtime hadn't ought to be listened to. Finns and Swedes are the only people I ever heard of who didn't have better sense."

"Maybe some of the Morrises are sick, Orland," Emma said. "I'll go see."

"Stay sat in your seat, woman. Even those Morrises have got better sense than to take to illness at mealtime."

The knocking became louder. The man out there was pounding on the storm door with a heavy oak walking stick.

Orland's wife turned and looked out the window behind her. It was still snowing. The wind had died down with nightfall and the flakes were floating lightly against the panes.

The stranger at the door was impatient. He opened the storm door and banged on the panels of the house door and against the clapboards with the knotted end of his walking stick, and then he turned and beat against the door with the heels of his studded boots. He was making a lot of noise out there for a stranger, more noise than Orland had ever heard at his door.

"I'll go see," Emma said again, rising from her chair at the other end of the table.

"You stay sat in your seat, woman," Orland told her.

Orland's wife sank back into the chair, but barely had she settled herself when suddenly the door burst open with a gust of snow and icy wind, and the strange man stood there glaring at them. He was wearing black leather breeches and a red and green mackinaw and a brown fur cap pulled so far down over his ears that only his eyes and nose were showing. Snow had clung to his eyelashes and had frozen in long thin icicles that reached almost to his mouth. He stomped and blew, knocking the snow from his boots and shaking it from his cap and mackinaw. The heavy oak walking stick rapped as loudly as ever against the door sill. The man had not entered the house, but the door was open and the frosty air blew inside.

Orland's back was turned to the door and the first that he knew of the man bursting in was when the icy blast of snow and wind struck him. His wife, Emma, had seen everything from the beginning, but she was afraid to say or to do anything until Orland turned around. She knew that a man who would burst open a door would not wait to be asked into the room.

"Holy Mother," the stranger who stood in the doorway muttered, "the bones of my body are stiff as ice."

He came into the room then, his mittens under his arm, and his hands full of snow that he had scooped from the doorstep. He shut the door with the heel of his boot and walked around the table at which Orland was sitting, and rubbed his hands with the new snow.

Orland had not said a word. He sat glaring at the heavily clothed man who had entered his house unbidden.

Emma asked the strange man, guardedly, if his hands were frozen. While she waited for him to answer, she glanced again at Orland.

"Holy Mother," the stranger said again, "the bones of my body are stiff as ice."

He continued to rub the new snow over the backs of his hands and around his fingers. He still did not go near the heater in the corner.

"My name is Phelps," he said, "and I come from the eastern country of Maine. Down there the townsmen take in cold men from the frost at night."

"Well," Orland said, pushing back his chair from the table, "the townsmen in this part of the state have got the sense to stay indoors when they have no good business out in a frosty night."

Emma went to the door and brought back a bowl of new snow. She placed the bowl on the carpet in front of the stranger who had said his name was Phelps. He began to unlace his boots while Emma got ready to take away the supper dishes.

"Freeze your toes, too?" Orland said. "Any man who would walk out and freeze his hands and feet ought to have them drop off with frostbite."

Phelps removed his boots and socks and began rubbing his toes with the new snow.

"Am a poor man," Phelps said, "and I'm not a house owner. My brother wrote me a letter to come over to New Hampshire and help him peel pulpwood. Started out walking, and I've got the high mountains yet to cross. Guess you will take me in and put me up for the night."

Orland filled his pipe and struck a match before he answered. He then waited until Emma had gone into the kitchen again.

"The country would be a heap better off without fools like you walking through the snow and frost to New Hampshire in dead of winter, and it's my duty to turn you out and let the frost finish its job of freezing you. That's what I ought to do to a man who would come into a neighbor's house without asking. The country has got too many like you in it now. But my wife would take on if I was to turn you out, so I'll have to let you stay for the night. Will give you warning, though; the next time your brother writes you to come over to New Hampshire to help him peel pulpwood, it had better be before winter sets in. You won't get aid here again. Won't stand to have strangers coming into my house unbidden."

Phelps took his feet out of the new snow and put them on the sheet of newspaper Orland's wife had spread for him. He made no effort to move or to thank Orland for permitting him to stay for the night. He just sat and stared at the snow falling against the window. He was an old man, much older than Orland. He looked to be at least eighty years old. His hair was almost white, but his body was firm and muscular. If he had been less than six feet tall, he would have appeared to be overweight.

Presently Emma came back into the room and carried out the bowl of melting snow and the damp newspaper, and then she handed the old man a clean bath towel. He dried his hands and feet and put his socks and boots on again.

"Show me the place to sleep, and good night," he said wearily.

"Guess you will want the use of the spare chamber," Orland said, scowling at the old man. "Well, you're going to get it. Could give you some blankets and put you on the carpet, but I'm not. Am giving you the use of the spare chamber. My wife will fix you a plate of breakfast in the morning, if you are in here on time. Nobody eats a breakfast in my house after six-thirty."

Emma lit a lamp and showed the old man to the spare chamber. When she returned, Orland had begun reading the paper and he had nothing to say to her.

Just before he got up to go to bed, Orland called his wife. "Give that man who said his name was Phelps a helping of beans and potatoes for breakfast," he said, "but don't give him but one plateful. Don't want to be the cause of prolonging the lives of people who walk through the snow and frost to New Hampshire in dead of winter."

Orland went to bed then, leaving Emma to clean the room and to set the chairs against the wall. He was asleep long before she had finished her work.

When Orland got up and lit the lamp the next morning at five-thirty, he listened for several minutes before calling Emma. He went to the wall that separated their room from the spare chamber and listened for a sound of the old man. The only sound that he could hear anywhere in the house was the breathing of Emma.

After calling his wife, Orland went to the kitchen range and opened the drafts and shook down the ashes. The firebox was ablaze in a minute or two, and he went to the next room and replenished the fire in the heater. Outside, it had stopped snowing during the night, and there were deep drifts of new snow.

Breakfast was ready at six-thirty, and Emma set the dishes aside on the range to wait until the old man came into the next room. She knew that Orland would call for his breakfast at almost any minute, but she delayed placing it on the table as long as she could.

"It's time for breakfast, Emma," Orland said. "Why haven't you got it ready?"

"Am putting it on the table right away," she said. "Maybe you had best go call Mr. Phelps while I'm doing it."

"Will be damned if I go call him," Orland said. "Told the old fool last evening what time breakfast was ready, and if he doesn't get up when it's ready, then I'm not going to wear out my shoes running to call him. Sit down and let's eat, Emma."

Emma sat down without a word.

After they had finished, Orland filled his pipe. He took a match from his coat pocket, but he waited a minute or longer before striking it.

"Clear away the dishes, Emma," he said.

Orland's wife carried out the dishes and plates to the kitchen. She placed the dish of beans on the range to keep them warm a while longer.

When she came back into the room for the rest of the tableware, Orland motioned to her to listen to him. "That old fool

from the eastern country and going to New Hampshire to help
his brother peel pulpwood had better be setting out toward the
high mountains. He's already missed the breakfast we had for
him. Will give him another ten minutes, and if he's not out of
the house by then, I'll throw him out, leather breeches and
all."

Emma went back into the kitchen to wash the dishes while
Orland filled the heater with maple chunks. One look at Orland's face was enough to frighten her out of the room.

Orland waited longer than ten minutes, and each second that
passed made him more angry. It was almost eight o'clock then,
an hour after breakfast was over. Orland got up and opened
the house door and the storm door. His face was aflame and
his motions were quick and jerky.

"Take care, woman," he said to Emma. "Take care!"

Emma came to the kitchen door and stood waiting to see
what Orland was going to do. She did not know what on
earth to do when Orland became as angry as he was then.

"Stand back, Emma," he said. "Stand back out of my way."

He began running around the room, looking as if he himself
did not know what he was likely to do that minute or the
next.

"Orland—" Emma said, standing in the kitchen door where
she could get out of his way if he should turn toward her.

"Take care, woman," he shouted at her. "Take care!"

.Orland was piling all the furniture in the corner of the
room beside the heater. He jerked up the carpet and the rugs,
pulled down the curtains, and carried all the old newspapers
and magazines to the fire. He was acting strangely, Emma
knew, but she did not know what on earth he was going to
do nor how to stop him. She had never seen Orland act like
that before in all her life, and she had lived with him for
almost fifty years.

"Orland—" she said again, glancing backward to the outside kitchen door to make certain of escape.

"Take care, woman," Orland said. "Take care!"

The furniture, rugs and carpet, and newspapers were blazing like a May grass fire within a few minutes. Smoke and
flame rose to the ceiling and flowed down the walls. Just when
Emma thought surely that Orland would be burned alive in
the fire, he ran out of the door and into the yard. She ran
screaming through the other door.

Emma's first thought when she saw the house burning, was
where would they live now. Then she remembered their other
house, the ten-room brick house down the road near the
village. Orland would not live in it because he had said that
the frame house would have to be worn out before they could
go to live in their brick house. He had been saying that for

twenty years, and during all of that time the fine brick house of ten rooms had been standing at waste. Now, at last, they could live in it.

There were no people passing along the road so early in the morning, but John White saw the smoke and flame from his house across the flats, and he came running over with a bucket of water. By the time he got there, all the water had splashed out of the bucket, and he set it down and looked at the fire.

"Am sorry to see that, Orland," he said.

"Save your pity for some who are in need of it," Orland said.

"Well, you've got good insurance on it, anyway," John said. "That will help a lot. When you collect the insurance money, you can go and live in your brick house in style and good comfort."

"Not going to collect the insurance," Orland said.

"You're not! Why won't you collect it?"

"Because I set fire to the house myself."

"Set fire to it yourself! Good God, Orland, you must have lost your mind and reason!"

"Had a blamed good reason for doing it."

John White walked away and turned around and came back where Orland was standing. He looked at Orland and then at the burning house and at Orland again.

Orland began telling John about the old man who had said his name was Phelps. He started at the beginning, when Phelps knocked on the storm door at mealtime. Then he told John about giving the old man permission to spend the night in the house after he had walked in unbidden.

"But I told him to get up in time for breakfast at six-thirty," Orland said. "I told him that, and the old fool heard me, too. When this morning came, I waited five, ten minutes for him to come and eat. He didn't even get up out of bed. He just stayed there, sleeping. Then I sat and waited a whole hour for him to get up, but he still just stayed in the spare chamber and slept. Am not the kind to allow the country to get cluttered up with men with no more sense than to start out walking to New Hampshire in dead of winter to peel pulpwood. That old fool said he started out from somewhere in the eastern country to walk over there through the snow and frost, and he hadn't even got as far as the high mountains. If I hadn't stopped him here, he'd have gone to some town and couldn't go further. Then he'd have been a burden on the state, because there's not a town down-Maine that would have claimed him, not even a town in the eastern country would have given him citizenship."

Suddenly, Emma screamed and fell down on her back. Orland ran to see what the matter with her was.

While he was away attending to Emma, John White saw something move behind one of the windows in the spare chamber. Before he could go closer to see what it was, the roof over that part of the building fell in, sending up a shower of sparks and fragments of black embers.

Orland came back beside John and stood watching the house as it sank lower and lower to the ground.

"Lived in this town a long time," John said, "almost any man's lifetime, I guess, but I never before saw a man burn his house down just for durn meanness. Don't guess you'd have done it, if it wasn't for the fact that you own a brick house that's a lot better shelter than this frame one was."

"That old fool said he was on his way to New Hampshire to help his brother peel—"

"Well, all I've got to say is that it looks to me like you could have asked him just once to get up out of bed and clear out of the house. Doesn't appear to me like a man ought to set fire to and burn down a good frame house just because a guest won't get out of bed in time for breakfast."

"Maybe I wouldn't have done it," Orland said, "but after I had thought all night about it, there wasn't any other way to treat him. Why, that old fool who said his name was Phelps opened my door and come in without my bidding, right when I was sitting at the table at mealtime. You don't guess I'd have gone and asked him to get out of bed, do you, after he had done a thing like that?"

"Guess you would have gone and told him to get up, all right, if you hadn't been trying for nearly twenty years to find a way to move into your brick house. This frame house was just about worn out, anyway, Orland. Wasn't no sense in burning him up just to get the house down and out of your way."

"Couldn't take the risk," Orland said. "This house has always been cussed mean. It was just hardheaded enough to have stood in good repair right up to the day I took ill and died."

(First published in *Story*)

Blue Boy

Two hours after dinner they were still sitting in the airtight, overheated parlor. A dull haze of tobacco smoke was packed in layers from the tabletop to the ceiling, and around the chairs hovered the smell of dried perspiration and stale perfume. The New Year's Day turkey-and-hog dinner had made the women droopy and dull-eyed; the men were stretched out in their chairs with their legs spread out and their heads thrown back, looking as if around each swollen belly a hundred feet of stuffed sausage-casing had been wound.

Grady Walters sat up, rubbed his red-veined face, and looked at his guests. After a while he went to the door and called for one of his Negro servants. He sent the Negro on the run for Blue Boy.

After he had closed the door tightly, Grady walked back towards his chair, looking at the drowsy men and women through the haze of blue tobacco smoke. It had been more than an hour since anyone had felt like saying anything.

"What time of day is it getting to be, Grady?" Rob Howard asked, rubbing first his eyes and then his belly.

"Time to have a little fun," Grady said.

Blue Boy came through the back door and shuffled down the hall to the parlor where the people were. He dragged his feet sideways over the floor, making a sound like soy beans being poured into a wooden barrel.

"We been waiting here all afternoon for you to come in here and show the folks some fun, Blue Boy," Grady said. "All my visitors are just itching to laugh. Reckon you can make them shake their sides, Blue Boy?"

Blue Boy grinned at the roomful of men and women. He dug his hands into his overall pockets and made some kind of unintelligible sound in his throat.

Rob Howard asked Grady what Blue Boy could do. Several of the women sat up and began rubbing powder into the pores of their skin.

The colored boy grinned some more, stretching his neck in a semi-circle.

"Blue Boy," Grady said, "show these white-folks how you caught that shoat the other day and bit him to death. Go on, Blue Boy! Let's see how you chewed that shoat to death with your teeth."

For several moments the boy's lips moved like eyelids a-flutter, and he made a dash for the door. Grady caught him by the shoulder and tossed him back into the center of the room.

"All right, Blue Boy," Grady shouted at him. "Do what I told you to do. Show the white-folks how you bit that pig to death."

Blue Boy made deeper sounds in his throat. What he said sounded more unintelligible than Gullah. Nobody but Grady could understand what he was trying to say.

"It don't make no difference if you ain't got a shoat here to kill," Grady answered him. "Go on and show the white-folks how you killed one the other day for me."

Blue Boy dropped on his hands and knees, making sounds as if he were trying to protest. Grady nudged him with his foot, prodding him on.

The Negro boy suddenly began to snarl and bite, acting as if he himself had been turned into a snarling, biting shoat. He grabbed into the air, throwing his arms around an imaginary young hog, and began to tear its throat with his sharp white teeth. The Howards and Hannafords crowded closer, trying to see the idiot go through the actions of a bloodthirsty maniac.

Down on the floor, Blue Boy's face was contorted and swollen. His eyes glistened, and his mouth drooled. He was doing all he could to please Grady Walters.

When he had finished, the Howards and Hannafords fell back, fanning their faces and wiping the backs of their hands with their handkerchiefs. Even Grady fanned his flushed face when Blue Boy stopped and rolled over on the floor exhausted.

"What else can he do, Grady?" the youngest of the Hannaford women asked.

"Anything I tell him to do," Grady said. "I've got Blue Boy trained. He does whatever I tell him."

They looked down at the small, thin, blue-skinned, seventeen-year-old Negro on the floor. His clothes were ragged, and his thick kinky hair was almost as long as a Negro woman's. He looked the same, except in size, as he did the day, twelve years before, when Grady brought him to the big house from one of the sharecroppers' cabins. Blue Boy had never become violent, and he obeyed every word of Grady's. Grady had taught him to do tricks as he would instruct a young puppy to roll over on his back when bidden. Blue Boy always obeyed, but sometimes he was not quick enough to suit Grady, and then Grady flew into him with the leather bellyband that hung on a nail on the back porch.

The Howards and Hannafords had sat down again, but the Negro boy still lay on the floor. Grady had not told him to get up.

"What's wrong with him, Grady?" Rob Howard asked.

"He ain't got a grain of sense," Grady said, laughing a little. "See how he grins all the time? A calf is born with more sense than he's got right now."

"Why don't you send him to the insane asylum, then?"

"What for?" Grady said. "He's more fun than a barrel of monkeys. I figure he's worth keeping just for the hell of it. If I sent him off to the asylum, I'd miss my good times with him. I wouldn't take a hundred dollars for Blue Boy."

"What else can he do?" Henry Hannaford asked.

"I'll show you," Grady said. "Here, Blue Boy, get up and do that monkeyshine dance for the white-folks. Show them what you can do with your feet."

Blue Boy got up, pushing himself erect with hands and feet. He stood grinning for a while at the men and women in a circle around him.

"Go on, Blue Boy, shake your feet for the white-folks," Grady told him, pointing at Blue Boy's feet. "Do the monkeyshine, Blue Boy."

The boy began to shuffle his shoes on the floor, barely raising them off the surface. Grady started tapping his feet, moving them faster and faster all the time. Blue Boy watched him, and after a while his own feet began going faster. He kept it up until he was dancing so fast his breath began to give out. His eyes were swelling, and it looked as if his balls would pop out of his head any moment. The arteries in his neck got larger and rounder.

"That nigger can do the monkeyshine better than any nigger I ever saw," Henry Hannaford said.

Blue Boy sank into a heap on the floor, the arteries in his neck pumping and swelling until some of the women in the room covered their faces to keep from seeing them.

It did not take Blue Boy long to get his wind back, but he still lay on the floor. Grady watched him until he thought he had recovered enough to stand up again.

"What else can your trained nigger do, Grady?" Rob Howard asked. "Looks like you would have learned him a heap of tricks in ten or twelve years' time."

"If it wasn't getting so late in the day, I'd tell him to do all he knows," Grady said. "I'll let him do one more, anyway."

Blue Boy had not moved from the floor.

"Get up, Blue Boy," Grady said. "Get up and stand on your feet."

Blue Boy got up grinning. His head turned once more on his rubbery neck, stretching in a semicircle around the room. He grinned at the white faces about him.

"Take out that blacksnake and whip it to a frazzle," Grady

told him. "Take it out, Blue Boy, and show the white-folks what you can do."

Blue Boy grinned, stretching his rubbery neck until it looked as if it would come loose from his body.

"What's he going to do now, Grady?" Rob Howard asked.

"You just wait and see, Rob," Grady said. "All right, Blue Boy, do like I said. Whip that blacksnake."

The youngest Hannaford woman giggled. Blue Boy turned and stared at her with his round white eyeballs. He grinned until Grady prodded him on.

"Now I reckon you folks know why I didn't send him off to the insane asylum," Grady said. "I have a heap more fun out of Blue Boy than I would with anything else you can think of. He can't hoe cotton, or pick it, and he hasn't even got enough sense to chop a piece of stovewood, but he makes up for all that by learning to do the tricks I teach him."

Once more Blue Boy's eyes began to pop in the sockets of his skull, and the arteries in his neck began to pump and swell. He dropped to his knees and his once rubbery neck was as rigid as a table leg. The grinning lines on his face had congealed into weltlike scars.

The Howards and Hannafords, who had come from five counties to eat Grady's New Year's Day turkey-and-hog dinner, gulped and wheezed at the sight of Blue Boy. He was beginning to droop like a wilting stalk of pigweed. Then he fell from his knees.

With his face pressed against the splintery floor, the grooves in his cheeks began to soften, and his grinning features glistened in the drying perspiration. His breathing became inaudible, and the swollen arteries in his neck were as rigid as taut-drawn ropes.

(First published in *Anvil*)

Evelyn and the Rest of Us

DURING the latter part of summer when the apples were ripening, Roy used to get a team of his father's horses and a surrey whenever he wanted them and all of us would go out to Quack's farm and bring back two or three sacks of apples. Then when we got back to town, we would go down into Johnny and Evelyn's cellar and make cider. The way we made it was like this: Johnny got one of his mother's sheets and we dumped a sack of apples on it and mashed them with bricks. When they were mashed just right, all of us helped to squeeze out the juice into glasses.

There was a boy whose name was Malcolm Streeter who lived down at the bottom of the hill near the West End school. When he began coming up and playing with us, he was about our size though several years older. Evelyn and Grace talked about him all the time but none of the rest of us liked him at all.

When the Streeter boy came up and drank our cider, we began playing tricks on him whenever we had a chance. Roy threw his cap up in a tree so he would have to climb after it before he could go home. He always got mad and said he was never coming up again, but he always came back in a day or two. We teased him a lot, too. We called him a sissy because he went to parties with girls. Evelyn and Grace were the only ones who liked the Streeter boy. He kept his hair parted all the time, and he gave them chewing gum. Both of them always took up for him whenever we talked about ducking him in the reservoir, or something like that.

"You mustn't throw him in the water," Grace and Evelyn begged us. "He doesn't mean any harm."

"I'd like to throw him overboard in the river and see what he would do," Quack said. "I'll bet he's a sissy just like a girl. I'll bet he couldn't swim out."

"He's just as good a swimmer as you are, Quack Hill!" Evelyn said. "I'll bet you can't swim across the river."

"Me! Can't swim across the river!" Quack said. "I can swim across the Atlantic Ocean without stopping even once."

Malcolm came up the hill the next afternoon while we were playing baseball in the lot. He stopped at the corner though, and sat on the stone wall around Johnny and Evelyn's house. We saw him sitting there, but nobody said anything to him.

Evelyn was in the house and Grace had gone downtown with her mother. If they had been there, they would have wanted him to play with us. We were glad they were not there, because the Streeter boy was a sissy.

Quack said something about stoning him; but the rest of us wanted to play baseball and we forgot all about him.

We played another hour and then went down to Johnny's for some of our apples in his cellar. Johnny and Evelyn kept the apples we brought from the country. When we wanted some to eat, or when we wanted to make cider, we went down into their cellar and got them.

We sat around in the cellar awhile eating apples and then we went upstairs to the kitchen for a drink of water. The cellar had two doors. One was at the side where the coal was brought in and the other was at the top of the steps and opened into the kitchen.

We went up the steps to the kitchen. Quack was in front and he opened the door. The rest of us were behind him. As soon as Quack opened the door all of us saw the same thing. The Streeter boy and Evelyn were lying together on the kitchen floor.

We had made a lot of noise down in the cellar, and a lot more when we went up the steps, but they had not heard us. We backed down the steps and closed the door without either of them hearing us or knowing that we had been there. We sat down in the cellar and ate some more apples. Quack said he wanted some cider, but nobody else wanted to make any. When we had eaten all the apples we could hold, we went out into the yard and sat on the stone wall in front of the house. Quack threw the baseball up in the air and caught it in his glove with one hand. Johnny socked his mitt with his fist and made a good pocket in it for the ball. Joe socked his glove and made a good pocket in it so he would not drop the ball when he ran after a fly in the outfield.

The Streeter boy came out of Johnny and Evelyn's house about half an hour before their mother came home from downtown. He jumped over the stone wall at the other side of the yard. He saw us sitting on the wall but he did not stop to say anything. He looked at us and put his thumb to his nose and wiggled his fingers at us. I don't know why we did not throw rocks at him. We usually did stone him when he left the hill and went home. Once we stoned him all the way down to the West End school until he ran up on his front porch. We had to stop throwing then because we would have broken a window. But this time none of us got up. Nobody felt like stoning him any more.

After he had gone Evelyn stayed in the house. Grace had come home with her mother from downtown but she was at home helping to cook supper. All of us sat on the wall until we had to go home. It was getting dark.

Nobody knew why it was, but we never played baseball or made any more cider after that. When school was over in the afternoon, Quack went downtown and stayed until suppertime; and Johnny got a job delivering the afternoon paper on a route in the East End. Grace and Evelyn went riding in the afternoon with boys from the high school and at night went to dances with them. Roy helped his father at the livery stable and drove the horses every afternoon for exercise. He stopped going to school the next year and began training horses. Soon after he stopped school he sold a pair of horses to a circus. He had trained them to stand on barrels and roll them around a ring while keeping time to music.

Nobody ever knew what happened to the Streeter boy. He went away when he was twenty years old and never came back. Evelyn said she didn't care if she never saw him again.

(First published in *American Earth*)

It Happened Like This

FOR five years before I put on long pants we lived just far enough away from the Mississippi River to be above flood level. Yet even there the creeks would back up after a big storm up the river and flood the pastures and corn lands. But as long as we lived there the Mississippi never touched us.

This was a queer country, all full of deep red gullies and low round hills with never a rock in sight. The earth was dark brown like delta silt, and it grew cornstalks so tall we had to break them down before the crop could be harvested. There were two or three Indian mounds near by, but nobody ever took the trouble to dig into them. People said they were filled with tomahawks and snake teeth and such things.

We lived on a small farm and had a Jersey cow, a big white horse, and a flock of Rhode Island Red chickens. My father got up early every morning and milked the cow and fed the horse six ears of corn before he took me to school. We drove the big white horse to the buggy and I was away until midafternoon. Then my father came for me and we went home. When we got there, we always had a hundred things to do. There was stovewood to chop, hay to throw down from the barn, water to pump, and dozens of other chores that had to be done every day.

We raised corn for the horse and chickens. For the cow we stripped the cornstalks of fodder and carried it to the barn in tight little bundles tied with binding twine. My father and I plowed the corn. The garden, though, was a different matter. We did not have the right kind of implements ourselves; so we hired Mr. Kates to cultivate the garden. Mr. Kates lived over the hill on his own farm. He had a daughter about my own age and her name was Lucy Kates.

Mr. Kates would come over and cultivate the garden and I would plow in the cornfield, while my father walked around to see if everything was going just right. Lucy came over too sometimes, with her father, and watched me plow the corn. She was a big girl with red hair and sunburned neck. She always wore low-necked dresses, and on a hot day in summer her breasts would be as red as fire. I said something to my father about Lucy getting sunburned.

"Why doesn't Lucy Kates cover up the front of herself as we do?" I asked him. "Why does she want to get sunburned like that?"

"She's getting to be a woman," my father said, "and women do all sorts of fool things."

I did not see that being a woman had anything to do with getting sunburned like a beet, but I never asked about it again.

It was shortly after this that our cow went dry and we were without milk for almost a year. My mother got mad at my father and did not speak to him for several months. The fact is, she did not speak to him until the cow began giving milk again. Just before she stopped speaking to him, she told him all she thought of him for letting our cow go dry. It was my father's fault. He let the cow go dry.

Going back just before this, Mr. Kates owned a fine bull. The bull was pastured on the creek land next to ours. There was a barbed-wire fence separating the two farms and an old gate that had once been used when both farms belonged to Mr. Kates' father. My father had bought a hundred-acre tract and built a house on it, and Mr. Kates nailed the gate up tight.

The dryness of our cow was due to trouble between my father and Mr. Kates. It was like this: Mr. Kates wanted twenty-five dollars for the services of his bull and my father thought fifteen dollars was about right. Mr. Kates stood firm at twenty-five.

Every time we saw Mr. Kates we asked him how much he wanted for the services of his bull, and it was always twenty-five and not a penny under. In the meantime, our cow was dry and getting fatter and lazier every day. My father missed his two glasses of milk every night for supper, but he did not say a word. My mother spoke only to me. When she had to have something of my father, I carried the message and returned the answer. They had never been like that before, and it was all because our cow went dry.

Finally my father could bear it no longer. It was bad enough not having two glasses of milk for supper, but my mother refusing to speak to him was too much. So, when he got the next opportunity with the cow, he went down to the pasture after supper one night and helped her into the next lot. He came home and went straight to bed. Early next morning he went down and helped the cow home and nailed the gate back as it had been before he took it down. The cow slept under a tree all that day and the following night.

Every morning when we left for school and when we returned in the afternoon, my father told my mother that we would have all the milk we wanted as soon as the cow got around to giving it. My mother looked at him as if to say she would not speak a word until the cow was actually giving milk twice every day.

Mr. Kates came over and plowed in the garden and asked my father if we wanted the services of his bull and my father shook his head. Mr. Kates went home wondering if he should let the bull's services go for fifteen dollars, but he could never make up his mind.

When our cow calved and Mr. Kates heard about it, he came over running. He knocked on our door and said he wanted to speak to my father. We went outside on the porch.

"I hear your cow calved the other night," he said to my father, still out of breath from running over.

"Yes, she calved the night before last, Mr. Kates," my father said proudly. "Do you want to take a look at them?"

Mr. Kates said he would like to see them. The truth was that was why he came over in such a hurry.

We got a lantern and went down to the barn and looked at the cow and her calf. Mr. Kates walked all around the calf, even climbing over the feed trough to get a better look at him. Mr. Kates was trying his best to trace the markings on the calf to see if they were anything like the ones on his bull.

"Well, Mr. Kates, what do you think of him?" my father asked, slowly wiping his face with a handkerchief.

"You got a pretty sturdy calf there, but it's a pity you didn't use my bull. My bull has got the best line of blood in this whole country, he has. Now, that calf won't make nothing but butcher-shop meat. Whereas, if you had bred to my bull you would have a calf worth a lot of money."

"I guess he's all right," my father answered, still holding the handkerchief over his face. "His sire is a prize-winning Jersey. He is one of the best bulls in this part of the country, they tell me."

Mr. Kates was trying his best to find out where our cow had been bred without coming straight out and asking point blank. He seemed to have a suspicion that his bull had been used, but he was not certain about it.

"Did you take your cow a pretty far piece to breed her?" he asked, looking straight at us.

"No, not far," my father answered. "Just a little distance away."

"Well, the next time you want to breed your cow you had better bring her to my bull. He's the best in the country."

We left the barn and walked up to the garden.

"I guess it wouldn't hurt your young vegetables any if I

was to come over tomorrow and run a cultivator over the rows lightly, would it?"

"You had better do that, Mr. Kates," my father replied. "The earth needs loosening after that shower we had yesterday."

"Well, I'll be going home now," Mr. Kates said, opening the gate. "And I'll be over the first thing in the morning to give those young vegetables a little cultivation."

"Just a minute, Mr. Kates," my father said, holding out several bills. "I owe you about this much for some work I haven't paid you for yet."

Mr. Kates took the money and counted it in the lantern light.

"There's fifteen dollars here—what's it for? I haven't got this much coming to me."

"Yes, you have. I've figured it out and—found that I still owe you that much for services I've never paid for."

My mother came out on the front porch and called us in to supper. My father and I washed up and sat down at the table. There was a big pitcher of milk at my father's place.

"Is Mr. Kates coming over to cultivate the garden tomorrow, Henry?" she asked my father.

"Yes, he'll be over early in the morning," said my father.

"Well, I'm glad of that," she said. "The potatoes need cultivation badly."

"Yes," my father said. "I'll tell him to plow the potatoes the first thing."

He poured himself two tumblers of milk and drank them down while he looked at me in a funny way over the rim of the glass.

(First published in *American Earth*)

Wild Flowers

THE mockingbird that had perched on the roof top all night, filling the clear cool air with its music, had flown away when the sun rose. There was silence as deep and mysterious as the flat sandy country that extended mile after mile in every direction. Yesterday's shadows on the white sand began to reassemble under the trees and around the fence posts, spreading on the ground the lacy foliage of the branches and the fuzzy slabs of the wooden fence.

The sun rose in leaps and bounds, jerking itself upward as though it were in a great hurry to rise above the tops of the pines so it could shine down upon the flat country from there to the Gulf.

Inside the house the bedroom was light and warm. Nellie had been awake ever since the mockingbird had left. She lay on her side with one arm under her head. Her other arm was around the head beside her on the pillow. Her eyelids fluttered. Then for a minute at a time they did not move at all. After that they fluttered again, seven or eight or nine times in quick succession. She waited as patiently as she could for Vern to wake up.

When Vern came home sometime late in the night, he did not wake her. She had stayed awake waiting for him as long as she could, but she had become so sleepy her eyes would not stay open until he came.

The dark head on the pillow beside hers looked tired and worn. Vern's forehead, even in sleep, was wrinkled a little over his nose. Around the corners of his eyes the skin was darker than it was anywhere else on his face. She reached over as carefully as possible and kissed the cheek closest to her. She wanted to put both arms around his head and draw him to her, and to kiss him time after time and hold his dark head tight against her face.

Again her eyelids fluttered uncontrollably.

"Vern," she whispered softly. "Vern."

Slowly his eyes opened, then quickly closed again.

"Vern, sweet," she murmured, her heart beating faster and faster.

Vern turned his face toward her, snuggling his head between her arm and breast, and moving until she could feel his breath on her neck.

"Oh, Vern," she said in a whisper.

He could feel her kisses on his eyes and cheek and forehead and mouth. He was comfortably awake by then. He found her with his hands and they drew themselves tightly together.

"What did he say, Vern?" she asked at last, unable to wait any longer. "What, Vern?"

He opened his eyes and looked at her, fully awake at last. She could read what he had to say on his face.

"When, Vern?" she said.

"Today," he said, closing his eyes and snuggling his head into her warmth once more.

Her lips trembled a little when he said it. She could not help herself.

"Where are we going to move to, Vern?" she asked like a little girl, looking closely to his lips for his answer.

He shook his head, pushing it tightly against her breasts and closing his eyes against her body.

They both lay still for a long time. The sun had warmed the room until it was almost like summer again, instead of early fall. Little waves of heat were beginning to rise from the weatherworn windowsill. There would be a little more of summer before winter came.

"Did you tell him—?" Nellie said. She stopped and looked down at Vern's face. "Did you tell him about me, Vern?"

"Yes."

"What did he say?"

Vern did not answer her. He pushed his head against her breast and held her tighter, as though he were struggling for food that would make his body strong when he got up and stood alone in the bare room.

"Didn't he say anything, Vern?"

"He just said he couldn't help it, or something like that. I don't remember what he said, but I know what he meant."

"Doesn't he care, Vern?"

"I guess he doesn't, Nellie."

Nellie stiffened. She trembled for a moment, but her body stiffened as though she had no control over it.

"But you care what happens to me, don't you, Vern?"

"Oh, God, yes!" he said. "That's all I do care about now. If anything happens—"

For a long time they lay in each other's arms, their minds stirring them wider and wider awake.

Nellie got up first. She was dressed and out of the room before Vern knew how quickly time had passed. He leaped out of bed, dressed, and hurried to the kitchen to make the fire in the cookstove. Nellie was already peeling the potatoes when he got it going.

They did not say much while they ate breakfast. They had to move, and move that day. There was nothing else they could do. The furniture did not belong to them, and they had so few clothes it would not be troublesome to carry them.

Nellie washed the dishes while Vern was getting their things ready. There was nothing to do after that except to tie up his overalls and shirts in a bundle, and Nellie's clothes in another, and to start out.

When they were ready to leave, Nellie stopped at the gate and looked back at the house. She did not mind leaving the place, even though it had been the only home she and Vern had ever had together. The house was so dilapidated that probably it would fall down in a few years more. The roof leaked, one side of the house had slipped off the foundation posts, and the porch sagged all the way to the ground in front.

Vern waited until she was ready to leave. When she turned

away from the house, there were tears in her eyes, but she never looked back at it again. After they had gone a mile, they had turned a bend in the road, and the pines hid the place from sight.

"Where are we going, Vern?" she said, looking at him through the tears.

"We'll just have to keep on until we find a place," he said. He knew that she knew as well as he did that in that country of pines and sand the farms and houses were sometimes ten or fifteen miles apart. "I don't know how far that will be."

While she trudged along the sandy road, she could smell the fragrance of the last summer flowers all around her. The weeds and scrub hid most of them from sight, but every chance she got she stopped a moment and looked along the side of the ditches for blossoms. Vern did not stop, and she always ran to catch up with him before she could find any.

In the middle of the afternoon they came to a creek where it was cool and shady. Vern found her a place to lie down and, before taking off her shoes to rest her feet, scraped a pile of dry pine needles for her to lie on and pulled an armful of moss from the trees to put under her head. The water he brought her tasted of the leaves and grasses in the creek, and it was cool and clear. She fell asleep as soon as she had drunk some.

It was late afternoon when Vern woke her up.

"You've been asleep two or three hours, Nellie," he said. "Do you think you could walk a little more before night?"

She sat up and put on her shoes and followed him to the road. She felt a dizziness as soon as she was on her feet. She did not want to say anything to Vern about it, because she did not want him to worry. Every step she took pained her then. It was almost unbearable at times, and she bit her lips and crushed her fingers in her fists, but she walked along behind him, keeping out of his sight so he would not know about it.

At sundown she stopped and sat down by the side of the road. She felt as though she would never be able to take another step again. The pains in her body had drawn the color from her face, and her limbs felt as though they were being pulled from her body. Before she knew it, she had fainted.

When she opened her eyes, Vern was kneeling beside her, fanning her with his hat. She looked up into his face and tried to smile.

"Why didn't you tell me, Nellie?" he said. "I didn't know you were so tired."

"I don't want to be tired," she said. "I just couldn't help it, I guess."

He looked at her for a while, fanning her all the time.

"Do you think it might happen before we get some place?" he asked anxiously. "What do you think, Nellie?"

Nellie closed her eyes and tried not to think. They had not passed a house or farm since they had left that morning. She did not know how much farther it was to a town, and she was afraid to think how far it might be even to the next house. It made her afraid to think about it.

"I thought you said it would be another two weeks . . . ?" Vern said. "Didn't you, Nellie?"

"I thought so," she said. "But it's going to be different now, walking like this all day."

His hat fell from his hand, and he looked all around in confusion. He did not know what to do, but he knew he had to do something for Nellie right away.

"I can't stand this," he said. "I've got to do something."

He picked her up and carried her across the road. He found a place for her to lie under a pine tree, and he put her down there. Then he untied their bundles and put some of their clothes under her head and some over her feet and legs.

The sun had set, and it was becoming dark. Vern did not know what to do next. He was afraid to leave her there all alone in the woods, but he knew he had to get help for her.

"Vern," she said, holding out her hand to touch him.

He grasped it in his, squeezing and stroking her fingers and wrist.

"What is it, Nellie?"

"I'm afraid it is going to happen . . . happen . . . happen right away," she said weakly, closing her eyes before she could finish.

He bent down and saw that her lips were bloodless and that her face was whiter than he had ever seen anyone's face. While he watched her, her body became tense and she bit her mouth to keep from screaming with pain.

Vern jumped up and ran to the road, looking up it and down it. The night had come down so quickly that he could not tell whether there were any fields or cleared ground there as an indication of somebody's living near. There were no signs of a house or people anywhere.

He ran back to Nellie.

"Are you all right?" he asked her.

"If I could go to sleep," she said, "I think I would be all right for a while."

He got down beside her and put his arms around her.

"If I thought you wouldn't be afraid, I'd go up the road until I found a house and get a car or something to carry you. I can't let you stay here all night on the ground."

"You might not get back—in time!" she cried frantically.

"I'd hurry as fast as I could," he said. "I'll run until I find somebody."

"If you'll come back in two or three hours," she said, "I'd

be able to stand it, I think. I couldn't stand it any longer than that alone, though."

He got up.

"I'm going," he said.

He ran up the road as fast as he could, remembering how he had pleaded to be allowed to stay in the house a little longer so Nellie would not have to go like that. The only answer he had got, even after he had explained about Nellie, was a shake of the head. There was no use in begging after that. He was being put out, and he could not do anything about it. He was certain there should have been some money due him for his crop that fall, even a few dollars, but he knew there was no use in trying to argue about that, either. He had gone home the night before, knowing they would have to leave. He stumbled, falling heavily, headlong, on the road.

When he picked himself up, he saw a light ahead. It was only a pale ray from a board window that had been closed tightly. But it was a house, and somebody lived in it. He ran toward it as fast as he could.

When he got to the place, a dog under the house barked, but he paid no attention to it. He ran up to the door and pounded on it with both fists.

"Let me in!" he yelled. "Open the door!"

Somebody inside shouted, and several chairs were knocked over. The dog ran out from under the house and began snapping at Vern's legs. He tried to kick the dog away, but the dog was just as determined as he was, and came back at him more savagely than before. Finally he pushed the door open, breaking a button lock.

Several Negroes were hiding in the room. He could see heads and feet under the bed and behind a trunk and under a table.

"Don't be scared of me," he said as calmly as he could. "I came for help. My wife's down the road, sick. I've got to get her into a house somewhere. She's lying on the ground."

The oldest man in the room, a gray-haired Negro who looked about fifty, crawled from under the bed.

"I'll help you, boss," he said. "I didn't know what you wanted when you came shouting and yelling like that. That's why I didn't open the door and let you in."

"Have you got a cart, or something like that?" Vern asked.

"I've got a one-horse cart," the man said. "George, you and Pete go hitch up the mule to the cart. Hurry and do it."

Two Negro boys came from their hiding places and ran out the back door.

"We'll need a mattress, or something like that to put her on," Vern said.

The Negro woman began stripping the covers from the bed,

and Vern picked up the mattress and carried it out the front door to the road. While he waited for the boys to drive the cart out, he walked up and down, trying to assure himself that Nellie would be all right.

When the cart was ready, they all got in and drove down the road as fast as the mule could go. It took less than half an hour for them to reach the grove where he had left Nellie, and by then he realized he had been gone three hours or longer.

Vern jumped to the ground, calling her. She did not answer He ran up the bank and fell on his knees beside her on the ground.

"Nellie!" he said, shaking her. "Wake up, Nellie! This is Vern, Nellie!"

He could not make her answer. Putting his face down against hers, he felt her cold cheek. He put his hands on her forehead, and that was cold, too. Then he found her wrists and held them in his fingers while he pressed his ear tightly against her breast.

The Negro man finally succeeded in pulling him backward. For a while he did not know where he was or what had happened. It seemed as if his mind had gone completely blank.

The Negro was trying to talk to him, but Vern could not hear a word he was saying. He did know that something had happened, and that Nellie's face and hands were cold, and that he could not feel her heart beat. He knew, but he could not make himself believe that it was really true.

He fell down on the ground, his face pressed against the pine needles, while his fingers dug into the soft damp earth. He could hear voices above him, and he could hear the words the voices said, but nothing had any meaning. Sometime—a long time away—he would ask about their baby—about Nellie's—about their baby. He knew it would be a long time before he could ask anything like that, though. It would be a long time before words would have any meaning in them again.

(First published in *Southways*)

Uncle Henry's Love Nest

AUNT JENNY was waiting at the front door, the letter crackling in her trembling hand, when Uncle Henry got off the street car at the corner that night and came up to the gate. The hinges squeaked a little more loudly than they ever had before when he came into the yard. Aunt Jenny stood stiffer and straighter than she ever had before in her life as she watched every step he took towards the house.

"Evening, Jenny," Uncle Henry said. He shut the gate, latched it, and came up the walk to the front door. "I didn't think I was late for supper. I'm a little earlier than usual, if anything."

Aunt Jenny still did not say anything. She stepped back a foot or two in order to give him plenty of room in which to pass by her.

The rest of us kept our seats around the living-room stove and tried not to make a sound. None of us knew what the letter was about, but it was easy to see that it had made Aunt Jenny madder than we had ever seen her about anything.

Uncle Henry came in, laid his hat and coat down, and stood by the stove, warming his hands. He nodded to all of us, and most of us said what we said every night: "Hello, Uncle Henry."

Aunt Jenny slammed the front door and strode through the room. When she got to the kitchen door, she stopped and told Uncle Henry she wanted to speak to him.

"I want to see you in the kitchen, Henry," she said, still stiff and straight. "Right away."

They went into the kitchen and shut the door. There was not much to hear for a while, and then we crept up to the door where we could listen. From the way it sounded to us, Uncle Henry must have sat down in the chair by the kitchen stove while Aunt Jenny stood up in front of him.

"Henry, I want you to tell me the meaning of this letter," she said in the same way she talked to us when we had done something she did not like.

"Well, what's the letter about, Jenny?" he said.

"Read it, and then you tell me what it's about."

There was not a thing to hear for a long time. After that, Uncle Henry's chair scraped a little, and then he laughed out loud. As soon as he did that, we could hear Aunt Jenny's foot tapping on the linoleum.

"What have you got to say for yourself, Henry?" she asked him.

"Nothing, Jenny. What is there to say about a thing like that? It's just a mistake. What else could it be? I haven't been on Centre Street in over a year."

"It's mighty funny, Henry, that this letter was addressed to you and a Mrs., when everybody in town knows where I live. I've never lived on Centre Street with you in my life."

From the way things sounded, Uncle Henry did not know what to say next. Aunt Jenny was doing all the talking, or most of it, anyway.

"No department store," she said, "is going to send out a letter thanking a customer for buying a suite of furniture unless somebody bought the furniture. And when the letter is addressed to you and a Mrs., and the post office forwards the letter addressed to Centre Street to my house here, it's time for you to do some explaining. How long has this been going on, Henry? Who are you living with, in your spare time, on Centre Street? What does she look like? How old is she?"

Uncle Henry did not say anything for a while. That made Aunt Jenny impatient.

"It would have been different if you had bought me a suite of furniture," she said evenly, "but the last stick of furniture you bought me was that dining-room table, and that was all of eight years ago."

"We'll call up the department store tomorrow and straighten this thing out," Uncle Henry said. "It's all a clerical mistake. All business offices make mistakes once in a while. It's a thing that can't be one hundred per cent perfect, Jenny."

"I wouldn't believe it if they did tell me it was a mistake," she said. "I've been thinking about the way you have been acting lately, anyway. It looks to me like you have been spending entirely too much time away from home, especially at night when you said you were going to a meeting."

"What in the name of common sense would I be doing with another—place?" he asked her. "I'm too old for a thing like that."

"That excuse won't do for me," Aunt Jenny said. "You will never be too old to go off and live with somebody younger and prettier than me, and leave me all alone."

It sounded for a minute as if Aunt Jenny was crying. We could hear Uncle Henry get up and take a few steps, and it sounded like he was trying to pat her on the back, or something.

"I've given you the best years of my life," she said, so low it was hard to hear what she was saying. "And all the thanks I get is this. I never thought you would leave me all alone in the world and go off to live with a younger and prettier woman, Henry."

"Now, Jenny," he told her, "you're just upset, that's all. Let's eat supper. You'll feel better then."

There was another long silence, and we thought it was time to get away from the door. Just when we got ready to leave, Aunt Jenny said something else.

"Is she a good cook, Henry?"

Uncle Henry laughed out loud. He laughed so loud he could be heard all over the house.

"Not as good as you are, Jenny," he said. "Not nearly as good."

We ran back to the stove and sat down and tried to act as if nothing had ever happened.

In another minute or two Aunt Jenny opened the kitchen door and began putting supper on the table. Uncle Henry helped her. We had never seen him do that before.

When it was time to go to the table, we all walked in and sat down without looking at either one of them. Uncle Henry started in talking like he always did, and we tried not to laugh at the funny things he said.

Every once in a while Aunt Jenny would tell one of us to pass Uncle Henry something, and she was getting up every few minutes to take him something herself. She had never done that before, especially when all of us were there to pass things.

"I have some good strawberry jam put away, Henry," she said. "I know you'd like some."

"No thanks, Jenny," he said. "I've had all I want now."

"But it's the best strawberry jam I ever made," she said. She got up and went to the closet and brought him a dishful. "I know you'll like it, Henry."

He ate a little and pushed the rest aside.

"I've got some fresh raisin bread, too," Aunt Jenny said. "I was saving it for Sunday, but you'd like it with strawberry jam, Henry."

Uncle Henry looked full to the limit. He pushed his plate back a little, shaking his head until she sat down again.

After we had all finished eating, Aunt Jenny nodded for us to leave the table while they drank their coffee. She sent us for the evening paper. When we brought it back from the porch, Aunt Jenny took it herself and got up and handed it to Uncle Henry. She even unfolded it and stood the paper up in front of his plate for him. We had never seen her do anything like that before, either.

Aunt Jenny almost choked when she saw the headline. She had to catch onto the chair to support herself for a moment. Uncle Henry, holding his coffee cup up to his mouth, dropped it, and coffee splashed over everything, and the cup rolled onto the floor.

The headline across the front page of the paper read: WIFE RAIDS LOVE NEST.

We did not know what was happening, but we thought we ought to go out into the yard and play awhile before dark.

(First published in the *Sunday Worker*)

Thunderstorm

SUNDAY afternoon came, and it was hotter than ever. If the heat kept up much longer, there would not be a blade of grass or stalk of corn alive in the whole country.

Will Tannet went to the front porch and looked at the thermometer. It was 105 degrees in the shade.

"People can't stand this much longer," he said.

He walked to the edge of the porch and looked at the sky. There was not a cloud to be seen anywhere.

His wife, Annie, came to the door behind him.

"Any sign of rain yet, Will?" she asked hopefully.

He shook his head.

When he turned around, she had gone.

"It's going to drive people crazy—or something," he said, looking up at the pale, faded blue sky. He unbuttoned his shirt another button, wiped his face, neck, and arms, and went to the barn to give the stock as much water as he could spare.

The girls, Nancy and Florabelle, were in their room changing their clothes. No matter how hot it got, they always had company on Sunday afternoons. Evans Waller had been there every Sunday afternoon for the past five or six months, to see Nancy, and two or three others generally came to call on Florabelle. Nancy and Evans were engaged, but they were keeping it a secret from Nancy's father until the drought was broken. They knew better than to say anything to Will until it rained.

Florabelle finished dressing and came out on the front porch first. She had on the white organdy dress that made her look cool even on the hottest day.

Her father came around the corner of the house, stopping when he saw her. He glared at her for a while before saying anything.

"What you up to now?" he said finally.

"Nothing, Pa," Florabelle said. "Nothing at all. Why?"

"I'd better not ever catch you at anything," he said. "I won't stand having no daughter of mine running wild. If I ever hear anything about you or Nancy, I'll thrash the hide off you both, even if you are nearly grown up."

"Why, Pa!" Florabelle said protestingly. "What on earth are you talking about? Now, you stop saying things like that about Nancy and me."

"Then remember what I told you," he said.

Will went into the house for his tobacco and came out again. He stopped at the corner of the house. "Tell your mother I'm going across the field to look at the spring," he said. He started off, but stopped after a few steps. "And don't you and your sister forget what I told you, either."

He went off out of sight around the house, going in the direction of the spring, a mile and a half away. The last time he was there, the spring looked as if it might run dry any day. It had never dried up before during the forty-six years he had lived on the farm; but it had never been so hot before since he could remember, and the land had never been without rain that long, either. It had not rained in that part of the country for seven weeks, and it was beginning to look as if it would never rain again. The earth was parched and cracked, the creek had dried up until there was only a dusty bed left to show for it, and the corn had curled up and dried a long time ago.

Half an hour after Will Tannet had left to look at the spring, Evans Waller drove up to the house in his car. Florabelle could see the dust being blown up in the road half a mile away before he got there, and she ran into the house. She was with Nancy in their room when Evans got out and came up on the porch.

"Hello, Nancy!" he called through the open door of the house. Then he sat down to wait. "Is Florabelle at home?"

Nobody answered him.

Mrs. Tannet came through the hall from the kitchen when she heard Evans's voice. She went into the room with her daughters.

"Now, Nancy," she began, "don't you and Evans drive off and leave Florabelle here by herself again. Every Sunday for the past two months you and Evans have gone for a ride and left her behind. She was here by herself last Sunday for almost two hours before any young man came to see her. I don't want you treating your sister like that again. You and Evans stay right here until Florabelle has company. Do you hear, Nancy?"

Nancy did not say anything. She went to the porch to see Evans.

"How about a ride?" he asked the first thing. "It's too hot to sit here."

"We'll have to wait until somebody comes to see Florabelle," Nancy said, sitting down on the bench beside him. "Is anybody coming that you know of? Is Harry coming today? Or Jimmy?"

Evans kicked the chair in front of him.

"Listen," he said, "why can't she look after her own self? Why do I have to—"

"Don't talk like that, Evans," Nancy pleaded. "You know how Mama is about Florabelle. It will only be—"

"I'm pretty tired of it, anyway," he said. "Every time I come here, I'm expected to sit around and wait for Florabelle to get a date. She can take care of herself, can't she? What's wrong with everybody here, anyhow?"

He got up and looked at the thermometer.

"God Almighty, it's a hundred and five here," he said, turning around and glaring at Nancy as though it was her fault it was so hot. "I'm going where it's cooler. Florabelle and you both can go to hell for all I care. I'm not going to sit here in this furnace and sweat myself to death. I have to sweat my hide off in the fields all week long, but I don't have to sit here and do it on Sunday, too. I'm leaving."

Evans got to the steps before Nancy caught him by the arm. He was about to jerk free of her when Florabelle came to the door.

"Hello, Evans," she said. "You look cooler than anybody I've seen all week."

"Hello," he said. He stood and glared at both of them for a long time. His gaze settled upon her bosom. "Hello," he said again.

He went back to the bench and sat down.

"Seen Jimmy Barker lately, Evans?" Florabelle said.

"No."

"Frank Littlefield?"

"No."

"Harry?"

"No."

Nancy jumped up and ran to the end of the porch.

"I'll bet that's Harry!" she said.

Florabelle smoothed out her dress and looked up the road. Evans got up and went down the steps to the yard.

"Come on, Nancy," he said. "Let's go. This is the hottest place in the world. Let's go somewhere and cool off."

He and Nancy got into his car and drove off, leaving Florabelle watching the cloud of dust being blown up by the car coming in the opposite direction.

She saw it was not Jimmy as soon as the car turned into the yard. It was Frank Littlefield. She had hoped it was Jimmy.

"Hot, ain't it?" he said, coming up on the porch and dropping into a chair.

"It must be the same everywhere," she said. "Or is it cooler on the other side of the ridge?"

"It's cooler than this place. Anywhere is cooler than it is

here. Why does your old man live in a hotbox like this, any-way?"

"Because it's our farm. We wouldn't have any place to live if we left here."

Frank got up and looked at the thermometer. It was still a hundred and five, but it was moving slowly toward a hundred and six. "If it gets any hotter, people are going to start acting like mad dogs," he said.

Florabelle fanned herself, keeping an eye on the road.

"How about going swimming down at Coulter's Mill?" Frank said. "That's what I'd like to do. How about it?"

Florabelle looked quickly in both directions to see if there were any signs of Jimmy Barker's coming. She began to wonder what she could do in order to make Frank wait a while longer. If Jimmy came, or Harry Cole, she wanted to get out of going with Frank.

"How about going swimming, I said!" he shouted. "Can't you hear anything—are you deaf?"

"It's early yet, isn't it?" she said.

"What's the matter with you, anyway?" he shouted. "Trying to stall me? I've got to go somewhere and cool off. I'll start foaming at the mouth if I have to sit here in this heat."

"Don't talk that way, Frank. You know I don't mean any-thing like that at all."

"If anybody asked me, I'd say you were the worst two-timer that ever lived. I didn't think I'd ever let myself get two-timed by a wench like you."

Florabelle's face flushed, but she tried to hide it from him. She turned away, watching the road at the same time.

"Well," Frank said, standing up in front of her, "if you won't go with me, you can go to hell."

He started down the steps. She ran and caught him by the arm in desperation.

"You wouldn't talk to me like that, Frank, if it wasn't for the heat. I know you don't mean what you say. As soon as it rains and turns cooler, you won't say things like that."

"It's never going to rain again," he said, pulling away from her and going toward his car.

Florabelle was about to run after him when she saw an auto-mobile coming down the road. She was sure it was either Harry or Jimmy Barker.

Frank started the engine and turned his car around. He almost ran head-on into the other car. Jimmy drove into the yard.

"What was Frank Littlefield so mad about?" Jimmy asked her.

"Oh, I don't know," Florabelle said. "He just couldn't stand the heat, I suppose."

They went up on the porch and sat on the bench.

"How about taking a little walk?" he asked her. "Just me and you off somewhere in the woods. It would be cooler in the woods."

Florabelle laughed.

"Pa wouldn't let me do anything like that," she said, looking shyly up at Jimmy.

"Go ask your mama, then," he said.

Florabelle's face flushed a little.

"Pa will be coming back soon," she said, "and if he didn't find me here, he'd go looking for me."

Jimmy stared at the thermometer hanging on the wall.

"It's too hot to stay here. Let's go somewhere."

Florabelle got up and went to him at the steps.

"If we didn't stay too long, it might be all right," she said slowly.

"Come on," he said, pulling her down into the yard.

They were halfway across the yard when another automobile came racing up the road. It suddenly slowed down and turned into the yard. Frank Littlefield jumped out.

"Putting me off, weren't you, just like I said?"

Before Florabelle could answer, Frank had hit Jimmy on the chin. Jimmy fell over backward, but was up on his feet again in a flash.

"Come on out behind the barn where I can do a good job," Frank said. He strode off in that direction, walking sideways and keeping his eyes on Jimmy. "Come on, if you ain't yellow."

Jimmy went after him, trying to catch up. They sparred at each other until they were out of sight behind the barn.

Florabelle did not know what to do. She stood where she was for a while, then she went to the porch and listened to the sounds that came across the yard.

First she could hear Frank's voice, then Jimmy's. Next she heard them shouting at the same time, and finally she could not distinguish between them any more. After a while there were no sounds that she could hear.

They had been behind the barn for such a long time that she began to wonder why they did not come back. It seemed to her as if they had been gone at least half an hour. She hoped they would make up and come back to the house before her father came home. She did not know what might happen if he came back and found them fighting out there like that.

Florabelle waited as long as she could. By that time she knew at least an hour had passed since Jimmy and Frank had disappeared from sight.

Just as she was getting ready to go and see what had happened to them, her father came up the path. She sank down into a chair when she saw him.

"That spring won't last much longer," he said. "It'll probably be gone by this time tomorrow. I don't know what I'm going to do about water when the spring goes dry."

He looked at the car nearest him in the yard.

"Whose is that?" he asked her.

"It's Jimmy Barker's," she said, trembling with fright.

"Where's he at?" he asked her.

"He and Frank Littlefield went out behind the barn," she said. She was unable to sit still any longer. "They've been out there an awfully long time, Pa."

"What did they go out there for?"

"They had an argument."

Without a word Will Tannet walked toward the barn. He picked up a good-sized stick along the way.

Presently he came around the corner of the barn and motioned to her. She went slowly toward her father. He did not take his eyes from her.

"What's the matter, Pa?" she asked when she got closer.

"Come here and look, and then maybe you can tell me what's the matter."

Florabelle peered cautiously around the corner of the barn. Both Jimmy and Frank were stretched out on the ground, lying motionlessly in the blazing sun. Before she shut her eyes and turned away, she saw the two pitchforks lying between them. She knew without another thought what had happened. She did not remember anything else after that.

When she opened her eyes, there was a thunder in her ears. It sounded as though the whole world was being broken apart. The sky outside was dark, but during the flashes of lightning she could see the outline of the room about her.

"What happened?" she asked.

Her mother was holding her hand, but she was crying so, she could not answer.

When Florabelle closed her eyes, she could hear her father's voice somewhere in the room. She tried to open her eyes again, but they would not open.

"It hasn't rained a drop yet," she heard him say. "With all this thunder and lightning, God would be serving us right if He never let it rain a single drop again."

She thought she heard other sounds, but she could not understand anything she heard after that. The thunder and lightning was louder than the screams of her mother and the curses of her father.

(First published in *College Humor*)

Meddlesome Jack

HOD SHEPPARD was in the kitchen eating breakfast when he heard one of the colored boys yell for him. Before he could get up and look out the window to see what the trouble was, Daisy came running into the room from the garden house in the field looking as if she had been scared out of her wits.

"Hod! Hod!" she screamed at him. "Did you hear it?"

He shook her loose from him and got up from the table. Daisy fell down on the kitchen floor, holding on to his legs with all her might.

"Hear what?" he said. "I heard one of the niggers yelling for me. That's all I heard. What's the matter with you, Daisy?"

Just then Sam, the colored boy, called Hod again louder than ever. Both Hod and Daisy ran to the back door and looked out across the field. The only thing out there they could see was the yellow broom sedge and the dead-leafed blackjack.

"What's all this fuss and racket about, anyway?" Hod said, looking at Daisy.

"I heard something, Hod," she said, trembling.

"Heard what? What did you hear?"

"I don't know what it was, but I heard it."

"What did it sound like—wind, or something?"

"It sounded like—like somebody calling me, Hod."

"Somebody calling you?"

She nodded her head, holding him tightly.

"Who's calling you! If I ever find anybody around here calling you out of the house, I'll butcher him. You'd better not let me see anybody around here after you. I'll kill him so quick—"

Sam came running around the corner of the house, his overall jumper flying out behind, and his crinkly hair jumping like a boxful of little black springs let loose. His eyes were turning white.

"Hey there, you Sam!" Hod yelled at him. "Quit your running around and come back here!"

"Sam heard him, too," Daisy said, standing beside Hod and trembling as if she would fall apart. "Sam's running away from him."

"Heard what—heard who! What's the matter with you, Daisy?"

Daisy held Hod tighter, looking out across the broom sedge. Hod pushed her away and walked out into the back yard. He stood there only a minute before the sound of Sam's pounding feet on the hard white sand grew louder and louder. Sam turned the corner of the house a second later, running even faster than he had before. His eyes were all white by that time, and it looked as if his hair had grown several inches since Hod had last seen him.

Hod reached out and caught Sam's jumper. There was a ripping sound, and Hod looked down to find that he was holding a piece of Sam's overall. Sam was around the house out of sight before Hod could yell at him to stop and come back.

"That nigger is scared of something," Hod said, looking in the doorway at Daisy.

"Sam heard him," Daisy said, trembling.

Hod ran to Daisy and put both hands on her shoulders and shook her violently.

"Heard who!" he yelled at her. "If you don't tell me who it was around here calling you, I'll choke the life out of you. Who was around here calling you? If I catch him, I'll kill him so quick—"

"You're choking me, Hod!" Daisy screamed. "Let me loose! I don't know who it was—honest to God, I don't know who it was, Hod!"

Hod released her and ran out into the yard. Sam had turned and was running down the road towards the lumber mill a mile away. The town of Folger was down there. Two stores, the post office, the lumber mill, and the bank were scorching day after day in an oval of baked clay and sand. Sam was halfway to Folger by then.

"So help me!" Daisy screamed. "There he is, Hod!"

She ran into the kitchen, slamming and bolting the door.

Out behind the barn Amos Whittle, Sam's father, was coming through the broom sedge and blackjack with his feet flying behind him so fast that they looked like the paddles on a water mill. He had both hands gripped around the end of a rope, and the rope was being jerked by the biggest, the ugliest, and the meanest-looking jack that Hod had ever seen in his whole life. The jack was loping through the broom sedge like a hoop snake, jerking Amos from side to side as if he had been the cracker on the end of a rawhide whip.

"Head him, Mr. Hod!" Amos yelled. "Head him! Please, sir, head him!"

Hod stood looking at Amos and the jack while they loped past him. He turned and watched them with mouth agape while they made a wide circle in the broom sedge and started back towards the house and barn again.

"Head him, Mr. Hod!" Amos begged. "Please, Mr. Hod, head him!"

Hod picked up a piece of mule collar and threw it at the

jack's head. The jack stopped dead in his tracks, throwing out his front feet and dragging his hind feet on the hard white sand. The animal had stopped so suddenly that Amos found himself wedged between his two hind legs.

Hod walked towards them and pulled Amos out, but Amos was up and on his feet before there was any danger of his being kicked.

"Where'd you get that jack, Amos?" Hod said.

"I don't know where I got him, but I sure wish I'd never seen him. I been all night trying to hold him, Mr. Hod. I ain't slept a wink, and my old woman's taken to the tall bushes. She and the girls heard him, and they must have thought I don't know exactly what, because they went off yelling about being scared to hear a sound like that jack makes."

The jack walked leisurely over to the barn door and began eating some nubbins that Hod had dropped between the crib and the stalls. One ear stood straight up, and the other one lay flat on his neck. He was the meanest-looking jackass that had ever been in that part of the country. Hod had never seen anything like him before.

"Get him away from here, Amos," Hod said. "I don't want no jack around here."

"Mr. Hod," Amos said, "I wish I could get him away somewhere where I'd never see him again. I sure wish I could accommodate you, Mr. Hod. He's the troublesomest jack I ever seen."

"Where'd you get him, Amos? What are you doing with him, anyway?"

Amos glanced at Hod, but only for a moment. He kept both eyes on the jack.

"I traded that old dollar watch of mine for him yesterday, Mr. Hod, but that jack ain't worth even four bits to me. I don't know what them things are made for, anyhow."

"I'll give you fifty cents for him," Hod said.

"You will!" Amos shouted. "Lord mercy, Mr. Hod, give it here! I'll sure be glad to get rid of that jack for four bits. He done drove my wife and grown girls crazy, and I don't know what mischief he'll be up to next. If you'll give me fifty cents for him, I'll sure be much obliged to you, Mr. Hod. I don't want to have nothing more to do with that jackass."

"I don't want him around, either," Hod said, turning to look through the kitchen window, "but I figure on making me some money with him. How old is that jack, Amos?"

"The man said he was three years old, but I don't know no way of telling a jack's age, and I don't aim to find out."

"He looks like he might be three or four. I'm going to buy him from you, Amos. I figure on making me a lot of money out of that jack. I don't know any other way to make money these days. I can't seem to get it out of the ground."

"Sure, sure, Mr. Hod. You're welcome to that jack. You're mighty much welcome to him. I don't want to have nothing more to do with no jackass. I wish now I had my watch back, but I reckon it's stopped running by now, anyhow. It was three years old, and it never did keep accurate time for me. I'll sure be tickled to get four bits for that jack, Mr. Hod."

Hod counted out fifty cents in nickels and dimes and handed the money to Amos.

"Now, you've got to help me halter that jack, Amos," Hod said. "Get yourself a good piece of stout rope. Plow lines won't be no good on him."

"I don't know about haltering that Jack, Mr. Hod. Looks like to me he's never been halterbroke. If it's all the same to you, Mr. Hod, I'd just as lief go on home now. I've got some stove-wood to chop, and I got to——"

"Wait a minute," Hod said. "I'll get the rope to halter him with. You go in the house and wake up Shaw. He's in the bed asleep. You go in there and get him up and tell him to come out here and help us halter the jack. Ain't no sense in him sleeping all morning. I'm damned tired of seeing him do it. When he comes home, he ought to get out and help do some work about the place."

Shaw was Hod's brother who had been at home seven or eight days on leave from the Navy. He was getting ready to go back to his ship in Norfolk in a day or two. Shaw was two years younger than Hod, and only a few years older than Daisy. Daisy was nineteen then.

"I'd sure like to accommodate you, Mr. Hod," Amos said, "but the last time you sent me in to wake up Mr. Shaw, Mr. Shaw he jumped out of bed on top of me and near about twisted my neck off. He said for me never to wake him up again as long as I live. Mr. Hod, you'd better go wake up Mr. Shaw your own self."

Hod reached down and picked up a piece of stovewood. He walked towards Amos swinging the stick in his hand.

"I said go in the house and get him up," Hod told Amos again. "That sailor had better stop coming here to stay in bed half the day and be all the time telling Daisy tales."

Amos opened the kitchen door and went into the house. Hod walked towards the barn where the jack was calmly eating red nubbins by the crib door.

When Hod reached the barnyard gate, the jack lifted his head and looked at him. He had two or three nubbins of red corn in his jaws, and he stopped chewing and crunching the grains and cobs while he looked at Hod. One of the jack's ears lay flat against the top of his head and neck, and the other one stood straight up in the air, as stiff as a cow's horn. The jack's ears were about fourteen or sixteen inches long, and they were as rigid as bones.

Hod tossed the piece of stovewood aside and walked to the opened gate for a piece of rope. He believed he could halter the jack by himself.

He started into the barnyard, but he had gone no farther than a few steps when boards began to fly off the side of the barn. The mare in the stall was kicking like a pump gun. One after the other, the boards flew off, the mare whinnied, and the jack stood listening to the pounding of the mare's hooves against the pine boards.

When Hod saw what was happening to his barn, he ran towards the jack, yelling and waving his arms and trying to get him to the leeward side of the barn.

"Howie! Howie!" he yelled at the jack.

As long as the mare got wind of the jack, nothing could make her stop kicking the boards off the barn from the inside. Hod jumped at the jack, waving his arms and shouting at him.

"Howie! Howie!"

He continued throwing up his arms to scare the jack away, but the jack just turned and looked at Hod with one ear up and one ear down.

"Howie! You ugly-looking son of a bitch! Howie!"

Hod turned around to look towards the house to see if Shaw and Amos were coming. He turned just in time to see Amos jumping out the window.

"Hey there, Amos!" Hod yelled. "Where's Shaw?"

"Mr. Shaw says he ain't going to get up till he gets ready to. Mr. Shaw cussed pretty bad and made me jump out the window."

The jack began to paw the ground. Hard clods of stableyard sand and manure flew behind him in all directions. Hod yelled at him again.

"Howie! Howie! You flop-eared bastard!"

The jack stopped and turned his head to look at Amos on the other side of the fence.

"Mr. Hod," Amos said, "if you don't mind, I'd like to have a word with you."

Hod yelled at Amos and at the jack at the same time.

"Mr. Hod," Amos said, "if I don't go home now and chop that stovewood, me and my folks won't have no dinner at all."

"Come back here!" Hod shouted at him.

Amos came as far as the gate, but he would not come any farther.

Suddenly the jack lifted his head high in the air and brayed. It sounded as if someone were blowing a trumpet in the ear.

The bray had no more than died out when the mare began pounding the boards with both hind hooves, the boards flying off the side of the barn faster than Hod could count them. He turned and looked to see what Amos was doing, and over his head he saw Daisy at the window. She looked as if she had completely lost her mind.

The jack brayed again, louder than ever, and then he leaped for the open barnyard gate. Hod threw the rope at him, but the rope missed him by six feet. The jack was through the gate and out around the house faster than Hod could yell. Amos stood as if his legs had been fence posts four feet deep in the ground.

The jack stopped at the open bedroom window, turned his head towards the house, and brayed as if he were calling all the mares in the entire county. Daisy ran to the window and looked out, and when she saw the jack no more than arm's length from her, she screamed and fell backward on the floor.

"Head him, Amos! Head him!" Hod yelled, running towards the jack.

Amos's feet were more than ever like fence posts. He was shaking like a tumbleweed, but his legs and feet were as stiff as if they had been set in concrete.

"Where in hell is that God damn sailor!" Hod yelled. "Why in hell don't he get up and help me some around here! If I had the time now, I'd go in there with a piece of cordwood and break every bone in his head. The son of a bitch comes home here on leave once a year and lays up in bed all day and stays out all night running after women. If that seagoing son of a bitch comes here again, I'll kill him!"

"Yonder goes your jack, Mr. Hod," Amos said.

Daisy stuck her head out of the window again. She was looking to see where the jack was, and she did not look at Hod. She was standing there pulling at herself, and getting more wild-eyed every second. She disappeared from sight as quickly as she had first appeared.

"Come on, you black bastard," Hod said; "let's go after him. I ought to pick up a stick and break your neck for bringing that God damn jack here to raise the devil. He's got the mare kicking down the barn, and Daisy is in there acting crazy as hell."

They started out across the broom sedge after the loping jack. The jack was headed for Folger, a mile away.

"If I ever get my hands on that jack, I'll twist his neck till it looks like a corkscrew," Hod panted, running and leaping over the yellow broom sedge. "Ain't no female safe around a sailor or a jack, and here I am running off after one, and leaving the other in the house."

They lost sight of the jackass in a short while. The beast had begun to circle the town, and he was now headed down the side of the railroad tracks behind the row of Negro cabins. They soon saw him again, though, when the jack slowed down at a pasture where some horses were grazing.

A hundred yards from the cabins they had to run down into a gully. Just as they were crawling up the other side, a Negro girl suddenly appeared in front of them, springing up from nowhere. She was standing waist-high in the broom sedge, and she was as naked as a pickaninny.

Hod stopped and looked at her.

"Did you see a jack?" he said to her.

"White-folks, I saw that jack, and he brayed right in my face. I just jumped up and started running. I can't sit still when I hear a jackass bray."

Hod started off again, but he stopped and came back to look at the girl.

"Put your clothes back on," he said. "You'll get raped running around in the sedge this close to town like that."

"White-captain," she said, "I ain't hard to rape. I done heard that jackass bray."

Hod turned and looked at Amos for a moment. Amos was walking around in a circle with his hands in his pockets.

"Come on," Hod told him, breaking through the broom sedge. "Let's get that jack, Amos."

They started towards the pasture where the jack had stopped. When the jack saw them coming, he turned and bolted over the railroad tracks and started jogging up the far side of the right-of-way towards Folger. Hod cut across to head him off and Amos was right behind to help.

There were very few men in town at that time of day. Several storekeepers sat on Coca-Cola crates on the sidewalk under the shade of the water-oak trees, and several men were whittling white pine and chewing tobacco. The bank was open, and RB, the cashier, was standing in the door looking out across the railroad tracks and dusty street. Down at the lumber mill, the saws whined hour after hour.

The jack slowed down and ran into the hitching yard behind the brick bank. When Hod saw that the jack had stopped, he stopped running and tried to regain his breath. Both he and Amos were panting and sweating. The August sun shone down on the dry baked clay in the oval where the town was and remained there until sunset.

Hod and Amos sat down in the shade of the depot and fanned themselves with their hats. The jack was standing calmly behind the bank, switching flies with his tail.

"Give me back my fifty cents, Amos," Hod said. "You can have that God-damn jack. I don't want him."

"I couldn't do that, Mr. Hod," Amos pleaded. "We done

made the trade, and I can't break it now. You'll just have to keep that jack. He's yours now. If you want to get shed of him, go sell him to somebody else. I don't want that jack. I'd heap rather have my old dollar watch back again. I wish I'd never seen that jack in all my life. I can do without him."

Hod said nothing. He looked at the brick bank and saw RB looking out across the railroad tracks towards the stores where the men were sitting on upturned Coca-Cola crates in the water-oak shade.

"Sit here and wait," Hod said, getting up. "I've just thought of something. You sit here and keep your eyes on that jack till I come back."

"You won't be gone long, will you, Mr. Hod? I don't mind watching your animal for you, but I'd sure hate to have to look at that jack any more than I'm compelled to. He don't like my looks, and I sure don't like his. That's the ugliest-looking creature that's ever been in this country."

"Wait here till I get back," Hod said, crossing the tracks and walking towards the brick bank.

RB saw Hod coming and he went back inside and stood behind his cashier's cage.

Hod walked in, took off his hat and leaned his arm on the little shelf in front of the cage.

"Hello, RB," he said. "It's hot today, ain't it?"

"Do you want to deposit money, or make a loan?"

Hod fanned himself and spat into the cuspidor.

"Miss it?" RB asked, trying to see through the grill.

"Not quite," Hod said.

RB spat into his own cuspidor at his feet.

"What can I do for you?" he said.

"Well, I'll tell you, RB," Hod said. "It's like this. You've got all this money here in the bank, and it ain't doing you much good where it is. And here I come with all my money tied up in livestock. There ain't but one answer to that, is there?"

"When did you get some livestock, Hod?" he asked. "I didn't know you had anything but that old mare and that gray mule."

"I made a trade today," Hod said, "and now just when my money is all tied up in livestock, I find a man who's willing to let me in on a timber deal. I need fifty dollars to swing my share. There ain't no use trying to farm these days, RB. That's why I'm going in for livestock and timber."

"How many head of stock do you own?"

"Well, I've got that mare, Ida, out there at my place, but I ain't counting her. And likewise that old mule."

"How many others do you own?"

"I purchased a high-class stud animal this morning, RB, and I paid out all my ready cash in the deal."

"A bull?"

"No, not exactly a bull, RB."

"What was it then?"

"A jackass, RB."

"A jackass!"

"Who in hell wants to own a jackass, Hod? I can't lend the bank's money on a jackass."

"You're in the moneylending business, RB, and I've got an animal to mortgage. What else do you want? I'm putting up my jack, and you're putting up your money. That's business, RB. That's good business."

"Yes, but suppose you force me to foreclose the mortgage —I'd have the jack, and then maybe I couldn't find a buyer. Jackass buyers are pretty scarce customers, Hod. I don't recall ever seeing one."

"Anybody would give you a hundred dollars for a good high-class jack, RB. If you knew as much about farming and stock-raising as you do about banking, you'd recognize that without me having to tell you."

"What does a jackass look like?"

"A jack don't look so good to the eye, RB, but that's not a jack's high point. When a jack brays—"

RB came running around from behind his cage and caught Hod by the arm. He was so excited that he was trembling.

"Is that what I heard last night, Hod?"

"What?"

"A jackass braying."

"Wouldn't be surprised if you did. Amos was out exercising him last night, and he said the jack brayed almost all night long."

"Come back here with me," RB said, still shaking. "I'm going to let you have that loan, and take a mortgage on that jack. I want to have a hand in it. If I'll let you have the loan, will you let me take the jack home and keep him at my house for about a week, Hod?"

"You're more than welcome to him, RB. You can keep him all the time if you want to. But why do you want to keep a jack at your house? You don't breed mules, do you?"

RB had Hod sign the papers before he replied. He then counted out five ten-dollar bills and put them into Hod's hand.

"This is just between me and you, Hod," he said. "Me and my wife haven't been on speaking terms for more than a month now. She cooks my meals and does her housework, but she's been mad at me about something and she won't say a word or have anything to do with me. But last night, sometime after midnight, we were lying there in the bed, she as far on her side as she could get without falling out, and all at once I heard the damnedest yell I ever heard in all my life. It was that jackass braying. I know now what it was, but I didn't know then. That jack was somewhere out in the sedge, and when he brayed, the first thing I knew, my wife was all over me, she was that scared, or something. That sounds like a lie, after I have told you about her not speaking to me for more than a month, and sleeping as far on her side of the bed as she could get without falling on the floor, but it's the truth if I know what the truth is. That jack brayed just once, and the first thing I knew, my wife was all over me, hugging me and begging me not to leave her. This morning she took up her old ways again, and that's why I want to stable that jack at my house for a week or two. He'll break up that streak of not talking and not having anything to do with me. That jack is what I am in need of, Hod."

Hod took the money and walked out of the bank towards the depot where Amos was.

"Where's the jack, Hod?" RB said, running after him.

"Out there behind your bank," Hod said. "You can take him home with you tonight when you close up."

Amos got up to meet Hod.

"Come on, Amos," Hod said. "We're going home."

Amos looked back over his shoulder at the jack behind the bank, watching him until he was out of sight. They walked through the broom sedge, circling the big gully, on the way home.

When they reached the front yard, Hod saw Sam sitting under a chinaberry tree. Sam got up and stood leaning against the trunk.

"What are you doing here?" Hod asked him. "What are you hanging around here for? Go on home, Sam."

Sam came forward a step, and stepped backward two.

"Miss Daisy told me to tell you something for her," Sam said, chewing the words.

"She said what?"

"Mr. Hod, Miss Daisy and Mr. Shaw went off down the road while you was chasing that jack. Mr. Shaw said he was taking Miss Daisy with him back to the navy yard, and Miss Daisy said she was going off and never coming back."

Hod went to the front porch and sat down in the shade. His feet hung over the edge of the porch, almost touching the ground.

Amos walked across the yard and sat down on the steps. He looked at Hod for several minutes before he said anything.

"Mr. Hod," he said, chewing the words worse than his son had before him, "I reckon you'd better go back to Folger and get your jack. Looks like that jack has a powerful way of fretting the womenfolks, and you'd better get him to turn one in your direction."

(First published in *We Are the Living*)

Molly Cotton-Tail

MY aunt had come down South to visit us and we were all sitting around the fireplace talking. Aunt Nellie did most of the talking and my mother the rest of it. My father came in occasionally for a few minutes at a time and then went out again to walk around the house and sit in the barnyard. He and Aunt Nellie did not get along together at all. Aunt Nellie was sure she was smarter than anybody else and my father did not want to get into an argument with her and lose his temper.

Aunt Nellie's husband had gone down to Florida on a hunting trip and she came as far as Carolina to see us while he was away. My uncle was crazy about hunting and spent all his spare time away from home gunning for game.

"Bess," Aunt Nellie asked my mother, "does Johnny like to hunt?" She nodded impersonally toward me where I sat by the fireplace.

My mother said I did not. And that was true. I like to catch rabbits and squirrels for pets but I did not want to kill them. I had a pet hen right then; she had been run over by a buggy wheel when she was growing up and one of her legs was broken. I hid her in the barn so my father would not know about her. She stayed there about two weeks and when the leg had healed I let her out in the yard with the other chickens. When my father did find her he said she would not have to be killed if I would take care of her and feed her because she could not scratch for worms like the other chickens. Her leg healed all right, but it was crooked and she limped every step she took.

"Well," Aunt Nellie said to my mother, "that is a shame. If he doesn't like to hunt he won't grow up to be a real Southern gentleman."

"But, Nellie," my mother protested for me, "Johnny does not like to kill things."

"Nonsense," Aunt Nellie said derisively. "Any man who is a real Southern gentleman likes to hunt. The Lord only knows what he will turn out to be."

My father would have taken up for me too if he had been

in the room just then. My father did not like to kill things either.

"I'm disappointed in having a nephew who is not a real Southern gentleman. He will never be one if he never goes hunting," Aunt Nellie always talked a long time about the same thing once she got started.

I was not greatly interested in being a real Southern gentleman when I grew up, but I did not want her to talk about me that way. Every summer she wrote my mother a letter inviting me up to her home in Maryland, and I wanted to go again this year.

My father heard what she said and went out in the back-yard and threw pebbles against the barn side.

I went into the dining room where the shotgun was kept and took it off the rack. The gun was fired off to scare crows when they came down in the spring to pull up the corn sprouts in the new ground. My father never aimed to kill the crows: he merely fired off the shotgun to make the crows so gun-shy they would not come back to the cornfield.

Taking the shotgun and half a dozen shells I went out the front door without anybody seeing me leave. I went down the road towards the schoolhouse at the crossroads. I had seen dozens of rabbits down at the first creek every time I went to school and came home. They were large rabbits with gray backs and white undercoats. All of them had long thin ears and a ball of white fur on their tails. I liked them a lot.

At the first creek I stopped on the bridge and rested against the railing. In a few minutes I saw two rabbits hop across the road ahead. Picking up the gun I started after them. A hundred yards from the bridge the road had been cut down into the hill and the banks on each side were fifteen and twenty feet high. At this time of year when there was nearly always a heavy frost each morning the bank facing the south was the warmer because the sun shone against it most of the day. I had seen several rabbits sitting in holes in the bank and I was sure that was where these rabbits were going now.

Sure enough when I got there a large gray-furred rabbit was sitting on the sunny bank backed into a hole. When I saw the rabbit I raised the shotgun to my shoulder and took good aim. The rabbit blinked her eyes and chewed a piece of grass she had found under a log somewhere. I was then only ten or twelve feet away but I thought I had better get closer so I should be certain to kill her. I would take the rabbit home and show my aunt. I wanted her to invite me to spend the summer at her house again.

I edged closer and closer to the rabbit until I stood in the drain ditch only three feet from her. She blinked her eyes and chewed on the grass. I hated to kill her because she looked as if she wanted to live and sit on the sunny bank chewing grass always. But my Aunt Nellie thought a boy should be a sportsman and kill everything in sight.

There was nothing else I could do. I would have to shoot the poor rabbit and take her back for my aunt to see.

I took steady aim along the center of the double-barreled shotgun, shut both eyes, and pulled the triggers one after the other. When I opened my eyes the rabbit was still sitting there looking at me. I was so glad after the gun went off that the rabbit was not dead that I dropped the gun and crawled up the bank and caught the rabbit by her long ears. I lifted her in my arms and held her tightly so she could not run away. She was so frightened by the gunshots she was trembling all over like a whipped dog. When I put her in my arms she snuggled her nose against my sweater and stopped quivering while I stroked her fur.

Holding the rabbit tight in my right arm I picked up the shotgun and ran home as fast as I could.

My father was still sitting in the back yard when I got there.

"What's that you've got under your arm?" he asked.

"A rabbit," I told him.

"How did you catch it?"

"I shot at her and missed her. Then I caught her by the ears and brought her home."

"Look here, Johnny," he said to me. "You didn't shoot at that rabbit while it was sitting down, did you?"

"I guess I did," I admitted; adding hastily, "but I didn't hit her, anyway."

"Well, it's a good thing you didn't hit it. A good sportsman never shoots at a rabbit while it is sitting down. A good sportsman never shoots at a bird until it flies. A real sportsman always gives the game he is after a chance for its life."

"But Aunt Nellie said I had to kill something and she didn't say not to kill things standing still."

"You stop paying any attention to your Aunt Nellie. She doesn't know what she's talking about anyway."

I let my father hold the rabbit while I fixed a box to keep her in. When I was ready I put her in it and shut her up tight.

"What are you going to do with the rabbit?" he asked me.

"Keep her."

"I wouldn't put it in a box," he said with a queer look on his face. "If it wants to stay it won't run off. And if it doesn't want to stay it will worry itself to death in that box all the time. Turn it loose and let's see what it will do."

I was afraid to turn my rabbit loose because I did not want her to run away. But my father knew a lot more about rabbits than I did. Just then Aunt Nellie and my mother came out on the back porch.

"What have you got there in the box?" Aunt Nellie asked me.

"A rabbit," I said.

"Where did you get it?"

"I shot at her with the gun but I didn't hit her and she didn't run away so I brought her home."

My aunt turned to my mother in disgust.

"There you are, Bess! What did I tell you?"

I did not hear what my mother said. But my father got up and went down to the barn. Aunt Nellie went into the house and slammed shut the door behind her. My mother stood looking at me for several minutes as if I had done the right thing after all.

Taking the rabbit out of the box I went down to the barn where my father was. He was sitting against the barn side shelling an ear of corn for half a dozen chickens around him. I sat down beside him and turned the rabbit loose. The rabbit hopped around and around and then sat down and looked at us.

"Why don't you name it Molly Cotton-Tail?" my father suggested, throwing a handful of shelled corn to the chickens.

"What does that mean?" I asked.

"There are two kinds of rabbits around here: jack rabbits and molly cotton-tails. That one has a cotton-tail—see the ball of white fur on its tail that looks like a boll of cotton?"

The rabbit hopped around and around again and sat down on her cotton-tail. The chickens were not afraid of her. They went right up to where she sat and scratched for corn just as if she had been a chicken too.

"Why don't you go into the garden and get a head of lettuce for it? Get a good tender one out of the hot-bed. All rabbits like lettuce," he said.

I got the lettuce and gave it to my rabbit. She hopped up to where we sat against the barn side, asking for more. I gave her all I had and she ate out of my hand.

"If you had killed that rabbit with the gun you would be sorry now," my father said. Anybody could see that he was beginning to like my rabbit a lot.

She hopped around and around in front of us, playing with the chickens. The chickens liked her, too.

"I'd lots rather have her living than dead," I said, suddenly realizing how much I liked her myself.

Molly hopped up between us and nibbled at my father's hand. He reached to stroke her fur with his hand but she hopped away.

"Whoa there, sooky," he soothed, reaching for our rabbit.

(First published in *American Earth*)

The Courting of Susie Brown

HALF an hour after the sun went down on the far side of the Mississippi, Sampson Jones was hurrying along the dusty road to Elbow Creek where Susie Brown lived all alone in her house behind the levee. Every once in a while he shifted the heavy shoe box from one arm to the other, easing the burden he was carrying.

When he jogged over the last rise of ground before reaching the levee, he saw the flickering light in Susie's window, and the sight that met his eyes made him hurry faster than ever.

Susie was inside her house, putting away the supper dishes. She was singing a little and brushing away the miller moths that swarmed around the light in the room.

Sampson rattled the rusty latch on the gate and hitched up his pants. Susie had never looked so good to him before.

"You look sweeter than a suck of sugar, baby," he shouted to her through the open window.

Susie spun around on her heels. The tin pan she was drying sailed out of her hands and clattered against the cookstove.

"What you want here again, Sampson Jones!" she cried, startled out of her wits. "What you doing down here off the high land!"

She had to stop and fan herself before she could get her breath back.

"You done found that out the first time, honey," he said, lifting the heavy shoe box and laying it before her eyes on the window sill. "Now why don't you just give up? Ain't no use spoiling it by playing you don't know why I come."

Susie studied the shoe box, wondering what it could hold. The sight of it made her hesitate. The last three times Sampson had come to court her, he had not brought her a single thing.

"I ain't got no time to waste on no sorry, measly-weight, trifling man," she said finally, turning her back on the shoe box.

"My trifling days is all over, honey," he said quickly. "I ain't trifling around no more."

Susie swung the dish towel on the line behind the cookstove and stole a quick glance at herself in the mirror over the shelf. Then she moved slowly across the room, watching Sampson and his shoe box suspiciously.

281

"When I get set and ready for a man, I'm going to get me a good one," she said, inspecting him disdainfully. "I ain't aiming to waste my good self on no short-weight plowboy."

Sampson grinned confidently at the scowling brown-skinned girl.

"Baby," he said, "what do you reckon I done?"

"What?" she asked, her interest mounting.

"I weighed myself at exactly two hundred and ten pounds just a little while ago previously."

He started to swing his legs through the window opening, but Susie gave him a shove that sent him dropping to the ground.

"I weigh my men on my own scales," Susie said stiffly. "I wouldn't take your weighing in any quicker than I would the next one who comes bragging along."

"What makes you think I'm lying about myself to you, honey?" he asked unhappily. "Why you crave to go and talk like that?"

"Because you don't weigh nowhere near two hundred pounds, that's why," she said sharply. "I done made up my mind over the kind of man I want when I get myself ready to want him, and you ain't the one I'm thinking about. It don't make no difference at all what you brings me in a shoe box, neither." She paused for a moment, getting her breath. "You hear what I say, Sampson Jones?"

"I hear you, honey," he said. "But it would make me downright awful sad if you was to make a bad mistake for yourself."

Susie leaned out the window and stared down at the box under his arm.

"Maybe if you was to find out what I brung you," he said, "you'd swing around to the other kind of talk. I sure has got a pretty thing for you, honey. I brung it all the way from Mr. Bob Bell's store at the big crossroads."

Susie glanced at the box, and then she straightened up and looked Sampson all over from head to toe. The white shoe box was tied tightly with heavy yellow twine. It gleamed enticingly before her eyes in the moonlight, only an arm's length away.

"How much you say you really sure enough weigh?" she asked continuing to look him up and down.

"I done told you two hundred ten, honey," he said hopefully. "Why you think I ain't telling you the whole lawful truth?"

Sampson watched her for a while, wondering if she were going to believe him this time. He had been coming down from the high land to see her for six months, trying his best every minute of the time he was there to court her into marrying him. Sometimes he succeeded in getting his arms around her for a little while, hugging her some around the waist and a little around the neck, but usually she kept him at a distance by making him stay outside on the ground while she sat on the porch, talking to him through the window.

No matter how well he argued with her, Susie had always said that the man she was going to take up with had to weigh two hundred pounds, or better. Sampson had never weighed more than a hundred and sixty pounds in his whole life, until he began courting her. Now he had managed to put on thirty additional pounds in six months' time after eating all the beans and fat pork he could put his hands on. But during the past month he had discovered that no matter how much he ate, he was not able to increase his weight a single pound over one hundred and ninety. And to make matters worse, his worry over that was causing him to lose weight every day. He had become desperate.

While he was standing there on the ground outside her window, Susie had moved away. Sampson hurried around to the front of the house. Susie had seated herself on the rocker on the porch, and she was sitting there placidly fanning her face.

Sampson set one foot on the bottom step hopefully.

"Don't you dare come one single more inch, Sampson Jones!" Susie said sharply. "I ain't satisfied in my mind with the weighing you said you done to yourself."

Sampson patted his expanded stomach and slapped his heavy thighs with his great brown hands.

"Woman," he said crossly, "you sure is one aggravating creature. Here I is with all this man-sized weight on my frame, and you act like you don't even see it at all. What's the matter with you, anyhow?"

He slammed the shoe box on the second step from the bottom, threw out his chest and thrust out his arms to show his bulging muscles.

"Why don't you get some scales and let me weigh you then, if you're all that sure?" she said. "You ain't scared to let me weigh you in, is you?"

Sampson stopped and thought it over carefully. After a while, he looked up at Susie.

"I'd be tickled to have you weigh me in, Susie," he said, "only I ain't got no scales to do it on. Has you?"

Before she could reply, he stooped down quickly and picked up the heavy shoe box.

"Drop that box, Sampson Jones!" she said sharply. "I know what you're up to. You're trying to trick me with that heavy box you've got there."

"No, I ain't, Susie," he said, startled. Sheepishly he put the box down on the step. "What makes you think a sorry thing like that about me?"

"Well," Susie said, rocking some more, "if you ain't lying in your talk, maybe you'll weigh in on my stillyerd."

Sampson's face fell.

"Has you got a stillyerd here, Susie, sure enough?"

Susie stood up.

"You stand right where you is now, and I'll bring it," she told him. "I'm getting all tired out from hearing all your boasting. The weighing in will settle it." She moved toward the door. "That is, if you ain't scared to show me your true weight."

"I ain't scared one bit, Susie," he said fearfully.

When she had gone out of sight into the house, Sampson ran out into the yard and began picking up all the rocks and stones he could put his hands on. He filled both hip pockets with the largest ones, and then began scooping up fistfuls of gravel and filling all his other pockets. Susie still had not returned, and so he hastily untied his shoes and stuffed them with all the sand he could get into them. He straightened up, trembling all over, when he heard Susie come toward him through the house. He was certain he had not succeeded in loading himself with the necessary ten pounds of stone, sand, and gravel. At the last moment, he found another stone and put it into his mouth.

Susie brought the weighing steelyard to the porch and hung it on a rafter. Then she looked around for Sampson.

Sampson went up the steps carrying the heavy shoe box under one arm. He thrust his other arm through the loop of rope dangling from the steelyard.

"Set the box on the floor," she ordered firmly.

He looked at her, pleadingly, for a few moments, but recognizing the determined expression on Susie's face, he dropped it.

"I been plowing hard all day in the cotton field, from sunrise to sunset," he began. "I wouldn't be taken back at all if I'd lost a heap of pounds, Susie."

"We'll see," she said harshly. "Hitch yourself up on that stillyerd."

Sampson thrust his arm through the loop and painfully swung himself clear of the floor. While he hung there, knowing his fate was in the balance, Susie stepped over and slid the weighing ball along the steel arm.

He tried to twist his head back in order to watch the weighing, but he was in such a cramped position that it was impossible for him to see anything overhead. He gave up and hung there by one arm, praying with every breath.

By the time Susie had satisfied herself that her weighing of him was accurate, Sampson was dizzy from strain and worry. He barely knew what he was doing when he heard Susie's voice tell him to set himself on his feet.

When his feet touched the floor, his knees began to sag, and he found himself staggering across the porch. He reached the wall and dug his fingernails into the rough weatherboarding in an effort to find support. Susie still had not said anything since she told him to get down from the steelyard, and he was too weak to ask her anything about it.

Presently he felt Susie's arms around his neck. The next moment he felt himself sliding downward to the floor.

When he regained his senses, Susie was kneeling beside him, hugging him with all her might. He struggled free of her grip and got his breath back. The stone he had been holding in his mouth was gone. He could not tell whether it had fallen out, or whether he had swallowed it. He was uneasy.

"Honey," Susie was saying to him, "I sure am happy about the big way you weighed in. Looks like you'd have done it for me sooner, instead of waiting all this long time."

"How much did I weigh in at, Susie?" he asked.

"Honey, you weighed exactly two hundred and fifteen pounds," she said delightedly. "And only a little while ago you said it was only two-ten. My, oh, my!"

Sampson closed his eyes.

When he looked up again, he saw Susie busily opening the heavy shoe box. She untied the string and took off the lid. Then she lifted out the ten-pound sadiron he had brought her with the hope that when he weighed for her he would be able to keep the box under his arm.

"It's the finest present I ever had in all my life, honey," she said sweetly, running the palm of her hand over the smooth surface.

She gazed at him admiringly.

While he waited for her to speak again, he glanced quickly up into her face, wondering how he was going to be able to rid himself of twenty-five pounds of stone before she discovered it on him.

(First published in *Coronet*)

The Picture

THE first question John Nesbit asked Pauline when she told him that she had employed a new maid and nurse for the children, was the same thing he had always said when another servant came to take the place of one that had left.

"Pauline, what kind of a—are you sure that she is a good Negress?"

"She is a splendid housemaid, John, and she knows how to care for the children. Both Jay and Claire love her, and they obey her to the last word. She had the best recommendations of any servant we've ever hired. Mamie is the kind of maid I have wanted ever since we were married."

"Yes, I know," John said; "but is this new maid a good Negress?"

"Her recommendations were perfect, John. I haven't any reason to suspect her of not being a suitable nurse for the children."

"Well, you have seen her, and I haven't. I'd much rather not have a servant in the house than to employ one who wasn't a good Negress. I've seen too many of them at the plantation, when I was a kid growing up, to have one of that kind in the house."

"Don't worry about Mamie, John," Pauline said. "I'm sure she is a good girl. If she isn't, we can always ask her to leave."

That settled the matter for the rest of the evening. The next afternoon, though, when he reached home from the mills, John saw the new maid on the lawn with Jay and Claire. He drove his car into the garage and walked down the driveway to the side entrance. Just before he reached the steps he looked back over his shoulder at the colored girl sitting on the bench under the cedar trees. Both Jay and Claire had left Mamie and were running to meet him. He had a second chance to look at the girl before the children reached him.

Mamie was a brown girl with straightened hair. She had the slender body of a young woman, and her long legs were straight and round-looking in the ash-colored stockings that covered them above her knees. John had noticed all that about her when he looked at her for the first time over his shoulder. When he looked the second time, he saw that Mamie was full-breasted.

After the children had become tired of climbing over his lap and had gone back outdoors to play on the lawn with their nurse, John asked Pauline again about the colored girl. John was the agent at the Glen Rock Cotton Mills, and he had grown to be unrelenting in questioning every man and woman to whom he gave employment. He expected Pauline to be the same about the colored servants she hired for the house.

"I saw that new nurse just now," he said.

"Don't you think she's all right?" she asked.

"That's for you to be certain about, Pauline. You have the opportunity of knowing her. Is she a good Negress? We certainly don't wish to have the other kind to nurse Jay and Claire. It would be better for us not to have any servants at all, than to have the kind that we do not want in the house."

"I wish you wouldn't worry so much about Mamie, John. I just know that she is all right. Please stop worrying about it. Leave her to me. If I find out that she is not a good girl, I'll discharge her. When you come home from the mills you should rest, and not let yourself be worried about the servants."

"I know I should, Pauline," he said, "but you don't know the colored people as I do. You were raised in the East, where the only colored people are the ones who are probably as good as the whites, but down here in Carolina it's different, and you haven't lived here long enough yet to be able to distinguish between the two kinds. I was raised on a plantation with colored people, and I grew up in a small town where more than half the population was colored. I know there are two kinds of them, just as you know there are at least two distinct classes of whites. The reason I ask about the servants as I do is that I want to be sure that you do not let them fool you. We wouldn't want the wrong kind of servants in the house caring for Jay and Claire."

"Of course, we don't," Pauline said. "Now, let's forget about that. We must get ready for dinner soon. There isn't much time left for us to dress. Don't forget, we have an eight o'clock invitation."

Neither of them mentioned the new maid or the cook for several days. Pauline believed that John was assured at last that Mamie was a good Negress.

Less than a week later, though, something happened. Pauline missed one morning the silver-framed photograph of John that had been on the dressing table in her room since the day they were married. Once each week, on Tuesdays, Pauline had cleaned the silver frame with cloth and paste, and on this Tuesday she could not find the picture anywhere in the house. She was not certain how long it had been missing from the table, because she had not consciously noticed it since Sunday. On Sunday she had dusted the silver and glass, and had put the silver-mounted photograph back on her dressing table. But on Tuesday it was missing.

The moment she realized that the picture was missing, she ran to the phone to call up John at his office at the mills. But while the operator was connecting them she suddenly realized that telling John about the picture was the last thing she should do. She hung up hurriedly, hoping that he would not suspect that it was she calling. She sat beside the telephone, her hands gripped together, waiting for the bell to ring. After five minutes she got up and ran from the room.

Pauline's first thought after leaving the room was, what in the world would John say to her if he should notice that the picture was missing! Suppose he should go to her room that

evening after dinner and see that the photograph was not on
her dressing table! He would surely ask her about it—what on
earth could she tell him! She ran from room to room, looking
over every inch of space in the house for the silver-framed
photograph, and when she had finished, she was still as helpless as she had been the moment that she discovered it was
missing. The picture was not in the house. Pauline was certain
of that. She had searched everywhere.

Della, the cook, was not there at that time of the afternoon,
and it was Mamie's day off. If they had been there she would
have run to them and asked if they had seen Mr. Nesbit's
photograph. She would even have asked them if either had
taken it and put it some place else. But there was no one there
then except herself and the children. It did not occur to her
to ask Jay and Claire if they had taken the photograph without
permission. They were then in the playhouse on the lawn.

She called to Jay and Claire as she ran to the garage for
her car. Seating them beside her, she backed out the automobile, turned around in the driveway, and drove out into
the boulevard. Pauline did not know where she was going until
she had driven several blocks down the boulevard. It was then
that she realized she had turned the car towards the Negro
quarter, and that in a short time she would be there.

Pauline passed Della's house without giving it more than
a glance. After she had passed Della's she wondered why she
had not stopped there to ask Della if she had seen Mr. Nesbit's
photograph that had always been on the dressing table in her
bedroom.

A block and a half farther down the street was Mamie's
house. Mamie lived there with her mother, Aunt Sophie, and
several older brothers and sisters.

Pauline slowed down her car before she could see the house,
and by the time she had reached it she had only to coast to
a stop and to jump out on the sandy sidewalk. Mamie's house
looked very much like most of the other houses in the Negro
quarter, but Pauline had seen it once before, and she needed
only to recognize the ivy-trellised porch to tell her that it was
the place where Mamie lived.

Several colored people were standing on the sidewalk, leaning against the whitewashed picket fence. None of them knew
her, and Pauline did not stop to speak. She ran through the
gate, up the steps to the open door. She knocked on the door
as rapidly as she could. She could not wait much longer. John
would be coming home from the mills at four o'clock, and
it was past three o'clock then. There was not a minute to
lose. She had to hurry.

Someone in the rear of the house opened a door and closed

it. The delay made Pauline frantic. She took several steps into the hall, listening for somebody to answer her knocking.

Pauline was in the center of the hall when Mamie opened a bedroom door and came out.

"Why! Miss Pauline!" Mamie said, astonished. "What's the matter, Miss Pauline?"

"Mamie, I came to ask—"

She stopped in the midst of her questioning and could go no further. Mamie had crossed the hall and was standing a few feet from her. Pauline sat down in a chair and looked at Mamie. Her heart was beating madly, and her head throbbed until she had to hold her hands over her face to ease the pain.

"Miss Pauline, ask me what? What's happened to you, Miss Pauline? You look scared, Miss Pauline."

Pauline opened her eyes slowly and looked at Mamie. She saw now exactly what John must have seen when he saw Mamie for the first time nearly two weeks before. She could see that Mamie was young and slender, that her hair was straight and glistening, and that her mixed blood had given her a kind of sensuous beauty that no white girl could ever possess. She saw that Mamie's legs were long and slender, and that Mamie was full-breasted. It was only then that she fully realized what John had meant when he asked her if Mamie were a good Negress. She could answer him now. She knew what to tell John the next time he asked her that about one of the colored servants.

"Mamie, I came to ask if you know—"

The door behind Mamie had been left open, and she looked into the bedroom for the first time. The sunshine came into the room, and a light breeze whipped the white curtains. The bedroom dresser was in full view.

Without waiting to finish what she was about to say, Pauline jumped from the chair and ran into Mamie's room. There on the dresser, just as it had sat on her own dressing table, was John's silver-framed photograph. She snatched the picture in her arms and ran back to Mamie.

"What made you—why—when did you take it—what did you do it for, Mamie!"

Mamie smiled. She did not try to run away, nor did she attempt to defend herself. She smiled.

Pauline leaned against the wall, hugging the silver-framed photograph to her breast. Her head had stopped throbbing, but she felt too weak to stand any longer. Just in time, Mamie ran and brought the chair to her mistress.

Outside in the back yard a group of Negroes were talking, and, as suddenly as she had first heard their voices, they began to laugh. They were not laughing about something that was humorous. That would be another kind of laughter; white-folks' laughing, Aunt Sophie called it. The laughter that now came from their throats was different from any other expression of emotion Pauline had ever heard. They were not laughing at anything nor with anyone; they were laughing as only Negroes can laugh about nothing.

Pauline did not know how long she had been there in Mamie's house when she opened her eyes. She felt as though she had been in a deep sleep for hours. The laughter in the back yard had stopped, but echoes of it rolled in her head, just as the smile on Mamie's face had been only the beginning. She knew then that she could never forget what she had seen and heard in a Negro's house. She knew she would never be able to explain it to John, nor would she ever be able to explain the smile on Mamie's face, and the laughter in Aunt Sophie's back yard.

The silence in the house frightened her, and she realized how late it was in the afternoon. Pauline knew that John was at home wondering where she and the children were. She jumped to her feet unsteadily and ran through the doorway. Mamie ran beside her, holding her arm and supporting her with her other arm around her waist. They got into the car and sped homeward, with Mamie on the rear seat beside Jay and Claire.

John was standing on the porch when she turned into the driveway from the boulevard. She stopped the car and ran to him.

"Where have you been?" he asked, kissing her.

"Hold me tight, John! Hold me till it hurts!"

For several minutes she lay in his arms, her eyes closed, and her body trembling. It was only when he put his hand under her chin and raised her head that she could look into his eyes.

"Why is Mamie here this afternoon, Pauline?" he asked her. "I thought this was her day off."

"It was her day off, John, but I couldn't get along without her. I went to her house and brought her back."

She knew the question that he had asked dozens of times was about to be asked of her again. She knew the question was coming, because he had always asked it of her. While she waited, she lowered her head again, tightening her arms around his neck, and closed her eyes tightly.

"Are you sure that we wish to keep Mamie?" he asked her. "Pauline, is she a good Negress?"

"Yes, John," she said, her body relaxing in his arms. "Mamie is a good girl."

(First published in the *New English Weekly*)

Memorandum

THE accident was unavoidable and I was set free, but nevertheless I am guilty. He was my friend.

I was hurrying home for lunch when I ran over Lazy-Bones. I blew my horn frantically, I jammed on the brakes, I shoved into reverse, and I shouted at Lazy-Bones with all the strength in my lungs. The poor fellow was reading the pink sports sheet of his newspaper and never looked up. If you had known Lazy-Bones as well as I had known him for more than twenty years perhaps you would understand why he did not look up and jump out of the way.

It was my fault. His death, I mean. In the first place I should not have been going home for lunch, and lastly, even though I was, I shouldn't have been speeding in such a breakneck hurry. At one o'clock for the past seventeen years I had lunched each noon in a small restaurant on Grand Street. But this day I had decided to go home for lunch because I needed a change of clothing. The suit I wore was damp and ill-smelling with perspiration. The day was hot. Over my desk the thermometer's crimson mercury had risen steadily all morning, at twelve-thirty reaching 103. Even in the shade 103 degrees Fahrenheit is hot. Outside in the street the heat scorched the canvas awnings and stewed the black asphalt. On the store fronts the thermometers were registering 116 and 117 degrees and upward. My linen coat and trousers, immaculately clean and fresh that morning, reeked with salty, odorous sweat.

It's always hot down here in Georgia though.

"Lazy-Bones," of course, was a nickname. Everybody, however, who knew him called him that. His weekly paycheck from the gas company was made out to the order of "Lazy-Bones." And when he went to the bank to cash it he scrawled "Lazy-Bones" on the back. I am not at all sure that Lazy-Bones remembered either his surname or his christened name.

Lazy-Bones worked for the local gaslight company. For twenty-three years he sacked coke. Many men of much greater stability would have walked out and joined the Navy or something of the sort. But not Lazy-Bones. Lazy-Bones loved his job.

Then one morning he was given a raise of two dollars a week and a bicycle and the job of delivering bills. He was proud of his promotion and of the increase in salary, and he lost no time in letting each and all of his friends know of his good fortune. Several times he told me, on each occasion proclaiming that his job was without exception the best in town. He said he liked it because he never had to hurry. When he sacked coke it was more or less a duty to fill at least ten or fifteen bags a day, but now he had an entire month of thirty days—he chuckled to himself—in which to deliver a handful of bills.

Lazy-Bones had a soft job.

And even though he was required to be at the office every day, he never worked—if anything Lazy-Bones ever did could be called work—more than a day or two in the week. He would take two or three bills Monday or Tuesday, or Wednesday or Thursday—never Friday or Saturday—stuff them somewhere in his breeches, then get out his wheel and roll it down the street two or three blocks before attempting to stride it. After he had perched himself precariously on the saddle he would finally get the bicycle straightened out and pedal and coast sluggishly around town.

And Lazy-Bones loved to dillydally along the way.

Occasionally he delivered a bill or two in our building. He would come perhaps two or three times in a year: invariably worming up the circular stairway instead of shooting up the elevator. When he slouched in to see me—and my office was on the seventh floor—he would be as fresh of breath after the backbreaking climb as I was after riding up the elevator. Lazy-Bones climbed stairways like an old, old man climbing a long ladder.

How could I ever forget the afternoon I stumbled over Lazy-Bones on the steps in front of the city hall? He was drooping on the stone steps, staring across the street, with those immobile eyes of his in stagnant study. I say "immobile" because he never moved his eyes: if he was compelled to change his gaze he merely moved his head an inch or so in that direction.

"Hello, Lazy-Bones," I called in friendly greeting.

Before he responded I had time to read through the headlines of the afternoon newspaper.

"Heh," he exhaled languidly without looking up.

"This has certainly been a hot day, Lazy-Bones, hasn't it?" I asked, moving into the shade of the building.

"Yeh," he drawled, after I had given up hope of hearing him speak again that afternoon. "Sure is a good old hot day."

I offered him a cigarette from my supply, but he declined at great length after muttering some pointed remarks on the sex of tailor-made smokes. When I had almost finished smoking, he took from his breeches' pocket a soiled little sack of tobacco and balanced it cautiously on his bony knee. After much trouble he found a packet of crumpled cigarette papers in another of his breeches' pockets and extracted them from the pocket one by one. I had finished my work for the day and was glad of the opportunity to stand in the shade of the city hall and feel the slight southeast breeze filtering through my clothing.

After replacing each paper in the crumbling packet he chose one and placed it between his lips while he returned the packet to his pocket. When that had been accomplished he held the mouth of the dirty little sack over the paper and allowed a few crumbs and flakes to dribble on the tissue.

I fanned my perspiring face with my straw. The sun would not go down for another hour yet. Lazy-Bones carelessly dangled the yellow drawstrings of the sack over his lips until one of them finally became fastened between his teeth. This success pleased him greatly. He glanced at me from the corner of his eye and smiled broadly.

"Sure is a good old hot day," he drawled again as though he loved the sound of the words. "Ain't it?"

"One of the hottest of the summer," I stated emphatically.

"You know, I like it when it's good and hot," he declared enthusiastically, the words punctuated with dabs at the tissue with the tip of his tongue.

Later he mined a soiled match. Apathetically he tested it on the seat of his breeches. He studied the purple tip and greenish base lovingly. Then he picked up one of his feet in his hand and critically examined the worn sole of his shoe. It was evident that its condition pleased him, because he drew the head of the match across its area several times, smiling from ear to ear. The match-head was damp. It crumbled to the steps with the first stroke, but Lazy-Bones did not know of the catastrophe until I burst out with the news in annoyance. Lazy-Bones was irritating at times.

I snatched a box of matches from my pocket and with a swift, continuous sweep of the hand lit one for him.

"Here! Lazy-Bones!" I called roughly. "Here's a light!"

Lazy-Bones motioned me aside with assurance.

"I've got a match somewhere what'll light up," he explained, chuckling.

In five minutes he found it and with magical operations was able to blaze its tip. However, he had to lick the cigarette paper again and while he was preoccupied with the tissue and his tongue the flame scorched his fingers. Of course he had to throw the match to the ground.

"Christ!" I mumbled under my breath.

Lazy-Bones at last, however, had what he would call a cigarette aglow.

"Sure is a good old hot day," he announced as though never before in all his life had he made the observation.

I lit another cigarette.

"Ain't it?" he demanded with explosive enthusiasm.

I smiled at Lazy-Bones, nodding with conviction.

He rubbed the ash from his cigarette and fixed his gaze on some insignificant object across the street. I loved the indolent fellow more than ever. He knew how to live, and he thoroughly enjoyed every hour of his sluggish existence.

Lazy-Bones presently got to his feet and stretched his arms and legs with an accompaniment of groans and grunts.

"Yes, sir," he yawned, "this sure has been a good old hot day."

Again I nodded, but nonetheless there came once more that familiar explosion from the depths of his body:

"Ain't it?"

Lazy-Bones lifted his bicycle from the pavement where several hours previously it had fallen when he slouched away from it. I waved farewell and started homeward. He motioned me to a stop.

"Well," he smiled with his eyes, his ears, his nose, his chin, and his yellowed teeth, "I'm going home now and drink a pint of gin and go to bed and dream about this good old hot day."

I smiled back at him, and with a wave of the hand started home once more.

"Sure has been a good old hot day. . . . Ain't it!"

I left him dillydallying with his wheel.

But that was a long, long time ago. . . .

When I finally got my car stopped I jumped out and pulled poor old Lazy-Bones's mangled body from the axle. I pulled him from under the car and prayed while I pulled that he wasn't dead. I picked his head up in my arms, thinning the gore on his white face with the perspiration running in streams down my forehead, and wiped away the blood with my white linen coat. I called his name, begging him to answer me.

"Lazy-Bones! Lazy-Bones!"

He did not answer. His head slipped through my fingers to the hot, sticky asphalt. Somebody jerked me away.

"Lazy-Bones! *Lazy-Bones!*"

An undertaker bore him away. His pink sports page, now a wet, red rag, was wrapped around his head.

As long as I live I shall remember Lazy-Bones. Knowing the sunny nature of the poor fellow as I did it seems incredible, but nonetheless in my hands, through his matted hair, his head had felt like a bag of freshly cracked ice.

(First published in *American Earth*)

Balm of Gilead

BACK in January, about the middle of the first week, Ned Jones received a letter from the fire insurance agent's office in Bangor. The letter said that the company, effective January 1st, last, had discontinued allowing a discount on premiums covering farmhouses and barns which were equipped with lightning rods. Therefore, the lettter said, the cost for protection on his buildings would be raised to twenty-two-fifty from twenty-fifty.

However, the letter went on, if the rods were already installed on the building, a lightning-rod expert would call and inspect the terminals, ground wires, brads, and so forth, and if the expert found them in first-class condition, the discount would be reinstated. The charge for all of this, the letter concluded, would be three dollars for the inspector's time.

"Thunderation," Ned said when he had finished reading the letter the third time. "Hell and thunderation!"

It did not take him long to figure out that he would save a dollar by not having the lightning rods inspected, but even so he could see that it was going to cost him two dollars a year more to keep his buildings covered by insurance.

"That's thunderation," he said.

His wife, Betty, was silent about the whole matter. She always froze up inside whenever something came up like that and threatened to cost an extra penny.

The insurance premium was not due and payable until February 1st, but a week before that time Ned got ready to make a trip to Bangor and pay a call at the insurance agent's office.

He and his wife started out to Bangor after breakfast, driving the old car slowly along the black-top road, taking care to stay as far on the right-hand side of the road as possible. The law was that a car owner would not have to carry liability and property-damage insurance as long as he did not have a mishap. Ned was set on not having that first accident on the highways that would force him to pay insurance premiums for the right to drive his car. It was an old car anyway, about twelve years old, and he did not intend buying another one when it was worn out.

They got to Bangor just before ten o'clock in the forenoon, and, after finding a safe place to park and leave the automobile, Ned and his wife went straight to the agent's office.

They sat down on a bench in the hall and waited for several minutes, and then a girl took them to see Mr. Harmsworth.

"Now, about that insurance on my stand of buildings out at Gaylord," Ned said, shaking his head and his finger at the agent.

"I take it you're upset about the new lightning-rod clause, effective January 1st, last," Mr. Harmsworth said, smiling at Ned and his wife. "You see Mr. Jones, and Mrs. Jones, the company at the home office in New Hampshire rewrites the contracts, and we agents have nothing whatever to do with the terms the company dictates."

"What do people in New Hampshire know about lightning rods anyway?" Ned said. "Now let me tell you. I once knew a man in New Hampshire who—"

"Let's not get off the subject, Mr. Jones, and Mrs. Jones," Mr. Harmsworth said. "After all, both my parents were born and raised in New Hampshire, and I'm sure there is a New Hampshire connection somewhere in your family, too."

He smiled at Mrs. Jones, beaming upon her all the force of what he knew was a sunny smile. Betty refused to be disarmed. She was frozen up inside, and she intended to remain unthawed as long as the insurance company refused to make an adjustment that would not cost them an extra penny.

"Now, I've lived down here in the State of Maine for all my life," Ned said, "and I'm sixty and more right now, and lightning rods are the only things in the world that'll keep lightning from striking and setting fire to the house or barn. All my life I've seen lightning strike a spire and run down the cable into the ground without even so much as smoking up the roof and clapboards. If it wasn't for lightning rods—"

"Are you sure lightning runs down lightning rods, Mr. Jones, and Mrs. Jones?" Mr. Harmsworth said. "I was under the impression it ran up the rods, or rather made contact on the point of the spire. However—"

"Lightning is lightning, whether it runs up or down, or slantwise, if it has a mind to," Ned said, rising up.

"I see you know a lot more about such things than I do," Mr. Harmsworth laughed, beaming upon Mrs. Jones. "I was raised here in the city, and I never had a chance to observe how lightning behaves when it comes in contact with a rod-equipped building. But, just the same, there's nothing either you or I can do about this here clause, because the home office rewrote the contract and sent us the printed forms, and I'm merely their representative. I carry out their orders, but I have no authority to alter a clause in a contract."

Ned looked at his wife, and she shook her head. That was all he wanted to know. No insurance company, with a home office in New Hampshire, run by New Hampshire people, was going to tell him whether they thought lightning rods were protection or not. He looked at his wife again, and shook his head. Betty tightened her mouth, freezing tighter inside, and nodded at Ned.

Mr. Harmsworth shuffled some papers on his desk, and, bringing one out with much crinkling and creasing, laid it before Ned.

"This is your bill for fire-protection coverage, due February 1st," he said, glancing quickly at Ned, but not looking at Mrs. Jones.

Ned pushed it back at him.

"Now, about this Balm of Gilead," Ned said, edging forward in his chair.

"What Balm of Gilead?" Mr. Harmsworth asked, startled. "What's that?"

Ned looked at his wife, and Betty nodded. That was what he wanted to know from her. He pulled his chair closer to the desk.

"My Balm of Gilead," he said. "I've got one in my dooryard, fourteen feet from the west wall of my dwelling house, and twenty-two feet from the east wall of my barn."

"What's a Balm of Gilead?" Mr. Harmsworth asked, still startled. "Wasn't that something in the Bible? How'd you get something that was in the Bible?"

Ned and Betty looked at each other, but neither of them made any motion of the head.

"Balm of Gilead is a tree," Ned said. "My Balm of Gilead was set out by my father, seventy-seven years ago, and it stands in my dooryard."

"What about it?" Mr. Harmsworth asked, wild-eyed.

"It's a lightning rod," Ned said. "It's the finest lightning rod on earth. After a Balm of Gilead—"

"You want us to give you a discount because you have a tree —" Mr. Harmsworth began, sitting forward in his chair.

"—passes its fiftieth year, it turns into a lightning rod," Ned continued doggedly. "Lightning won't strike any other thing within fifty yards of it. Lightning strikes the Balm of Gilead every time."

"I don't know what you're driving at exactly," Mr. Harmsworth said, "but I wouldn't suppose you expect to get any discount on your fire insurance for having a tree like that."

Betty stiffened her backbone.

"I don't know why not," Ned said. "Why shouldn't I get a discount when I've got a Balm of Gilead located almost halfway between my two buildings, and the farthest is twenty-two feet from it. A tree like that is two or three times more protection than rods on the buildings. Why, it even makes the buildings proof against lightning! I figure I'm due five or six dollars discount for having that tree where it is."

Mr. Harmsworth scratched his head and took a swift look at Mrs. Jones. He had time to see that her mouth was drawn in a tight line across her face. He did not look at her again.

"If you insist upon it," he said, "I'll take it up with the home office in New Hampshire. I won't be able to do a thing until I hear from them. But I shouldn't think they would allow anybody a discount on fire insurance for having a Balm of Gilead tree."

"If they wasn't those New Hampshire people," Ned said, "they'd know how much protection a tree like that is."

"I'll write you a letter and let you know what the home office has to say just as soon as I get their answer," he said, standing up.

Ned and Betty got up and went out into the hall. Mr. Harmsworth followed them trying to shake hands with at least one of them. Betty kept her hands clasped tightly across her waist. Ned outwalked the agent to the street.

"Ignorant young cuss," Ned said. "Associates with New Hampshire people."

Betty nodded her head.

They bought a few things in a store, and then got into their car and drove home. Neither of them mentioned the insurance during the rest of the day.

During the remainder of the week, and through the first three days of the following one, both Ned and his wife watched the mail for the letter from the agent in Bangor. On the third day the letter came.

They went into the kitchen and sat down in the chairs by the window before opening it. Ned first took out his glasses and carefully polished the lenses. Betty put her handkerchief to her nose, and then put it away. Ned read the letter aloud.

DEAR MR. JONES:

I have taken up the matter of the Balm of Gilead tree in your dooryard with the home office in New Hampshire, and I am herewith advising you of their decision. It seems that the company thought it was all a joke or something because, in their own words, they wished to know if your Balm of Gilead tree would "catch mice, scare crows away, and cure painter's colic." Further along in their letter they state most emphatically that under no circumstances would a discount on fire-insurance premiums be allowed for possession of a Balm of Gilead tree. . . .

The letter did not end there, but Ned read no farther. He

handed the letter to his wife, and she laid it aside on the table, drawing her mouth into a thin straight line across her face.

"I never did waste any feelings for the people of New Hampshire," Ned said, putting away his glasses, getting his hat, and standing up.

His wife did not say a word when he left the kitchen and went out into the dooryard.

When she saw him come out of the woodshed with the ax and the crosscut saw, she put on her jacket and went out to help him.

First he cut a notch in the Balm of Gilead on the side in order to fell it in the direction where he wanted it to fall. When that was done, he picked up one end of the crosscut, and Betty picked up the other end. They began sawing silently, their faces bright but drawn in tight lines, and both hoping that an electrical storm would come early in the spring, and each of them praying silently that lightning would strike the house and burn it to a heap of ashes on the ground.

(First published in *Story*)

A Very Late Spring

MARY JANE knew Dave was up to some kind of mischief, but to save her soul she could not find out what it was. Dave had been acting queerly for more than a month. He was nervous and restless when he came in the house and she had a hard time making him finish his meals. Dave said he was just not hungry, but Mary Jane knew that was not the real reason. He was up to some kind of mischief.

Dave blamed it all on the weather. Here it was the last of April and almost the first of May, he said, and it was still winter. There should have been a thaw three or four weeks ago, but instead there were nineteen inches of snow and ice on the ground and the thermometer never went above the twenties. And it looked like more snow right then.

Mary Jane reminded him of the winter three years before when the spring thaw did not come until the first week in May. She said she was certain the lake ice would go out almost any day now.

Mary Jane could not see how the weather had anything to do with the way he was acting.

Instead of getting over his restlessness, Dave got worse.

When he came home at night, after working all day in the lumber mill, he wanted to go out again before he finished eating his supper. There was a dance at the Grange hall every Tuesday night, and the moving pictures every Friday night, but there was no place to go during the rest of the week. Mary Jane went to the pictures on Friday nights and to the dance whenever there was one, and the other evenings she was in the habit of staying at home and doing her lacework. Dave wanted to go somewhere every night now.

"Why can't you sit by the fire and read the newspapers like you used to do, Dave?" she asked, with her worried frown that he had once liked so much.

"I want to go somewhere," was his answer. It was the same answer each time she asked him.

She placed supper on the table and Dave sat down in his chair.

"You act like a twelve-year-old boy, Dave," she stated accusingly. "You used to want to stay at home when I wanted to go to the dance or the pictures at the Grange hall. Now you want to go off and leave me by myself every night. What makes you so restless lately?"

"Maybe the winters are getting worse," he mumbled to himself. "I wish I lived out in California or down in Florida, where they don't have to put up with snow and ice half the whole year."

Mary Jane gave up trying to talk to Dave. Every time she asked him what made him so restless at night he always cursed the winters and said he was going where there were none. It did no good to try to talk to him. Dave did not pay any attention to her. He was always thinking about something else.

Two days later there was a four-inch snowfall. It began to snow at about eight o'clock in the morning just after Dave went to the lumberyard. By six o'clock that night it had almost stopped, but there were four inches of it on the ground—on top of the nineteen inches already there.

Mary Jane waited all day for night to come. Not because she wanted it to come, but because she dreaded it more than anything in the world. She knew Dave would come home cursing the winters and the snow. And then before he was halfway through supper he would get up and want to go somewhere. She knew exactly what he would say about it.

Just as she knew he would do, that evening Dave stopped eating in the middle of his meal and got up from the table. She watched him go to the next room for his hat and mackinaw. Then he went to the hall and put on his heavy shoes. When he did that, she could stand it no longer. She ran to him.

"Where are you going, Dave?"

"I'm going out to walk around awhile," he said nervously. "I'm going out. I'll be back after a while."

Dave went out the door and closed it behind him. She could hear the crunch of the snow under his feet while he walked down the path to the road. When he got there, the sound stopped. She knew he was walking in the deep snow and cursing about the winters.

After the dishes had been washed and the kitchen put in order, Mary Jane went to the next room and sat down in front of the fire. She had been doing a lot of thinking for the past two weeks or more, and the more she thought, the more uneasy she became. There was something that disturbed her. She could not help thinking about it because every time Dave got restless and went out it made her think about it all the more.

She had been doing a lot of thinking lately about the schoolteacher the Maxwells were boarding. The teacher had been living there all winter, but Mary Jane had not seen her until about the middle of January. The girl was too young to teach school and she was too pretty to live in the village. Her name was Flora Dunn. She remembered when Dave told her. He said she was not much more than seventeen or nineteen years old. That was all he said about her, but ever since then Mary Jane had been thinking a lot. The teacher who was there the year before had been asked not to come back because she put too much coloring on her face. The Dunn girl was not like that. She was so young she was pretty without coloring.

Mary Jane suddenly sprang up and put on all her heavy clothes and went to the barn and hitched the horse to the sleigh. When that was done, she carefully took off all the harness bells. She had enough to distract her without hearing a lot of tinkling little bells on the horse. And besides, she did not want the bells on tonight, anyway. She took the bells off and laid them on the carriage seat.

She drove down the road past the Maxwells' house. Then she drove up and down in front of the house six or seven times. She stopped by a tree the last time and hitched the horse to it. After that she walked up and down the road to keep warm.

After waiting twenty minutes in the road Mary Jane saw Flora go upstairs to bed and turn out the light. In two minutes a figure came from the house and through the snow to the road. Mary Jane knew it was Flora. She was certain of that.

While she waited beside the horse and sleigh, Flora crossed the road and went down the hillside toward the cannery at the lake. Mary Jane followed her across the snow. There was no moon visible, but the clouds were so thin the moon gave enough light to enable her to follow Flora.

When Flora reached the cannery, she opened the unlocked door and went inside for a few minutes. Then she came back and stood in the doorway, looking out over the lake as though she expected somebody to come across the ice.

Mary Jane waited beside a tree. Presently she could hear a low whistle out on the lake somewhere, and almost instantly followed an answering whistle from Flora. Mary Jane waited. She knew it was Dave walking across the ice on the lake. And she knew he was coming to the cannery.

Dave came across the ice and went up the steps to the cannery door. Flora stepped back inside just as he came up, and Mary Jane could not see what they were doing. She lost no time in getting to the cannery. Then cautiously she went up the steps. The door had been closed but not locked. She opened it easily without a sound. Dave and the girl had lighted a candle and put it on the peeling-table. The light it gave was not strong enough to see everywhere inside, but she could easily distinguish Dave and the girl. They were whispering together in the corner behind the boiling-tubs.

Mary Jane slammed the door and reached for a piece of rope she saw hanging on the wall.

"Who is that?" she heard Dave's anxious voice.

Flora screamed.

Mary Jane ran across the cannery floor to the corner. She slashed Dave's face with the rope and struck Flora around her legs.

"For God's sake, Mary Jane," Dave pleaded, when he recognized her face in the candlelight. "Mary Jane, please don't do that!"

"So you got tired of waiting for the winter to pass, didn't you?" she shouted at him. "The winter made you restless, didn't it?"

She stung him again and again with the rope across his face and shoulders. She did not hit Flora again.

Flora clung to Dave's arm and would not leave him. Mary Jane got more angry when she saw Flora hanging to Dave. She drew back to strike the girl, but Dave jerked the rope from her hand.

"What's the matter with you, Mary Jane?" he shouted. "You stop trying to hurt her!"

"You shut your mouth, Dave! I'm going to teach her a lesson so she'll never bother a married man again as long as she lives!"

Dave caught her arms and held her. As soon as he touched Mary Jane she relaxed and almost fell to the floor.

"If you'll promise not to see Dave again I won't tell on you," she said to Flora. "But if you don't promise, I'll take both of you up to the house and tell the Maxwells exactly where you were and what you were doing. If I did that, you'd have to leave your school tomorrow—and anyway, you'll have better sense than to apply for this same school again next year, won't you?"

"I promise," Flora begged. "I promise I won't see him again! Please don't tell Mr. Maxwell, or anybody!"

"Well, we're going home now," Mary Jane said. "Come on."

They walked up the hill to the road. Dave walked in front, Mary Jane behind him, and Flora last. When they reached the road, Flora ran to the house without looking back.

"Come on home, Dave," Mary Jane said.

She led him to the horse and sleigh.

Neither said a word while they rode through the village. At the barn Dave unharnessed the horse while Mary Jane went into the house.

When Dave came into the room, Mary Jane was looking at something in the almanac. Dave pretended not to be interested in what she was doing.

"Dave," Mary Jane said, handing him the almanac opened at the month of April, "Dave, the almanac says there's going to be a big spring thaw in northern New England beginning the 20th—and tomorrow's the 20th. Did you know that?"

"Where does it say that?" he asked anxiously, taking the almanac and holding it so the light could fall on the print. "Does it say we're going to start the spring thaw tomorrow, sure enough?"

(First published in *Scribner's*)

Joe Craddock's Old Woman

JULIA CRADDOCK was thirty-five and not once in her life had she been pretty and charming. Thirty-five years had passed— youth and maturity—and still no beauty or charm. And the older she became the uglier she was. Her body was hard and muscular from fifteen years in the kitchen and over the wash tubs. Her hair was coarse, stringy, and dingy. Her face had creased into lines of toil and hideousness and her breasts had fallen flat to her chest like saddle flaps. No man had ever seen in Julia anything but the repugnant suggestion of a female. Not even Joe, her husband. She to him had always been Old Woman.

And now she was dead.

Death was her compensation. As it came it was a compensation for the ugliness of her face and body, and of her life. She had been miserable while she lived—eleven children, fourteen cows, and a flock of chickens.—And eight stinking hogs. Not once had Julia left the farm in over ten years. Work, work, work, from four in the morning till nine at night; never a vacation, a trip to town, nor time to bathe all over. Joe worked all the time, too. Yet his labor returned nothing but an aching back, heartbreak, and poverty. The harder he worked the poorer he became. If he made twenty bales of cotton in the fall the price would drop to where he could barely pay for the fertilizer—usually not even that. Or if the price went up to thirty cents a pound he would, by the curse of too much rain or not enough rain, have no cotton to sell. There with Joe and Julia life wasn't worth living very long.

And now Julia was dead. And she had never been pretty, nor had she ever felt as though she were. Not once had she had silk against her skin, powder on her nose, a glow on her cheeks, or all the dirt removed from the underside of her fingernails.

The undertaker came and carried her body away. The next morning he brought it back prepared for the burial that afternoon in the cemetery beside the camp-meeting grounds.

But what a body he brought back!

For a long time Joe wouldn't believe it was Julia. But he found the photograph she had given him a few weeks before they were married and then he knew it was Julia. She looked like a young girl again.

Julia had been bathed all over, and her hair had been shampooed. Her hands were white, and the fingernails manicured; her face was clean and smooth with powder and rouge, and cotton in her mouth levelled the hollows of her cheeks. For once Julia was beautiful. Joe couldn't take his eyes from her. He sat all day by the casket, silent, weeping, worshiping her beauty. She was clothed in silk—stockings and chemise—and over that a sea-blue dress. The silk dress was sleeveless and cut low in the bust. The undertaker had made her look like a beautiful young girl.

That afternoon she was buried with her beauty in the cemetery at the camp-meeting grounds. Joe begged at the last minute to have the funeral postponed until the next day, but the undertaker wouldn't listen to him. And neither did he understand.

Julia's children, with the exception of the oldest two, were not certain of what had become of their mother. It was several years before they could believe that the body the undertaker brought back was that of Julia their mother.

"But that woman in the coffin was a beautiful lady," they would say.

"Yes," Joe told them, "Julia—your mother—was a beautiful lady."

Then he would go to the dresser drawer and take out the photograph for them to see.

(First published in *Blues*)

An Evening in Nuevo Leon

IT WAS ten o'clock in the starlit desert evening when we drove into Nuevo Leon. After winding through the adobe-walled streets for a while we found the hotel and stopped in front of the entrance. There were few persons out that late, and the only sounds we could hear were the gurgling of the fountain in the plaza across the street and the desert breeze in the tall palms, making a sound like rustling taffeta.

While we were taking some of our things from the car, the proprietor of the hotel came out bowing and smiling. He helped us with a couple of the bags and led us into the lobby.

"It is an honor to have you come into my hotel," he said, stopping in the center of the lobby and bowing again. "I am very pleased to have you as my guests. The Reforma Hotel is honored."

We smiled in return. It made us feel good to be welcomed in such a manner.

The proprietor backed behind the desk. Then he placed the register in front of me and handed me the freshly dipped pen.

"The house is yours, Señor," he said graciously. "Have you been long in Mexico?"

We were tired and dusty, and far from being in a talkative mood. It had been a hard trip across the desert and mountains from the coast. Although the distance was less than three hundred miles, it had taken us since five that morning to reach Nuevo Leon.

I scrawled my name on the register, adding "y Sra." On the next line I wrote out my wife's maiden name in full.

The proprietor leaned over the register and looked at the two entries closely.

"The señorita?" he inquired, looking at us.

"There are only two of us," I said, indicating my wife and myself.

He bent over the register, this time taking out his glasses and perching them on his nose. After several moments he straightened up and removed the glasses, shaking his head emphatically.

"No, Señor," he said unsmilingly.

My wife nudged me with her elbow.

"Here is how it is, Señor," I spoke up. "I signed my name, and added 'y Sra.' for my wife. Then on this next line I wrote out my wife's name in full, her professional name. That was to make everything plain."

"But where is the señorita?" he asked, unshaken. "I did not see her arrive here at the hotel with you." He looked at my wife and me, counting us on two fingers of his hand. "Where is the señorita?"

"There is no señorita," I said quickly. "My wife and the señorita are one and the same person."

A broad smile lighted the proprietor's face.

"That is wonderful!" he said, bowing to my wife.

"What is?" I asked.

"You and the señorita are to be married! It is wonderful!"

My wife and I leaned wearily against the desk. It was almost eleven o'clock by then and we had been up since four that morning. We were envious of all the other guests in the Reforma who had long since retired.

"Señor, let me explain," I began. "It is a custom of us crazy Norteamericanos. When a man's wife has a professional name, we sometimes sign both her married name and her professional name at a time like this. She may be receiving telegrams under both names."

"No, Señor," he spoke up. "That is impossible."

"Why?" I asked.

"The telegraph office is closed."

"Never mind, then," I said, glancing at my wife. She had dropped her head wearily on the desk. "We don't want to receive any telegrams tonight, anyway. Just give us a room and let us go to sleep."

The proprietor nodded his head gravely.

"It is all right now," he said. "I misunderstood. I offer my apologies. I am very sorry. I will now give you two rooms where you may retire to sleep immediately."

My wife raised her head from the desk.

"One room," she said sleepily.

"That is impossible," he said sternly.

My wife's head dropped back into the comfort of her arms on the desk.

"Why is it impossible?" I asked.

"I cannot give you one room, because you and the senorita may not sleep together in the Reforma Hotel. It is impossible. I will give you two separate rooms, Señor y Señorita."

My wife held up her hand, showing him her wedding ring. He looked at it uncertainly.

"We have been married for only seven long, long years, Señor," she said wearily.

"My apologies, Señora," he said gravely. "I am deeply humiliated by my behavior. I offer you my apologies time and time again."

My wife and I backed away, relieved. After we had gone halfway to the stairs we turned and discovered that the proprietor was still behind the desk. He was bent over the register, with his glasses perched on his nose again, reading the entries I had made.

"There has been a serious mistake," the proprietor said, looking at us accusingly. "Señora, your husband has not yet arrived at the hotel. When do you expect him?"

My wife and I looked at each other confusedly.

"What are you talking about?" she said, going back to the desk. "This is my husband here, Señor!"

He looked at the names written on the register once more. Then he straightened up, shaking his head sternly.

"It is impossible," he said.

"Why?" she asked.

"Your husband has not yet registered at the Reforma Hotel. When he arrives, he must sign his name in this book before he may share your room with you, Señora."

He looked at us more sternly than ever.

"What in the world are we going to do?" my wife asked perplexedly, turning to me.

"I don't know," I told her. "I don't know what we can do."

While we stood there, the proprietor took two keys from the rack behind the desk and led the way to the stairs. We followed in silence, fearing to utter a word even in whisper.

When we reached the hall on the second floor, the proprietor unlocked a door and bowed my wife into the room. Before I could follow her inside he stepped into the doorway, blocking my entrance.

"No, Señor," he said, shaking his head at me. "It is impossible."

I could see my wife standing on tiptoes looking at me over his shoulder. She was speechless.

Dropping the luggage, I went up to him.

"Let me explain once more, Señor," I began, trying my best to conceal my impatience. "We are married to each other. My wife is wearing her wedding ring. We wish to enter our room and retire for the night. We are very tired. We drove all the way across the desert from the coast today."

He turned and looked at my wife. She gazed at him appealingly.

After several moments of indecision, he shrugged his shoulders and stepped aside, bowing deeply.

"I must apologize for my error," he said. "Sometimes I do not always understand the customs of the Norteamericanos. Please accept my apologies."

He bowed backward down the hall until he reached the stairway. I ran into the room, shut the door, and locked it securely before anything further could happen.

We stood at the door listening to his footsteps until we were certain he had gone down to the lobby.

It was not long before we were startled by a sudden rapping on the door. We waited, holding our breath. After a moment the knocking began again, louder than before. It could not be ignored after that.

"Who is it?" I shouted in the darkness.

"I am the proprietor, Señor," he said. "Please open the door immediately."

"Don't do it," my wife said. "We'll never get any sleep tonight if we have to argue with him again."

"But he may break down the door," I said.

"Let him break it down," she said wearily. "It's his door."

We were quiet, not making another sound.

The renewed knocking shook the whole building. It continued unceasingly.

"We may as well find out what he wants," I said. "We can't sleep with that going on."

"Don't let him start another argument, whatever you do," my wife said. "Tell him it is too late to argue now, but that we will argue with him in the morning after breakfast."

I turned on the light.

"What do you want, Señor?" I asked at last.

"The door must be opened immediately," he said, raising his voice above the knocking.

I got up and unlocked the door. The proprietor stood in the doorway. He did not cross the threshold.

"It is impossible!" he said excitedly.

"What's impossible?" I asked.

"You may not sleep with the señorita!" he said loudly.

"Oh, my goodness!" my wife cried. "He's started that again!"

I could hear doors opening along the hall. Everybody in the hotel had been aroused by the clamor.

"Look here!" I said crossly. "I am not sleeping with a señorita! This is my wife!"

"It is impossible!" he said, raising his voice above mine.

"Why is it impossible?" I shouted.

"You must occupy a separate room, Señor!" he commanded. "Tomorrow you may become married to the señorita, if she wishes to be married, and then tomorrow night you will not be required to occupy separate rooms. But tonight you must!"

I glanced toward my wife helplessly.

"What are we going to do?" I asked.

"Goodness knows," she said. "Won't he listen to reason at all?"

I turned round and faced the proprietor, opening my mouth to speak. Before I could utter a sound he had already spoken.

"It is impossible, Señor," he said, pushing himself between me and the room.

I found myself being directed down the hall, past several persons standing sleepily in the doorways of their rooms. He opened a door and turned on the light.

"Please accept my apologies, Señor," he said, bowing low. "It is to my deep regret. But it was impossible."

He closed the door, quickly turning the key in the lock on the outside. After he had withdrawn it, I heard him walking briskly down the hall to the stairway.

(First published in *Harper's*)

Ten Thousand Blueberry Crates

No one in the village had ever heard of a wood-turning mill called the Yankee Dowel Company when the stranger asked to be directed to it. He said he was positive the plant was in the town of Liverpool, because he had a letter in his pocket with the postmark on it and the name and address of the company printed on the letterhead. There were six or seven mills of that kind in the town, the largest being over in East Liverpool and owned by Walt Brown.

"Who signed the letter you got there?" Nate Emmonds asked him.

"A man by the name of Brown," he said, looking at the letter again. "Walter J. Brown."

"Walt Brown, eh?" Nate said, glancing around at the men in the store. "Walt Brown signed the letter, and he calls himself the Yankee Dowel Company. I wonder what he could be up to now?"

A knowing wink passed from man to man around the stove.

"He used to be the Eastern Barrel Hoop Corporation," someone said, slapping his hands on his knees and having a good laugh with the other men, "but I ain't heard much about that corporation since wooden flour barrels went out of use. Walt's been doing his durndest trying to sell me a load of barrel hoops to stake tomato plants with. He thinks up the queerest notions to get rid of his hoops of any man I ever saw. Who ever heard of staking tomato plants with barrel hoops, anyhow?"

It was several minutes before the crowd stopped laughing at Walt. He had been up to some crazy schemes in his lifetime. Only a month or two before that, he was all excited over a plan of his to make a new kind of wooden clothespin at his mill. Now there was something else up his sleeve. The trouble with Walt was he was always letting somebody get the better of him when it came to business deals. He got along all right as long as he stuck to his lumber business, but whenever he tried to branch out into fancy woodwork he was always licked from the start. Everybody thought he had learned his lesson after losing a lot of money in the barrel-hoop deal, and believed that he would stick to his planing and stop trying to get rich by taking up fancy doweling. Apparently, though, he was going in for it again.

"Sure," Nate said, "I know Walt Brown. But what's your name, and what do you want to see him for?"

The man looked at Nate and then at the crowd around the stove before he said anything. He knew the men would not tell him how to find the mill until he told them his name and business.

"I'm Bullock," he said, "from over at the Falls. I buy and sell wooden products."

Androscoggin Falls was a town forty-five miles northeast of Liverpool. There were several shoe factories there, with a dozen or more mills turning out wooden products of various kinds.

Nate slapped his hands on his knees and winked at the men around him.

"So you're a Bullock from over at the Falls, eh? I don't guess you give milk then, do you?"

Everybody in the store broke out laughing again. The man from the Falls could not keep from laughing either.

"No," he said, suddenly getting red in the face and looking angry. "No, I don't give milk, but I'm a damn hard butter when I get wild and loose."

The crowd took it all in without a sign. The men knew Nate had run up against a man every bit as sharp-witted as he was. Nate looked at Bullock very hard for a moment, but he had nothing to say to that answer.

"Come on outside," Nate told him, "and I'll show you how to find Walt Brown's mill."

When they were out in the street, Nate offered him some

smoking tobacco and admired his automobile. It was not long before both of them were laughing and telling each other jokes.

Bullock said finally that he was in a hurry to find the mill and get back to the Falls. Nate told him to take the upper lake road three miles to East Liverpool. Walt's mill was at the end of the lake where the State road crossed the stream.

It did not take him long to go the three miles in his car. When he reached East Liverpool, he walked into the mill and found Walt operating one of the wood-turning machines. There were five or six other men working in the plant with him.

"You're Walter Brown, aren't you?" Bullock asked him.

"I'm the one," Walt said. "What do you want?"

"I'm Bullock, from over at the Falls. You sent me some prices on cider-jug handles last week. I came over to talk business with you."

Walt brightened up immediately. He shut off the machine he was running and took Bullock to his office in the house across the street.

"That's a fairly good price you gave me on fifty gross," Bullock said. "I've got a chain store begging for some right away, so if I were to double that number could you shade the price a little?"

"Well, I guess maybe I can," Walt said. "And I guess maybe we can do business together."

Walt was very much excited over the prospect of getting a big order for wooden handles. When he had sent Bullock the quotation the week before, he had not expected it to amount to anything. Some people said his prices were too high, and that his plant was too far away from the railroad for him to get much business without offering f.o.b. shipments like the rest of the mill men. It cost a lot of money to truck twenty-seven miles to the depot.

Bullock signed the order for a hundred gross of the jug handles and gave Walt shipping directions. He knew he would have to pay trucking costs in addition to the freight, but he had figured all that into the cost before he left the Falls. Even then he was getting the handles cheaper than ever before, and he was pleased with Walt's price. The wooden jug handles had been costing him from fifty to seventy-five cents more a gross from the mills at the Falls.

When he was about to leave, he happened to see a stack of barrel hoops in the mill. He asked Walt if he turned out hoops too. Walt explained that it was some leftover stock he had been unable to sell because people had stopped buying flour in barrels as they used to and bought it now in sacks instead.

Bullock went in and looked the lot over. Walt watched him break one of the hoops over his knee to inspect the grain in the wood. Bullock's business was dealing in wooden products on commission, but he had not had a hoop to pass through his hands in more than three years.

"I can't do anything with barrel hoops either, these days, but I'll tell you one thing I've never been able to get enough of."

"What's that?" Walt asked quickly.

"Blueberry crates," he said. "I can't get enough of them. I could have sold five hundred only last week to a man over in New Hampshire if I could have got my hands on some. The blueberry-crate business is better this year than it ever has been. Everybody wants crates this year to ship berries to market."

Walt thought a while about blueberry crates and walked around in circles. He had made almost everything in wooden products during his lifetime, but a blueberry crate was one thing he had never thought of. He knew he could do it, though, because his machines would turn out practically anything.

"I can make blueberry crates," he said.

"If you can make delivery of them by the end of this month I can use them," Bullock said. "I'll pay the ruling price on them at the time you make delivery, too. That's a better deal for you than setting a price beforehand, because the market will be up when the season opens. I'll take as many as you can get out in that time, too. But they'll have to be ready before the end of the month, because after that the season will be too far advanced."

Walt went to his office to get an order blank for Bullock to sign, but when he came back to the mill Bullock had gone. Walt did not like that, because he never wanted to make up an order when it hadn't been signed for in advance. In that case he could not bring suit to collect if the man refused to take the lot. But Bullock looked all right, and he talked as if he meant to take them. In the matter of blueberry crates a signed order did not mean much anyway, because if a man decided to cancel an order all he had to do was to claim the crates were not up to standard specifications.

Walt went ahead with his plans for making the crates anyway. But first he started getting out the wooden jug handles and had his men begin work on them right away. They would finish that job in a few days, and in the meantime they could begin getting the machines ready for the crates.

He went to the village the next morning to buy some nails with which to put the crates together. He had made a sample crate the night before, and with the weight of the nails he used he had figured out an estimate for the entire lot.

When he reached the village he went to Pat Hobb's store and told Pat he wanted some crate nails. Pat talked awhile about the road money, and how it was being wasted by putting in a gravel fill by the North Schoolhouse. Walt was on the town road commission but he did not have much to say. He was in a hurry for the nails so he could get back to the mill.

Pat went over to the keg and picked it up. There were not more than ten pounds of nails in it.

"How many do you want?" he asked Walt.

"How many have you got?"

"About eight to ten pounds, maybe twelve."

"I want all of those, and I'll need a lot more besides."

"But I can't sell you all I've got, Walt. Suppose somebody else came in and said they wanted some?"

"Good God, I can't help that," Walt said. "You've got them to sell ain't you? Well, sell them to me. I'm the one that wants to buy them."

"I couldn't do that, Walt," Pat said, putting the keg on the floor again. "I wouldn't have none left if I sold them all to you."

"Good God," said Walt, "ain't you in the selling business? What do you keep store for if it ain't to sell?"

"I know, but somebody—"

"Good God, Pat, don't make me mad. You can get some more nails, can't you? I'll want a lot more myself before I'm done buying. Why, do you know how many blueberry crates I'm going to make?"

"No," Pat said. "How many?"

"Ten thousand."

"Ten thousand blueberry crates?"

"That's what I said."

"Good God, Walt, that's a heap of blueberry crates. I never heard of a man making ten thousand of them before. What are you going to do with them?"

Walt did not know just then, himself. When he had said *ten thousand* it was done to impress Pat, so he could get all the nails he wanted, but when he began to think it over he was not sure that Bullock could take that many. It would take a lot of quart baskets of blueberries to fill that many crates, and there were other mills making crates too. But Walt knew he could never back down now. Pat would tell Nate Emmonds about it, and that would make Nate take back a lot of the things he had been saying about Walt and his wooden-products business.

"I've got an order from Bullock over at the Falls for that many. Maybe more, too."

Pat remembered Bullock's coming into the store and asking for Walt a few days before that. He would tell Nate about the big number of crates Walt was making as soon as he came into the store again.

"I'll take what nails you got there, Pat," Walt said. "And I'll be back in a few days for a lot more. I'll need a pile of nails to put all those crates together."

"All right," Pat agreed, "you can take them. But I know I ain't doing best. Somebody will be sure to come in and ask for crate nails and I won't have none at all."

"You order some right away. I'll be in again soon for two or three kegs full."

Walt went back to the mill and got to work on the crates. The wooden handles for the cider and vinegar jugs would be ready by the end of the next day. After he got them off to Bullock he could put all his men to work on the crates.

Everybody in town had heard about the large number of blueberry crates Walt was going to make, and by the middle of the following day men began coming in to ask Walt for a job helping make them. Walt took on fifteen new men and went to work. By the end of the week they were turning crates out at the rate of a thousand a day. The stack in the millyard got higher and higher, and it was not long before crates were piled twenty feet high in every available place.

The piles of crates attracted the attention of a man passing through East Liverpool in his car late Tuesday afternoon of the following week. He stopped, turned around, and drove back to the mill where Walt was. Walt was too busy to stop work.

"What kind of crates are those?" he asked Walt.

"Blueberry," Walt said without turning around,

"If you had said raspberry, I couldn't have told the difference. Raspberry crates are exactly like those. And I ought to know, because raspberry crates is my business."

"What do you want?" Walt asked him. "I can't waste time talking when I've got work to do."

"I want to buy those crates," the man said. "I had just started on a buying trip to get raspberry crates for my customers. I buy and sell wooden products on commission, and if you'll meet my offer halfway we can do business. I'll take all the crates you've got and haul them away in my own trucks starting tomorrow. You'll sell them to me, won't you?"

"Nope," Walt said, "I won't sell them to you. And those ain't raspberry crates, either—them are blueberry crates. And anyway, they are already bargained for. I'm making them on order."

Walt could not understand why the man called them raspberry crates. If he had learned the business of making crates before he jumped into it, he would have known that blueberry crates had to be made up in bundles because most of them were shipped several hundred miles down East on the coast, while raspberry crates were usually nailed together at the time they were made because they were used in this section of the state

TEN THOUSAND BLUEBERRY CRATES 315

and it was cheaper and a saving of time to truck them to the
fields directly from the mills. A distance of fifty miles was all
that was necessary at times to change the name and use of a
crate.

"This is the first time I ever saw blueberry crates put together at the mill. All the blueberry people I know want the
parts shipped to them in bundles, and then they knock the
crates together right in the fields where—"

"When you've been in the wooden-products business for as
long a time as—"

"Then you're not going to sell me those raspberry crates
even if I—"

"These blueberry crates are already bargained for. And if
they was raspberry crates I wouldn't sell—"

"I've got to be going," the man said. "I can't waste my time
standing here talking all day to a blundering fool."

"If you don't get going I'll have to waste some of my time
looking for a piece of four-by-four to start you off with."

The man knew he could never persuade Walt to sell the
crates, no matter what name he called them by, so he went
back to his car and drove away. He had been dealing with mill
men in that section of the state for thirty years, and he knew
that whenever one of them talked as Walt did there was never
anything but time and temper lost in trying to buy something
from him.

Two days before the crates would be finished, Walt wrote
Bullock a letter telling him when they would be ready and
asking for shipping instructions.

Bullock drove over from the Falls the same day he received
Walt's letter. He did not know what to do with the crates
just then, because the season would be over in another week
or two. But he figured that Walt would have only two or three
or, at the most, five hundred crates, and he could take them
to the Falls and carry them over to the next season and still
make a good profit.

When he reached East Liverpool and saw the millyard, he
almost had a heart attack. He had never seen so many blueberry crates in all his life, and he had been dealing in them
for twenty years.

When he had first talked to Walt about making crates, he
had no idea Walt intended making them, at least not in such
quantities, and he was certain he had not signed an order for
them. But he wanted to continue getting wooden jug handles
at the good price Walt had made him. There was no other mill
in the whole state that would sell handles to him at that figure.
Bullock knew if he told Walt he had not ordered the crates,
Walt would be angry about it and perhaps refuse to sell him
any more cider-jug handles.

Before Walt came out of the mill, Bullock had a few minutes to think about what he was going to say. He knew it would ruin him to take that many blueberry crates merely to please Walt.

Walt came out of the mill and met Bullock at his car. Bullock was sitting on the running board looking at the crates in the millyard stacked higher than the buildings themselves.

"Well, Bullock," Walt said, shaking his hand, "they're ready. The last durn one of them. There's ten thousand waiting for you."

"Ten thousand!" Bullock gasped. "Ten thousand what?"

"Crates, man—blueberry crates."

"Ten thousand blueberry crates?"

"Sure," Walt said. "When I undertake a job I finish it. I made ten thousand of them for you, and I could get out half that many more by the end of the week if you want them. I've got fifteen extra men helping at the mill."

"Ten thousand," Bullock said again, still unable to realize that there were that many blueberry crates in the world.

"What's your shipping instructions? Where do you want them sent—over to the Falls?"

Bullock rose to his feet and supported himself against the side of his automobile.

"Good God," he said, wiping his face with the back of his hand.

"What's the matter?" Walt asked him.

"I'm afraid there's been a mistake," he said. "A pretty bad mistake, too. I guess probably I should have told you about it in the first place, because I've found that nearly every mill man in the state makes the same mistake when he undertakes to make blueberry crates. And naturally it's pretty hard on the mill man."

"What do you mean? There ain't no mistake. You said you wanted as many crates as I could make, didn't you? You said you'd take all I made. There's no mistake on my part."

"Yes, it's a bad mistake," Bullock said, gravely shaking his head from side to side. "You see, your business is in dowels principally, isn't it? And going back to the bottom of things, you are in the lumber business. That's your main business. All this kind of work making crates and hoops and jug handles is a sort of side line with you. Well, that shows you're not a blueberry-crate man at all. That's why you didn't know you were making a mistake. A blueberry-crate man would never have done that."

"Done what?" Walt begged. "What's the matter with the crates I made?"

"Your crates are put together. They would have to be knocked down and bundled before they would be of any use to me. Why, man, it would cost a fortune to truck those empty crates to the depot and ship them by freight to my customers all over the state. That many empty crates would take up more space than the railroad has got boxcars to put them in. That's the mistake. You'll have to knock them down before I can use them."

"But this other man said he would haul raspberry crates away just like they stand now, if—"

"Good God, man," Bullock said, "we're talking about blue-berry crates. I didn't say anything about raspberry—"

"That's right," Walt said. "I just got mixed up in what I was saying."

Walt wished Bullock would go away and leave him alone. He felt very cheap there with Bullock, having all those crates on his hands, whatever kind they were now. But no matter how hard he tried to think his way out of the trouble he was in, he still knew the crates had been thrown back on him. If he hired the men to knock the crates down and bundle them he would lose at least two or three hundred dollars on the deal. He could not afford that. And he knew he could not force Bullock to take them, because there was no signed contract. He remembered about the pile of barrel hoops stacked up in the mill, too. They had been left on his hands because he nailed them together. Instead of nailing the ends together they should have been bundled and shipped flat. And now there was no market for hoops of any kind. Then his mind raced back to the crates. He wished he had asked the man who wanted to buy them for raspberry crates to leave his name and address. He could ask Bullock to put him in touch with the raspberry-crate man, because Bullock would prob-ably know every wooden-products buyer in the State, but Walt didn't want to do that. The other man had been angry when he left, and he would probably refuse to have anything to do with Walt after being ordered away from the mill.

"Well, I guess I'll keep them," Walt said. "I don't want to knock them down. There wouldn't be any sense in doing that."

"Suit yourself," Bullock said. "But I can't use them as they are now. They would have to be knocked down and bundled. Now, if I was in the *raspberry*-crate business I could take every one you've got. Raspberry crates—"

"These ain't raspberry crates," Walt said stiffly. "Them are blueberry crates."

Walt went back into the mill. Bullock followed him, saying something about signing an order for fifty gross of cider-jug handles that he wanted added to the first order. Walt brought him an order blank and watched him fill it in and sign it. The moment Bullock finished writing his signature he got into his automobile and started towards the Falls as fast as he could.

When Bullock was out of sight, Walt went to the millyard and looked at the stacks of blueberry crates awhile. Then he went back into the mill and looked at the barrel hoops. He was wondering what Nate Emmonds would say about him this time.

(First published in *American Earth*)

New Cabin

PART way across the swamp, Davi Millard stopped and washed his hands and face in the clear water that trickled in a shallow stream under the log path. Every night when he stopped there on his way home from work, he could see how much smaller the stream had become since the evening before.

Two months before, when he started hewing logs for new cabin, the water rushed down the sandy course with enough force to carry small limbs and chunks of swamp-rotted logs. But since then, the winter rains had stopped and the swamp was once more a mire of soft, depthless mud, harmless-looking in its covering of tangled vegetation. The green ferns and running vines that grew through the spring and summer covered the mire-holes with the appearance of solid earth.

Davi had lived all his life on the edge of the swamp and he knew almost instinctively how dangerous it was.

After treading his way carefully over the chained logs to the other side of the swamp, Davi began running the rest of the way home. It was no more than a mile from the swamp to old cabin, but the path was crooked and narrow as it wound through the thick growth of turpentine pines.

The moon was shining, and it was almost as bright as day in the woods. When he saw the clearing ahead, he ran faster.

The place was as still and quiet as the pine forest around it. There was not even a thin wisp of smoke coming from the chimney, and if he had not seen the place before, at night, he would have declared it was deserted.

Opening the front door noiselessly, Davi listened for a moment. Through the broken window shutter, a faint ray of moonlight entered the dark room and fell across the foot of the bed. Closing the door behind him, he went silently to the middle of the room. From there he could see the outlines of the table, the chairs, and the bed. In the gloom everything looked as if it were covered with a foot-thick coating of dust.

Davi went to the wood box and fumbled in the dark until he had found a pine lighter. He struck a match to it, the dripping pitch flared up instantly, then he tossed the blazing knot into the fireplace. When he turned around, the whole room was alive with yellow, flickering light. The table, chairs, and bed looked as bright as they were the day he brought them.

Jeanie sat up in bed nervously, the covers falling from her shoulders. Even before she could open her eyes, she was smiling at Davi. He crossed the room and watched her while she brushed the hair from her face.

"How long have you been asleep, Jeanie?" he asked her. She smiled at him, shaking her head.

"I guess I was a little late tonight, again," he said, appealingly. "The moon came up just at sundown, and I kept on working awhile. I want to finish new cabin as quick as I can."

Jeanie threw aside the covers and slid to the side of the bed, touching the chilly floor with the tips of her toes.

"I kept the fire going in the stove as long as I could," she said, "but I was so sleepy I couldn't stay awake any longer. I'm afraid your supper is cold now, Davi."

He stood where he was, a grin leaping from the corners of his mouth to all his face, and watched her stand up. When Jeanie took the first step towards the kitchen, Davi picked her up with a sweep of his arms and carried her back to bed. He held her at the side of the bed for a moment; then, hugging her so tightly she could barely breathe, he kissed her on the mouth and dropped her on the bed. She caught her breath when she fell, and she felt as if she were dropping a dozen feet instead of only two.

"Don't bother about my supper," Davi said, laughing at her. "I'll eat it cold."

He left her and went to the kitchen and felt around in the darkness until he found the bread and potatoes. He brought back a cake of corn bread and a gourd-sized sweet potato and sat down on the side of the bed. Jeanie was wide awake by then.

"Is new cabin pretty near finished now, Davi?" she asked him. "I get awfully lonesome here all day long."

"It'll be ready to move into in about a week, or maybe less time than that," he told her, nodding slowly. "As soon as I can get the floor laid, we'll move in. The window shutters can wait till after we move. It'll only take a couple of days to make those, anyway."

The pine lighter in the fireplace flickered, blazed, and died down. The knot was almost burned up.

Davi carried the potato skins back to the kitchen. When he got back, he undressed quickly and got into bed.

They lay together for a long time not saying anything. Jeanie moved closer to his side several times, and Davi buried his face in her hair.

When he was almost asleep, Jeanie whispered something.

"I can't hear you," he said, turning his head a little.

"That meddlesome old Bony King came here again, today," Jeanie said in a muffled whisper.

Davi turned over and raised himself on his elbow. He looked through the darkness into Jeanie's face.

"What did he want?"

"I told him I didn't want anything to do with him, no matter what he wanted."

"What did he say?"

"I didn't pay any attention to anything he said. I told him to go away and mind his own business, but he just laughed at me and stayed anyway."

Davi sank down upon the pillow, jerking his elbow from under him.

"Maybe Bony thinks I'm getting ready to move off and leave you," Davi said slowly, pausing between each word to draw his breath sharply. "Maybe he thinks I'm building new cabin over on the other side of the swamp for me and a new somebody."

Jeanie snuggled under his arm, worming her head until her face was pressed tightly against his neck.

"I don't care what he thinks," she said, shivering. "I don't want him coming here every day and sitting and looking at me all the afternoon. It upsets me so, I don't know what to do sometimes. Today, I felt like picking up a stick and whaling him for all he was worth."

Davi raised himself on both elbows and stared through the darkness of the room. Jeanie lay silently beside him. He did not say a word until Jeanie shivered again.

"The next time Bony comes here, tell him I said that if he don't quit bothering you, I'll tend to him all right, all right."

"One of the things he says every time he comes is, don't I feel sorry for myself because I married you instead of him?"

"What do you tell him to that, Jeanie?"

"I told him today that if I couldn't be married to you, I wouldn't be married to anybody else in the country."

Davi put his arms around her and drew her tightly to him. Jeanie whimpered for a while, and then she lay quiet and still. Davi could feel her relax while her breathing became lighter. He pressed his lips against her cheek, closing his eyes.

It was long after midnight when Davi woke up with a sudden consciousness. He was wide awake in a second, wondering what had made him wake up like that. He listened, raising his head from the pillow, but he could hear nothing. Outside the room, the pine barrens extended mile after mile in all directions. Nobody lived closer than twelve miles, and the only sound Davi had ever heard there was the occasional muffled crash of a dead falling tree or the faraway whine of a bobcat. This time he could hear nothing at all.

After a while he lay down again, but he could not go back to sleep. He lay as still as he could so he would not wake Jeanie.

While he lay there, wondering how long it was until dawn, he began to wonder if Bony King had anything to do with his waking up in the middle of the night. The more he thought about it, the more he realized that Bony was the cause. He turned over and looked through the crack in the window shutter at the moonlit pines at the edge of the clearing beyond the garden.

For the past year Bony King had been trying to make trouble for him, but Davi had always thought it would die down when Bony saw he could not make Jeanie leave and go to live with him. Davi remembered then that every day for almost three weeks Jeanie had told him of Bony's coming to old cabin while he was away building new cabin.

Bony was a turpentine worker who lived in a shanty on the East Arm of Ogeechichobee Swamp. He had started out by telling Jeanie he was not going to stop trying to get her until she left Davi and came to live with him. Once when Davi was at the store near East Arm, Bony had told him the same thing. Davi had laughed it off then. But for the past few weeks, Bony had been coming to old cabin every day.

During the rest of the night Davi lay awake wondering what he could do about it. He could not move away from the swamp, because that was the only home he and Jeanie had.

Just before daybreak he got up and dressed without waking Jeanie. He went to the kitchen and ate some more of the cold corn bread and sweet potatoes. By then, the sun was coming up. He looked into the next room before leaving, and Jeanie was still asleep. He tiptoed out of the kitchen and started down the path for another day's work on new cabin, three miles away.

Jeanie did not wake up until almost an hour later. She turned over, first, to see if Davi was awake, and when she found he was gone, she leaped out of bed and ran into the kitchen. When she had reached the front yard, she was awake enough to know that Davi had left and gone to work.

After cooking her breakfast and cleaning the house, she went out into the garden. It was then only in the middle of the morning, and she began digging at the weeds with the blunt-bladed hoe. The vegetables she and Davi had planted nearly a month before were up and thriving in the damp earth and warm sunshine. She dug and chopped with the dull hoe until there was not a single weed left in the first row.

Just before noon, she looked up and saw Bony King sitting on a pine stump at the end of the garden. He did not say a word when she looked at him for the first time, and she had no way of knowing how long he had been sitting on the stump watching her. Jeanie's first thought was to drop the hoe and run into the kitchen. When she was just about to run, she happened to think that Bony would surely follow her now, no matter where she went. She decided quickly that the best thing to do was to stay where she was.

During the next half hour she did not glance even once in Bony's direction. She knew he was still sitting on the stump, because she could see his shadow out of the corner of her eye, but she was determined not to look at him, if he stayed there all day.

Finally, she could bear it no longer. Bony had been sitting there for the past hour or more, whittling on a stick and smiling at her. Jeanie dropped the hoe and stared him full in the face.

"What do you want here again today, Bony King?" she cried at him, stamping her feet and beating her fists against her hips.

He did not say a word. He only smiled more broadly at her.

"I wish you would keep away from here and let me and Davi alone," she said angrily. "We don't like you one bit!"

"Davi don't, but you do," Bony said, shifting his crossed legs. "Now, ain't that so, Jeanie?"

"That's a whopping big old lie!" she cried. "You're just trying to make it hard for me because I married Davi, and wouldn't you!"

Bony brushed the shavings from his overalls.

"You ought to change over, Jeanie," he said. "Now's a pretty good time to do it, too. I've already got my new cabin built, and Davi hasn't."

"That's another of your whopping old lies," Jeanie said. "You even haven't started to build one yourself, and you know it."

"How do you know so much about what I do and what I don't do?" he said.

"Davi tells me."

"Davi didn't tell you the truth about that, because I'm starting on mine already."

Jeanie could not keep from answering him, even though she knew he was saying things like that just to make her talk to him.

"Davi's got ours pretty near finished, and you haven't even started on yours, Bony King."

Bony got up and crossed the garden. He came down the row and stopped at the end of her hoe handle.

"It won't be finished if Davi slips off the log path through the swamp, some night," Bony said, nodding his head at her. "It's pretty dangerous for a man to cross the swamp at night, anyway. If a cloud was to come up all of a quick one of these moonlight nights while a man was halfway through the swamp, he wouldn't be able to see the rest of the way, especially on that slippery log path. If he was in a hurry, and tried to follow the log path out, he might slip off into one of those mire-holes that's all covered over with pretty ferns and vines. I've seen it get so dark in the middle of the swamp that you couldn't even follow your hand in front of you."

Jeanie reached down to pick up the hoe, but Bony set his foot on the handle, and she could not lift it.

"That was no story I was trying to dress up for you," he said, shaking his head at her. "That's the truth."

"Davi will take care of himself," Jeanie said slowly.

"Not if he was to trip and fall off that chained-log path into a mire-hole, on a pitch-black night," Bony said, swinging his head from side to side. "I've seen it happen before."

Jeanie closed her eyes for a moment, promising herself to make Davi stop staying at new cabin after dark.

"Some folks won't learn a lesson till it's too late," Bony told her.

He had already taken two or three steps toward her, and before she realized what was happening, he had taken another step and grabbed her. Jeanie tried to jerk away from him, but her dress was so old and worn she was afraid it would be torn if she tried to struggle with Bony. Bony put both arms around her and tried to kiss her.

"You wouldn't try to do that if Davi was here," Jeanie said.

"Why wouldn't I?" he laughed. "What's he got to do with it now?"

She pulled away from him, holding him off with her elbows stiff, and then she hit him as hard as she could. All he did was laugh at her.

"I like a girl with plenty of fight in her," Bony said.

He caught her with both hands. Her dress tore like a sheet of newspaper. While she struggled to cover herself she realized how much strength was bound up in a man's muscles.

"The more you fight, the more you'll wear yourself out," he told her, laughing at her while she tried to hold the torn dress together. The dress had been torn down her back to her waist, and she could feel the hot sun burning her bare body. "And more than that," Bony said, "when you fight, it just naturally makes your dress rip more and more."

Jeanie stepped closer to Bony. A moment later, she had

pushed with all her strength, and he went tumbling backward. The last she saw of him then was when his feet went kicking into the air over his head. He had ruined nearly two whole rows of onions and cabbages.

Running with all her might, and holding her dress behind her, Jeanie reached the safety of the kitchen. She slammed the door shut and pushed the table against it.

Bony walked around the house several times like a dog circling a strange animal he was afraid to strike at. He looked in the windows, first at the front and then at the rear, but he did not try to open them. After a while, he sat down on a stump only half a dozen steps from the front door.

"I could get in if I wanted to," he shouted at Jeanie. "I could smash open one of these windows with no trouble at all. That's all I'd have to do to get in, if I wanted to. But I guess I'll wait awhile."

Jeanie huddled on the floor beside the bed, shivering and crying.

Some time later, she thought she heard a sound of some kind outside the room. She crept on her hands and knees to the window and looked out through the broken shutter. Bony was walking slowly down the path toward the swamp. He did not look back.

With the strength she had left, she crawled back to the bed and fell across it. She cried until she lost consciousness.

It was completely dark when she woke up. Running to the window, she could see by the sky that the sun had set a long time before. Overhead were dark patches of clouds drifting toward the moon.

By then she was fully awake. She went to the door, and back to the window. She did not know how many times she went back and forth, looking. Each time she crossed the room she felt weaker. Then she fell on the floor sobbing and shivering, too weak to get to her knees.

At last Jeanie opened the door and looked searchingly into the moonswept yard. There was still no sign of Davi out there. At first she ran in circles about the place, trying to make up her mind what to do. Then she turned down the path and ran with all her might toward the swamp.

A few yards from the edge of the swamp, where the single log path began, she stopped suddenly. Before her lay the tangled swamp over which Davi had always carried her. She started slowly, testing each step of the footing on the slippery, barkless, chained logs. Before she had gone the length of the first log, she felt herself being lifted off her feet.

She could not turn around, but she could feel the strange arms around her waist, and she knew then that it was Bony who had caught her up. She did not cry out when he lifted her off her feet and carried her back to the solid ground at the end of the log.

Bony put her down, turning her around to look into her face. He was smiling at her in the same way he had looked while sitting on the stump in the garden that afternoon.

"You're up mighty late," he said.

"Where's Davi?" Jeanie cried.

"Davi?" Bony repeated. "I was thinking the same thing myself only a little while ago. To tell the truth exactly, I don't know where he's at."

"You do know, Bony! Where's Davi?"

He held her more tightly, gripping his fingers around her arms.

"I've got an idea, but I wouldn't swear to it," he said. "The reason I wouldn't swear to it is because I didn't see it with my own eyes. It's so dark in here every time a cloud passes under the moon that it's hard to see your own hand in front of you."

"You tell me where Davi is!" Jeanie cried, beating her hands against him.

"I'd say that maybe Davi started across the swamp and tripped up. It was mighty foolish of him to start across the swamp on a cloudy night. I'd be afraid of falling into one of those mire-holes, if it was me."

Jeanie tore herself away from Bony. He ran after her, but she managed to slip out of his grasp, and she ran toward the swamp. Bony lost sight of her completely after half a dozen steps. He could hear the sounds she made, but it was almost impossible to tell the true direction they came from.

"Jeanie!" he shouted. "Jeanie! Come back here, you fool! You can't cross the swamp! Come back here, Jeanie!"

Jeanie did not answer him, and he started treading his way along the first log of the path. He stopped when he found he could not see or feel his way any farther. He listened, and he could not hear anything of Jeanie. In desperation, he got down on his hands and knees and felt his way forward along the slippery logs. Every once in a while he stopped and called to Jeanie, listened for some sound of her, and felt in the mire-holes beside the path.

Towards morning, mud-caked and helpless, Bony reached the firm ground at the end of the path. He sat down to wait for daylight, wondering how long it would take to find some trace of Jeanie, or of Davi.

(First published in *College Humor*)

Mamma's Little Girl

"I'M afraid," Arlene whispered, closing her eyes tightly. "I am so afraid, honey."

In the next room, Miss McAllister lifted the heavy lid and rattled half a hod of dusty coke into the firebox. The cookstove was already red-hot on top, and the heat from it sang in the stifling air.

Before replacing the lid on the stove, Miss McAllister walked over to the table by the window and picked up a piece of gauze that had been lying there on the white oilcloth ever since she had finished sterilizing the blue and white enameled pan. She carried the cloth to the stove and dropped it into the flame. There was a sizzling sound, a leaping tongue of purple fire, a puff of blackish smoke, and the gauze had been incinerated.

Miss McAllister shook down the ashes for the third time.

"I'm so afraid," Arlene said again, her lips trembling more than ever. "Honey, don't—don't let anything happen to me!"

"It will be all right," I said, looking away from the eyes that burned through me. "Nothing could ever happen to you, Arlene. He promised nothing would. Everything will have to be all right."

Her fingers stiffened.

"I told Mamma we were going for a ride into the country this afternoon. I told her we would not be back in time for dinner tonight. I told Mamma not to worry, because I would be with you."

The heat from the next room was swimming before my eyes. All the doors and windows had been closed tightly, and there was not a breath of fresh air anywhere. Overhead, beads of pitch dropped from the pine ceiling and fell on the bare floor at our feet.

"What did she say?" I asked Arlene. "Did she say anything?"

"She said that would be all right. She said she knew you would bring me home safely."

"What did you say?"

"What did I say then? Why, I've forgotten now. Though I suppose I told her we would be back early. Why?"

Miss McAllister came into the room and looked at us. She stood close to the other door, turning around to look at us.

She was wearing a stiffly starched white skirt with broad straps over the shoulders, and white cotton stockings and white canvas shoes with flat heels. The blouse she was wearing was pink georgette, and it was so thin that I could see the brown mole on her skin just above her waist.

"Where is he now?" I asked her.

"He'll be here any minute now," Miss McAllister said, looking at Arlene. "He phoned that he was on his way."

Arlene's fingers squeezed mine.

"You don't suppose he will be delayed, do you?" I asked. "Do you think there'll be anything to make him late? Will he get here in time?"

"Of course he will come," Miss McAllister said, smoothing the pink georgette over her breasts and laughing deeply within her chest when she looked at Arlene.

A bead of glistening brown pitch fell from the ceiling to the toe of Miss McAllister's right shoe, missing the tip of her nose by a hair's breadth and dropping between the hollow of her breasts. Somebody was coming up the squeaky stairs.

Arlene was about to whisper something to me when the door opened and Doctor Anderson came in. He paused a moment to look at us. He smiled at Arlene, waved his hand at me, and then turned to Miss McAllister. She closed the door, bolted it with the thumb lock, and took Doctor Anderson's hat and hung it on the tree behind her. They walked into the next room, side by side, talking to each other.

Doctor Anderson wet his finger on his tongue and tapped the top of the stove with it. We could hear the sizzle in the room where we were.

"I like your regulation blouse," Doctor Anderson said. "At the next meeting of the board, I'm going to propose that we adopt your style of uniform for all the nurses at the hospital."

Miss McAllister unbuttoned his vest and helped him with his long white coat.

"I forgot to bring the other one with me today," she said. "I was in such a rush all morning that I didn't have time to look for a regulation blouse."

"How did you feel this morning? All right?"

"I had a little wobble in my walk for an hour or so. When I first got up, I felt like I was walking on stilts."

"My wife asked me what kind of a case I had last night. I told her it was an emergency call."

There was a quick step, a moment's silence, and an almost inaudible sucking of lips.

Doctor Anderson stepped into the doorway.

"All right, Miss—" he said. "We're ready now."

Arlene turned her face from him and buried her head against me.

"I'm afraid, honey," she whispered. "I'm so afraid."

I could not release her, and after a while Doctor Anderson came over and pulled us apart. He said something to Miss McAllister that I did not hear.

"Kiss me just once more, honey, and I'll not be afraid to go," Arlene said, holding her lips up to mine. "I'll not be afraid to go."

Doctor Anderson stepped back a moment. He waited for several minutes, fingering his stethoscope.

"All right, Miss——" he said. "We're ready now."

"I'm not afraid any longer," Arlene said, standing.

Doctor Anderson took her by the arm and led her into the next room. I saw them enter the kitchen and I could hear Miss McAllister shaking down the ashes in the red-hot cookstove for the fourth time. It was so hot by then that the air in both rooms smelled scorched.

After a few minutes, Doctor Anderson came to the door. His sleeves were rolled above his elbows and his face and hands were so inflamed by the heat in the kitchen that the skin looked as though it had been smeared with blood.

He beckoned to me.

"You may come in for just a moment, Mr.——" he said. "But please do not touch anything on the table with your hands or body."

He stepped back and I walked unsteadily into the room with them. Miss McAllister had opened a can of ether, and the odor had already permeated the air. It made me a little sick to smell it, even though the odor was still faint.

"I'm not afraid at all now," Arlene said, smiling up at me from the white oilcloth on the table top. "Kiss me just once more, and I'll be all right, honey."

Miss McAllister stepped over to the table and drew the sheet over Arlene, folding back the hem at her throat. When she turned to go, she looked at the three of us through tight lips.

Doctor Anderson stepped over to the table and drew the sheet from Arlene, jerking it off in a single motion, and throwing it on a chair beside the cookstove. He came back and stood on the other side of the table looking down at Arlene.

I kissed her until Doctor Anderson laid his hand on my back and pulled me away from her. Her face was bloodless.

"That will be too much excitement for the patient, Mr——" he said, pushing me away.

Miss McAllister was standing impatiently beside me with the ether cone in her hands. She caught Doctor Anderson's eyes and nodded her head in the direction of the door. He turned me around and pushed me towards the other room.

When I looked back at Arlene and saw her for the last

time, she raised her head just a little and said something. I
stopped and waited until she could repeat what I had not
heard.

"Please call up Mamma," she said, smiling, "and tell her I'll
not be home tonight."

"I will, Arlene," I promised, starting back into the room
where she lay. "I'll do anything in the world for you, Arlene."

Miss McAllister tapped her foot impatiently while she
waited for Doctor Anderson to send me out.

"That's sweet of you to say that, honey—and don't forget to
call up Mamma and tell her I'll not be home tonight. And—
honey, if—if I never see you again—you will always love me,
won't you—you'll always remember me, won't you?"

Before I could run to her, Doctor Anderson had grabbed
me by the arms and had pushed me into the next room. Miss
McAllister ran and shut the door between us, bolting it with
the thumb lock. Already the sickening odor of ether had entered that room, and I ran to the other door and down the
stairs for fresh air.

On the front porch the old man was still sitting there smoking his pipe. The tobacco had burned out, but he puffed on
the stem just as though it were lit. He glanced up when I ran
out on the porch, and looked at me over the rim of his
spectacles.

"I can't remember that I've ever seen your face before, son,"
he said, squinting at me. "When did you move in?"

My head was swimming and I could not understand anything he was saying. I leaned against the rooms-for-rent sign
on the wall, closing my eyes as I felt myself slide slowly downward to the porch floor.

(First published in *Contact*)

Honeymoon

NEVER mind what put Claude Barker up to getting married.
Nearly everybody does something like that sometime or other.
They'll be going along minding their own business for months
at a time, and then all at once they come across a girl that
sort of—well, never mind about that, either.

If it had been anybody else than Claude, nobody would
have thought much about it. He was one of the bunch that had
been hanging around town, mostly at the poolroom, doing

nothing most of the time, for five or six years, maybe ten or twelve. Claude said he was waiting for a job at the filling station, but everybody else who wasn't working said that, too.

Jack and Crip were sitting in the sun in front of the filling station when Claude went by the first time. That was about ten o'clock that morning, and Claude was on his way to the courthouse to get a license.

"What's Claude up to?" Crip said.

The car Claude had borrowed early that morning from Jack sounded as if it would never make the trip to the courthouse and back.

"Search me," Jack said. "Maybe he thinks he knows where he can find a job."

"Yeah," Crip said, spitting. "But whoever would have thought of borrowing a car to run away from it? If a job ever hears of Claude, it'll wish it hadn't by the time it catches up with him. He'd turn around and fan its tail all the way from here to Atlanta and back again. His old man . . ."

Claude's old man, sitting on the bench in front of the post office, said he thought he knew why Claude had suddenly taken it into his head to get married. Everybody was waiting for the cotton-gin whistle to blow so he could go home to dinner. Claude had been to the courthouse and back, and somebody had seen him drive out to the preacher's house on the edge of town half an hour before.

Claude's old man said he reckoned he knew why Claude was getting married. "By God, it wouldn't pain a man much to make a guess like that," somebody said. "No, but it would be a hell of a come-off if there were no more girls like Willeen Howard left in the country." "That ain't no lie," somebody else said. "When that time comes, I'll be ready to turn the country over to the niggers and boll weevils and screwworms and sell out from here."

The ginnery whistle down the railroad tracks blew for the twelve-thirty layoff. Claude's old man stood up to go home to see what his wife had cooked up for dinner.

"I'll tell you people what put the marrying bug on Claude. The boy is young yet, and he wasn't used to fooling around with white girls. He's been of the habit . . ."

The crowd broke up like a rotten egg hitting the side of a barn.

"Claude's been in the habit . . ."

Old man Barker didn't have time to finish. He had to hurry home and eat his meal before his wife let the victuals get cold.

Downtown at the noon hour was quiet except for a handful of Negroes from the country who were sitting on the shaded railroad-station platform eating rat-trap cheese and soda crackers. Occasionally an automobile would plow through town on its way to Atlanta or Savannah, leaving the air tasting like ant poison for half an hour afterward.

Claude and Willeen came rattling down the street, across the square, Jack's old car hitting the railroad irons with a sound like a brick running through a cotton gin. Claude drove up to the filling station and stopped. Crip woke up and ran out to see who it was. Claude had lifted the seat and was unscrewing the gas-tank cap.

"Boy, you need lots of gas today," Crip said, putting the nozzle into the tank and looking at Willeen at the same time.

"Give me two gallons," Claude said.

"What you two going to do now?" Crip asked, turning the pump crank.

"That ain't no lie," Claude said, winking at Willeen.

Crip hung up the hose while Claude was counting out the change for the gasoline. He took a quick look into the back seat to see if Claude and Willeen had any baggage for a trip. There was not a thing. He looked again to be sure.

Crip did not have time to do any more looking around, because he had to have one more look at Willeen before Claude drove off with her. It was too late then to ask her why she had not told him something about it. If he had known about it in time, he could have asked her himself. It would not have been any trouble for him to get married. He could have done it just as easily as Claude did. But, God Almighty, what a funny feeling Willeen gave you when you looked at her real hard. It made you feel as if you were eating a clingstone peach and had got down almost to the last of it, and the more you sucked it, and bit the stone, the better the peach tasted, and you began to feel sort of hoggish but didn't give a damn how you acted when you couldn't get enough of it.

Willeen got back into the front seat and sat down. Claude grabbed up the water bucket and began filling the radiator.

It would have been easy enough to have married her, if you had only thought about it before Claude did. You'd make a monkey of yourself, all over the place, any day of the week, for some of that. By that time your eyes felt dry and stuck in your head when you had blinked them for so long, and when you shut them for a moment to get them moistened, you were ready to start all over again. After that you couldn't help seeing all the pretty things she had and you forgot all about tending the filling station and got to thinking that maybe I could fix it up someway or other. It wasn't so long ago that Willeen told you you could throw her down if you wanted to. You were a damn fool not to do it when she gave you the chance. But that wasn't now by a long shot.

They drove off down the street leaving Crip standing there looking like a cow mired in quicksand.

Claude drove around the square seven or eight times, warming up the engine, and finally stopped in front of the poolroom. It made him itch all over when he thought of having a cue stick in his hands. There was no reason why he should not take time to shoot a couple of games. He might be able to win half a dollar, and then he could buy another couple gallons of gas. They could ride twice as far if they had two more.

It was time for the one-thirty ginnery whistle to blow, and people were already on their way back from dinner. A game was just starting when Claude went inside, and he grabbed a cue stick from the rack and got in. They played five rounds of three-handed straight, and Claude came out even, after all.

Somebody in the street was blowing an automobile horn. Upton Daniels came in, and Claude started a two-handed game of rotation with him. Claude broke, and made the seven and the fifteen ball.

"Boy, what a shot!" he said. "I wouldn't take dollars for this stick of mine. There's never been one like it before."

Upton made a face by pushing out his mouth.

"You ought to have seen me ring them in last night," said Claude. "Seven and eleven were pay balls, and I rang them in nine games in a row. It takes a good man to do that."

"Pig's butt," Upton said.

Upton shot and missed an easy one. He banged his cue stick on the floor and made another face with his mouth.

Claude ran in three balls, missed the fourth, but Upton was left sewn up behind the fourteen. Upton jerked up his cue and scattered the balls with the heavy end.

"That gives a man away every time," Claude said, chalking his cue tip. "The first thing I learned about shooting pool was to keep my head. That's why I'm the best shot in town. If you was as good as I am, you could make yourself a little money now and then off the drummers who come to town. I know you've made runs of thirty-seven and thirty-eight every once in a while, but that was just luck."

"Pig's butt," Upton said.

The horn out in the street started blowing again. When they finished the game, Claude went out to the front of the poolroom and looked into the street to see who was making so much racket. He had missed a couple of easy shots just on that account.

When he saw Willeen sitting in the car, he shoved his cue stick at Upton and ran outside. Willeen looked angry.

"God Almighty," Claude said under his breath, getting into the car and driving off.

It was about five o'clock in the afternoon then, and there were only two gallons of gasoline in the tank. Ten miles out of town, Claude turned around and came back. When they reached his house, it was time for supper.

"I'll go inside and fix things up first," he told Willeen. "It won't take long."

He got out and started up the steps. Willeen called him back, and he went to the car.

"I'd like to go home first and get a few things, Claude," she said. "You wouldn't mind, would you?"

"Sure, that's all right," he said, starting the car. "By the time you're ready, I'll have got things fixed up here. I'll be by for you about ten o'clock."

"You don't have to wait that long, Claude," Willeen said. "I'll be ready in just a few minutes."

"I've got to see a fellow downtown," Claude said. "It might take me a couple of hours to find him. We'd better make it ten o'clock, like I said. I've got to take this car back where I got it from, for another thing."

On his way back after leaving Willeen at her father's house, Claude stopped at the poolroom a minute. Somebody gave him a drink of corn, and after that he decided to shoot a few games of pool with Upton before going home to fix things up for Willeen.

Claude's old man was downtown early the next morning. When he passed the filling station, Jack and Crip asked him where Claude was.

"He and Willeen are still asleep," Claude's old man said. "But I reckon you'll be seeing Claude most any time now. Is there anything in particular you boys want to see him about? Is that job ready for him?"

"He's still got my car," Jack said. "He ought to bring it back. I only let him have it for a couple hours yesterday, and he kept it all day and all night."

"Don't worry about your car, son," old man Barker said. "It's standing up there in the front yard of the house right this minute. Claude'll be coming downtown with it before very long."

He went across the square and sat down in the shade in front of the post office. There were three or four men over there who had been talking about the news in the morning paper.

After he had sat down, somebody asked him how Claude was getting along now that he was married to Willeen Howard. Old man Barker nodded his head. Somebody else spat into the dust. "This would sure-God be a puny country if it got cleaned out of girls like that. If the time ever comes when they don't invite a throw-down, then it's time to let the niggers and boll weevils and screwworms run wild." Claude's old man sort of chuckled to himself. The boy wasn't up when he left home. "What did Claude have to say when he woke up this morning? I'll bet it was the same thing I said' when I was in his place once," the fellow said, winking.

About an hour later Claude drove Jack's car down to the filling station. They were waiting for him.

"How's everything, Claude?" Jack said.

"Couldn't be better," Claude told him.

"It's a funny feeling, though, I bet," Jack said.

Claude turned and looked at Crip a moment. Crip looked straight at him, but he had nothing to say to Claude.

"Funny?" Claude said, laughing a little and going to the gas pump and leaning against it. "Funny ain't no name for it, Crip."

Crip looked at him between the eyes.

"I still can't seem to get over it somehow," Claude said. "This morning I woke up and opened my eyes and I saw a bare arm lying over me. When I saw it, I was scared to death. I jumped out of bed in a hurry, thinking to myself, 'What in hell am I doing sleeping in bed with a white girl?'"

Crip kicked at the tires on Jack's old car to see how well they were holding up. He walked all the way around it a couple times. Nobody had said anything after Claude finished talking.

After a while Claude walked off down the street towards the poolroom. Jack pushed the car behind the filling station where it would be out of the way. While he was back there, he took the cap off the gas tank to see if Claude had left any gas in it. There was almost a whole gallon inside. Jack thought that was funny, because Claude had started off into the country as if he had figured on taking a trip somewhere.

(First published in *Kneel to the Rising Sun*)

The Grass Fire

DURING the last week of April nobody with any sense at all would have gone out and deliberately set fire to a hayfield. There had been no rainfall since the March thaw and the country was as dry as road dust in midsummer. The farmers who had fields that needed burning over were waiting for a heavy shower of rain to come and soak the ground thoroughly before they dared begin the spring firing.

Carl Abbott had been in the habit of burning over his fields the last week of April for the past thirty years and he said that he was not going to start that late in his life letting his new crop hay be ruined by raspberry bushes and gray-birch seedlings if he knew anything about it. The people in the town thought he was merely talking to himself again to make himself heard, and that he really had the good sense to keep fire away from dry grass until a hard rain had come. Carl was always talking about the way he stuck to his lifelong habits, and people never paid much attention to him any more, anyway.

It was late in the afternoon when Carl got ready to fire the field on the north side of his farm. He carried two buckets of water with him, and a broom, and went up the side road to the north field.

When he reached the gate, he saw Jake Thompson come driving down the backroad. Carl tried to get through the gate and behind the stone wall before Jake saw him, but he could not hide himself quickly enough because of the two buckets of water he was carrying, and his wooden leg.

"Hey there!" Jake called, whipping up his horse. "What you doing in that hayfield?"

Carl waited until Jake drove up to the gap in the wall. He put the buckets down and leaned against the broom handle.

"I'm standing here looking at you," Carl told him. "But I'm already tired of doing that, and so now I'm going in here and fire my hayfield."

"Why! you damned old fool," Jake said, "don't you know that you'll burn up your whole farm if you do that now? Feel that wind—it'll carry flame down across that meadow and into that wood lot before you know which way to look. Nobody with any sense would fire a hayfield until after a good heavy rain comes and soaks the ground."

"I didn't ask for the loan of any of your advice," Carl said.

"And I don't generally pass it around to every damn fool I meet, either," Jake said, "but I hate to have to sit here and see a man burn up all he's got and ever will have. The town's not going to raise money to waste on supporting you. There's too many just like you living on the town already."

"Guess I can live on the town if I've a mind to. Been paying taxes for thirty years and more."

"If it was left up to me," Jake said, "I'd dig a big hole in the ground and cover you up in it. And I'm man enough left to do it, too."

Carl stooped over and picked up the water buckets.

"Didn't you hear about that grass fire over in the east part of town day before yesterday?" Jake asked. "A man over there set fire to his hayfield and it got loose from him and burned up his wife."

"That's nothing to concern me," Carl said. "Haven't got a wife, and never felt the need for one. It's people with wives who do all the fool things in the world, anyway."

"Guess you're right about that," Jake said. "I was about to let it slip my mind that your daddy had a wife."

Carl turned around with the water buckets and walked a dozen yards out into the field. The dead grass was almost waist high, and it cracked and waved in the wind like chaff in a hay barn. Each time Carl took a step in the dead grass a puff of dust rose up behind him and blew away in the wind. Carl was beginning to believe that Jake was right after all. He had not realized how dry the country really was.

Jake drove his horse and buggy to the side of the road and crossed his legs. He sat back to wait and see how big a fool Carl Abbott really was.

"If you go and fire that hayfield, you'd better go take out some insurance on your stock and buildings. They won't be worth a dime otherwise; though I guess if I was hard put to it, I could give you a dollar for the ashes, including yours. They'd make the finest kind of top dressing for my potato field this year."

"If you've got any business of your own, why don't you go and attend to it?" Carl said. "Didn't invite you to stay here."

"By God, I pay just as many taxes for the upkeep of the town's roads as you do, Carl Abbott. Shall stand here until I get good and ready to go somewhere else."

Carl always said something or did something to make Jake angry whenever they got within sight or hearing distance of each other.

Jake crossed his legs again and snapped the leaves off a birch seedling with his horsewhip.

The wind was coming down from the northeast, but it shifted so frequently that nobody could have determined its true direction. In the month of April there was no way of finding out which way the wind was blowing. Jake had said that in April the wind came in all directions, except straight up, and that if man were to dig a hole in the ground it would come that way, too.

Carl stooped over in the grass and struck a match on the seat of his pants. He held the flame close to a tuft of grass and weathered it with his hands.

The flame flared up so quickly and so suddenly that it jumped up through his arms and singed his whiskers before he could get out of the way. The wind was true in the east just then, and it was blowing at about thirty miles an hour. The flame died down almost as suddenly as it had flared up, and a column of white smoke coiled straight upward for a few feet before it was caught in the wind and carried down over the meadow. The fire was smoldering in the dead grass, and the white smoke showed that it was feeding on the crisp dry tufts that grew around the stems like powder puffs. A hayfield could never be burned over completely if it were not for the small coils of grass that curled in tufts close to the ground. When the tufts blazed, the long waist-high stems caught and burned through. Then the tall grass fell over as if it were being mown with a scythe, and the fire would be under way, feeding itself far faster than any number of men could have done.

Jake Thompson watched the white smoke boil and curl in the air. He saw Carl walk over to one of the buckets and souse the broom in the water, taking all the time he wished. Then he went back to the fire and stood looking at it smolder in the tufts.

A fairly new, well-sewn house broom and a pail or two of water was the finest kind of fire-fighting equipment in a hayfield. But farmers who burned over hayfields rarely undertook such a task without having three or four men to help keep the fire under control. Six men who knew how to souse a broom in a bucket of water at the proper time, keeping it sufficiently wet so the broom-straw would not catch on fire, could burn over the largest hayfield in the state. Water alone would not even begin to put out a grass fire; it was the smothering of the flame with the broad side of the broom that kept it from spreading. But nobody with any sense at all would have thought of firing a field that year until a rain had come and made the ground moist and dampened the grass tufts. Under those conditions a field would have burned so slowly that one man could have kept it under control.

Jake knew that Carl did not have a chance in the world of being able to check that fire once it had got under way.

The white smoke was boiling upward in a column the size of a barrelhead by that time. The wind had shifted again, circling around Carl's back and blowing down across the meadow from a new angle. The grass tops bowed under the force of the wind, and the wind was changing so frequently that it kept the field waving first in one and then in some other direction. Carl looked around and overhead as if by that he were doing something that would cause the wind to die down into a breeze.

Jake crossed his legs again and waited to see what was going to happen next. Carl Abbott was without doubt the biggest fool he had ever known.

Suddenly the flames shot into the air higher than Carl's head and began leaping across the field towards the meadow like a pack of red foxes let loose. Carl jumped backward, stumbling, and overturning one of the buckets of water. The flames bent over under the force of the wind until they looked as if they were lying flat on top of the grass. That made the field burn even faster still, the leaping flame setting fire to the grass quicker than the eye could follow. It had been burning no longer than two or three minutes, but in that short time it had spread out into the shape of a quarter cut of pie, and it was growing larger and larger each second. Carl ran around in circles, his wooden leg sticking into the ground and tripping him with nearly every step. He would have to stop every step or two and take both hands to pull the wooden peg out of the ground.

"Hey there, Carl Abbott!" Jake shouted at him above the roar of the burning grass. "What in hell are you doing out there! Get away from that fire!"

Carl heard Jake but he paid no attention to what he said. He was trying to beat out the fire with his wet broom, but his work was not checking the flames in any direction. He was so excited that, instead of beating at the flames, most of the time he was holding the broom in the fire, and hitting the water buckets with his wooden leg. The broom caught on fire, and then he did not know which way to turn. When he did succeed in hitting at the fire with the broom, as fast as he smothered one tuft of grass it caught fire again almost immediately. In the meantime two or three fresh ones blazed up beside it.

"Come out of there, you damn fool!" Jake shouted at him. "You'll be cooked and ready to eat if you don't get out of that fire!"

Carl's hat had fallen off and had already burned into a handful of gray ashes. His whiskers were singed close to his face, making him appear at a distance as if he had had a shave, and his peg leg was charred. If he had stood still all the time he would not have been hurt, because the fire would have burned away from him; but Carl ran right into the hottest part of it, almost out of sight in the smoke and flame. His woolen pants were smoking, his coat was dropping off in smoking pieces, and a big black circle was spreading on his shirt where a spark had ignited the blue cotton cloth.

Jake jumped out of his buggy and ran into the hayfield calling Carl. He could not sit there and see a man burn himself alive, even if the man was Carl Abbott.

He grabbed Carl and dragged him away from the flame and threw him down on the ground where the grass had already burned over. Carl's wooden leg was burned completely through, and as he fell to the ground it broke off in half. All that was left of it was a charred pointed stub about six or eight inches long. Carl had made the peg himself, and, instead of using oak as Jake had advised him to do, he had made it out of white pine because, he said, it would be lighter to carry around. Jake dragged him by the collar to the gap in the stone wall and dumped him in the road. Carl tried to stand up, forgetting the burned-off peg, and he tumbled over into the drain ditch and lay there helplessly.

"You would go ahead and act like a damn fool, after all, wouldn't you?" Jake said. "It's a pity I didn't let you stay out there and make ashes. They would have been worth more than you are alive. Meat ashes make the finest kind of dressing for any kind of crop."

Carl sat up and looked through the gap in the stone wall at the smoking hayfield. The fire line had already reached the wood lot, and flame was beginning to shoot from the top of the pines and hemlocks. Two hundred yards farther away were Carl's buildings. He had a team of horses in the barn, and a cow. There would be no way in the world to save them once the fire had reached the barn and caught the dry hay.

Jake tossed Carl a stick and watched him hobble the best he could down the road towards his house and buildings.

"What are we going to do?" he begged Jake. "We can't let my stock and buildings burn up, too."

"What we?" Jake said. "You and who else? You're not talking to me, because I'm having nothing to do with all this mess. I told you what not to do when you came up here a little while ago, but you were so damn smart I couldn't get anything through your head. That's why I'm having nothing at all to do with all this mess."

Carl protested feebly. He tried to get up and run down the road, but he fell each time he attempted to stand up.

"Why! do you think I'd have people saying that they passed your place and saw me helping you put out a grass fire when nobody with any sense at all would ever have started one in this kind of weather? People in this town know I don't associate with crazy men. They know me better than that. That's why I don't want them to think I've lost my mind and gone plumb crazy with you."

Carl opened his mouth, but Jake had not finished.

"I wouldn't even spit on a blade of witch grass now if I thought it would help check that fire you started. Why! the townspeople would think I had a hand in starting it, if I went and helped you check it. Nobody would believe me if I tried to tell them I begged you not to fire your field in the beginning, and then went right out and helped you fight it. The townspeople have got better sense than to believe a tale like that. They know I wouldn't do a fool thing like you went and did. They know that I have better sense than to go out and start a fire in a hayfield when it hasn't rained yet this spring. I'm no fool, Carl Abbott, even if it does appear that I'm associating with one now."

"But you can't let my stock and buildings burn up," Carl

said. "You wouldn't do that, would you, Jake? I've been a fair and honest friend of yours all my life, haven't I, Jake? And didn't I cast my vote for you when you wanted to be road commissioner?"

"So I can't, can't I? Well, you just stand there and watch me try to save your stock and buildings! And this is no time to be talking politics, either. Wouldn't help you, anyway, not after the way you did there in that hayfield. I told you not to go and fire that field, and you went right ahead like a damn fool and struck a match to it, just as if I had been talking to myself away over in another part of town. No! I'm not going to do anything about it—except talk. When the townspeople ask me how your farm and buildings came to catch on fire and burn up your stock and wood lot, I'll tell them you fired it."

Carl found a heavier stick and hobbled down the road towards his house and buildings. The fire had already run through the wood lot by that time, and, as they came around the bend in the road, flame was licking at the house and barn.

Jake walked behind Carl, coming down the road, and led his horse instead of riding in the buggy. He watched Carl try to run, and he thought once of putting him into the buggy, but he did not like the idea of doing that. Townspeople would say he was riding Carl around in his horse and buggy while the stock and buildings burned up.

When they got closer to the house, the roof was ablaze, and the barn was smoking. The hay in there was dry, and it looked as if it would burst into flame any second. Carl hobbled faster when he saw his buildings burning.

"Help me get my stock out, Jake," he begged. "You won't let my stock burn up, will you, Jake?"

Jake tied his horse to a tree beside the road and ran across the yard to the barn. He could not stand there and see a team of horses and a cow burn alive, even if they did belong to Carl Abbott. He ran to the barn and jerked open the stall doors.

An explosion of smoke, dust, and flame burst into his face, but the two horses and the cow bounded out the moment the stall doors were thrown open. The horses and cow ran across the yard and leaped over the brush by the roadside and disappeared into the field on the other side.

Jake knew it was a stroke of chance that enabled him to save the stock, because if the horses and cow had been farther in the barn, nothing could have induced them to leave it. The only way they could have been saved would have been to blindfold them and lead them out, and there would have been no time for that. The flame had already begun to reach the stalls.

Carl realized by that time that there was no chance of saving anything else. He saw the smoke and flame leap through the roof of the barn the moment that Jake had opened the stall doors. He felt terribly sick all over.

Jake went over to the tree and untied his horse. He climbed into the buggy and sat down. Carl stood looking at his burning buildings, and he was trying to lean on the big stick he had found up the backroad.

Jake whipped up his horse and started home. Carl turned around and saw him leave, but he had nothing to say.

"Whoa!" Jake said to his horse, pulling on the reins. He turned around in the buggy seat and called to Carl. "Well, I guess you'll have better sense than to do a thing like that again, won't you? Next time maybe you will be anxious to take some advice."

Carl glared at Jake, and turned with nothing to say to stand and watch the fire. Then suddenly he shouted at Jake.

"By God, the hayfield is burned over, ain't it?" he said, hobbling away. "Well, that's what I set out to do at the start."

Jake whipped up his horse and started for home. When he looked back for the last time, he saw Carl whittling on a pole. Carl had cut down a young pine and he was trimming it to replace the peg that had burned off in the hayfield. He wished to make the new one out of oak, but oak was the kind of wood that Jake had told him to use in the first place.

(First published in *We Are the Living*)

Where the Girls Were Different

NOBODY could ever explain exactly why it was, but the girls who lived in all the other parts of Oconee County were different from the ones in our section. All the girls in Woodlawn, which was the name of the town where we lived, were the sassy kind. They were always slapping and biting, too. I suppose all of them were tomboys. That's about the worst thing you can call a girl when she is growing up. But the girls who lived at Macy's Mill, and at Bradford, and especially in Rosemark, were a different kind. We used to talk about it a lot, but nobody knew why it was.

"How are the Rosemark girls different?" I asked Ben, when we were talking about it one day.

"Jiggers," he said, "I don't know exactly."

I never went around like Ben and the other boys did, because I had a girl who lived in town and I went to see her two or three times a week, and that was as many nights as my folks would let me go out. They did not believe in letting me go all over the county to see girls. So I stayed at home and went to see Milly pretty often.

But those girls in other parts of the county were not like the ones at home. The other boys used to go off nearly every night to see girls at Bradford and Macy's Mill and Rosemark, Rosemark especially. I don't know why that was, either. There was just something about those girls down in Rosemark that made a man act kind of funny.

Ben went down to Rosemark three or four nights every week to see girls. The strange part of it was he rarely went to see the same girl more than once. He had a new girl almost every time he went down there. The other boys did the same way, too. They had a new girl every time. Shucks, I had to stay at home and go to see Milly and nobody else.

I asked Ben in a confidential way what it was about the girls down in Rosemark that made them so different from the ones around home.

Ben was my first cousin and I didn't mind asking him personal questions.

"Jumping jiggers!" he said. "You've never been down there to see a Rosemark girl, have you, Fred?"

I told him how it was about Milly. I did not want to go to see her all the time, but I never had a chance to go down to Rosemark like the other boys.

"Well," he said, "you are a fool to go to see her all the time. She's just like all the other girls around here. You've got to go down to Rosemark and see some real girls. They're not like these around Woodlawn."

"What are they like, Ben?" I asked him again. Everybody said they were different, but nobody ever said in what way they were different. "What do they do that's different?"

"Well, that's hard to say. They act just like all girls do— but they are different."

"Tell me about them, Ben."

"I'll tell you this," he said. "You got to be careful down there. Every girl in Rosemark that's got an old man or a brother is watched pretty close. I guess that's because they are pretty wild."

"How are they wild?" I asked him. "What do they do?"

"That's hard to say, too. You can't put your finger on it exactly—they are just different. You've got to go down there."

"But how can I get a date with one of them?"

"Oh, that's easy," he said. "You just go down there some Sunday night and wait outside a church until they come out. Then pick one out and ask her to let you take her home. That's the way to do it."

"Can I do that? Would she let me take her home?"

"Sure. That's one way they are different. You can get any girl you want if you ask her before somebody else does. You go down Sunday night and try it. Jiggers, Fred, you got to see those Rosemark girls! The ones around here aren't fit to fool with."

I hated to tell my folks the next Sunday night that I was going to see Milly when I wasn't, but—gee—I had to go down to see those girls in Rosemark. I drove the old car down and got there just before the churches let out.

I picked out the biggest church I could find and waited outside the door. I figured that the bigger the church the better chance I would have because there would be more girls in it.

Shucks, it wasn't any trouble at all. I asked the first girl that came out by herself if I could take her home and she said, "Sure," just as nice. Gee, this was the way to see girls. Up at home the girls acted sassy about letting you take them home. These Rosemark girls were different that way.

"Where do you live?" I asked her.

"About five miles out in the country," she said. She talked nice and soft like all girls would if they knew what was good for themselves. "Do you want to take me?"

"You bet I do," I told her. "I don't care how far it is."

Five miles wasn't anything. It was fine, because I'd have a longer time to find out about her. I could tell right away she was different.

She showed me the way to go and we started out. The old car was running good, but there was no hurry to get there.

"What's your name?" I asked her.

"Betty," she said.

No girl up in Woodlawn had a name like that. I was beginning to see why all the boys at home liked to come down to Rosemark.

Gee, she was different! She sat real close to me and sort of hunched her shoulders forward like she was awfully pleased. I had never seen a girl act so nice in all my life. She put her arm through mine and sort of leaned against me a lot and I had a devil of a time trying to keep our old car in the road.

As soon as we got outside of town a little distance another automobile came up behind us real close. I drew over to the side of the road so it could pass, but whoever was running it wouldn't try to pass. I thought that was funny, because I was driving only about ten miles an hour and making a lot of dust behind, too. The man who was running the other car was crazy not to pass us and go on ahead.

Betty sat closer and closer all the time and was so nice I didn't know what to make of it.

"The devil," I said to myself, "I'm going to take a chance and kiss her."

That was a reckless thing to do, because all the girls I knew up home were pretty particular about things like that and they didn't mind slapping you good and hard, either.

Gee whiz! I reached down and kissed her and she wouldn't let me stop. The old car rocked from one side of the road to the other as dizzy as a bat. I couldn't see to steer it because Betty wouldn't let me stop kissing her, and I had to wait until we ran into a ditch almost before I knew which way to turn the wheel. Gee whiz! The girls in Rosemark were certainly different, all right.

Finally I got away from her and got back my breath and saw which way to guide the old car.

"Don't you like to kiss me?" she asked, hunching her shoulders forward again like a girl does when she wants to make you feel funny.

Shucks, I couldn't let her get away with that! I reached my right arm around her and kissed her as hard as I could. She didn't mind how rough I was, either. I guess she liked it, because she put both of her arms around my neck and both of her legs across my lap and hugged the life out of me. *Gee whiz!* I didn't know girls did like that! Ben said the girls down in Rosemark were different, but I didn't expect anything like this to happen to me. Holy cats! The girl was sitting on my lap under the steering wheel and I was having a devil of a time trying to kiss her for all I was worth and steer the old car at the same time.

Right then I knew I was coming down to Rosemark again as soon as I could get away. Ben sure knew what he was talking about when he said the girls down here were nothing like the ones at home. Shucks, those old girls up at home were not anything.

By this time we had got to the place where she lived and she looked up just at the right moment to tell me where to turn in. Before I could steer the old car into the driveway the automobile that had been behind us all the time beat me to it and I had to jerk on the brakes to keep from running smack into it.

"Who is that fool?" I asked Betty.

"That's Poppa," she said.

I started to say something pretty mean about him for doing a thing like that but I thought I had better not if I wished to come back to see her. I was going to ask her for a lot of dates as soon as we got in the yard.

She took her arms down and moved over to her side of the seat just as if nothing in the world had happened.

I shut off the engine and reached over and opened the door.

for her. She jumped out just as nice and I was right behind her. I got as far as the running board when the man who had beaten us to the gate pushed me back into the seat. He shoved me so hard I hurt my spine on the steering wheel.

"Where do you think you're going?" he growled at me. "Start up that car and get away from here and don't ever let me see you again."

He came closer and shoved me again. I then saw for the first time that he had a great big rusty pistol with a barrel about a foot and a half long in his other hand.

"If I ever catch you around Betty again I'll use this gun on you," he said.

I didn't lose any time getting away from there. I hated to go away and not see Betty again, so I could ask her for a lot of dates next week, but it wouldn't do any good to have dates if I couldn't come back.

I drove the old car back home and went to bed. I knew now why Ben never went to see the same girl twice. He knew what he was doing, all right. And I knew why he said the girls down there were different. They sure were different. It was hard to say what the difference was, but if you ever went down there it was easy to feel it all over yourself.

The next morning I saw Ben and told him about going down to Rosemark the night before. After a while I told him about the way Betty kissed me and how she wanted to sit on my lap under the steering wheel.

"What!" he said, his eyes wide open.

I told him about it again, and how she wouldn't let me stop kissing her and how she put her legs across my lap.

"Jumping jiggers, that's funny. None of them ever let me kiss her, and none of them ever sat on my lap."

"Gosh, Ben," I said, "then why did you think they were different?"

"Jumping jiggers!" he said again, frowning all over. "I don't know."

(First published in *American Earth*)

The Sunfield

FOR the first time in more than an hour a light breeze blew through the open windows of the cottage and whipped the white curtains feebly. Myrtle Lewis ran from the window where she had been gazing vacantly at the treeless horizon and threw herself upon the bed. Even with her eyes pressed tightly against the counterpane, she could still see the countless chains of shimmering heat.

The phonograph was running endlessly in the last groove of the record. The machine had been wound tightly, and the needle was sharp and new. It sounded like the blare of a muted saxophone.

Wha whoo wha . . . Wha whoo wha . . . Wha wha wha . . .

The wail filled the house, every crack and joint of it. It seeped like thin oil into the fiber of the doors, floors, and sills. The sounds that escaped through the open windows floated over the surrounding sunfield, that endless expanse of bare smooth earth, until at last they were driven by the heat into the hard clay.

Myrtle tried to shut the sound from her ears by locking her arms around her head, but it was not so easy to do as that. The sound was as penetrating as stabs of sharp pain. After passing through her, it moved through the windows, and there she thought she could see it join the waves of heat that zig-zagged upward and upward toward the summit of the deep blue sky.

At the front of the cottage somebody was banging on a door, but Myrtle did not hear the sound in the phonograph's painful blare. She began tossing from side to side, still holding her arms tightly around her head. It was no use trying to keep herself from crying; she could not stop no matter how hard she tried.

The phonograph was running down. The needle began to scratch, and the last wail of the saxophone solo was only a thin cry without pain. It made her cry all the more.

By the time the sound had died out, the banging on the front door had stopped.

While she rolled from side to side, squeezing her head with the right embrace of her arms, the bedroom door opened and Sid came in. He looked at Myrtle for several moments before closing the door behind him. He went several steps forward.

"Myrtle," he called, glancing around the room to make certain no one else was there.

She made no sign of having heard him, and she continued to toss and roll from one end of the bed to the other. She had begun to cry hysterically, and her white dress was crumpled and damp.

Sid ran to the side of the bed, knelt on the floor beside her, and tried to take her arms from around her head. She did not know anyone was there until she felt his hands grasping her.

"Who's that?" she cried in surprise, choking back the sobs

in her throat and trying to pull herself away. "Who's that?" she asked again.

She had stopped crying, but she had cried too long to be able to stop altogether. Before Sid could answer her she was crying and sobbing again.

"It's Sid, Myrtle," he said, shaking her a little. "It's Sid. What's the matter? What happened?"

The sun was full on her face, blazing hotly through the window beside the bed, and she could not see anything. After she had recognized Sid's voice, she stopped trembling except for occasional shudders that she could not control.

Myrtle opened her eyes a little. When she saw Sid, she threw herself into his arms clutching him frantically. Until she had stopped crying entirely, Sid did not try to make her talk. He held her, stroking her hair, and tried to help her as gently as he could. She clung to him.

An automobile shot past the house, fifty feet away on the wide hot concrete highway, and the house shook with the vibration of the air. The car was making seventy miles an hour.

Long after the sound of the speeding automobile had died out, Myrtle opened her eyes and looked up at Sid. He smiled down at her, stroking her heavy brown hair and brushing it away from her forehead with thick rough fingers.

"Hello, Sid," she said, smiling happily. "I haven't seen you in a long time, have I?"

He shook his head and turned her face toward his. She tried for a moment to turn away, but he held her tightly with his hand against her cheek, and she did not struggle any more after he had begun to kiss her. She closed her eyes until she felt his lips withdrawn from hers. She looked into his face.

"What were you crying about, Myrtle?"

"I wasn't crying, Sid."

"You are still crying a little."

She sat up and wiped the tears from her face. She pushed her hair back and tried to smile. Sid got up from the floor and sat down on the bed beside her. With her back to him, she ran her fingers over the knuckles of his hand. He caught her and held her.

"There's nobody here, is there?" he asked, looking around the room for a second time.

"No," she said. "There's nobody here."

"What was wrong? What happened?"

"Nothing, Sid," she smiled, her gaze falling away. "Nothing happened."

"Then what made you cry, Myrtle?"

Myrtle turned away from him and looked at the phonograph on the table. It had run down while they were talking, but she could see the needle pointed into the last groove of the record. She got up, went to the table, and closed the top.

"Aren't you going to tell me, Myrtle?" Sid insisted.

"There's nothing to tell," she said, shaking her head. "Honest, there isn't. I'm just foolish sometimes, I guess. That's all."

Sid got up and stood at the window, holding aside the white curtains. As far as the eye could see, the land was flat and treeless. The summer heat danced in layer after layer, and the air was as motionless as the earth underneath.

"Did you want something?" Myrtle asked, startling him.

He turned around and walked toward her at the door that led into the front room. Just before he got to her, she turned and went through the door. He followed her.

"I was going into town, and I stopped to get a pack of cigarettes," he said at last. "I knocked for a long time, but you didn't answer."

"I knew," she said. "I must have been asleep."

She laughed before he could say anything.

Sid laid a quarter on the table, and she gave him the cigarettes and the change.

"I'd better take a drink, too," he said, breaking open the pack of cigarettes.

Myrtle took a bottle of beer from the cooler and opened it. Sid shook his head about the glass.

"Forget it, will you Sid?" she begged, leaning over the table towards him. "Won't you, Sid?"

He gulped down several swallows.

"Why should I, even if I could?"

Myrtle sat down on the table.

"It won't help anybody for you to remember," she said, not looking up.

He drank some more beer.

"How about moving into town, then?" he asked. "You would do just as well there as you can here, maybe better. Everybody who stops here will look you up in town, Myrtle. You've got a lot more friends than you think you have. The boys will look you up no matter where you are. And I know people in town who would rather drop into your place than go anywhere else."

"Sure about that, Sid?" she laughed.

Before he could answer her, she had jumped down from the table and crossed the room to the front door. She stood there looking out across the wide white concrete highway. Over there the flat land was broken by a fringe of pines and oaks that bordered a meandering creek. There were no other trees between the horizons.

"It's not safe, either," Sid said, coming up behind her. "I don't like to say that every time I see you, but it's true."

"I'm not afraid," Myrtle said. "I've never been afraid, Sid. What is there to be afraid of, anyway?"

She continued to stare at the sunfield; the passing of another automobile, going seventy miles an hour or more, did not draw her gaze from it.

"Look here, Myrtle," he said, turning her partly around, "it might be different if you were older, but you're not twenty-five yet. That makes a big difference."

She turned completely around, and for a moment Sid thought she was going to begin crying again. She fought the tears back, biting her lips a little.

"I swear I'm not going to let anybody else marry you, Myrtle," he said, his voice trembling. "And you've either got to get away from here and go into town where it's safe, or else . . ."

She came to him, and he thought by the expression on her face that she was going to say something, but instead she pressed her head upon his chest.

"Where are you going, Sid?" she asked. "Where had you started when you stopped here?"

"I've got to see a man in town," he said. "I've got a little business to attend to."

She stepped back, out of his reach.

"What do the boys do in town, Sid?" she asked. "You know, the boys who drop in here for cigarettes and beer sometimes."

He stepped back a little in order to get a better look at her. She had succeeded in fighting back the tears.

"Nothing much," he said. "They don't do much, I guess."

Myrtle ran across the room and stopped behind the table.

"That's a lie, Sid Temple!" she cried. "Sid Temple, you know it's a lie!"

Sid caught her before she could run from the room.

"Now, listen here, Myrtle," he said, shaking her. "You've got to get away from here. You'll go crazy. This is no place for you, staying here by yourself and making a halfway living selling drinks and cigarettes. I'm not going to let you stay."

"I wouldn't marry you or anybody else in the world!" she cried. "I'd die before that. I wanted to once, but it's different now. Everybody I know is a cheap rat—you too, Sid!"

They both looked up to see standing in the doorway Jim Lyon and Jack Randlett and two or three others.

"What's the matter?" Jim asked, coming inside.

"Nothing," Sid said.

"Was he bothering you, Myrtle?" Jim asked her, coming between them.

"Why should he?" she laughed.

Jack Randlett and the others came inside. Everyone looked first at Sid, and then at Myrtle. She crossed the room and stopped at the cooler. Jim followed her and stood beside her at the table. Sid sat down in a chair.

"What'll it be this time?" Myrtle asked, smiling at them.

Nobody said anything then.

"Don't be bashful," she said. "What will you have, Jim? It looks like you'll have to order for the rest of them this time."

"Anything," Jim said.

"Beer?"

"Beer?"

"Beer?"

"No," he said, shaking his head. "No beer for me this time. Give me a soda."

Myrtle took several bottles from the cooler and put them on the table. While she was opening them, Jim sat down on the table where he could get a good look at her.

"Was Sid Temple getting in your way?" he whispered.

"Of course not," she said, laughing. "We were just having a little argument. It wasn't anything."

"I'm glad I had some business in town today, anyway," he said. "I wouldn't have been coming by here."

Myrtle looked at him until their eyes met.

"So you're going into town on business?" she said.

"Sure," he said. "We're going to pour a concrete dam across a creek over home and make a fish pond. We're going to have fish all the time. All you'll have to do will be go out and drop a line in the water and pull one out."

Myrtle sat down on the table.

"And I suppose you're going into town to buy twenty sacks of cement?"

"Sure," he said, "only it will take about twenty-five."

Myrtle turned around and looked at Jack Randlett.

"What are you going into town for, Jack?"

Jack looked as if he did not know what to say at first. Myrtle had never before asked him what he was going to town for, and he was too surprised to answer.

"To buy a pair of shoes?" Myrtle said.

"Well, I don't know," he said, hesitating. "Do you think I need a new pair?"

Everybody in the room laughed at Jack and, before he knew it, he was stammering and his face was red.

Myrtle's expression changed completely, and she was glaring at Jack and Jim and the others.

"You're a liar, Jim! And you're a liar, Jack Randlett!" She jumped down from the table. "All of you are liars! You're going into town to spend the evening on St. Mary's Street!"

There was no sound or motion in the room. Each person there stared at another, and back again at Myrtle.

"I didn't know you knew anything about St. Mary's Street, Myrtle," Jim said. "How did you find out anything about—?"

"Shut up, Jim," Jack Randlett said.

The expression on Myrtle's face frightened them all.

"All of you come in here on your way to town and spend a few dimes and say you've got some business to attend to, and expect me to believe you. When you leave here, you go straight to St. Mary's Street and buy hard drinks and start talking to those girls sitting in the windows. Then you come back by here and stop for a soft drink and try to make me believe something else. All of you do that—married, unmarried, or what not. You think you can come in here and buy a pack of cigarettes and make me believe you. You're all a bunch of cheap rats—every last one of you. I was engaged to one of you once—not anybody in this room, but one of your bunch— and all the time we were engaged he was going into town and spending the night on St. Mary's Street. Then he'd come back the next day and think I didn't know. Why shouldn't I know? You think just because I don't see you on St. Mary's Street that I won't know you were there. Well, go ahead and think what you want to, but don't expect me to believe it."

Sid came across the room to the table where Myrtle was sitting. He stood close to her and looked down into her face.

"I asked you to marry me, Myrtle," he said, "and I'm going to do it again. Tell Jack and Jim and the rest of them to go outside so I can talk to you."

"They are my customers," Myrtle said. "Why should I drive them out?"

"Because I said so."

Myrtle laughed.

"This is a respectable roadhouse; this is no dive. People can come and go as they please, and in broad daylight too. Somebody seems to have got a bad impression of my place."

Sid turned around and said something to Jack Randlett, and all of them went outside. Presently Myrtle heard an automobile start, and after it had left, Sid came back into the room.

"Let's close up the front so you can lie down and rest some, Myrtle," Sid said, taking her by the arm. "You need a rest. The heat out here in the middle of this sunfield is enough to get anybody down."

She jerked her arm from his fingers and pushed him away from her.

"You're a fool, Myrtle," he said. "Just because the fellow you were engaged to was a cheap rat, that's no sign everybody else is too. You know that. You've got to know it, Myrtle."

"Why don't you go on into town like you started to, on business?" she laughed.

"Everybody isn't like that, Myrtle. I'm not."

"You are a liar, Sid. You know you are a liar."

"You've known me for nearly five years now, Myrtle. In all that time you know good and well I've always been just like I am now."

"I don't care what you've been. I won't have anything to do with you."

She ran from the room, slamming the door behind her.

Sid went to the front door and stepped outside. The sun was slanting full in his face, but he did not notice it. Several automobiles raced past the cottage on the hot concrete highway, but he did not hear them. After walking around for a while, he sat down on the running board of his car, holding his head in his hands.

When he looked up and blinked his eyes in the bright sunshine, he heard Myrtle's phonograph begin playing. Whatever the name of the piece, it was the only one he had ever heard her play.

Wha whoo wha . . . Wha whoo wha . . . Wha wha wha . . .

He sat on the step of the car listening to the music, trying to decide whether to go on into town without trying to see Myrtle until he came back, or whether to go into the house and try to talk to her again then.

The sound from the phonograph through the open windows seemed to become louder and louder, as though the machine had suddenly been regulated to issue its greatest volume. A speeding automobile passed, but its sound was drowned in the deafening blare from the house.

He jumped to his feet and ran up the steps to the front door. The door into Myrtle's room was still closed, and he opened it soundlessly and stepped into the bedroom.

He expected to find her lying across the bed, rolling and tossing from one end to the other as he had found her earlier in the afternoon. He was sure she would be crying again.

When he stepped into the room, he saw Myrtle lying motionlessly on the bed. The phonograph blared in his ears until he could not see straight.

Running to the bed, he saw Myrtle lying on her back with her eyes closed, and in her open hand lay her revolver. There was not even a tear on her cheek.

He bent over her, calling her nàme and trying to speak to her. The phonograph ran on and on, the sound filling the house with its grating blare. When he grasped her shoulders, Myrtle opened her eyes and looked straight into his. There was a faint smile on her lips that stayed there after her eyes had closed again. He could not arouse her after that.

The phonograph had run into the last groove on the record. It was running in the circle, the needle screeching a little, and making the same sounds over and over again.

Wha whoo wha . . . Wha whoo wha . . . Wha wha wha . . .

Sid jumped to his feet and knocked the phonograph from the table. It went flying across the room and crashed against the wall. It still ran on and on, making a whir, but the needle was no longer touching the groove on the record.

He went to the window, pulling the white curtains back, and looked across the sunfield. The heat was as intense as ever, and it seemed to him that the waves that rose in layer after layer each carried the sound of Myrtle's phonograph when it ran in the last groove in the record, on and on.

(First published in *Southways*)

The Sick Horse

BENTON came running around the corner of the house yelling for me to come quick. I didn't have a chance to ask him then what the trouble was, but when we got to the barn, I heard Benton saying that something was the matter with King. I had been looking for that, and I wasn't a bit surprised. If a man ever got the worst end of a bargain, I sure thought it was Benton the Friday before, when he swapped Jim Dandy for King and a durn rusty mowing machine.

All I could think of then was that maybe the best thing for the new horse was a stiff dose of medicine. I didn't have a chance to mention that to Benton until after we got inside and had opened the stall door.

Benton was blocking the door and I couldn't see the horse right away.

"Is he down yet, Benton?" I said, pushing past him.

Benton jumped aside as if somebody had jabbed him in the ribs.

"He don't have to get down for me to know he's sick, Clyde," he said. He put his hand on King's bony rump and stared at the scrawny tail. "I should have had the sense to have found out before I traded if he was taken to sick spells. But somehow I was thinking of something else—"

Benton stood back and I had a good look at King. I'd seen him in the sunlight the day the trade was made, and I never thought I'd see a worse-looking nag, but when I took a good look at him this time, I knew I'd never seen a bundle of horse-hide like that in all my life. King was standing on four legs that looked like they had been—well, to tell the whole truth, that horse looked for all the world like one of those playthings the kids make by sticking match stems into a potato.

"I reckon we should have kept Jim Dandy," Benton said, stopping short and looking at the horse. "But I had a feeling at the time—"

"He needs medicine, Benton," I said. "He needs it bad."

Jim Dandy was the finest horse we'd ever had. I guess Benton was thinking that too, because he kept glancing over to the next stall where Jim Dandy's halter was still hanging. Benton had made up his mind to swap, though, and he got a mowing machine to boot. I could tell by looking at King that he'd never last long enough to eat the hay that mower cut.

"Clyde," Benton said, "what had we better do?"

"He's real sick," I said. "He needs bracing up or something right away."

Benton didn't say anything for a while, and I looked around, and the minute I saw his face I knew what he was thinking. He was standing there looking at King and wondering what the visitors who were always dropping in to see the horses would say about that one. I'd seen ones a lot better-looking than King led off to the boneyard, and so had Benton, too.

"Better go get the castor oil, Clyde," Benton said, sitting down on the harness bench.

He was almost as sick as King was, but there was nothing I could do for him.

"Maybe we'd better wait and see if he won't get better first," I said. "That horse looks now like he might not be able to stand castor oil yet, Benton."

"Go get the castor oil like I said, anyway," Benton told me.

I went through the barn door and on into the house where the medicine was kept. When I got back, Benton had got up and gone around to the other side of King, and the horse looked just as sickly on that side as he did from any other direction. I knew that if he ever got rid of him we'd have to make a trade sight unseen.

I set the medicine on the harness bench. Right then King looked like he'd never live to stomach it.

"Give it to him, Clyde," Benton said weakly.

"Benton," I said, "I wouldn't try to force King in the shape he's in. He looks kind of white around the gills."

"Give it to him, anyway. If he won't get well, I don't want him standing around here looking like that."

Right then and there I had a feeling that the better use of the castor oil was to take it out behind the barn and pour it over the rust on the mowing machine, but there was no way to talk Benton out of giving it to King.

I went over to the harness room and got the gun and filled it with the castor oil like Benton said to. Benton did not make a move to help me. When I got back and was ready to give it to King, I motioned to Benton, and he came over and helped me get the horse's head up.

When it was all over, instead of helping me with the hay, Benton went into the house and sat down. He took a seat by the front window hoping, I guess, to be able to shy visitors away from the barn if any should stop in that afternoon.

I went on about finishing up my work and didn't have a chance to see Benton again until late in the afternoon. I had heard one car stop in front of the house, but whoever it was got headed off by Benton at the front gate and didn't get a chance to come to the barn where the sick horse was.

About five o'clock I walked around to the front of the barn and sat down to wait for Benton to come out. I knew he would be there before feeding time to look at King, and I did not want to miss seeing if the medicine had helped any. I couldn't get it out of my head all that time about trading Jim Dandy for King and the rusty mower. It was a fool trade, if there ever was one, and I couldn't figure out what had made Benton go and do it. Jim Dandy was just about the finest horse a man could hope to own. He was a good height and just about perfect in weight, and he had the finest mane and tail I ever expect to see again on a horse.

I'd always rubbed him down twice a day, and I had even got so I would rather do that than take a day off and go to town. I'd curry him and brush him until his sides were as shiny as new paint. The cold weather always ruffled up his hide, and when I started in, it would be as fuzzy as a kitten's. By the time I had finished, it looked like he'd just stepped out of the show ring with a blue ribbon. Then I'd start on his tail and mane and spend another hour working over that. I'd comb him carefully first, and then I'd begin brushing them. His mane was as silky and smooth as a young girl's hair, and those waves would come out and shine just like they had been put there with a curling iron.

But it was his tail that showed up the wavy streaks so well. His tail reached all the way down to the ground, and after you'd worked over it three quarters of an hour and stood back to let the sunshine play on it, it looked exactly like a frozen lake that had locked up with the frost when the wind was high. You can see the same thing in November before the snow falls by standing on a hilltop somewhere and looking down a mile or two away and see one of those sheets with the waves locked up in the ice. I tell you, there's not a prettier sight anywhere than that, and that's exactly how the curly waves in Jim Dandy's mane and tail looked.

I don't know how long I'd been sitting there in the sun thinking about Jim Dandy when Benton opened the house door and came down toward the barn. Just then a car drove up, but Benton was too busy thinking about something else to hear it; and two men got out and came on down toward the barn where we were.

Benton had his head down, and I couldn't motion to him till he got to the barn door, and then it was too late. Henry Trask and Fred Welch were too close to the barn by then to head off. I couldn't do a thing but just stand there and pray that they would never get inside to see King.

"Well," Benton said, "I guess we'd better go take a look."

It wasn't till then that he heard Henry and Fred behind him. Benton jumped like he was trying to get out of his skin.

"I heard you've got a new horse, Benton," Henry said. "Trying to keep it a secret? Tell Clyde to lead him out and let us get a look at him. And don't go trying to tell me he's a better horse than Jim Dandy, Benton."

Benton didn't know what to say then. He knew there was no way to get Henry and Fred away before they saw the horse. They had already got to the door, and nothing in the world could stop them then. They'd come eight miles to take a look at King.

"Henry," Benton said, "I wish you and Fred hadn't come here today."

"Why?" Fred asked. "What's the trouble, Benton? Your wife ailing or something?"

"My horse is sick," Benton said, reaching out for the side of the barn to find support. Nobody could have looked more sick than Benton did right then, but somehow both Henry and Fred failed to notice it.

"That's all right, Benton," Henry said. "You won't have to lead him out. We'll go inside and look at him in the stall."

We all walked inside and went down through the harness room and opened the door to the stall. Benton stood back. He acted like he never wanted to look at King again. Anyway, he opened the door and stepped back instead of leading the way inside as he usually did when he was proud to show the horse he owned.

"There's no horse in here, Benton," Henry said, coming back through the door. "Is this a joke or something? The stall's as empty as a Baptist church at blueberrying time."

Both me and Benton stepped to the door and looked inside. Sure enough, King wasn't there. We didn't know what to think.

"He was there right after noontime," Benton said excitedly, "because me and Clyde came in here and gave him a gunful of castor oil, didn't we, Clyde?"

"Sure as I've got legs to stand on," I said. "And he couldn't have got out, because this door has been latched all day long."

We ran inside, Benton and me. Then we saw what had happened. The side of the stall next to the areaway had been kicked down. All but the two bottom boards had been smashed to pieces.

Henry and Fred were standing behind us.

"That's the quickest I ever saw a horse get well," Benton said. "Here I've been all day trying to keep people from coming in to see King, and here he goes and gets well and kicks the side of the stall down."

Benton was all excited, thinking that King had turned out to be a fine spirited horse, after all, in spite of his looks.

"Come on," Benton said, leaping over the splintered boards. "He's back in the areaway. I know he's not out, because all the doors stay locked."

The four of us ran out into the areaway, where all the harnessing is done, but King wasn't anywhere in sight. The outside door was shut and latched just like Benton had said it was and just like I knew it was. But King wasn't in the areaway, either.

"Maybe he got into another stall or into the grain room," Henry said.

We went down toward the other end of the barn.

"He couldn't have got into another stall," Benton said, "because the rest of the stalls are on the other side of the one he was in. There's no other way for him to go, that I can see. The grain-room door is shut tight."

Just the same, to make sure, I opened it and looked around inside, but King wasn't there and hadn't been there.

It was the strangest thing I'd ever seen. I was stumped. Benton didn't know what to do next, either.

"What's that door lead into?" Henry said, walking to the door beyond the grain room.

"Shucks," Benton said, "there's no sense opening that door, because that's just a sort of privy me and Clyde use in the winter when we're working in the barn."

Henry took a couple of steps, and stopped short around the corner of the grain room.

"There's no sense in opening the door, all right," Henry said. "It's already open."

The rest of us ran down so we could see what he was talking about.

Right then—well, I don't know what anybody said after that. It was—I had to look three or four times myself before

I knew what I was doing, and even then—sometimes I still can't believe what I saw. Benton—if Benton—but there's no use in trying to tell what Benton said. The whole thing—

We all finally got outside the barn someway. Benton sat down on a bench and looked off across the hills. Both Fred and Henry were laughing too much to talk sense any more. First they'd say something about Benton's new horse, and then they'd look at each other, and then they'd break out laughing all over again.

"Benton," Henry said after they had quieted down some, "it was worth your losing a horse just to know that your stock is the smartest in the country, wasn't it? I've seen horses do smart things, but this is the first time I ever saw or heard of one being smart enough to go to the privy when he took sick."

Benton got up.

"But King died in there, though," he said. "I've lost him, Henry."

"That's just it, Benton," Fred said. "Any horse that had enough sense to back in there and die on the bench proves that even when your horses are nothing to look at, they are still the smartest in the country."

Benton could not see it in that light then. He was still worried to think that the tale would hurt his reputation as a horseman. Henry and Fred left soon afterward, still laughing like I knew they would be for the next four or five days, and I didn't see much of Benton till late in the evening.

At bedtime Benton came upstairs while I was undressing to pass the night. He walked across the room and back before he said anything.

"I wouldn't have had that to happen for anything in the world, Clyde," he said. "I'd a heap rather have a horse of mine drop dead in the show ring—than that."

"I don't know, Benton," I said. "It takes a smart animal to do a thing like that. Maybe King figured that he had to make up someway for his lack of looks."

Benton came over to the table.

After a while he looked up at me. A change had come over his face.

"You're right, Clyde," he said. "It just goes to prove what I've felt ever since I was ten years old, when I started handling horses, and that is that there's no bad horses. Some of them have good looks, some have good sense, and the ones that don't have looks have the other, because all horses have some sense."

"Well, King didn't have any looks, but he sure had horse sense," I said.

Benton jumped to his feet.

"That's it, Clyde! Horse sense! I knew as well as I knew

my name that that fellow I traded with thought he had stung
me, and so did you and everybody else; but I could tell by
watching King that day that he had what every horse worth
his currycomb ought to have. By God, Clyde, King had horse
sense!"

(First published in *Esquire*)

The Rumor

To George Williams went the distinction of being the first
to suggest making Sam Billings the new town treasurer. The
moment he made the nomination at the annual town meeting
there was an enthusiastic chorus of approval that resulted
in the first unanimous election in the history of Androscoggin.
During the last of the meeting everybody was asking himself
why no one had ever thought of Sam Billings before.

The election of Sam to the office of town treasurer pleased
everybody. He was a good businessman and he was honest.
Furthermore, the summer-hotel property that he owned and
operated on the east shore of Androscoggin Lake paid about a
tenth of the town's total tax assessment, and during the season
he gave employment to eighty or ninety people whose homes
were in the town. After he was elected everybody wondered
why they had been giving the office to crooks and scoundrels
for the past twenty years or more when the public money
could have been safe and secure with Sam Billings. The retiring treasurer was still unable to account to everybody's
satisfaction for about eighteen hundred dollars of the town's
money, and the one before him had allowed his books to get
into such a tangled condition that it cost the town two hundred
and fifty dollars to hire an accountant to make them balance.

Clyde Ballard, one of the selectmen, took George aside to
talk to him when the meeting was over. Clyde ran one of the
general stores in the village.

"You did the town a real service today," he told George.
"Sam Billings is the man who should have been treasurer all
the time. How did you come to think of him?"

"Well," George said, "Sam Billings was one of my dark
horses. The next time we need a good selectman I'll trot another one of them out."

"George, there's nothing wrong with me as a selectman,
is there?" Clyde asked anxiously.

"Well, I'm not saying there is, and I'm not saying there's not. I'm not ready to make up my mind yet. I'll wait and see if the town builds me a passable road over my way. I may want to buy me an automobile one of these days and if I do I'll want a lot of road work done between my place and the village."

Clyde nodded his head understandingly. He had heard that George Williams was kicking about his road and saying that the selectmen had better make the road commissioners take more interest in it. He shook hands with George and drove back to the village.

The summer-hotel-season closed after the first week in September and the guests usually went home to Boston and New York Tuesday or Wednesday after Labor Day. Sam Billings kept his hotel open until the first of October because there were many men who came down over the week-ends to play golf. In October he boarded up the windows and doors and took a good rest after working hard all summer. It was two or three weeks after that before he could find out what his season's profits were, because he took in a lot of money during July and August.

That autumn, for the first time in two or three decades, there was no one who spoke uneasily concerning the treasurer or the town's money. Sam Billings was known to be an honest man, and because he was a good businessman everybody knew that he would keep the books accurately. All the money collected was given to Sam. The receipt of the money was promptly acknowledged, and all bills were paid when presented. It would have been almost impossible to find a complaint to make against the new treasurer.

It was not until the first real snow of the winter, which fell for three days during the first week in January, that anything was said about the new town treasurer. Then overnight there was in general circulation the news that Sam Billings had gone to Florida.

George Williams drove to the village the same afternoon the news reached him over on the back road. He happened to be listening to a conversation on the party line when something was said about Sam Billings having gone to Florida, otherwise George might possibly have waited a week or longer before somebody came by his place and told him.

He drove his horse to the village in a hurry and went into Clyde Ballard's store. They were talking about Sam Billings when George walked in.

George threw off his heavy coat and sat down in a chair to warm his feet against the stove.

"Have you heard about it yet, George?" Clyde asked him.

"Sure I have, and God never made a bigger scoundrel than

Sam Billings," he answered. "I wouldn't trust him with a half-dollar piece of my money any farther than I can toss a steer by the tail."

"I heard you was one of Sam's principal backers," one of the men said from the other side of the stove. "You shouldn't talk like that about your prime candidate, George."

Clyde came up to the stove to warm his hands and light a cigar.

"George," he said, winking at the other men around the fire, "you told me that Sam Billings was your dark-horse candidate—you must have meant to say *horse-thief*."

Everybody shouted and clapped his knees and waited for George to say something.

"I used to swear that Sam was an honest man," George began seriously, "but I didn't think then that he would turn around and run off to Florida with all the town's money in his pants. At the next election I'm going to vote to tie the town's money around my old black cow's neck. I'd never again trust an animal that walks standing up on his hind legs."

"Well, George," Clyde said, "you ain't heard it all, about Sam yet. Can you stand a little more?"

"What else did he do?" George stood up to hear better.

"He took Jenny Russell with him. You know Jenny Russell —Arthur Russell's oldest girl. I guess he's having plenty of good times with her and the town's money down in Florida. I used to think that I had good times when I was younger but Sam Billings's got me beat a mile when it comes to anything like that."

George sat down again. He filled his pipe and struck a match.

"So he made off with a woman too, did he? Well, that's what they all do when they get their hands on some money that don't belong to them. Those two things go hand in hand— stolen money and women."

"He picked a good-looker while he was about it," another of the men said. "He'd have to travel a far piece to find a better-looker than Jenny Russell. And if he don't have a good time with her he ought to step aside for a younger man."

George grunted contemptuously and sucked the flame into the bowl of his pipe. He remembered the time when he had had an eye on Jenny Russell himself.

"I heard it said this morning that Sam was going to have his hotel property fired so he could collect the insurance on it," Clyde said from behind the counter where he was waiting on a customer. "If he does that, the whole town assessment will have to be changed so we will be able to collect enough tax money to keep the roads repaired and the schools running."

Nobody said anything for several minutes. George glared

at each man around the stove. The raising of the tax rate stared everybody full in the face.

Clyde came over to the stove again and stood beside it, warming his hands.

"My wife heard it said over the party line last night—" He paused and looked from face to face. Everybody in the store leaned forward to hear what Clyde was going to say. "She heard that Sam Billings murdered one of those rich men from New York in his hotel last summer. I guess he killed him to get his money. He wouldn't stop at anything now."

"Well, I always said that Sam Billings was the biggest crook that ever lived in the town of Androscoggin," George said disgustedly. "The last time I saw Sam I thought to myself, 'Now, how in hell is Sam Billings going to keep the town's money from getting mixed up with his own?' I know now that I was right in thinking that. We ought to catch him and have him sent to the Federal prison for the rest of his life."

"He'll be a slick eel to catch," Clyde said. "Men like Sam Billings figure out their getaway months beforehand. He's probably laughing at us up here now, too. That's the way they all do."

"The Federal government knows how to catch men like Sam Billings," George said. "They can catch him if they start after him. But I don't suppose they would bother with him. We can send him to the State prison, though."

The men around the stove agreed with George. They said that if they ever got their hands on Sam they would do their best to have him sent to prison for as long a time as the law would allow.

A few days later George saw another of the selectmen and asked him about Sam Billings. George's plan of action was to get the Florida police to locate him and then have the sheriff send a deputy down to bring him back for trial. The selectman was in favor of getting Arthur Russell to have the Federal government go after Sam on the charge of taking his daughter Jenny out of the state. In that case, he explained to George, they could get Sam back without it costing the town any of its own money.

George was in favor of any plan just so long as Sam Billings was brought back and tried for stealing the money.

Later in the winter somebody told George that Sam had taken Jenny Russell and gone to Cuba with her. After that was generally known, there was nobody in the whole town who would take up for Sam or speak a word in his behalf. He had taken the town's money and made off with it. That was all there was to it.

"I never did take any stock in that Billings," George said in Clyde's store in the village. "He made so much money out of his hotel he couldn't be satisfied with what he had of his own, but had to go and take the town's money too. And if I was Arthur Russell I'd get the Federal law after him for taking Jenny off like he did. If she was my daughter and Sam Billings took her off to Florida for a good time, or wherever it was he went to, I'd get him arrested so quick it would scare the hide off his back."

"We made a big mistake when we trusted all the town's money to him," Clyde admitted. "It will take us ten years to wipe out that loss. He had almost a thousand dollars when he left."

"You were one of the fools that voted for him," George said. "It's a pity the voters ain't got more sense than they have about such things."

"If I remember correctly," Clyde retorted, "you nominated Sam Billings for town treasurer."

George went outside and unhitched his horse. He drove home without answering Clyde Ballard.

Nothing further was heard either directly or indirectly from Sam during the remainder of the winter. There were no bills that had to be paid right away though, and the town was not yet suffering because the funds were in Sam's possession.

Early that spring, when Sam usually began getting his hotel into shape for the season that opened in June, everybody in town heard one day that he was back home. Sam Billings had been seen in the village early one morning hiring a crew of carpenters and laborers. He had always made repairs on his hotel property at the same time each year.

And Jenny Russell was back home too, and everybody knew about it the same day.

There was a crew of twenty men at work around the hotel Monday morning, getting it ready for the coming season. The boards were removed from the windows and doors, and a new boathouse was being built beside the landing float in front of the hotel. All the unemployed men in town went to the hotel and applied for jobs, because everybody knew that Sam Billings paid good wages and settled promptly every Saturday night.

Sam went about his business just as he had always done each spring. No one told him of the things that had been said about him during the past winter, and he knew nothing about the charges that Clyde Ballard and George Williams and practically everybody else in town had talked about all winter.

George went to the village the first of the week and heard that Sam was back in town for the summer. He went into Clyde's store and sat down on the counter.

"Well, I guess the town's money is safe enough," he told

Clyde. "Sam Billings is back home, and I hear that Jenny Russell is too."

"I heard over the party line last night that Sam bought a big hotel down in Florida last autumn," Clyde said. "He hired Jenny Russell to go down there with him to see that the chambermaids kept it clean and orderly. Jenny Russell is a good worker, and I guess Sam figured that she was a better supervisor than he could get anywhere else. She keeps his hotel here clean and orderly all the time."

"Sure, Jenny is a good supervisor," said George. "There's no better worker anywhere than Jenny Russell. I used to think I'd hire her for my housekeeper, and maybe marry her some day. Sure, she is a fine supervisor. Sam Billings is a good businessman and he knows the kind of help he needs for his two high-class hotels."

"There's no sense in worrying about the town's money," Clyde said. "Sam Billings is an honest man."

"Sure, Sam is. There never was a more honest man alive than Sam Billings. I've known Sam all my life. The town's money is just as safe with him as it would be in my own hands. Sam Billings is an honest man, Clyde."

(First published in *American Earth*)

August Afternoon

VIC GLOVER awoke with the noonday heat ringing in his ears. He had been asleep for only half an hour, and he was getting ready to turn over and go back to sleep when he opened his eyes for a moment and saw Hubert's woolly black head over the top of his bare toes. He stretched his eyelids and held them open in the glaring light as long as he could.

Hubert was standing in the yard, at the edge of the porch, with a pine cone in his hand.

Vic cursed him.

The colored man once more raked the cone over Vic's bare toes, tickling them on the underside, and stepped back out of reach.

"What do you mean by standing there tickling me with that dad-burned cone?" Vic shouted at Hubert. "Is that all you can find to do? Why don't you get out in the field and do something to them boll weevils? They're going to eat up every boll of cotton on the place if you don't stop them."

"I surely hated to wake you up, Mr. Vic," Hubert said, "but there's a white man out here looking for something. He won't say what he's looking for, but he's hanging around waiting for it."

Vic sat up wide awake. He sat up on the quilt and pulled on his shoes without looking into the yard. The white sand in the yard beat the glare of the sun directly into his eyes and he could see nothing beyond the edge of the porch. Hubert threw the pine cone under the porch and stepped aside.

"He must be looking for trouble," Vic said. "When they come around and don't say anything, and just sit and look, it's trouble they're looking for."

"There he is, Mr. Vic," Hubert said, nodding his head across the yard. "There he sits up against that water-oak tree yonder."

Vic looked around for Willie. Willie was sitting on the top step at the other end of the porch, directly in front of the strange white man. She did not look at Vic.

"You ought to have better sense than to wake me up while I'm taking a nap. This is no time of the day to be up in the summertime. I've got to get a little sleep every now and then."

"Boss," Hubert said, "I wouldn't never wake you up at all, not at any time, but Miss Willie just sits there high up on the steps showing her pretty and that white man has been out there whittling on a little stick a long time without saying nothing. I'm scared about something happening when he whittles that little stick clear through, and it's just about whittled down to nothing now. That's why I waked you up, Mr. Vic. Ain't much left of that little whittling-stick."

Vic glanced again at Willie, and from her he turned to stare at the stranger sitting under the water-oak tree in his front yard.

The piece of wood had been shaved down to paper thinness.

"Boss," Hubert said, shifting the weight of his body uneasily, "we ain't aiming to have no trouble today, is we?"

"Which way did he come from?" Vic asked, ignoring the question.

"I never did see him come from nowhere, Mr. Vic. I just looked up, and there he was, sitting against that water oak out yonder and whittling on that little stick. I reckon I must have been drowsy when he came, because when I opened my eyes, there he was."

Vic slid down over the quilt until his legs were hanging over the edge of the porch. Perspiration began to trickle down his neck as soon as he sat up.

"Ask him what he's after, Hubert."

"We ain't aiming to have no trouble today, is we, Mr. Vic?"

"Ask him what he wants around here," he said.

Hubert went almost halfway to the water-oak tree and stopped.

"Mr. Vic says what can he do for you, white-folks?"

The man said nothing. He did not even glance up from the little stick he was whittling.

Hubert came back to the porch, the whites of his eyes becoming larger with each step.

"What did he say?" Vic asked him.

"He ain't said nothing yet, Mr. Vic. He acts like he don't hear me at all. You'd better go talk to him, Mr. Vic. He won't give me no attention. Appears to me like he's just sitting there and looking at Miss Willie on the high step. Maybe if you was to tell her to go in the house and shut the door, he might be persuaded to give some notice to what we say to him."

"Ain't no sense in sending her in the house," Vic said. "I can make him talk. Hand me that stillyerd."

"Mr. Vic, I'm trying to tell you about Miss Willie. Miss Willie's been sitting there on that high step showing her pretty and he's been looking at her a right long time, Mr. Vic. If you won't object to me saying so, Mr. Vic, I reckon I'd tell Miss Willie to go sit somewhere else, if I was you. Miss Willie ain't got much on today, Mr. Vic. Just only that skimpy outside dress, Mr. Vic. That's what I've been trying to tell you. I walked out there in the yard this while ago to see what he was looking at so much, and when I say Miss Willie ain't got much on today, I mean she's got on just only that skimpy outside dress, Mr. Vic. You can go look yourself and see if I'm lying to you, Mr. Vic."

"Hand me that stillyerd, I said."

Hubert went to the end of the porch and brought the heavy iron cotton-weighing steelyard to Vic. He stepped back out of the way.

"Boss," Hubert said, "we ain't aiming to have no trouble today, is we?"

Vic was getting ready to jump down into the yard when the man under the water oak reached into his pocket and pulled out another knife. It was about ten or eleven inches long, and both sides of the handle were covered with hairy cowhide. There was a spring button in one end. The man pushed the button with his thumb, and the blade sprang from the case. He began playing with both knives, throwing them up into the air and catching them on the backs of his hands.

Hubert moved to the other side of Vic.

"Mr. Vic," he said, "I ain't intending to mess in your business none, but it looks to me like you got yourself in for a peck of trouble when you went off and brought Miss Willie back here. It looks to me like she's got up for a city girl, more so than a country girl."

Vic cursed him.

"I'm telling you, Mr. Vic, you ought to marry yourself a wife who hadn't ought to sit on a high step in front of a stranger, not even when she's wearing something more than just only a skimpy outside dress. I walked out there and looked at Miss Willie, and, Mr. Vic, Miss Willie is as bare as a plucked chicken, except for one little place I saw."

"Shut up," Vic said, laying the steelyard down on the quilt beside him.

The man under the water oak closed the blade of the small penknife and put it into his pocket. The big hairy cowhide knife he flipped into the air and caught it easily on the back of his hand.

"Mr. Vic," Hubert said, "you've been asleep all the time and you don't know like I do. Miss Willie has been sitting there on that high step showing off her pretty a long time now, and he's got his pecker up. I know, Mr. Vic, because I went out there myself and looked."

Vic cursed him.

The man in the yard flipped the knife into the air and caught it behind his back.

"What's your name?" he asked Willie.

"Willie."

He flipped the knife again.

"What's yours?" she asked him, giggling.

"Floyd."

"Where are you from?"

"Carolina."

He flipped it higher than ever, catching it underhanded.

"What are you doing in Georgia?"

"Don't know," he said. "Just looking around."

Willie giggled, smiling at him.

Floyd got up and walked across the yard to the steps and sat down on the bottom one. He put his arms around his knees and looked up at Willie.

"You're not so bad-looking," he said. "I've seen lots worse-looking."

"You're not so bad yourself," Willie giggled, resting her arms on her knees and looking down at him.

"How about a kiss?"

"What would it be to you?"

"Not bad. I reckon I've had lots worse."

"Well, you can't get it sitting down there."

Floyd climbed the steps on his hands and feet and sat down on the next to the top step. He leaned against Willie, putting one arm around her waist and the other under her knees. Willie slid down the step beside him. Floyd pulled her to him, making a sucking sound with his lips.

"Boss," Hubert said, his lips twitching, "we ain't aiming to have no trouble today, is we?"

Vic cursed him.

Willie and Floyd moved down a step without loosening their embrace.

"Who is that yellow-headed sapsucker, anyhow?" Vic said. "I'll be dadburned if he ain't got a lot of nerve—coming here and fooling with Willie."

"You wouldn't do nothing to cause trouble, would you, Mr. Vic? I surely don't want to have no trouble today, Mr. Vic."

Vic glanced at the eleven-inch knife Floyd had stuck into the step at his feet. It stood on its tip, twenty-two inches high, while the sun was reflected against the bright blade and made a streak of light on Floyd's pants leg.

"Go over there and take that knife away from him and bring it to me," Vic said. "Don't be scared of him."

"Mr. Vic, I surely hate to disappoint you, but if you want that white-folk's knife, you'll just have to get it your own self. I don't aim to have myself all carved up with that thing. Mr. Vic, I surely can't accommodate you this time. If you want that white-folk's knife, you'll just be bound to get it your own self, Mr. Vic."

Vic cursed him.

Hubert backed away until he was at the end of the porch. He kept looking behind him all the time, looking to be certain of the exact location of the sycamore stump that was between him and the pine grove on the other side of the cotton field.

Vic called to Hubert and told him to come back. Hubert came slowly around the corner of the porch and stood a few feet from the quilt where Vic was sitting. His lips quivered and the whites of his eyes grew larger. Vic motioned for him to come closer, but he would not come an inch farther.

"How old are you?" Floyd asked Willie.

"Fifteen."

Floyd jerked the knife out of the wood and thrust it deeper into the same place.

"How old are you?" she asked him.

"About twenty-seven."

"Are you married?"

"Not now," he said. "How long have you been?"

"About three months," Willie said.

"How do you like it?"

"Pretty good so far."

"How about another kiss?"

"You just had one."

"I'd like another one now."

"I ought not to let you kiss me again."

"Why not?"

"Men don't like girls who kiss too much."

"I'm not that kind."

"What kind are you?"

"I'd like to kiss you a lot."

"But after I let you do that, you'd go away."

"No, I won't. I'll stay for something else."

"What?"

"To get the rest of you."

"You might hurt me."

"It won't hurt."

"It might."

"Let's go inside for a drink and I'll show you."

"We'll have to go to the spring for fresh water."

"Where's the spring?"

"Just across the field in the grove."

"All right," Floyd said, standing up. "Let's go."

He bent down and pulled the knife out of the wood. Willie ran down the steps and across the yard. When Floyd saw that she was not going to wait for him, he ran after her, holding the knives in his pocket with one hand. She led him across the cotton field to the spring in the pine grove. Just before they got there, Floyd caught her by the arm and ran beside her the rest of the way.

"Boss," Hubert said, his voice trembling, "we ain't aiming to have no trouble today, is we?"

Vic cursed him.

"I don't want to get messed up with a heap of trouble and maybe get my belly slit open with that big hairy knife. If you ain't got objections, I reckon I'll mosey on home now and cut me a little firewood for the cook-stove."

"Come back here!" Vic said. "You stay where you are and stop making moves to go off."

"What is we aiming to do, Mr. Vic?"

Vic eased himself off the porch and walked across the yard to the water oak. He looked down at the ground where Floyd had been sitting, and then he looked at the porch steps where Willie had been. The noonday heat beat down through the thin leaves overhead and he could feel his mouth and throat burn with the hot air he breathed.

"Have you got a gun, Hubert?"

"No, sir, boss," Hubert said.

"Why haven't you?" he said. "Right when I need a gun, you haven't got it. Why don't you keep a gun?"

"Mr. Vic, I ain't got no use for a gun. I used to keep one to shoot rabbits and squirrels with, but I got to thinking hard one day, and I traded it off the first chance I got. I reckon it was a good thing I traded, too. If I had kept it, you'd be asking for it like you did just now."

Vic went back to the porch and picked up the steelyard and hammered the porch with it. After he had hit the porch four or five times, he dropped it and started out in the direction of the spring. He walked as far as the edge of the shade and stopped. He stood listening for a while.

Willie and Floyd could be heard down near the spring. Floyd said something to Willie, and Willie laughed loudly. There was silence again for several minutes, and then Willie laughed again. Vic could not tell whether she was crying or laughing. He was getting ready to turn and go back to the porch when he heard her cry out. It sounded like a scream, but it was not exactly that; it sounded like a shriek, but it wasn't that, either; it sounded more like someone laughing and crying simultaneously in a high-pitched, excited voice.

"Where did Miss Willie come from, Mr. Vic?" Hubert asked. "Where did you bring her from?"

"Down below here a little way," he said.

Hubert listened to the sounds that were coming from the pine grove.

"Boss," he said after a little while, "it appears to me like you didn't go far enough away."

"I went far enough," Vic said. "If I had gone any farther, I'd have been in Florida."

The colored man hunched his shoulders forward several times while he smoothed the white sand with his broad-soled shoes.

"Mr. Vic, if I was you, the next time I'd surely go that far, maybe farther."

"What do you mean, the next time?"

"I was figuring that maybe you wouldn't be keeping her much longer than now, Mr. Vic."

Vic cursed him.

Hubert raised his head several times and attempted to see down into the pine grove over the top of the growing cotton.

"Shut up and mind your own business," Vic said. "I'm going to keep her till the cows come home. Where else do you reckon I'd find a better-looking girl than Willie?"

"Boss, I wasn't thinking of how she looks—I was thinking of how she acts. That white man came here and sat down and it wasn't no time before she had his pecker up."

"She acts that way because she ain't old enough yet to know who to fool with. She'll catch on in time."

Hubert followed Vic across the yard. While Vic went towards the porch, Hubert stopped and leaned against the water oak where he could almost see over the cotton field into the pine grove. Vic went up on the porch and stretched out on the quilt. He took off his shoes and flung them aside.

"I surely God knowed something was going to happen when

he whittled that stick down to nothing," Hubert was saying to himself. "White-folks take a long time to whittle a little piece of wood, but when they whittle it down to nothing, they're going to be up and doing before the time ain't long."

Presently Vic sat upright on the quilt.

"Listen here, Hubert—"

"Yes, sir, boss!"

"You keep your eye on that stillyerd so it will stay right where it is now, and when they come back up the path, you wake me up in a hurry."

"Yes, sir, boss," Hubert said. "Are you aiming to take a little nap now?"

"Yes, I am. And if you don't wake me up when they come back, I'll break your neck for you when I do wake up."

Vic lay down again on the quilt and turned over on his side to shut out the blinding glare of the early afternoon sun that was reflected upon the porch from the hard white sand in the yard.

Hubert scratched his head and sat down against the water oak, facing the path from the spring. He could hear Vic snoring on the porch above the sounds that came at intervals from the pine grove across the field. He sat staring down the path, drowsy, singing under his breath. It was a long time until sundown.

(First published in *Esquire*)

Masses of Men

HUGH MILLER worked for the street-railway company. Hugh had a silver button, a gold button, a bronze watch fob made like a trolley car, and a small tin disk with the numeral 7 almost worn off. He had worked for the company for twenty-six years repairing tracks, and the company had once told him that some day he would be retired with a comfortable pension.

After all those years, Hugh was still trying to get along in the world. He still hoped to be made superintendent of construction. For some reason, though, he had never got far. He was still repairing tracks, replacing switch frogs, and jacking up the rails to put in new crossties.

Even though there were other men who were stepped ahead when the time came to fill up the ranks, Hugh kept his job as a laborer, repairing the tracks year after year, and hoped he would be made superintendent of construction before he got too old to work any longer.

"I'll get it yet," he told himself. "I'll get it as sure as shooting. They've got to promote me some day, and I've been working long enough now to get it. I'll get it as sure as shooting."

Hugh had put off marrying Cora until he was promoted. Cora told him that she did not mind waiting a little longer, because she was working herself then in a store in town and earning as much as Hugh himself was. But after the twelfth year, Hugh decided that if he ever was going to get married, he ought to do it without further delay. He was growing old and though Cora was still as youthful in appearance as she was when they became engaged, she was beginning to complain of the long hours she had to stand on her feet behind the counter in the variety store.

"We'll get married right now," Hugh told her one Saturday night while they were riding home from downtown on his company pass. "There's no sense in waiting any longer. If you are ready, we'll be married next week. I've been thinking about it a long time, and there's no sense in waiting till I get promoted."

"I'd love to, Hugh," she said, clutching his arm in the crowded car. "I think it's silly to put it off any longer. I've been hoping for it to happen for I don't know how long. We don't have to wait until you get promoted. It would be all the nicer to have the promotion come while we are married."

They got off the car at the boulevard stop and walked home slowly. They lived next door to each other, in boardinghouses, and there was no hurry since it was Saturday night.

That was the beginning. They walked slowly down the dark street talking about next week, and Hugh kept saying to himself under his breath that he would surely get promoted the next time the company filled up the ranks. He was certain of it. He told Cora he was. She believed him.

After they were married, Hugh rented a five-room house not far from the carbarn. It was just a step down the alley from the tree-lined street where the trolleys passed all day and most of the night. It was a good house, for the money, and it was comfortable. Having their doorstep in an alley did not really matter much after all. They did not mind that. The house was almost on the corner, and the upstairs windows looked out over the tree-lined street. They could step out the front door, walk a few steps, and be in the street. It was not a bad place to live, and Cora liked it.

First there was a girl; they named her Pearl. Later there was a boy, John; after another year there was another girl, and they named her Ruby.

Hugh still looked forward to the time when he would be

made superintendent of construction for the street-railway company, but after Ruby was born, he did not think about it any more. He somehow got out of the habit of thinking about it. Cora had stopped working in the variety store downtown; she stayed at home and attended to the house and cared for the children. She was beginning to wonder what she could do to her skin to keep it from turning so dark; in the meantime she hid her face when people came to the door for some reason or other. She knew there was nothing wrong with her skin; it was merely becoming darker and darker every day. But she wished she knew what to do about it. Her hair already had a wide streak of gray in it.

She never mentioned it to Hugh, but Hugh never talked any more, anyway. When he came home from work, he ate his supper and went to bed. She did not have a chance to tell Hugh anything like that. He was too tired to listen to her.

When Pearl, the oldest girl, was nine, Hugh was knocked down by an automobile one day, while he was jacking up a rail to replace a rotten crosstie, and run over and killed. The company sent his body home that evening, when the rest of the workers got off at five o'clock, and Cora did not know what to do. After she had put the children to bed, she went out and walked down the street until she met a policeman. She told him what had happened to Hugh, and he said he would have the body taken away early the next morning. She went back home and looked at Hugh, but she could not notice any difference in him; at home, Hugh was always asleep.

Cora knew there would be a little money coming in from the company. She was certain there would be something, but she was afraid it would not be enough for them to live on until she could find work of some kind. When she thought about it more, she was afraid there would not even be enough to pay for Hugh's funeral and burial.

The policeman had the body taken away the next morning, and it was buried somewhere. Cora did not know where, but she did know there was nothing else to do about it. The children had to have food, and they had to have a little heat in the house.

She waited a month for the money to come from the street-railway company, and it still did not come. After that she went to the office and asked for it. There was no one there who seemed to know anything about the matter. Nobody in the big brick building had ever heard of Hugh Miller, and when they looked up the name in their records, no one was certain which Hugh Miller she was inquiring about. Cora stayed there all day, but when the people in the building went home at dark, she did not know what else to do except to go home, too.

After that she did not bother the people at the street-railway company any more. She did not have time to go there, for one thing, and she had a lot to do at home. The three children had to be taken care of, and she had to go out every day and find enough food to keep them from being hungry. Sometimes it took her all day long to get enough to feed them for just one small meal; other times she could find nothing at all for them to eat, but she kept on walking because the children had to be fed.

Pearl was going on ten. She was the oldest, and Ruby was still just a baby. But Pearl was growing up. She had long yellow hair and a blue gingham dress, and she tried to help her mother all she could. She cared for the other children while Cora was out trying to get some food, and at night she helped her mother put them to bed. After they were asleep, Cora would tell her about her father, Hugh.

"Your father worked for the street-railway company," she told Pearl. "The company would help us out, but they are so busy up there they can't seem to find time to do anything about it now. They would help us if they could get all the Hugh Millers who have worked for them straight in their minds. Your father was just one of them, and it's hard for the company to tell them apart."

"I can work," Pearl told her mother. "I'm old enough now. I'll see if I can find something to do. You take me with you, Mamma, and I'll ask about it. John and Ruby can take care of each other if we lock them in a room before we go out."

"You're not very big for your age," Cora said. "People wouldn't believe you when you told them you were going on ten."

"But I can work. I'll show them how much I can do."

"Hugh worked for the street-railway company, Pearl. He was your father. Some day the company will help us out. They're busy right now. I don't like to bother them so much when they act like they are so busy."

Pearl went to bed telling her mother that she was old enough to work. Cora did not say anything else to her, but she could not think of any kind of work that Pearl was capable of doing.

The next morning John and Ruby went out early to bring back some wood for the stove. They had no shoes to wear, and their coats were not warm enough. It was midwinter, but the ground was bare of snow. When they came back that afternoon, their feet were bleeding around the toes and their heels had cracked open in several places.

"Where's the firewood, John?" Cora asked him.

"We couldn't find any."

Cora put on her cloak, pulling it up around her head and

shoulders, and went out into the alley. There was no wood of any kind there, but up at the other end there was a coal bin that sometimes overflowed into the narrow way. She filled her apron with coal and ran back to the house. The children huddled around the stove, shivering and whimpering, while she kindled the fire.

"I'm hungry, Mamma," Ruby said.

"I'll get you something to eat," Cora promised her.

"When are we going to have something to eat again?" John asked her.

"I'll bring you something when I come back."

Cora put on her cloak and went out into the alley. She ran to the street and stood there indecisively for several moments until she could make up her mind which direction she would take. She turned down the street this time, instead of going up it.

After she had run and walked for five or six blocks, she came to a cluster of one-story suburban stores. There were several men standing at the curb in front of the buildings. They were waiting for a streetcar to take them downtown. The men turned and looked at Cora when they saw that she was running towards them.

"Mister, give me half a dollar for my children," she pleaded.

The men turned all the way around and looked her up and down. One of them laughed at her.

"Sister," one of them said, "I wouldn't give a dime for you and a dozen more like you."

The others laughed at what he had said. The trolley was coming down the street, its bell clanging. The men stepped out into the street and stood beside the tracks waiting for it to stop and take them aboard. Cora followed them into the middle of the street.

"Mister," she said to the man who had spoken to her, "Mister, what would you—"

"Don't call me 'Mister,'" he said angrily. "I don't like it. My name's Johnson."

The others laughed at her again. Johnson stepped forward and looked down at her while his friends continued laughing at her.

"Mr. Johnson," Cora said, "what would you give me half a dollar for?"

"What would I give you half a dollar for?" he asked.

"Yes, Mr. Johnson. What would you give it to me for?"

He turned around and winked at the other men before answering her. They urged him on.

"Have you got a girl at home?" he asked her.

"Yes, sir. I've got Pearl, and Ruby, too."

"Well, I couldn't give you half a dollar, but I might be able to give you a quarter."

The streetcar stopped and the door sprang open. The motorman had a tin disk pinned to his coat that looked just like the one Hugh had.

The other two men hopped on, calling to Johnson to hurry. He looked at Cora for a moment longer, his hand on the streetcar, but when she continued to stand there with her mouth open, unable to say anything, he turned and jumped aboard.

Cora was left standing beside the tracks. When the car started, she stood on her toes and tried to see the man inside who had spoken to her. She called to him frantically, trying to make him understand her, and she waved her arms excitedly, attempting to attract his attention. All three of them ran to the rear end of the car and pressed their faces against the glass to see her better. Cora ran down the middle of the street, between the streetcar rails, calling to them and trying to stop them, but the car was soon out of sight and she was left standing in the car tracks. She went to the sidewalk and walked back up the street until she had reached the corner in front of the stores where the men had been standing when she first saw them. When she got to the corner, she sat down on the curb to wait.

Cora did not know how long she had waited, but she had promised the children she would bring back some food when she returned, and she had to wait no matter how long the time was. But Johnson finally came back. He got off the streetcar and walked towards her at the curb. He was surprised to see her there, and he stopped before her and looked down at her in amazement. Cora was glad the other men had not come back with him.

She led him up the street, running ahead and urging him to hurry. Even though he followed her without protest, he did not walk fast enough to please Cora, and she was continually asking him to hurry. He stopped once and struck a match for his cigarette against an iron street-light pole, and Cora ran back and pulled at his coat, begging him to follow her as fast as he could.

When they got to the house, Cora awakened Pearl. The man stood close to the door, debating with himself whether to remain and see what happened or whether to leave before something did happen. Cora got behind him and held the door shut so he could not leave.

"How old is she?" he asked Cora.

"She's almost ten now."

"It's cold as hell in this house. Why don't you have some heat in here? You've got a stove there."

"Give me a quarter, and I'll try to get some coal somewhere," Cora said.

"Tell her to stand up."

"Stand up, Pearl," Cora told her.

Pearl shrank against the foot of the bed; she was bewildered and frightened. She wished to run to her mother, but the strange man was between them. She was afraid he would catch her before she could reach the door where Cora stood.

"You're lying to me," Johnson said. "She's nowhere near ten."

"I swear to God, Mr. Johnson, she's almost ten," Cora said. "Please, Mr. Johnson, don't go off now."

"Christ, how do I know this's not a shakedown?" he said, shivering and shaking.

"I swear before God, Mr. Johnson!"

Johnson looked around the room and saw John and Ruby asleep under the quilts on the bed.

"How old is the other girl?"

"She's going on eight."

"Christ!" he said.

"What's the matter, Mr. Johnson?"

"I don't believe you. You're lying to me. Neither one of them is over seven or eight."

"Pearl's almost ten, Mr. Johnson. I swear before God, she is. Please give me the quarter."

He walked across the room towards Pearl. She tried to run away, but Cora caught her and made her stand still beside the foot of the bed. Cora waited behind Johnson.

"Tell her to turn around," he said.

"Turn around, Pearl," Cora told her.

"Christ!" Johnson said, rubbing his face and neck with both hands.

"What's the matter?" Cora asked him.

"It's too damn cold in here," he said, his hands trembling. "My feet are frozen already. Why don't you build a fire in the stove?"

"If you'll give me the quarter, I'll try to get a little coal somewhere."

"How do I know you're on the level?" he asked her. "How do I know this is not a shakedown? I'm afraid of you. You don't look right to me. How do I know you won't go yelling for a cop the first thing?"

"I wouldn't do that. Give me the quarter."

"I'd be in a pretty fix, caught like that. They'd give me twenty years at hard labor. I'd never get out alive."

"I won't tell anybody, Mr. Johnson. I swear before God, I won't. Just give me the quarter."

Johnson pushed his hands into his pockets and looked at Pearl again. His hands were cold; his feet were, too. His breath looked like smoke in the cold house.

"Tell her to let me see her," he said.

"Let him see you, Pearl," Cora said.

Johnson waited, looking at her and at Cora. He could not stand there freezing to death while waiting for Cora to make her obey.

"Hurry up, Pearl, and let him see you," Cora urged.

Pearl began to cry.

"They'd give me life for that," Johnson said, backing towards the door. "You'd get a cop after me before I could get out of the house. I don't like the way you look. Why don't you have some heat in here? You've got a stove."

"Honest to God, Mr. Johnson, I wouldn't tell on you," Cora pleaded. "Give me the quarter, and you can trust me."

"Get some heat in here first," he said. "My feet are freezing solid."

"I can't get any coal until you give me the quarter."

"You can go steal some, can't you?"

"Give me the quarter first, Mr. Johnson."

"How do I know you're on the level? I don't like the way you look. How do I know this's not a shakedown?"

"I swear to God, I won't tell on you, Mr. Johnson."

Johnson lit a cigarette and inhaled the smoke in the manner of a man gasping for breath. With his lungs and mouth and nostrils dense with smoke, he dropped the cigarette into the stove and thrust both hands back into his pants pockets.

"Tell her to come over here," he said.

"Go over there, Pearl."

Johnson bent down and looked at Pearl in the dim light. He straightened up once for a moment, and bent down again and looked at her more closely.

"They'd hang me before tomorrow night if they caught me," he said unevenly.

"Give me the quarter, Mr. Johnson, and I swear before God I won't tell anybody."

"Tell her to stand still."   .

"Stand still, Pearl."

"For God's sake get some heat in here."

"Give me the quarter first, Mr. Johnson," Cora begged.

"And then go out and tell a cop?" he said shrilly.

"Just give me the quarter first."

"You're crazy," he shouted at her. "I don't like the looks of you. How do I know what you'll do? You might run out of here the first thing yelling for a cop."

"Give me the quarter, and I'll get a little coal."

"And tell a cop."

"I swear I won't do that, Mr. Johnson. Give me the quarter, and I'll get some coal."

Johnson turned his back on Cora and went closer to Pearl.

He took his hands out of his pants pockets and blew into them.

"Tell her to stop that crying."

"Stop crying, Pearl."

Johnson reached down and put his hands under Pearl's thick yellow hair, but the moment he touched her, she whirled around and ran to Cora.

"They'd screw my head off my neck so quick I wouldn't have a chance to think about it."

"Give me the quarter, Mr. Johnson, and I swear to God I won't tell on you."

He hesitated a moment; looking at Pearl, he shoved his hand into his pants pocket and brought out a twenty-five-cent piece. Cora grabbed it from his hand and bolted for the door.

"Wait a minute!" he shouted, running and catching her. "Come back here and tell her to keep still before you go."

"Keep still, Pearl," her mother told her.

"Hurry up and get some coal before I freeze to death in this place. And if you tell a policeman, I'll kill the last one of you before they take me. I ought to have better sense than to let you go out of here before I do. I don't like the way you look."

Cora ran to the door and into the alley before he could say anything more to her. She slammed the door and ran with all her might to the end of the alley. Without losing a moment, she raced down the street towards the one-story stores.

After she had gone a block, she stopped and carefully placed the quarter on her tongue and closed her lips tightly so she would be sure not to drop it or lose it on the dark street.

One of the grocery stores was still open. She took the coin out of her mouth, pointing at the bread and pressed meat, and placed the money in the clerk's hand. He dropped the wet silver piece as though it were white-hot steel and wiped his hands on his apron.

"What's this?" he said. "What did you do to it?"

"Nothing," Cora said. "Hurry up!"

When Cora got back, the children were asleep. John and Ruby were rolled tightly in the quilts, and Pearl was lying on the bed with her coat over her. Her gingham dress was lying on the floor, marked with brown streaks of footprints. She had been crying, and the tears had not fully dried on her cheeks; her eyes were inflamed, and her face was swollen across the bridge of her nose.

Cora went to the side of the bed and threw the coat from her and looked down at her. Pearl had doubled herself into a knot, with her arms locked around her knees, and her head was thrust forward over her chest. Cora looked at her for a while, and then she carefully replaced the coat over her.

After unwrapping the bread and pressed meat, she stuffed the paper into the stove and struck a match to it. She drew her chair closer, and bent forward so she could stretch her arms around the sides of the stove and feel the heat as much as possible before the wrapping paper burned out.

When the stove became cold again, Cora laid the bread and pressed meat on a chair beside her and rolled up in her quilt to wait for day to come. When the children woke up, they would find the food there for them.

(First published in *Story*)

The Corduroy Pants

Two weeks after he had sold his farm on the back road for twelve hundred dollars and the Mitchells had moved in and taken possession, Bert Fellows discovered that he had left his other pair of corduroy pants up attic. When he had finished hauling his furniture and clothes to his other place on the Skowhegan road, he was sure he had left nothing behind, but the morning that he went to put on his best pair of pants he could not find them anywhere. Bert thought the matter over two or three days and decided to go around on the back road and ask Abe Mitchell to let him go up attic and get the corduroys. He had known Abe all his life and he felt certain Abe would let him go into the house and look around for them.

Abe was putting a new board on the doorstep when Bert came up the road and turned into the yard. Abe glanced around but kept right on working.

Bert waited until Abe had finished planing the board before he said anything.

"How be you, Abe?" he inquired cautiously.

"Hell, I'm always well," Abe said, without looking up from the step.

Bert was getting ready to ask permission to go into the house. He waited until Abe hammered the twenty-penny into the board.

"I left a pair of corduroys in there, Abe," he stated preliminarily. "You wouldn't mind if I went up attic and got them, would you?"

Abe let the hammer drop out of his hands and fall on the step. He wiped his mouth with his handkerchief and turned around facing Bert.

"You go in my house and I'll have the law on you. I don't give a cuss if you've left fifty pair of corduroys up attic. I bought and paid for this place and the buildings on it and I don't want nobody tracking around here. When I want you to come on my land, I'll invite you."

Bert scratched his head and looked up at the attic window. He began to wish he had not been so forgetful when he was moving his belongings down to his other house on the Skowhegan road.

"They won't do you no good, Abe," he said. "They are about ten sizes too big for you to wear. And they belong to me, anyway."

"I've already told you what I'm going to do with them corduroys," Abe replied, going back to work. "I've made my plans for them corduroys. I'm going to keep them, that's what I'm going to do."

Bert turned around and walked toward the road, glancing over his shoulder at the attic window where his pants were hanging on a rafter. He stopped and looked at Abe several minutes, but Abe was busy hammering twenty-penny nails into the new step he was making and he paid no attention to Bert's sour looks. Bert went back down the road, wondering how he was going to get along without his other pair of pants.

By the time Bert reached his house he was good and mad. In the first place, he did not like the way Abe Mitchell had ordered him away from his old farm, but most of all he missed his other pair of corduroys. And by bedtime he could not sit still. He walked around the kitchen mumbling to himself and trying to think of some way by which he could get his trousers away from Abe.

"Crusty-faced Democrats never were no good," he mumbled to himself.

Half an hour later he was walking up the back road toward his old farm. He had waited until he knew Abe was asleep, and now he was going to get into the house and go up attic and bring out the corduroys.

Bert felt in the dark for the loose window in the barn and discovered it could be opened just as he had expected. He had had good intentions of nailing it down, for the past two or three years, and now he was glad he had left it as it was. He went through the barn and the woodshed and into the house.

Abe had gone to bed about nine o'clock, and he was asleep and snoring when Bert listened at the door. Abe's wife had been stone-deaf for the past twenty years or more.

Bert found the corduroy pants, with no trouble at all. He struck only one match up attic, and the pants were hanging on the first nail he went to. He had taken off his shoes when he climbed through the barn window and he knew his way through the house with his eyes shut. Getting into the house and out again was just as easy as he had thought it would be. And as long as Abe snored, he was safe.

In another minute he was out in the barn again, putting on his shoes and holding his pants under his arm. He had put over a good joke on Abe Mitchell, all right. He went home and got into bed.

The next morning Abe Mitchell drove his car up to the front of Bert's house and got out. Bert saw him from his window and went to meet Abe at the door. He was wearing the other pair of corduroys, the pair that Abe had said he was going to keep for himself.

"I'll have you arrested for stealing my pants," Abe announced as soon as Bert opened the door, "but if you want to give them back to me now I might consider calling off the charges. It's up to you what you want to do about it."

"That's all right by me," Bert said. "When we get to court I'll show you that I'm just as big a man as you think you are. I'm not afraid of what you'll do. Go ahead and have me arrested, but if they lock you up in place of me, don't come begging me to go your bail for you."

"Well, if that's the way you think about it," Abe said, getting red in the face, "I'll go ahead with the charges. I'll swear out a warrant right now and they'll put you in the county jail before bedtime tonight."

"They'll know where to find me," Bert said, closing the door. "I generally stay pretty close to home."

Abe went out to his automobile and got inside. He started the engine, and promptly shut it off again.

"Come out here a minute, Bert," he called.

Bert studied him for several minutes through the crack in the door and then went out into the yard.

"Why don't you go swear out the warrant? What you waiting for now?"

"Well, I thought I'd tell you something, Bert. It will save you and me both a lot of time and money if you'd go to court right now and save the cost of having a man come out here to serve the warrant on you. If you'll go to court right now and let me have you arrested there, the cost won't be as much."

"You must take me for a cussed fool, Abe Mitchell," Bert said. "Do I look like a fool to pay ten dollars for a hired car to take me to county jail?"

Abe thought to himself several minutes, glancing sideways at Bert.

"I'll tell you what I'll do, Bert," he proposed. "You get in my car and I'll take you there and you won't have to pay ten dollars for a hired car."

Bert took out his pipe and tobacco. Abe waited while he thought the proposition over thoroughly. Bert could not find a match, so Abe handed him one.

"You'll do that, won't you, Bert?" he asked.

"Don't hurry me—I need plenty of time to think this over in my mind."

Abe waited, bending nervously toward Bert. The match-head crumbled off and Abe promptly gave Bert another one.

"I guess I can accommodate you that little bit, this time," he said, at length. "Wait until I lock up my house."

When Bert came back to the automobile Abe started the engine and turned around in the road toward Skowhegan. Bert sat beside him sucking his pipe. Neither of them had anything to say to each other all the time they were riding. Abe drove as fast as his old car would go, because he was in a hurry to get Bert arrested and the trial started.

When they reached the courthouse, they went inside and Abe swore out the warrant and had it served on Bert. The sheriff took them into the courtroom and told Bert to wait in a seat on the first row of benches. The sheriff said they could push the case ahead and get a hearing some time that same afternoon. Abe found a seat and sat down to wait.

It was an hour before Bert's case was called to trial. Somebody read out his name and told him to stand up. Abe sat still, waiting until he was called to give his testimony.

Bert stood up while the charge was read to him. When it was over, the judge asked him if he wanted to plead guilty or not guilty.

"Not guilty," Bert said.

Abe jumped off his seat and waved his arms.

"He's lying!" he shouted at the top of his voice. "He's lying —he did steal my pants!"

"Who is that man?" the judge asked somebody.

"That's the man who swore out the warrant," the clerk said. "He's the one who claims the pants were stolen from him."

"Well, if he yells out like that again," the judge said, "I'll swear out a warrant against him for giving me a headache. And I guess somebody had better tell him there's such a thing as contempt of court. He looks like a Democrat, so I suppose he never heard of anything like that before."

The judge rapped for order and bent over towards Bert.

"Did you steal a pair of corduroy pants from this man?" he asked.

"They were *my* pants," Bert explained. "I left them in my house when I sold it to Abe Mitchell and when I asked him for them he wouldn't turn them over to me. I didn't steal them. They belonged to me all the time."

"He's lying!" Abe shouted again, jumping up and down. "He stole my pants—he's lying!"

"Ten dollars for contempt of court, whatever your name is,"

the judge said, aiming his gavel at Abe, "and case dismissed for lack of evidence."

Abe's face sank into his head. He looked first at the judge and then around the courtroom at the strange people.

"You're not going to make me pay ten dollars, are you?" he demanded angrily.

"No," the judge said, standing up again. "I made a mistake. I forgot that you are a Democrat. I meant to say *twenty-five dollars.*"

Bert went outside and waited at the automobile until Abe paid his fine. In a quarter of an hour Abe came out of the courthouse.

"Well, I guess I'll have to give you a ride back home," he said, getting under the steering wheel and starting the engine. "But what I ought to do is leave you here and let you ride home in a hired car."

Bert said nothing at all. He sat down beside Abe and they drove out of town toward home.

It was almost dark when Abe stopped the car in front of Bert's house. Bert got out and slammed shut the door.

"I'm mighty much obliged for the ride," he said. "I been wanting to take a trip over Skowhegan way for a year or more. I'm glad you asked me to go along with you, Abe, but I don't see how the trip was worth twenty-five dollars to you."

Abe shoved his automobile into gear and jerked down the road toward his place. He left Bert standing beside the mailbox rubbing his hands over the legs of his corduroy pants.

"Abe Mitchell ought to have better sense than to be a Democrat," Bert said, going into his house.

(First published in *Scribner's*)

Crown-Fire

WHEN I stood up the next time, I saw Irene coming around the bend in the road, swinging her wide-brimmed hat beside her. Her face was flushed and her cheeks were the color of ripe oranges. Over her shoulders her long hair fell in waves, rippling like the mane of her father's sorrel mare pacing along the cowpath in the pasture.

The moment I first saw her, I sat down quickly, trying to hide myself in the tall roadside grass. I was afraid she would see me before she reached the place where I was, and would turn and run across the field before I could speak to her.

Irene was walking slowly, looking backward every few steps at the fires on the eastern ridge. The whole world seemed to have been on fire that day. The air was dense with blue wood-smoke, and, now that evening had come, the flames on the ridge began to color the sky. There had been no rain for almost a month, and the fields and woods were burning night and day. No one tried to stop the fires; only rain could stop the flames from eating over the earth eastward and westward.

I did not know what Irene was going to do when I jumped up and surprised her. I did not want her to run away from me again; each time I had tried to walk home with her in the evening she had run so fast that I could not keep up with her. But I had to see her and to talk with her. I had wished all that summer to be able to walk along the road with her. Once she had said she did not hate me; but no matter what I said to her, she continued to run away from me, leaving me alone in the road.

Just as she reached the place where I was, I pushed aside the tall grass and sprang to the road beside her. I was certain I could hear the beating of her heart; she was so frightened she did not know what to do.

"Please, Irene," I begged, catching her arm and holding it tightly in my hands, "please let me walk part of the way home with you. Will you? Please let me, Irene."

She was still too frightened to speak or to move. Her heart was beating as madly as that of a captured rabbit.

"Irene," I said, trembling until my voice sounded as though it were hundreds of miles away, "please let me, this one time. Will you?"

Her breath was becoming slower. The rise and fall of her bosom was slower and more even, and the trembling of her lips had stopped.

"Please stop holding me, Sidney," she said.

"Let me walk part of the way home with you, Irene. Please let me, this one time."

"Why do you ask to do that?"

She continued to look at me while I tried to think of something to tell her. I could think of no reason, except that I wanted to go with her. I had waited all summer for the time to come when she would let me walk with her; but now when she had asked me why I wished to go with her, I did not know what to say.

"I've got to go with you, Irene," I said, clutching her arm tighter. "I've got to walk home with you."

"I can't let you do that," she said. "You mustn't."

"Why, Irene? Tell me why. Why won't you let me?"

She turned her head and looked back at the red sky over the ridge. There was no sound of shouting men, no cracking of falling pines; there was only the deepening red of the sky at night.

Because I had been waiting all summer, ever since school was out in June, for the time to come when I might walk along the road with her in the evening—because I had lain awake night after night, staring at the blackness, thinking of her—because I could not keep myself from touching her—I released her arm and pressed my hand over her bosom. There was a period of time, an interval so short I knew of no way of measuring its length, when she did not move. Her head was turned towards the fires on the ridge when I clutched her, and she closed her eyes tightly, and, her lips parting, her breath again came quick. Then as suddenly as I had placed my hand over her breasts, she jerked away from me and ran down the road towards home.

"Please, Irene," I begged, running after her; "please come back. I didn't mean to make you run away. Let me go with you."

She was running swiftly, but not so swiftly as I was. I caught her arm again and pulled her back. I could not force her to stop, and we walked along the road while I held her.

"I'm going to tell your father, Sidney," she said. "You just wait and see if I don't. I'm going to tell him what you did to me. You just wait and see if I don't tell your father."

I did not know what to say. I did not mind so much the whipping he would give me as I did my father's knowledge of what I had done to her. I did not know what to do. I was afraid to release her arm, and I was afraid to continue holding her.

"I'm going to tell your father on you, Sidney," she kept on saying. "You just wait and see if I don't. I'm going to tell him what you did to me in the road."

When we reached the churchyard where the path was that made a short cut to Irene's house, we both stopped. It had become darker, and the reflection of the fires against the sky was so bright I could even see the tears in Irene's eyes when she turned her head towards me. Both of us stood in the churchyard trembling, and looking at the red sky and at each other.

"Why did you do that, Sidney?" she asked.

"When I went to the road to wait for you, Irene, I didn't think of doing anything like that. I only wanted to see you and walk home with you. But—when I caught you—I couldn't keep from touching you. I had to. I just had to hold you."

The fires on the ridge drew her gaze towards them once more. She could not keep from looking at the smoke and flame and at the dull red glow overhead.

Suddenly she turned and looked directly at me.

"Sidney, if you don't let me go," she said, "I'll scream. I'll scream until everybody hears me."

At any other time I would have put my hand over her mouth; this time I clutched her in my arms, holding her more desperately than I had the first time. She did not move. She stood still, looking backward at the fires on the ridge. The night was almost light as day by that time. The shadows were long and gray, and the air was filled with blue woodsmoke. We stood in the churchyard path, waiting.

Wind on the ridge had risen, and the flames were leaping higher into the night. While we watched them, we could see the flames climbing into the treetops and burning the pine needles. A little later, the fire in the underbrush and in the grass had almost died out; but in the tops of the pines it burned faster and brighter than ever.

"It's a crown-fire now," Irene said. "Look—the pine tops are burning!"

The sight we saw made us tremble. We were standing close to each other, holding each other. Irene's face was more flushed than ever, and her bosom rose and fell faster than it had in the road when I sprang at her from the tall grass.

"A crown-fire can't be stopped until it burns itself out," she said. "I'm afraid of crown-fires."

She placed her hands over my hands and pressed them tightly against her. Then she leaned against me, and I could feel the soft warmth of her body touching mine. Her heart beat so madly that I could feel with my hands its throb through her body, and her breath came so quickly that, even though I held her firmly, her breasts trembled as her lips were doing.

I did not know for how long a time I had held my face against the soft warmth of her throat when she suddenly raised my head and kissed my lips and tore herself out of my arms. It was much later though, because the crown-fire had burned off into the distance, almost out of sight.

"I've got to go home now, Sidney," she said; "if I don't go now, they'll be coming after me."

I ran after her, and stopped. We were then on the other side of the churchyard, at the end of the path. Through the trees I could see the lights of her house.

"Will you let me walk home with you tomorrow evening, Irene, and every evening?" I asked.

She stopped a moment and looked back at me. I waited, shaking all over, to hear her reply. I was afraid that she would say she would not allow me to come with her again.

While I waited, clutching at a tree beside me, she looked off into the distance towards the ridge where the fire had been. There was no light in the sky then, and the air was clearing of woodsmoke. I went a step nearer, gripping the rough bark of the pine tree between my fingers.

"Will you, Irene?"

Without a word, she turned and ran through the grove towards the lights in her home. After she had gone, I stood beside the tree listening. I had hoped so much that she would promise to let me come with her again the next evening, and every evening after that, that I could not believe she had gone away without an answer.

Later I walked back through the dark churchyard, out of the path, and up the road past the tall grass where I had lain that afternoon. There was no longer a light in the sky over the ridge. The crown-fire had burned itself out at the edge of the cleared field. Until there was again fire on the ridge, perhaps not again until the next summer, I knew she would run away from me each time I tried to stop her. Every day when I wanted to see her, I should have to hide in the tall roadside grass and look at her while she passed. I knew I could never again catch her as I had done that evening, because ever after she would be on guard against me, and if I should spring from the tall grass and succeed in catching her, she would surely tell my father of what I had done to her.

Long before I reached home I had made up my mind to catch her again some day and to hold her as I had done for nearly an hour that night. I knew I should never again be happy until I held her again and could feel her soft warm lips kiss mine; I should never again be happy until she pressed my hands against her to hold tighter the trembling of her breasts. Some day, that year or the years following, there would again be a crown-fire on the ridge. New pines would spring up to take the places of the burned ones, and someone would drop lighted matches in the dry underbrush.

(First published in *Lion and Crown*)

Runaway

MRS. GARLEY was seated at the head of the table drinking coffee and reading the paper after breakfast when she heard a plate fall and break on the kitchen floor. The boarders had eaten and left, and she was alone in the room. Garley had left the house too.

When she ran to the kitchen door, threw it open, and looked inside at Lessie, the little Negro girl was cringing in the corner behind the range.

"So you broke another one of my dishes, did you?" Mrs. Garley said evenly. Her anger was slowly rising; the longer she stood and looked at Lessie, the madder she could become. "That makes two you've broken this month, Lessie. And that's two too many for me to stand for."

The nine-year-old colored girl moved inch by inch farther into the corner. She never knew what Mrs. Garley might do to her next.

"You come out here in the middle of this floor, Lessie," the woman said. "Come this minute when I speak to you!"

The girl came several steps, watching Mrs. Garley and trembling all over. When she was halfway to the center of the room, Mrs. Garley ran to her and slapped her on both sides of her face. The blows made her so dizzy she did not know where she was or what she was doing. She threw her arms around her head protectingly.

"You stinking little nigger!" Mrs. Garley shouted at her.

Before Lessie could run back to the corner behind the stove, Mrs. Garley snatched up the broom and began beating her with it, striking her as hard as she could over the head, shoulders, and on her back. The girl began to cry, and fell on the floor. Mrs. Garley struck her while she lay there screaming and writhing.

"Now, you get up from there and get to work cleaning this house," she told Lessie, putting the broom away. "I want every room in this house as clean as a pin by twelve o'clock."

She left the kitchen and went into the front of the house.

II

Lessie had complained about the work. She had complained about washing so many dishes and cleaning so many rooms in the boardinghouse. She said she was too tired to finish them every day. Mrs. Garley had slapped her for every word she uttered.

"If that nigger has run away," she told her husband, "I'll whip her until there's nothing left of her."

"You can't expect too much of her," Garley said. "She's not big enough to do much heavy work."

"You talk like you're taking up for her," his wife said. "I feed her, give her clothes, and keep her. If she won't be grateful of her own accord, I'll make her be grateful."

Lessie had run away, and Mrs. Garley knew she had. Mrs. Garley had been expecting it to happen for some time, but she believed she had frightened the girl enough to keep her there. Lessie had been brought into town from the country when she was four years old, and for the past three years she had done all the housework.

"It's about time to let her go, anyway," Garley said. "You wouldn't be able to keep her much longer without paying her something."

"There you go, taking up for her again! I pay her with her meals and bed. That's all she should have. I wouldn't give her a red cent besides that."

Garley shook his head, still not convinced. For one thing, he was afraid there might be trouble if they kept her any longer. Everybody in town knew they kept Lessie there to do the work, and somebody might want to make trouble for them. His wife worked the girl harder than a grown person.

"Well, I want Lessie back, and I want you to bring her back," his wife said. "I want her back by tomorrow morning at breakfast time."

Garley looked at his wife but said nothing. He depended upon her for his living. Without her and the boardinghouse, he did not know what he could do. She ran the boardinghouse and paid all the bills. When she told him to do something, he could not say he would not do it. He got up and went through the house to the back porch.

There was a small room behind the kitchen, only long enough and wide enough for a cot that had been cut in half for Lessie. There never had been much in the room, except the bed, and now there was nothing else there. Even the two or three dresses his wife had made for Lessie by cutting down some of her old clothes were gone. Garley looked under the cot, and found nothing there. Lessie had run away, and there was nothing to show that she might have intended coming back. She had taken all she possessed.

When Garley saw his wife half an hour later, she stopped him in the hall, hands on hips.

"Well?" she said. "Do you expect to find her hiding under a chair somewhere in the house?"

"Where can I look?" he asked. "How do I know which way she went?"

"How do I know?" Mrs. Garley said. "If I knew, I'd go there and find her myself. You find Lessie and bring her back here by breakfast time tomorrow morning, if you know what's good for you. If you don't . . . if you don't . . ."

Garley found his hat and went out the front door. He turned down the street in the direction of the Negro quarter of town. That was the only likely place for Lessie to be hiding, unless she had gone to the country.

III

As soon as he passed the first Negro house in the quarter, Garley had a feeling that everybody in the neighborhood was watching him from behind doors, windows, and corners of buildings. He turned, jerking his head around quickly, and tried to catch somebody looking at him. There was nobody to be seen anywhere. The place looked completely deserted.

"Lessie wouldn't know any of these darkies," he said to himself. "She never left home, and nobody ever came there to see her. I wouldn't be surprised if nobody knew she was alive, except my wife and me. Lessie wouldn't come down here among strangers when she ran away."

He walked on, trying to think where he could look for her. He decided she would not have gone to the country, because she would have been too afraid to do that. The only other place for her to be hiding, after all, was in the quarter. If he did find her, he believed he would come across her hiding behind some Negro woman who had taken her in.

Garley had half made up his mind to go back home and tell his wife he had looked through every house in the quarter without finding Lessie. But when he stopped and started back, he began to think what his wife would say and do. She might even take it into her head to turn him out of house and home if he went back without Lessie, or word of her.

Turning down an alley, he picked out a house at random. The door and the windows were open, but there was no sign of anyone's being there. There was not even smoke in the chimney.

Garley hesitated, and then went to the house next door.

He knocked and listened. There was no sound anywhere, even though there was a fire under a washpot in the yard. He stepped into the doorway and looked inside. In the corner of the room sat a large Negro woman, rocking unconcernedly to and fro in a chair. On her lap, all but hidden in the folds of her breasts, sat Lessie. The girl was clinging to the woman and burying her head deeper and deeper under the woman's arms.

"Hello, Aunt Gracie," Garley said, staring at them.

"What do you want down here, Mr. Garley?" Aunt Gracie asked stiffly.

"Just looking around," Garley said.

"Just looking around for what?" the woman asked.

"Well, Lessie, I guess."

"It won't do you a bit of good," Aunt Gracie said. "You'll just be wasting your time talking about it."

"I didn't know where she was, to tell the truth," he said.

"And it won't do you no good to know where she is, either," Aunt Gracie said, "because you can go tell that wife of yours that she's going to stay where she is at."

Garley sat down in a chair by the door. The Negro woman hugged Lessie all the tighter and rocked her back and forth. Lessie had not looked at him.

"To tell the truth," Garley said, "my wife has been pretty hard on Lessie for the past three or four years. She's been a little harder than she ought to have been, I guess."

"She won't be again," Aunt Gracie said. "Because the child's going to stay right here with me from now on. You white people ought to be ashamed of yourselves for treating darkies like you do. You know good and well it couldn't be right to make Lessie work for you all the time and not give her something more than a few old rags made over from your wife's clothes when she is done with them, and what scraps get left over from the kitchen."

Garley hoped Aunt Gracie would not begin next about the way his wife had slapped and beat Lessie with the broom. He hoped nobody knew about that.

"When you get home," Aunt Gracie said, "tell your wife I've got Lessie, and that I'm going to keep her. Tell her to come down here herself after her, if she dares to, but I don't reckon she will, because she knows what I'll say to her will make her ears burn red."

Garley got up, taking one more look at Lessie. He had never known she was so small before. Even though she was nine years old, she looked no larger than a six- or seven-year-old girl. He backed to the door, not saying a word.

Outside in the alley again, he turned towards home. It would soon be time for supper, and meals were served on time. He looked at his watch as he hurried up the street through the quarter. On the way he cut across a vacant lot, to make certain that he got there in plenty of time.

His wife was standing on the front porch.

"Well, did you find Lessie?" she demanded.

"She'll be back by breakfast time," Garley said. "You told me that was when she had to be back, didn't you?"

"That's what I said, and if she's not here then, you can get ready to do some stirring around for yourself."

"I'll do the best I can," he said, hurrying through the hall behind her to the dining room, where the boarders had already sat down at the table.

Garley slipped into the room and got into his seat unnoticed. He was just in time to get a helping from the first dish that was passed down his side of the table.

(First published in *Southways*)

The People *v.* Abe Lathan, Colored

UNCLE ABE was shucking corn in the crib when Luther Bolick came down from the big white house on the hill and told him to pack up his household goods and move off the farm. Uncle Abe had grown a little deaf and he did not hear what Luther said the first time.

"These old ears of mine is bothering me again, Mr. Luther," Uncle Abe said. "I just can't seem to hear as good as I used to."

Luther looked at the Negro and scowled. Uncle Abe had got up and was standing in the crib door where he could hear better.

"I said, I want you and your family to pack up your furniture and anything else that really belongs to you, and move off."

Uncle Abe reached out and clutched at the crib door for support.

"Move off?" Uncle Abe said.

He looked into his landlord's face unbelievingly.

"Mr. Luther, you don't mean that, does you?" Uncle Abe asked, his voice shaking. "You must be joking, ain't you, Mr. Luther?"

"You heard me right, even if you do pretend to be half deaf," Luther said angrily, turning around and walking several steps. "I want you off the place by the end of the week. I'll give you that much time if you don't try to make any trouble. And when you pack up your things, take care you don't pick up anything that belongs to me. Or I'll have the law on you."

Uncle Abe grew weak so quickly that he barely managed to keep from falling. He turned a little and slid down the side of the door and sat on the crib floor. Luther looked around to see what he was doing.

"I'm past sixty," Uncle Abe said slowly, "but me and my family works hard for you, Mr. Luther. We work as hard as anybody on your whole place. You know that's true, Mr. Luther. I've lived here, working for you, and your daddy before you, for all of forty years. I never mentioned to you about the shares, no matter how big the crop was that I raised for you. I've never asked much, just enough to eat and a few clothes, that's all. I raised up a houseful of children to help work, and none of them ever made any trouble for you, did they, Mr. Luther?"

Luther waved his arm impatiently, indicating that he wanted

393

the Negro to stop arguing. He shook his head, showing that he did not want to listen to anything Uncle Abe had to say.

"That's all true enough," Luther said, "but I've got to get rid of half the tenants on my place. I can't afford to keep eight or ten old people like you here any longer. All of you will have to move off and go somewhere else."

"Ain't you going to farm this year, and raise cotton, Mr. Luther?" Uncle Abe asked. "I can still work as good and hard as anybody else. It may take me a little longer sometimes, but I get the work done. Ain't I shucking this corn to feed the mules as good as anybody else could do?"

"I haven't got time to stand here and argue with you," Luther said nervously. "My mind is made up, and that's all there is to it. Now, you go on home as soon as you finish feeding the mules and start packing the things that belong to you like I told you."

Luther turned away and started walking down the path toward the barn. When he got as far as the barnyard gate, he turned around and looked back. Uncle Abe had followed him.

"Where can me and my family move to, Mr. Luther?" Uncle Abe said. "The boys is big enough to take care of themselves. But me and my wife has grown old. You know how hard it is for an old colored man like me to go out and find a house and land to work on shares. It don't cost you much to keep us, and me and my boys raise as much cotton as anybody else. The last time I mentioned the shares has been a long way in the past, thirty years or more. I'm just content to work like I do and get some rations and a few clothes. You know that's true, Mr. Luther. I've lived in my little shanty over there for all of forty years, and it's the only home I've got. Mr. Luther, me and my wife is both old now, and I can't hire out to work by the day, because I don't have the strength any more. But I can still grow cotton as good as any other colored man in the country."

Luther opened the barnyard gate and walked through it. He shook his head as though he was not even going to listen any longer. He turned his back on Uncle Abe and walked away.

Uncle Abe did not know what to say or do after that. When he saw Luther walk away, he became shaky all over. He clutched at the gate for something to hold on to.

"I just can't move away, Mr. Luther," he said desperately. "I just can't do that. This is the only place I've got to live in the world. I just can't move off, Mr. Luther."

Luther walked out of sight around the corner of the barn. He did not hear Uncle Abe after that.

The next day, at a little after two o'clock in the afternoon, a truck drove up to the door of the three-room house where Uncle Abe, his wife, and their three grown sons lived. Uncle

Abe and his wife were sitting by the fire trying to keep warm in the winter cold. They were the only ones at home then.

Uncle Abe heard the truck drive up and stop, but he sat where he was, thinking it was his oldest boy, Henry, who drove a truck sometimes for Luther Bolick.

After several minutes had passed, somebody knocked on the door, and his wife got up right away and went to see who it was.

There were two strange white men on the porch when she opened the door. They did not say anything at first, but looked inside the room to see who was there. Still not saying anything, they came inside and walked to the fireplace where Uncle Abe sat hunched over the hearth.

"Are you Abe Lathan?" one of the men, the oldest, asked.

"Yes, sir, I'm Abe Lathan," he answered, wondering who they were, because he had never seen them before. "Why do you want to know that?"

The man took a bright metal disk out of his pocket and held it in the palm of his hand before Uncle Abe's eyes.

"I'm serving a paper and a warrant on you," he said. "One is an eviction, and the other is for threatening to do bodily harm."

He unfolded the eviction notice and handed it to Uncle Abe. The Negro shook his head bewilderedly, looking first at the paper and finally up at the two strange white men.

"I'm a deputy," the older man said, "and I've come for two things—to evict you from this house and to put you under arrest."

"What does that mean—evict?" Uncle Abe asked.

The two men looked around the room for a moment. Uncle Abe's wife had come up behind his chair and put trembling hands on his shoulder.

"We are going to move your furniture out of this house and carry it off the property of Luther Bolick. Then, besides that, we're going to take you down to the county jail. Now, come on and hurry up, both of you."

Uncle Abe got up, and he and his wife stood on the hearth not knowing what to do.

The two men began gathering up the furniture and carrying it out of the house. They took the beds, tables, chairs, and everything else in the three rooms except the cookstove, which belonged to Luther Bolick. When they got all the things outside, they began piling them into the truck.

Uncle Abe went outside in front of the house as quickly as he could.

"White-folks, please don't do that," he begged. "Just wait a minute while I go find Mr. Luther. He'll set things straight. Mr. Luther is my landlord, and he won't let you take all my furniture away like this. Please, sir, just wait while I go find him."

The two men looked at each other.

"Luther Bolick is the one who signed these papers," the deputy said, shaking his head. "He was the one who got these court orders to carry off the furniture and put you in jail. It wouldn't do you a bit of good to try to find him now."

"Put me in jail?" Uncle Abe said. "What did he say to do that for?"

"For threatening bodily harm," the deputy said. "That's for threatening to kill him. Hitting him with a stick or shooting him with a pistol."

The men threw the rest of the household goods into the truck and told Uncle Abe and his wife to climb in the back. When they made no effort to get in, the deputy pushed them to the rear and prodded them until they climbed into the truck.

While the younger man drove the truck, the deputy stood beside them in the body so they could not escape. They drove out the lane, past the other tenant houses, and then down the long road that went over the hill through Luther Bolick's land to the public highway. They passed the big white house where he lived, but he was not within sight.

"I never threatened to harm Mr. Luther," Uncle Abe protested. "I never did a thing like that in my whole life. I never said a mean thing about him either. Mr. Luther is my boss, and I've worked for him ever since I was twenty years old. Yesterday he said he wanted me to move off his farm, and all I did was say that I thought he ought to let me stay. I won't have much longer to live, noway. I told him I didn't want to move off. That's all I said to Mr. Luther. I ain't never said I was going to try to kill him. Mr. Luther knows that as well as I do. You ask Mr. Luther if that ain't so."

They had left Luther Bolick's farm, and had turned down the highway toward the county seat, eleven miles away.

"For forty years I has lived here and worked for Mr. Luther," Uncle Abe said, "and I ain't never said a mean thing to his face or behind his back in all that time. He furnishes me with rations for me and my family, and a few clothes, and me and my family raise cotton for him, and I been doing that ever since I was twenty years old. I moved here and started working on shares for his daddy first, and then when he died, I kept right on like I have up to now. Mr. Luther knows I has worked hard and never answered him back, and only asked for rations and a few clothes all this time. You ask Mr. Luther."

The deputy listened to all that Uncle Abe said, but he did not say anything himself. He felt sorry for the old Negro and his wife, but there was nothing he could do about it. Luther Bolick had driven to the courthouse early that morning and secured the papers for eviction and arrest. It was his job to serve the papers and execute the court orders. But even if it was his job, he could not keep from feeling sorry for the Negroes. He didn't think that Luther Bolick ought to throw them off his farm just because they had grown old.

When they got within sight of town, the deputy told the driver to stop. He drew the truck up beside the highway when they reached the first row of houses. There were fifteen or eighteen Negro houses on both sides of the road.

After they had stopped, the two white men began unloading the furniture and stacking it beside the road. When it was all out of the truck, the deputy told Uncle Abe's wife to get out. Uncle Abe started to get out, too, but the deputy told him to stay where he was. They drove off again, leaving Uncle Abe's wife standing in a dazed state of mind beside the furniture.

"What are you going to do with me now?" Uncle Abe asked, looking back at his wife and furniture in the distance.

"Take you to the county jail and lock you up," the deputy said.

"What's my wife going to do?" he asked.

"The people in one of those houses will probably take her in."

"How long is you going to keep me in jail locked up?"

"Until your case comes up for trial."

They drove through the dusty streets of the town, around the courthouse square, and stopped in front of a brick building with iron bars across the windows.

"Here's where we get out," the deputy said.

Uncle Abe was almost too weak to walk by that time, but he managed to move along the path to the door. Another white man opened the door and told him to walk straight down the hall until he was told to stop.

Just before noon Saturday, Uncle Abe's oldest son, Henry, stood in Ramsey Clark's office, hat in hand. The lawyer looked at the Negro and frowned. He chewed his pencil for a while, then swung around in his chair and looked out the window into the courthouse square. Presently he turned around and looked at Uncle Abe's son.

"I don't want the case," he said. "I don't want to touch it."

The boy stared at him helplessly. It was the third lawyer he had gone to see that morning, and all of them had refused to take his father's case.

"There's no money in it," Ramsey Clark said, still frowning. "I'd never get a dime out of you niggers if I took this case.

And, besides, I don't want to represent any more niggers at court. Better lawyers than me have been ruined that way. I don't want to get the reputation of being a 'nigger lawyer.'"

Henry shifted the weight of his body from one foot to the other and bit his lips. He did not know what to say. He stood in the middle of the room trying to think of a way to get help for his father.

"My father never said he was going to kill Mr. Luther," Henry protested. "He's always been on friendly terms with Mr. Luther. None of us ever gave Mr. Luther trouble. Anybody will tell you that. All the other tenants on Mr. Luther's place will tell you my father has always stood up for Mr. Luther. He never said he was going to try to hurt Mr. Luther."

The lawyer waved for him to stop. He had heard all he wanted to listen to.

"I told you I wouldn't touch the case," he said angrily, snatching up some papers and slamming them down on his desk. "I don't want to go into court and waste my time arguing a case that won't make any difference one way or the other, anyway. It's a good thing for you niggers to get a turn on the 'gang every once in a while. It doesn't make any difference whether Abe Lathan threatened Mr. Bolick, or whether he didn't threaten him. Abe Lathan said he wasn't going to move off the farm, didn't he? Well, that's enough to convict him in court. When the case comes up for trial, that's all the judge will want to hear. He'll be sent to the 'gang quicker than a flea can hop. No lawyer is going to spend a lot of time preparing a case when he knows how it's going to end. If there was money in it, it might be different. But you niggers don't have a thin dime to pay me with. No, I don't want the case. I wouldn't touch it with a ten-foot pole."

Henry backed out of Ramsey Clark's office and went to the jail. He secured permission to see his father for five minutes.

Uncle Abe was sitting on his bunk in the cage looking through the bars when Henry entered. The jailer came and stood behind him at the cage door.

"Did you see a lawyer and tell him I never said nothing like that to Mr. Luther?" Uncle Abe asked the first thing.

Henry looked at his father, but it was difficult for him to answer. He shook his head, dropping his gaze until he could see only the floor.

"You done tried, didn't you, Henry?" Uncle Abe asked.

Henry nodded.

"But when you told the lawyers how I ain't never said a mean thing about Mr. Luther, or his daddy before him, in all my whole life, didn't they say they was going to help me get out of jail?"

Henry shook his head.

"What did the lawyers say, Henry? When you told them how respectful I've always been to Mr. Luther, and how I've always worked hard for him all my life, and never mentioned the shares, didn't they say they would help me then?"

Henry looked at his father, moving his head sideways in order to see him between the bars of the cage. He had to swallow hard several times before he could speak at all.

"I've already been to see three lawyers," he said finally. "All three of them said they couldn't do nothing about it, and to just go ahead and let it come up for trial. They said there wasn't nothing they could do, because the judge would give you a turn on the 'gang, anyway."

He stopped for a moment, looking down at his father's feet through the bars.

"If you want me to, I'll see if I can find some other lawyers to take the case. But it won't do much good. They just won't do anything."

Uncle Abe sat down on his bunk and looked at the floor. He could not understand why none of the lawyers would help him. Presently he looked up through the bars at his son. His eyes were fast filling with tears that he could not control.

"Why did the lawyers say the judge would give me a turn on the 'gang, anyway, Henry?" he asked.

Henry gripped the bars, thinking about all the years he had seen his father and mother working in the cotton fields for Luther Bolick and being paid in rations, a few clothes, and a house to live in, and nothing more.

"Why did they say that for, Henry?" his father insisted.

"I reckon because we is just colored folks," Henry said at last. "I don't know why else they would say things like that."

The jailer moved up behind Henry, prodding him with his stick. Henry walked down the hall between the rows of cages toward the door that led to the street. He did not look back.

(First published in *Esquire*)

The Dream

For six or seven years Harry had been telling me about a dream. I thought nothing of it, because nearly everyone has dreams; some of them are pleasant, others very disagreeable, but, otherwise, I could never see anything in a dream to become upset about. Each time I dreamed I remembered what happened in the dream for a day or two, and afterwards never

thought of it again. But Harry had been having the same dream
regularly each month all that time. Exactly the same thing happened on each occasion, the time and place were invariably
the same; and the two people had not changed in dress or appearance since the beginning. Harry was one of them; the
other was a young girl.

Harry, while he was at home the winter before, had con-
sulted a psychiatrist. The man had a reputation for correcting
and curing practically every case of minor mental disorder he
had undertaken, and Harry felt certain that if there was anything wrong with him the psychiatrist could help him. He
went, however, to see him only once. Harry explained that the
dream was recurrent each month, but the psychiatrist said
there wasn't anything to it. He said it was all utterly silly. He
told Harry to forget it.

Probably that was his method of curing Harry. But, anyway, Harry said he lost all confidence in him after that, and
he never went back again. His reason for doubting the ability
of the psychiatrist to help him was that the man had said something about the impossibility of a dream's occurring more than
once. But Harry's dream was recurrent. It came back again the
following month, the next, and the next.

It was late June when I saw Harry the first time that summer, and he had just had his monthly dream. He told me all
about it again. It was precisely the same thing he had told me
the year before.

We were at the boathouse and Harry was putting a new
coat of green paint on his canoe. While he was retelling the
dream I was sitting against a tree. As he neared the close of
the dream his paintbrush moved faster and faster, and when he
reached the end the brush was moving so swiftly he could not
keep enough paint in the bristles to coat the canvas.

"You finish it for me," he said, his eyes ablaze and his hands
jerking nervously. "There isn't much more to paint, anyway."

I took the brush from him, and before I could reach for the
paint bucket he had disappeared in the woods behind the boathouse. I did not see him again that day.

Harry's condition worried me more then than it had since
he first began dreaming. It seemed to me that there must be
something that could be done to help him, and perhaps cure
him completely. I did not believe for a moment, however, that
he would become insane. Neither did Harry. He had always
been normal, and as far as I could see he was still normal. We
both looked upon the dream as something temporary that
would pass away at any moment.

We had known each other for ten years. Each summer we
came up to Maine with our families and stayed through the
season. Our camps were on the same lake, and we saw each

other almost every day. We went on fishing trips together, and we went swimming two or three times a day. Once a week we went somewhere to a dance, and more frequently, over to the village to the movies. Whenever we talked about the dream Harry always said it was as bad as ever. He said the fact that he continued having the recurrent dream was what was bad; the dream itself, however, was very pleasant.

The intensity of the dream was as memorable as the events of it. Nothing really happened, he said; it was the feeling and lifelike reality that caused him so much worry. He had told me about it so many times I believed I knew how he felt. Each time, he was walking along a lonely road through a forest in northeastern Maine. The moon was out, but a thin veil of grayish clouds darkened everything and left the road and forest in a dull glow like the soft light of a shaded lamp. After he had walked a mile and a half along the road he came to a bridge over a stream. It was a timber bridge, about four and a half feet wide. He had not heard a sound or seen a single living thing until he reached the bridge. But the moment he put his foot on the bridge he heard someone call his name very softly. He looked up, and in front of him, in the center of the gravel road, was a young girl. She was about eighteen. She stood in the road ahead of him, bathed in this dull yellowish light of the clouded moon. He stopped on the bridge and looked at her.

"What do you want?" he asked her.

"I am waiting for Harry," she said.

Harry said he begged her to tell him her name and where she lived, but she would never answer either question.

"I'm Harry," he then told her.

"Then I'll turn around and go back."

"Let me go with you," he said to her. "I'm Harry, and if you are looking for me I'll go with you."

"No," she said. "No, I must go back alone."

Harry said he ran after her and nearly killed himself trying to catch her. She was always the same distance ahead of him, no matter how hard he ran to catch her. After they had gone three miles, he suddenly woke up and jumped out of bed. After that, no matter how much he wanted to go back to sleep and recapture the dream, he was always wide awake until morning. Each time this happened he had to get up in the middle of the night, dress, and walk around the camp until daylight. He was never sleepy after the dream, although he usually slept each morning until eight-thirty or nine.

I saw Harry again the next day, but we did not speak about his dream for almost a month. Then one morning he told me he had had the dream for July. He told me about it again. It was the same as it had always been.

Then he told me something else. He said that recently, since he had been at camp that summer, he had been having the dream while he was awake. The daytime dream, as he called it, did not come at regular intervals like the one in sleep, but it was the same dream nevertheless. He would be driving his car along the country road to the village, wide awake and singing or whistling, when suddenly he saw this young girl standing in the road. When he was almost upon her, she turned and ran down the road in the direction he was going. He was never able to catch her then either, although once he speeded his car up to eighty miles an hour. She disappeared from sight three miles from the place where he first saw her. Several times he stopped the car, got out, and ran into the woods calling her. He knew that was foolish, but he said the intense attraction she held for him impelled him to go after her.

"I'm going crazy if I don't stop seeing her," he said. "The only thing that will help me now will be catching her or finding her somewhere. I've passed the point where I could forget her even if the dream should suddenly stop and never come back again. The only hope I have of remaining normal for the rest of my life is that of possessing her. That doctor said it was nothing to worry about, but I've gone beyond that now. I don't worry any longer. I've got to get her. If I don't I'll be insane in another year. It's not too late yet to save myself, because last winter and spring at home I went around with a crowd of boys and girls, had dates, went to dances, and acted perfectly naturally. But as soon as the time came to have another dream I went all to pieces."

"Maybe you saw a girl like her once, and she's your love-ideal," I said jokingly, trying to make him stop thinking about it so seriously. "You ought to try to find her when you go home this fall."

But he would never laugh about the dream. He was always serious about it, as if it were something sacred.

"There's no other girl like her. There couldn't be. No other girl could have such a voice. The sound of it is perfect, and there is a distinct meaning in the musiclike notes."

"Just the same," I said, "if I were you I'd try to find one like her when you go home. You would be all right then. It would be all over. The dream would probably never come back again."

Harry walked away without answering me. The expression on his face told me that he believed I could never understand.

Near the end of August, a few days after the time for him to have the monthly dream, I went over to Harry's camp early one morning. He was sitting very still in a deep canvas camp chair under the pine trees.

When he saw me, he jumped up and ran to meet me.

"I had that dream again the other night," he said excitedly.

His hands were shaking even more than they did the day he was painting the canoe at the boathouse. "The same dream came back again the other night."

"That's too bad," I said. "The thing for you to do now is to try every psychiatrist in the country until you are cured. Surely there is one somewhere who can help you."

"No," he said, "I don't want it to stop now. I want it to keep on coming back, because it will turn into reality. I'm going to find that girl. Last night while I was having the dream I saw a signboard nailed to a tree beside the bridge. It was there for the first time. Somebody recently put it up. It was a new sign, freshly painted and lettered. There was a big arrow on it, such as highway signs have, and over that was lettered *Lost Lake—20 Miles*."

"What does that mean?"

"That means that I will find the girl living at Lost Lake, of course. That is where she lives."

"How do you know she lives there?" I was undecided whether he was joking at last about the dream, or if he was really serious and believed that.

"Because the sign said that lake is twenty miles from the bridge. And Lost Lake is twenty miles from Rangeley, isn't it? Well, that means that the bridge is near Rangeley too. I'm going up there to find her. I might not find her the first day, but I will before I come back. She's living in a camp somewhere on Lost Lake. I know that. I'm too certain about it to be wrong."

I could not understand how he could believe that girl was up there, at least one that would be enough like her to make him believe she was the same.

"There is probably more than one lake with that name," I said. "The one you are looking for may be on the other side of the continent."

He ignored me entirely.

"I'm not certain where that bridge is, but it is of no importance, because I can start from Rangeley, or from any other direction and get to the lake. You see how that could be, don't you? The important thing is to get to the lake. Then I'll start walking around it and ask at each camp for the girl. It may take me a week to go around the lake, because there is no road along the shore, but I won't be surprised if I find her at the first camp I stop at."

I was almost as excited as Harry, in spite of myself. His explanations of the sign on the tree and his interpretations of the dream would have convinced me that the girl was actually alive if my better sense had not told me it was impossible. However, I wanted to go with him, for the adventure.

"When are you starting, Harry?" I asked him. "I want to go along."

"I'm starting in the morning," he said, "but I can't take you along. I'm sorry. But you see, as soon as I find her I'm going to marry her. That's what I've been waiting for all these seven years."

"Good Lord, Harry," I said, "you don't mean to say that you believe you are going to find a girl actually enough like the one in the dream to make you think she is the same one, do you?"

He took two rings from his pocket and held them in the palm of his hand for me to see. One was a diamond solitaire, the other a wedding ring.

"I've had these for more than two years," he said. "I didn't have the nerve to show them to you before, because I knew you would laugh at me. But since I've found her I don't mind showing them to you."

"But you haven't found her yet, Harry. She may not be at Lost Lake, after all."

Harry did not say anything for several minutes. He looked at me as if he were wondering how anyone could doubt that such a girl as he had dreamed of was not alive that moment.

"If you don't believe what I've told you," he said, "then why don't you bet me that I won't find her?"

Whatever doubt was then left in my mind was slowly leaving me. Even at that moment I thought I saw her standing up there in the woods, at a camp on the lake, waiting for Harry to come.

"Do you want to do that?" he insisted.

"No," I said. "I'd rather not."

(First published in *American Earth*)

A Small Day

GOVERNOR GIL was standing astride the path, knocking heads off the weeds, when Walter Lane came up the hill from the spring. A wide circle of wilted weeds lay on the ground around him, and his walking stick was still swinging. It looked as if he had been waiting there for half an hour or longer.

"It's been mighty hot today," Walter said, stopping and lowering the two pails of water to the ground.

"It's a small day when the sun don't shine," Governor Gil said. "Where's the rest of your family, and the girl?"

"My wife and the young ones went over to visit her folks

this afternoon," Walter told him. "They'll be coming home some time tonight after supper." He turned around and looked down the path behind. "Daisy's coming up the path any minute now. She's down at the spring filling a bucket."

Governor Gil looked down the path, but Daisy was not within sight. It was almost a hundred yards from the crown of the slope down to the bottom of the hill, where the spring was.

"I reckon I can wait here," he said, taking a new grip on his walking stick and bending forward to reach the weeds farthest away. "It's a small day when I can't afford to spend a little time waiting."

Walter watched the heads tumble off the stalks of weeds. Governor Gil went about it as if he were determined not to let a weed in the whole county go to seed that year. Every once in a while he shifted his position a little, stamping down the wilted weeds and reaching for new ones to whack at. Sometimes he started out in the morning, after breakfast, on horseback to see how his cotton and cane crops were growing, but before he got out of sight of home he always got off his horse and started whacking away at the weeds with his walking stick. He hated weeds worse than he did boll weevils or screwworms. However, for some reason or other, he never paid any attention to the weeds that grew in the yard around his house; they were so rank there that sometimes his hunting dogs got lost in the growth and had to backtrack their way out.

"Did you want to see me, Governor Gil, or was it Daisy you asked about?" Walter said, wondering.

Instead of answering, Governor Gil stopped a moment and glanced down the path. He nodded his head in that direction, and returned to swinging his stick at the weeds.

Governor Gil Counts had once, for a term, been governor of the state, about twenty-five or thirty years before, and the title suited him so well that nobody ever thought of calling him anything else. He ran his farm with the help of Walter Lane and several other tenants, and never left it. He had not been out of the county since the day he came home from the governor's office, and he had said he would never leave home again. He lived a quarter of a mile up the road in a big three-story mansion, from which the white paint had peeled while he was serving his term in office. The once-white, three-story columns rising from the front porch were now as dark and rough as the bark on a pine tree.

"There's no sense in standing out here in the sun," Walter said. "Come on to my house and take a seat in the porch shade, Governor Gil. Daisy'll be along to the house just about as soon as she'll get here."

"This'll do," he said, stopping and looking down the path. "I haven't got time to sit down now."

He went past Walter and started down the path toward the spring. Walter left his pails and followed behind. Heads of weeds tumbled to the right and left of them.

At the crown of the slope they saw Daisy coming up. She was carrying a pail of water in one hand and fanning herself with a willow branch.

"I may as well tell you now, Walter," Governor Gil said, stopping. "It's time for your girl to marry. It's dangerous business to put it off after they get a certain age."

Walter took half a dozen steps around Governor Gil and stopped where he could see his face.

"Who ought she to marry?" Walter said.

Governor Gil let go at some pigweeds around his knees, whacking his stick at them just under the seed pods. The heads flew in all directions.

"I've arranged for that," he said. "I sent my lawyer a letter today telling him to get a license. It'll be here in a few days."

Walter looked again at Governor Gil, and then down the path. Daisy had come over the crown of the slope.

"That might be all right," Walter said, "but I don't know if she'll be tamed. Right now she's just about as wild as they come. Of course, now, I'm not raising any serious objections. I'm just going over in my mind the drawbacks a man might run into."

"A year from now there might be plenty of drawbacks," Governor Gil said. "Right this minute drawbacks don't count, because she's reached the marrying age, and nothing else matters. If I had a daughter, Walter, I'd want to do the right thing by her. I'd want her to marry before drawbacks had a chance to spoil her. I'm ready to marry her without an argument."

"You damned old fool," Daisy said, dropping her pail, "what put that into your head?"

Governor Gil had drawn back to let go at a clump of weeds swaying in the breeze beside the path, but he never finished the stroke. His stick fell back against his knees and the clump of weeds continued to sway in the wind.

"Now, that's what I was thinking about," Walter said. "I had an idea she wouldn't be willing to be tamed just yet."

"Why, I've been counting on this for a pretty long time," Governor Gil said excitedly. "I've just been biding my time all this while when you were growing up, Daisy. I've had my eyes on you for about three years now, just waiting for you to grow up."

"You damned old fool," Daisy said, stooping down for her pail and starting around them in the path.

Walter did not try to stop her. He looked at Governor Gil to see what he had to say now.

They watched her for a moment.

"She'll tame," Governor Gil said, nodding his head at Walter and following her up the path to the house.

When they got to the back door, Daisy put the pail on the shelf and sat down on the doorstep. She sat and looked at them with her knees drawn up under her elbows and her chin cupped in her hands.

"Maybe if you could just wait—" Walter began. He was waved aside by a sweep of the walking stick.

"I'm going to have the handseling tonight," Governor Gil said, nodding his head at Daisy and flourishing the stick in the air. "The marrying can wait, but the handseling can't. The license will be along from my lawyer in a day or two, and that's just a matter of formality, anyway."

Walter looked at Daisy, but she only stared more sullenly at them.

"I reckon we ought to wait till my wife gets back from visiting her folks," Walter said. "She ought to have a little say-so. For one thing, she'll have to make Daisy some clothes first, because Daisy hasn't got much to wear except what she's got on, and that's so little it wouldn't be decent if we weren't homefolks. Just about all she's got to her name is that little slimsy gingham jumper she's wearing. My wife will want to make her a petticoat, if nothing else. It would be a sin and a shame for her to get married like she is now. If she had something to wear under what she's got on, it might be different, but I won't be in favor of sending her out to get married in just a slimsy jumper between her and the outside world."

Governor Gil shook his walking stick in the air as if to wave away any possible objection Walter might mention.

"That's all right for the marriage," he said, "but that won't be for a few days yet. Your wife will have plenty of time to make up a petticoat for her if she wants to. But she won't even have to do that, because I'll buy her whatever she'll need after the marriage. And what she'll need for the handseling won't be worth mentioning."

He stopped and turned around to look at the sun. It was already setting behind the pine grove in the west.

"Had your supper yet?" he asked, looking at Walter and nodding at Daisy.

"Not yet," Walter said. "We didn't stop work in the cotton until about half an hour ago, and the first thing that needed doing was carrying up the water from the spring. Daisy, you go in the kitchen and start getting something ready to eat. Maybe Governor Gil will stay and eat with us tonight."

"No," he said, waving his stick at Daisy, "don't do that, Daisy. You just come up to my house and get your meal there tonight. There's no sense in you getting all worn out over a hot stove now. There's plenty to eat up there."

He turned to Walter.

"If your wife won't be home until late tonight, you just come up to my house and go around to the kitchen, and the help will set you out a good meal, Walter."

He started walking across the yard toward the road. When he got to the corner of the house, he stopped and found that neither Daisy nor her father had made a move to follow him.

"What's the matter?" he said impatiently.

"Well, now," Walter said, "I can make Daisy go up to your house, Governor Gil, but I can't be held responsible for what she does after she gets there. I wish you would wait till my wife came back tonight before you took Daisy off, but if your mind is made up not to wait, then all I can say is you'll have to charge her yourself after she gets there."

"She won't need any charging," Governor Gil said. "I've yet to know the wildest one of them that wouldn't tame when the time comes to handsel."

He turned around and started walking toward the road that led to his house, a quarter of a mile away.

Walter looked down at the doorstep, where Daisy still sat sullen and motionless.

"You ought to be tickled to death to have the chance to marry Governor Gil," he told her. "Who else is there in the county who'll treat you nice and give you all you want? I'll bet there's many a girl who'd jump at the chance to marry him."

"The damned old fool," Daisy said.

"Well, you'd better," he told her. "I'll bet your mother will make you, if I can't. She's no fool, either. She knows how well off you'll be, not having to go hungry for something to eat, and having enough clothes to cover your nakedness, neither one of which you've got now, or ever will have, if you don't go on up there like you ought to."

Walter sat down on the bottom step and waited for Daisy to say something. The sun had set, and it would be getting dark soon. If she did not go right away, Governor Gil might get mad and change his mind.

Presently he turned around and looked at her.

"What's the matter with you, Daisy? You won't even say anything. What's got into you, anyway?"

"What does he want me to go up there tonight for?" she asked. "He said the license wouldn't be here for two or three days."

"That's just Governor Gil's way, Daisy. He makes up his mind to do something, and nothing stops him once it's made up. He wants to marry you, and he wants to right now. There's no sense in putting it off, anyway. The best thing for you to do is to start right in before he changes his mind. If you don't, you'll live to be sorry, because tomorrow you'll have to go right back to the field again—tomorrow and every day as long as cotton grows."

Daisy got up without saying anything and went into the house. She was in her room for ten or fifteen minutes, and when she came to the door it was dark outside. She could barely see her father sitting on the steps at her feet.

"Now, that's what I call sense," Walter said. "I thought you'd change your mind after you got to thinking about all these hot days in the sun out there in the cotton."

She went down the steps past him and crossed the yard without a word. She started up the road in the direction of Governor Gil's mansion.

After Daisy had gone, Walter began to wonder what his wife would say when she came home. He was certain she would be glad to hear that Governor Gil wanted to marry Daisy, but he was not so sure of what she would say when he told her that the marriage license would not come for another two or three days. He decided it would be best not to say anything about that part to her. Just as long as she knew Governor Gil had come to the house to ask Daisy to marry him, she would be satisfied.

It was pitch-dark when he got up and went into the kitchen, made a light, and looked around for something to eat. He found some bread left over from dinner, and he did not have to build a fire in the cook-stove after all. He sat down at the kitchen table and ate his fill of bread and sorghum.

After he had finished, he blew out the light and went to the front porch to sit and wait for his wife to come home.

Up the road he could see lights in Governor Gil's house. There was a light in the kitchen, as usual, and one in the front part of the house too. Upstairs, two or three rooms were lighted for the first time since he could remember.

Just when he was expecting his wife and children to get there any moment, he heard somebody running down the road. He got up and listened as the sound came closer. It was somebody running fast, because the sound came closer every second.

He ran out to the road to see who it was. At first he thought it might be Daisy, but he soon knew it wasn't, because a boy called out to him.

"Mr. Walter! Mr. Walter!"

"Who's that?" he shouted back.

A Negro houseboy stopped, panting, in the road beside him.

"What's the matter, Lawson?"

"Mr. Walter, Governor said to tell you if you ever raise another hellcat like Miss Daisy, he'll chop your head off. Now,

Mr. Walter, I didn't say it! Please, sir, don't think I said it! It was Governor who told me to tell you that! You know I wouldn't say that myself, don't you, Mr. Walter?"

"What's the matter up there, Lawson?" Walter asked the boy.

"I don't know exactly, Mr. Walter, except that Governor started yelling upstairs a while ago, and he hasn't stopped yet. He told me to telephone for the doctor and the lawyer to come in a hurry. He hardly stopped yelling long enough to tell me, either. Soon as I telephoned for them, he told me to run down here as fast as I could and tell you what I told you."

"Was Miss Daisy up there then?" Walter asked.

"I reckon it was Miss Daisy who made him yell," Lawson said hesitatingly.

"Why?"

"I don't know if Governor wants me to tell you," Lawson said. "He only told me to tell you what I already told you, Mr. Walter."

"You'd better tell me, Lawson. What was it?"

"Miss Daisy flew into him and pretty near bit the daylights out of him. Governor was yelling and nursing his hurt so much, he didn't have time to say much else."

Walter started back to the porch to sit down and wait for his wife to come home. He could not keep from laughing a little, but he tried to hold himself back so he could laugh all the more with his wife when she got there.

Lawson was still standing outside the yard. He turned around to tell the boy to go on back.

"What else did Governor Gil say, Lawson?" he asked him.

"I didn't hear him say much else, except Governor said it'll be a mighty small day when he tries to handsel a hellcat like Miss Daisy again."

Walter went to the porch and sat down. He leaned back and started to laugh. He could not wait for his wife any longer. He leaned back and laughed until he slid out of the chair.

(First published in the *New Yorker*)

Indian Summer

THE water was up again. It had been raining for almost two whole days, and the creek was full to the banks. Dawn had broken gray that morning, and for the first time that week the sky was blue and warm.

Les pulled off his shirt and unbuckled his pants. Les never

had to bother with underwear, because as soon as it was warm enough in the spring to go barefooted he hid his union suit in a closet and left it there until fall. His mother was not alive, and his father never bothered about the underclothes.

"I wish we had a shovel to dig out some of this muck," he said. "Every time it rains this hole fills up with this stuff. I'd go home and get a shovel, but if they saw me they'd make me stay there and do something."

While Les was hanging his shirt and pants on a bush, I waded out into the yellow water. The muck on the bottom was ankle deep, and there were hundreds of dead limbs stuck in it. I pulled out some of the largest and threw them on the other bank out of the way.

"How's the water, Jack?" Les asked. "How deep is it this time?"

I waded out to the middle of the creek where the current was the strongest. The yellow water came almost up to my shoulders.

"Nearly neck deep," I said. "But there's about a million dead limbs stuck in the bottom. Hurry up and help me throw them out."

Les came splashing in. The muddy water gurgled and sucked around his waist.

"I'll bet somebody comes down here every day and pitches these dead limbs in here," Les said, making a face. "I don't see how else they could get here. Dead tree limbs don't fall into a creek this fast. Somebody is throwing them in, and I'll bet a pretty he doesn't live a million miles away, either."

"Maybe Old Howes does it, Les."

"Sure, he does it. He's the one I'm talking about. I'll bet anything he comes down and throws limbs in every day."

Les stepped on a sharp limb. He held his nose and squeezed his eyes and ducked under and pulled it out.

"You know what?" Les said.

"What?"

"Old Howes told Pa we scared his cows last Saturday. He said we made them run so much he couldn't get them to let down their milk Saturday night.

· "This creek bottom isn't his. Old Howes doesn't own anything down here except that pasture on the other side of the fence. We haven't even been on the other side of the fence this year, have we?"

"I haven't seen Old Howes's cows all summer. If I did see them, I wouldn't run them. He just told Pa that because he doesn't want us to come swimming in the creek."

Pieces of dead bark and curled chips suddenly came floating down the creek. Somewhere up there the trash had broken loose from a limb or something across the water. I held my arms V-shaped and caught the bark and chips and threw them out of the way.

Les said something, diving down to pull up a dead limb. The muck on the bottom of the creek was so deep we could not take a step without first pulling our feet out of the sticky mud; otherwise we would have fallen flat on our faces in the water. The muck had a stink like a pig pen.

Les threw the big limb out of sight.

"If Old Howes ever comes down while we're here and tells us to get out of the creek, let's throw muck at him. Are you game, Jack? Wouldn't you like to do that to him just once?"

"That's what we ought to do to him, but we'd better not, Les. He would go straight and tell my folks, and your pa."

"I'm not scared of Old Howes," Les said, making a face. "He hasn't got me buffaloed. He wouldn't do anything. He's scared to tell anybody. He knows we'd catch him some time and mud-cake him."

"I don't know," I said. "He told on me that time I caught his drake and put it in that chicken run of his."

"That was a long time—" Les stopped and listened.

Somebody had stepped on a dead limb behind the bushes. The crack of the wood was loud enough to be heard above the splashing and gurgling of the creek.

"What's that?" both of us said.

"Who's that?" Les asked me.

"Listen!" I said. "Duck down and be quiet."

Behind the bushes we could hear someone walking on dead twigs and dry leaves. Both of us squatted down in the water until only our heads were above it.

"Who is it?" Les whispered to me.

I shook my head, holding my nose under the water.

The yellow water swirled and gurgled through the tree roots beside us. The roots had been washed free of earth by the high waters many years before, and now they were old-looking and covered with bark.

Les squatted lower and lower until only his eyes and the top of his head were showing. He held his nose under the water with both hands. The water was high, and its swiftness and muddy-heaviness made gurgling sounds that echoed up and down the creek.

Suddenly the bushes parted, and Jenny came through. When Les saw her, his eyes popped open and he jerked his head above the water to get his breath. The noise he made when the water bubbled scared all three of us for a moment.

Jenny was Old Howes's daughter. She was about our age, possibly a year or two older.

Les saw her looking at our clothes hanging on the bushes. He nudged me with his elbow.

"What are you doing down here?" Les said gruffly, trying to scare her.

"Can't I come if I want to?"

"You can't come down here when we're in swimming. You're not a boy."

"I can come if I wish to, smarty," Jenny said. "This creek doesn't belong to you."

"It doesn't belong to you, either," Les said, making a face. "What are you going to do about that?"

"All right," Jenny said, "if you are going to be so mean about it, Leslie Blake, I'll take your clothes and hide them where you'll never find them again as long as you live. What are you going to do about that?"

Jenny reached for the clothes. She grabbed Les's pants and my shirt and union suit.

Les caught my arm and pulled me towards the bank. We couldn't hurry at first, because we had to jerk our feet out of the muck before we could move at all.

"Let's duck her, Jack," Les whispered. "Let's give her a good ducking. Come on."

We crawled up the bank and caught Jenny just as she was starting to run through the bushes with our clothes. Les locked his arms around her waist and I caught her arms and pulled as hard as I could.

"I'll scream!" Jenny said. "If you don't stop, I'll scream at the top of my lungs. Papa is in the pasture, and he'll come right away. You know what he'll do to both of you, don't you?"

"We're not afraid of anybody," Les said, scowling and trying to scare her.

I put my hand over her mouth and held her with one arm locked around her neck. Together we pulled and dragged her back to the bank beside the creek.

"Don't you want to duck her, Jack?" Les said. "Don't you think we ought to? She's been telling Old Howes tales about us. She's a tattletale tit."

"We ought to duck her, all right," I said. "But suppose she goes and tells on us about that?"

"When we get through ducking her, she won't tell any more tales on us. We'll duck her until she promises and crosses her heart never to tell anybody. She's the one who's been throwing dead limbs into the creek every day. I'll bet anything she's the one who's been doing it."

Jenny was helpless while we held her. Les had her around the waist with both arms, and I still held her neck locked in the crook of my left arm. She tried to bite my hand over her mouth, but every time she tried to hurt me, I squeezed her neck so hard she had to stop.

I was a little afraid to duck Jenny, because once we had

ducked a colored boy named Bisco, and it had almost drowned him. We ducked Bisco so many times he couldn't breathe, and he became limp all over. We had to stretch him out on the ground and roll him over and over, and all the time we were doing that, yellow creek water was running out of his mouth. I was afraid we might drown Jenny. I didn't know what would happen to us if we did that.

"I know what let's do to her, Les," I said.

"What?"

"Let's mud-cake her."

"What's the matter with ducking her? It will scare her and make her stop throwing dead limbs into the creek. It'll stop her from telling tales about us, too."

"We'd better not duck her, Les," I said. "Remember the time we ducked Bisco? We nearly drowned him. I don't want anything like that to happen again."

Les thought a while, looking at Jenny's back. She was kicking and scratching all the time, but she couldn't begin to hurt us, and we had her so she couldn't get loose.

"All right," Les said. "We'll mud-cake her then. That's just as good as ducking, and it'll teach her a lesson. It'll make her stop being a tattletale tit."

"She's going to tell on us anyway, so we'd better do a good job of it this time. But it ought to make her stop throwing dead limbs into the swimming hole, anyway."

"She won't tell on us after we get through with her," Les said. "She won't tell anybody. She won't even tell Old Howes. Ducking and mud-caking always stops kids from telling tales. It's the only way to cure it."

"All right," I said. "Let's do it to her. She needs ducking, or mud-caking, or something. Somebody has got to do it to her, and we're the right ones to make a good job of it. I'll bet she won't bother us again after we get through with her."

Les threw Jenny on the ground beside the bank, locking her arms behind her back and holding her face in the earth so she couldn't make any noise. Les had to straddle her neck to keep her still.

"Take off her clothes, Jack," Les said. "I've got her. She can't get away as long as I'm holding her."

I reached down to pull off her dress, and she kicked me full in the stomach with both feet. When I fell backward and tried to sit up, there was no breath left in me. I opened my mouth and tried to yell at Les, but I couldn't even whisper.

"What's the matter, Jack?" Les said, turning his head and looking at me.

I got up on both knees and doubled over, holding my stomach with both arms.

"What's the matter with you, Jack?" he said. "Did she kick you?"

Les's back had been turned and he had not seen what Jenny had done to me.

"Did she kick me!" I said weakly. "It must have been her, but it felt like a mule. She knocked all of the wind out of me."

"Sit on her legs, then," Les said. "She can't kick you if you do that."

I ran down to the side of the creek and came back with a double handful of yellow muck. When I dug it out of the creek, it had made a sucking sound, and the odor was worse than any that ever came out of a pig pen. The muck in the creek stank worse than anything I had ever smelled. It was nothing but rotted leaves and mud, but it smelled like decayed eggs and a lot of other things.

I got Jenny's dress off and tossed it on the bushes so it would not get covered with muck. Les was able to hold her arms and cover her mouth at the same time by then, because she was not nearly so strong as either of us.

"She's got underwear on, Les," I said.

"Sure she has," Les said. "All girls wear underclothes. That's what makes them so sissy."

"You're not talking about me, are you?" I said, looking at him. "Because if you are—"

"I'm talking about her," Les said. "I know you have to wear the stuff because your people make you do it. But girls like to have it on. They don't want to go without it. That's why girls are so sissy."

"All right," I said, "but don't try to get nasty with me, because I'll—"

"You won't do anything, so shut up. Hurry and take her clothes off."

"Are we going to strip her naked?" I said.

"Sure," Les said. "We've got to. We can't mud-cake her if we don't strip her, can we?"

"I know that," I said, "but suppose Old Howes came down and saw us—"

"Old Howes wouldn't do nothing but spit and slip up in it. Who's scared of him, anyway? I'm not."

After we had struggled with Jenny a while longer, and after her underclothes were finally off, Les said he was tired of holding her. He was puffing and blowing as if he had been running five miles without stopping to rest.

I took Jenny's arms and put my hand over her mouth and sat on her neck. Les picked up a big handful of muck and threw it at her. The muck struck her on the stomach, making a sound like slapping water with a plank. He threw another handful. It splattered all over us.

While Les was running to the creek for another load, I turned Jenny over so he could smear some on her back. She did not struggle any more now, but I was afraid to release my grip on her arms or to take my hand off her mouth. When I had turned her over, she lay motionless on the ground, not even kicking her feet any more.

"This'll fix her," Les said, coming back with his hands and arms full of yellow muck. "She's had it coming to her for a long time. Maybe it'll stop her from being a tattletale tit."

He dropped the mass on her back and ran back for some more.

"Rub that in while I'm getting another load, Jack," he said. "That's what she needs to make her stop throwing dead limbs into the creek. She won't tell any more tales about us, either."

I reached over and with one hand smeared the muck up and down Jenny's back, on her legs, and over her arms and shoulders. I tried not to get any of it in her hair, because I knew how hard it was to try to wash it out with yellow creek water.

"Turn her over," Les said, dropping down beside us with a new load of muck. "We're just getting started on her."

I turned Jenny over again, and she did not even try to get loose from me. Les had begun to spread the muck over her, rubbing it into her skin. He took a handful and smeared it over her legs and thighs and stomach. Then he took another handful and rubbed it over her shoulders and breasts. Jenny still did not attempt to move, though she squirmed a little when Les rubbed the most tender parts of her body with the mass of rotted leaves and mud. Most of the time she lay as still as if she had been sound asleep.

"That's funny," I said.

"What's funny?" Les asked, looking up.

"She's not even trying to get loose now."

"That's because she's foxy," Les said. "She's just waiting for a good chance to break away. Here, let me hold her awhile."

Les took my place and I picked up a handful of muck and began spreading it over her. The muck was not sticky any longer, and when I smeared it on her, it felt slick and smooth. When my hands moved over her, I could feel that her body was much softer than mine, and that parts of her were very soft. When I smeared the slick mud over her breasts, it felt so smooth and soft that I was afraid to touch her there again. I glanced at her face, and I saw her looking at me. From the way she looked at me, I could not help thinking that she was not angry with us for treating her like that. I even thought that perhaps if Les had not been there she would have let me mud-cake her as long as I wished to.

"What are you doing, Jack?" Les said. "That's a funny way to spread muck on her."

"We've got enough on her, Les. Let's not put any more on her. Let's let her go home now. She's had enough."

"What's the matter with you?" Les said, scowling. "We're not half finished with her yet. We've got to put another coat of muck on her."

Jenny looked up when Les said that, and her eyes opened wider. She did not have to speak to tell me what she wished to say.

"That's enough, Les," I said. "She's a girl. That's enough for a girl."

I don't know, but somehow I believed that Les felt the same way I did, only he did not want to admit it. Now that we had stripped her and had smeared her all over with muck, neither of us could forget that Jenny was a girl. We had treated her as though she were a boy, but she remained a girl still.

"If we let you up now, will you promise not to tell?" Les asked her.

Jenny nodded her head, and Les dropped his hand from her mouth.

We both expected to hear her say what she was going to do, and what she was going to tell, because of the way we had treated her; but the moment she was freed she sat up quickly and tried to cover herself with her arms, without once speaking.

As soon as we saw that she was not going to call for Old Howes, Les and I ran to the creek and dived head-on into it. We squatted down until only our heads were showing above the water and began scrubbing the muck off us. Jenny looked at us, covering herself as much as she could.

She still had not said anything to us.

"Let's get dressed and run for home," Les said. "Pa would tear me up into little pieces if he caught me down here now, with her like that."

Jenny covered her eyes while we dashed out of the water and grabbed our clothes. We ran behind the bushes to dress. While we were standing there, we could hear Jenny splashing in the creek, scrubbing the muck from her.

Les had only his shirt and pants to put on, and he was ready to go before I could even straighten out my union suit. He buckled his pants and started backing off with his shirt tail hanging out while he tried to find the right buttons for the buttonholes. I had been in such a hurry to jump in the creek when we first came that I had tangled my union suit, and when I would get the arms straight, the legs would be wrong side out. Les kept backing farther and farther away from me.

"What's the matter?" he said. "Why don't you hurry?"

"I can't get this union suit untangled."

"That's what you get for wearing underclothes in summer."

"I can't help it," I said, "and you know it."

"Well, it's not my fault, is it?"

"Aren't you going to wait for me?"

"I can't, Jack," he said, backing away faster. He suddenly turned around and began running. "I've got to go home."

"I thought you said you weren't scared of Old Howes, or of anybody else!" I yelled after him, but if he heard me, he pretended not to understand what I had said.

After Les had gone, I took my time. There was no need to hurry, because I was certain that no matter what time I got home, Jenny would tell Old Howes what we had done to her, and he would come and tell my folks all about it. I wished to have plenty of time to think of what I was going to say when I had to face everybody and tell the truth.

Jenny had left the creek by the time I was ready to button my shirt, and she had only to slip her underclothes over her head and to put on her dress to be ready to go home. She came through the bushes while I was still fumbling with my shirt buttons.

"What's the matter, Jack?" she asked, smiling just a little. "Why didn't you run off with Leslie?"

"I couldn't get dressed any quicker," I said.

I was about to tell her how my union suit was so tangled that I had had to spend most of the time struggling with that, but I thought better of saying it.

She came several steps closer, and I started to run from her.

"Where are you going?" she said. "What are you running for?"

I stopped, turned around, and looked at Jenny. Now that she was dressed, she looked the same as she had always looked. She was the same in appearance, but somehow I knew that she was not the same, after what had happened beside the creek. I could not forget the sensation I had felt when my hands, slick with mud, had touched the softness of her body. As I looked at her, I believed I felt it again, because I knew that without the dress and the underclothes she would always remain the same as she was when I had first touched her.

"Why don't you wait for me, Jack?" she said.

I wanted to run away from her, and I wanted to run to her. I stood still while she came closer.

"But you're going to tell, aren't you? Aren't you going to tell what we did to you?"

She had come to where I stood, and I turned and walked beside her, several feet away. We went through the bushes and out through the woods to the road. There was no one in sight, and we walked together until we reached her house.

Just before we got to the gate I felt my hand touch hers. I don't know, but somehow, whether it was true or not, I believed she had taken my hand and held it in hers for a moment. When I suddenly looked to see, because I wanted to know if she really had taken my hand and squeezed it, she turned the other way and went through the gate.

I waited in the middle of the road until she walked up the front steps and crossed the porch. She stopped there a moment and brushed her dress with her hands, as if she wanted to be sure that there was no muck clinging to it. When she opened the door and went inside, I was not certain whether she had glanced at me over her shoulder, or whether I merely imagined she had. Anyway, I believed she had, because I felt her looking at me, just as I was sure that she had held my hand for a moment.

"Jenny won't tell," I said, running up the road towards home. "Jenny won't tell," I kept saying over and over again all the way there.

(First published in *Story*)

A Swell-Looking Girl

NOTHING much ever happened in the upper part of Pine County until Lem Johnson went over into the next county and married a swell-looking girl named Ozzie Hall. About eight or ten years before there had been a shotgun wedding in the lower part of the county, it's true; but Pine County was so large nobody in the upper part ever took much interest in what those countrymen down there were doing.

Lem Johnson was a farmer. He worked a two-horse crop with a Negro called Dan. Lem lived by himself in a four-room house. The Negro, Dan, lived across the road in a cabin with his wife and half a dozen pickaninnies. Dan, the Negro, worked for Lem on shares.

When Lem went over into the next county and married Ozzie Hall, it was the biggest event that had taken place in the Lucyville section of Pine County since anybody could remember. A man could live a lifetime and never see a thing like that happen again. She was a swell-looking girl, all right.

Before Lem went over and married Ozzie Hall he was the biggest sport in the whole county. He like to go out with the girls and have a good time. He had always gone somewhere every Saturday night, again all day Sunday, and Sunday night.

Sometimes he would drive up in front of a girl's house and call for her. She would come out and stand by the buggy while Lem sat back with his feet on the dashboard and had a good time with her. Other times he would drive up and ask a girl to go riding with him. All the girls liked that, too.

And all this time Lem was anxious to get married.

When he went to town on Saturday afternoon, he always said something about getting married. The boys teased Lem a lot about wanting to marry a girl.

"I'm a-rearing to get married," Lem told them.

"Want a woman all-time, eh, Lem?" they teased him.

"That's right," he said earnestly, "I don't want to have to wait all week for Sunday."

The boys sat in front of the store and wondered what girl Lem was going to marry.

"Say, Lem," one of them yelled after him down the road as he was leaving, "you ain't going buggy-riding every night when you get married, are you?"

Everybody whooped and shouted and Lem prodded the mule and drove away blushing.

All the girls in the Lucyville section knew Lem was thinking of getting married, too. But Lem did not ask any of them to marry him. They were not classy enough to suit him. He wanted a swell-looking girl. He had seen pictures of the kind of girl he wanted in the mail-order catalogues.

Lem heard that there was a girl just like he wanted over in the next county. One Saturday morning he hitched up the mule and drove away. It was late in the afternoon when he got there, but sure enough there she was, as classy as any girl he had ever seen in the mail-order catalogues.

Lem got her to marry him right away, and brought her home to Pine County Sunday night.

Ozzie had a lot of fine clothes and silk stockings and she certainly was good-looking. And she had a lot of things just like Lem had seen in the mail-order catalogues, besides some things he had never seen before.

Lem went right out the first thing and told everybody about Ozzie. He told everybody how good-looking she was and how much silk underwear she had.

Right there was where he made the biggest mistake of his life. All the boys began coming around at once to take a look at Ozzie, hoping to get a chance to see some of the things Lem talked about so much. They rode up three in a buggy, two on horseback, and a lot of them walked.

Lem took Ozzie out on the front porch to show her off. The boys had come a long way to see her.

"Well, Lem," Tom said, "you sure got yourself a swell-looking girl, ain't you?"

"Listen, Tom," Lem whispered confidentially, "Ozzie here is the swellest-looking girl in the whole country. You ought to see all the pink little things she's got."

Ozzie sat down in a chair and looked at the boys. There were twenty or more sitting on the edge of the porch looking up at her. Some of them said a lot of awfully fresh things when Lem was not listening.

"What kind of pink little things?" Tom asked him.

"All sorts of things, Tom. There's a lot I ain't learned the names of yet."

"I don't believe it," Tom stated.

"You don't believe it?" Lem asked in surprise. "You don't believe she's got some of those things on now?"

"Naw, I don't. The girls in this part of the county don't wear things like that. City girls do. Country girls like the ones around here don't. The girls in this part of the county wear underwear made out of ten-cents-a-yard cotton mill-ends."

"Ozzie don't!"

"I'll bet she does, too. All country girls wear mill-end underclothes. They buy the cloth at ten cents a yard."

"Ozzie don't!"

"Sure she does. Ain't she a country girl, too?"

"I'll prove she don't!"

"How?" Tom wanted to know. "Where?"

"Hell, right here!" Lem was good and mad at Tom for not believing what he told him.

Ozzie sat looking at the boys, with her legs crossed high. The boys were having the time of their lives looking at Ozzie from where they sat. She was a swell-looking girl, all right.

Lem walked over to Ozzie and told her to stand up. The boys crowded around to see what Tom and Lem were up to now.

Lem reached down and lifted the hem of Ozzie's skirt above her knees. Her stockings ended there, but there was no pink thing to be seen. All the boys could see where Ozzie's stockings ended. Tom could see, too; but he still did not believe she wore the things Lem said she did. Ozzie covered her face with her hands and peeped at the boys through her fingers.

Tom poked Lem with his thumb, nodding his head. Lem lifted her dress a little higher, looking for something pink. There was not anything yet, except more of her legs showing. Lem was determined to prove to Tom that Ozzie did not wear ten-cents-a-yard cotton mill-end underclothes. He lifted her dress a little higher and a little higher. Nothing appeared that would prove to Tom the things Lem had said on the other end of the porch were true. The boys crowded closer and closer to Ozzie.

Lem was sweating all over. The perspiration popped out on

his hands and face and he felt a ticklish sensation running up and down his back. He was beginning to wish he had never started to prove to Tom what he said about Ozzie. But there was no way out of it now. He had to keep it up until he proved that he knew what he was talking about.

Tom poked him again with his thumb.

"By God, Tom, I know what I'm talking about!" he shouted, jerking Ozzie's dress over the top of her head. "Now look!"

Lem stood there, staring popeyed at Ozzie while she was fighting to get her dress down and cover up her nakedness. The boys were making little whistling sounds and rubbing their eyes to make sure they were seeing right. Ozzie had on nothing at all under her dress. She ran into the house as fast as she could.

Tom took Lem by the arm and they went to the other end of the porch. The boys were out in the yard now, standing around talking and whispering in groups of twos and threes. They had a lot to talk about. She was a swell-looking girl, all right.

"Well, Lem," Tom said, swallowing hard two or three times, "you sure got mixed up that time, didn't you?"

"Tom, I swear before God she had a lot of those pink little things on last night."

"Maybe she wears them some days, and some days she don't wear nothing at all," Tom said.

Lem was trying hard to think about it, trying hard to figure out some sort of answer. To save his soul he could not understand why she did not wear the things all the time. He sat down on the edge of the porch, thinking as hard as he could about it.

"Well, she's a swell-looking girl, Lem. How did you ever find one like that?"

Lem did not bother to answer Tom. He sat on the edge of the porch trying to figure out why Ozzie wore those things one day and took them off the next.

Tom jumped to the ground and stood close to Lem.

"Lem, if I was you I'd keep her just like she is," he whispered. "Ten-cent mill ends ain't good enough for a girl like you got in there."

Tom went out in the yard where the rest of the boys were. They stood around in front of the house talking for two or three hours until the sun went down. Then they began to leave.

(First published in *American Earth*)

Uncle Jeff

UNCLE JEFF was a pretty good all-around carpenter, and he could drive a tenpenny nail into a board without making hammer marks on the wood, but he had been lazy ever since he was a boy, and he did not work at his trade any more than he was compelled to.

"All of those Newsomes are lazy," people said, "and it's unfair to single out Jeff for not being an exception."

Uncle Jeff's wife, though, never let up scolding him for being so downright lazy. Aunt Annie said he was too lazy to turn over in bed when he got tired sleeping on one side, and that she had to do it for him so he would stop moaning and go back to sleep.

But more than that, she had said a hundred times, if she had said it once, that she was going to leave him if he did not change his ways. Every time that came up, Uncle Jeff put his arm around her and promised to do every single thing she wanted him to do. When he said that, Aunt Annie usually weakened and said she would stay.

"I don't know what got into me," Aunt Annie said. "When I was young, I had the chance of marrying some of the finest men in town. I turned them all down for you, Jeff Newsome."

"Now, Annie," Uncle Jeff told her, "that's no way to look at it. You must have had a pretty good reason for marrying me when you did."

"Maybe I did then," she said, "but I've got more sense now, and I wouldn't do it again."

"I've tried to be a good husband to you, Annie," Uncle Jeff said. "I may make mistakes sometimes, but I mean well."

When Uncle Jeff talked like that, Aunt Annie could not keep back the tears. She had a good cry and did not scold him again for another week or ten days.

The boarders always noticed the difference after Aunt Annie and Uncle Jeff had had one of their talks up in her room. At supper she always picked out the best pieces of meat for Uncle Jeff's plate, and she gave him an extra large helping of dessert. That period lasted, generally, for two or three days; then she would begin scolding him for little things for another two or three days; and then toward the end she found fault with everything he did or did not do, and Uncle Jeff was in for another bawling out.

During those times when Aunt Annie was not speaking to him, Uncle Jeff told one or two of the boarders that toothache or a sneezing spell had kept her awake all night, and that if she appeared to be out of sorts, just not to pay any attention to it.

That was when Uncle Jeff usually went away from home for a day or two, sometimes three days at a time. He figured that Aunt Annie would appreciate him more when he came back. Sometimes she did, and sometimes she did not.

When Uncle Jeff left home, he caught a ride in a truck or automobile to Savannah and stayed with a friend of his. There was nothing wrong with his doing that, because Emma's house, where he stayed, was clean and orderly. It did not have a bad reputation like some of the houses had. He had known Emma for a long time, for fifteen or eighteen years at least, and Emma treated him like a favorite brother. She had partitioned off the right wing of the house for private use, and Uncle Jeff was always welcome to sleep in the guest room.

Every time he went to visit Emma, he wondered what would happen if the house were raided while he happened to be there. He was fairly certain that Emma saw to it that things were taken care of in the proper places, but nonetheless there was always a chance of a slip somewhere, and if that ever did happen, he was just as sure that he would be taken to the police station with Emma and the girls and booked. He did not mind that, but he was thinking what a shock it would be to Annie for her to see his name in the paper that way, and wondering what he would say if it ever happened.

"Another spat, Jeff?" Emma asked him when she opened the door. "It's been less than two weeks this time, hasn't it?"

"About the same as usual," he said. "Annie's got me worried good and plenty this time about her leaving me, though. She says it like she means it."

He went inside, and Emma took him through the hall to the dining room where she was eating supper. She brought a plate for him, and she helped him to the baked fish and vegetables.

"Annie won't leave you, Jeff," she said, patting him on the shoulder. "Don't let her talk upset you. A woman isn't going to drive a man out, or go away herself, unless it's something like the world coming to an end. You and Annie won't fall out that bad."

After supper they talked awhile in the dining room, and then Uncle Jeff took the evening paper and went upstairs to bed. Emma brought him a cold bottle of beer, and an extra pillow for his head while he was reading, and turned the covers back.

"My husband spoiled me something awful," Emma said as she was bending over the bed smoothing the sheets. "Before he died he used to let me take care of him like a baby. I've never got used to it since."

Jeff turned around to answer her, thinking she was talking to him, but after he had taken one look at her, he realized she was talking to herself. He watched her while she folded the covers back and smoothed them out several times until she was satisfied with the way they looked. After that she patted and pushed the two pillows around until she had them just right. When she finished, she opened the bottle of beer and poured it into a glass for him. He walked to the window and looked outside.

She had gone as far as the door before he knew she was leaving. He turned around and thanked her for bringing him the bottle of beer.

Emma did not say anything for a moment, and then she came back into the middle of the room.

"I'd hate to have you stop coming here, Jeff," she began. There was a long pause while she seemed to be thinking what to say next. "But I've been wondering about something."

"What?" he asked.

"How would you like to find a way to make you and Annie stop having these spats—something that would put you back where you were when you got married?"

"How would you do that?" he asked quickly.

"I think I know a way," she said, looking at him and nodding her head slowly. She put her hand against her face absent-mindedly. "I think I know just what would do it."

"What is it?" he asked. "How do you go about it?"

"Annie needs jolting, Jeff," she said. "A good, hard, teeth-rattling jolt."

"You don't mean for me to go home and shake her hard, or hit her, do you?"

"No," she said. "Of course not."

"How can she be jolted then?"

"I have a pretty good idea in my mind," she said. "But I'm not going to tell you now. You're going to stay innocent of the whole thing. This is something just between Annie and me."

She turned and walked out of the room, closing the door behind her. Uncle Jeff stood staring at the door, wondering what in the world Emma was talking about. He heard her go down the stairs and heard a door slam in the hall on the first floor. After wondering about what she had said for a while, he gave up finally and started undressing. When he was ready to get into bed, he picked up the evening paper and propped up against the pillows Emma had fixed for him. He always liked to read before going to sleep.

It was early in the evening, not much more than nine-thirty, and the house was quiet. Far in the other wing of the building he could hear a radio faintly, and occasionally one of the girls laughed loud enough for him to hear.

Half an hour later the light was out and he was sound asleep.

Suddenly in the middle of the night he sat up in bed, shaking and perspiring. He had had a terrible dream. He jumped out of bed, turned on the light, and looked at the room to see where he was. He did not waste any more time standing there.

Jerking on his clothes the easiest way they would go on, he turned out the light and opened the door cautiously. He could not hear anyone downstairs, and so he tiptoed down the hall and out the private door into the alley. Even when he got there, he did not feel safe. He walked on his toes to the end of the alley and when he got there he stopped and looked carefully in all directions before going any farther. He did not see anyone, and he walked away as fast as he could.

Uncle Jeff did not know what time of night it was until he had got to the edge of the city. When he was outside the light cast by the last street lamp, he took out his watch, struck a match, and looked at the time. It was still early, only a quarter past one. He started walking toward home without any waste of time.

There were not many trucks on the highway at that time of night, and Uncle Jeff was beginning to be afraid he would not get a ride at all. It was a long distance home, sixty-five or seventy miles, and he would never be able to walk it before morning. He looked behind him every few yards to see if there were any sign of a truck or automobile.

While he walked along the dark hard highway toward the north, he began to wonder if it were possible for a person to dream what he had not been able to think of while he was awake. He decided it would not be possible, for him at least, because he was sure that his dream about Emma was going to come true. He was so certain about it that he told himself that his waking up was the best piece of luck he had ever had in his whole life. He was not angry with Emma, because he knew she meant well, but he was just as certain in his own mind that the scheme he thought she had planned would do him ten times more harm than good. He whistled over every step of ground for the next two miles.

Three hours later he stopped and built a fire in the ditch beside the highway to warm his hands and feet. Automobiles passed him, and trucks, too, but none of them had stopped to give him a ride. He did not mind that this time, because he was so glad to be out of Savannah and on his way back home that he did not care if he had to walk every step of the way there.

He huddled over the fire warming himself until the last embers had died out. Then he got up, stretched himself comfortably, and started walking toward home.

It was after daylight before he finally got a ride in a truck, and it was midmorning before he reached the house. He walked around the block once before going in. There was no reason for his doing that this morning, but the habit was more than he could overcome in one day.

Aunt Annie was in the dining room setting the table for dinner when he walked in the front door. He hung his hat on the hat tree the boarders used and walked down the hall. When he passed the dining-room door, he saw Aunt Annie standing by the table looking at him. She did not say a word then.

"Hello, Annie, darling," Uncle Jeff said. "It's a fine spring day outside today, isn't it?"

She did not answer him.

He walked cautiously to the door.

"What's the matter, Annie darling?" he said.

She was holding the morning paper in her hands behind her back. Suddenly she drew her arm up as though she were fighting mosquitoes and slammed the paper on the table. Then she took several steps toward Uncle Jeff. Uncle Jeff backed into the hall.

"Of all the humiliating, scandalous, low-down—" she began.

"What is it?" he asked anxiously.

"This!" she cried, beating the newspaper against the palm of her hand. "What will my boarders think of me? How long do you think the schoolteachers will be allowed to board in my house after this? What will the respectable, honest, God-fearing citizens of this town think of me after this? How can I walk along the street and hold my head up now? Oh, why did I ever marry you in the first place!"

Uncle Jeff stared at her in amazement.

"What happened, Annie?" he asked.

She took one more look at him, gripped the paper in both hands, and marched to the stairs. She stopped there for a moment, looked at him again before bursting into tears, and then ran upstairs to her room. She slammed the door shut but did not lock it. Uncle Jeff went up the stairs behind her and walked noiselessly into the room. She had thrown herself across the bed, on her face, and she was crying hysterically. Once during the time he stood not knowing what to do, she turned her face and looked to see if he were in the room. As soon as she saw him, she turned her face away again, and cried.

Uncle Jeff sat down on the bed beside her and tried to ease the newspaper out of her hand. When she felt it move, she gripped it so tight he could not get it from her.

"Now, Annie," Uncle Jeff begged, "you ought to tell me what all the trouble is about."

Aunt Annie sat up and glared at him. The tears were dripping down her cheeks and disappearing into the fabric of the counterpane.

"Why did you do it, Jeff?" she asked at last, weakly and hopelessly. "Oh, Jeff, why did you?"

"Do what?" he said. "Why did I do what?"

"Go to that house in Savannah and be arrested and have your name printed in the paper like this," she said quickly. "You have deceived me, Jeff. You have done this to me—brought all this pain and humiliation to me."

"I didn't get arrested, Annie," he said confusedly.

She opened the paper and read aloud how the police had raided a house on Webster Street and had arrested Emma Weeks, nine girls, and a man who gave the name of Jeff Newsome.

When she finished, she looked at Uncle Jeff curiously.

Uncle Jeff shook his head bewilderedly.

"Did you go to Savannah?" she asked coldly.

"Yes, but—"

"Did you go to Emma Weeks's house on Webster Street?"

"Yes, I went there, but—"

Aunt Annie closed her lips tightly while he was trying to explain. Each time she spoke, she opened her mouth only enough to pronounce the words.

"Were you arrested and taken to jail?"

"I dreamed about it," he said in confusion. "I dreamed I was in jail. But I wasn't arrested at all, or put in jail."

"You're lying as big as the broad daylight, Jeff Newsome!" Aunt Annie said. "You are sitting there telling me the biggest, blackest lie of your life! You got out on bail somehow, and now you sit there and lie to me about it. It looks to me like you would have sense enough to admit it when it's all here in the Savannah paper."

Instead of trying to protest any more, he wondered how he would ever succeed in convincing anybody in town that he had not been arrested in the raid on Emma's house. He knew Emma well enough to figure out that she had had her own house raided in order to have him booked at the police station, and he knew now that she had done it in order to jolt Annie. He was convinced that when Emma discovered he had left her house, she had persuaded somebody to give his name to the police so her plan to jolt Annie could be carried out. Emma was smart enough to think that fast. And besides, Emma liked to have her house raided every few months, anyway; it was the best advertising she could get.

Aunt Annie was looking at him coldly.

He did not know how to go about trying to explain the thing so she would believe him.

"Well, what have you got to say for yourself?" Aunt Annie demanded.

"Now, Annie," he began, casting about in his mind for some method of handling the thing, "it's not like you think it is. I didn't—"

Aunt Annie suddenly leaned forward and grasped Uncle Jeff's hand. Her face was flushed and there was a kind of softness in her eyes that he had not seen in a long time. She smiled at him, too.

"Jeff," she said slowly, "I haven't been a good wife to you lately. I don't know what got into me. I've done nothing but scold and find fault. Being like that has made me miserable, and I did more scolding trying to cover up how bad I felt. The last time I kicked you out of bed and made you sleep in another room I hated myself so much I wanted to die. I didn't tell you how I felt then, because I was all the time hating myself so much I couldn't admit it. But I can tell you now, because I feel—"

Her eyes were so soft they looked as if they would melt any second.

"Will you forgive me, Jeff?"

"Me? Forgive you?" he asked unbelievingly.

She nodded, holding his hand tightly.

"Well, I guess so," he said, "but—"

"Never mind saying any more, Jeff," she said.

"But I don't know how to explain—"

"What kind of a woman is Emma Weeks, Jeff?" she broke in. "How old is she? How long have you known her?"

Uncle Jeff settled back on the pillows Aunt Annie propped up for his head and wondered how Emma had known all this was going to turn out as it had in the end. The more he thought about it, the more confused he became. It was a mystery bigger than life itself to him.

Aunt Annie unlaced his shoes, lifted his feet onto the bed, and smiled down at him. Uncle Jeff wiggled his toes and waited for her to come into his arms. He had already decided it would be better if he never attempted to convince her that actually he had not been arrested in Emma's house and had not been booked with the girls at the police station.

(First published in *Jackpot*)

The Visitor

No one knew it except ourselves, but some day Laura and I were going to be married. Laura was only seventeen then, while I was a few years older, and we had plenty of time to talk about it before her mother would even think of letting us marry. First of all, of course, I would have to go away to Richmond or Washington or Baltimore and get a good job and begin making enough money for both of us. Laura and I were certain that we would not have to wait longer than another two or three years. She had just finished her second year away at boarding school.

Since the middle of June, when Laura came home from school to spend the summer, we had been having the most wonderful time together that any two people could possibly have. She had been at home only a week or ten days and I had been to see her almost every night, and, of course, Sundays. Her father's peaches began to ripen after the first week in June, and since his orchard was only a mile or two away we went there every Sunday afternoon and sat under the trees eating the fruit, or else we went down to the pasture with my hat full of peaches and ate them beside the brook water.

The next Wednesday I had to go away with my uncle for a few days into another county, and when we came home late Saturday night I went to bed right away so I could be up in time to see Laura early the next morning. Before we went away on my uncle's business trip I told Laura that I would certainly be back home by Sunday and that I would come over in the morning and stay all day. In the afternoon we planned to go to the orchard and stay there until dark.

Laura was waiting for me in the porch swing when I went over to see her the next morning. I was about to run up the steps and kiss her quickly before anybody saw us, but before I could reach her a strange girl opened the screen door and came out on the porch. I had never seen the girl before and Laura had not said anything to me about her coming. There was something about her that was so nice I did not know what to say. I stood staring at her awkwardly until Laura turned around and put her arm around the girl's waist and introduced us to each other. I don't know what it was unless it could have been the clothes she wore, but she was so different from Laura that I could not stop staring at her. Laura's clothes were just like hers, but there was something about the way her dress fitted her that made me unsteady on my feet. I felt lightheaded for a few minutes and my arms and legs had very little life in them. I was so confused by the way she looked that I did not hear her last name, but when Laura called her Drusilla I went closer to her, repeating the name under my breath over and over again. I had never heard of anyone named Drusilla before, and the girl was so lovely and her eyes so blue and her dress fitted her so smoothly that I did not know what to say. I shook hands with her though, and then I went with them to the porch swing.

I sat down between them and held my hands together in a way that I had never done before.

"Drusilla and I are roommates at school," Laura said to me, trying to reach my hands with her fingers.

I sat still and did not say anything. I had been looking forward for a whole week to this Sunday when we should be alone together and Laura's friend had come so unexpectedly, to me at least, that I not only resented her being there but actually hated Laura just a little for having her in her home. But I still could not forget the way she looked when I first saw her standing at the screen door.

"Laura has told me a lot about you," Drusilla said, leaning toward me. "But she did not say half enough. I expected you to look like a high-school boy, but you really look and act like a college man."

Laura laughed and leaned against my shoulder.

"Drue," she said, "I made you promise not to try to take Bob away from me—if you must have somebody to talk to like that we'll get Bob to bring one of his friends over to see you."

I sat up erectly then, looking first at Laura and then at Drusilla. I had wondered ever since I came why Laura had not invited one of the other boys over to see Drusilla.

"Don't bother," Drusilla laughed, winking shyly at me, "I'm perfectly pleased with the company we have."

Both of them laughed, and began talking about something else. I sat silently between them trying to decide if I wanted another boy to come and talk to Drusilla. I was bending forward with my elbows on my knees while they talked to each other behind me, Laura leaning lightly against my shoulder and Drusilla facing her with her legs pressed tightly against me. I remembered that I had been looking forward to Sunday for a whole week, when Laura and I could go to the orchard together and be alone all day.

As soon as dinner was over we started to the orchard. Laura ran ahead, trying her best to make both of us run with her, but I did not feel like running, and I hung behind as far as I could. Drusilla kept a few paces in front of me all the time.

Just as we reached the top of the hill Laura suddenly stopped and turned around. All three of us stood still for a moment and listened. Laura's mother was calling her. I did not hear what she said.

"What does she want, Laura?" Drusilla asked her.

"I've got to go back and take her into town," Laura said, pouting just a little. "I forgot that she wants me to drive her some place this afternoon. But I've got to go. You and Bob can go to the orchard anyway, and wait for me there. I'll be back as quickly as I can. Maybe I can get back in an hour or two. I'll hurry."

Without waiting any longer she turned around and ran back to the house. Drusilla and I stood watching her for several minutes.

"Don't eat all the peaches—save a few for me!" she called back over her shoulder. "I'll be back soon."

We turned around in the path and walked slowly down the hill toward the orchard gate. It was hot, just as the clear days in summer always were in Carolina.

"Now, I suppose you will have a dull time this afternoon," Drusilla said seriously without looking at me.

"Why?" I asked, thinking of Laura.

"Oh, because Laura isn't with us—and because you think you must be nice to me for politeness." She turned her eyes in my direction. What she did with her eyes when she looked at me was not exactly winking. I could not understand just what it was.

"If you were anybody else I would probably feel like that," I said earnestly, "but it's different with you."

Drusilla had run ahead and she did not hear what I said. When I realized that she had not heard what I said, I wanted to catch up with her and tell her again. I wanted to be nice to her because she was Laura's friend, and I certainly did not want her to feel that I did not want her to be there. I ran to catch up with her.

She had reached the gate leading into the orchard and had gone inside before I got there.

"Wait a minute, Drusilla," I called. "I'll show you where the best peaches are."

"All of them look delicious to me," she smiled. "I think I'll eat one of these first."

She reached overhead and pulled a sun-reddened peach from the nearest limb.

"There are the best ones down there," I pointed toward a tree a hundred yards farther in the orchard. "Let me get you one of those."

She came behind me, eating the peach she had pulled from the tree by the gate.

"Try this one," I offered, handing her the best one I could find on the tree. "I'll bet you will like it. This is Laura's favorite tree."

She took a bite from the one I gave her and came toward me under the tree.

"Oh, the fuzz tickles, doesn't it?" she laughed, rubbing her fingers over her cheeks. "Why does it have such fuzzy skin?"

"All good peaches are fuzzy," I told her. "The ones that haven't any fuzz aren't much good."

We stood under the tree close together for a while, eating peaches.

"Oh, I see a beautiful one," she said, pointing over my head.

Before I could find the peach she had seen overhead she had pulled the limb down and reached for it. I was about to help her get it when suddenly she dropped the peach she was holding and cried out. I knew at once what had happened. A bee had stung her.

"Hurry, Drusilla," I said, "let's run to the house and put something on it that will stop it from hurting."

I ran towards the gate, but when I turned around to see if she were coming, I saw her sit down under the tree. I ran back to her.

"What's the matter, Drusilla? Aren't you coming to the house?"

"I can't," she said, tears dropping down her cheeks. "It hurts too much."

"But what are we going to do?" I begged her. "It will swell up and hurt more and more if we stay here."

"Can't you do something to it, Bob?" she asked, looking up into my eyes. "Can't you make it stop hurting just a little bit?"

I remembered once when I had been bitten by a snake that an old Negro man sucked the poison out and put tobacco juice on it. I did not have any tobacco, but I knew I could suck the poison out of a bee sting if it were possible.

I got down on my knees beside her and asked her where the bee had stung.

"Right here," she said, pointing to her shoulder. "Can't you see where it's swelling now?"

"You will have to roll up your sleeve," I said. "I can't get to it unless you do."

Instead of rolling up her sleeve she began to unfasten a pin that held her dress together over her chest.

"Here's the place—see?" she said, pushing back the dress from her shoulder.

I squeezed the flesh between my fingers until I saw the stinger and then I pulled it out. Leaning over her I put my mouth over the swelling and sucked as hard as I could, and then I spat the poison on the ground. I kept that up for almost five minutes before I was certain I had sucked out as much of the poison as I could.

"Does it feel any better now, Drusilla?" I asked her, breathless. "Does it hurt as much as it did before?"

"Oh, it barely hurts at all now," she said, looking up at me bending over her. "But you had better do that some more. Maybe it will keep it from swelling now."

I bent over her again and sucked as hard as I could. She

had fallen backward until she was lying on the ground and my arm was under her head. Then suddenly I forgot all about the bee-sting. I felt my lips tight over her skin and my hands gripping her shoulders. She was lying on her back, and her head had turned sideways against my head. I could not see her face, but I felt her hands holding tightly to me as if she were afraid she would fall if she took them away. I don't know how long we lay there, but it seemed that the more I sucked the bee sting the less I could think about it. I had forgot to spit out the poison and I was kissing her shoulder far away from the place where the bee had stung her. I knew that she had forgotten all about the sting too, and that she did not feel the pain any more, because her cheeks were tight against my face and she was kissing me. The peach fuzz still clung to her and we both felt it tickle when our faces were close together. And then our lips were pressed together and our arms were around each other as tightly as we could clasp them. After a while it seemed as if we had been there in the orchard a long time together. The sun was setting behind the peach trees and we were already damp with the early dew. The peach fuzz was all over us but neither of us minded it any more.

"We must go now, Bob," she said. "It's very late."

I waited, but she did not move.

"Where do you live, Drusilla?" I asked quickly.

She told me the address. I closed my eyes and repeated the street number over and over to myself until I was certain I would never forget it.

The stars were coming out when we got up and walked across the field to the house. And because it was dark we walked side by side in the narrow path with our arms around each other. When we reached the top of the hill I lifted her in my arms and carried her down to the bottom where the last gate was. She put her arms tightly around my neck and held her face close to mine until we were within sight of the house.

Laura was waiting for us on the front porch. She jumped up and ran to meet us when we went up the steps.

"Where have you been all this time—did something happen?" she asked.

We told her about the bee that had stung Drusilla.

"But it doesn't hurt now," Drusilla said.

I went across the porch to the swing and waited until they came.

"I got back from town so late that I decided to wait here for you," Laura explained. "But if I had known you were going to stay this late I would have come down to the orchard and walked home with you."

I sat down for a few minutes and then got up to go home. Laura went to the gate with me.

"I'm sorry I ran away like I did this afternoon and made you entertain Drue all day—but she is leaving in the morning and you can come back soon, Bob."

"Is she going home tomorrow?" I asked quickly. "I'd better tell her good-by, then."

I ran back to the porch where we had left Drusilla in the swing, but she had gone into the house. I walked back to Laura and asked her to tell Drusilla that I went to tell her good-by but that she had left the porch.

"Good night, Bob," Laura said, squeezing my hand.

I opened the gate and went out.

"Good night," I said.

Laura waited several minutes at the gate while I ran down the road towards home. I forgot that I had not kissed her until I had gone into the house.

When I went upstairs to my room I was angry with Laura for having Drusilla down to visit her, and I was just a little angry with Drusilla for making me like her more than I did Laura. I tried not to think about it very much, but I knew I liked Drusilla more than I loved Laura.

As soon as I could find the ink bottle I began writing a letter.

Dearest Drusilla: I am coming to Baltimore to look for a job and I want to see you as soon as I get there. I know I'll like to live there because I . . .

I stopped and wondered how I could say everything I wanted to in a letter.

(First published in *American Earth*)

Handy

NOBODY knew where Handy came from, and nobody knew where he would go if he left, but if he had not killed Grandpa Price, he could have stayed another ten years or more.

Grandpa Price was old, and he was peevish, and he did nothing but fuss and find fault all day long. If he had been let alone, he would not have lived much longer, anyway.

But Handy hit Grandpa Price with a windlass, and the old man died that night. Handy had to pack up the little that belonged to him and get ready to go somewhere else to live.

"You ought to have had better sense," Harry Munford told him.

"It wasn't sense that had to do with it," Handy said.

"Just the same, it wasn't a good thing to do."

"A man oughtn't be an out-and-out troublemaker," Handy said. "People who spend their lives building things don't have time to find fault with others."

"Even so," Harry said, "you shouldn't have done what you did to Grandpa Price."

A whole day could be spent counting up the downright troublemaking things Grandpa Price had said and done during the past ten or fifteen years. When he ran out of the ordinary things to find fault with, such as not enough gravy on the chicken or too much sweetening in the custard, he would go around quarreling about the time of day it happened to be. Sometimes when it was morning, he would say it ought to be afternoon, and when it was noon, he would say it ought to be dawn, and then rant and rave if anybody said noon was as good as anything else for it to be. Only a few days before he died, he got after Harry because the chimney might not be in plumb. That made Harry so mad he almost lost his head. "What if it ain't?" he shouted at the old man. "Because if it ain't, it ought to be," Grandpa Price said. Harry was so mad by then that he went for a plumb line and dropped it on the chimney. The chimney was only an eighth of an inch out of plumb. "That ought to make you shut your mouth from now on!" Harry shouted at him. "I won't shut my mouth, because the chimney is out of plumb and you know it. It ought to be torn down and built up again right," Grandpa Price said. "Over my dead body," Harry told him. Grandpa Price fussed about the chimney being out of plumb all the rest of the day, and even through supper until he went to bed that night. He called Harry and all the Munfords lazy, good for nothing, and slipshod. He followed Harry around the place the next day saying anybody who would take up for an out-of-plumb chimney was not a good citizen.

"The more I think about it, Handy, the more I think you shouldn't have done it," Harry said. "Any number of times I've felt like picking up a brick or a crowbar and doing the thing myself, but a man can't go around the world hitting old men like that, no matter how provoked he is. The law's against it."

"I just couldn't stand it no longer, Mr. Harry," Handy said. "I'm sorry about it now, but it just couldn't be helped at the time."

Handy had lived there ten or twelve years. When he walked into the front yard for the first time, it was in the middle of the cotton-picking season. He came in and said he was looking for something to do. It was at a time when Harry needed cotton pickers if he ever needed them. He was glad to see anybody who came up and said he wanted a job. Harry was all ready to hire Handy. He told Handy he was paying sixty cents a hundred in the fields.

Handy shook his head as though he knew exactly what he wanted. Cotton picking was not it. "No sirree, bob. I don't pick no cotton," Handy said. "I haven't got any need for any-body else these days," Harry told him. "The cotton is falling on the ground, going to waste faster every day, and that's all I'm concerned about now." "You always got need for some-thing new, or something made of something old." "What do you mean?" "I make things," Handy said. "I just take what's thrown away and make it useful. Sometimes I like to make a thing just because it's pretty, though."

He picked up a stick of wood about a foot long and two or three inches thick. Nobody paid much attention to what he was doing, and Harry was sizing him up to be a tramp. He asked Handy if he had ever worked in the fields, and Handy said he had not. He asked him if he had worked on the river steamers, and Handy said, No. In the cotton mills. Not ever. Railroads. No. Harry shook his head. He put Handy down a tramp. Han-dy scraped the wood with the knife blade and handed it to Harry. It was the smoothest-whittled wooden spoon anybody had ever seen. It looked as if it had been sandpapered and polished with soapstone. It had taken Handy only the length of time he was standing there to do it, too. Harry turned the spoon over and over in his hands, felt of it, and smiled at Handy. Anybody who could do a thing like that deserved a better jack-knife than Handy had. Harry took his own out of his pocket and gave it to him.

Nobody said anything more to him about picking cotton in the fields. Handy walked around the yard looking at things for a while, and then he went around to the back of the house and looked inside the barn, the woodshed, the smokehouse, and the chicken run. He looked in all the hen nests, and then he began carving nest eggs out of some blocks of wood he found in the barn. They were smooth and brown, and the laying hens liked them better than any other kind.

After he had made six or eight nest eggs, he found some-thing else to do. He never asked Harry or anybody if it was all right for him to do a thing, or if they wanted something made; he just went ahead and made whatever he felt like doing. The chairs Handy made were the most comfortable in the house, the plowstocks were the strongest on the farm, and the weather vanes were the prettiest in the country.

"The trouble with Grandpa Price, he wasn't like me and you, Handy," Harry said. "The reason me and you are alike is that I crave to get things growing in the field, and you to make things with your hands. Grandpa Price didn't have that feeling in him. All he wanted was to find fault with what other people grow or make."

Handy was sad and dejected. He knew it would take him a

long time to find another place where the people would let him
stay and make things. He would be able to stop along the road
now and then, of course, and make a chicken coop for somebody or build a pigpen; but as soon as he finished it, they would
give him a leftover meal or a pair of old pants and tell him to
go on away. He knew all about the trouble he was going to have
finding somebody who would let him stay and just make things.
Some of them would offer him a job plowing in the fields, or
working on a river steamer. "I want to make things out of
pieces of wood," Handy said. "I want to build things with my
fingers." The people were going to back away from him; they
would shut the door in his face. He could not sit still. His hands
began to tremble.

"What's the matter, Handy?" Harry asked him. "What
makes you shake like that? Don't let what happened to Grandpa Price untie you."

"It's not that, it's something else."

"What else?"

"I'm going to find it hard not having a place to live where I
can make things."

"I hate like everything to see you go," Harry said. "Somehow or other it don't seem right at all." It hurt him so much to
think about Handy's leaving that he tried not to look at him.
"But," he said, "the sheriff will make it hard for me if I fail
to tell him what happened." It was already the day after Grandpa Price had died, and the sheriff had to be told about it before
Grandpa Price could be buried in the cemetery. "But I don't
want to do it, just the same," Harry said sadly. "It means
driving you off, Handy, and I'd drive you off a dozen times
before I'd let the sheriff find you here when he comes."

It hurt Harry so much to think about it he could not sit there
and look at Handy. He got up and walked away by himself.

When he came back, Handy was not there. But presently he
saw Handy's head bobbing up and down behind the barn fence,
and he was relieved. After a while he went into the house to
change into clean overalls and shirt. He had to change before
he could go into town, anyway. There was nothing to stop him
from taking as much time as he wanted, though. He looked at
two or three pairs of overalls before deciding which to put on.
He liked to have a person like Handy around, because Handy
was always making something, or getting ready to make something. That was what he liked about Handy. He was like the
children when they came home from school, or on holidays.
They were busy at something, play or work, every minute they
were awake. He was afraid, though, that when they grew up
they would get to be like Grandpa Price, that they would spend
their time finding fault instead of making things.

When Harry finally came out into the yard, it was late in the afternoon.

"I don't like to go to town at this time of the day," he said, looking toward the barn where Handy was, up at the sky, and back again toward the barn. "It would mean coming back long after dark."

Harry walked around the house, to the garden several times, and finally toward the barnyard. He wondered more and more all the time what Handy was spending so much time down there for. Several times he had seen Handy come to the barn door, throw some trash and shavings outside, and then disappear again.

It grew dark soon, and he did not see Handy again until the next morning. Handy was at the table eating breakfast when Harry came in and sat down.

"What's this?" Harry asked, standing up again suddenly.

"A little present for Grandpa Price," Handy said.

"But Grandpa Price is dead—"

"I only made it to hang around his neck in the grave," Handy said. "I always wanted to make something for him, but I thought he'd find so much fault with it if he was alive that I went ahead and made it all wrong just to please him."

It was a wooden chain about two feet long, each link about the size of a fingernail, and each one a different object. Handy had carved it from beginning to end since the afternoon before, sitting up all night to finish it.

"If Grandpa Price was alive, he'd be so tickled to get it he wouldn't want to find any fault with it, Handy. As it is, I don't know that I've ever seen a finer-looking present."

Harry sat down and picked up the chain to look at it more closely. The first link he looked at was a miniature chair with three legs shorter than the fourth one.

"I didn't think anybody but me remembered about that time when Grandpa Price quarreled so much about one of the chairs having one leg shorter than the others. I said one leg was shorter. Grandpa Price said three were short and one was long. Up to that time, that was about the biggest quarrel me and him ever had, wasn't it, Handy?"

Handy nodded.

Harry bent over to see what some of the other objects were. One was carved to look like a piece of the sky with the sun and stars shining at the same time. Another was a picture in a frame that looked upside down no matter which way it was turned.

Handy pushed back his chair and got up.

"This is too fine a thing to put in a grave, Handy," Harry said. "It would be a sin to bury a thing like this in the ground where nobody could ever see it again."

"I made it for a present to hang around Grandpa Price's neck," Handy said. "That's why I made it."

"Well," Harry said, shaking his head, "that being the case—I guess you've got the right to say—But it does seem a shame—"

Handy went out through the kitchen, down the steps, and across the yard to the barn. As soon as he got inside the barn door, he fired the shotgun.

Harry jumped to his feet, carrying the chain for Grandpa Price's neck with him.

"What did Handy shoot for?" he said.

He looked out the window for a minute, then he went down to the barn.

When he came back, he was slow about it. He looked sad, but there was another look on his face at the same time. One moment he felt so good he had to grin about it. "Handy won't have to go now, after all." He grinned all over his face. "If Handy had stayed alive, I'd never have seen him again," he said to himself. He walked up on the porch and began looking at the chain again, picking out a link here and a link there to stare at and feel with his fingers.

"Grandpa Price can be buried in the cemetery if he wants to," he said, aloud, "but Handy is going to be buried right here in the back yard."

He felt the chain with all the fingers of both hands and held it up to gaze at in the sunlight.

"I want to have him around," he said.

(First published in the *New Republic*)

An Autumn Courtship

AMOS WILLIAMS had been carrying a jug of his last year's cider over to Esther Tibbetts's every Sunday night for two months or more and he thought it was about time for something to happen. Amos had been trying all summer to marry Esther, but Esther owned a good farm and a fine set of buildings and she thought she was very well off just as she was. Every Sunday night Esther seemed to be ready to say she would marry Amos, but by that time the cider was all gone and he had to go away and wait for another week to pass before he could try again.

When he went back to work at the skewer mill Monday morning, the other men wanted to know if anything had happened the night before. Everybody in the mill knew that Amos was trying his hardest to marry Esther before winter and cold weather came. Amos had begun taking Esther a jug of cider because one of the men there had said that if a woman drank enough hard cider she would marry anybody.

"What did Esther say last night, Amos?" one of the men asked him, winking at the others. "Did she say she would get married to you?"

Amos said nothing for a few minutes. The mill was turning out candy sticks for all-day suckers this week because there was a big stock of meat skewers on hand and a large order for candy sticks had been received over the week end. Amos picked up a wrench and adjusted the turning-machine on his bench while everybody stood around waiting to hear about Esther.

"The cider gave out too quick, I guess," he said. "I thought for a while she was going to say she would get married, but I guess there wasn't enough cider."

"What you should do, Amos," another of the men said seriously, "is to take two jugs of cider with you next Sunday night. When I was courting my wife, I couldn't do a thing with her until I began taking two jugs with me when I went to see her. You should take two jugs of cider, Amos. That will make things happen, all right."

"I'll have to do something about it," Amos said. "My cider barrel is getting low. I've only got five or six gallons left in it now. And winter is coming on, too. If Esther don't marry me pretty soon, I'll have to buy some new blankets."

"You take Esther two jugs next Sunday night, Amos, and if all that cider won't make something happen for you I'll give you five gallons out of my own barrel."

Amos pulled the belt on his machine and went to work turning candy sticks. He was getting uneasy now that winter was coming. He had planned to marry Esther before it began to be cold at night so he would not have to buy any new blankets. His sister had taken all his quilts when she was married that past spring and now he could not get them away from her. Esther had a lot of quilts and if he could marry her they would use hers that winter. Everything would work out just fine if Esther would only say she would marry him. He would live in Esther's house because it was a mile closer to the skewer-mill than his own, and he would not have to walk so far when he went to work.

By the end of the week Amos was desperate. Since Tuesday there had been a heavy frost every night and the only bed covering he had was the old yellow quilt his sister said she would not have. It would have been a foolish waste of money to go to the store and buy two or three sets of blankets, considering the fact that Esther had dozens and dozens of quilts which they would use if she would only marry him before winter and cold weather came.

Early Sunday evening Amos filled two jugs with his last-year's cider and took them with him to see Esther. When he got there, he wanted Esther to begin drinking with him right away. Esther liked cider, especially when it was a year old, and they drank one jug empty before nine o'clock. Amos had not said a word the whole evening about marrying. He figured that it would be better to wait and talk about that when they started on the second jug.

Esther took a good stiff drink from the new jug and danced a few steps before she sat down again.

"This is good cider, Esther," he said preliminarily.

Esther put her hand over her mouth and swallowed two or three times in quick succession.

"You always have good apple juice, Amos," she smiled at him.

Amos rubbed the palms of his hands nervously over his knees, trying to erase the indigo stain of white birch from the skin. He liked to hear Esther praise his cider.

"The boys at the skewer mill promised to give me a whole barrel of cider when I get married," he lied shamelessly.

He glanced at Esther, hoping to find on her face some sign of the effect the carefully planned story should have had on her. Esther looked blankly at the ceiling, as though she did not know why Amos came to see her every Sunday night with his last-year's cider. Amos poured her another glass from the jug.

While she drank the cider, Amos studied the pile of thick quilts and comforters on the foot of her bed in the next room. Seeing Esther's quilts made him more than ever determined to marry her right away. He could see no sense in his coming to her house every week and bringing her his good cider when, if she would marry him, he could be there every night and have all his cider for himself.

And this time, when he brought two jugs, he knew he had the best opportunity of his life. If Esther drank both jugs of cider and still continued to say that she would not marry him, then there would be no use in wasting any more of his cider on her.

Esther finished the glass and gave it to Amos. He put it on the table and turned around just in time to see Esther lifting her skirt near the hem with a thumb and forefinger and carelessly throwing one leg across the other. He knew at once that the second jug was doing all it should do, because Esther had never crossed her legs so gaily during all the other times he had been bringing one jug. He poured her another glass, and rubbed his birch-stained hands together enthusiastically while she was placing the glass to her lips.

"Esther, I've got more than seven thousand dollars in the savings bank," he began. That was the first thing he said each time he asked her to marry him. "My farm and buildings are worth three thousand dollars and I haven't any debts."

Esther lifted her eyelids and looked at Amos. Her eyes were sleepy-looking but she was wide awake.

"I don't want to be married," she said, beginning to giggle a little for the first time. "I want to stay like I am, Amos."

This was the only time he had ever been with Esther when she had a cider-giggle. He watched her anxiously, startled by her prompt refusal.

"But blankets—" he cried out nervously.

"What blankets?" she asked, raising herself on her elbow and guiding herself across the room. The cider-giggle was getting beyond her control.

"Winter is coming—cold weather!" he shouted desperately.

"What about cold weather, Amos?" she giggled again.

"I was just thinking about blankets," he said hopelessly.

Esther went to the door and looked into her bedroom. Amos came and stood behind her.

"I haven't any blankets, Amos," she giggled, "but I've got a lot of quilts and comforters."

Amos looked hopefully over her shoulder at the pile of quilts and comforters on her bed.

"I want us to get married, Esther," he said thickly. "How would you like to marry me?"

Esther pushed Amos roughly aside and went back into the room. She was giggling so foolishly she could not speak.

Amos went to the table and poured her another glass of cider. While she drank it he glanced at the almost empty jug, realizing that he would have to hurry Esther if he was to get her consent before all the cider was gone.

When she handed him the empty glass, Amos put it on the table and caught her hands before she could jerk away from him. Then, holding her arms so she could not push him away, he kissed her. Knowing that she would try to push him away when he did that, he put his arms around her and held her while he talked to her about marrying him.

"I want that you should marry me, Esther," he struggled with her strength, "because if you don't I'll have to buy some blankets for the winter."

Esther pushed and scratched but Amos held her all the tighter. He could see that she was mad, but at the same time she could not keep from giggling just as sillily as ever. Amos poured out the last glass of cider for her while he held her with one hand.

Still holding her with one hand he tried to force the cider into her mouth. Suddenly she shoved Amos with all her might, and both of them fell on the floor. Amos was not hurt, but Esther struck her knee on a chair and cut a deep gash in her leg. The blood ran through her stocking and dripped on the floor beside them.

"Esther, I want that you should marry me right away before—" he began a second time.

Before he could say another word Esther had grabbed the nearest cider jug and hit him over the head with it. The blow was glancing, and the jug only stunned him for a moment. She had swung the jug so hard, though, that it was jerked from her fingers and crashed against the cast-iron stove. She immediately reached for the second jug, but Amos was too quick for her. He ran to the door and out into the yard before she could throw it at him. When he got to the road, she had reached the door, and with all her strength she hurled the stone jug at Amos. Amos dodged out of the way and ran down the road toward his house.

When he got home, there was nothing to do but drink some cider and go to bed. He was so mad about the way things turned out that he drank almost three times as much cider as he usually did when he went down into his cellar.

By the time Amos started to the skewer mill the next morning he was resigned to his inability to marry Esther. His only regrets now were that he had wasted all his last-year's hard cider on her and would have to buy two or three sets of blankets, after all.

When he got to the mill, a stranger was standing in the doorway. The man made no effort to move when Amos tried to enter.

"Your name is Amos Williams, isn't it?" he asked.

"Amos Williams it's been ever since I can remember," Amos said sourly, trying to get into the mill.

"Well, you will have to come along with me to the county jail," he said, holding out a folded paper.

"What for?" Amos demanded.

"The paper says 'Assault on the Person of Esther Tibbetts.'"

The man who had promised Amos five gallons of cider the week before, when he suggested that Amos take Esther two jugs, came up the road to the mill door. He asked Amos what the trouble was and Amos told him.

"You got me into all this trouble," Amos swore at him. "You said two jugs would make her marry me, and now she's had me arrested for assault."

"Well, it's too bad you've got to go to jail and lose all that time here at the mill, Amos, but it was all your own fault."

"How was it my fault?"

"It's like this, Amos. There are three kinds of women. There are one-jug, two-jug, and three-jug women. You should have told me at the start that Esther was a three-jug woman. If you had done that, I could have told you to take her three jugs of cider instead of only two."

(First published in *This Quarter*)

Midsummer Passion

MIDDLE-AGED Ben Hackett and the team, Cromwell and Julia, were haying to beat hell when the thunderstorm broke on the east ridge. Ben knew it was coming, because all morning the thunder had rumbled up and down the river; but Ben did not want the storm to break until he had drawn the hay to the barn, and when the deluge was over he felt like killing somebody. Ben had been sweating-hot before the storm came and now he was mad. The rainwater cooled him and took some of the anger out of him. But he still swore at the thunderstorm for ruining his first-crop hay.

The storm had passed over and the sun came out again as hot as ever, but just the same he had to throw off the load of hay he had on the rack. Swearing and sweating. Ben unloaded and drove Cromwell and Julia across the hayfield into the lane. Ben filled his pipe and climbed up on the hayrack. Clucking like a hen with a new brood of chicks, Ben urged the team toward the highroad half a mile away. The sun was out, and it was hot again. But the hay was wet. Damn it all!

"If God knows all about making hay in this kind of weather, He ought to come down and get it in Himself, by Jesus," Ben told Cromwell and Julia.

Cromwell swished his horsehairs in Ben's face and Julia snorted some thistledown out of her nose.

Glaring up at the sky and sucking on his pipe, Ben was almost thrown to the ground between the team when Cromwell and Julia suddenly came to a standstill.

"Get along there, Cromwell!" Ben growled at the horse. "What's ailing you, Julia!"

The horse and mare moved a pace and again halted. Ben stood up, balancing himself on the hayrack.

"By Jesus!" he grunted, staring down the lane.

An automobile, unoccupied, blocked the narrow trail.

Ben climbed down, swearing to Cromwell and Julia. He paced around the automobile uncertainly, inspecting it belligerently. No person was in sight.

"Damn a man who'd stand his auto ablocking the lane,"
Ben grumbled, glancing at Cromwell and Julia for confirma-
tion. "I guess I'll have to push the thing out of the way myself.
By Jesus, if whoever left it here was here I'd tell him something he wouldn't forget soon. Not by a damn sight!"

But Ben could not move the car. It creaked and groaned
when he pushed and when he pulled, but it would not budge
a single inch. Knocking out his pipe and wiping his face,
Ben led the team around the automobile through the undergrowth. When he got back into the lane, he stopped the horses
and went back to the car. He glanced inside for the first time.

"By Jesus!" Ben exclaimed high-pitched.

Hastily glancing up the lane and down, he opened the door
and pulled out a pair of silk stockings.

Ben was too excited to say anything, or to do anything.
Still fingering the stockings he presently looked in the driver's
seat, and there, to his surprise, under the steering wheel sat
a gallon jug of cider almost empty. Ben immediately pulled
the cork to smell if it was hard. It was. He jabbed his thumb
through the handle hole and threw the jug in his elbow. It
was hard all right, but there was very little of it left.

"Cromwell," he announced, smacking his lips with satisfaction, "that's pretty good cider, for a windfall."

As he carefully replaced the jug under the steering wheel,
Ben saw a garment lying on the floor. It was entangled with
the do-funnys that operated the car. Carefully he pulled the
garment out and held it before his eyes. He could not figure
out just what it was, yet he knew it was something women
wore. It was pinkish and it was silkish and it looked pretty.
And there was very little of it. Ben stared openmouthed and
wild-eyed.

"By Jesus, Cromwell," Ben licked his mustache lip, "what
do you know about that!"

Cromwell and the mare nibbled at the road grass, uncon-
cerned.

Ben fingered the drawers a little more intimately. He turned
them slowly around.

"It's a female thing, all right, Cromwell." Ben danced excitedly. "It's a female thing, all right!"

Holding the garment high in his hands, Ben climbed on the
hayrack and drove down the lane into the highroad. The
garment was nice and soft in his hands, and it smelled good,
too.

He rode down the road thinking about the drawers. They
filled him with the urge to do something out of the ordinary
but he didn't know what he could do. When he reached Fred
Williams's place, he drew up the team. Fred's wife was stoop-

ing over in the garden. Ben pushed the garment carefully into his pants pocket.

"Nice day, today, Mrs. Williams," he called airily, his voice breaking foolishly. "Where's Fred?"

"Fred's gone to the village," she answered, looking around bent over her knees.

Ben's hand stole into the pocket feeling the garment. Even in his pocket out of sight it made him feel different today.

Hitching the team to the horse rack, Ben went into the garden with Fred's wife. She was picking peas for supper. She wasn't bad-looking. Not by a damn sight!

Watching her while she pulled the peas from the vines, Ben strode around her in a circle, putting his hand into the pocket where the pink drawers were. The woman did not say much, and Ben said nothing at all. He was getting so now he could feel the drawers without even touching them with his hands.

Suddenly Ben threw his arms around her waist and squeezed her excitedly.

"Help!" she yelled at the top of her voice, diving forward. "Help!" she cried. "Help!"

When she dived forward, both of them fell on the pea vines, tearing them and uprooting them. She yelled and scratched, but Ben was determined, and he held her with all his strength. They rolled in the dirt and on the pea vines. Ben jerked out the pink drawers. They rolled over and over tearing up more of the pea vines. Ben struggled to pull the drawers over her feet. He got one foot through one drawers leg. They rolled down to the end of the row tearing up all the pea vines. Fred would raise hell about his pea vines when he came home.

Ben was panting and blowing like a horse at a horse-pulling, but he could not get the other drawers leg over the other foot. They rolled up against the fence and Fred's wife stopped struggling. She sat up, looking down at Ben in the dirt. Both of them were brown with the garden soil and Ben was sweating through his mask.

"Ben Hackett, what are you trying to do?" she sputtered through the earth on her face.

Ben released her legs and looked up at her. He did not say anything. She stood up, putting her foot in the empty leg, pulling the drawers up under her skirt. That was where he had been trying all this time to put them. Damn it!

Ben got up dusting his clothes. He followed her across the garden into the front yard.

"Wait here," she told him.

When she returned, she carried a basin of water and a towel.

"Wash the dirt off your face and hands, Ben Hackett," she directed, standing over him, wearing the pink drawers.

Ben did as he was told to do. When he finished washing his face and hands, he slapped some of the dirt out of his pants.

"It was mighty nice of you to bring the towel and water," he thanked her.

"You are halfway fit to go home now," she approved, pinning up her hair.

"Good day," Ben said.

"Good day," said Fred's wife.

(First published in *Transition*)

A Day's Wooing

WHEN Tuffy Webb woke up that morning, the first thing he saw was his new straw hat hanging on the back of the cane-bottomed chair beside the bed. The red, orange, and blue silk band around the hat looked as bright in the sunshine as the decorations in the store windows in town on circus day. He reached out and felt the rough crown and brim, running his fingers over the stiff brown straw. He would never have to step aside for anybody, in a hat like that. That was all he needed, to get the world by the tail.

"Maybe that won't knock a few eyes out!" Tuffy said, throwing off the covers and leaping to the floor. "They'll all be cross-eyed from looking at it."

He placed the hat carefully on his head and walked over to the mirror on the wall. The new straw hat looked even finer Sunday morning than it had Saturday night, when he tried it on in the store.

"When Nancy sees this lid, she'll come tumbling," Tuffy said, stepping back and tilting the hat a little on one side of his head and winking at himself under the brim.

He walked past the mirror several times, free and easy in his loose knee-length nightshirt, turning his eyes to see himself in passing. It was easy to get up courage in a hat like that.

"I could have all the girls after me now if I wanted them," he said to himself.

Tuffy got dressed in a hurry and made a fire in the cook-stove. He pulled the hat down carefully over his head so it would not fall off and hit the floor while he was cooking breakfast.

During all the time he was in the kitchen he kept thinking to himself that he would not have to keep bach much longer after that, not after Nancy saw him in his new hat. She would be tickled to death to marry him now, the first time she saw him walking up to her house with the straw sailor tilted over one ear, sort of like a cock's comb that always looked like it was going to fall off but never did.

After breakfast Tuffy had to drive the cows to the pasture on the other side of the creek because it had become time for them to have a change of feed, and the Johnson grass over there was ready for grazing.

He started off with his hat on his head, but he got to thinking about it and finally decided he ought to leave it at the house. Sometimes a yearling took to heels and bolted off into a thicket, and he did not like to think of taking any chances of having the hat fall off into the briers and mud, and maybe being trampled by the cows. Now that he was thinking about it, he remembered seeing a cow chew up a straw hat once and swallow it.

He hurried back to the house and hung the hat on the cane-bottomed chair beside the bed.

Tuffy got back from the pasture at about eleven o'clock, and he changed his clothes right away, putting on his coat and the hat. After that he still had almost an hour to wait before he could leave home, because he did not wish to get to the Millers' while they were eating dinner. If he did that, one of the Millers would be certain to say that he had got there then to get something to eat.

He walked out on the porch and leaned against the railing for a while. The sun was almost directly overhead, and there was not a cloud in sight. He knew he could not have chosen a finer day to go calling on Nancy in a new straw hat. There was not a single drop of rain in the whole sky above.

"This would be a dandy time to speak to Nancy about us getting married," he said, going out into the yard and walking first around the chinaberry tree and then around the willow. "All I'd have to do would be to ask her, and I know already what Nancy'll say. She's just as willing as I am, and she knows it. It wouldn't do her any good to try to show otherwise."

Tuffy leaned against the willow, picking at the bark with his thumbnail.

"If I go right up to her and say, 'Nancy, how about me and you hitching up together?' she'll say, 'When, Tuffy?' and I'll say, 'The sooner the better suits me.' Then she'll say, 'Nothing would please me more.' That's all there will be to it, and it'll be all planned and settled. All I'll have to do is get a preacher to marry us, and then me and Nancy'll be married for a fare-you-well. Getting married wouldn't take long, maybe no longer than tomorrow noon. We'll probably start right in tomorrow some time. That's none too soon for me, and I know it won't be none too soon for Nancy."

Tuffy went over and sat on the woodpile.

"I'll go over there to old Berry Miller's and walk right up to where they're all sitting on the porch and lose no time about it. Berry'll probably want to know what I came for, all dressed up like this in a coat and a new straw hat, and I'll soon tell him, too. 'Well,' I'll say, 'I came to marry Nancy, Berry. How do you like that? Me and her are getting married right off.' He won't scare me a bit, no matter what he says. He might have some little fault to begin with, but there's no objection I know about that's good enough to stop me from going ahead and getting married to Nancy. I'll walk right up to where she's sitting on the porch and put my arm around her and show those Millers I mean business and don't mean maybe."

Tuffy picked up a piece of stovewood and began tearing splinters out of it with his fingernails. He piled the splinters in a little stack between his feet.

"If old Berry Miller makes any show of getting his bristles up, I'll reach right down and kiss her in front of all the Millers, and then pick her up and walk off with her without so much as looking back at them even once. That'll show Berry that when I set out to get married, I don't let nothing in the whole wide world stop me. Those Millers can't put the scare into me."

He hurled the stick of stovewood across the yard. It narrowly missed hitting one of his hens asleep in a dust hole under the chinaberry tree. The hen woke up and ran squawking for her life. The other chickens got scared and followed her under the house.

Tuffy took out his handkerchief and wiped the sweatband of his new straw hat. It was a scorching hot day, especially out in the sun at midday, and the heavy wool coat had never felt so tight before.

"If I had thought to get the license yesterday, me and Nancy could have got married today," he said disgustedly, kicking at the ground. "Now, why didn't I think about that yesterday? I'll have to wait till tomorrow before I can go to the courthouse now."

He got up and walked to his car. He had not intended getting inside, because it was still about half an hour too soon for him to leave, but he could not wait any longer. He would have to drive around ten or fifteen miles an hour, and maybe stop at the creek and wait awhile, but he was too anxious to be on his way to Nancy's house to wait around home any longer. He started the car and drove off, pushing the new straw hat tightly on his head so the wind could not blow it off.

It was half past twelve o'clock when Tuffy Webb drove up to the Berry Miller place and stopped his car in the shade. He had not got there a minute too soon, because the Millers were at that minute coming out on the porch from the dinner table. It was getting hotter all the time, and Tuffy sat in his car for several minutes trying to cool off before getting out and going up to the house.

Before looking at the Millers on the porch, he took out his handkerchief and tried to wipe off some of the perspiration that trickled down his cheeks and down the back of his neck. When he finished, he took off his hat and wiped the sweatband good and dry.

Old man Berry Miller waved at him from the porch. One of the Miller boys rose up on his elbow from the porch floor to see what Tuffy was doing.

Tuffy got out and walked stiff and erect across the yard to the house. He was uncomfortable all over, and it made his face flush red when he realized what he was doing there. The Millers had a way of staring at him that made him forget what he was doing sometimes.

"Come on in on the porch out of that hot sun and have a slice of watermelon fresh out of the bottom of the well," Berry Miller said. "There's not much left, but what there is, you're welcome to it. It's only the leavings."

Berry brushed away the flies with his hat. They swarmed around the porch for a few moments and then settled back again on the rinds and watermelon seed scattered about on the floor.

"Well, howdy, folks," Tuffy said.

One of the boys waved his arm at Tuffy, and both the girls giggled. Berry's wife rocked back and forth in her chair without saying a thing. A watermelon seed had stuck to her chin and was drying there. Tuffy wondered why nobody told her to brush it off.

"Mighty hot day today," he said, flushing red again when his eyes swept the porch and saw the two girls.

Their white dresses were starched so stiffly that they looked as if corset stays had been sewn into the cloth.

"Sort of," Berry said. "Can't complain, though. Heat's due us."

The boys on the other end of the porch sat up.

"What are you all dressed up for, Tuffy?" Henry asked him. "Going somewhere?"

Tuffy's eyes dropped and he dug the toe of his shoe into the sandy yard.

Nancy, the oldest girl, giggled again.

Tuffy looked up quickly, hoping to see her plain.

"You're dressed up fit to kill, ain't you, Tuffy?" Henry said.

Berry kicked a piece of watermelon rind off the porch.

"That's a mighty fine-looking straw hat you've got on there, Tuffy," Berry said. "You must have bought that at a big store somewhere, and paid a lot of money for it, in the bargain. A pretty all-colored band like that don't come on everyday hats."

Tuffy nodded his head.

The other Miller boy on the porch, Clyde, scraped up a handful of watermelon seed and began shooting them between his fingers. Presently one of the seed hit Tuffy in the face, making him jump as if somebody had taken a slingshot and hit him in the eye with a hickory nut. Tuffy would not look at Clyde, because he and Clyde never had got along any too well. They had had several fist fights already that summer.

Berry's wife moved to and fro in her rocker, looking disinterestedly at Tuffy. The watermelon seed had dried on her chin and was stuck there for good. He glanced at her, and their eyes met. Whenever she looked at him, it always made Tuffy feel as if she were looking at some object directly behind him. She had never spoken a word to him in all her life.

Nancy smoothed out the skirt of her starched white dress, bending the stiff hem down over her knees. He could still see where her stockings ended on her legs. Nancy's sister looked at Tuffy and giggled.

"I just thought I'd drop by," Tuffy said at last. "I didn't have much else to do today."

"Had any watermelon today so far?" Berry asked him.

"No," Tuffy said.

"If you don't mind eating the leavings," Berry said, waving his hand at the rind-strewn porch, "you're welcome to have some."

Tuffy looked to see what Nancy was doing, but he could not see the expression on her face when his eyes were watching the black and white garter-line on her legs. She bent the starched hem over again, but when she leaned back, it straightened out again and her legs above the stocking tops were as bold as ever.

"Ain't you staying?" Berry asked.

"I don't care if I do," Tuffy said. "I was just riding around, and I thought I'd stop by."

Clyde picked up a piece of rind and threw it at the tree in the yard.

"It's been quite a while since I last saw you all dressed up like that," Berry said. "If I remember correctly, the last time was at the baptizing over at the church about a month ago. Wasn't you all dressed up that day, Tuffy?"

Nancy giggled and hid her face against her sister's shoulder. Tuffy blushed again.

"I didn't have this new hat then, though," he said.

"So you didn't!" Berry said. "That is right, aint it? That hat looks so natural on your head that I forgot all about it. But you did have on a coat that day, didn't you?"

Tuffy nodded, digging the toe of his shoe into the yard.

"I wish you had come by a little sooner," Berry said. "It's pretty late now to get any of the good part of the melons. The leavings ain't much to offer a body. But of course, now, if you ain't particular, just go ahead and help yourself."

One of the boys kicked a piece of rind across the porch and it fell into the yard near Tuffy's feet. He looked at it, all covered with sand.

"Where you going, Tuffy?" Henry asked him.

"Nowhere much," Tuffy said.

"How about me and you going off a piece?" Henry said, winking. "There's some easy pickings on Sunday afternoons over beyond Hardpan."

Tuffy glanced at Nancy. There was a peculiar look on her face that made him uneasy. The garter-line on her legs wavered in his sight when she rocked slightly in her chair. He dropped his eyes to the ground once more.

"I don't reckon I can right now," he told Henry, blushing red all over.

The two girls began whispering to each other. Every once in a while Nancy glanced up at Tuffy, and then she quickly looked the other way.

Tuffy took off his hat and fanned his face with it.

"It's about time to do some thinking about a little fox-hunting, ain't it, Tuffy?" Berry said. "These nights now are beginning to have a little nip in them, along about midnight, and the foxes will be running before you know it. Anyway, it don't hurt none to sort of warm up the hounds. They've been laying around here all summer and have got as lazy as can be. I been thinking lately of going out some night pretty soon and giving them a short run."

Tuffy nodded his head, but he did not say anything.

"I been thinking about making a trade of some kind for a couple more hunters," Berry said. "That Blackie is still a little lame from last year, and that Elsie is weighted down with pups. That Rastus looks like he takes to cold-trailing more and more every year, and I'm a little upset. I don't reckon it would do any harm to make a trade of some kind, if I could find exactly what I'm looking for. I've got a mule that's stove-up pretty bad, and I figure I need hunting dogs a lot more now than I do a blamed stiff-legged mule."

Tuffy glanced up at Nancy, looking as if he were bursting with something to say. He looked at her so desperately that she reached over and bent the starched hem and held it down. He could do no more than swallow hard and flush red all over.

It made his skin feel prickly under the heavy coat when she looked at him.

Clyde sat up and slid down to the edge of the porch. He sat swinging his legs over the edge and looking at Tuffy. Tuffy was becoming more and more uncomfortable. He had been standing for half an hour in the hot sun, and he caught himself swaying on his feet.

"I sure admire that new straw hat of yours, Tuffy," Berry said. "Especially that all-colored pretty band around it."

Tuffy looked desperately at Nancy, and then glanced at the rest of the family. Everyone, except Nancy, stared right back at him. Nancy hung her head when their eyes met.

Henry crossed the yard between him and the house, taking something out of his pocket. He began pulling on it, making it snap like elastic. When he stopped in front of Tuffy, Tuffy looked to see what Henry was playing with. It was a girl's garter, bound in pink silk, and tied in a bow with a red rosebud sewn into it. Tuffy jumped as if he had been pricked with a pin.

Tuffy backed off, taking short steps towards his car.

"Not going so soon?" Berry said. "Why, it hardly seems like more than a minute ago when you got here."

Tuffy stopped. Henry had kept up with him, snapping the garter. He put one end against Tuffy's arm, pulled the other end back a foot or two, and turned it loose. Tuffy jumped when the elastic stung him.

"Where you going, Tuffy?" Henry asked him.

Tuffy looked at the porch where Nancy was. She had sat upright in the chair, leaning slightly forward, and stopped rocking. The starched flare of her skirt had straightened out once more, and he was glad she wore yellow garters.

He started backing away again. Henry followed him, springing the elastic rosebud-trimmed garter at him.

"Let's me and you ride over beyond Hardpan, Tuffy," Henry urged. "It won't be no trouble at all to find us a couple of girls, and we can make a lot of headway on a Sunday afternoon. How about it, Tuffy, huh?"

Tuffy backed away faster, shaking his head. When he got to the tree where his car was, he turned around and jumped into the front seat.

Nancy ran into the house. She could be heard crying all the way to the back porch.

When Tuffy got his car started, Berry got up and walked out into the yard. He watched the automobile disappear over the hill, trying to turn his ear away from Henry's cursing.

"I hate to see a man rush off like that," Berry said. "I'd have swore he came here for some purpose to begin with."

He stood with his back to the house while Clyde left the

orch and crossed the field to get some more watermelons
o cool in the bottom of the well.

First published in *Redbook*)

Summer Accident

IT was a hot night, and the heat was singing.

I knew something was going to happen, and I should have
had the sense to stay at home. But that was the trouble. I let
myself be talked into it. I went down to the Square and met
Stumpy and Verne at seven o'clock.

Almost everyone was sitting on his front porch when I
walked down the street, and I was certain I could hear people
saying something about me. "There goes Herbert downtown
again tonight," they were saying. "One of these days those
boys are going to get into trouble so deep they'll never get out
to see daylight again." I walked faster.

When I reached the Square, Stumpy was sitting on the curb
in front of the bank. He got up and stretched.

"Where's Verne?" he asked. "Isn't he coming like he said
he would?"

"He said he'd be here as soon as he finished eating supper.
I haven't seen him since he went home."

"We'll wait a little while," Stumpy said. "But we can't wait
all night. Weathers will be leaving soon."

"Let's wait until some other time, Stumpy. I don't want to
get into trouble, and I can't help feeling that something's
going to happen. I just know it is. Let's go home."

"You're just like all the rest of them, Herb," Stumpy said.
"If I was troubled with cold feet, I'd cut them off. I wouldn't
go around complaining about them all the time."

I did not know what to say. Stumpy wasn't afraid of anything, as far as I knew, and he had a way of making me feel
ashamed of myself for being afraid. But I couldn't help it
that time. I knew something was going to happen. I could feel
it deep down inside of me.

Just then Verne came up behind us, and all three of us
turned and walked slowly up Maple Street. Verne was the one
who had started it. He had talked Stumpy into helping him,
and Stumpy had made me go along.

"Now is the time to get him," Stumpy said. "There's never
going to be a better time than this."

"I'm ready," Verne said, his lower jaw trembling a little.
"Where is he?"

"Wait a minute," Stumpy said. "Now, here is what we'll do. I'll creep up behind him and grab him around the neck. He's around there in the parking lot beside the bottling plant sitting in his cut-down. Verne, you come right behind me, and as soon as I've got a good grip around his neck, you get his feet and hold on for all you're worth. We'll hold him while Herb cranks up the cut-down and drives out of the lot toward the country. It'll be easy to do, because once I get a good grip around his neck, there's no way for him to get loose. Look, this will keep him quiet after we get him out of town."

He pulled out the revolver he had told us about that afternoon. It was pearl-handled, and it was a five-shooter. The barrel, trigger, and hammer were so rusty that the whole gun looked as if it had been painted red. Stumpy had said the gun was fifteen years old, and it looked as if it had been buried in soggy ground during all that time. The rust dropped off in scales every time Stumpy turned it over in his hands.

Stumpy went ahead, and Verne and I followed at his heels. Before we realized it, Stumpy had grabbed Weathers, and a moment later he was shouting for Verne to grab his feet. I cranked up Weathers's cut-down and turned it around. We were out of the lot and on Maple Street speeding toward the country before much more than a minute had passed. During all the time we were going up Maple Street, Weathers was kicking and grunting. I knew that Stumpy and Verne could hold him if anyone could, but I wished then, more than ever, that we had left Weathers alone. I knew something was going to happen before the night was over.

Two miles out of town, Stumpy shouted at me. The muffler was disconnected and the cut-down was making so much noise that I could not understand a word he said. I slowed down.

"Turn off the road toward Dean's Pond," Stumpy said.

I turned into the lane, and we bumped over the rough road for half a mile. There was not a light to be seen anywhere. When we reached the pond, I shut off the motor and switched off the lights.

"Why don't you stay away from here?" I heard Verne ask Weathers.

"Who's going to make me?" Weathers said.

"I'll make you—won't I, Stumpy?"

"Shut up, Verne," Stumpy said. "You'll make him mad in a minute. Shut up."

"Well, he came up to the house to see my sister, didn't he?"

"You ought not to have a sister, and he wouldn't have bothered her. Look at me. I haven't got a sister. That's why he never steps on my toes."

While they were talking and arguing, I sat down on the

running board, and looked out across the pond. I could hear water spilling over a dam, but I could not see a thing. Every minute I stayed there, I became more certain that something was about to happen. I knew it was.

Stumpy and Verne were the ones who wanted to beat up Weathers. I never had wanted to, but they had argued me into helping them, and I had said I would. They did not like Weathers because he had been coming to town since early in the spring and getting dates with every girl he saw. He would drive into town early in the afternoon and hang around the Square, waiting for a chance to make a date for the night. When a girl walked past him, he would turn and look at her. If he liked the way she looked, he would whistle and catch up with her. Most of the girls had given him dates; a few of them had allowed him to see them several times.

Weathers had been beaten up, kicked out of houses, and shot at more times than anyone could remember, but nothing like that had ever stopped him from coming back to town the next time he wanted a date. Whenever he came to town, he boasted that there was not a girl in the whole county worth looking at, if she hadn't had a date with him. That was what had made Stumpy and Verne so angry. He had a date with Dolly Bennett, and tied her to the sofa in the parlor. Dolly's father shot at him as he was jumping through the window, but he missed hitting Weathers. After that, Stumpy and Verne said they were going to beat him up. Before they did anything about it, though, Weathers went to see Verne's sister. As soon as Stumpy found out about it, he said he had seen enough of Weathers loafing in the Square, wearing his orange-striped shirt and smoking a long brown cigar, while he waited for a girl to come along and take up with her. They had made up their minds after that to catch Weathers and beat him up.

Stumpy and Verne were still arguing, with Weathers butting in whenever he had a chance. I got up and walked around to the other side of the cut-down where I couldn't hear the water.

"Papa said he'd shoot the balls off you, if you ever come back to our house again," Verne told Weathers.

"Hell, I'm not scared of your old man, or anybody's old man," Weathers said. "Bring him out here, if you want to see me hammer him down to size."

"Shut up, Verne," Stumpy said, "or else come up here and hold him a while. I'm tired doing all the holding while you sapsuckers do nothing but talk."

"Hell, you'd be mad, too, if he came to see your sister and threw her down on the floor."

"I haven't got a sister," Stumpy said, "so cut out all the talk and come up here and do your share of holding him for a while."

"He went into the parlor with her and locked the door and threw the key out the window. Then he took out his knife and split her drawers off. When Papa broke in, he had her naked down on the floor. He didn't even get up and run, and Papa had to beat him off of her with a chair."

"I wish you sapsuckers would cut out the arguing," Stumpy said. "I'm going to turn him loose in a minute, if you don't. I don't care what he did to your sister. Shut up."

"What did you bring him out here for, then?"

"I brought him out here to beat up," Stumpy said, "but if you don't shut up, I'm going to turn him loose and let him beat you up. I'm tired of listening to you."

"Papa had to take her to a doctor the next morning," Verne said. "The doctor said Papa chased Weathers off just in time."

"Shut up, you sapsucker," Stumpy said.

Verne called me.

"Reach in Stumpy's pocket and hand me that gun, Herb," he said. "There's no sense in holding Weathers like this when all we have to do is to point Stumpy's gun at him and make him stand still."

I went around to the side where Stumpy was and put my hand on the rusty barrel. It was like picking up a handful of sand; the rust scaled off and I had trouble in holding the barrel.

"No, you don't!" Stumpy said, hitting me with his knee. "I'm the only one who handles that gun. Get away."

"Get it, Herb," Verne said. "Go ahead and get it. Don't pay any attention to Stumpy."

"I wish you sapsuckers would hurry and get tired of playing," Weathers said. "I've got a date for eight o'clock."

"Verne wants the gun, Stumpy," I said, reaching for it again.

"Grab it, Herb," Verne said. "Don't be scared of Stumpy. He can't turn Weathers loose."

I reached around Stumpy's back and caught the barrel again and held on to it with all my might. Stumpy tried to push me away, and he tried to kick me with his knee, but I held the barrel, and slowly I could feel it coming out of his pocket. Just when I thought I had it, Stumpy released Weathers and turned around to take the gun away from me. Verne made a dive for it, too. All three of us twisted and pulled, and fell in a heap on top of Weathers. He yelled when we fell on him.

I never knew how it happened, but the first thing I knew there was an explosion like a stick of dynamite under a tin can. There was a blinding flash of white light, a choking cloud

of black smoke, and a moment later somebody was yelling as
if he was being killed.

All of us were too stunned to move after the shot was fired,
and we lay there on top of Weathers, trying to think what had
happened. I could not feel the gun in my hand, but I was certain I had my fingers gripped around it the moment when the
shot was fired.

"Get up, Herb," Stumpy said. "You're sitting on my foot."

I crawled away from them, and Verne came behind me.
Stumpy got up holding his hand. It was red with blood.

"What happened?" I said.

Verne turned around and looked at Weathers. He jumped
to his feet a second later, clutching at Stumpy.

"Look at him!" Verne shouted. "Stumpy, look at him!"

We ran over to where Weathers lay. There was a stream of
blood coming from his chest, seeping through the orange-
striped shirt that Stumpy hated so much.

Verne got down beside him.

"I didn't do it, Weathers," he said. "Honest to God,
Weathers, I didn't do it! It wasn't me, Weathers. I swear it
wasn't me, Weathers."

"Shut up, Verne," Stumpy said. "Somebody did it."

"I didn't do it—I swear I didn't do it, Weathers!" Verne
said.

"Shut up, Verne," Stumpy said.

I crawled over on my hands and knees to where Weathers
lay. I could see his eyes open for a moment, and then slowly
close.

Stumpy walked around to the other side of him and sat
down on the ground. I could still hear water somewhere, but
I could not see it.

"What happened?" Weathers asked, his eyes still closed.

Nobody answered.

Verne began looking in the grass for the revolver. It was
getting dark, but the white and orange and scarlet red of
Weathers's shirt could be seen at any distance.

"It shot me," Weathers said.

Stumpy sat up on his knees, looking down into Weathers's
face. Stumpy still did not say anything.

Verne found the revolver. He picked it up, holding it at
arm's length, and walked toward the pond. He was gone for
nearly five minutes. When he came back, the revolver was
not in his hands. We sat and stared at each other.

Finally, Stumpy got to his feet. Weathers's eyes had opened
again, but they had remained open this time.

Verne waited beside Weathers until Stumpy and I had
walked to the other side of the cut-down. A little later he came

over to where we were. Without any of us speaking of it, we started walking back to town.

Stumpy started out walking fast.

"We didn't have any business bothering Weathers," Verne said. "He wouldn't be dead if we hadn't brought him out here to beat up. It's our fault. We should have let him alone. He wasn't hurting anybody."

"Shut up," Stumpy said, walking ahead.

"I never heard of him really hurting a girl, anyway. He didn't mean to do any harm to any of them, not even Dolly Bennett or my sister."

"Shut up," Stumpy said, walking faster.

"He would be alive now, if we had minded our own business, instead of trying to butt into his. God knows what will happen to us now. Maybe all of us will be electrocuted. That's what they'll do to us for killing him."

I ran and caught up with Stumpy and tried to keep up with him. He was walking faster and faster.

The perspiration began to run down my face, wetting the collar of my shirt. The heat was singing.

"Weathers wasn't doing anybody any harm," Verne said. "And maybe the girls didn't mind it much, because they always gave him dates when he asked for them. Maybe they even liked him, and wanted him to come around. He had a date with some girl for tonight, too. We ought to have let him alone, because they all acted like they were tickled to have him date them. I never heard any of them say she didn't want Weathers to come to see her. Even my sister never said that, not even after he got her naked in the parlor that time."

"Shut up, Verne," Stumpy said, walking faster. "God damn it, shut up!"

(First published in *Contempo*)

The Walnut Hunt

WHEN Church came up the street after dinner, he had one of his father's oat sacks that was large enough to hold a barrelful of walnuts. I had got a forty-eight-pound flour sack, and was waiting for him at the corner.

"We'll break our backs carrying these big sacks full of walnuts," I said when Church stopped and showed me his. "Why didn't you get a smaller one?"

"Why didn't you?" Church said.

"It's the only one I could find. We don't have to get them

full, anyway. I'd be satisfied with mine half full this time."

"Same here," he said. "Come on. We won't have time to find even a pocketful if we don't hurry. I'll bet somebody's out there in the woods beating us to them right this minute."

We went up to the end of the street and crossed the cotton field behind P. G. Howard's barn bordering the road. The field was about half a mile wide, and beyond the field were the woods where we hunted walnuts every fall. There were lots of walnut trees there, but the woods were so large that sometimes it took a long time to find any.

"I hope we get some whoppers this time, Ray," Church said, running down the cotton rows and jumping over the dried-up stalks. "I'd like to take home enough to fill a wash tub, after they're hulled and dried out."

The year before we brought home three or four loads of them, and after they had been hulled and spread out in the sun to ripen, we put away enough to last us almost all winter.

"How about last year?" I said. "If we get that many again, we ought to sell some and make a little money."

"There's no fun in that," Church said, picking up a rock and throwing it ahead of us as far as he could. "I'd rather eat them, any day."

We crossed one of the lateral drain ditches that ran from the lower end of town to the creek. The ditch was dry at that time of year, because it carried water off only during the winter rains. Down on the sandy bottom of the ditch were a lot of rabbit tracks. From the way it looked, rabbits must have learned to use the ditches when they were going somewhere so they could keep out of sight of the dogs that were always prowling around the cotton and oat fields looking for them.

Church stood on the side of the ditch and kicked some dirt down to the bottom.

"I'll bet rabbits have a hard time getting out of there when they fall in," he said. "I'd hate to be a rabbit."

"They have a better time than we do," I said. "And, anyway, they have steps and paths they can use when they want to get out."

Church kicked some more dirt down into the ditch. Like all the drain ditches that had been dug near town, it was about six feet deep and two or three feet wide at the bottom. It was not hard to jump across any of them, but dogs and rabbits fell in sometimes when they were not watching what they were doing.

Church walked backward and got a running start and jumped across, and I followed him. The woods were not far away then, and we did not stop again until we had got there. The oak trees were so tall that they hid all the other trees from sight, and it was hard work looking for walnut trees. After we had gone almost to the other side of the woods, we found a walnut tree, a big one, too; but somebody had beat us to it, and there was not a single one left on the tree or ground. Whoever it was had taken the crop, and they had even hulled some of them there instead of taking them home first.

"That's what I was afraid of," Church said, throwing down his sack and looking at the hulls on the ground. "But I'd like to know who's been getting walnuts in these woods, just the same."

"They couldn't have found them all," I said. "I'll bet there are a hundred more trees all around us."

I started off, and Church picked up his sack and came behind. It was easy to see that he was angry because we had not come sooner. When we got to the other side of the woods, we had not found a single walnut.

"What do you know about that, Ray?" he said, kicking his father's oat sack around on the ground.

"Let's try the grove on the other side of that field," I told him. "There are bound to be walnuts somewhere."

Church picked up his sack and came along, dragging it on the ground behind him.

We had gone halfway across the field towards the second grove when we came to another drain ditch. We were about to jump over it when I happened to see somebody lying on the sandy bottom a dozen yards away. I caught Church by the sleeve before he could jump, and pulled him back.

"What's the matter, Ray?" Church asked.

"Don't talk so loud," I told him, pulling him back out of sight of the ditch. "There's somebody down in there, Church."

"Where?" he said, looking scared.

I pointed where I had seen somebody.

"What are we going to do?" he asked, trembling a little. "We'd better go back home, hadn't we?"

I got down on my hands and knees, and Church dropped beside me, keeping as close as he could.

"Wait till I see who it is," I told him. "I'm going to crawl up there and find out. It's funny for somebody to be out here lying in the bottom of a ditch like that."

Church would not follow me until I had got almost to the edge of the ditch. Then he came hurrying up behind me.

"Don't let anybody see us, Ray," he said. "They might shoot, or something."

I crawled slowly to the side, holding my breath, and looked down at the bottom. Annie Dunn was lying on her back on the sand, staring straight up into the blue sky. Her clothes were knotted around her, and she was covered with streaks of red clay that looked like fresh blood in the sunshine. She was as still as the silence all around us then, but she looked as if she had been having a terrible fight with somebody down there.

Annie lived around the block from us, and she was always going somewhere or coming back. She never stayed at home much after her father got killed in the flour mill, and sometimes her mother came to our house to ask if any of us had seen Annie.

Church caught my sleeve and tried to pull me away. I shook my head and pulled away from him. After a while he stopped trying to make me leave and came back to where I was at the edge of the ditch. Annie had not moved an inch since we first saw her.

"Hello, Annie," I said.

Some pieces of earth broke loose from the side of the ditch and fell tumbling down upon her. She looked straight into our faces.

"What's the matter, Annie?" Church said, so scared he could hardly be still long enough to look at her.

Annie looked straight at us but did not say a word.

"What are you doing down there in the bottom of that ditch, Annie?" I asked her. "You look like you've been fighting somebody down there, Annie."

Annie closed her eyes, and a moment later her face was as white as a boll of cotton. While we watched her, she doubled up into a knot; then she began kicking the sides of the ditch with her feet. One shoe had come off, and the sole of her stocking on her foot was caked with damp red clay. Church backed off a little, but when Annie screamed, he hurried back to see what the matter was with her.

When she had quieted down again, Church looked at her with his mouth hanging open. "Are you hurt, Annie?" he said. "What's hurting you to make you scream like that? Why won't you say anything, Annie?"

"Why don't you get up from there and go home, Annie?" I asked her.

Annie screamed again, and then she lay still for a while, not making a sound or a motion. Some of the color came back to her face, and she opened her eyes and looked up at us in the same way she had the first time.

"Don't tell anybody, Ray, you and Church," she said weakly. "I don't want anybody to know."

She sounded so much like someone begging you to do something for her that you could not keep from making a silent promise.

"You'd better get up from there, now," Church said.

"I can't," Annie said. "I can't get up, Church."

"Don't you want to?" Church said.

Annie shook her head as much as she could.

"I'm going to tell your mamma, Annie," he said. "If you don't get up from the bottom of that ditch and go home, I'm going straight and tell your mamma."

Annie's face suddenly became white again, and she dug her hands into the sides of the ditch, squeezing the moist red clay until it oozed between her fingers. She began screaming again.

"I'm going home," Church said. "I'm not going to stay here."

I was scared, too, but I did not think we should go away and leave Annie lying there screaming in the bottom of the ditch. I caught Church's sleeve and held him.

Some more dirt broke loose under our hands and fell tumbling down into the ditch upon Annie. She seemed not to notice it at all.

When she stopped screaming and opened her eyes and looked up at us, she did not look like Annie at all. The color had not come back to her cheeks.

"Don't tell anybody, Ray, you and Church," she said weakly. "Will you promise?"

"Why not, Annie?" Church said. "Why don't you want us to tell anybody?"

"I'm having a baby," she said, closing her eyes.

Church leaned so far forward that a whole armful of clay and sand broke loose and fell down into the ditch. Some of it covered one of her legs.

We backed away from the ditch, not getting up from our hands and knees until we were a dozen yards away.

"Let's get away from here," Church said, holding his breath between the words. "I want to go home."

We ran across the field. When we were halfway across, I happened to think about our walnut sacks that we had left at the drain ditch, but I did not say a word to Church about them. When we reached the grove, Church was all out of breath, and we had to stop a minute and lean against some of the trees to get our wind back.

"Do you think Annie's going to die, Ray?" he said, holding his breath between the words and almost choking each time he said one of them.

I did not know what to say. I started running again, and Church began crying because he was behind. By the time we had got to the field behind P. G. Howard's barn, Church was crying so much he could not see where to run. He fell down and tumbled head over heels two or three times, but I did not stop to wait for him to catch up. I kept on running until I got on our front porch.

(First published in *Kneel to the Rising Sun*)

Priming the Well

WHEN I was a little fellow my mother, who was half dam-yankee, used to tell me the story about wooden nutmegs. Even now I can clearly remember her picturing the early peddlers with pouches of painted nutmegs going from farm to farm along the Potomac, selling the spice with all the solemnity of a Methodist circuit rider. That the nutmegs were easily sold and eagerly bought is beside the story; the wonder is that we Southerners were so dumb we did not know the difference.

For some reason I never fully understood, my mother and father, when I was still quite young, went down East and bought a farm in the Kennebec River Valley. Then, when I was eleven years old and my sister nine, they decided that they would sell the farm and move back to Virginia. This was the easiest phase of the decision, because finding somebody who wanted to invest six thousand dollars in a Maine farm was a problem difficult to solve. Even when we did find a purchaser it was by mere accident that the sale was so easily made.

It was a three-months drought that finally brought a buyer to us. And that was chance, too; because droughts for more than three or four weeks were uncommon where we were.

In the late spring, about four months before the drought came to an end—the last rain fell on the first day of June—there were two men who were very anxious to buy our farm. The price either of them was willing to pay at that time, how-ever, was not much more than one half the figure my father had placed on it. Mr. Geroux, a Frenchman, was one of the prospective purchasers, and Elisha Goodwin the other. Mr. Geroux was a native of New Brunswick, but he had lived in Maine thirty years or longer. He had become unusually pros-perous in recent years because of the rising market for seed potatoes, and during all that time he had been acquiring that same cautious mind Elisha Goodwin had inherited from six generations of forefathers. Both of these men, however, realized the value of our farm and both knew it was worth every dollar of six thousand. Neither of them was willing, though, to pay the price asked until he was sure it could not be bought for less. And, as we were told afterwards, Mr. Geroux would have paid almost anything up to ten thousand for the farm, because its improvements, fertility, and location were making it increasingly valuable.

In the month of August, the beginning of the last month of the terrible drought, both Mr. Geroux and Elisha Goodwin came to see my father in regard to purchasing our farm. They did not come together, of course, because each of them wanted to buy it before the other did. At the same time, each of them wanted to close the deal before he was forced to bid against the other. The month of August was the dryest ever to be recorded in the State of Maine. Everyone was certain of that. No rain had fallen since the first of June. The Kennebec River was so low that it was out of the question for the paper mills to float pulpwood, and all of those which were not importing Scandinavian baled pulp had to close down. Even the lakes in the back country were so low that at least fifty per cent of the fish had already died. There was nothing that could be done about the weather, though, and everybody just had to wait for fall to come, bringing rain or snow. Towards the end of the month the water famine was becoming dangerous. The farmers, whose wells had gone dry and who had been drawing water from the river and lakes, were faced with additional danger when the river went completely dry along with most of the lakes. The stock on every farm was dropping dead day and night. There had been no milk in the valley for nearly a month, and the horses, steers, and sheep were hungry and thirsty. The month of August was without exception the most damaging month in the history of the entire Kennebec River Valley.

There was a deep lake on our farm about a mile and a half from the buildings and we were fortunate in having some water for our stock and ourselves. We drew water to the house every day from the lake. Our well had gone dry just as quickly as all the other wells in the valley.

We had been drawing water in three barrels every day from the lake. After six weeks of this my father became tired of having to go to the lake every day. He decided that we would draw twenty-five or thirty barrels one day a week and store it on the farm. This would save us the trouble of having to go every day and give us time to do some other work that was needed. The real problem, however, was where and how to store a week's supply of water. It would have been foolish to buy twenty-five or thirty barrels, or even half that many, when we could use them at the most only two or three weeks longer. Then they would have to be stored away and they would dry and warp until they were valueless. I believe it was my mother who made the suggestion of storing the water in the well. At least, it was she who said it was the only place she knew about. At first my father was of the opinion that the water would run or seep out of the well faster than we could haul it, but he was willing to try it, anyway. The plan worked, much to my mother's joy. All of us—my father, my sister, and myself— congratulated her on making such a wise suggestion.

We went to work at once and all that day we drew water from the lake and poured it into the well. By late afternoon we had transferred about thirty or thirty-five barrels of lake water to the well. That evening all we had to do was lower the bucket and bring up as much water as we needed for the stock. The next it was the same. The water was still there and apparently none had seeped away. It was a great improvement over the way we had been doing before.

It was by accident that Elisha Goodwin stopped at our house that afternoon. His horse had thrown a shoe and he came up to the barn to draw out the nails so the hoof would not be injured. He came up to the barn where we were at the time.

"Well, Mr. Langley," he said to my father, "what are we going to do about this here drought? The whole State of Maine will be ruined if this keeps up another two weeks. There ain't a drop of water on my whole farm."

"The drought is terrible," my father said. "I won't have even a peck of potatoes out of the whole farm to sell this year. But, strange to say, I've got plenty of water in my well."

"What?" Mr. Goodwin shouted unbelievingly. "You say you got water in your well?"

"Plenty of it."

"Well, I don't believe it. Nobody else has got any water in their wells. How comes it you got water in your'n?"

"I water my stock from it twice a day and we have plenty of water for the kitchen besides. It's just as full as it's ever been."

Elisha Goodwin thought we were joking with him about having plenty of water in the well, but he went over to see for himself just the same. My father sent my sister into the house.

Elisha Goodwin picked up three or four pebbles and leaned far over the well looking down into it and trying to see the water. He dropped one of the pebbles into the well and cocked his head sideways, listening for the *ker-plunk* the stone made when it struck the water. He repeated this as long as his pebbles lasted. Then he stood up and looked at us. By watching his face we could tell that he was getting ready to say something important.

He stood up looking at us and scratching the top of his head with three of his fingers while his hatbrim was held tightly by the other two. His chin-whiskers moved up and down faster than I could count.

"How much is it you're asking for this place of your'n?"

My father told him how much we were holding it for.

"You haven't closed a deal with anybody yet, have you?"

"Well, not exactly," my father stated. "Though Mr. Geroux has asked me to give him a two-month option on the place."

"Did you let him have it?" Elisha Goodwin asked hurriedly.

"I'm to let him know tomorrow about it," my father said.

"You come with me to the village," Elisha Goodwin said. "We'll fix up a sale before sundown. I'm going to buy your place. It's the only farm in the whole gol-darned State that's got any well water on it."

"Are you sure you want to buy it, Mr. Goodwin?" my father asked him. "You know the price and terms. It's six thousand dollars cash."

"I don't give a gol-darn what your terms are. I'm going to pay you six thousand dollars in cash for it as soon as you go to the village with me and draw up a bill of sale and turn over the deed. I ain't going to let that good-for-nothing Canuck get his hands on the best farm in the whole gol-darned country. Come on to the village and get it settled right away."

Instead of driving to the village in the buggy, he and my father went in our automobile. He left his horse and buggy hitched at our barn. They were gone about two hours.

When they came back, they shook hands with each other and Elisha Goodwin drove home at a fast clip. He must have forgotten about his horse throwing a shoe.

My mother came out with my sister and asked us what agreement had been made. My father told her all about it. She smiled a little but did not say anything just then. While I carried water to the stock and while my sister went down into the cellar to get some potatoes for supper, they walked across the pasture talking to themselves about something they did not want us to overhear. When they came back, we all went into the kitchen while supper was cooking.

"Well, we are moving back to Virginia next week," my father told us, smiling at my mother. "As soon as we can pack everything we want to take with us we're leaving."

He called my sister to him and lifted her on his knee. He stroked her curls absent-mindedly several times.

"Louise," he smiled at her, "tell me: are you a little Virginia girl, or are you a little New Englander?"

My sister answered without a moment's hesitation.

"I'd rather be a little Virginia lady."

"But your mother is a damyankee—don't you want to be like her?"

He always smiled to himself when he called my mother a damyankee.

Before my sister could reply, my mother came over where we were and lifted her to the floor from my father's lap.

"Louise, you and Tommy run out into the yard and play until supper is ready. Run along, now."

We left the kitchen and went out on the porch. Hardly before we were down the front steps, we heard two people laughing as though they had just seen the funniest thing in the world. We tiptoed to the kitchen window and looked in to see what was so funny. Both my mother and father were standing in the middle of the kitchen floor holding on to each other and laughing so hard I thought they would burst open if they kept it up much longer.

My sister pulled me by the arm and pointed down the river. The sky down there was the blackest I have ever seen. The black clouds were coming closer and closer all the time, like somebody covering you with a big black blanket at night. Away down the valley we could see the tops of trees bending over so far that many of them broke off and fell to the ground.

"Look!" my sister said, clutching my arm. She was trembling all over. "Look!"

Holding each other tightly by the hand, we ran into the house as fast as we could.

(First published in *American Earth*)

The Shooting

SOMEBODY fired a pistol two or three times, and the reports shook dust loose from the canned goods on the grocery shelves and woke up some of the flies in the display windows.

There had not been so much excitement in town since the morning three years before when the bloodhounds tracked the post-office robbers to the vestry of the Methodist church.

The sound of the pistol shots was still ringing in people's ears when two or three dozen men and boys burst out of the stores and poolrooms and made a beeline for the center of the square, where they could see what was going on. When they got there, most of them were in such a hurry to see something happen that they began running around in circles trying to find it.

"I'd swear that was a .45 that went off," somebody said. "But I don't know a single soul in town who owns anything better than a .38."

Just then a man ran out of the building between the bank and the barbershop, and some of the boys followed him through the square until he stopped, with his back against the brick wall, in front of the drugstore. The building he had run out of was a walk-up hotel with a lot of dead flies in the front windows.

Either somebody had telephoned him, or else he had heard the shooting all the way at home, because it was not more than three or four minutes before Toy Shaw, the town marshal, came running down the street with his suspenders hanging loose.

"It's still pretty early in the day for anybody to be practicing with a gun, or even playing with it," somebody said. "I know I never got up after breakfast to do anything like that."

By that time the housewives who had been downtown doing early shopping were slipping out the back doors of the grocery stores and trying to get home before any more shooting took place. A lot of them always wore boudoir caps when they came down to the stores around nine and ten o'clock to do the buying for the day, and it was a peculiar sight to see them tiptoeing through the back alleyways with a bag of groceries in one hand and their skirts held high with the other.

Toy Shaw ran up to the crowd in the square, pulling out his revolver and pinning his marshal's badge on his shirt at the same time.

"What's all this shooting about?" Toy said, puffing and blowing.

Somebody pointed at the man across the square against the drugstore brick wall. Nobody remembered ever seeing him before, but he looked a lot like most of the fruit-tree salesmen who came through the country about that time of the year.

"I don't know who did the shooting," the fellow said, "but that's the one who did the running."

"Has he got a gun on him?" Toy asked.

Nobody knew about that. They kept on shaking their heads.

"Well, then," Toy said, putting his gun away and moving his badge to the other side of his shirt. "There's nothing to be scared about."

Just then, when the crowd started to follow Toy over to the drugstore, a woman ran down the stairs of the walk-up hotel and dashed into the street.

People everywhere scurried into the buildings. When the barbershop was full, they began crowding into the bank and poolroom.

The woman, who really did not look to be more than an eighteen-year-old girl, had a long-barrel, blue-steel revolver.

Somebody nudged Toy Shaw, and Toy stuck his head out the barbershop door and ordered her to disarm herself.

"Pitch that gun on the ground, lady," he said, ducking back inside.

The girl leveled the pistol at the wall of the barbershop and fired it stiff-armed. The pistol recoiled so strongly that she almost toppled over backward. After a while she took her finger out of her ear and looked all around to see if she had hit anybody or anything.

"What's the matter, Toy?" somebody asked him. "You ain't scared to disarm a woman, are you?"

Toy pulled up his suspenders and looped them over his shoulders.

"That's one of these gunwomen," he said, keeping back out of sight.

"Shucks, Toy," somebody said, "she's just a girl. She couldn't hit a barn door."

Toy stuck his head through the door once more, and drew it back after he had taken a hasty look outside.

"It's funny the way a woman thinks about a gun before she does anything else when she gets a little peeved about something or other," he said. "It looks like men would've learned by this time that it don't pay to leave firearms laying around where their womenfolks can lay hold of them."

The man across the square had not moved an inch the whole time. He was as motionless as a telephone pole against the drugstore wall.

"What kind of a marshal are you, anyway, Toy," a fellow said, "if you're scared to disarm a woman?"

"I don't remember that being in the bargain," Toy said. "When I took the oath, it only mentioned armed housebreakers and bankrobbers and other men. It didn't say a single word about these gunwomen."

The girl backed across the street, still searching the doorways and windows with her eyes for the man who had run out of the walk-up hotel. When she got to the center of the square, she turned around for the first time and saw the man backed up against the drugstore wall. He looked too scared even to turn and run out of sight.

"Now's your chance, Toy," somebody said, shoving him to the door. "Go on out there and slip up behind on her, and she'll never know what grabbed her."

Toy tried to stay where he was for the present, but the crowd kept on shoving and pushing, and he found himself outside in the street. Somebody slammed the door shut, and unless he turned tail and ran, there was nothing he could do but go in the direction of the girl.

He tiptoed across the street behind her, trying not to make a sound. With every step he took, she took one in the same direction. For a while he did not gain a single inch on her. When she stopped a moment to pull up her stocking, Toy went a little faster.

Just when he was within twenty feet of her, one of the foxhounds that had been asleep under the water-oak tree woke up, scared to death by all the silence around town, and howled.

The girl was as scared as the hound, or Toy, or anyone else. She turned around to see what had happened.

"Don't shoot, lady," Toy begged. "Don't shoot, whatever you do!"

The girl stuck her finger into her ear and fired in Toy's direction. The bullet zipped through the leaves and branches of the tree over his head.

"I never shot at a lady in all my life," Toy said, his voice shaking and thin. "And, lady, I sure don't want to have to do it now."

He pointed at his marshal's badge on his shirt without taking his eyes from her.

"Lady," he said, "whatever you do do, don't shoot that gun again. It's against the ordinance to fire off a gun inside the town limits."

The girl flared up.

"Shut your mouth!" she cried. "Don't you try to tell me what to do!"

Toy glanced behind him to see if any of the crowd was close enough to have heard what she said to him.

"Lady," he said, "I'm just telling you that you're going to have that thing all shot out in another minute or two, and then what are you going to do?"

The girl turned her back on Toy and ran towards the man in front of the drugstore. Toy went after her, hoping to be able to stop a murder, if he could get there in plenty of time.

The man was too scared to move an inch, even to save his life. He looked as if he would have given anything he had to be able to run, but it was easy to see that he could not move his feet an inch in any direction.

The girl leveled the gun at the trembling man's chest.

"Don't shoot him!" Toy yelled at her. "Shoot up in the air!"

The girl pointed the gun into the sky and fired the remaining bullets. When the hammer clicked on an empty chamber, she dropped the revolver at her feet.

Toy dashed up and grabbed her around the waist. It looked from the other side of the square as if she sort of swooned in Toy's arms. He had to hold her up when she gave way all at once.

The man sank to the pavement, beads of perspiration jumping like popcorn on his forehead.

By that time the crowd began pouring out of the stores and running across the square.

Toy dragged the girl to the wall beside the white-faced man, and set her down gently. She fainted away again with her head on the man's shoulder.

Somebody ran up and slapped Toy on the back. He jumped to his feet.

"I guess we've got a pretty brave marshal, after all," the

fellow said. "There's not many men who would walk right
out in broad daylight and disarm a woman."

"It wasn't anything at all," Toy said, standing back and
letting the crowd have a chance to look at him. "It was just as
simple as falling off a log."

The girl began to regain consciousness. She opened her
eyes and shrank in fright when she saw the crowd of strange
men all around her. She clutched at the fellow beside her,
throwing her arms around his neck and squeezing him tightly
to her. The fellow swallowed hard.

"Are you hurt, honey?" she asked him, turning his face to
hers with her hands.

The fellow swallowed hard again.

Toy pushed his way through the crowd. The men and boys
fell back to let him pass through. When he got past them, he
ran his thumbs under his suspender straps and threw them off
his shoulders.

He knew what was coming, and he knew there was nothing
he could do to stop it. Somebody followed him a few steps to
the corner.

"You'd better hurry home and rest up awhile now, Toy,"
the man said. "I know you must be all wore out after taking a
gun away from that thin little girl."

The crowd broke out in laughter. The men were soon so
noisy he could not hear anything more that was said to him.
He hurried around the corner as fast as he could.

(First published in *Scribner's*)

The Fly in the Coffin

THERE was poor old Dose Muffin, stretched out on the corncrib floor, dead as a frostbitten watermelon vine in November, and a pesky housefly was walking all over his nose.

Let old Dose come alive for just one short minute, maybe
two while about it, and you could bet your last sock-toe dollar
that pesky fly wouldn't live to do his ticklish fiddling and
stropping on any human's nose again.

"You, Woodrow, you!" Aunt Marty said. "Go look in that
corncrib and take a look if any old flies worrying Dose."

"Uncle Dose don't care now," Woodrow said. "Uncle Dose
don't care about nothing no more."

"Dead or alive, Dose cares about flies," Aunt Marty said.

There wasn't enough room in the house to stretch him out
in. The house was full of people, and the people wanted plenty

of room to stand around in. There was that banjo-playing fool in there, Hap Conson, and Hap had to have plenty of space when he was around. There was that jigging high-yellow gal everybody called Goodie, and Goodie took all the room there was when she histed up her dress and started shaking things.

Poor old Dose, dead a day and a night, couldn't say a word. That old fly was crawling all over Dose's nose, stopping every now and then to strop its wings and fiddle its legs. It had been only a day and a night since Dose had chased a fly right through the buzz saw at the lumber mill. That buzz saw cut Dose just about half in two, and he died mad as heck about the fly getting away all well and alive. It wouldn't make any difference to Dose, though, if he could wake up for a minute, maybe two while about it. If he could only do that, he would swat that pesky fly so hard there wouldn't be a flyspeck left.

"You, Woodrow, you!" Aunt Marty said. "Go like I told you do and see if any old flies worrying Dose."

"You wouldn't catch me swatting no flies on no dead man," Woodrow said.

"Don't swat them," Aunt Marty said. "Just shoo them."

Back the other side of the house they were trying to throw a make-shift coffin together for Dose. They were doing a lot of trying and only a little bit of building. Those lazybones out there just didn't have their minds on the work at all. The undertaker wouldn't come and bring one, because he wanted sixty dollars, twenty-five down. Nobody had no sixty dollars, twenty-five down.

Soon as they got the coffin thrown together, they'd go and bury poor old Dose, provided Dose's jumper was all starched and ironed by then. The jumper was out there swinging on the clothesline, waving in the balmy breeze, when the breeze came that way.

Old Dose Muffin, lying tickle-nosed in the corncrib, was dead and wanted burying as soon as those lazy, big-mouthed, good-for-nothing sawmill hands got the grave dug deep enough. He could have been put in the ground a lot sooner if that jabbering preacher and that mush-mouthed black boy would have laid aside their jawboning long enough to finish the coffin they were trying to throw together. Nobody was in a hurry like he was.

That time-wasting old Marty hadn't started washing out his jumper till noon, and if he had had his way, she would have got up and started at the break of day that morning. That banjo-playing fool in the house there, Hap Conson, had got everybody's mind off the burial, and nobody had time to come out to the corncrib and swat that pesky fly on Uncle Dose's nose and say howdy-do. That skirt-histing high-yellow in

there, Goodie, was going to shake the house down, if she didn't
shake off her behind first, and there wasn't a soul in the world
cared enough to stop ogling Goodie long enough to come out
to the crib to see if any pesky flies needed chasing away.

Poor old Dose died a ragged-pants sawmill hand, and he
didn't have no social standing at all. He had given up the
best job he had ever had in his life, when he was porter in the
white-folks' hotel, because he went off chasing a fly to death
just because the fly lit on his barbecue sandwich just when
he was getting ready to bite into it. He chased that fly eight
days all over the country, and the fly wouldn't have stopped
long enough then to let Dose swat him if it hadn't been starved
dizzy. Poor old Dose came back home, but he had to go to
work in the sawmill and lost all his social standing.

"You, Woodrow, you!" Aunt Marty said. "How many times
does it take to tell you go see if any old flies worrying Dose?"

"I'd be scared to death to go moseying around a dead man,
Aunt Marty," Woodrow said. "Uncle Dose can't see no flies
no way."

"Dose don't have to be up and alive like other folks to
know about flies," she said. "Dose sees flies, he dead or alive."

The jumper was dry, the coffin was thrown together, and
the grave was six feet deep. They put the jumper on Dose,
stretched him out in the box, and dropped him into the hole
in the ground.

That jabbering preacher started praying, picking out the
pine splinters he had stuck into his fingers when he and that
mush-mouthed black boy were throwing together the coffin.
That banjo-playing Hap Conson squatted on the ground, picking at the thing like it was red-hot coals in a tin pan. Then
along came that Goodie misbehaving, shaking everything that
wouldn't be still every time she was around a banjo-plucking.

They slammed the lid on Dose, and drove it down to stay
with a couple of rusty twenty-penny nails. They shoveled in
a few spades of gravel and sand.

"Hold on there," Dose said.

Marty was scared enough to run, but she couldn't. She
stayed right there, and before long she opened one eye and
squinted over the edge into the hole.

"What's the matter?" Marty asked, craning her neck to see
down into the ground. "What's the matter with you, Dose?"

The lid flew off, the sand and gravel pelting her in the face,
and Dose jumped to his feet, madder than he had ever been
when he was living his life.

"I could wring your neck, woman!" Dose shouted at her.

"What don't please you, Dose?" Marty asked him. "Did I
get too much starch in the jumper?"

"Woman," Dose said, shaking his fist at her, "you've been

neglecting your duty something bad. You're stowing me away in this here ground with a pesky fly inside this here coffin. Now, you get a hump on yourself and bring me a fly swatter. If you think you can nail me up in a box with a fly inside of it, you've got another think coming."

"I always do like you say, Dose," Marty said. "You just wait till I run get the swatter."

There wasn't a sound made anywhere. The shovelers didn't shovel, Hap didn't pick a note, and Goodie didn't shake a thing.

Marty got the swatter fast as she could, because she knew better than to keep Dose waiting, and handed it down to him. Dose stretched out in the splintery pine box and pulled the lid shut.

Pretty soon they could hear a stirring around down in the box.

"Swish!" the fly swatter sounded.

"Just hold on and wait," Marty said, shaking her head at the shovelers.

"Swish!" it sounded again. "Swat!"

"Dose got him," Marty said, straightening up. "Now shovel, boys, shovel!"

The dirt and sand and gravel flew in, and the grave filled up. The preacher got his praying done, and most of the splinters out of his fingers. That banjo-playing fool, Hap Conson, started acting like he was going to pick that thing to pieces. And that behind-shaking high-yellow, Goodie, histed her dress and went misbehaving all over the place. Maybe by morning Hap and Goodie would be in their stride. Wouldn't be too sure about it, though, because the longer it took to get the pitch up, the longer it would last.

(First published in *Mid-Week Pictorial*)

Slow Death

ALL day we had been sitting in the piano box waiting for the rain to stop. Below us, twenty feet away, the muddy Savannah River oozed past, carrying to the sea the dead pines and rotted mule collars of the uplands.

Overhead, the newly completed Fifth Street Bridge kept us dry. We had stacked piles of brickbats under the corners of the piano box to keep the floor of it dry, and the water that drained from the bridge and red-clay embankment passed under us on its way to the swollen river.

Every once in a while Dave got up on his hands and knees and turned the straw over. It was banana straw, and it was soggy and foul-smelling. There was just enough room for the two of us in the crate, and if the straw was not evenly strewn, it made lumps under our backs and sides that felt as hard as bricks.

Just behind us was a family of four living in a cluster of dry-goods boxes. The boxes had been joined together by means of holes cut in the sides, like those of doghouses, and the mass of packing cases provided four or five rooms. The woman had two Dominique hens. These she kept in the box with her all the time, day and night, stroking their feathers so they would be persuaded to lay eggs for her. There were a dozen or more other crates under the South Carolina side of the bridge; when old men and women, starved and yellow, died in one of them, their bodies were carried down to the river and lowered into the muddy water; when babies were born, people leaned over the railings above and listened to the screams of birth and threw peanut shells over the side.

At dark the rain stopped. The sky looked as if it would not clear before morning, and we knew it would drizzle all night. Dave was restless, and he could not stay in the box any longer.

"Come on, Mike," he said. "Let's get out of here and dig up something to eat somewhere."

I followed him through the red mud up the side of the embankment to the pavement above. We walked through puddles of water, washing the sticky red clay from our feet as we went.

Dave had fifty cents in his pocket and I was determined not to let him buy me anything to eat. He had baled waste paper in a basement factory off and on for two weeks, and when he worked, he made fifty cents a day. He had worked the day before in the basement, and the money had been kept all that time.

When we crossed the river into Georgia, I turned sharply to the right and started running up the levee away from Dave. I had gone fifty yards when he caught me by the sweater and made me stop. Then he took the fist out of his pocket and showed me the fifty-cent piece.

"Don't worry about me, Dave," I told him, catching his wrist and forcing his hand back into his pocket. "I'll get by till tomorrow. I've got the promise of a half-day job, and that ought to be good for a dollar—a half, anyway. Go on and buy yourself a good meal, Dave."

"No," Dave said, jerking the fist out of his pants. "We'll split it."

He pulled me along with him towards the city. We broke through the levee grass and went down the embankment to the pavement. There was a dull orange glow in the low sky ahead of us, and the traffic in the streets sounded like an angry mob fighting for their lives.

We walked along together, splashing through the shallow puddles of rainwater on the pavement, going towards the city. Suddenly Dave stopped squarely in the middle of a sheet of rainwater that had not drained off into the sewers.

"You're young, Mike," he said, catching my sweater and shaking it as a dog does a pillow. "I'm old, but you're young. You can find out what to do, and come back and tell me, and we'll do it."

"What's the matter, Dave?" I asked him. "What are you talking about?"

He waved his arm in an arc that took in most of the world.

"Somewhere there's people who know what to do about being down and out. If you could find out from them, and come back, we could do it."

"It'll take more than two of us, Dave. We'll have to get a lot more on our side first."

"Don't worry about that," he said. "As soon as the people know what to do, and how to do it, we can go up and run hell out of those fat bastards who won't give us our jobs back."

"Maybe it's not time yet, Dave."

"Not time yet! Haven't I been out of my job two years now? How much time do you want? Now's the time, before all of us starve to death and get carried feet first down into that mud-slough of a river."

Before I could say anything, he had turned around and started up the street again. I ran and caught up with him. We splashed through the puddles, dodging the deepest-looking ones.

Dave had had a good job in a fertilizer plant in South Augusta two years before. But they turned him out one day, and they would not take him back. There were seventy men in the crowd that was laid off that time. Dave would never tell me what had happened to the rest of them, but I knew what had happened to Dave. After he had run behind in house rent for six or seven months, the landlord told him to move out. Dave would not do it. He said he was going to stay there until he got back his job in the fertilizer plant in South Augusta. Dave stayed.

Dave stayed in the house for another four months, but long before the end of that time the window sashes and doors of the building had been taken out and carried off by the owner. When winter came, the rain soaked the house until it was as soggy as a log of punkwood. After that, the cold winds of January drove through the dwelling, whistling through the wide slits of the house like a madman breathing through clenched teeth. There was no wood or coal to burn in the fireplaces. There were only two quilts and a blanket for Dave and his wife and three children. Two of the children died before the end of January. In February his wife went. In March there was a special prayer service in one of the churches for Dave and his eleven-year-old daughter, but Dave said all he got out of it was a pair of khaki pants with two holes the size of dinner plates in the seat.

Dave did not know whether his remaining daughter had died, or whether she was being taken care of by charity, or whether she had been taken in to live at a whorehouse. The last time he had seen her was when a policeman came and took her away one morning, leaving Dave sitting in a corner of the windowless house wrapped in the two quilts and a blanket.

We had reached Seventh Street by that time. The Plaza was hidden in fog, and all around it the tall hotels and government buildings rose like century-old tombstones damp and gray.

"Go on and eat, Dave," I told him again. "When you get through, I'll meet you here, and we'll walk back to the river and get in out of the cold."

"I'm not going a step till you come with me."

"But I'm not hungry, Dave. I wouldn't lie to you. I'm not hungry."

"I'm not going to eat, then," he said again.

The night was getting colder and more raw all the time. Some drain water in the gutter at our feet lay in a long snake-like stream, and it looked as if it would freeze before much longer. The wind was coming up, blowing the fog down the river and stinging our backs. A moment later it had shifted its course and was stinging our faces.

"Hurry up, Dave," I begged him. "There's no sense in our standing here and freezing. I'll meet you in half an hour."

Dave caught my sweater and pulled me back. The roar of speeding automobiles and the crashing rumble of motor trucks made such a din in the street that we had to shout to make ourselves heard.

Just as I was about to try again to make him get something to eat for himself, I turned around and saw a black sedan coming around the corner behind us. It was coming fast, more than forty miles an hour, and it was on the inside, cutting the corner.

I pulled at Dave to get him out of the way, because his back was turned to the sedan and he could not see it.

He evidently thought I was trying to make him go to the restaurant alone, because he pulled away from me and stepped backward out of my reach. It was too late then to try to grab him and get him out of the way, and all I could do was to shout at him as loud as I could above the roar in the street. Dave must still have thought I was trying to make him go to the restaurant alone, because he stepped backward again. As he stepped backward the second time, the bumper and right front mudguard on the sedan struck him. He was knocked to the sidewalk like a duckpin.

The man who was driving the big sedan had cut the corner by at least three feet, because the wheels had jumped the curb.

There was a queer-looking expression on Dave's face.

The driver stopped, and he walked back to where we were. By that time people had begun to gather from all directions, and we were surrounded on all sides.

"Are you hurt, Dave?" I asked him, getting down on the sidewalk with him.

The driver had pushed through the crowd, and when I looked up, he was standing at Dave's feet looking down at us, scowling.

"Mike," Dave said, turning his face towards me, "Mike, the half-dollar piece is in my right-hand pants pocket."

His fingers were clutching my hand, and he held me tight, as though he were afraid he would fall.

"Forget the half, Dave," I begged him. "Tell me if you're hurt. If you are, I'll get a doctor right away."

Dave opened his eyes, looking straight up at me. His shoulders moved slightly, and he held me tighter.

"There's nothing wrong with him," the driver of the sedan said, pushing the crowd away from him with his elbows. "There's nothing the matter with him. He's faking."

The man stood erect above us, looking down at Dave. His mouth was partly open, and his lips were rounded, appearing to be swollen. When he spoke, there was no motion on his lips; they looked like a bloodless growth on his mouth, curling outward.

"Mike," Dave said, "I guess I'll have to give up trying to get my job back. It's too late now; I won't have time enough."

The man above us was talking to several persons in the crowd. His lips seemed to be too stiff to move when he spoke; they looked by that time like rolls of unbaked dough.

"He's faking," he said again. "He thinks he can get some money out of me, but I'm wise to the tricks of these bums. There's nothing wrong with him. He's no more hurt than I am."

I could hear people all around us talking. There was one fellow in the crowd behind me talking loud enough for everyone to hear. I could not see his face, but no one could have failed to hear every word he said.

"Sure, he's a bum. That's why they don't take him to the hospital. What in hell do they care about a bum? They wouldn't give him a ride to the hospital, because it might cost them something. They might get the Goddam sedan bloody. They don't want bum's blood on the Goddam pretty upholstery."

I unbuttoned Dave's sweater and put my hand under his shirt, trying to find out if there were any bones broken in his shoulder. Dave had closed his eyes again, but his fingers were still gripped tightly around my wrist.

"He's faking," the driver said. "These bums try all kinds of tricks to get money. There's nothing wrong with him. He's not hurt. He's faking."

The fellow behind us in the crowd was talking again.

"Why don't you take him to the hospital in your sedan, Dough-Face?"

The man looked the crowd over, but he made no reply.

I drew my hand out from under Dave's shirt and saw blood on my fingers. It had not come from his shoulder. It came from the left side of his chest where he had struck the pavement when the sedan knocked him down and rolled over him. I put my hand inside again, feeling for broken bones. Dave's body on that side was soft and wet, and I had felt his heart beating as though I had held it in the palm of my hand.

"How about taking him to the hospital?" I said to the driver looking down at us. "He's been hurt."

"That's the way these bums fake," the driver said, looking from face to face in the crowd. "There's nothing wrong with him. He's not hurt. If he was hurt, he'd yell about it. You don't hear him yelling and groaning, do you? He's just lying there waiting for me to throw him a ten or a twenty. If I did that and drove off, he'd jump up and beat it around the block before I could get out of sight. I know these bums; all they want is money. That one down there is faking just like all the rest of them do. He's no more hurt than I am."

I tried to get up and lift Dave in my arms. We could carry him to the hospital, even if the driver wouldn't take him in the sedan.

The driver was facing the crowd again, trying to convince the people that Dave was attempting to hold him up for some money.

"He's faking!" he said, shouting between his dead lips. "These bums think they can get money by jumping in front of an automobile and then yelping that they're hurt. It's a good lesson for them; maybe they'll stop it now. I'm wise to them; I know when they're faking."

Dave opened his eyes and looked at me.

"Wait a minute, Mike," he said. "Put me down. I want to tell you something."

I laid him on the sidewalk as carefully as I could. He lay there looking up at me, his hand gripping my wrist.

"I just want to make sure you know where the half is, Mike," he said. "The half is in my right-hand pants pocket."

I was about to tell him again that it was all right about the fifty cents, and to forget it, when suddenly his grip on my wrist loosened and his eyes clouded.

During all the time I knelt there holding him in my arms I was trying to think of something to say to Dave before it was too late.

Before I could think of anything to tell him, the driver of the sedan elbowed closer and looked down at us.

"He's faking," he said. "The dirty bum's faking."

He elbowed his way out of the crowd and went toward his sedan. When he reached it, he shouted back over the heads of the people.

"There's nothing wrong with him! He can't put nothing over on me! I'm wise to these dirty bums. All they want is some money, and then they get well quick enough. The dirty bum's faking!"

"Sure, he's a bum," the fellow behind me said, his voice ringing as clear as a bell. "He might get some bum's blood on your Goddam pretty upholstery."

Just then a policeman came running up, attracted by the crowd. He pushed the people away and poked me with his nightstick and asked what the trouble was. Before I could tell him, he struck me on the back with the billy.

"What the hell you guys blocking the street for?"

I told him Dave was dead.

He bent down and saw Dave for the first time.

"That's different," he said.

He turned around and walked half a block to a call box and rang up the city hospital for an ambulance. By the time he had come back, the man who was driving the sedan had left.

"Why didn't you take him to the hospital in the car that knocked him down?" the policeman asked, whirling his nightstick and looking down the street at a woman in front of a show window.

"Hell, can't you see he's a bum?" the fellow behind me said. "We didn't want to get bum's blood all over the Goddam pretty upholstery."

The policeman stopped and looked at the fellow and me. He took a step forward.

"On your way, bums," he said, prodding us with his billy. "Clear out of here before I run you both in."

I ran back beside Dave and stood over him, a foot on each side of his body. The policeman jumped at me, swinging his billy and cursing.

All at once the street lights went black, and when I could

see again, the fellow who had stayed with me was dragging me down the street towards the freightyards. As we passed under the last street light, I looked up into his face gratefully. Neither of us said anything.

(First published in the *New Masses*)

Hamrick's Polar Bear

AFTER the cold winter was over, most people stopped worrying about Hamrick's polar bear. Just as soon as the sun began glowing warm again, and when the buds started swelling, people all over the country, both white and colored, laughed about Hamrick's fooling everybody about the bear. It was no joking matter, though, during that cold winter. It got so cold that a polar bear was about the only animal that could stand being out of doors. It was the coldest winter that had ever struck Georgia.

"Hush!" Doc said. "Folks will believe anything if you tell it to them under the precise right circumstances. I've got a level head myself, and I don't believe every fool story that comes down the road."

Doc Barnard was like nearly everyone else after the winter had passed. Now that warm spring had come, he was telling one and all that he never had believed there was a big white polar bear over at Hamrick's.

"Hush!" he said. "The first time I heard about that bear, I thought then that there was going to be a lot of folks fooled into believing that there was a polar bear over there."

In April, Hamrick said the bear was still there, and if anybody did not want to take his word for it, then all he had to do was go down into the woods below his pasture and look.

Nobody paid much attention to Hamrick, because warm weather had started and people had forgotten how cold it had been the past winter. They were thinking about fox hunting then, and fishing.

During the early part of May, early one morning after breakfast, the bear stepped up on Mrs. Felix Howard's kitchen porch. All the men had left the house to plow on the other side of the farm, and Mrs. Howard was alone. She was sweeping out her kitchen when the polar bear came up on her porch.

She said afterwards that she had a lot on her mind that morning and was busy at the time thinking about some new curtains for her parlor. She swept the litter out of the kitchen, through the door, and out on the porch. She had just about finished when she saw the big white polar bear.

"Scat!" she said, hitting the bear on the head with her broom. "Get off my porch!"

The bear jumped off the porch, cleared the fence, and ran out of sight around the house. He was a big animal, weighing close to three hundred pounds, but he was light on his feet.

Mrs. Howard went back into the kitchen and sat down to think about what she was going to cook for dinner. She had got as far as boiled onions, when it suddenly dawned upon her that the animal she had hit over the head a few minutes before was a bear.

"My heaven above!" she cried. "Hamrick's polar bear!"

She began to scream at the top of her voice while she was running through the house and down the road to her brother's filling station and store. She was breathless when she got there.

"What's the matter with you, Emma?" her brother Ed asked her. "You act like you saw a ghost, or something."

"Hamrick's polar bear, Ed!" she yelled at him. "The creature came up on the kitchen porch while I was sweeping out, and I hit him over the head with the broom."

"Doc Barnard says there ain't no such thing as Hamrick's polar bear, Emma."

"You tell Doc Barnard that bear came to my kitchen door, and he was as big as a year-old calf."

Ed got a shotgun and some shells.

"You stay here at the store, Emma," he said uneasily. "I'm going over to Hamrick's."

On the way to Hamrick's he stopped and asked several Negroes if they had seen or heard anything of the polar bear. They had all heard about the bear, but none of them had seen a trace of the animal.

Walter Hamrick was sitting in his barn doorway shelling seed corn when Ed got there.

"Emma came running down to the store a little while ago, saying a big white bear was on her kitchen porch," Ed told Hamrick. "It looks to me like she's either seeing things, or else that polar bear you've been telling about all winter is running wild."

"He ate a six-months-old calf in the pasture one night last week," Hamrick said. "I didn't say much about it because people still think I'm a liar for ever mentioning that durn bear. I wish you folks would quit calling me a liar, and join up with me to track him down and shoot him."

Ed sat down, watching the shelled corn fall from Hamrick's hand into the bucket.

"I'll be dogged if I don't believe you are right about that

bear, after all," Ed told him. "Emma must have seen him, because I've never seen her so excited before."

"That durn bear is hungry," Hamrick said. "He's been mostly sleeping all winter. But now that it's too warm for him to sleep, he's wanting a lot to eat. He must have smelled chickens or something at your sister's, to make him go up on her porch like that. Next thing, he'll be killing cows and mules to eat, and humans."

Ed got up to go back to the store.

"How do you figure a polar bear ever got to this part of the country?" he asked.

"I've been telling you folks all winter about that durn bear, but everybody thinks I'm a liar. Liar or not, I'd say that durn bear broke away from a circus or carnival last fall, and hid in the woods. He might have even broke loose two or three hundred miles from here, and traveled this far before settling down to sleep out the cold weather."

"I'm going over after the Howards, and maybe Doc Barnard," Ed said. "The thing for us to do is to put on a bear hunt, and stay on it till we track the animal down and shoot him."

He left Hamrick shelling corn in the barn doorway. On the way back to the store, he saw Hunnicut Branch running across his cotton field. When Hunnicut saw Ed, he turned and ran to the road to meet him.

"What's the matter, Hunnicut?" Ed asked him. "See a bear?"

"I sure did, Mr. Ed!" Hunnicut said, panting. "A great big white bear! A great big polar bear like Mr. Walter Hamrick's been talking about all the past winter!"

"Where's the bear now?"

"My old woman hit him over the head with a stick of stove-wood, and that bear lit out for the woods."

"It looks like the womenfolks will be the ones to beat that bear to death, after all."

"I told my old woman she must have lost her mind to go hitting a bear on the head, but she said she was so mad at him for nibbling off her sweet-potato vines in the garden that she didn't stop to be scared of him."

"That bear killed one of Walter Hamrick's young cows last week," Ed said. "He would make short work of a human."

"I reckon he would, Mr. Ed," Hunnicut said, stepping back and looking around behind him. "I sure reckon he would."

Ed hurried down the road to his store and filling station. His sister rushed out and met him in the middle of the road.

"Mrs. Barnard phoned down here just a minute ago and said Hamrick's bear came up to her house. She said she had locked herself in the room and was scared to go out. She said something about her girls, but she was so excited I couldn't make out what she was trying to tell about them."

Ed did not wait to ask any questions. He ran down the road toward Doc Barnard's place. It was about a quarter of a mile away. Once he stopped and broke open his shotgun to make certain both barrels were loaded.

When he got to the Barnards', there was not a person to be seen anywhere. There was no sign of Hamrick's polar bear, either.

He knocked on the door. Presently he heard Mrs. Barnard move some chairs around, and then she raised a window several inches.

"Where's that bear, Mrs. Barnard?"

"The good Lord only knows!" she cried out. "Where are my girls?"

The two Barnard sisters, who were between eighteen and twenty, were living at home that year. They had taught school for a year or two, but the fall before they came back home and were trying to get jobs in town.

"Are Nellie and Gussie in the house, or out?"

"They were in here until that bear came," Mrs. Barnard said. "They were in their room dressing to go to town, when the bear walked in the house. I guess they jumped through the window, they were that scared. Only the good Lord knows what's become of them!"

Ed went out into the yard to look down the road to see if anybody was coming to help look for the bear. He had forgotten to tell Emma to phone for help, but he thought she would keep enough of her senses to know to do that. He could not see anybody, so he walked around the corner of the house, holding the shotgun ready in case he saw Hamrick's polar bear.

The whole back yard was covered with white and red chicken feathers. It looked as if somebody had ripped open two or three feather beds and thrown the feathers into the yard. Hamrick's bear had cleaned out the chicken yard. By the looks of the feathers blowing around the yard, he must have killed and eaten twenty or twenty-five hens and pullets.

Ed found what he believed were bear tracks leading across the cotton field toward a little grove of woods three or four hundred yards away. The ground was soft, and the bear was easy to track.

He had just got to a thicket at the edge of the grove when he heard a rustling of some kind. He threw his gun to his shoulder, ready to take aim the second the bear reared up and showed himself.

"Don't shoot, Mr. Ed!" somebody yelled at him. "Please don't shoot me!"

Ed dropped the gun a little.

"Who's that?"

"It's me, Mr. Ed! It's Hunnicut Branch!"

"What's the matter, Hunnicut?"

"I'm just near about scared to death, Mr. Ed!"

Ed dropped the gun butt on the ground and tried to see Hunnicut through the thicket. The Negro was crouching on his knees in the thicket, holding onto a sapling.

"What scared you?" Ed asked him.

"That great big white polar bear again, Mr. Ed! That polar bear scared me!"

"Where did you see him this time?"

"Right here! Right in here! Here in this thicket, Mr. Ed. I saw him loping across the field from Mr. Barnard's house, and I ran and hid in this here thicket. First thing I know, he was in here too! He wrestled me!"

"Wrestled you!"

"He sure did! That was the wrestlingest bear I ever heard about. He didn't appear to be hungry to eat me at all—just playful, like he had been used to it all his life. He came in here and put those long paws around me and made me wrestle. I didn't want to wrestle a bit, but he made me wrestle!"

"You're a liar, Hunnicut," Ed said. "You're a big black liar."

"I swear I'm telling you the truth, Mr. Ed," Hunnicut pleaded. "You know I wouldn't want to lie to you. That bear made me wrestle with him until he got me down on my back, and then he stood up on his hind legs and held one of his paws up in the air just like the real wrestlers do in town when one of them wins."

Ed pushed through the thicket until he found where the brush had been flattened down and broken off.

"You go get all the Howards, Hunnicut, and tell Miss Emma at the store to phone everybody she can think of to come help track down that bear."

When Ed left the thicket, he followed a log road running down the side of the hill. At the edge of the clearing at the bottom was a field house. There was not a sound anywhere about the field house, but he thought he ought to look inside while he was there. He stuck his head inside, and fell back three or four steps before he could catch his balance.

"What's—who's—?" he stammered.

Presently the older Barnard girl peeped around the corner of the opening. She drew her head back out of sight.

"Is that you, Nellie?" he asked. "Who's that with you?"

Gussie peeped around the corner.

"Did the bear chase you girls in there?"

"He certainly did," Nellie said. "We'd still be running if he hadn't turned around and gone back into the cornfield."

"Well, come on out," Ed told them. "You can go home now.

There's nothing to be scared of. I'm after the bear to shoot him."

"We can't," Nellie said faintly.

"Why can't you?"

"The bear came in the house while we were dressing, and we didn't have time to get our clothes on."

"Well," he told them, "you'll either just have to stay here till somebody brings you something to put on, or else go back without anything. I don't have anything to spare, or I'd share with you."

He turned and walked across the cornfield, looking in the soft earth for tracks of the bear. When he was a hundred feet away, he glanced back over his shoulder at the field house.

"That field house hasn't got a sign of a door on it, Nellie," he called. "And if that polar bear should take it into his head to come back this way, there wouldn't be a thing to keep him from coming inside."

He started out across the cornfield again. Suddenly he heard a commotion behind him. Turning, he saw Nellie and Gussie flying around the corner of the field house, running toward the woods. They did not have a stitch of clothes on, except their stockings. Before he could bat his eyes, they were out of sight in the woods.

Part way across the cornfield, he saw the top of a persimmon tree shaking violently. He crept forward, gun raised, watching the tree. When he was fifteen feet away, he saw Hamrick's polar bear near the top with his forelegs around the tree, shaking it with all his might. The bear acted as if he had climbed up and eaten a green persimmon, and had got so mad he was trying to shake all the green ones down.

Ed leveled his gun, but just then the bear saw him and slid down to the ground a few feet from Ed. Ed found the bead just in time to pull the trigger before the bear could plunge for him.

Nothing happened. Ed pulled the other trigger, and still nothing happened. The bear was on him by then, knocking the gun out of his hands, and locking his forelegs around him. Ed fell to the ground, kicking, yelling, and scratching. The bear was making awful-looking faces, as if he were trying to get the taste of green persimmons out of his mouth.

Just when Ed thought his time had come, he happened to think of Hunnicut. Ed squirmed around on his back, stretching out his arms on the ground. As soon as he did that, the bear rose up on his hind legs and held his right paw high in the air over his head.

The Howards, Walter Hamrick, and a lot of others were running across the cornfield toward him. Ed got to his feet, waving his arms and yelling for them not to shoot. Taking off

his belt, Ed looped it around the bear's neck and led him toward the men.

"All he wanted was somebody to wrestle with him," Ed
said, pushing their guns aside. "He's a trained, wrestling bear.
He won't hurt anybody. If he's fed, and wrestled with once
in a while, he'll be as gentle as you please. I reckon he must
have been starved for something to eat, and a little wrestling."

The crowd stared after Ed, not knowing what to say. Ed
led the way toward the road with his belt looped around the
bear's neck. Hamrick's polar bear trotted along beside him,
as meek as a kitten.

(First published in *Redbook*)

We Are Looking at You, Agnes

THERE must be a way to get it over with. If somebody would
only say something about it, instead of looking at me all the
time as they do, when I am in the room, there wouldn't be
any more days like this one. But no one ever says a word
about it. They sit and look at me all the time—like that—but
not even Papa says anything.

Why don't they go ahead and say it—why don't they do
something—They know it; everyone knows it now. Everybody looks at me like that, but nobody ever says a word
about it.

Papa knows perfectly well that I never went to business
college with the money he sent me. Why doesn't he say so—
He put me on the train and said, Be a good little girl, Agnes.
Just before the train left he gave me fifty dollars, and promised
to send me the same amount monthly through October. When
I reached Birmingham, I went to a beauty-culture school and
learned how to be a manicurist with the money he sent me.
Everybody at home thought I was studying shorthand at the
business college. They thought I was a stenographer in Birmingham, but I was a manicurist in a three-chair barbershop.
It was not long until in some way everybody at home found
out what I was doing. Why didn't they tell me then that they
knew what I was doing— Why didn't they say something
about it—

Ask me, Papa, why I became a manicurist instead of learning to be a stenographer. After you ask me that, I'll tell you
why I'm not even a manicurist in a three-chair barbershop any
longer. But say something about it. Say you know it; say you

know what I do; say anything. Please, for God's sake, don't sit there all day long and look at me like that without saying something about it. Tell me that you have always known it; tell me anything Papa.

How can you know what I am by sitting there and looking at me— How do you know I'm not a stenographer— How am I different from everybody else in town—

How did you know I went to Nashville—ask me why I went there, then. Say it; please, Papa, say it. Say anything, but don't sit there and look at me like that. I can't stand it another minute. Ask me, and I'll tell you the truth about everything.

I found a job in a barbershop in Nashville. It was even a cheaper place than the one in Birmingham, where the men came in and put their hands down the neck of my dress and squeezed me; it was the cheapest place I had ever heard about. After that I went to Memphis, and worked in a barbershop there awhile. I was never a stenographer. I can't read a single line of shorthand. But I know all about manicuring, if I haven't forgotten it by this time.

After that I went to New Orleans. I wished to work in a fine place like the St. Charles. But they looked at me just like you are doing, and said they didn't need anyone else in the barbershop. They looked at me, just like Mamma is looking at me now, but they didn't say anything about it. Nobody ever says anything about it, but everybody looks at me like that.

I had to take a job in a cheap barbershop in New Orleans. It was a cheaper place than the one in Memphis, or the one in Nashville. It was near Canal Street, and the men who came in did the same things the men in Birmingham and Nashville and Memphis had done. The men came in and put their hands down in the neck of my dress and squeezed me, and then they sat down and talked to me about things I had never heard of until I went to Birmingham to be a stenographer. The barbers talked to me, too, but nobody ever said anything about it. They knew it; but no one ever said it. I was soon making more money on the outside after hours than I was at the table. That's why I left and went to live in a cheap hotel. The room clerk looked at me like that, too, but he didn't say anything about it. Nobody ever does. Everyone looks at me like that, but there is never a word said about it.

The whole family knows everything I have done since I left home nearly five years ago to attend business college in Birmingham. They sit and look at me, talking about everything else they can think of, but they never ask me what I'm doing for a living. They never ask me what company I work for in Birmingham, and they never ask me how I like stenography. They never mention it. Why don't you ask me about my boss—

But you know I don't work for a company. You know everything about me, so why don't you say something to me about it—

If somebody would only say it, I could leave now and never have to come back again once a year at Christmas. I've been back once a year for four years now. You've known all about it for four years, so why don't you say something— Say it, and it then will be all over with.

Please ask me how I like my job in Birmingham, Mamma. Mamma, say, Are your hours too long, Agnes—have you a comfortable apartment—is your salary enough for you— Mamma, say something to me. Ask me something; I'll not tell you a lie. I wish you would ask me something so I could tell you the truth. I've got to tell somebody, anybody. Don't sit there and look at me once a year at Christmas like that. Everyone knows I live in a cheap hotel in New Orleans, and that I'm not a stenographer. I'm not even a manicurist any longer. Ask me what I do for a living, Mamma. Don't sit there and look at me once a year at Christmas like that and not say it.

Why is everyone afraid to say it—I'll not be angry; I'll not even cry. I'll be so glad to get it over with that I'll laugh. Please don't be afraid to say it; please stop looking at me like that once a year at Christmas and go ahead and say it.

Elsie sits all day looking at me without ever asking me if she may come to visit me in Birmingham. Why don't you ask me, Elsie—I'll tell you why you can't. Go ahead and ask if you may visit me in Birmingham. I'll tell you why. Because if you went back with me you'd go to New Orleans and the men would come in and put their hands down the collar of your frock. That's why you can't go back to Birmingham with me. But you do believe I live in Birmingham, don't you, Elsie— Ask me about the city, then. Ask me what street I live on. Ask me if my window in Birmingham faces the east or west, north or south. Say something, Elsie; isn't anyone ever going to ask me anything, or say something—

I'm not afraid; I'm a grown woman now. Talk to me as you would to anyone else my age. Just say one little something, and I'll have the chance to tell you. After that I'll leave and never come back again once a year at Christmas.

An hour ago Lewis came home and sat down in the parlor, but he didn't ask me a single question about myself. He didn't say anything. How does he know—Lewis, can you tell just by looking at me, too— Is that how everyone knows— Please tell me what it is about me that everyone knows. And if everyone knows, why doesn't someone say something about it— If you would only say it, Lewis, it would be all over with. I'd never have to come home again once a year at Christmas and be made to sit here and have everyone look at me like that but never saying anything about it.

Lewis sits there on the piano stool looking at me but not saying anything to me. How did you find it out, Lewis— Did someone tell you, or do you just know— I wish you would say something, Lewis. If you will only do that, it will be all over with. I'd never have to come back home once a year at Christmas and sit here like this.

Mamma won't even ask me what my address is. She acts as though I went upstairs and slept a year, coming down once a year at Christmas. Mamma, I've been away from home a whole year. Don't you care to ask me what I've been doing all that time— Go ahead and ask me, Mamma. I'll tell you the truth. I'll tell you the perfect truth about myself.

Doesn't she care about writing to me—doesn't she care about my writing to her— Mamma, don't you want my address so you can write to me and tell me how everyone is— Every time I leave they all stand around and look at me and never ask when I'm coming back again. Why don't they say it— If Mamma would only say it, instead of looking at me like that, it would be better for all of us. I'd never have to come back home again, and they'd never have to sit all day and look at me like that. Why don't you say something to me, Mamma— For God's sake, Mamma, don't sit there all day long and not say a word to me.

Mamma hasn't even asked me if I am thinking of marrying. I heard her ask Elsie that this morning while I was in the bathroom. Elsie is six years younger than me, and Mamma asks Elsie that but she has never asked me since I went to Birmingham five years ago to study shorthand. They don't even tell me about the people I used to know in town. They don't even say good-by when I leave.

If Papa will only say something about it, instead of looking at me like that all the time, I'll get out and stay out forever. I'll never come home again as long as I live, if he will only say it. Why doesn't he ask me if I can find a job for Lewis in Birmingham— Ask me to take him back to Birmingham and look after him to see that he gets along all right from the start, Papa. Ask me that, Papa. Please, Papa, ask me that; ask me something else then, and give me a chance to tell you. Please ask me that and stop sitting there looking at me like that. Don't you care if Lewis has a job— You don't want him to stay here and do nothing, do you— You don't want him to go downtown every night after supper and shoot craps until midnight, do you, Papa— Ask me if I can help Lewis find a job in Birmingham; ask me that, Papa.

I've got to tell somebody about myself. You know already,

but I've got to tell you just the same. I've got to tell you so I can leave home and never have to come back once a year at Christmas. I went to Birmingham and took the money to study manicuring. Then I found a job in a barbershop and sat all day long at a little table behind a screen in the rear. A man came in and put his hand down the neck of my dress and squeezed me until I screamed. I went to Nashville, to Memphis, to New Orleans. Every time I sat down at the manicurist's table in the rear of a barbershop, men came in and put their hands down my dress.

If they would only say something it would be all over with. But they sit and look, and talk about something else all day long. That's the way it's been once a year at Christmas for four or five years. It's been that way ever since I took the money Papa gave me and went to Birmingham to study stenography at the business college. Papa knows I was a manicurist in a barbershop all the time I was there. Papa knows, but Papa won't say it. Say something, Papa. Please say something, so I can tell you what I do for a living. You know it already, and all the others, too; but I can't tell you until you say something about it. Mamma, say something; Lewis, say something. Somebody, anybody, say something.

For God's sake, say something about it this time so I won't have to come back again next year at Christmas and sit here all day in the parlor while you look at me. Everybody looks at me like that, but nobody ever says it. Mamma makes Elsie stay out of my room while I'm dressing, and Papa sends Lewis downtown every hour or two. If they would only say something, it would be all over with. But they sit all day long in the parlor, and look at me without saying it.

After every meal Mamma takes the dishes I have used and scalds them at the sink. Why don't they say it, so I'll never have to come back—

Papa takes a cloth soaked in alcohol and wipes the chair I've been sitting in every time I get up and leave the room. Why don't you go ahead and say it—

Everyone sits in the parlor and looks at me all day long. Elsie and Lewis, Mamma and Papa, they sit on the other side of the room and look at me all day long. Don't they know I'll tell them the truth if they would only ask me— Ask me, Papa; I'll tell you the truth, and never come back again. You can throw away your cloth soaked in alcohol after I've gone. So ask me. For God's sake, say something to me about it.

Once a year at Christmas they sit and look at me, but none of them ever says anything about it. They all sit in the parlor saying to themselves, We are looking at you, Agnes.

(First published in *Clay*)

A Knife to Cut the Corn Bread With

THE sun opened Roy's eyes. Through the curtainless window-opening, a four-by-four hole in the side of the house which could be closed by a wooden door in stormy weather, he could see the sun rolling over the top of the sandhill half a mile away. Behind him in the other room of the house he could hear Nora working over the fire in the kitchen stove.

The early morning air was chill and damp. A dull coating of mist had settled on the room, and even the quilt felt moist and watery.

"You awake yet, Roy?" Nora asked through the door in her soft girlish way.

"Just about," he said, listening for the sound of her bare feet in the room. "The sun looks like it's going to set the whole world on fire today. Look out the window at it."

She came out of the kitchen and stood beside the bed, one hand resting on the rattly iron headpiece, looking pale and fragile in the first clear light of the morning. She did not smile when she looked at him, but he could see in her eyes the sparkle that lingered there yet after two years.

"There's nothing like the sun to stir things awake," he said, looking neither at her nor away from her. "Every time I see it come up like it did just a while ago—like the world on fire—it does something to me inside."

Her eyes wandered away as his had done, seeing only their own stare.

"All the fat-bacon is gone," she said, her lips trembling almost imperceptibly. "I guess we'll just have to eat the bread without it."

Roy did not say anything. His eyes turned back toward the sun, which looked like a house on fire in the middle of the night. The red ball was over the crest of the sandhill, moving swiftly over the tops of the stunted pines and scrub oak.

Nora had left before he knew it. He did not know she had gone until he heard the soft tread of her bare feet in the room behind him.

"Maybe Mr. Gene will let us have a little piece of fat-bacon today," he said, raising his voice for her to hear. "I know it's early in the week, but you've already worked two whole days for him. He ought to let us have a little piece today."

A little while later he heard her go to the well for a bucket of fresh water. When she came back, he waited for her to say something, but there was no reply. She opened the oven door and looked to see how the corn bread was cooking. When she closed the oven door, she went out on the back porch and threw a pan of dishwater into the yard.

In a few minutes she brought in the plate of hot corn bread and the pot of coffee and set them on the floor beside the bed. Then she sat down and poured him a cupful of coffee.

Roy could manage to hold the cup in his hand once Nora had placed it there. Then by bending his head a little he could sip the coffee whenever he wished to. Nora, though, always watched carefully so he would not spill it. He could have fed himself the corn bread, once it was placed in his hand and his hand placed on his chest, because he could bend his head down far enough to bite it with his teeth. But Nora always sat beside him where she could help him, and she could not keep from feeding him with her own hand every once in a while.

Nora had finished eating and was ready to go. She gave him a second cup of coffee while she was there, and then she went to the back porch to comb her hair again.

"How many more days of hoeing have you got up there in Mr. Gene's cotton?" he asked her.

"Maybe three, and there might be four. Two of the colored hands didn't come yesterday. If they don't come today, it will take us four days to finish the piece."

"You'll have six days' pay coming to you then, won't you?" he asked. "When you see Mr. Gene today, tell him we're all out of fat-bacon, Nora. Tell him we'd like to get a little two-pound piece."

She did not say anything for a while. She went into the kitchen, and came back into the room with him.

"Suppose he won't let us have it?" she asked.

"But Mr. Gene ought to do that for us," he told her.

She had left before he realized it. He had closed his eyes for a few moments and, when he opened them again, she was no longer there. He supposed she thought he had dropped off to sleep again, and had gone to hoe cotton without waking him.

He was wide awake. He looked out the window again, but the sun had traveled so far he could not see it any longer.

There was another whole day before him. Until sundown that night he would lie there on his back, unable to move a single limb of his body. He could move his head a little, because his neck was not limp like his arms and legs. But still he could not move out of the position he was in. He had lain there, except for the times when Nora half dragged, half carried him across the room or to the porch, for the past eight months.

It had been eight months, not the eight years it seemed to him, since the bale of cotton had fallen on him when he was helping Mr. Gene and a Negro to store the ginned crop in the shed beside Mr. Gene's barn. Nobody had ever said whose fault it was that the bale had fallen off the truck and had knocked him flat on the ground, landing on top of him. Roy did not know himself. It might have been an accident, or one of the others might have toppled the bale over just to see what he would do. But whatever the reason was, he had not seen the bale fall until it was too late to get out of the way. It struck him, knocking him flat on the ground, and then fell on him, landing on his back. He had not been able to move a hand or foot since. Mr. Gene had said it was just an act of God, and could not be helped. He had said many times since then that there was nothing he could do about it.

For a while Mr. Gene had wanted him to move off the farm. He told Roy there was nothing he could do any more, and that he needed the house for another tenant to take his place. But Roy and Nora had said they had nowhere else to go, and that since Roy had been paralyzed while working for him, they thought he ought to let them stay. Mr. Gene finally agreed to that, but he told Nora she had to work out the rent, and the bread and meat and coffee. She went to work with the Negroes in the fields, doing the best she could with what little strength she had.

Ever since then Roy had tried to get off his back. The doctor came once, soon after he had got hurt, and said that he would never walk again, much less work, and that he probably would be flat on his back for the rest of his life. If it had not been for Nora, Roy did not know what would have happened to him. There was nobody else to take care of him. He and Nora had been married only two years. She was fifteen when they were married and came there to live, and even at seventeen she was not fully grown. She was still a little girl.

Sometimes the Negroes who lived in the tenant houses farther down the road stopped and talked to him, and most of them brought things from their gardens when they had enough to spare. On rainy days, and sometimes on Sundays, Ernest Mann, who lived with his wife and children in the closest Negro tenant house, came by and stopped to talk a while. Ernest would tell him everything that was happening on the farm, and Roy was glad of that, because there were many things that Nora never got a chance to find out about.

Roy did not know what was going to happen to them. He was afraid that Mr. Gene was going to put them off the place almost any day. He knew it would happen sooner or later. When it did happen, he did not know what they would do. It was difficult for Nora to earn a living for both of them, even there; if they moved away, he did not know what she could find to do that would bring in enough to pay house rent and buy food and provide clothes now and then. He worried about that all the time; but he could find no answer that seemed to satisfy him. Several times he had told Nora he wanted her to go away and leave him, because he did not wish her to break herself trying to support him. Nora would never let him talk about it when she could stop him.

There did not seem to be much he could do about things. There was nothing much to live for; all he had was his love for Nora, and hers for him.

After all those months in bed he could determine almost to the quarter-hour the time when Nora would come home. He watched the sun's rays shining through the windows as though they were hands on a clock.

Nora came up on the front steps while he was looking through the door. He had been expecting her any minute. She looked more tired and weary than ever when he saw her. It was painful to see her coming home at night like that. He could not help feeling like somebody who with a whip was forcing a seventeen-year-old girl to go out and do a man's work in the hot sun for ten and eleven hours every day.

"That's you, isn't it, Nora?" he said, trying to see her plainly.

"Yes, Roy," she answered.

Nora came into the room and sat down on the bed beside him. The old stockings that she wore over her hands to protect them from the sun and to keep the wooden hoe handle from blistering her fingers were in shreds. She took them off and dropped them weakly on the floor at her feet.

"Have you been all right today, Roy?" she asked. A smile broke the corners of her mouth, but she was too tired to let it go any farther across her cheeks. "Are you all right now, Roy?"

He smiled at her and turned his face as close to hers as he could. She bent over and placed her mouth against his while he kissed her. Her eyes closed slowly while he kissed her hungrily. She did not move for a long time.

"Did you ask Mr. Gene for the piece of fat-bacon?" he said after a while.

She nodded her head.

"Wouldn't he let you have it?"

She shook her head.

"Why not?"

"He said we'd have to wait until Saturday before he could let us have anything. He said we ought to make out with what he lets us have once a week."

Roy could feel himself trying with all his mind to make his body move. He felt as though he had been strapped hand and foot with iron bands. Every time he strained his hands he felt as though some force were beating him over the head and face with heavy chains.

"I don't care if he did say that; that's not fair at all," he said as loud as he could. "You work for him by the day just like anybody else works, and he ought to give you enough to eat, besides the house rent."

Nora fell across his chest, her arms squeezing him tightly. He could feel her breast jerk with sobs, but she did not make any sounds. He closed his eyes and tried to think of something he could do. It was driving him mad to have to lie there and see her suffer like that.

Presently she stopped crying and sat up.

"I'll go cook some corn bread and make the coffee," she said. She stood up, but her hands were still on his face. "I'll hurry and cook us something to eat, Roy."

He let her go without saying anything more. He could hear her bare feet on the kitchen floor, and he could hear the frail house shake and tremble each time she took a step.

It was dark by then. The twilight had gone quickly, lasting, it seemed, only a few minutes.

Out on the steps he heard somebody knock.

"Who's that?" he called through the door.

"Ernest."

"Come in, Ernest," he said.

Roy could not see the Negro in the dark, except for a moment when he passed through the door. When he got there, he sat down on the floor, his back against the wall.

"What have you been doing today, Ernest?" Roy asked him.

"Chopping cotton like everybody else," Ernest said.

"Be finished soon?"

"Maybe Friday night, in that field, maybe Saturday noon."

"That's what Nora thought, too," Roy said.

Neither of them said anything for a while. Presently Ernest shuffled his feet on the floor, but he did not get up.

"I heard Miss Nora ask the white-boss for a piece of fat-bacon tonight," Ernest said. "I sure felt something or other, too."

"Mr. Gene wouldn't let us have a piece," Roy said. "He told Nora we'd have to wait till Saturday."

"I know it," Ernest said. "I was standing right there and I heard it all. I never felt like doing something more in all my life, either. I sure had a feeling come over me."

Nora could be heard opening the oven door and sliding the bread pan inside.

"I reckon you know all about the way the white-boss goes to church every Sunday morning down at that church on Swift Creek, don't you?" Ernest said.

"I used to see him down there sometimes," Roy said. "Before I got hurt."

"They tell me he's the biggest-talking man in the church now. They say he talks the loudest, prays the loudest, sings the loudest, and makes the most noise when he puts money in the collection box."

"That's the way I remember him," Roy said. "He makes a big to-do about going to church. He always was a religious man. He told me once I was going to hell for sure because I didn't go to church like him."

Ernest shuffled his feet on the floor some more.

"He's all that religious-acting, but he won't give his tenants a little piece of fat-bacon until Saturday afternoon."

Roy lay still for a while. He was hungry, hungry as could be. He could smell the coffee boiling, and he could hear Nora taking the pan of hot corn bread from the oven, but he was so hungry for a little piece of meat he felt as though he would be willing to cut a slice out of his numb legs if he dared. He had never thought of doing that before, and he wondered what would happen to him if he did. He did not believe he would feel any pain. He had not been able to feel anything at all in his arms and legs for eight months. The blood, if there was any, could be stopped by tying a piece of cloth tightly around it. He wondered what Nora would do—he would not be able to eat any himself if she refused to. But he would not have to tell her where it came from. She could think Ernest, or one of the other Negro tenants, gave it to him. His mind felt as if it was racing like a bird in flight. His own hunger pained him, but he knew that Nora's, after she had been working day after day in the fields doing a man's work, was even greater than his. If he could only feed her, he would be able to lie there day after day without straining to do something but feeling as helpless as a man bound hand and foot with iron bands.

In the midst of it, he heard Ernest saying something. He listened with one ear.

"You white-folks call him Mr. Gene," Ernest said, "but do you know what I call that white-boss?"

"What?" Roy said.

"I call him Mr. Jesus. When he's not around to hear me. That's it. Mr. Jesus."

Something struck Roy's mind like a pinprick. He could see Mr. Gene—Mr. Jesus now—standing up in Swift Creek Church and shouting out a prayer. He could see him taking the preacher home to dinner and sitting down to a table piled high with chicken and pork and sweet potatoes and white bread. He could see his own self lying there in bed with a knife slicing off pieces of his leg. He could see—

Nora had come in and sat down on the bed beside him. He felt her hand on his forehead, cool and soft.

"Did you bring a knife to cut the corn bread with?" he asked her.

"No, Roy," she said in surprise. "Do you want me to get a knife?"

He was thinking that he could keep the knife beside him in bed until the next day, when she would be away chopping cotton in the field.

"You never wanted a knife before, Roy. Do you want me to get one now?"

"The sharpest knife," he said. "The sharpest knife to cut the corn bread with."

The moment she took her hand from his forehead he could remember nothing. He closed his eyes and lay there waiting for her to come back. He did not know how he would ever again be able to let her leave him, even for so short a time as a second or two.

(First published in *Direction*)

The Man Who Looked Like Himself

EVERYTHING that Luther Branch touched was wont to crumble in his hands like so much desiccated clay. It had always been like that. He was barely able to keep himself alive, and his clothes were always in rags. But no man could truthfully say that Luther had not tried and was not still trying to make a decent living. He worked harder, day in and day out, than any other man in town.

Several years before, one of his efforts to get ahead had been selling fire insurance to storekeepers and house owners. He failed in that just as he did in everything else he tried to do. It looked as though it were impossible for him to make a dollar.

Once, while he was trying his best to sell insurance, somebody came right out and told Luther that he was not suited to that line of work.

"Luther," the man said, "I can't buy fire protection from you. You don't look like an insurance man."

There was nothing Luther could say, because he knew he did not look like the other men who sold insurance. And, for that matter, he knew he did not look like anyone else in town.

"That's the whole trouble, Luther. You don't look like an insurance man ought to look."

"What do I look like, then?" Luther asked.

"I'll be jumped if I know, Luther. If I could see you in the right job, I'd know for sure; but to save my life I can't figure you out. I suppose you just look like yourself."

Luther Branch did look like himself. Everybody had been saying that since he was a boy, and now that he was past forty, that was all there was to it.

He went into Ben Howard's grocery store early one morning to have a word with Ben. He had been going in there for the past ten or fifteen years to see if Ben had anything to tell him. Ben told him that he ought to start out that same hour and try every kind of known way there was to make money, and to jump from one to the other just as fast as he discovered that he was not suited to a particular line of work.

"It's the only way I know to tell you how to do," Ben said. "I've known you all my life, and we live on the same street, and go to the same church every Sunday, and I want to do everything possible to help you. I've always tried to be your friend. That's why I say the best thing to do is to try everything there is until you find the work you were cut out for. If I could think of a better scheme, I'd certainly tell you about it the minute I heard about it."

"I guess I'll try selling fruit from door to door," Luther said. "It might just as well be that as anything else. It's one line I haven't tried yet. I'll sell fruit."

He went home and got out a pushcart from under the shed and bought it full of oranges and tangerines and grapefruit. He started out trying to sell fruit.

At the first house he stopped he hesitated for a moment at the door before ringing the bell. He had suddenly had a feeling that fruit-selling was not his life-work, either. He started to turn around and go back home without even making an effort to sell anything. He would take the fruit back to the store where he had got it on credit and turn it all back.

"Good morning, Mr. Branch," somebody said.

He was half-way down the steps when he heard the woman speaking to him. He stopped and looked around at her standing in the doorway.

"What have you for sale today, Mr. Branch?" she asked pleasantly.

"Fruit, Mrs. Todd," he answered.

"What kind of fruit? Citrus?"

Luther knew by the tone of Mrs. Todd's voice that she was in the market for citrus fruit. He felt better then, because he was certain he would be able to make a sale. He ran out to the street and brought back several baskets and set them down in front of her on the porch. He stepped back, taking off his hat, and waited for her to select the fruit she wished to buy.

"The oranges are nice-looking," Mrs. Todd said, rolling one in her hand. "And I've been looking for some large juicy grapefruit. How much are they, Mr. Branch?"

"The grapefruit are . . ."

She looked up at Luther then, waiting for him to quote prices to her. Their eyes met for a second, and Luther choked on something in his throat. He coughed and rubbed his neck, but he could not force a single word from his lips after that. Mrs. Todd had averted her eyes, but she looked up into his face again. He knew at that moment that it was hopeless. It had always been like that. It did not matter whether it was insurance, fruit, soap, china doorknobs, or second-hand automobiles that he was attempting to sell. When people stopped and looked at him, the deal was off. He had never yet looked like the thing he was trying to sell.

There was a long period of silence when nothing was said. Mrs. Todd stepped back towards the door, glancing at Luther. Luther picked up the baskets and backed down the steps in the direction of the pushcart in the street. By the time he had reached it, the woman had gone into the house and had closed the door behind her.

On the way home with the empty cart, after having returned the unsold fruit to the store, Luther felt as if there was not any use in his trying to make a living any longer. The best thing for him to do, he told himself, was to apply for admittance to the county poor farm. That was all that was left for him to do. He was ready to quit after almost a lifetime of trying to make a living.

The next day he stopped at Ben Howard's store for a moment. Ben was busy at the time, but he motioned to Luther to wait until he was free. Luther waited until the customer had left the store, and Ben came up to him in front of the candy counter.

"How did you make out selling oranges and grapefruit yesterday, Luther?"

Luther shook his head, allowing it to fall forward until his eyes were staring at the oiled floor at Ben's feet.

He was getting ready to tell Ben that he had decided to go to the county poor farm when Ben slapped him heavily on the shoulder, causing him to forget what he had in mind to say.

"Now, Luther, you might think it was none of my business again, but I'm your friend and I want to help. This is what I've got to say, Luther. I've thought of something else for you to try. Go get yourself a—"

Somebody burst through the door, throwing it wide open, and ran up to the counter where Ben and Luther were standing.

"What's the trouble, Henry?" Ben asked as soon as he could

see who it was. "You ran in here like something was after you behind. What's the matter?"

"I've got to find somebody quick to butcher a hog for me, Ben. One of my five-hundred-pounders broke out of the barn and got run over in the street by a truck just a few minutes ago. I've got to find somebody to butcher it for me right away. The weather's too hot for me to waste any time over it. Who can I get to help me?"

"Why don't you get Jim Hall, down at the market, to do it for you, Henry?" Ben said. "That's his trade."

"I just now spoke to Jim, but he's all alone in the market today, and he can't close up. I've got to find somebody else. I've got to have a man in a hurry. He needn't be a finished butcher, because I can help do some of the work myself. But I need somebody to pitch in right away!"

Luther started for the door, leaving them both silent while they searched their minds for a butcher. Just as he got to the door, Ben caught up with him.

"Looks like you ought to know somebody in town, Luther, who could help Henry with his hog."

Henry came forward and stared Luther in the face. His mouth hung open for several moments while he stared. Ben, too, had begun to stare at Luther by that time. Luther looked from one to the other bewilderedly. He thought they were going to accuse him of having run down the fattening hog and killed it.

"Well, I'll be a son of a gun!" Henry said, stepping back to survey Luther from head to toe. I'll be a son of a gun if I won't!"

Luther stood at the door, not knowing what to do. He waited for one of them to say what it was that had caused them both to stare at him so hard.

Presently, Henry glanced at Ben and walked up to Luther, putting his hand on his shoulder.

"You're the man, Luther. I'll be a son of a gun if you aren't."

"He's right, Luther," Ben said. "Henry's dead right. You're the man."

Luther started to protest.

"I didn't run over a hog in the street, Ben. I don't even own a truck. And you know good and well I couldn't even kill a chicken with that little pushcart of mine."

"No! No! Luther," Henry protested. "I didn't try to accuse you of killing my hog. You're all mixed up. You're the man I'm looking for to butcher it for me. Why, Luther, you even look like a butcher!"

Both men had become excited.

"All your troubles are over now, Luther," Ben said. "You

won't have to worry again for the rest of your life. You'll own your own market before the year is out, and everybody in town will be buying their meat from you. It's going to be hard on Jim Hall, but there's no help for that. Maybe, after you get started, you can hire Jim to help you. But don't let him stay up front. It's your place to stay up front in full view where the people can see you."

Henry was nodding his head emphatically.

"When people buy something, Luther," Henry said, "they want the man who's selling it to look like the thing they're buying. It hasn't failed to be true since the world began."

"But I haven't any money to start a meat market," Luther protested.

"You let me take care of that part," Ben said. "You don't have to worry about anything any more. You just stay like you are."

Luther shoved his hands deep into his pockets where his gripped fingers would be safe from sight. He was even trembling a little.

"Why didn't you tell me that before, Ben?" he asked shakily. "Here I am, past forty years old, and I've been a failure all my life. If I had known about that twenty years ago, I wouldn't be in the fix I'm in now. Why didn't you say it sooner?"

"I didn't know it myself, Luther, till just now when Henry started talking about a butcher. I suppose it needed just something like what Henry said to bring it out. But there's no mistaking it now, Luther. I know what I see when I see it."

Henry went to the door.

"Let's hurry, Luther. We've got to get that hog quartered before night."

Luther went out on the sidewalk in front of the store and stopped to look across the street towards Jim Hall's meat market. His head went up erectly, his shoulders went back, and his thick, heavy body stiffened. He was still looking at the market when Henry caught him by the sleeve and pulled him up the street.

As they turned the corner, Luther looked back over his shoulder once more, and then he started walking briskly up the street with Henry at his side. He was walking so fast by that time that Henry was finding it difficult to keep up with him.

(First published in the *American Mercury*)

The Mating of Marjorie

HE was coming—he was coming—God bless him! He was coming to marry her—coming all the way from Minnesota!

Trembling, breathless, Marjorie read the letter again and again, holding it desperately in the ten fingers of her hands. Then at last, her eyes so blurred she could no longer see the handwriting, she placed the letter against the bareness of her breasts where she could breathe into it all the happiness of her heart. All the way from Minnesota he was coming—coming all that great distance to marry her!

The letter's every word, every mark of careless punctuation, was burned inerasably on her memory. The thought of the letter was like a poem running through her—like the chill of sudden warmth—fragments of lines repeating themselves like the roar in a furnace pipe.

His letter was not a proposal of marriage, but he did say he liked the way she looked in the picture she sent him. And why should he be coming all the way from Minnesota if he did not intend asking her to be his wife? Surely he wanted her.

Marjorie had his picture, too. She could actually feel the untiring strength of the lean muscles stretching over his face to the chin. Her fingers stole over his face excitedly, filling her with passion for the man with whom she would mate. He was a strong man. He would do with her as he pleased.

Surely he would like her. He was a mature man, and men who are mature seek beauty of soul and body when they marry. Marjorie was beautiful. Her beauty was her youth and charm. He wrote Marjorie that her eyes and her face and her hair were the loveliest he had ever seen. And her body was beautiful, too. He would see that when he came. Her slender limbs were cool and firm like the young pine trees in winter. Her heart was warm and eager. He would like her—surely he would.

Should she please him, and should he want her, and naturally he would when he saw her, Marjorie would give him her soul. Her soul would be her greatest gift to him. First she would give him her love, then her body, and at last her soul. No one had ever possessed her soul. But neither had her body or her love been possessed.

He had written frankly in all his letters. He said he wanted a wife. It was lonely, he said, living alone in Minnesota. Marjorie was lonesome, too. She had lived the long five years since her mother's death, alone. She understood. She had always been lonesome.

Marjorie prepared a room for him and waited his coming. She laundered the linen sheets and pillowcases three times. She dried the linen each time on the limbs of the fir trees and ironed it in the early morning while it was still damp with the pine-scented air.

The day of his coming Marjorie was awake long before the sun rose. The sun rose cool and swift.

Before laying out the new clothes she would wear for him, she ran to the room and patted the pillows and smoothed the coverlet for the last time. Then hurriedly she dressed and drove to the depot nineteen miles away.

He arrived on the noon train from Boston. He was much larger than she had expected him to be, and he was much more handsome than she had hoped.

"Are you Marjorie?" he asked huskily.

"Yes," Marjorie answered eagerly. "I am Marjorie. You are Nels?"

"Yes," he smiled, his eyes meeting hers. "I am Nels."

Marjorie led Nels to the automobile. They got in and drove away. Nels was a silent man, speaking crisply and infrequently. He looked at Marjorie all the time. He looked at her hands and face intently. She was nervous and self-conscious under his noncommittal scrutiny. After they had gone several miles he placed his arm across the back of the seat. Only once or twice did Marjorie feel his arm. The bumpy roads tossed them both as the car sped across the country. Nels's arms were as strong and muscular as a woodsman's.

Late that afternoon Marjorie and Nels walked down through the wood to the lake. There was a cold icy wind out of the northeast and the lake rose and tossed as if a storm were upon it. While they stood on a boulder at the lakeside watching the waves, a sudden gust of wind threw her against his shoulder. Nels braced her with his steellike arms and jumped to the ground. Later she showed Nels the icehouse and pointed out to him the shed where the boats were stored in winter. Then they walked home through the pines and firs.

While Marjorie prepared supper Nels sat in the parlor smoking his pipe. Several times Marjorie ran to the open door for a hurried glimpse of the man she was to marry. The only motion about him was the steady flow of tobacco smoke boiling from the bowl of his pipe. When the meal was ready, Marjorie quickly changed her dress and called Nels. Nels enjoyed the meal before him. He liked the way she had prepared the fish. Her skin was so hot she could not bear to press her knees together. Nels ate with full appetite.

After Marjorie had hastily carried the dishes to the kitchen she again changed her dress and went into the room where Nels sat by the fireplace. They sat in silence until she brought him the album and showed him the pictures. He looked at them silently.

All through the evening she sat hoping he would soon take her in his arms and kiss her. He would later, of course, but she wanted now to be in his arms. He did not look at her.

At ten-thirty Nels said he would like to go to bed. Marjorie jumped up and ran to his room. She turned back the pine-scented covers and smoothed the pillows. Bending over the bed, she laid her flushed cheek against the cool soft linen. Tearing herself away, she went back into the room where Nels sat silently by the fire.

After Nels had gone to his room and closed the door behind him, Marjorie went to her own bedroom. She sat down in a rocking chair and looked out upon the lake. It was after midnight when she got up and undressed. Just before retiring she tiptoed to the door of Nels's room. She stood there several minutes listening intensely. Her fingers touched the door softly. He did not hear her. He was asleep.

Marjorie was awake at five. Nels came into the kitchen at seven while she prepared breakfast. He was freshly clean, and under his loose tweed suit she all but felt the great strength of his body.

"Good morning," he said.

"Good morning, Nels," she greeted him eagerly.

After breakfast they sat in the parlor while Nels smoked his pipe. When he finished smoking, he stood up before the fireplace. He took out his watch and glanced at the time. Marjorie sat hushed behind him.

"What time does the train leave for Boston?" he asked.

With stilled breath she told him.

"Will you take me to the train?" he asked her.

She said she would.

Marjorie immediately went into the kitchen and leaned heavily against the table. Nels remained in the parlor refilling his pipe. Marjorie ran toward the parlor several times, but each time she turned back when she reached the door. She wanted to ask Nels if he were coming back. She picked up a plate and it crashed to the floor. It was the first piece of china she had broken since the morning of her mother's death. Trembling, she put on her hat and coat. Of course he was coming back! How foolish it was to think he would not! He was probably going to Boston to get some presents for her. He would come back—of course he would!

When they reached the depot, Nels held out his hand. She placed her hand in his. It was the first time his skin had touched her skin.

"Good-by," he said.

"Good-by, Nels," she smiled at him. "I hope you enjoyed your visit."

Nels picked up his traveling bag and started towards the waiting room.

Marjorie's arms and legs had the numbness of death in them. She started the motor uncertainly. He had not said he would return!

"Nels!" she cried desperately, gripping the door of the automobile with bloodless fingers.

Nels stopped and turned around, facing her.

"Nels, you are welcome to come back any time you want to," she begged unashamedly.

"Thank you," he replied briefly, "but I'm going home to Minnesota and I'll not be back again."

"What!" she cried, her lips quivering so violently she could barely make them speak. "Where are you going—?"

"To Minnesota," he replied.

Marjorie drove home as fast as her car would take her. As soon as she reached the house she ran to Nels's room.

In Nels's room Marjorie stood by the side of the bed and looked at the crumpled sheets and pillows with tear-blinded eyes. With a sob she threw herself between the sheets where Nels had lain. In her arms she hugged the pillows and dampened them with her tears. She could feel his body against hers. She kissed his face and held her lips for him to kiss.

It was night when she arose from the bed. The sun had gone down and the day was over. Only the cool clear twilight was left to shadow the room.

Throwing a blanket around her shoulders, Marjorie jerked the sheets and pillowcases from the bed and ran blindly to her own room. She opened the cedar chest and tenderly folded the crumpled sheets and pillowcases. She laid the linen in the chest and dragged the chest to the side of her bed.

Marjorie turned out the light and lay down between the sheets of her own bed.

"Good night, Nels," she whispered softly, her fingers touching the smooth lid of the cedar chest at her side.

(First published in *Scribner's*)

Martha Jean

WE had got booted out of a flat in the West End where we had caught up with one of the floating crap games, and instead of making the rounds on a raw night like that, we took a short cut across town to Nick's Place. Sleet was falling, and the wind was as sharp as knife blades. We met two or three men on the way; everybody was bent almost double against the icy wind, holding his hat and coat with numb fingers.

"What did you let them throw us out for, Hal?" The Type said. "There's no law against a man following a public crap game. I've gone broke in better flats than that one, anyway."

The Type bumped into a lamp post. He turned around and kicked the iron pole with his foot.

"Winter's a hell of a time of year," he said. "Let's go home."

"Nick's Place will be heated up," I said. "Come on, and we'll look in there for a while."

The usual all-night crowd was standing around the stove in Nick's Place, warming their fingers against the red-hot sides of the blast heater. Como, the Negro porter, stoked the fire and kept his back turned on the sleet that slashed against the door and windows.

When The Type and I walked in, Nick ran up from somewhere and met us halfway.

"I'm going to close up early tonight," Nick said. "You boys will have to go home for a change. Won't your folks be surprised to see you, though?"

"You mean you're telling us to get out?" The Type said.

"There's no money in keeping open on a night like this," Nick argued. "I'd just be wasting heat and light, and getting nowhere at all."

"Hello, Nick," I said. "How about lending me a dollar till sometime next week? Here's how it is. I started out—"

"No loans tonight, boys," he said. "I'm going to close up right away."

Como shivered.

"If it's all the same to you, Mr. Nick," Como said, "I'd just as lief stay and sleep right here on the floor by the stove tonight. Way out where I live, my old woman—"

"And burn up half a ton of coal," Nick said.

"I won't burn but one little shovelful the whole night long," Como pleaded. "A black man like me would die of pneumonia if I had to go out in that cold sleet tonight."

"You drag yourself out of here in half an hour, Como," Nick told him. "After you sweep out, I don't care where you go. You can go home if you want to."

The crowd around the stove pressed a little closer at the prospect of having to leave a warm room.

Nick came around the stove behind me. He shoved his thumb into my ribs.

"Wake up, Hal," he said. "What's the matter with you? Broke again? No drinks, no eats, no playing the machines?"

"I'm cleaned out tonight, Nick," I told him. "If I hadn't got kicked out of a game over in the West End, I'd have been on my feet."

Nick shrugged his shoulders and walked over to the wall where the row of slot machines stood on the tables. He shoved his fingers into the cups at the bottom of the machines where sometimes he found a nickel or a quarter somebody left behind.

"You boys are pretty bum sports," Nick said, coming back to the stove. "Why don't you go out and raise some money to play the machines with? The Type hasn't had a dime in his pocket this week."

"What's the matter with you, Nick?" The Type said. "What do you want me to do? Go out and crack the First National Bank?"

"I'm carrying you for six dollars now," Nick said. "I've got to have a pay day soon."

"I'll see what I can do," The Type told him.

Como was dumping a scuttle of coal into the stove when the front door burst open in a whirl of sleet and icy air. Everybody turned and looked in that direction just as a girl's head was seen outside. She stepped into the doorway.

"Shut the door," Nick said.

Como ran to the front and closed the door.

Everybody looked surprised at the sight of a girl in Nick's Place. I had never seen one there before; I had never heard of a girl entering the place. Nick's was a hangout for men and boys, and there was nothing there except the slot machines and pool tables. The lunch counter was hardly a place to come for a meal. Nick and Como had drinks and a few sandwiches, but that was all.

The forlorn-looking girl stood at the front of the room, shivering a little. The sleet on her hair and coat began to melt in the warm air, but her slippers were wet.

"Who's that?" The Type said. "She doesn't look like one of the girls around the corner to me. I never saw her before."

Como came back and dumped another scuttleful of coal into the iron heater. It was red-hot all over.

"I'll bet she ran away from home," The Type said.

Nick had gone up to the girl, and he was looking at her closely. She drew away from him, and he had to go stand with his back against the door to keep her from running out into the street.

"This is a hell of a place for a runaway country girl to land," The Type said.

"She won't stay in here long," I said. "As soon as she sees what she's got into, she'll leave."

The Type looked at the faces in the crowd around the stove. "I'd hate to see . . ."

Nick said something to the girl, and The Type stopped to hear what it was.

"If anybody starts getting fresh with her," I said, "I'm going to start swinging. I'm not going to stay here and see her get ganged."

The Type did not pay any attention to what I had said. He walked a little closer to the front in order to hear what Nick was saying to her.

The girl found her handkerchief and wiped the tears that sprang into her eyes.

"What do you want?" Nick said.

She shook her head.

"What did you come in here for if you don't want anything?" Nick asked her. "What's up?"

She shook her head again. She was a girl about fifteen or sixteen, and a lot prettier than any of the girls in the house around the corner. To look at her reminded you of the girls you had seen going to Sunday school on Sunday mornings.

"Hungry?" Nick asked her.

She made no reply, but it was easy to see that she had come in for something to eat, thinking that Nick's Place was a café.

"Como," Nick yelled, "bring us up some coffee and a couple of sandwiches. Get a hump on!"

"Yes, sir!" Como said, patting the warmth of the stove before hurrying to the lunch counter.

Nick led the girl to the counter and made her sit down on one of the stools. He sat down beside her, between her and the door.

The boys around the stove began winking at each other, nodding their heads at Nick and the girl.

When Como had the coffee hot, Nick asked her what her name was.

"Martha Jean," she said without hesitation.

Nick sat a little closer.

"Where you live?"

Martha Jean shook her head, tears springing to her eyes once more. Nick was satisfied. He did not ask her any more questions.

"When she finishes, give her a slice of cake, Como," Nick said, getting up.

Como shook his head.

"There ain't no cake, Mr. Nick," Como said.

Nick flared up.

"I said give her cake, Como, you shoeshine African!" he shouted. "When I say give her cake, I mean give it to her!"

"Yes, sir, boss!" Como said, shaking his head.

Nick came over towards the stove, walking sideways while he tried to keep his eyes on Martha Jean, and washing his hands in the air. When he got to the stove, he looked the crowd over, and picked on The Type to glare at as usual.

"All right now, you boys beat it somewhere else. Go on home, or somewhere. I'm closing up for the night."

Nobody made a move to leave.

Nick shoved The Type away from the stove.

"The next time you come back, have that six dollars you owe me," Nick told him, pushing.

"What the hell, Nick?" The Type said. "You've never hurried me for anything on the books like this before. What's the matter with you?"

"I had a bad dream last night," Nick said. "I dreamed that they hauled you off to a big stone-wall building and you got electrocuted. I've got to look out for myself now."

Some of the crowd moved away from the stove, but nobody left the room.

Nick shoved me with a stiff-arm.

"What's the big hurry, Nick?" I said to him.

"That's my business," Nick said. "Get a hump on."

"When is the girl going?"

"Martha Jean's staying."

"You can't do that, Nick," I said. "She came in here to get something to eat. She's nothing to me, but I hate to see her get pushed about like one of the girls around the corner."

"You're going to talk yourself out of a good thing, Hal," he said. "Don't I lend you money every time you ask for it, almost? Don't I keep you posted on good things? Don't I bail your brother-in-law every time he's picked up? What's the matter with you?"

Nick shoved me again, harder than before.

"What are you going to do with her?" I said.

"That's Nick's business," he answered. "If you know what's good for you, Hal, you'll get out of here before you talk too much."

The rest of the crowd was standing around the door, watching the girl. The Type was buttoning up his coat to leave.

Nick shoved me with his stiff-arm again.

"When you get home tonight, Hal," he said, pushing and shoving me towards the door, "tell your folks to give you something to do if they're not going to give you any spending money. I can't be having you hanging around my place if you don't have any money to play the machines with."

Nick turned his back on me and went over to where the girl was seated at the counter. She had finished eating, and Nick took her arm and pulled her towards the stove. She tried to pull away from him, but during all that time she had not raised her eyes to look at anybody in the room.

He dragged her to the stove.

"Cold, Martha Jean?" he asked her, putting his arms around her.

Some of the crowd had already left. Nearly all the fellows were letting Nick drive them out because they were afraid he would stop making loans when they were broke. Besides that, there were the tips Nick was always passing out when he got news of a sure thing to bet on. If Nick stopped letting us in on sure things, nearly everybody would stop getting spending money. Nick always got it all back, sooner or later, in the slot machines. Nick's crowd was afraid not to do what he told them to do.

The Type and I stood at the door watching Nick and Martha Jean at the stove.

"Got a place to stay tonight?" he asked her.

She answered him with a shake of her head and with a shiver that convulsed her whole body.

"How long have you been in town?" he asked.

"I came today," Martha Jean said.

"Looking for a job?"

"Yes."

Nick squeezed her with his arm.

"You don't have to worry about that any more," he told her, trying to raise her face up to his. "I'll fix everything for you."

Martha Jean tried again to get away from him, but Nick put both arms around her and held her tight to his side.

"Como," Nick said, "go upstairs and fix a place for Martha Jean. Fix up the front room for her, the one with the new bed and chairs in it. Get a hump on!"

"Yes, sir, boss!" Como said, tapping the red-hot stove with his fingers.

Martha Jean looked up for the first time. There was a startled expression in her eyes. When she turned towards The Type and me, I could not keep from going to her. She looked as helpless as a rabbit that had been caught in a steel trap for two or three days.

Nick turned around and glared at me.

Como could he heard stamping around upstairs in the room overhead. He was fixing things in a hurry so he could get back downstairs to the red-hot stove.

"Do you want to stay here with him?" I said to her, edging closer. "Or do you want to leave?"

Martha Jean started to say something. Her tears began flowing again, and she fought Nick desperately.

"What did I tell you, Hal?" Nick said angrily. "You wouldn't believe me, would you?"

He turned around and shook his head at me.

"Didn't I tell you you'd talk yourself out of a good thing? You wouldn't believe me, would you?"

He turned the girl loose for a moment, and swung around on his heels. Before I had a chance to duck, his fist flew at my head. The next thing I knew I was on the floor, unable to tell which was up and which was downside.

I could not see what The Type was doing, but I knew he was not helping me. Nick went back to Martha Jean, unbuttoning her coat and putting his arms under it. He held her so tight that she cried with pain.

By the time I could get to my feet, I did not know what to do next. After Nick had knocked me down, I began to realize there was nothing I could do to stop him. If The Type had helped me, it would have turned out differently. But The Type was thinking about Nick's loans and racetrack tips. He stood at the door ready to leave.

When I was on both feet again, Nick stepped over and shoved me towards the door with his stiff-arm. I went flying across the room, falling against The Type. The Type opened the door and tried to push me out into the street.

I fought him off and came back inside the door.

Nick picked up Martha Jean and started for the stairway with her. She began to scratch and fight, and Nick had a hard time keeping her from hurting him. She finally succeeded in scratching his face with her fingernails, and Nick dropped her like a hot brick.

"Como!" he yelled.

Como came tumbling down the stairs.

"Put him out and lock the door, Como," Nick ordered. "Throw him out, if he won't get out."

Nick grabbed Martha Jean again. She was such a little girl, and so young, she did not have much chance with Nick. All he had to do to hold her was to lock one arm around her neck, and cover both her hands with his other one.

Como picked up the iron stove poker and came towards me. He was scared to death. I knew he would never hit me, but I could see that he was so scared of Nick that he had to pretend to be trying to drive me out the door. The Type had gone.

"Throw that poker down, Como," I said.

"Mr. Hal," Como said, "you'd better leave Mr. Nick alone when he's mad. There ain't no telling what he's liable to do when he gets good and mad at you."

"Shut up, Como," I said.

Nick picked Martha Jean up once more and carried her as

far as the stairway. There he put her down quickly and ran towards me. I tried to meet him with my fists, but he jumped up into the air and came down on top of me. My bones felt as if they were being crushed like eggshells. When I woke up, I was lying on my face on the icy pavement.

The door was locked, and all but one light downstairs had been turned off. In the rear of the room, under one light, I could see Como throwing a hod of coal into the stove and trying to see through the window to the street outside at the same time.

I crossed the street, shielding my face against the sleet and wind that raced down the street. While I waited, I called for The Type two or three times. He did not answer, and I knew he had gone. There was nobody else on the street on a night like that.

Upstairs in the room Como had opened up, Nick had taken off his coat and was trying to make Martha Jean take off hers. She ran from him, from one side of the room to the other. Nick finally gave up trying to catch her, and picked up his coat and swung it at her.

At first she tried to cover her face and head against the stinging blows of the coat, but when Nick struck her across the back with it, she fell on the floor. All I could see was Nick bending over her and picking her up. When she was on her feet again, she got away from him. Nick swung at her with his coat, and struck the electric-light bulb hanging on a cord from the ceiling. The room suddenly became as black as the night outside.

I stood shaking and trembling in the street. The stinging, whipping, cutting sleet and wind blinded my eyes, and it was hard to open them after the light in the room went out. After a while, when Como had put out the last light downstairs, I turned and walked heavily up the street.

Once I thought I heard Martha Jean scream, but when I stopped and listened in the stinging sleet, I could not hear it again. After that I did not know whether it was she or whether it was only the wind that cried against the sharp corners of the buildings.

(First published in *Esquire*)

Big Buck

WHEN the sun went down, there were a heap of people just tramping up and down the dusty road without a care in the whole wide world. It was Saturday night and the cool of the evening was coming on, and that was enough to make a lot of folks happy. There were a few old logging mules plodding along in the dust with a worried look on their faces, but they had a right to look that way, because they had worked hard in the swamp all week and suppertime had come and gone, and they were still a long way from home.

It was the best time of the whole year for colored people, because it was so hot the whites didn't stir around much, and a colored man could walk up and down in the big road as much as he wanted to. The women and girls were all dressed up in starched white dresses and bright silk hair bows, and the men had on their Sunday clothes.

All at once a hound dog somewhere down the road started barking his head off. You could look down that way, but you couldn't see anything much, because the moon hadn't come up yet. The boys stopped in the middle of the road and listened. The old dog just kept on barking. They didn't say much, but they knew good and well those old hound dogs never took the trouble to get up and bark unless it was a stranger they smelled.

"Take care of yourself, nigger!" the black boy in the yellow hat yelled. "Stand back and hold your breath, because if you don't, you won't never know what hit you."

"What you talking about, anyhow?" Jimson said.

"I just turned around and looked down the road," Moses said, "and I saw a sight that'll make your eyes pop out of your head."

"What you see, nigger?" Jimson asked, trembling like a quiver bug. "You see something scary?"

"I seen Big Buck," Moses said, his voice weak and thin. "I seen him more than once, too, because I looked back twice to make sure I saw right the first time."

The two Negroes backed off the road into the ditch and pulled the bushes around them. They squatted there a while listening. Farther up the road people were laughing and singing, and talking loud. The old hound dog down the road was barking like he just wouldn't give up.

"Ain't no sense in Big Buck scaring the daylights out of folks the way he does," Jimson said. "It's a sin the way he keeps on doing it."

"Big Buck don't exactly aim to set out to scare folks," Moses said. "People just naturally get the shakes when he comes anywhere around, that's all. It ain't Big Buck's fault none. He's as gentle as a baby."

"Then how come you're sitting here, squatting in these bushes, if he ain't nothing to be scared of?"

Moses didn't say anything. They pulled the bushes back a little and looked down the road. They couldn't see much of

Big Buck, because it had been dark ever since sundown; but they could hear his feet flapping in the dusty road as plain as cypress trees falling in the swamp in broad daylight.

"Maybe he once was gentle, when he was a baby himself," Jimson said. "Maybe he is now, when he's asleep in his bed. But last Saturday night down at the crossroads store he didn't act like no baby I ever knew."

"What did he do down there?" Moses asked.

"He said he liked the looks of the striped band on my new straw hat, and then he slapped me so hard on the back I hit the ground smack with my face. That's how like a baby Big Buck is. I know, I do."

"Quit your jabbering," Moses whispered. "Here he comes!"

They pulled the bushes around them and squatted closer to the ground so they wouldn't be seen. They took off their hats and ducked down as far as they could so their heads wouldn't show. They were mighty glad it had got as dark as it was.

"Just look at that courting fool," Jimson whispered. "Ain't he the biggest sport you ever did see? He's all dressed up in yellow shoes and red necktie ready to flash them colors on the first gal he sees. That courting fool can do courting where courting's never been done before. Man alive, don't I wish I was him! I'd get me a high yellow and—"

"Shut your big mouth, nigger!" Moses whispered, slamming Jimson in the ribs with his elbow. "He'll jump us here in these bushes sure, if you don't shut that big mouth of yours."

Big Buck swung up the road like his mind was made up beforehand just exactly where he was headed. He was whistling as loud as a sawmill engine at Saturday afternoon quitting time, and throwing his head back and swinging his arms like he was sitting on top of the world. He was on his way to do some courting, it was plain to see.

The colored boys in the bushes shook until their bones rattled.

Then right square in front of the bushes Big Buck stopped and looked. There wasn't no cat that could see better than him in the dark. His big black face only had to turn toward what he wanted to see, and there it was as plain as day in front of his eyes.

"You niggers is going to shake all the leaves right off them poor bushes," Big Buck said, grinning until his teeth glistened like new tombstones in the moonlight. "Why you boys want to go and do that to them pretty little trees?"

He reached an arm across the ditch and caught hold of a woolly head. He pulled his arm back into the road.

"What's your name, nigger?" he said.

"I'm Jimson, Mr. Big Buck," the colored boy said. "Just Jimson's my name."

Big Buck reached his other arm into the bushes and caught hold of another woolly head. He yanked on it until Moses came hopping out into the road. He and Jimson stood there under Big Buck's arms trembling worse than the leaves on the bushes had done.

"What's your name, black boy?" Big Buck said.

"This is little Moses," he answered.

"Little Moses how-many?"

"Just little Moses March."

"That's a funny name to have in August, boy," Big Buck said, shaking him by the hair until Moses wished he'd never been born. "What you quivering like that for, boy? Ain't nothing to be scared of if you change your name to August."

"Yes, sir, Mr. Big Buck," Moses said. "I'll change it. I'll change my name just like you said. I'll do just like you told me. I sure will, Mr. Big Buck."

Big Buck turned Moses loose and laughed all over. He slapped Jimson on the back between the shoulders and, before Jimson knew what had happened, the ground rose up and smacked him square in the face. Big Buck looked down at Jimson and raised him to his feet by gripping a handful of woolly hair in his hand. He stood back and laughed some more.

"You peewees don't have to act like you is scared out of your mind," Big Buck said. "I ain't going to hurt nobody. You boys is my friends. If it wasn't so late, and if I wasn't on my way to do some courting, I'd stop a while and shoot you some craps."

He hitched up his pants and tightened up his necktie.

The boys couldn't help admiring his bright yellow shoes and red necktie that looked like a red lantern hanging around his neck.

"Which-a-way is it to Singing Sal's house from here?" he asked.

"Whoses house?" Jimson asked, his mouth hanging open. "Whoses house did you say?"

"I said Singing Sal's," Big Buck answered.

"You don't mean Singing Sal, does you, Mr. Big Buck?" Moses asked. "You couldn't mean her, because Singing Sal ain't never took no courting. She's mule-headed——"

"You heard me, peewee," Big Buck said. "I say what I mean, and I mean Singing Sal. Which-a-way does she live from here?"

"Is you fixing to court her, sure enough?" Moses asked.

"That's what I'm headed for," he said, "and I'm in a big

hurry to get there. You peewees come on and show me the way to get to where that gal lives."

Jimson and Moses ran along beside him, trotting to keep up with the long strides. They went half a mile before anybody said anything.

Every time they met a knot of people in the road, the folks jumped into the ditches to let Big Buck pass. Big Buck didn't weigh more than two hundred and fifty pounds, and he wasn't much over seven feet tall, but it looked like he took up all the space there was in a road when he swung along it. The women and girls sort of giggled when he went by, but Big Buck didn't turn his head at all. He kept straight up the big road like a hound on a live trail.

It wasn't long before Jimson and Moses were puffing and blowing, and they didn't know how much longer they could keep up with Big Buck if he didn't stop soon and give them a chance to get their breath back. The folks in the road scattered like a covey of quail.

When they got to the fork in the road, Big Buck stopped and asked them which way to go.

"It's over that way, across the creek," Jimson said, breathing hard. "If you didn't have no objection, I'd like to tag along behind you the rest of the way. Me and Moses was going over that way, anyway."

"I don't aim to waste no time knocking on wrong people's doors," Big Buck said, "and I want you boys to lead me straight to the place I want to go. Come on and don't waste no more time standing here."

They swung down the right-hand way. There weren't many houses down there, and they didn't lose any time. Big Buck was away out in front and the boys had a hard time keeping up.

They passed a couple of houses and went up the hill from the bridge over the creek. Big Buck started humming a little tune to himself. He didn't mind climbing a hill any more than walking on level ground.

When they got to the top, Big Buck stopped and hitched up his pants. He wiped the dust off his new yellow shoes with his pants' legs, and then he tightened up the red necktie until it almost choked him.

"That's the place," Jimson said, pointing.

"Then here's where I light," Big Buck said. "Here's where I hang my hat."

He started toward the cabin through the gap in the split-rail fence. He stopped halfway and called back.

"I'm mighty much obliged to you boys," he said.

He dug down into his pants and tossed a bright dime to them. Jimson got it before it was lost in the dark.

"You boys helped me save a lot of time, and I'm mighty much obliged," he said.

"You ain't going to try to court that there Singing Sal, sure enough, is you, Mr. Big Buck?" Jimson asked. He and Moses came as far as the fence and leaned on it. "Everybody says Singing Sal won't take no courting. Some say she ain't never took not even a whiff of it. Folks have even got themselves hurt, just trying to."

"She just ain't never had the right man come along before and give it to her," Big Buck said. "I've heard all that talk about how she won't take no courting, but she'll be singing a different tune when I get through with her."

Big Buck took a few steps toward the cabin door. Moses backed off toward the road. He wasn't taking no chances, because Singing Sal had a habit of shooting off a shotgun when she didn't want to be bothered. Moses backed away. Jimson stayed where he was and tried to get Moses to come closer so they could see what happened when Big Buck started inside.

"There ain't nothing to be scared of, Moses," Jimson said. "Big Buck knows what he's doing, or he wouldn't have come all the way here like he done."

Big Buck hitched up his pants again and picked his way around the woodpile and over an old wash tub full of rusty tin cans. He put one foot on the porch step and tried it with his weight to see how solid it was. The step squeaked and swayed, but it held him up.

Out in the yard by the sagging split-rail fence Jimson and Moses hung onto a post and waited to see. When Big Buck rapped on the door, their breath was stuck tight inside of them. There wasn't time to breathe before a chair fell over backward inside the cabin. Right after that a big tin pan was knocked off a table or shelf or something, and it fell on the floor with a big racket, too. She sure had been taken by surprise.

"Who's that at my door?" Singing Sal said. "What you want, whoever you is?"

Big Buck kicked the door with one of his big yellow shoes. The whole building shook.

"Your man has done come," he said, rattling and twisting the door knob. "Open up and let your good man inside, gal."

"Go away from here, nigger, while you is good and able," Singing Sal said. "I ain't got no time to be wasting on you, whoever you is. Now, just pick up your feet and mosey on away from my house."

"Honey," Big Buck said, getting a good grip on the knob, " I done made up my mind a long time back to start my courting while the victuals is hot. Just set me down a plate and pull me up a chair."

Before he could move an inch, a blast from Singing Sal's shotgun tore through the flimsy door. It didn't come anywhere near Big Buck, but it did sort of set him back on his heels for a minute. Then he hitched up his pants and yanked on the knob.

"Put that plaything down before you hurt yourself, honey," he shouted through the hole in the door. "Them things don't scare me one bit."

He gave the knob a jerk, and it broke off, and the lock with it. The door opened slowly, and the yellow lamplight fell across the porch and yard as far as the woodpile. He strutted inside while Singing Sal stared at him wild-eyed. Nobody had ever come through her door like that before. He acted like he wasn't scared of nothing in the world, not even double-barrel shotguns.

"Who's you?" she asked, her eyes popping.

He started grinning at her, and his whole mouth looked like it was going to split open from one ear to the other.

"I'm your man, honey," he said, "and I've come to do you some courting."

He walked on past her, looking her over from top to bottom while she stood in a daze. He walked around her to get a good look at her from behind. She didn't move an inch, she was that up in the air.

Jimson and Moses crept a little closer, going as far as the woodpile. They stayed behind it so they would have a place to dodge in case Singing Sal got hold of herself and started shooting again.

"I'm Big Buck from the far end of the swamp, honey," he said. "You must have heard of me before, because I've been around this part of the country most all my life. It's too bad I've been this long in getting here for some courting. But here I is, honey. Your good man has done come at last."

He pulled up a chair and sat down at the table. He wiped off the red-and-yellow oilcloth with his coat sleeve and reached to the cookstove for a skillet full of pout-mouthed perch. While he was getting the fish with one hand, he reached the other one over and picked up the coffeepot and poured himself a cupful. When that was done, he reached into the oven and got himself a handful of hot biscuits. All the time he was doing that, Singing Sal just stood and looked like she had just woke up out of a long sleep.

"You sure is a fine cook, honey," Big Buck said. "My, oh my! I'd go courting every night if I could find good eating like these pout-mouthed perches and them hot biscuits."

After Big Buck had taken a bite of fish in one gulp and a whole biscuit in another, Singing Sal shook herself and reached down on the floor for the shotgun she dropped when she shot it off the first time. She brought it up and leveled it off at Big Buck and squeezed one eye shut. Big Buck cut his eyes around at her and took another big bite of perch.

"Honey, shut that door and keep the chilly night air out," he told her, pouring another cup of coffee. "I don't like to feel a draft down the back of my neck when I'm setting and eating."

Singing Sal raised one ear to hear what he was saying, and then she sighted some more down the barrel of the shotgun, but by then it was waving like she couldn't draw a bead any more. She was shaking so she couldn't hold it at all, and so she stood it on its end. After she had rested a minute, she clicked the hammer until it was uncocked, and put the shotgun back under the bed.

"Where'd you come from, anyhow?" she asked Big Buck.

"Honey, I done told you I come from back in the swamp where I cut them cypress trees all week long," he said. "If I had known how fine it is here, I wouldn't have waited for Saturday to come. I'd have gone and been here a long time back before this, honey."

He took another helping of fish and poured himself some more hot black coffee. All the biscuits were gone, the whole bread pan full. He felt on the oilcloth and tried to find some crumbs with his fingers.

Singing Sal walked behind his chair and looked him over good from head to toe. He didn't pay no attention to her at all. He didn't even say another word until he finished eating all the fried fish he wanted.

Then he pushed the table away from him, wiped his mouth, and swung a long arm around behind him. His arm caught Singing Sal around the middle and brought her up beside him. He spread open his legs and stood her between them. Then he took another good look at her from top to bottom.

"You look as good as them pout-mouthed perch and hot biscuits I done ate, honey," he said to her. "My, oh, my!"

He reached up and set her down on his lap. Then he reached out and kissed her hard on the mouth.

Singing Sal swung her nearest arm, and her hand landed square on Big Buck's face. He laughed right back at her. She swung her other arm, but her fist just bounced off his face like it had been a rubber ball.

He reached out to grab her to him, and she let go with both fists, both knees, and the iron lid cover from the top of the skillet. Big Buck went down on the floor when the iron lid hit him, and Singing Sal landed on top of him swinging both the iron lid and the iron water kettle with all her might. The kettle broke, and pieces of it flew all over the room. Big Buck pushed along the floor, and she hit him with the skillet, the coffeepot, and the top of the table. That looked like it was enough to do him in, but he still had courting on his mind. He reached out to grab her to him, and she hit him over the head with the oven door.

Singing Sal had been stirring around as busy as a cat with fur on fire, and she was out of breath. She sort of wobbled backward and rested against the foot of the bed, all undone.

She was panting and blowing, and she didn't know what to pick up next to hit him with. It looked to her like it didn't do no good to hit him at all, because things bounced off him like they would have against a brick wall. She hadn't ever seen a man like him before in all her life. She didn't know before that there was a man made like him at all.

"Honey," Big Buck said, "you sure is full of fire. You is my kind of gal to court. My, oh, my!"

He reached up and grabbed her. She didn't move much, and he tugged again. She acted like she was a post in a post-hole, she was that solid when he tried to budge her. He grabbed her again, and she went down on top of him like a sack of corn. She rolled off on the floor, and her arms and legs thrashed around like she was trying to beat off bees and hornets. Big Buck got a grip on her and she rolled over on her back and lay there quiet, acting like she hadn't ever tussled with him at all. Her eyes looked up into his, and if she had been a kitten she would have purred.

"How did you like my fried fish and hot biscuits, Big Buck?" she asked, lazy and slow. "How was they, Big Buck?"

"The cooking's mighty good," he said. "I ain't never had nothing as good as that was before."

The wind blew the door almost shut. There was only a little narrow crack left. Jimson and Moses stood up and looked at the yellow lamplight shining through the crack. After that they went to the gap in the fence and made their way to the big road. Every once in a while they could hear Singing Sal laugh out loud. They sat down in the ditch and waited. There wasn't anything else they could do.

They had to wait a long time before Big Buck came out of the house. The moon had come up and moved halfway across the sky, and the dew had settled so heavy on them that they shivered as bad as if they had fallen in the creek.

They jumped up when Big Buck came stumbling over the woodpile and through the gap in the fence.

From the door of the house a long shaft of yellow lamplight shone across the yard. Singing Sal was crouched behind the door with only her head sticking out.

"What you boys hanging around here for?" Big Buck said. "Come on and get going."

They started down the hill, Big Buck striking out in front

and Jimson and Moses running along beside him to keep up with him.

They were halfway down the hill, and Big Buck hadn't said a word since they left the front of the house. Jimson and Moses ran along, trying to keep up with him, so they would hear anything he said about courting Singing Sal. Any man who had gone and courted Singing Sal right in her own house ought to be full of things to say.

They hung on, hoping he would say something any minute. It wasn't so bad trying to keep up with him going downhill.

When they got to the bottom of the hill where the road crossed the creek, Big Buck stopped and turned around. He looked back up at the top of the hill where Singing Sal lived, and drew in a long deep breath. Jimson and Moses crowded around him to hear if he said anything.

"Them was the finest pout-mouthed perches I ever ate in all my life," Big Buck said slowly. "My, oh, my! Them fried fish, and all them hot biscuits was the best eating I ever done. My, oh, my! That colored gal sure can cook!"

Big Buck hitched up his pants and started across the bridge. It was a long way back to the swamp, and the sun was getting ready to come up.

"My, oh, my!" he said, swinging into his stride.

Jimson and Moses ran along beside him, doing their best to keep up.

(First published in *College Humor*)

Kneel to the Rising Sun

A SHIVER went through Lonnie. He drew his hand away from his sharp chin, remembering what Clem had said. It made him feel now as if he were committing a crime by standing in Arch Gunnard's presence and allowing his face to be seen.

He and Clem had been walking up the road together that afternoon on their way to the filling station when he told Clem how much he needed rations. Clem stopped a moment to kick a rock out of the road, and said that if you worked for Arch Gunnard long enough, your face would be sharp enough to split the boards for your own coffin.

As Lonnie turned away to sit down on an empty box beside the gasoline pump, he could not help wishing that he could be as unafraid of Arch Gunnard as Clem was. Even if Clem was a Negro, he never hesitated to ask for rations when he needed something to eat; and when he and his family did not get enough, Clem came right out and told Arch so. Arch stood for that, but he swore that he was going to run Clem out of the country the first chance he got.

Lonnie knew without turning around that Clem was standing at the corner of the filling station with two or three other Negroes and looking at him, but for some reason he was unable to meet Clem's eyes.

Arch Gunnard was sitting in the sun, honing his jackknife blade on his boot top. He glanced once or twice at Lonnie's hound, Nancy, who was lying in the middle of the road waiting for Lonnie to go home.

"That your dog, Lonnie?"

Jumping with fear, Lonnie's hand went to his chin to hide the lean face that would accuse Arch of short-rationing.

Arch snapped his fingers and the hound stood up, wagging her tail. She waited to be called.

"Mr. Arch, I—"

Arch called the dog. She began crawling towards them on her belly, wagging her tail a little faster each time Arch's fingers snapped. When she was several feet away, she turned over on her back and lay on the ground with her four paws in the air.

Dudley Smith and Jim Weaver, who were lounging around the filling station, laughed. They had been leaning against the side of the building, but they straightened up to see what Arch was up to.

Arch spat some more tobacco juice on his boot top and whetted the jackknife blade some more.

"What kind of a hound dog is that, anyway, Lonnie?" Arch said. "Looks like to me it might be a ketch hound."

Lonnie could feel Clem Henry's eyes boring into the back of his head. He wondered what Clem would do if it had been his dog Arch Gunnard was snapping his fingers at and calling like that.

"His tail's way too long for a coon hound or a bird dog, ain't it, Arch?" somebody behind Lonnie said, laughing out loud.

Everybody laughed then, including Arch. They looked at Lonnie, waiting to hear what he was going to say to Arch.

"Is he a ketch hound, Lonnie?" Arch said, snapping his finger again.

"Mr. Arch, I—"

"Don't be ashamed of him, Lonnie, if he don't show signs of turning out to be a bird dog or a foxhound. Everybody needs a hound around the house that can go out and catch pigs and rabbits when you are in a hurry for them. A ketch hound is a mighty respectable animal. I've known the time when I was mighty proud to own one."

Everybody laughed.

Arch Gunnard was getting ready to grab Nancy by the tail. Lonnie sat up, twisting his neck until he caught a glimpse of Clem Henry at the other corner of the filling station. Clem was staring at him with unmistakable meaning, with the same look in his eyes he had had that afternoon when he said that nobody who worked for Arch Gunnard ought to stand for short-rationing. Lonnie lowered his eyes. He could not figure out how a Negro could be braver than he was. There were a lot of times like that when he would have given anything he had to be able to jump into Clem's shoes and change places with him.

"The trouble with this hound of yours, Lonnie, is that he's too heavy on his feet. Don't you reckon it would be a pretty slick little trick to lighten the load some, being as how he's a ketch hound to begin with?"

Lonnie remembered then what Clem Henry had said he would do if Arch Gunnard ever tried to cut off his dog's tail. Lonnie knew, and Clem knew, and everybody else knew, that that would give Arch the chance he was waiting for. All Arch asked, he had said, was for Clem Henry to overstep his place just one little half inch, or to talk back to him with just one little short word, and he would do the rest. Everybody knew what Arch meant by that, especially if Clem did not turn and run. And Clem had not been known to run from anybody, after fifteen years in the country.

Arch reached down and grabbed Nancy's tail while Lonnie was wondering about Clem. Nancy acted as if she thought Arch were playing some kind of a game with her. She turned her head around until she could reach Arch's hand to lick it. He cracked her on the bridge of the nose with the end of the jackknife.

"He's a mighty playful dog, Lonnie," Arch said, catching up a shorter grip on the tail, "but his wagpole is way too long for a dog his size, especially when he wants to be a ketch hound."

Lonnie swallowed hard.

"Mr. Arch, she's a mighty fine rabbit tracker. I—"

"Shucks, Lonnie," Arch said, whetting the knife blade on the dog's tail, "I ain't ever seen a hound in all my life that needed a tail that long to hunt rabbits with. It's way too long for just a common, ordinary, everyday ketch hound."

Lonnie looked up hopefully at Dudley Smith and the others. None of them offered any help. It was useless for him to try to stop Arch, because Arch Gunnard would let nothing stand in his way when once he had set his head on what he wished to do. Lonnie knew that if he should let himself show any anger or resentment, Arch would drive him off the farm before sundown that night. Clem Henry was the only person there who would help him, but Clem . . .

The white men and the Negroes at both corners of the filling station waited to see what Lonnie was going to do about it. All of them hoped he would put up a fight for his hound. If anyone ever had the nerve to stop Arch Gunnard from cutting off a dog's tail, it might put an end to it. It was plain, though, that Lonnie, who was one of Arch's sharecroppers, was afraid to speak up. Clem Henry might; Clem was the only one who might try to stop Arch, even if it meant trouble. And all of them knew that Arch would insist on running Clem out of the country, or filling him full of lead.

"I reckon it's all right with you, ain't it, Lonnie?" Arch said. "I don't seem to hear no objections."

Clem Henry stepped forward several paces, and stopped.

Arch laughed, watching Lonnie's face, and jerked Nancy to her feet. The hound cried out in pain and surprise, but Arch made her be quiet by kicking her in the belly.

Lonnie winced. He could hardly bear to see anybody kick his dog like that.

"Mr. Arch, I . . ."

A contraction in his throat almost choked him for several moments, and he had to open his mouth wide and fight for breath. The other white men around him were silent. Nobody liked to see a dog kicked in the belly like that.

Lonnie could see the other end of the filling station from the corner of his eye. He saw a couple of Negroes go up behind Clem and grasp his overalls. Clem spat on the ground, between outspread feet, but he did not try to break away from them.

"Being as how I don't hear no objections, I reckon it's all right to go ahead and cut it off," Arch said, spitting.

Lonnie's head went forward and all he could see of Nancy was her hind feet. He had come to ask for a slab of sowbelly and some molasses, or something. Now he did not know if he could ever bring himself to ask for rations, no matter how much hungrier they became at home.

"I always make it a habit of asking a man first," Arch said. "I wouldn't want to go ahead and cut off a tail if a man had any objections. That wouldn't be right. No, sir, it just wouldn't be fair and square."

Arch caught a shorter grip on the hound's tail and placed the knife blade on it two or three inches from the rump. It looked to those who were watching as if his mouth were watering, because tobacco juice began to trickle down the corners of his lips. He brought up the back of his hand and wiped his mouth.

A noisy automobile came plowing down the road through the deep red dust. Everyone looked up as it passed in order to see who was in it.

Lonnie glanced at it, but he could not keep his eyes raised. His head fell downward once more until he could feel his sharp chin cutting into his chest. He wondered then if Arch had noticed how lean his face was.

"I keep two or three ketch hounds around my place," Arch said, honing the blade on the tail of the dog as if it were a razor strop until his actions brought smiles to the faces of the men grouped around him, "but I never could see the sense of a ketch hound having a long tail. It only gets in their way when I send them out to catch a pig or rabbit for my supper."

Pulling with his left hand and pushing with his right, Arch Gunnard docked the hound's tail as quickly and as easily as if he were cutting a willow switch in the pasture to drive the cows home with. The dog sprang forward with the release of her tail until she was far beyond Arch's reach, and began howling so loud she could be heard half a mile away. Nancy stopped once and looked back at Arch, and then she sprang to the middle of the road and began leaping and twisting in circles. All that time she was yelping and biting at the bleeding stub of her tail.

Arch leaned backward and twirled the severed tail in one hand while he wiped the jackknife blade on his boot sole. He watched Lonnie's dog chasing herself around in circles in the red dust.

Nobody had anything to say then. Lonnie tried not to watch his dog's agony, and he forced himself to keep from looking at Clem Henry. Then, with his eyes shut, he wondered why he had remained on Arch Gunnard's plantation all those past years, sharecropping for a mere living on short rations, and becoming leaner and leaner all the time. He knew then how true it was what Clem had said about Arch's sharecroppers' faces becoming sharp enough to hew their own coffins. His hands went to his chin before he knew what he was doing. His hand dropped when he had felt the bones of jaw and the exposed tendons of his cheeks.

As hungry as he was, he knew that even if Arch did give him some rations then, there would not be nearly enough for them to eat for the following week. Hatty, his wife, was already broken down from hunger and work in the fields, and his father, Mark Newsome, stone-deaf for the past twenty years, was always asking him why there was never enough food in the house for them to have a solid meal. Lonnie's head fell forward a little more, and he could feel his eyes becoming damp.

The pressure of his sharp chin against his chest made him

so uncomfortable that he had to raise his head at last in order to ease the pain of it.

The first thing he saw when he looked up was Arch Gunnard twirling Nancy's tail in his left hand. Arch Gunnard had a trunk full of dogs' tails at home. He had been cutting off tails ever since anyone could remember, and during all those years he had accumulated a collection of which he was so proud that he kept the trunk locked and the key tied around his neck on a string. On Sunday afternoons when the preacher came to visit, or when a crowd was there to loll on the front porch and swap stories, Arch showed them off, naming each tail from memory just as well as if he had had a tag on it.

Clem Henry had left the filling station and was walking alone down the road towards the plantation. Clem Henry's house was in a cluster of Negro cabins below Arch's big house, and he had to pass Lonnie's house to get there. Lonnie was on the verge of getting up and leaving when he saw Arch looking at him. He did not know whether Arch was looking at his lean face, or whether he was watching to see if he were going to get up and go down the road with Clem.

The thought of leaving reminded him of his reason for being there. He had to have some rations before suppertime that night, no matter how short they were.

"Mr. Arch, I . . ."

Arch stared at him for a moment, appearing as if he had turned to listen to some strange sound unheard of before that moment.

Lonnie bit his lips, wondering if Arch was going to say anything about how lean and hungry he looked. But Arch was thinking about something else. He slapped his hand on his leg and laughed out loud.

"I sometimes wish niggers had tails," Arch said, coiling Nancy's tail into a ball and putting it into his pocket. "I'd a heap rather cut off nigger tails than dog tails. There'd be more to cut, for one thing."

Dudley Smith and somebody else behind them laughed for a brief moment. The laughter died out almost as suddenly as it had risen.

The Negroes who had heard Arch shuffled their feet in the dust and moved backwards. It was only a few minutes until not one was left at the filling station. They went up the road behind the red wooden building until they were out of sight.

Arch got up and stretched. The sun was getting low, and it was no longer comfortable in the October air. "Well, I reckon I'll be getting on home to get me some supper," he said.

He walked slowly to the middle of the road and stopped to look at Nancy retreating along the ditch.

"Nobody going my way?" he asked. "What's wrong with you, Lonnie? Going home to supper, ain't you?"

"Mr. Arch, I . . ."

Lonnie found himself jumping to his feet. His first thought was to ask for the sowbelly and molasses, and maybe some corn meal; but when he opened his mouth, the words refused to come out. He took several steps forward and shook his head. He did not know what Arch might say or do if he said "No."

"Hatty'll be looking for you," Arch said, turning his back and walking off.

He reached into his hip pocket and took out Nancy's tail. He began twirling it as he walked down the road towards the big house in the distance.

Dudley Smith went inside the filling station, and the others walked away.

After Arch had gone several hundred yards, Lonnie sat down heavily on the box beside the gas pump from which he had got up when Arch spoke to him. He sat down heavily, his shoulders drooping, his arms falling between his outspread legs.

Lonnie did not know how long his eyes had been closed, but when he opened them, he saw Nancy lying between his feet, licking the docked tail. While he watched her, he felt the sharp point of his chin cutting into his chest again. Presently the door behind him was slammed shut, and a minute later he could hear Dudley Smith walking away from the filling station on his way home.

II

Lonnie had been sleeping fitfully for several hours when he suddenly found himself wide awake. Hatty shook him again. He raised himself on his elbow and tried to see into the darkness of the room. Without knowing what time it was, he was able to determine that it was still nearly two hours until sunrise.

"Lonnie," Hatty said again, trembling in the cold night air, "Lonnie, your pa ain't in the house."

Lonnie sat upright in bed.

"How do you know he ain't?" he said.

"I've been lying here wide awake ever since I got in bed, and I heard him when he went out. He's been gone all that time."

"Maybe he just stepped out for a while," Lonnie said, turning and trying to see through the bedroom window.

"I know what I'm saying, Lonnie," Hatty insisted. "Your pa's been gone a heap too long."

Both of them sat without a sound for several minutes while they listened for Mark Newsome.

Lonnie got up and lit a lamp. He shivered while he was putting on his shirt, overalls, and shoes. He tied his shoe-laces in hard knots because he couldn't see in the faint light. Outside the window it was almost pitch-dark, and Lonnie could feel the damp October air blowing against his face.

"I'll go help look," Hatty said, throwing the covers off and starting to get up.

Lonnie went to the bed and drew the covers back over her and pushed her back into place.

"You try to get some sleep, Hatty," he said; "you can't stay awake the whole night. I'll go bring Pa back."

He left Hatty, blowing out the lamp, and stumbled through the dark hall, feeling his way to the front porch by touching the wall with his hands. When he got to the porch, he could still barely see any distance ahead, but his eyes were becoming more accustomed to the darkness. He waited a minute, listening.

Feeling his way down the steps into the yard, he walked around the corner of the house and stopped to listen again before calling his father.

"Oh, Pa!" he said loudly. "Oh, Pa!"

He stopped under the bedroom window when he realized what he had been doing.

"Now that's a fool thing for me to be out here doing," he said, scolding himself. "Pa couldn't hear it thunder."

He heard a rustling of the bed.

"He's been gone long enough to get clear to the crossroads, or more," Hatty said, calling through the window.

"Now you lay down and try to get a little sleep, Hatty," Lonnie told her. "I'll bring him back in no time."

He could hear Nancy scratching fleas under the house, but he knew she was in no condition to help look for Mark. It would be several days before she recovered from the shock of losing her tail.

"He's been gone a long time," Hatty said, unable to keep still.

"That don't make no difference," Lonnie said. "I'll find him sooner or later. Now you go on to sleep like I told you, Hatty."

Lonnie walked towards the barn, listening for some sound. Over at the big house he could hear the hogs grunting and squealing, and he wished they would be quiet so he could hear other sounds. Arch Gunnard's dogs were howling occasionally, but they were not making any more noise than they usually did at night, and he was accustomed to their howling.

Lonnie went to the barn, looking inside and out. After walk-ing around the barn, he went into the field as far as the cotton shed. He knew it was useless, but he could not keep from calling his father time after time.

"Oh, Pa!" he said, trying to penetrate the darkness.

He went farther into the field.

"Now, what in the world could have become of Pa?" he said, stopping and wondering where to look next.

After he had gone back to the front yard, he began to feel uneasy for the first time. Mark had not acted any more strangely during the past week than he ordinarily did, but Lonnie knew he was upset over the way Arch Gunnard was giving out short rations. Mark had even said that, at the rate they were being fed, all of them would starve to death inside another three months.

Lonnie left the yard and went down the road towards the Negro cabins. When he got to Clem's house, he turned in and walked up the path to the door. He knocked several times and waited. There was no answer, and he rapped louder.

"Who's that?" he heard Clem say from bed.

"It's me," Lonnie said. "I've got to see you a minute, Clem. I'm out in the front yard."

He sat down and waited for Clem to dress and come outside. While he waited, he strained his ears to catch any sound that might be in the air. Over the fields towards the big house he could hear the fattening hogs grunt and squeal.

Clem came out and shut the door. He stood on the doorsill a moment speaking to his wife in bed, telling her he would be back and not to worry.

"Who's that?" Clem said, coming down into the yard.

Lonnie got up and met Clem halfway.

"What's the trouble?" Clem asked then, buttoning up his overall jumper.

"Pa's not in his bed," Lonnie said, "and Hatty says he's been gone from the house most all night. I went out in the field, and all around the barn, but I couldn't find a trace of him anywhere."

Clem then finished buttoning his jumper and began rolling a cigarette. He walked slowly down the path to the road. It was still dark, and it would be at least an hour before dawn made it any lighter.

"Maybe he was too hungry to stay in bed any longer," Clem said. "When I saw him yesterday, he said he was so shrunk up and weak he didn't know if he could last much longer. He looked like his skin and bones couldn't shrivel much more."

"I asked Arch last night after suppertime for some rations— just a little piece of sowbelly and some molasses. He said he'd get around to letting me have some the first thing this morning."

"Why don't you tell him to give you full rations or none?"

Clem said. "If you knew you wasn't going to get none at all, you could move away and find a better man to sharecrop for, couldn't you?"

"I've been loyal to Arch Gunnard for a long time now," Lonnie said. "I'd hate to haul off and leave him like that."

Clem looked at Lonnie, but he did not say anything more just then. They turned up the road towards the big house. The fattening hogs were still grunting and squealing in the pen, and one of Arch's hounds came down a cotton row beside the driveway to smell their shoes.

"Them fattening hogs always get enough to eat," Clem said. "There's not a one of them that don't weigh seven hundred pounds right now, and they're getting bigger every day. Besides taking all that's thrown to them, they make a lot of meals off the chickens that get in there to peck around."

Lonnie listened to the grunting of the hogs as they walked up the driveway towards the big house.

"Reckon we'd better get Arch up to help look for Pa?" Lonnie said. "I'd hate to wake him up, but I'm scared Pa might stray off into the swamp and get lost for good. He couldn't hear it thunder, even. I never could find him back there in all that tangle if he got into it."

Clem said something under his breath and went on towards the barn and hog pen. He reached the pen before Lonnie got there.

"You'd better come here quick," Clem said, turning around to see where Lonnie was.

Lonnie ran to the hog pen. He stopped and climbed half-way up the wooden-and-wire sides of the fence. At first he could see nothing, but gradually he was able to see the moving mass of black fattening hogs on the other side of the pen. They were biting and snarling at each other like a pack of hungry hounds turned loose on a dead rabbit.

Lonnie scrambled to the top of the fence, but Clem caught him and pulled him back.

"Don't go in that hog pen that way," he said. "Them hogs will tear you to pieces, they're that wild. They're fighting over something."

Both of them ran around the corner of the pen and got to the side where the hogs were. Down under their feet on the ground Lonnie caught a glimpse of a dark mass splotched with white. He was able to see it for a moment only, because one of the hogs trampled over it.

Clem opened and closed his mouth several times before he was able to say anything at all. He clutched at Lonnie's arm, shaking him.

"That looks like it might be your pa," he said. "I swear before goodness, Lonnie, it does look like it."

Lonnie still could not believe it. He climbed to the top of the fence and began kicking his feet at the hogs, trying to drive them away. They paid no attention to him.

While Lonnie was perched there, Clem had gone to the wagon shed, and he ran back with two singletrees he had somehow managed to find there in the dark. He handed one to Lonnie, poking it at him until Lonnie's attention was drawn from the hogs long enough to take it.

Clem leaped over the fence and began swinging the single-tree at the hogs. Lonnie slid down beside him, yelling at them. One hog turned on Lonnie and snapped at him, and Clem struck it over the back of the neck with enough force to drive it off momentarily.

By then Lonnie was able to realize what had happened. He ran to the mass of hogs, kicking them with his heavy stiff shoes and striking them on their heads with the iron-tipped singletree. Once he felt a stinging sensation, and looked down to see one of the hogs biting the calf of his leg. He had just enough time to hit the hog and drive it away before his leg was torn. He knew most of his overall leg had been ripped away, because he could feel the night air on his bare wet calf.

Clem had gone ahead and had driven the hogs back. There was no other way to do anything. They were in a snarling circle around them, and both of them had to keep the single-trees swinging back and forth all the time to keep the hogs off. Finally Lonnie reached down and got a grip on Mark's leg. With Clem helping, Lonnie carried his father to the fence and lifted him over to the other side.

They were too much out of breath for a while to say any-thing, or to do anything else. The snarling, fattening hogs were at the fence, biting the wood and wire, and making more noise than ever.

While Lonnie was searching in his pockets for a match, Clem struck one. He held the flame close to Mark Newsome's head.

They both stared unbelievingly, and then Clem blew out the match. There was nothing said as they stared at each other in the darkness.

Clem walked several steps away, and turned and came back beside Lonnie.

"It's him, though," Clem said, sitting down on the ground. "It's him, all right."

"I reckon so," Lonnie said. He could think of nothing else to say then.

They sat on the ground, one on each side of Mark, looking at the body. There had been no sign of life in the body beside them since they had first touched it. The face, throat, and stomach had been completely devoured.

"You'd better go wake up Arch Gunnard," Clem said after a while.

"What for?" Lonnie said. "He can't help none now. It's too late for help."

"Makes no difference," Clem insisted. "You'd better go wake him up and let him see what there is to see. If you wait till morning, he might take it into his head to say the hogs didn't do it. Right now is the time to get him up so he can see what his hogs did."

Clem turned around and looked at the big house. The dark outline against the dark sky made him hesitate.

"A man who short-rations tenants ought to have to sit and look at that till it's buried."

Lonnie looked at Clem fearfully. He knew Clem was right, but he was scared to hear a Negro say anything like that about a white man.

"You oughtn't talk like that about Arch," Lonnie said. "He's in bed asleep. He didn't have a thing to do with it. He didn't have no more to do with it than I did."

Clem laughed a little, and threw the singletree on the ground between his feet. After letting it lie there a little while, he picked it up and began beating the ground with it.

Lonnie got to his feet slowly. He had never seen Clem act like that before, and he did not know what to think about it. He left without saying anything and walked stiffly to the house in the darkness to wake up Arch Gunnard.

III

Arch was hard to wake up. And even after he was awake, he was in no hurry to get up. Lonnie was standing outside the bedroom window, and Arch was lying in bed six or eight feet away. Lonnie could hear him toss and grumble.

"Who told you to come and wake me up in the middle of the night?" Arch said.

"Well, Clem Henry's out here, and he said maybe you'd like to know about it."

Arch tossed around on the bed, flailing the pillow with his fists.

"You tell Clem Henry I said that one of these days he's going to find himself turned inside out, like a coat sleeve."

Lonnie waited doggedly. He knew Clem was right in insisting that Arch ought to wake up and come out there to see what had happened. Lonnie was afraid to go back to the barnyard and tell Clem that Arch was not coming. He did not know, but he had a feeling that Clem might go into the bedroom and drag Arch out of bed. He did not like to think of anything like that taking place.

"Are you still out there, Lonnie?" Arch shouted.

"I'm right here, Mr. Arch. I—"

"If I wasn't so sleepy, I'd come out there and take a stick and—I don't know what I wouldn't do!"

Lonnie met Arch at the back step. On the way out to the hog pen Arch did not speak to him. Arch walked heavily ahead, not even waiting to see if Lonnie was coming. The lantern that Arch was carrying cast long flat beams of yellow light over the ground; and when they got to where Clem was waiting beside Mark's body, the Negro's face shone in the night like a highly polished plowshare.

"What was Mark doing in my hog pen at night, anyway?" Arch said, shouting at them both.

Neither Clem nor Lonnie replied. Arch glared at them for not answering. But no matter how many times he looked at them, his eyes returned each time to stare at the torn body of Mark Newsome on the ground at his feet.

"There's nothing to be done now," Arch said finally. "We'll just have to wait till daylight and send for the undertaker." He walked a few steps away. "Looks like you could have waited till morning in the first place. There wasn't no sense in getting me up."

He turned his back and looked sideways at Clem. Clem stood up and looked him straight in the eyes.

"What do you want, Clem Henry?" he said. "Who told you to be coming around my house in the middle of the night? I don't want niggers coming here except when I send for them."

"I couldn't stand to see anybody eaten up by the hogs, and not do anything about it," Clem said.

"You mind your own business," Arch told him. "And when you talk to me, take off your hat, or you'll be sorry for it. It wouldn't take much to make me do you up the way you belong."

Lonnie backed away. There was a feeling of uneasiness around them. That was how trouble between Clem and Arch always began. He had seen it start that way dozens of times before. As long as Clem turned and went away, nothing happened, but sometimes he stayed right where he was and talked up to Arch just as if he had been a white man, too.

Lonnie hoped it would not happen this time. Arch was already mad enough about being waked up in the middle of the night, and Lonnie knew there was no limit to what Arch would do when he got good and mad at a Negro. Nobody had ever seen him kill a Negro, but he had said he had, and he told people that he was not scared to do it again.

"I reckon you know how he came to get eaten up by the hogs like that," Clem said, looking straight at Arch.

Arch whirled around.

"Are you talking to me . . . ?"

"I asked you that," Clem stated.

"God damn you, yellow-blooded . . ." Arch yelled.

He swung the lantern at Clem's head. Clem dodged, but the bottom of it hit his shoulder, and it was smashed to pieces. The oil splattered on the ground, igniting in the air from the flaming wick. Clem was lucky not to have it splash on his face and overalls.

"Now, look here . . ." Clem said.

"You yellow-blooded nigger," Arch said, rushing at him. "I'll teach you to talk back to me. You've got too big for your place for the last time. I've been taking too much from you, but I ain't doing it no more."

"Mr. Arch, I . . ." Lonnie said, stepping forward partly between them. No one heard him.

Arch stood back and watched the kerosene flicker out on the ground.

"You know good and well why he got eaten up by the fattening hogs," Clem said, standing his ground. "He was so hungry he had to get up out of bed in the middle of the night and come up here in the dark trying to find something to eat. Maybe he was trying to find the smokehouse. It makes no difference, either way. He's been on short rations like everybody else working on your place, and he was so old he didn't know where else to look for food except in your smokehouse. You know good and well that's how he got lost up here in the dark and fell in the hog pen."

The kerosene had died out completely. In the last faint flare, Arch had reached down and grabbed up the singletree that had been lying on the ground where Lonnie had dropped it.

Arch raised the singletree over his head and struck with all his might at Clem. Clem dodged, but Arch drew back again quickly and landed a blow on his arm just above the elbow before Clem could dodge it. Clem's arm dropped to his side, dangling lifelessly.

"You God-damn yellow-blooded nigger!" Arch shouted. "Now's your time, you black bastard! I've been waiting for the chance to teach you your lesson. And this's going to be one you won't never forget."

Clem felt the ground with his feet until he had located the other singletree. He stooped down and got it. Raising it, he did not try to hit Arch, but held it in front of him so he could ward off Arch's blows at his head. He continued to stand his ground, not giving Arch an inch.

"Drop that singletree," Arch said.

"I won't stand here and let you beat me like that," Clem protested.

"By God, that's all I want to hear," Arch said, his mouth curling. "Nigger, your time has come, by God!"

He swung once more at Clem, but Clem turned and ran towards the barn. Arch went after him a few steps and stopped. He threw aside the singletree and turned and ran back to the house.

Lonnie went to the fence and tried to think what was best for him to do. He knew he could not take sides with a Negro, in the open, even if Clem had helped him, and especially after Clem had talked to Arch in the way he wished he could himself. He was a white man, and to save his life he could not stand to think of turning against Arch, no matter what happened.

Presently a light burst through one of the windows of the house, and he heard Arch shouting at his wife to wake her up.

When he saw Arch's wife go to the telephone, Lonnie realized what was going to happen. She was calling up the neighbors and Arch's friends. They would not mind getting up in the night when they found out what was going to take place.

Out behind the barn he could hear Clem calling him. Leaving the yard, Lonnie felt his way out there in the dark.

"What's the trouble, Clem?" he said.

"I reckon my time has come," Clem said. "Arch Gunnard talks that way when he's good and mad. He talked just like he did that time he carried Jim Moffin off to the swamp—and Jim never came back."

"Arch wouldn't do anything like that to you, Clem," Lonnie said excitedly, but he knew better.

Clem said nothing.

"Maybe you'd better strike out for the swamps till he changes his mind and cools off some," Lonnie said. "You might be right, Clem."

Lonnie could feel Clem's eyes burning into him.

"Wouldn't be no sense in that, if you'd help me," Clem said. "Wouldn't you stand by me?"

Lonnie trembled as the meaning of Clem's suggestion became clear to him. His back was to the side of the barn, and he leaned against it while sheets of black and white passed before his eyes.

"Wouldn't you stand by me?" Clem asked again.

"I don't know what Arch would say to that," Lonnie told him haltingly.

Clem walked away several paces. He stood with his back to Lonnie while he looked across the field towards the quarter where his home was.

"I could go in that little patch of woods out there and stay till they get tired of looking for me," Clem said, turning around to see Lonnie.

"You'd better go somewhere," Lonnie said uneasily. "I know Arch Gunnard. He's hard to handle when he makes up his mind to do something he wants to do. I couldn't stop him an inch. Maybe you'd better get clear out of the country, Clem."

"I couldn't do that, and leave my family down there across the field," Clem said.

"He's going to get you if you don't."

"If you'd only sort of help me out a little, he wouldn't. I would only have to go and hide out in that little patch of woods over there a while. Looks like you could do that for me, being as how I helped you find your pa when he was in the hog pen."

Lonnie nodded, listening for sounds from the big house. He continued to nod at Clem while Clem was waiting to be assured.

"If you're going to stand up for me," Clem said, "I can just go over there in the woods and wait till they get it off their minds. You won't be telling them where I'm at, and you could say I struck out for the swamp. They wouldn't ever find me without bloodhounds."

"That's right," Lonnie said, listening for sounds of Arch's coming out of the house. He did not wish to be found back there behind the barn where Arch could accuse him of talking to Clem.

The moment Lonnie replied, Clem turned and ran off into the night. Lonnie went after him a few steps, as if he had suddenly changed his mind about helping him, but Clem was lost in the darkness by then.

Lonnie waited for a few minutes, listening to Clem crashing through the underbrush in the patch of woods a quarter of a mile away. When he could hear Clem no longer, he went around the barn to meet Arch.

Arch came out of the house carrying his double-barreled shotgun and the lantern he had picked up in the house. His pockets were bulging with shells.

"Where is that damn nigger, Lonnie?" Arch asked him. "Where'd he go to?"

Lonnie opened his mouth, but no words came out.

"You know which way he went, don't you?"

Lonnie again tried to say something, but there were no sounds. He jumped when he found himself nodding his head to Arch.

"Mr. Arch, I—"

"That's all right, then," Arch said. "That's all I need to know now, Dudley Smith and Tom Hawkins and Frank and

Dave Howard and the rest will be here in a minute, and you can stay right here so you can show us where he's hiding out."

Frantically Lonnie tried to say something. Then he reached for Arch's sleeve to stop him, but Arch had gone.

Arch ran round the house to the front yard. Soon a car came racing down the road, its headlights lighting up the whole place, hog pen and all. Lonnie knew it was probably Dudley Smith, because his was the first house in that direction, only half a mile away. While he was turning into the driveway, several other automobiles came into sight, both up the road and down it.

Lonnie trembled. He was afraid Arch was going to tell him to point out where Clem had gone to hide. Then he knew Arch would tell him. He had promised Clem he would not do that. But try as he might, he could not make himself believe that Arch Gunnard would do anything more than whip Clem.

Clem had not done anything that called for lynching. He had not raped a white woman, he had not shot at a white man; he had only talked back to Arch, with his hat on. But Arch was mad enough to do anything; he was mad enough at Clem not to stop at anything short of lynching.

The whole crowd of men was swarming around him before he realized it. And there was Arch clutching his arm and shouting into his face.

"Mr. Arch, I—"

Lonnie recognized every man in the feeble dawn. They were excited, and they looked like men on the last lap of an all-night fox-hunting party. Their shotguns and pistols were held at their waist, ready for the kill.

"What's the matter with you, Lonnie?" Arch said, shouting into his ear. "Wake up and say where Clem Henry went to hide out. We're ready to go get him."

Lonnie remembered looking up and seeing Frank Howard dropping yellow twelve-gauge shells into the breech of his gun. Frank bent forward so he could hear Lonnie tell Arch where Clem was hiding.

"You ain't going to kill Clem this time, are you, Mr. Arch?" Lonnie asked.

"Kill him?" Dudley Smith repeated. "What do you reckon I've been waiting all this time for if it wasn't for a chance to get Clem. That nigger has had it coming to him ever since he came to this county. He's a bad nigger, and it's coming to him."

"It wasn't exactly Clem's fault," Lonnie said. "If Pa hadn't come up here and fell in the hog pen, Clem wouldn't have had a thing to do with it. He was helping me, that's all."

"Shut up, Lonnie," somebody shouted at him. "You're so

excited you don't know what you're saying. You're taking up for a nigger when you talk like that."

People were crowding around him so tightly he felt as if he were being squeezed to death. He had to get some air, get his breath, get out of the crowd.

"That's right," Lonnie said.

He heard himself speak, but he did not know what he was saying.

"But Clem helped me find Pa when he got lost looking around for something to eat."

"Shut up, Lonnie," somebody said again. "You damn fool, shut up!"

Arch grabbed his shoulder and shook him until his teeth rattled. Then Lonnie realized what he had been saying.

"Now, look here, Lonnie," Arch shouted. "You must be out of your head, because you know good and well you wouldn't talk like a nigger-lover in your right mind."

"That's right," Lonnie said, trembling all over. "I sure wouldn't want to talk like that."

He could still feel the grip on his shoulder where Arch's strong fingers had hurt him.

"Did Clem go to the swamp, Lonnie?" Dudley Smith said. "Is that right, Lonnie?"

Lonnie tried to shake his head; he tried to nod his head. Then Arch's fingers squeezed his thin neck. Lonnie looked at the men wild-eyed.

"Where's Clem hiding, Lonnie?" Arch demanded, squeezing.

Lonnie went three or four steps towards the barn. When he stopped, the men behind him pushed forward again. He found himself being rushed behind the barn and beyond it.

"All right, Lonnie," Arch said. "Now which way?"

Lonnie pointed towards the patch of woods where the creek was. The swamp was in the other direction.

"He said he was going to hide out in that little patch of woods along the creek over there, Mr. Arch," Lonnie said. "I reckon he's over there now."

Lonnie felt himself being swept forward, and he stumbled over the rough ground trying to keep from being knocked down and trampled upon. Nobody was talking, and everyone seemed to be walking on tiptoes. The gray light of early dawn was increasing enough both to hide them and to show the way ahead.

Just before they reached the fringe of the woods, the men separated, and Lonnie found himself a part of the circle that was closing in on Clem.

Lonnie was alone, and there was nobody to stop him, but

he was unable to move forward or backward. It began to be clear to him what he had done.

Clem was probably up a tree somewhere in the woods ahead, but by that time he had been surrounded on all sides. If he should attempt to break and run, he would be shot down like a rabbit.

Lonnie sat down on a log and tried to think what to do. The sun would be up in a few more minutes, and as soon as it came up, the men would close in on the creek and Clem. He would have no chance at all among all those shotguns and pistols.

Once or twice he saw the flare of a match through the underbrush where some of the men were lying in wait. A whiff of cigarette smoke struck his nostrils, and he found himself wondering if Clem could smell it wherever he was in the woods.

There was still no sound anywhere around him, and he knew that Arch Gunnard and the rest of the men were waiting for the sun, which would in a few minutes come up behind him in the east.

It was light enough by that time to see plainly the rough ground and the tangled underbrush and the curling bark on the pine trees.

The men had already begun to creep forward, guns raised as if stalking a deer. The woods were not large, and the circle of men would be able to cover it in a few minutes at the rate they were going forward. There was still a chance that Clem had slipped through the circle before dawn broke, but Lonnie felt that he was still there. He began to feel then that Clem was there because he himself had placed him there for the men to find more easily.

Lonnie found himself moving forward, drawn into the narrowing circle. Presently he could see the men all around him in dim outline. Their eyes were searching the heavy green pine tops as they went forward from tree to tree.

"Oh, Pa!" he said in a hoarse whisper. "Oh, Pa!"

He went forward a few steps, looking into the bushes and up into the treetops. When he saw the other men again, he realized that it was not Mark Newsome being sought. He did not know what had made him forget like that.

The creeping forward began to work into the movement of Lonnie's body. He found himself springing forward on his toes, and his body was leaning in that direction. It was like creeping up on a rabbit when you did not have a gun to hunt with.

He forgot again what he was doing there. The springing motion in his legs seemed to be growing stronger with each step. He bent forward so far he could almost touch the ground with his fingertips. He could not stop now. He was keeping up with the circle of men.

The fifteen men were drawing closer and closer together. The dawn had broken enough to show the time on the face of a watch. The sun was beginning to color the sky above.

Lonnie was far in advance of anyone else by then. He could not hold himself back. The strength in his legs was more than he could hold in check.

He had for so long been unable to buy shells for his gun that he had forgotten how much he liked to hunt.

The sound of the men's steady creeping had become a rhythm in his ears.

"Here's the bastard!" somebody shouted, and there was a concerted crashing through the dry underbrush. Lonnie dashed forward, reaching the tree almost as quickly as anyone else.

He could see everybody with guns raised, and far into the sky above the sharply outlined face of Clem Henry gleamed in the rising sun. His body was hugging the slender top of the pine.

Lonnie did not know who was the first to fire, but the rest of the men did not hesitate. There was a deafening roar as the shotguns and revolvers flared and smoked around the trunk of the tree.

He closed his eyes; he was afraid to look at the face above. The firing continued without break. Clem hugged the tree with all his might, and then, with the faraway sound of splintering wood, the top of the tree and Clem came crashing through the lower limbs to the ground. The body, sprawling and torn, landed on the ground with a thud that stopped Lonnie's heart for a moment.

He turned, clutching for the support of a tree, as the firing began once more. The crumpled body was tossed time after time, like a sackful of kittens being killed with an automatic shotgun, as charges of lead were fired into it from all sides. A cloud of dust rose from the ground and drifted overhead with the choking odor of burned powder.

Lonnie did not remember how long the shooting lasted. He found himself running from tree to tree, clutching at the rough pine bark, stumbling wildly towards the cleared ground. The sky had turned from gray to red when he emerged in the open, and as he ran, falling over the hard clods in the plowed field, he tried to keep his eyes on the house ahead.

Once he fell and found it almost impossible to rise again to his feet. He struggled to his knees, facing the round red sun. The warmth gave him the strength to rise to his feet, and he muttered unintelligibly to himself. He tried to say things he had never thought to say before.

When he got home, Hatty was waiting for him in the yard.

She had heard the shots in the woods, and she had seen him stumbling over the hard clods in the field, and she had seen him kneeling there looking straight into the face of the sun. Hatty was trembling as she ran to Lonnie to find out what the matter was.

Once in his own yard, Lonnie turned and looked for a second over his shoulder. He saw the men climbing over the fence at Arch Gunnard's. Arch's wife was standing on the back porch, and she was speaking to them.

"Where's your pa, Lonnie?" Hatty said. "And what in the world was all that shooting in the woods for?" Lonnie stumbled forward until he had reached the front porch. He fell upon the steps.

"Lonnie, Lonnie!" Hatty was saying. "Wake up and tell me what in the world is the matter. I've never seen the like of all that's going on."

"Nothing," Lonnie said. "Nothing."

"Well, if there's nothing the matter, can't you go up to the big house and ask for a little piece of streak-of-lean? We ain't got a thing to cook for breakfast. Your pa's going to be hungrier than ever after being up walking around all night."

"What?" Lonnie said, his voice rising to a shout as he jumped to his feet.

"Why, I only said to go up to the big house and get a little piece of streak-of-lean, Lonnie. That's all I said."

He grabbed his wife about the shoulders.

"Meat?" he yelled, shaking her roughly.

"Yes," she said, pulling away from him in surprise. "Couldn't you go ask Arch Gunnard for a little bit of streak-of-lean?"

Lonnie slumped down again on the steps, his hands falling between his outspread legs and his chin falling on his chest.

"No," he said almost inaudibly. "No. I ain't hungry."

(First published in *Scribner's*)